Indian Drama in English Translation

Basavaraj Naikar

PUBLISHERS & DISTRIBUTORS (P) LTD

Published by
ATLANTIC
PUBLISHERS & DISTRIBUTORS (P) LTD
7/22, Ansari Road, Darya Ganj, New Delhi-110002
Phones : +91-11-40775252, 40775214, 23273880, 23275880
Fax : +91-11-23285873
Web : www.atlanticbooks.com
E-mail : orders@atlanticbooks.com

Printed & bound in India by Atlantic Print Services

Dedicated to

Dr. R.K. Dhawan

For his selfless service to literature

Preface

In this anthology I have collected as many as twenty nine articles on the Indian regional plays available in English translation that I have written over the last four decades as part of my academic teaching and personal interest. Within this limited number of plays there is a lot of variety. The themes of these plays range from the ancient to the modern; from the mythological to the historical; from the religious to the secular; from the social to the psychological or identitarian; from the rational to the absurd and from the classical to the folk. These articles are hoped to be useful to all the students of English Departments of Indian Universities, where Indian Drama in English Translation as part of the wider subject, Indian Literature in English Translation is studied widely along with Indian English Literature. As compared with the Indian English Drama, the Indian Regional Drama in English Translation is conspicuously vaster and more varied with its multiple voices, themes, techniques and styles. But it is unfortunate that all the significant plays in the regional languages of India are not yet available in English translation due to the lethargy and indifference of our academic scholars who have sold their souls to the west. I was sadly surprised to notice that many significant Hindi plays were not available in English translation, when I was eagerly searching for them for prescription in our University. I simply do not understand whatever has happened to our scholars.

There has not been a systematic project of publishing regional plays in English translation undertaken by our so called well-known publishers who are brazenly commercial in their outlook and lack the academic vision. Likewise our academics have not yet opened their eyes to the rich dramatic tradition of India and in building up a critical tradition of their own backed up by the tenets of Bharata's *Natyasastra* and the local theories of folk drama. It is the bounden duty of Indian scholars especially in English Departments to combine the studies of classical, contemporary and folk drama through English translation and evolve a critical tradition free from the clutches of western theories. This field is so vast that no single scholar can ever do justice to it sufficiently as it needs a team work supported by willing scholars, translators and standard and enlightened publishers, who are free from mere commercial concerns. The next stage is to bring out histories of Indian Regional Drama in English Translation written by various scholars from different languages and compiled together in a meaningful manner. I believe and hope that my present anthology will pave the way for that difficult though not impossible ideal.

Basavaraj Naikar
bsnaikar@yahoo.com

Contents

1

The Little Clay Cart: A Tragicomedy of Noble Love

Although Sanskrit drama is generally known for its mythical element, Sudraka's *The Little Clay Cart* (*Mṛcchakatika*) happens to be an exceptional play on account of its socio-political setting, contemporary element and realistic treatment. Though written in ancient time, the play appears to be so modern and relevant to the twentieth-century readers because of its universality of vision. In fact, it can easily be compared with modern films or tele-films because of its treatment of common theme of man-woman relationship so dear to humanity at large. It is, therefore, possible to interpret it not only from the technical point of view of Sanskrit dramaturgy, but even from the modern Western perspective as well.

The most refreshing aspect of *The Little Clay Cart* is that its protagonist is not a king but an ordinary merchant like Carudatta. It is this ordinariness of Carudatta, which helps the modern spectator or reader to achieve a quick rapprochement with him. The elevation of an ordinary man and not a king or queen to the level of a protagonist of the play is evidence of remarkable originality and courage shown by Sudraka against the background of Sanskrit drama, which is full of gods, demons, natural, and supernatural elements. Plays dealing with social aspects of human life happen to be very rare in Sanskrit drama, as contrasted with the Western dramatic tradition generally known for its social realism. That is why this play is more popular than any other Sanskrit play in Russia and other countries.

The social aspect of the Hindu society is reflected in the present condition of the protagonist, Carudatta. He is a Brahmin and, therefore, represents the Hindu taxonomy of *varnas* or castes. A Brahmin is at the top of the *varna*-hierarchy in India, generally known for his love of knowledge and practice of virtue. Thus, the 'Brahmin' character happens to be a major stereotype in Sanskrit drama, especially in the play under discussion. Carudatta is classified as *Dhiraprasanta* (hero quiet) in Sanskrit dramaturgy. But such a virtuous or noble Brahmin has unfortunately fallen on bad days. Once upon a time, he was a rich man in Ujjayini who had given shelter and help to a large number of poor people. He was known as a paragon of virtue and an incarnation of generosity. But the vices of his virtue, i.e. generosity, have reduced him to the level of an impecunious person. In simple terms, once a rich man has been converted into a poor man, there is no end to his suffering in life. That explains the unhappiness and humiliation of Carudatta. The dramatist, obviously, wants to show how a man suffers from the tragic flaw of limitlessness of his qualities, even if it is a good quality like generosity. A poor man, according to him, may live apparently, but metaphorically he as good as dead. A man of self-respect as he is, he says, "If I had a choice between poverty and death, I should choose death. Death is but a brief pain, but poverty means suffering without end" (p. 56). He is also aware of the changes in social relationships brought about by poverty, "Still, poverty brings a man not only cares, but the contempt and even hostility of strangers, the disgust of his friends, the hatred of his kinsfolk, the contempt of his wife, till he decides to depart for the woods" (p. 57). He, thus, articulates the universal economic philosophy of life by highlighting the importance of wealth or money in human life. As a householder, it is his duty to reserve some money for his livelihood and not squander it indiscriminately. He is expected to be practical about the economic necessities of his life. But Carudatta has not followed this principle of economic self-sufficiency because of his error of over-generosity.

In spite of his poverty, Carudatta has not lost his nobility of character and the beauty of his behaviour. That is exactly why he remains an admirable character in the play. That again is the reason why Vasantasena, the famous courtesan of Ujjayini has fallen in love with him. Although she belongs to a brothel and caters to the sexual needs of a variety of people, she has reserved her deep love for the paragon of virtue, Carudatta in spite of his dire poverty. The love between Carudatta and Vasantasena is characterized by immaculate purity cutting across the barriers of caste, status or economic factor. The dominant sentiment or *rasa* happens to be erotic or *sringara*.

The theme of pure love is highlighted by the playwright by contrasting it with that of lust represented by Samsthanaka (or Sakara), brother-in-law of King Palaka of Ujjayini. When Samsthanaka sees Vasantasena, he is easily drawn to her physical beauty and tries to follow her and forces her to love him. He knows that she is a famous courtesan in the local brothel and therefore, reasons that she has no choice in entertaining men, who are in need of her. His notion of a prostitute is highly limited and he, therefore, considers her only as a commodity or sex object and never as a human being with her own will and inclinations. Libertine, the assistant of Samsthanaka makes it very clear, "Look here, ma'am, living in the District means living with young men. You are a courtesan: think of yourself as a vine on the roadside, for everyone to pluck. The body you wear is up for sale and auctioned off. And you serve equally, my dear girl, the ones you like and the ones you hate. In the same pond bathe the wisest Brahmin and the most stupid pariah. The same blossoming vine bends under the peacock, bends under the crow. The boat that ferries high-caste, ferries outcaste. You are a courtesan, and like the pond, the vine and the boat you must accompany everybody" (p. 61). He is also angry to learn that Vasantasena has been in love with the impecunious Carudatta and refuses to love himself, who is 'a Man Divine, Vasudeva himself.' He tells his assistant Libertine, "Master, this born slave girl has been in love with that penniless Carudatta ever since they met in the court of Kama temple and she does not want me. The fellow's home is just on the left side here, so please don't let her slip from our fingers"

(p. 61). Samsthanaka's attitude to Vasantasena is very commercial and he does not recognize the fact that even a courtesan has her own likes and dislikes transcending her profession of flesh-trade.

Vasantasena's love for Carudatta is born out of her respect for his nobility of character, generosity and cultured behaviour. She also knows that she cannot love Samsthanaka, although he is a rich man with high political connections. Love is a matter of the heart and a voluntary affair and it cannot be forcibly bought with money and power. Even though Vasantasena is forced by the contingencies of her life to surrender her body to rich customers, she cannot surrender her heart also to anyone so mechanically and indiscriminately. Love can happen only between two like-minded beings. Being a cultured lady and a connoisseur of music and dance, she simply cannot love a brainless ruffian like Samsthanaka, though he is rich and politically powerful. The grammar of love presented in the play is so universal and convincing that it holds good even in the twentieth century and can be seen parallel to the similar stories of love and lust presented in modern literature and films. Such a situation is very common in modern Indian films.

Whereas Samsthanaka's attraction for Vasantasena borders on shameless lust, the relationship between Vasantasena and Carudatta is a matter of pure love supported by mutual trust and respect. That is why she keeps her jewelry in Carudatta's custody in order to escape from the possible robbery of the same by Samsthanaka and his gang. She says to Carudatta: "If your honour is disposed to favour me, then I wish to leave my jewelry in your home. Those bandits pursued me because of my jewels" (p. 69). Samsthanaka symbolizes evil whereas Carudatta symbolizes good in the context of the play. Carudatta escorts Vasantasena to her house. Vasantasena likes his graceful behaviour so much that she begins to pine for him and tries to articulate her admiration for him by drawing a portrait of him.

The path of love is never smooth. It is always beset with countless hindrances and ordeals. When, for example, Carudatta is away from home to attend a musical concert at night, he is shocked to learn that the jewelry of Vasantasena kept in his house as a trust has been stolen. He does not know how to convince

Vasantasena. He is worried about the loss of his credibility on account of his poverty, "Who will believe the truth? Everybody will suspect me. For in the world poverty has no dignity and excites suspicion. Oh, disaster! If fate has so far shown its favour to my wealth, why must it now also cruelly sully my honour? (p. 90). Although reduced to pauperism, Carudatta has not lost his integrity and principles. His wife, who is a sensitive lady, understands his anxiety and volunteers to offer her own pearl necklace, which Carudatta sends to Vasantasena through his assistant, Maitreya. His integrity and trustworthiness are evident in his instructions to Maitreya, "Maitreya, take this necklace and go to Vasantasena. Tell her in my name that in all good faith I have mistaken her gold box for mine and lost it in a game of dice; she must accept this pearl necklace in its stead.... She charged us with it because she trusted us, and I merely pay this as the price of her great trust. By the body I touch, Maitreya. I conjure you not to return before you have made her accept it (pp. 91-92).

While Vasantasena understands Carudatta's problem, she admires his integrity and extraordinary credibility. Her love for him increases all the more. She is happy to know that Carudatta has not lost his innate nobility in spite of his present impecuniosity. That is why she inwardly compares him to a mango tree, "The mango tree has lost its bloom, but still the juice of its fruits drips down" (p. 106). Her intense love for him propels her to visit his house and return to him the gold box that she has got from Sarvilaka, who had stolen it from Carudatta's house. Carudatta's nobility is matched by Vasantasena's. Unable to control his passionate love for her, Carudatta embraces her to his heart's content. The passionate hug is further sweetened by the break of rain and thunder. Carudatta waxes poetic when he says, "May the thunder rage, the lightning flash for a hundred years, for I am embraced by a girl, who is rare to a man like me. Blessed are the lives of those, who may press to theirs the moist and rain-chilled bodies of mistresses that hastened to their houses! Vasantasena, my darling.... Look darling, the rainbow! Is it not as though all of heaven seems to yawn and stretch drowsily, flicking its lightning tongue between the gaping jaws of the clouds and stretching the rainbow like its arms?

(pp. 118-19). The passionate private encounter between Carudatta and Vasantasena easily brings to our mind similar situations in modern literature and films.

That night Vasantasena stays in Carudatta's house as a family guest. The next morning she sees Rohasena, Carudatta's little son refusing to play with the clay cart and demanding a golden cart like the one of his neighbouring friends. Vasantasena understands the dire effect of poverty on Carudatta's family and therefore, offers her jewelry to Rohasena asking him to buy a golden cart with it. So far the course of true love between Vasantasena and Carudatta runs smooth.

But henceforth it takes a different turn and is beset with many hindrances. The conflict between good (represented by Carudatta) and evil (represented by Samsthanaka or Sakara) begins to develop slowly into a climax. When, for example, Vasantasena wants to see Carudatta privately in the Puskakarandaka Park, evil comes into operation without her knowledge. Instead of getting into Vardhamana's cart she gets into Sthavaraka's cart by mistake. When she reaches Puspakarandaka Park, she is welcomed by Samsthanaka and his assistant, Libertine instead of by Carudatta. On realizing her mistake of coming in the wrong cart, she requests Samsthanaka for protection. But ruffian as he is, Samsthanaka begins to talk bombastically about himself and pesters her with his request for love. His bombastic words easily bring Ben Jonson's characters like Brainworm and Bobadil to our mind. The more he appeals to her, the more irritated she grows. As he goes near her cart eager to help her alight from it, she kicks him thereby insulting him and hurting his ego. The power of evil embodied in Samsthanaka is enraged by Vasantasena's rejection of his love. He, therefore, bursts out, "With these two hands that boast ten beautiful nails, with these two hands that are as ready to caress as to whip, I shall drag you out of my carriage, pretty girl, by your hair, just as Jatayu did to Valin's mistress" (p. 141). Samsthanaka wants to execute his evil desire as early as possible. He, therefore, asks his assistant, Libertine to kill her. But the Libertine refuses to do so on moral grounds. Then he asks the coachman Sthavaraka to kill her. But he also refuses to oblige him on moral grounds. Then Samsthanaka sends both of them away from the spot. He tries in vain to cajole her and wean her love for him. But when she invokes the name of Carudatta thereby rejecting his offer, he throttles her. Consequently, Vasantasena loses her consciousness and sags to the ground. Obviously, evil reaches its climax here. Samsthanaka mistakes her to be really dead and boasts of his 'heroic' act joyfully,

> That crooked vessel of misconduct, witch
> That wallowed in inequity, who came
> On time to love whoever came to love
> Need I rebuke my arms' heroic acts?
> Even her breath died.... Mother, she is dead!
> As dead as Sita in the *Bharata*!
> I wanted her; she loathed me, and my rage
> Has killed her off in this deserted park
> Puskpakarandaka—the noose of Death
> Fell suddenly to frighten her to death.
> Poor dad and brother kept at court to miss this!
> Poor mother like another Draupadi
> To miss this spectacle of resolute
> Heroic bravery of me, her son! (p. 145)

Samsthanaka, evil incarnate, does not stop his evil action at this point. He tries to shift the blame of the so-called murder of Vasantasena on to his assistant, the Libertine, who returns to the park after some interval of time. The Libertine is outraged morally so much that he leaves his service and goes away from there. Then Samsthanaka covers the unconscious Vasantasena with dry leaves and clears away from the park.

Samsthanaka is so angry with Carudatta for being the object of Vasantasena's love and admiration that he wants to wreak vengeance on him by inculpating him with the murder of Vasantasena. One may easily see here how the power of evil is systematically working through Samsthanaka. He goes to the court and lodges a complaint of murder against Carudatta. He argues that Carudatta has murdered Vasantasena to rob her of her golden ornaments and jewelry. Carudatta, who is an embodiment of good, feels utterly shocked and helpless. Evil seems to be in the ascendant and good totally helpless. When Carudatta is summoned by the jury to the court, he cannot defend himself properly on account of lack of proper evidence in his favour. Unfortunately for Carudatta, all the statements of Samsthanaka are confirmed by circumstantial evidences. Vasantasena's mother confesses that her daughter had gone to Carudatta's house for a rendezvous but not returned. As per the instructions of the judge, a court official goes to the park and returns to confirm that the dead body of Vasantasena is lying in the park. Samsthanaka seems to be triumphant with his evil accusation of Carudatta, "Bah, woman-killer! You murdered a woman like Vasantasena with her hundred ornaments of gold, and now you turn hypocrite and deny everything.... You lured her to the Puspakarandaka Park, my very own park to boot, and strangled her with your own hands for her money! Yes, and now you say she went home!" (p. 150). One may see how evil is at its climax at this point of the play. Even the judge is not convinced by the accusation, as he knows the innate goodness of Carudatta. He says to himself, "Accusing Carudatta is like lifting the Himalayas, crossing the ocean, catching the wind!" (p. 158). But the legal system being what it is, it has its own limitations. Carudatta is so much humiliated by his unkind fate that he cannot defend himself cleverly against Samsthanaka. The judge, much against his wish, has to yield to the pressure of circumstantial evidences and declare Carudatta as a murderer. The court decision is referred to King Palaka for the necessary punishment. The royal order of King Palaka prescribes death punishment for the criminal, who has murdered Vasantasena. Good embodied in Carudatta is totally powerless at this juncture and reduced to tragic victimization. Consequently, Carudatta is led to the hanging place for execution. His assistant Maitreya and others wail and cry helplessly for their master. When Carudatta wants to see his son Rohasena for the last time before his execution, the officers get Rohasena, who implores them to kill him instead of his father. The executioners, who have to hang Carudatta to death, are ready to accomplish their unpleasant task. Up to this point the play follows a tragic course and reaches its climax.

Thus, when Carudatta is at the lowest ebb of his life and in the most helpless condition, there comes about a very unexpected reversal in his life. The tragic pattern is reversed by a quirk of his fate. The power of Good being awakened, it begins to assert itself and expose Evil. When Samsthanaka is eager to enjoy the sight of Carudatta being hanged, his evil desire is frustrated in a very unexpected manner. Sthavaraka, who has seen Samsthanaka killing Vasantasena in the park, has been kept in a dovecote as a prisoner. He is surprised at the strange course of events. Feeling utterly sorry for Carudatta's plight, he wants to die by jumping from the roof. He, therefore, jumps but does not die. On the contrary, his fetters are broken. These unexpected and strange events help to expose and thwart the path of evil, as it generally happens in *Shakespeare's Last Plays*. He boldly declares to the pariahs that it was he, who took Vasantasena by mistake to the park, where Samsthanaka murdered her when she refused to love him. The pariahs and the people are surprised by the revelation of truth by Sthavaraka. Unlike in *Shakespeare's Last Plays*, where truth is revealed by the supernatural or divine agency, in *The Little Clay Cart* it is revealed through the human agency itself—a fact that redounds to Sudraka's extraordinary talent as a realistic dramatist. Samsthanaka is also nonplussed by the revelation of truth and therefore tries to bribe Sthavaraka with gold. But Good cannot be corrupted by Evil any longer. Sthavaraka refuses to accept the bribe and exposes the hypocrisy and murderous ness of Samsthanaka. The unexpected turn of events brings a ray of hope in the utterly helpless Brahmin, Carudatta. He thanks Sthavaraka for telling the truth. Although Samsthanaka is forcing the executioners to hasten the process of hanging, the latter is deliberately delaying the process. The power of Good is operative in their moral philosophy that the delay may turn in favour of the culprit. In fact, it is proved beyond doubt when Vasantasena and the Buddhist monk come there. Now Evil is completely exposed by Good. The executioners are puzzled by the living presence of Vasantasena and everybody realizes the falsity of the charge of murder. Samsthanaka realizes his folly and starts running away from there. Carudatta is really surprised and confounded simultaneously by the strange turn of events. He stares at Vasantasena first with doubt and then with confidence. The play reaches the stage of denouement when Vasantasena reveals the truth that it was Samsthanaka, who tried to kill her and that it was the Buddhist monk (the former Masseur), who helped her by giving shelter to her in the monastery.

At this juncture, the emotional problem of Carudatta gets entangled with the political life of the kingdom. Some change has taken place in the political order of the kingdom thereby rendering things favourable to Carudatta. For example, Sarvilaka comes there and declares that he has killed King Palaka and enthroned Prince Aryaka. He also confesses before Carudatta that it was he, who had stolen Vasantasena's jewels kept in Carudatta's custody. Now Carudatta's moral stature is supported by political power unlike in the immediate past. Sarvilaka, who has become a kingmaker, now orders that Samsthanaka should be arrested. One can easily see the reversal of positions. Good has grown powerful and Evil has become powerless. Sarvilaka asks for Carudatta's opinion about the punishment to be given to Samsthanaka. But Samsthanaka, who is shameless as well as opportunistic, seeks mercy from Carudatta who, because of his innate nobility, grants amnesty to his adversary instead of wreaking vengeance. He even goes to the extent of recommending his release. Samsthanaka is happy to be released. Carudatta, thus becomes an embodiment of the highest Hindu values of life like forgiveness. Like Prospero in *The Tempest* he believes in the philosophy that there is greater heroism in forgiveness than in vengeance. Carudatta attains the stature of a saint in civil dress. At the end of the play, all the good people are rewarded properly. Accordingly, Vasantasena is declared as the wife of Carudatta. Carudatta's wife is so great in her attitude to life that she never creates any problem about her husband's taking a second wife. Vasantasena, the courtesan is promoted to the status of a respectable wife (*kulavadhu*). The monk is promoted as the abbot of all the monasteries in the Kingdom. The *pariahs* are made the Chiefs of their castes whereas Candalaka is promoted as the Chief Constable and Samsthanaka is continued in his old position. Thus, everything ends on a happy note thereby affirming the moral order of the world. The tragic events have been transformed into happy ones like marriage, promotion, forgiveness, and reconciliation thereby extending the joy of life and taking sorrow in their stride.

Thus, in *The Little Clay Cart* is depicted the victory of pure love over lust; of good over evil; of truth over falsity; of moral law over legal law; of nobility, truthfulness and forgiveness over jealousy, hauteur, meanness and revenge. The play undoubtedly intensifies our faith in the moral order of the universe and enhances our sense of beauty and meaningfulness of life. Such a beautiful moral vision has been very artistically expressed in dramatic terms by Sudraka, who therefore, belongs to the galaxy of the great dramatists of the world like Shakespeare, Kalidasa and Bhavabhuti. The play is a dramatic presentation and affirmation of the Hindu philosophy, which believes in the view that truth ultimately triumphs over falsehood (*Satyameva Jayate*).

Reference

Sudraka, *The Little Clay Cart* in *Two Plays of Ancient of India*, English Translation by J.A.B. van Buitenan, New Delhi: Motilal Banarasidass, 1965. (All the page references to the play are from this edition.)

• • • • •

2

The Recognition of Sakuntala: A Sublime Comedy

The Recognition of Sakuntala (*Abhijnana Sakuntala*)[1] is world famous play written by the Sanskrit playwright, Kalidasa. The Western scholars have praised it wholeheartedly. The German poet's admiration for *Sakuntala* is quite well known. It depicts the love between the young girl of sixteen, Sakuntala and King Dusyanta, their painful separation and their final happy union. It shows the principle that all is well that ends well. But whatever happens in the middle is worth noting, as it poses several problems for the protagonist, if not for her lover, King Dusyanta. Perhaps that is one of the reasons why Europeans prefer Sudraka's *The Clay Cart* (*Mricchakatika*) to Kalidasa's *Sakuntala*. There are a few conspicuous differences between *The Clay Cart* and *Sakuntala* as far as setting, theme, and philosophy of life are concerned. *The Clay Cart* has a realistic setting and a strong dose of social element in it, which is not to be seen in *Sakuntala*. But what are to be admired in the case of Kalidasa are his feminist leanings, which makes him name the play after a girl instead of naming it after King Dusyanta. Kalidasa's originality and greatness could be seen in the working out of his theme, which he borrowed from earlier sources, in the manner in which Shakespeare borrowed his stories from earlier sources, but converted them into his own excellent dramatic visions. A bit of a comparative picture of Sakuntala as depicted in the *Mahabharata* and in Kalidasa's play will help us to understand his artistic inventiveness and creative talent.

In the Sakuntala episode of the *Mahabharata*, King Dusyanta meets Sakuntala by chance when Sage Kanwa is away from his hermitage for gathering fruits. He instantly falls in love with her and marries her according to the Gandharva mode by reasoning with her. Although she demurs at having to marry him in the absence of her foster father, she is forced by the king to marry her. So she agrees to marry him on condition that her child should be the future heir of his kingdom and he agrees to the condition due to his infatuation for her.

Kalidasa follows this source almost closely by making King Dusyanta go to the hermitage of Kanwa during his hunting trip. When he is about to shoot the animals, an inmate of the hermitage tells him not to shoot any animal on the sacred campus of the hermitage. So King Dusyanta controls his urge for hunting the animal, but later he hunts the innocent and forlorn girl, Sakuntala metaphorically. The king wants to pay his respects to the sage, but as the sage is away from the hermitage, he chances to see the sixteen year young Sakuntala, overhears her conversation with her friends and meets her on some pretext on the bank of River Malini. Naturally, he acts like a romantic boy, who is infatuated with any young and beautiful girl. Sakuntala is duty bound to entertain him as she is pressurized by her friends to do so. In this close meeting, both of them begin to respond to each other amorously. There is some age gap between the two. Whereas Sakuntala is a girl of just sixteen years, he must be past his thirty or forty years as he already has his queens in his gynaeceum. When he asks her about her identity, she reveals to him her half-human and half-supernatural element by narrating how she was born to the Apsara, Menaka by the Sage Viswamitra (of Ksatriya varna) and abandoned by her mother, but nourished by the *sakunta* birds and picked up by sage Kanwa and brought up by him as his foster daughter. Thus, Sakuntala does not belong to the human worldly entirely, as she is half-human (on the father's side) and half-divine (on her mother's side). Thus, right from the beginning Kalidasa gives an epic atmosphere of interrelatedness of the human and the divine world. To that extent he violates the law of probability and rules of a realistic modern drama. Here another detail may be noticed. Although Sakuntala is half-human and half-divine, King Dusyanta confirms to himself that even in her half-humanness she happens to be a daughter of a Ksatriya father, Viswamitra and hence goes ahead with his philandering. As he is an upholder and protector of *varnasrama-dharma* he finds no fault in his courting and winning Sakuntala according to the *Gandharva* code of marriage.

In the meanwhile Kalidasa invents a few occasions to increase the impact of love on Sakuntala. For example, she wishes to see King Dusyanta on the pretext of removing the thorns from her hands. Similarly, he makes Dusyanta come near Sakuntala to ward off a bumblebee which is torturing her by going round her face. One may see an irony here. The bumblebee collects honey from a variety of flowers. King Dusyanta wards off the bumblebee but metaphorically becomes a bumblebee himself and sucks the honeyed beauty of her youth and marries her in haste as per the convention of Gandharva marriage. So the bee-motif plays an important ironical role in the play. Such details are not in the source material in the *Mahabharata*. Just as King Dusyanta falls in love with Sakuntala, she also falls in love with him according to the biological law of Nature. She even writes a love letter to King Dusyanta, which is discovered by her friends like Anasuya and Priyamvada, who pave the way for their private meeting.

Another detail invented by Kalidasa is the curse-motif, which is not in the source. When Sakuntala neglects Sage Durvasa on his coming to the hermitage of Sage Kanwa, as she is brooding over her love for her lover, he curses her that she should not be remembered by the man about whom she is brooding. But when her friends approach Sage Durvasa to withdraw his course on humanitarian grounds, he says that his curse cannot be cancelled, but can only be modified. He says that Sakuntala could be remembered by the man (her lover) on her producing a memento (ring). Her friends think that that is some relief at least. Now the curse seems to have come into operation. Kalidasa's originality lies in the introduction of this curse motif and ring motif, which are interrelated. Both these are crucial to the play to highlight the theme of amnesia and memory. Some scholars opine that Kalidasa was influenced by the Kashmir Saivism which teaches the doctrine that man has come to this mortal world after forgetting his celestial world and has to return to his original world after the veil of *maya* (or phenomenal illusion) and forgetfulness is removed from him. This philosophical doctrine may have influenced Kalidasa, but it cannot be applied empirically to all the details of the play's action.

Another small detail that Kalidasa brings into the play is that King Dusyanta is not in his royal costume and panoply but in a simple robe of a noble man and a connoisseur of women. He displays his philandering habit by trying to talk with Sakuntala on some pretext or the other. According to Sanskrit dramaturgy, King Dusyanta happens to be hero-noble (*dhirodatta*) type. His nobility of behavior is reveled to the reader at a later stage of his life in the play. But Sakuntala also begins to feel some kind of amorous attraction for him as it is quite natural to her age. But the main problem here is that although King Dusyanta marries her according to the Gandharva mode of marriage, he has committed a great mistake in marrying her without the permission of her foster father and without the approval of some well-wishers and elders, in other words, without any social approval. Another grave error that he commits is that having married her in haste and impregnated her; he should have taken her to his palace right then, but he leaves her back at the hermitage on the pretext of sending his officers and army to take her back. If he had wanted the social or public approval, he should have waited for some time to solemnize his marriage and consummate his love, but he has not done that at all. On the other hand, he has behaved in a high-handed and arrogant manner by throwing the norms to winds due to his uncontrollable philandering. Then Sakuntala also displays her foolish innocence by believing in whatever he says and yielding to his urgent amorous demands. Thus, both of them are in the wrong, but King Dusyanta's crime is greater than Sakuntala's because he happens to be a responsible man at the helm of royal affairs.

Another notable difference between the source in the *Mahabharata* and Kalidasa's play happens to be the departure of Sakuntala to King Dusyanta's court immediately after the arrival of Sage Kanwa to his hermitage. In the source, Sakuntala returns to King Dusyanta's court after her son, Bharat is born and becomes eligible to be declared as the heir-designate of the kingdom. But in Kalidasa's play Sakuntala goes to the court of King Dusyanta when she is still pregnant and asks him to accept her as his wife and her would-be son as his heir. This becomes rather difficult for the king to accept. Since the curse, an invention of Kalidasa, has come into operation, the king's memory is clouded and consequently he suffers from oblivion. Hence, he fails to recognize Sakuntala with whom he has dallied and made her big with child. Here Kalidasa's invention of a curse by Sage Durvasa and its operation is part of the supernatural machinery, which may not be palatable to the taste of modern readers. It clearly violates the law of probability and goes against the principles of modern psychology. Likewise when Sakuntala is to go to her husband's palace, she has no proper cloths to wear, but she is offered some gifts or ornaments and cloths by the trees, which clearly violates the law of probability and therefore does not look credible and acceptable to the modern reader. But the reader is rather helpless and has to willingly suspend his disbelief in order to understand the overall intention of Kalidasa, who belonged to an early age.

The reaction of Sakuntala to King Dusyanta's rejection due to his amnesia is also to be examined in some detail. In the source (the *Mahabharata*), Sakuntala argues vehemently with King Dusyanta and even quotes the scriptural authorities about the duties of a king and convinces him about his past action, i.e. Gandharva marriage with her and succeeds in getting his approval. But in Kalidasa's play, Kalidasa has made her rather soft and helpless. King Dusyanta tells Sarngarava and Saradvata, "O hermits, rich in holiness, try as I might, I cannot recall to my mind accepting the hand of this lady in marriage at any time. Seeing that she is plainly pregnant, how can I receive her when I have doubts about being her husband?" (p. 237). As she has no witnesses to speak in her favour, she grows rather helpless when he fails to remember her marriage with him. He asks her to produce a memento so that he could remember the past. In fact, she wants to produce the memento, i.e. ring on her finger. But when she feels for the ring on her finger she learns that unfortunately she has lost in the water of the lake when travelling in a boat and playing with water. This loss of the ring in the water is also an invention of Kalidasa to support his curse-motif, which holds mirror to his creative talent. The ring is lost simply because the supernatural curse is in operation. When rejected by King Dusyanta, Sakuntala grows helpless and follows her companions, Sarngarava and Saradvata, who leave her at the king's court. It is surprising that Kalidasa has depicted her as docile, obliging and *sattvik*-natured girl, although she happens to be the daughter of a Ksatriya sage. She seems to be the exact opposite of the modern radical and aggressive feminist, who rants about her identity and shouts for gender equality and justice.

Here we may notice how Kalidasa has made her a docile and helpless girl, who is part of the Indian (Hindu) patriarchal society. Although he has given her the central place in the title of the play, he seems to have marginalized her in the central action of the play. But on the way she is lifted up to Heaven by some angel, *apsara* and left at the hermitage of Sage Marica. This incident of her being whisked away to the upper world is not to be seen in the source, but seems to be an invention of Kalidasa. Such a supernatural happening is certainly not palatable to the modern reader or spectator. Again it violates the law of probability and distances us from the theme.

But Kalidasa's invention of the fisherman episode is quite realistic and interesting. When the fisherman finds the ring in the belly of a fish that he is cutting for his food, he is tempted to sell it in the market and gets caught by two policemen, who take him to the palace of King Dusyanta for trial and think that the fisherman will be punished severely. But on the contrary King Dusyanta learns the details of how he managed to get hold of the ring, he convinced of the veracity of the event and easily connects it with Sakuntala. The very sight of the ring seems to remove the curse of Sage Durvasa on him and helps him remember Sakuntala and realize his folly. He rewards the fisherman amply instead of punishing him as expected by the two policemen who had caught and brought the fisherman to the presence of the king. He repents over his crime and consequently cancels the Spring Festival. Not only that. He even tries to look at a painting of Sakuntala that he has drawn without showing it to his queen and feels nostalgic about her. His Chief Queen Vasumati feels jealous of seeing the portrait of Sakuntala. This entire episode is quite realistic and of human interest, though it comes as a complement to the supernatural event of sage Durvasa's curse. Kalidasa's originality and knowledge of human nature are easily displayed here.

In the same mood of repentance, King Dusyanta is able to understand the sufferings of other human beings more sensitively. On learning about the shipwreck of Dhanamitra, a merchant of Saket, he does not wish to annex the latter's property to his kingdom, but has an enquiry conducted about Dhanamitra's surviving wife. Again on learning that she is pregnant before the death of her husband in the shipwreck, King Dusyanta displays his humanitarian approach by declaring that the property of the dead Dhanamitra should go his child growing in the womb of his wife and therefore cannot be annexed by the kingdom. In such decisions, King Dusyanta's deep humanism and understanding of the subtle legal problems is exhibited, thereby holding mirror to Kalidasa's insight into human nature.

Another supernatural event is added by Kalidasa. When King Dusyanta is deeply depressed by the sight of Sakuntala after getting hold of the ring from the fisherman, he hears the frightened voice of Madhavya (the Jester/Vidusaka), who is snatched away from the palace of clouds by some supernatural being, who is invisible. Madhavya complains that somebody is trying to break his neck as if he is sugarcane and crying for help. Then King Dusyanta hears the voice and learns from his chamberlain Parvatayana that Madhavya has been whisked off from the palace of clouds by somebody. He also hears the threatening voice of the invisible being that he is thirsty for the blood of the victim. Then King Dusyanta takes his bow and arrow and gets ready to shoot at the invisible being. Then the invisible voice manifests itself as Matali (Lord Indra's charioteer) and asks him not to shoot his arrow at the envoy sent by Lord Indra and tells him further that Lord Indra wants the help of King Dusyanta to fight the war against the demons that have been creating a lot of problems for them. Matali asks King Dusyanta to mount the celestial chariot and go to the celestial world to fight with the demons there. King Dusyanta feels honoured by the Lord of Heaven's invitation and readily climbs the chariot and goes to oblige the Great Lord of Immortals. This whole incident is supernatural and discounts the human interest of the play. It is not palatable to the modern reader, who has lost faith in the supernatural world and spiritual themes. Perhaps what Kalidasa wants to show through this supernatural event is that King Dusyanta has fulfilled his primary duty of fighting on the battlefield with demons at the invitation of Lord Indra and proved his kingly responsibility, which in a way balances his philandering habit.

We learn from King Dusyanta's dialogue with Matali that this is his second visit to Indraloka; that Lord has bestowed upon him great honour by making him sit on his own seat and garlanded him with the Mandara garland. He asks Matali to explain the celestial route that they are following now. Matali tells him that they are following the Celestial Path including the Path of Seven Winds, the Path of the Wind Pravaha, the Path of the Clouds, the range of Mountains called Hema-Kuta, which is the home of Kimpurusas and where the parents of Lord Indra, Sage Marica and his consort Aditi practice hard penance in their hermitage. All this celestial setting and characters belong to the mythical and divine world and lend a cosmic and epic atmosphere to the play, but certainly violate the law of probability and therefore cannot attract the attention and admiration of a modern reader. King Dusyanta's journey into the celestial world of Indra reads like a modern spaceship or rocket sent to moon or Mars or like a chunk of modern science fiction. Obviously, it adds to the romantic and idealistic element of the play thereby violating the laws of realistic drama to that extent. Hence, the modern reader feels rather alienated by the sight or description of such a celestial world.

But when King Dusyanta enters the hermitage of sage Marica and his spouse, Aditi, the parents of Lord Indra, he finds a boy playing with a lion cub there and forcing it to show its teeth to him. As King Dusyanta asks for the boy's name a hermit lady replies that it is Sarvadamana. On seeing the boy the king feels a strange tenderness towards him, perhaps due to his biological affinity to him and admires his heroism. He also sees the mark of a Sovereign on the boy's palm. The boy refuses to leave teasing the lion cub. Then the hermit lady requests King Dusyanta to release the lion cub from the iron grip of the boy. As the king tries hard to release the lion cub from the boy's grip, the armlet comes loosened and falls on the ground. Here Kalidasa provides another supernatural truth to the armlet. According to him, Sage Marica has tied this armlet around the arm of the boy to protect him from possible danger from crooked people like demons, etc. The moment somebody tries to harm the boy the armlet instantly becomes a serpent and bites the enemy. But the armlet does not become a serpent to bite King Dusyanta when he tries to pick it up in his hand it does not become a serpent at all. Then the hermit lady recognizes that there is something strange about the entire event. She also realizes that the boy does not shy away from King Dusyanta as from any stranger, but takes naturally to him. Then she brings a toy peacock, the boy starts playing with it. Such supernatural events help the playwright to pave the way for the revelation or truth. In fact, this scene may be said to be a denouement. King Dusyanta enquires the hermit lady about the mother of the boy and learns that she is a daughter of an *apsara*, Menaka by name and abandoned by her in the mortal world, but she was nourished by *sakunta* birds and later brought up by sage Kanwa as a foster-daughter. The hermit lady refuses the spell the name of Sakuntala's husband who abandoned her unjustly. Though King Dusyanta feels ashamed of himself, he is confirmed in his guess that Sarvadamana is none other than his own son and that Sakuntala is none other than his own beloved whom he had married secretly according to the Gandharva convention. Another problem that teases the modern reader is how come King Dusyanta could not have any progeny in spite of having two queens like (Chief) Vasumati and (Junior) Hamsamati.

Now Sakuntala, who comes to know the strange happenings in the hermitage of Sage Marica, feels that her luck is turning. She is happy to learn that King Dusyanta has relented and she is surprised when he falls at her feet and seeks her forgiveness for his crime. The king shows her the ring which restored his memory and wants to slip it on her finger, but she refuses to accept it as she does not want to trust it, which caused so much agony to her. He then tells her how he recovered it. Then she curses not the king, but her past *karma* and accepts the situation as part of her destiny. By then Matali enters and enheartens the King, "Indeed. Fortune has blessed you, gracious lord, by granting you the happiness of meeting again your lawful wife and of seeing the face of your son" (p. 277). Then Sage Marica blesses the couple. When King Dusyanta prostrates at his feet, the sage blesses him, "My son, long may you protect the Earth" (p. 278). Aditi blesses him, "Be invincible in battle, my child" (p. 278). King Dusyanta feels a sense of fulfillment after he is blessed by the Parents of the Universe. Then Sage Marica tells the King that Menaka, the mother of Sakuntala stays in his hermitage and serves him. He explains further how the king suffered due to the loss of memory due to Sage Durvasa's curse and Lord Indra knew it all. He then sends Galava through the aerial path to Sage Kanwa to tell him about the happy union of King Dusyanta and Sakuntala.

Thus, there is family reunion and reconciliation after a long period of misunderstanding, forgetting and painful separation. The separation seems to have ripened them and made them wiser than earlier and readied them to accept the contingency of their life. King Dusyanta's repentance after discovering the ring from the fisherman seen in his painting the picture of Sakuntala on a canvass and his cancellation of the spring festival indicates his mental agony. But Sakuntala's separation from him for about seven years is indicated and her emaciation is mentioned, but her suffering is not presented at all, as she lived at the hermitage of Marica quite comfortably under somebody's protection. They are united in the hermitage of Sage Kanwa, separated from each other from the court of King Dusyanta but are reunited in the hermitage of sage Marica. Thus, there is a pattern of union, separation and reunion and reconciliation, which easily brings to our mind the last plays or romances of Shakespeare. Thus, all suffering ends up in happiness thereby making the would-have-been tragedy a romantic comedy. But it is not an ordinary comedy but an epical comedy and a sublime comedy. The union of lovers is crowned with the birth of Sarvadamana or Bharata, who is the would-be king of Bharatavarsa and takes away the mere romantic attraction between man and wife, but has paved the way for the fulfillment of the higher, procreative purpose of God. In a way the German poet, Goethe is right when he describes the pattern of loss and gain. As Romila Thaper says, "Hence did Goethe rightly say that *Sakuntala* combines the blossoms of spring with the fruits of autumn, it combines Heaven and Earth. Truly in *Sakuntala* there is one Paradise Lost and another Paradise Regained."[2]

***

Although modern readers may find fault with some details in the play and its action, Kalidasa has to be complimented for his strict observance of most of the conventions of Sanskrit Dramaturgy. The use of *Nandi* at the beginning, and *Bharatavakya* or Benediction at the end of the play, the employment of a character like Vidusaka for providing humourous element and the poetic descriptions of the details of hunting, which was a popular pastime of the kings in the ancient days and of the beauty of Nature, etc., are in conformity with the tenets of Sanskrit Drama. He has composed it as a *Nataka*, a special genre among the ten kinds of drama mentioned in Bharata's *Natyasastra*. Likewise he has portrayed the amorous love (*sringara rasa*) in union (*sambhoga*) and separation (*vipralambha*). We have no quarrel with or objection to Kalidasa's artistic skill in his observance of the rules of Sanskrit dramaturgy. But our problems begin to trouble us when we try to understand the play from a modern point of view influenced by our Western education.

***

Many foreign critics like Goethe and Max Muller (German) Monier-Williams and Frazer (British) have admired the play for various reasons. They have paid glowing tributes Kalidasa's imaginative faculty and mastery over the dramatic technique. For example, Monier-Williams says, "No composition of Kalidasa displays more the richness of his poetical genius, the exuberance of his imagination, the warmth and play of his fancy, his profound knowledge of the human heart, his delicate appreciation of its most refined and tender emotions, his familiarity with the workings and counter-workings of its conflicting feelings—in short more entitles him to rank as the Shakespeare of India."[3] Indian critics like Rabindranath Tagore and Sri Aurobindo appreciate everything contained in *Sakuntala* by saying that it is in line with the tenets of Hindu philosophy, which teaches the lesson that everybody should his duty (*svadharma*) for the smooth functioning of the society. Such critics seem to be more patriotic than critical in their views.

But some Western critics like A.B. Keith and Walter Ruben find fault with Kalidasa's limited vision of life. For example, Keith complains that Kalidasa "shows no interest in the great problems of life and destiny. The admiration of Goethe...must not blind us to the narrow range imposed on Kalidasa's interests by his unfeigned devotion to the brahmanical creed of his time.... Assured as he was, that all was governed by a just fate which man makes for himself by his own deeds, he was incapable of viewing the world as a tragic scene, of feeling any sympathy for the hard lot of the majority of men, or appreciating the reign of injustice in the world. It was impossible for him to go beyond his narrow range; we may grateful that, confined as he was, he accomplished a work of such enduring merit and universal appeal as *Sakuntala*."[4] One cannot help agreeing with Keith for his opinion about Kalidasa's *Sakuntala* as it confines itself to the man-woman relationship and does not go beyond that to recognize the variegated socio-political life or an element of evil or negative aspects of life. The characterization of almost all the major characters is marked by some kind of idealism and sublimity untainted by the negative feelings of human life. Everything is good and ideal and hence goody-goody and no chance for the recognition of evil in life at all. The play begins at the hermitage of Kanwa and ends up in the hermitage of Sage Marica.

Kalidasa has shown the transformation of the earthly love into spiritual love in a very subtle manner. There is no controversy about that at all. But most of them do not accept or appreciate the supernatural and mythical element employed in the play as it violates the law of probability. They also complain that Kalidasa does not reveal any historical details of his age in his play, which therefore seems to be an artistic enclosure without any connection with the outer and wider world.

But critics whether Western or Eastern, have whole-heartedly appreciated Kalidasa's description of the various moods of Nature and showing the interconnection between human life and Nature. Henry Wells[5] appreciates Kalidasa by saying that he is a poet of Nature par excellence. Nobody can fail to notice that there is an epic atmosphere in the play in the sense that the human world, the natural world and the divine world are interconnected. For example, Sakuntala herself is half-divine or angelic as she happens to be the daughter of the Apsara Menaka. Then King Dusyanta is also metaphorically divine in the sense that kings were considered to be gods on the earth. Then Sakuntala is deeply connected with nature emotionally. She is very intimate with the trees, creepers and antelopes in the hermitage complex. She waters the creepers regularly, feeds and tends the deer affectionately with *ingudi* oil when its mouth is wounded by the sharp blades of *darbha* grass. When she departs to her husband's palace, all the animals refuse to have their food and seem to be crying. She tells her friends to send word to her after the pregnant deer is delivered of its baby. The trees love her so much that they offer gifts of silk robes and ornaments to her. This emotional attachment of Sakuntala to Nature is very delicate, convincing, and poetic, although a bit of it is improbable. In fact, she may be said to be a daughter of Nature. Then Lord Indra inviting King Dusyanta to help him defeat the demons and King Dusyanta going to Heaven hold mirror to the epical atmosphere of interaction between the human world and the divine world. This interrelatedness between Man, Nature, and gods is believed by the Hindu critics to be a holistic vision of life (*purna dristi*), which is generally characteristic of epic vision of life all over the world.

Theatre History

Although *Sakuntala* is a world famous play and is studied at the undergraduate and post graduate levels in Indian Universities at least in regional translations, if not in original Sanskrit, we do not have any information of its being performed regularly or annually in our country simply because perhaps it happens to be an unwieldy play running into seven acts and requiring more than three to four hours of performance. And another difficulty with the play is that it requires rich and expensive costumes of royal costumes and paraphernalia like a chariot, horses, hermitage atmosphere containing antelopes and their peculiar robes and garments, the Indian directors of drama and organizers do not dare invest huge amount of money in its performance just for a couple of shows, until some government agency sponsors it out of cultural necessity and prestige. Thus, the play remains to be a reading play rather than an easily performable one.

Another important thing that is missing in Indian cultural world is the absence of the film versions of not only Kalidasa's *Sakuntala* but also of other Sanskrit playwrights' famous plays. I have not heard, let alone seen any films of *Sakuntala* either in Sanskrit or in regional languages produced attractively for the students and teachers of India. By contrast, we may see many plays of Shakespeare in their film versions which are watched by the people all over the world. It only shows our intellectual poverty and lack of passion for excellence and adventure in the field of art and culture.

***

In India, there have been great Sanskrit scholars like S.K. De, P.V. Kane, R.G. Bhandarkar and K. Krishnamoorthy and many more. Some of them have translated *Sakuntala* and other Sanskrit plays into English with ample notes and introduction, etc. and have done great service to Indian academic life. But the main problem with most of these scholars is that their English language employed in their translations is rather quaint, stilted and artificial and hence not modern and readable. As Sanskrit language is characterized by passive voice, these Sanskrit scholars employ this passive voice in their sentence structures quite often without understanding the fact that it is not relished and liked by the modern or Western readers. Even Monier Williams' language is not free from such kind of artificiality as he uses a number of brackets to clarify the obscure ideas in the original

Sanskrit. Such translations tend to be unreadable and a scholar has to wade through them laboriously and patiently. As far as I know it and sincerely too, the modern translation of *Sakuntala* by Ms. Chandra Rajan, published by Penguin India is the best one, not only for its modern and readable translation but also offering a wide comparative and critical perspective on the play. Such modern and readable translations of other Sanskrit plays of Bhasa, Bhavabhuti, Visakhadatta, Harsha and so on are eagerly awaited, but none knows when it will be possible simply because it requires an ideal combination of a modern scholar like Chandra Rajan, a modern publisher like Penguin with its resident language editor and the avid and eager reader who longs for such translations.

***

Many of the Sanskrit critics of India are known for their deep scholarship, but when it comes to analyzing a play like *Sakuntala*, they concentrate on the explication of minute textual details and showing the text's conformity with the rules laid down by the *Natyasastra* rather mechanically without thinking about the theme independently. They may explain the niceties of language and description of Nature and aspects of characterization, but do not go beyond that. Their patriotism makes them appreciate everything written by Kalidasa and defend it somehow or the other without viewing it from different angles. They do not find fault with the timeless mythical setting and characters of the play. They feel extremely satisfied with their highly limited approach to Kalidasa. Hence, all their criticism does not cross the limits of formalistic criticism at all. For example, no Sanskrit critic has analyzed *Sakuntala* from a sociological or Marxist point of view. Hence, any scholar educated in English Literature cannot appreciate and benefit from the writings of Sanskrit scholars on *Sakuntala*.

***

There have been many English translations of *Sakuntala* right from Monier Williams, through Barbara E. Stoler down to the present scholars like Chandra Rajan (wife of Dr. Balachandra Rajan, the great Milton scholar from India). There is a great need for English scholars (for this is not the field meant for Sanskrit scholars) to undertake a comparative study of all these English translations against the background of modern theories of translation. This adventure requires an active knowledge of modern theories of translation as well as a good grounding in Sanskrit. Scholars with such rare combination of talents are very rare in India.

(Incidentally, it may be mentioned here that there are more than half a dozen Kannada translations of *Sakuntala*, beginning with Sri Basavappa Sastri's (1883) up to Churamari Sesagirirao (1934). But the Kannada scholars have not undertaken a comparative study of these translations as they are not armed with the knowledge of modern theories of translation.)

***

As I have already mentioned the modern reader does not appreciate the supernatural and mythical element in *Sakuntala*. I have often wondered as to why not rewrite *Sakuntala* in a modern style by removing the unnecessary descriptions, mythical setting and supernatural things and events. Bertrolt Brecht has rewritten many of Shakespeare's plays according to his epic theatre technique. Dr. M.V. Rama Sarma (another Milton scholar from India) has already attempted such a modern version of *Sakuntala* which is quite appreciable.

***

It is unfortunate that good critical anthologies on *Sakuntala* like the Case Studies and Critical Heritage Series so common in America are not available in India, simply because in our country there is no organic connection between universities, researchers, publishers, and distributors due to lack of proper academic enlightenment. Such a series requires a coordinated work of Sanskrit and English scholars, which is not prevalent in India yet.

References

1. Kalidasa. *The Loom of Time: A Selection of His Plays and Poems*. Tr. Chandra Rajan. New Delhi: Penguin Books, 1980. (All the page references are to this edition.)

2. Romila Thapar, *Sakuntala: Texts, Readings, Histories*. New York: Columbia University press, 2011, p. 248.
3. Kalidasa, *Abhijnanasakuntalam*. Ed. M.R. Kale. Delhi: Motilal Banarasidass. Reprint. 1980, p. 14.
4. A.B. Keith. *History of Sanskrit Drama*. Delhi: Motilal Banarasidass. 1972, p. 160.
5. Henry W. Wells. *The Classical Drama of the Orient*. Bombay: Asia Publishing House, 1965, p. 168.

• • • • •

3

Three Mythological Plays of Kuvempu

Kuvempu, an acronym of Dr. K.V. Puttappa (1904-94) is a well-known poet, critic, playwright, essayist, educationist and epic poet. His magnum opus, *Sri Ramayana Darshanam* won the Jnanpith Award for him in 1967. His two epic novels like *Kanuru Heggditi* and *Malegalalli Madumagalu* are known for the depiction of the provincial and feudal life of South Karnataka. He has written fourteen poetic plays dealing with the themes connected with the Hindu epics like the *Ramayana* and the *Mahabharata*. Six out of them are purely mythological plays, three are semi-historical, two are social and two are children's plays. All his plays are poetic and easily bring to our minds the poetic plays of W.B. Yeats or of Rabindranath Tagore. In these poetic plays, he employs the almost medieval but poetic and picturesque Kannada tinctured with Sanskrit phraseology.

Dr. Prabhushankara has translated his three plays into English for the benefit of the non-Kannada readers. The first among them is *A Throat for a Thumb*, which deals with the life of Ekalavya and his devotion to his Guru Acharya Drona. Kuvempu has been a champion of the downtrodden in his philosophy of life. He has upheld the dignity and sanctity of the Sudras as against the Brahmins in the Indian context. His play, *Ekalavya* holds mirror to his subaltern vision of life. The very fact that he has chosen this theme shows the politics of creative writing. He has problematized the burning issues of Hindu society like caste-hierarchy and class conflict prevalent in India right from the ancient days. His revolutionary thinking and writing perhaps owe something to his early training in the Ramakrishna Ashrama of Mysuru. As all of us know the *Mahabharata* upholds the *varnashrama dharma*, which may be acceptable to the high caste people, but certainly not acceptable to the low-caste people or the non-brahmins in these days of democracy.

In the present play, *A Throat for a Thumb* Kuvempu has borrowed the outline of the story from the Mahabharata, but has filled with flesh and blood by highlighting the psychological dilemmas, tensions, and politics of emotions like jealousy, which have a universal appeal. Ekalavya the protagonist of the play belongs to the low caste hunter community, who was trained in archery by Acharya Drona efficiently in the past. Acharya Drona was full of appreciation for Ekalavya's achievement in his bowmanship, in spite of his being denied the privileges and luxuries of royal life. That is why Ekalavya has developed great respect for his guru and is ready to offer his fee to his preceptor (*gurudaksina*) at the right time. The play is set in a thick forest with a waterfall in the background and known for its sublime beauty and grandeur. Kuvempu displays his special love and capacity for the description of Nature in all its pretty and ferocious aspect.

The central conflict depicted in the play is the one between Acharya Drona's moral dilemma and his disciple, Ekalavya's unalloyed devotion and dedication to his guru. This conflict is shown on the stage directly, whereas the conflict between Arjuna's jealousy and Ekalavya's high achievement in his archery is depicted indirectly.

The play begins with his remembrance of his guru and his reverential gratitude to him. He has painted an image of his Guru on the face of a rock in the forest, which happens to be his place of action (*karmabhumi*). He has the highest concept of his guru, which is in line with the Hindu concept of a guru in general. He offers his salutations to his guru as follows:

The Guru is Brahma, the Guru is Visnu,
The Guru is Maheswara,
The Guru himself is the Para-Brahman,

I bow my head to the Guru.
I bow down my head to the Guru
Who opened the eyes of one like me—
Who was blind through ignorance—
By prying my eyes with his eye-stick
And applying the balm of knowledge. (p. 3)

He acknowledges his debt to his guru, who has offered him the knowledge of the Almighty God and of his own self, and burnt the bonds of his *karma*. Thus, he considers his guru as an embodiment of absolute knowledge and who is beyond all the triple *gunas*.

When he is in the thick of the forest and reminiscing about his guru, his mother comes there to offer him his lunch. But he plays a few franks and surprises her by hiding himself behind the rock and the waterfall and calls her. But she mistakes it to be the voice of a ghost or a spirit of the waterfall. She reveals in her surprised mood how her son is a forlorn and lonely boy, who has neither brother nor sister and who has lost his father at an early age. She remembers her past sorrow of having lost her husband and having brought him up with great care and deep concern. All these details, obviously, reveal Ekalavya's dire conditions of life. Unlike the royal personages like Arjuna and the Pandavas, he has no comforts of life and no emotional anchorage except the love of his mother. That is why he has great respect for his mother. He says:

While your love is the light of my life,
Bird and beast, mountain and ravine,
Sky and forest—everything is bright.
Sans you everything is naught. (p. 14)

He tells her further how he has achieved expertise in different skills of martial art like *jala-stambhana* and *sabdavedhi*, etc. He tells her with great confidence how he has achieved them:

Long ago have I left behind that crawling stage,
Thanks to my preceptor that art is at my finger's tips;
Tiger or lion, cobra or mighty elephant,
Be it near or far, or even unseen,
I but bend the bow, aim the arrow,

Think of my Guru, and shoot,
Know for certain, never can I miss my mark!
Did I not tell you the other day
Of an incident that occurred a while ago? (p. 15)

He tells her about how he is expecting the arrival of his guru, Acharya Drona and wants to have his lunch only after treating his guru.

But Acharya Drona is in a great moral dilemma, which he cannot reveal to his own son, Ashwatthama, who accompanies him to the forest, where they are to meet Ekalavya, the hunter boy. Then Ashwatthama suspects something sinister in the intention of his father. Acharya Drona asks his son not to be present when he meets his disciple, but Ashwatthama is really puzzled by this strange request by his father. Acharya Drona attributes his moral dilemma to his Fate. As he had to teach the martial arts like archery and others, he was trapped in a labyrinth of obligation of some kind. As Arjuna had carried out Acharya Drona's order, the latter had promised him to grant him whatever boon the former had desired from his guru. Acharya Drona's order to Arjuna smacked of his concealed pride and trapped him in an inescapable shackle of obligation:

Our ego is the root cause of all our sins.
Were it not so, why did I, as Arjuna's preceptor,
Give room in my heart to the devil of my pride,
Cause Arjuna to go and humiliate Drupada
And drag him and drop him at my feet—thus falling
Under the obligation of that ambidextrous youth?
Why would I have given him my word,
That I would make of him a bowman
Unequalled in all the three worlds?
And now that fellow is all possessed
With the devil of a longing after fame:
Name, name, nam!
The madness that his own name
Should be matchless in all the three worlds!
What pride these Princes have!

Pride of a name, nothing but puddles of blood!
Arena of battle, and agony for the world!
A name forsooth! It's nothing but mire,
A bloody, gory mire! (p. 36)

He broods about how pride and knowledge vitiate a man's morals and how even a prince like Arjuna suffers from professional jealous due to his obsession with name and fame in the world. Arjuna does not like a hunter lad like Ekalavya to be equal to him in the art of archery and in the expertise in *sabdavedhi* and other special skills. Nor does he want to invite the hunter lad and challenge him for a competition as he thinks it below his dignity to fight and compete with a boy of the low class and of hunter community. Thus, the class consciousness and caste considerations occupy the mind of Arjuna. He therefore refuses to fight with Ekalavya and defeat him thereby proving his own matchlessness. He wants to take advantage of his guru's promise to him to make him matchless in the world; he traps his guru, Drona in his own promise. Acharya Drona self-scrutinizes and makes his inner dilemma quite explicit to the audience as follows:

Drupada had been humbled,
And the flame of my pride had been fanned.
In that joyful moment I said to him;
"Arjuna, in appreciation of your action,
I take this pledge: I will impart
To you such mastery over bowmanship
That there will be none to equal you
In all the three worlds; I will raise your name
Too the very heavens; and I will carve it
In letters of blood on the foreheads of all the
Elephants that are stationed in all the directions carrying the earth.
It will be your fame that Acharya Drona
Has no other disciple who can excel you." (p. 42)

It is this promise to Arjuna that entangles him in a moral dilemma. He attributes his dilemma to the invisible Fate. Although Arjuna is ambidextrous (*savyasachi*), he is jealous and afraid of

Ekalavya who has mastered all the specialized skills in archery. That is why Acharya Drona honestly expresses the cause of his moral dilemma to Ekalavya himself:

> It's by displaying on that day
> Your mastery of *sabdavedhi* to that son of Pandu
> That you have entangled me in this moral dilemma. (p. 52)

Now that Ekalavya has achieved expertise in his archery thereby stealing a march over Arjuna, Acharya Drona's pledge is broken. But he has got to keep the word that he has given to Arjuna. That is why he has come to the forest to helplessly ask for his fee (or *gurudaksina*).

Ekalavya has such great respect for his guru that he is willing to sacrifice anything for him. He waits for the guru's request or rather order:

> What then is the course for me? Pray tell me Acharya.
> I offer to the Guru what he himself has given me.
> Can that be called an act of sacrifice? No, it is the highest gain. (p. 53)

Then Acharya Drona tells him about his moral dilemma and asks him not his life but just a thumb as his *gurudaksina*:

> For *daksina* I ask your *daksina* thumb!
> That thumb which is the very life of your bowmanship,
> That thumb which mounts the arrow and draws the bowstring!
> Why are you silent? Are you upset my boy? (p. 54)

Although Ekalavya is shocked by the Guru's request, he soon composes himself and recounts his dream that he saw the previous night and his readiness to offer anything to the Supreme Spirit. Now Acharya's Drona's demand for the thumb has come as a corollary to that dream. Ekalavya's reverence to his guru is so great that he readily chops off his right thumb with the sharp edge of his arrow on a piece of rock and offers it to him:

> Pray accept Gurudev, this is your *daksina*.
> This *daksina* thumb of mine!
> Bless me, Gurudev, and save this child of yours. (p. 57)

Although Acharya Drona has received his *daksina* from Ekalavya and fulfilled his promise to Arjuna, he knows that he has entered the chain fatal causality. He knows that he cannot escape from the consequences of his *karma*. He looks rather depressed and tells Ekalavya, "A throat for a thumb/ My head for the thumb, my son!" (p. 58). He seems to see his own future forecast ominously in the mirror of blood. As he tells Ekalavya:

> But I saw quite another sight, my boy,
> A horrible sight!
> After you were gone, I came and sat by the blood;
> To pick up the severed thumb I bent down a little,
> And I saw my own shadow in that mirror of blood;
> Even as I was dismayed at the distortion of my face,
> A giant hand, clutching a sword, pounced upon me
> And cut off the throat of that shadow of mine!
> My severed head rolled down! I saw....
> My trunk without a head! Seeing that sight, I cried out to you!
> What is in store for me?
> Only Fate knows. And Fate seems to have decided
> To sever my head for the thumb I have severed! (p. 59)

He attributes his action to the consequences of his *karma* and expresses his helplessness in the working out of the Fate of man in general. His so-called crime has prepared him to receive the proper punishment at the right time in future. Thus, action and reaction goes on moving on in a chain fashion, almost like in any Greek tragedy.

When Ekalavya's mother discovers the stains of blood on his robes and the pool of blood on the rock she forces him to tell what exactly has happened to him. He then tells her that the thumb is his. But the mother guesses what might have happened and cannot simply tolerate such a sacrifice demanded by his guru. She therefore curses the man:

> He, who has, as sacrifice, my son's thumb extracted,
> Let that sinner's head as sacrifice similar, be severed! (p. 64)

But Ekalavya tells her a lie that his thumb was severed by accident and requests her to go home. He then wants to seek his

Guru's pardon. He picks up the severed thumb from the rock and flings it down into the deep gorge. He sprinkles the water of the waterfall and washes away the blood on the rock. Then he prostrates before the Drona-image and then sits down with crossed legs in the meditative posture. He prays to the Preceptor Divine for dispelling his inner darkness. The play ends at this point.

Though the outline of this play is borrowed from the *Mahabharata*, it is known for its excellent poetry and highlighting the moral dilemma of Chary Drona, Prince Arjuna's jealousy and class consciousness and Ekalavya's highest regard for his Guru microscopically. Arjuna never comes on the stage, although his presence is felt all through it. In a way, this is not a full-length play with a complex plot, but a short play concentrating on one significant episode in the *Mahabharata*. It touches the chords of our heart due to its depiction of the subtleties of human emotions and moral dilemmas. Like Rabindranath Tagore, Kuvempu was poetic and romantic whenever there is a chance for him to describe Nature. For example, in this play he offers lengthy description of trees, creepers, rock and the waterfall and the cries of wild animals.

This play is staged quite often by the amateur actors and actresses in many Youth Festivals of Universities in Karnataka. It easily captures the attention of the audience due to its poetic beauty and stylized action.

***

Kurukshetra, the Graveyard happens to be his second play in this anthology translated into English. The outline of this theme is also borrowed from the *Mahabharata*. It depicts the horrible effect of Kurukshetra war on the last day of the war that lasted for eighteen days continuously. It shows the horror of a battlefield being converted into a graveyard and holds mirror to the inevitable transformation of the joys of life into the sad silence of death. It retrospectively shows how this tragedy happened to due to the greed of the King of Kauravas, Duryodhana and his negligence of the principle of *dharma* or righteousness. Kuvempu offers a heightened psychological picture of the characters of both parties of Pandavas and Kauravas in a very convincing manner. It has the element of sublime horror reminding us of the cosmic drama of creation, protection and destruction following one another. As Kuvempu has explained in his prefatory note, "This play is a symbol. It is the very image of the tragedy of war—of its injustice and cruelty; the destruction it causes and the folly that spurs it; its inescapability; and the destruction of culture" (p. 68).

As we all know Kurukshetra war is the central but terminal event of the *Mahabharata*. It shows the brotherly hostility and jealousy between the Pandavas and the Kauravas, who symbolize the forces of Good and Evil respectively. The same conflict is seen retrospectively on the battlefield which has turned out to be the graveyard now. So the very sepulchral setting of the graveyard creates a somber and dismal atmosphere and makes Man (as also the audience) aware of the final dissolution (or *pralaya*) of life and indicates the end of an era, Dwapara Yuga. In the grave battle of Kurukshetra, the cousin brothers like the Pandavas and the Kauravas have fought with each other for the sake of land and power (and woman) and prestige, the vicious ones like the Kauravas have been vanquished by the virtuous ones like the Pandavas thereby showing the triumph of Truth and righteousness over falsehood and vice.

The battleground of Kurukshetra provides the setting of the play, which begins with Dwapara Yuga-Purusha, who is a personification of Dwapara Yuga, the third in a series of four Yugas. The graveyard is conspicuous for its unbearable silence. So Dwapara comments upon this ultimate silence following the clamorous conflict between human beings; between enemies and inimical forces. The very invention of the character like a personification of Dwapara Yuga holds mirror to Kuvempu's fertile creative imagination and provides a cosmic background to the whole event. Dwapara asks a few pertinent questions, which happen to be the fundamental questions of life in general:

> How is it, that today this Kurukshetra of the Bharata War
> Wears the silence of a cremation ground?
> The blaring of the war trumpets penetrating all the quarters,

The dreadful clamour of the taunts of impetuous, hilarious warriors,
And the clang of the clashing swords of valiant fighters—
All these sounds which I used to hear every day
Are heard no more. (p. 70)

He misses the twang of bowstrings, the clash of swords, the whinnying of horses and the trumpeting of elephants. He misses gigantic heroes like Bhima and others. He comments on the nature of the battlefield very philosophically and seriously:

Until today Kurukshetra was the battleground
Of kings; it has now become the blasted field
Bearing stacks of corpses due to rot!
But yesterday this was the playground for mighty heroes;
Today it is the graveyard for specters to play on!
What are battlefields but a vast graveyard.
And what is a battle but a mass massacre?
What is victory? It is the lament of the vanquished
And the gloating of the victors. (p. 71)

He mentions how the great heroes like Duryodhana, Karna and others have been vanquished by the enemies and lying dead on the battlefield. Dwapara Yuga feels sad that Kali Yuga should meet him on the Kurukshetra battlefield in order to charge of the age from the former. But Kali Yuga tells Dwapara Yuga philosophically not to grieve over it as the processes of creation, evolution, and destruction have to follow each other in a cyclical sequence:

All the divine sport of creation
Lives in evolution and dissolution.
Why grieve over it? Of the treasure seen in a dream
Vanished upon waking, it's not proper to cry over it. (p. 75)

As Dwapara Yuga grieves over the death of great *brahmacharis* like Bhishma and heroes and givers of charity like Karna, Kali Yuga consoles him by saying that in Kali Yuga greater heroes will be born and greater achievements will be accomplished by people in science and knowledge, endowed with a wider outlook, although they may be pigmies in physical stature. He reminds

Dwapara Yuga that there is a new creation dormant if destruction and that there is a new life latent in death and that Time will roll on cyclically. Now that Dwapara Yuga is convinced or rather silenced by Kali Yuga, he gives charge of the Age to Kali Yuga by presenting him his crown and sword formally thereby symbolically showing the transfer of power to the latter.

At that time an enormous number of relatives of the dead warriors are moving towards the Kurukshetra battlefield to trace their kith and kin and take away their dead bodies for proper cremation. The battlefield has become "a storehouse of corpses and the domain of nocturnal specters" (p. 79).

In the next scene Girvana, Chanura and Nilaksha the three loyal servants of Duryodhana, the king of Kauravas, are searching for the dead body of their master and his close associate, Karna the great giver of charity. Chanura remembers King Duryodhana's love and concern for his servant like himself with a sense of deep gratitude.

Like the royal servants, an ordinary woman, the wife of an ordinary foot soldier also has come to the battlefield along with her child to trace the dead body of her husband, who had gone to the battlefield to fight and return triumphant. But now she is shocked to see that her husband is lying like a rotting corpse in the graveyard, which has become his home. She philosophizes that "He is now neither father nor husband, neither relative nor friend nor foe! He is now no one's elder or younger brother" (p. 84). The child's innocent questions and the mother's sorrowful answers rally touché the chords of our heart deeply. Kuvempu has displayed his knowledge of human nature and psychology microscopically and beautifully in a heart-rending manner.

In the next scene, three Devils visit the graveyard in order to feed on the dead bodies of the warriors, but appreciate their heroism and attribute the mass massacre to the sport of Fate. By that time a ripe Old Woman visits the graveyard in search of her dead son, Narayana and laments his death by remembering him sadly and nostalgically. Then Krishna and Vidura come there. On Vidura's asking him a few fundamental questions, Krishna replies to him that he would release whoever (whether friend or foe) utters his name at the time of his death, from the cycle of mortality and grant him salvation. Thus, Krishna displays his divine compassion. At the same time he makes his omniscience and omnipresence and perfection known to Vidura as follows:

> Vidura, you are a *Bhaktiyogin*,
> The *Vedas* and the *Sastras* are the voice
> Of but a part of me, they are not the whole truth.
> My heart is larger than the *Vedas* and *Sastras*,
> Than the voice of the *Yogins* and of the *Munis*.
> There is room—nay, happiness—in my heart for
> Sinners whom the *Vedas* refuse to harbor,
> Whom the *Sastras* do not permit even to approach,
> Whom *Siddhas* and the *Yogins* will not receive.
> There is no one whom I shun—
> There is room in me for all.
> Listen to this secret: I do not recognize Don'ts.
> Morality, Truth and Dharma are my ornaments,
> They are not fetters that bind me.
> Noblest among my devotees,
> I am not a mere bundle of Principles;
> Nor am I a mere Person;
> Know this of me—I am the Primeval Consciousness,
> The Primeval Bliss Incarnate! (p. 91)

Thus, Lord Krishna makes it quite clear to Vidura that the entire human drama is part of His cosmic Drama or Frolic Play (*Lila*). Obviously, it becomes clear that Kuvempu has presented not the pastoral and romantic Krishna but the metaphysical Krishna, who is identical with the Lord Supreme or the Brahman.

In the next scene, Dhritarashtra, the blind king and his wife Gandhari, who is blindfolded come to the battlefield accompanied by Sanjaya in search of their son, Duryodhana. Dhritarashtra wishes to be dead as well as he has been blind and grieves over the death of his beloved son. Likewise Bhanumati, the Queen of Duryodhana also comes there accompanied by a maid in search of her husband's body. The whole scene is heart-rending due to the irreparable loss of lives of the beloved ones.

In the next scene, the Pandavas like Dharmaraja, Bhima, Arjuna, Draupadi and others enter the Kurukshetra graveyard seeking their children and relatives like Ghatotkacha, Abhimanyu, and others. Dharmaraja exclaims sadly about the park of Dharma being burnt up in the fire of Bhima's might. And Bhima replies that there is nothing to lament about as the park of *adarma* is being burnt up by *dharma*. At that time an anonymous soldier, who is dying, cries for water, but Bhima wants to know if the soldier belongs to his party or to the enemy's. But Dharmaraja scolds him by asking him to shed his enmity after the enemy is vanquished and show some humanitarian mercy to the soldier. Accordingly, Bhima offers some water to the soldier, who drinks the water but feels sad to have received it from the enemy's hand thereby displaying his loyalty to his master, Duryodhana. In such situations Kuvempu has shown his remarkable insight into the human nature and the psychology of political loyalty. Even Bhima appreciates the anonymous soldier's loyalty to his master.

In the next scene, Duryodhana, the Kaurava Emperor requests Ashwatthama to cremate Karna with him as they want to be united in death as in life. Then he thinks about his plight in life. He accuses Acharya Bhishma and Acharya Drona:

> By trusting you all, I deceived myself!
> O Granddad Bhishma! O my Acharya!
> Did not all of you belong to my side?
> To me you gave but your body,
> But to them you gave your mind and heart!
> Just for the sake of bread—
> Not because you loved me, I know that well—
> Purely for the sake of bread.
> You were on my side, and for the sake of appearances,
> You pretended to fight for me, did you not?...
> Wearing the guise of *Dharma*, all of you tricked me! (pp. 102-03)

By then Dwapara meets the Kaurava Emperor and tells him that his reign ends that day, that he has transferred his power to Kali and that he has come to bid him farewell. Then Duryodhana talks ironically about Krishna and their entire group and Krishna's so-called treachery and making a mockery of *dharma*. By then Krishna himself comes there meets Duryodhana and clarifies his doubts:

O King of kings, I am not the foe
Who destroyed your empire;
Is it not you yourself who destroyed yourself?
I am not the sinner who, out of envy and spite,
Deceived the Pandavas under the pretext of playing dice
And drove them away to the forest.
Nor am I the sinner who provoked Dharma
By trying to outrage the modesty of Draupadi
In the open court, before the every eyes of all dignitaries.
Nor yet am I the sinner who lit up the flames of war
By turning a deaf ear to me
When I begged of you to give a tiny bit
Of land to the sons of Pandu,
Scorning the grand counsel of all elders
You yourself are the cause of your ruin!
Behold how this war of Kurukhetra
Has now become the veritable domain of Lord Rudra,
Through your own folly. Is it not through you
That Bhishma, Drona and others—
The priceless gems of the Dwapara age—
Have all been smashed to smithereens? (pp. 105-06)

Then Lord Krishna pardons Duryodhana in spite of the latter's accusation and complaint against former and tells him that everybody is an actor in the Cosmic Drama and that Duryodhana has played his part well and that even Karna has played his part quite well. This part of the scene looks like a dream vision. After this is broken Dhrutarashtra, Gandhari and Sanjaya see the dead body of Emperor Duryodhana and lament over it bitterly.

In the next scene, Krishna and Vidura visit the battlefield of Kurukshetra and tells Vidura that "The mother who threw away the baby from the cradle has come to see her darling son in the graveyard" (p. 110). Then we see Mother Kunti coming to the same battlefield searching for her darling son, Karna. She has to tell her son Sahadeva that Karna is also her son born before her marriage. She suggests to him that Karna was her adulterine son, although she does not reveal the details. Sahadeva is really puzzled by the revelation of the truth by his mother, but cannot do anything about it, "It is Karna, the apple of my eye, who was the offspring of my maidenly love! My eldest son, eldest of all of you" (p. 111). She feels a deep sense of embarrassment in owning her adulterine son, Karna the giver of charity and displays her maternal affection and bereavement. Kuvempu has shown his great creative talent in analyzing the psychology of Mother Kunti and her moral dilemma.

In the next scene, Kuvempu has depicted another interesting scene wherein he has shown the mutual horror perpetrated by the soldiers of two inimical groups. An Old Woman and a Young Mother search for their relatives on the battlefield and at last find the corpses of both of them. The irony is that both the son of the Old Woman and the husband of the Young Mother are dead by stabbing each other. The Young Mother says, "Alas, grandma, look you here: this wretch has stabbed my husband to death. Alas!... Accursed by the Kauravas!" (p. 117). The Old Woman bursts out, "Alas, alas, your husband has stabbed my son to death...accursed by the Pandavas!" (p. 117).

In the next scene, Dharmaraja and Bhima visit the battlefield and find the dead bodies of Ghatotkacha and Abhimanyu. Bhima grieves over the loss of his beloved son Ghatotkacha and then understands the agony of King Dhritarashtra and Queen Gandhari who have lost all of them hundred and one sons. By then Kunti and Sahadeva bring the dead body of Karna and Kunti asks Bhima to cremate the body of Karna. But Bhima hates to do that as Karna the wretch has killed his sons on the battlefield. But then Sahadeva gently brings to their mind that Karna is none other than their own eldest brother and Kunti supports that truth in a vague manner, but requests them to cremate Karna properly. Then Dharmaraja and Bhima are surprised by the revelation of the harsh truth. Then Arjuna blames Krishna for lying to him and making him kill his own eldest brother, Karna. Mother Kunti blames herself as a sinner who was the cause of the murder of her own beloved eldest son. This scene, obviously, shows the irony of human life, which is brought out by Kuvempu in a convincing and touching manner.

The last scene is very interesting for its philosophical conclusion and prophesy about the Kali Yuga that is about to begin. It holds mirror to Kuvempu's originality and creative imagination. In this scene Rudra, the destructive aspect of Lord Siva appears on the battlefield-turned-graveyard and has a dialogue with Lord Krishna. Rudra suggests that all creation followed by protection comes at last to the stage of destruction by way of completing one circle and paving the way for the next cosmic cycle. He says rightly:

> All charities, all vows
> Come here at last,
> All come to me!
> All vices, all virtues
> Turn to ashes at last
> At one laugh of mine. (p. 123)

He says further that the creation, which came into being out of his mad impulse will at last become his morsel, to his mad impulse; and that this is the beginning of the world and the final terminal end. Then Lord Krishna acknowledge Rudra's final act of tragedy and appreciates him for successfully completing his cosmic duty of destruction. Likewise Lord Rudra also appreciates Lord Krishna for playing his Cosmic Drama so well and perfectly along with its beauty and terror and being replete with all the nine *rasas*. Then Lord Krishna acknowledges and welcomes the onset of Kali Yuga at the termination of Dwapara Yuga and predicts about the arrival of great religious men, poets, emperors, and great historical happenings. Here Kuvempu has shown his remarkable views on the world historical movements by bringing them up to the present contemporary age of twentieth century. He makes Lord Krishna predict the arrival of great religious leaders like Bhagavan Buddha, Jesus Christ, Muhammad, Acharya Shankara, and Ramakrishna Paramahamsa; the Greek and Roman Empires, the British Empire, the Mughal Empire; Maharashtra, the Kannada Land, the Vijayanagara Empire; the great world wars, revolutions, breakdown of imperialism, progress in science and technology; universal democracy, enthronement of the Common Man, world peace and prosperity. Kuvempu's prediction about the modern Kali Yuga is both negative and positive, and both fearful and hopeful. He has thus brought the mythological theme up to the present age and made it a part of his wish-fulfillment. It holds mirror to Kuvempu's discovery of relevance of the *Mahabharata* mythology to the present age.

The play is known for its sublime theme having the cosmic dimensions and philosophical height. At the same time is known for its beautiful poetry. Kuvempu may be easily compared and contrasted with Bhisham Sahani in the depicting the sublime and serious theme of the *Mahabharata* in their plays like *Kurukshetra, the Graveyard* and *Andh Yug* respectively.

The Sudra Ascetic happens to be his last play in this anthology of translated plays. It holds mirror to Kuvempu's subaltern vision and reversion and revision of the *Ramayana* theme in an intelligent and creative manner. In the *Ramayana* of Valmiki, the protagonist, Rama is shown to be an upholder of caste hierarchy (*varnasrama dharma*). But Kuvempu, like any rational man, refuses to believe in it as Rama happens to be divine figure and cannot be said to be partial only to the upper caste Brahmins and against the *sudras*. He thinks that this passage in the epic must be an interpolation inserted by some later writers to support their own belief in *varnasrama dharma*. He therefore has shown his courage of conviction by revising the passage according to his humanist vision thereby showing Rama in a better light, as a supporter of merit rather than of mere caste.

He therefore invents beautiful characters like Bhairava, the Tree Spirit and Death in the manner of English Morality Plays and sets the theme in motion. The first scene is set in a thick forest where Sage Sambuka, a Sudra ascetic has been practicing his severe penance and is immersed in his yogic trance so much that anthills have grown around him. Bhairava, the Tree Spirit has been guarding the forest in order to protect the ascetic from wild beasts. By then Death itself comes there in order to save the ascetic. Their dialogue is very interesting:

BHAIRAVA: (*In a terrible voice*)

By Sage Sambukadeva I charge you,
Stop you there like a stone!

DEATH: Hearken O fool!

At the behest of the goddess of *Dharma*

It is to save the honour of Sage Sambuka
That I have come here.
You are but his body-guard;
But I am the guard of his very self-respect!
Now that you have learnt the truth,
Make way for me. Do not become a laughing stock. (p. 132)

Then Death tells Bhairava how Sri Ramachandra has come to the forest to rectify the wrong done to a Brahmin, who says he has lost his son because of the sacrilege committed by a *sudra* Sambuka by engaging himself in penance. According to the Brahmin plaintiff this sacrilege should not have been committed in Sri Rama's Land of Righteousness.

In the second scene, we are shown the Brahmin going to the palace of Rama at night. Then he praises Rama as the guardian of Ayodhya, King of the solar Line, embodiment of love, righteousness and forgiveness and sublime like Mount Meru. When Sri Rama comes out of his palace and asks him about the purpose of his meeting him the Brahmin complains to him about the loss of his son due to the sacrilege committed by Sambuka:

What else?
Is it not enough that Dharma
Incensed by the penance of that Sudra
Has sent a curse? (p. 136)

He requests King Rama to rectify the wrong and restore the life of his son. He requests Rama to accompany him to the forest where his son's corpse is lying. Sri Rama asks him if there has been a violence of Dharma in his kingdom of righteousness. Then the Brahmin accuses Sri Rama himself as the cause of the unfortunate event, i.e. the death of his son. Then Sri Rama exclaims:

Am I the sole cause of all wrongs?
That day the washerman blamed me,
And today this Brahmin is doing likewise. (p. 142)

Then the Brahmin takes Sri Rama's to the forest known as Sambuka's Hermitage and tells him that a Sudra bearing the name of Sambuka and an infidel has been practicing penance in the guise of an ascetic much against the injunctions of the Sastras. Sri Rama ponders for a little while and asks the Brahmin if he has done his obeisance to the ascetic. But the Brahmin refuses to do obeisance to a Sudra ascetic and explains it further:

> It is to the unrighteousness
> Committed by a Sudra
> By performing penance
> And transgressing the law of *varnasrama*
> That one of your body-subjects became the victim...
> He died of snake-bite! (*Weeps*) (p. 144)

Then Sri Rama understands the mean and heinous attitude of the Brahmin and thinks about it inwardly thus:

> How shall I teach a lesson to this old fool,
> Who is blinded by the arrogance of caste
> And has misunderstood the scriptures?
> Sambuka is a great Yogi.
> Incensed by the great dishonor done to the ascetic,
> Dharma has brought about the untimely death
> Of this old man's darling son in my very kingdom.
> This man who cannot realize his own wrong doing
> Is indirectly blaming me
> And directly abusing Yogi Sambuka. (pp. 144-45)

Then Sri Rama asks the Brahmin to show him the forest so that he may invoke Dharma to rectify the wrong:

> O twice-born, show me the Sambuka forest.
> Let us go there and wipe out unrighteousness.
> In Rama's kingdom, unrighteousness itself is death,
> And the destruction of unrighteousness is victory over death:
> The victory of Dharma is the defeat of death!
> If righteousness is restored, your son will be revived. (p. 145)

But when the Brahmin takes Sri Rama to the spot where the anthill stands covering Sage Sambuka, Sri Rama's reaction is contrary to the Brahmin's expectation. Sri Rama feels hurt by the Brahmin's complaint but yet inwardly he compares Sambuka to Valmiki, who was also a Sudra:

That seer-poet, too, even like this Sambuka,
Is a Sudra, is he not?
One who had been a hunter,
But, performing austere penance,
Rose to the status of a Maharshi?
Is there anything that can match
The power of penance? (p. 149)

Thus, Sri Rama reasons with the Brahmin about the greatness of penance. But the Brahmin defends himself and his *varnasrama dharma* by saying that the Vedas have forbidden a Sudra from practicing penance and that though milk is life-giving, the milk of a bitch is forbidden and so on and so forth. Sri Rama tells the Brahmin that an ordinary weapon will not be able to kill Sambuka as he happens to be a great sage, but the Brahmin urges him to use his Brahmastra on Sambuka. Thus, Sri Rama helplessly uses his Brahmastra, but to the Brahmin's chagrin the deadly weapon begins to circumambulate around Sage Sambuka humbly instead of harming him. Not merely that. Sri Rama gives him a hint that his Brahmastra, which could not harm Sage Sambuka, will have to pursue the Brahmin for his sacrilege of maligning the great yogi. He says:

Obeying my command will not suffice.
You must open your eyes of true judgement;
Then the father shall survive,
And the son, too, shall survive. (p. 153)

Now the Brahmin understands that his own life is in danger and realizes his folly and caste-arrogance and requests Sri Rama to save his life by repenting over his arrogance. Then Sri Rama makes it more explicit by saying that the sanction of the *Sastras* is not needed to do the right deed by the right mind. Sri Rama's words are supported by an invisible voice from Heaven, which declares that no decision should be reached without reason and that any irrational decision will be tantamount to the undoing *Dharma*. Now the Brahmin is really frightened by Sri Rama's words and realizes his folly and confesses it openly:

O thou wise one, I am now enlightened.
You have truly taught me a proper lesson—
Me who was hidebound in old custom,
Who had thoroughly misread the Sastras,
Who was blinded in caste-arrogance?
Whatever may be the kind of tree,
Does it make any difference?
Could there be discrimination between fire and fire?
Does a spreading blaze show any discrimination?
Worthy of veneration are all ascetics,
What matters it who are
That are hallowed by penance.
Prostrating to them is indeed a blessing,
And scorning them a foul, heinous sin! (p. 154)

Then Sri Rama is happy to notice the Brahmin's repentance and realization of his folly and explains the mystery and greatness of penance to him further:

You will presently realize, sir,
That, however you may honour them,
It will bring great merit.
Can the sublime ever confess
A poor fruit? Even as the sugarcane,
The more it is crushed, the sweeter its juice,
Even as the ocean
The more it is churned, the sweeter the nectar it yields,
So too shall good befall you;
For now you are a God-like vipra! (p. 155)

Thus, the transformation brought about by the *brahmastra* wielded by Sri Rama has effected the much required change of heart and mental attitude in the Brahmin. He, therefore, like a chastened soul, moves step by step and falls at the feet of Maharshi Sambuka. Consequently, the entire wood is a stir with joy and there is a shower of blossoms. The trumpet of Heaven blares. The spirit of Death runs away, fast, faster until it disappears from sight. Now the Brahmin's dead son gets up as he is revived by the blessings of Sri Rama and of Sage Sambuka. Sri Rama asks the boy to:

Bow down to that great ascetic, O son of the twice-born,
By the sage's grace, you are now, verily a twice-born.
Penance, even from where is it performed
Has far-reaching consequences!
May your hands be my own hands
That have raised you up!
May all prosper!
May the country be free from all impediments!
May the Cosmic Law prosper! (p. 156)

Now the Brahmin folds his hands to the sage Sambuka, whose hands emerge from the thicket and bless them. Then the melody of Heaven fills the atmosphere and there is a shower of blossoms from the heavens.

The play thus shows the final triumph of rationality and the extraordinary importance of penance and defeat of narrow-minded caste discrimination and irrationality practiced by the superstitious Brahmin during the reign of Sri Rama. Obviously, the play holds mirror to Kuvempu's creative imagination, rational approach, subaltern vision and the courage of conviction to revise and correct the interpolated version of the *Ramayana* thereby making it relevant to the modern democratic world.

In all these three poetic plays, Kuvempu has remarkable originality and giving flesh and blood to the outline stories of the *Mahabharata* and the *Ramayana* respectively, not only by revising them in the light of modern knowledge of life, but also making them relevant to our life. The poetic beauty and the elaborate descriptions of Nature and the lyrical melody found in the original Kannada plays easily brings to our mind Rabindranath Tagore's poetic and symbolic plays in many aspects.

Reference

Kuvempu, *Three Plays*. Tr. Prabhushankara. Bangalore: Kannada and Culture, Government of Karnataka.1989. (All the page references are from this edition.)

• • • • •

4

The Vision of Darkness in *Andha Yug*

Dharmavir Bharati (1926-97) the Hindi author was born in Allahabad, Uttar Pradesh. He studied there and participated in the anti-British Quit India movement. He earned a doctorate in Siddha saint literature in 1947, and then became a full-time journalist, editing the weekly *Dharma Yug* from 1960 to 1989. His journal was a war correspondent in Bangladesh in 1971, made a tremendous impact. He was also a poet, novelist and essayist. His two novels, *Gunahonka Devata* (*The God of Sins*) and *Suraj Ka Satvan Ghoda* (*The Seventh Horse of the Sun*) are classics of Hindi literature. He has published five one-act plays under the title *Nadi Pyasi Thi* (*The River was Thirsty*, 1954), often produced by schools, colleges and amateur groups.

He wrote only one full-length play *Andha Yug* (*Blind Age*, 1954), originally as radio drama, now recognized as a classic of modern Hindi theatre. "Set late in the *Mahabharata*, it concerns the eternal values of life that are damaged or broken and re-established again and again." Bharati was deeply perturbed about the perpetual problem of war becoming global and destroying humanity. Obviously reflecting nuclear conflict, his play also interrogated the received wisdom of Krishna's assurances. An epic drama in blank verse, it applied various forms such as folk theatre, Parsi theatre, *Katha-gayan* (singing of tales), and Western tragedy as required. The use of symbols and imagery provided a new dimension to the theme. It was a challenge to directors because the text's poetry and dramatic beauty is not easy to convey. Thus, the premiere had to wait till 1962, produced by Satyadev Dubey on Theatre Unit's rooftop stage in Bombay. Subsequently, the National School of Drama performed it in 1963, directed by Alkazi, and revived it several times. Many directors in other languages, like Ajitesh Bandyopadhyay (Bengali, 1970) and Ratan Thiyam (Manipuri, 1993), also staged important versions.[1]

His play, *Andha Yug*, translated into English by Alok Bhalla, deals with the epical theme of the conflict between the Kauravas and the Pandavas culminating into climax on the eighteenth day of Kurukshetra war. Although the theme is borrowed from the last part of Vyasa's *Mahabharata*, Dharmavir Bharati has accentuated it in such a way that it remains relevant even today. It was written immediately after the Partition of India, but it appeals to the reader even in the twenty-first century, which is vitiated by international terrorism and fundamentalism. Though the story of Kauravas and Pandavas is incidental to it, it achieves the universality of appeal by highlighting the metaphysical conflict between Good and Evil. It is on account of its universality that it becomes relevant in every age and nation.

The play begins with a prologue, which foreshadows the theme in advance. It says that the play is concerned with the age of darkness as described in *Vishnu Purana* in which there would be a decline in prosperity and *dharma* and the whole earth would slowly perish; the one, who has wealth, would rule; the one, who wears a false mask, would be honoured; the one, who is greedy, would be a king; the people, weary of misrule, would hide in dark caves and wait for their days of misery to end. It says further that it was only Lord Krishna, who was dispassionate and detached, whereas all the others were blind and self-absorbed and that the play is the story of enlightenment through the life of the benighted and the blind.

The first at begins with the narrator commenting on the central event and its negative nature, "Both sides in the war/ violated/ the code of honour/ smashed it/ ripped it into shreds/ and scattered it—/ the Kauravas perhaps more than the Pandavas" (p. 27).[2] He comments further that it is a strange war in which both sides are doomed to fail; that blindness rules this age and not reason and that blind fear, blind love, blind power and blind justice shall prevail in the end. The Kurukshetra war is obviously an archetypal one as it suggests the metaphysical war between Good and Evil. Whereas the Kauravas represent Evil, the Pandavas represent Good. The war is necessitated by the blindness of the Kauravas and consequently the Pandavas have suffered countless sorrows. But in the war there has been a reversal of situation. So far Good was helpless against the force of Evil. But Good is slowly gaining victory over Evil. As a consequence of this unwanted war the common people feel that their whole life has become meaningless. For example, the two guards express their opinion, which voices that of the common people. They say that they are very tired but yet they have to march up and down guarding these desolate corridors. They are unhappy to learn that the Kaurava queens, who once wandered gracefully like the fragrant breeze, have become widows now. They are sad to notice that the Kaurava Kingdom is ruled by an old and blind ruler and therefore all their actions are meaningless. Now the guards are surprised to see the Kaurava Kingdom is overcast with thousands and thousands of ravenous vultures, which are eager to feed on the dead. The guards consider them as a bad and dreadful omen. The shadow of the vultures indicates physical darkness symbolizing other kinds of darkness like ocular, psychological and one moral ones. King Dhritarashtra's blindness is indicative of ocular darkness. Queen Gandhari's voluntary blindfolding of her eyes shows her extraordinary loyalty to her husband. But both of them, in addition to being physically blind (or blindfolded) are morally blind also because of their blind affection for and attachment to their children, i.e. Kauravas. The different kinds of blindness unfold themselves as the play proceeds forward.

When Vidura comes to see King Dhritarashtra, the guard tells him that the king could not see the terrifying scene of war, as he is physically blind. He is waiting for the latest news bulletin to be brought by Sanjaya. But when Vidura meets the king, the latter confesses that he is afraid for the first time in his life. Vidura tells him,

Afraid?
The fear you experience today
Had gripped others years ago. (p. 33)

Vidura reminds the king that the latter had been warned by Bhishma and Dronacharya and that Krishna had also advised him,

Do not violate the code of honour.
If you violate the code of honour
It will coil around the Kaurava clan
Like a wounded python
And crush it like a dry twig. (p. 33)

But King Dhritarashtra had not bothered to listen to this advice. On the contrary his physical blindness was accentuated by the moral blindness caused by his filial attachment to his sons,

My sons were the flesh of my flesh
They were the final arbiters of truth for me.
My love for them was my law
My code of honour. (p. 34)

In other words, his attachment to his sons is an extension of his selfishness, which prevents him from understanding the world from a wider perspective. He has realized his mistake rather belatedly,

Today
I realized
That there is a truth
That lies beyond the boundaries
Of my selfhood.
I realized that only today. (p. 35)

He feels terrified by what he has learnt today. Queen Gandhari also feels that the ideals like *dharma*, duty and honour are mere illusions; that there is a ferocious beast in each man; that everyone is hypocritical and self-interested. She does not have any faith in Krishna. That is why she has blindfolded herself. In the seventeen days of war, all her sons except Duryodhana have been killed one by one. Now she desperately hopes that Duryodhana will be victorious in the war. Thus, when both King Dhritarashtra and Queen Gandhari are waiting for the latest news from Sanjaya, there comes a mendicant, who confesses that his prediction (that the Kauravas shall be victorious) has proved to be false due to the intervention of a stranger man like Krishna. The same view is corroborated by the Guard 2, who says, "And the one they worship as their Lord takes the responsibility for all of them!" (p. 43). But those, who have no faith in the moral order symbolized by Krishna, happen to be the blind King Dhritarashtra and his blindfolded Queen Gandhari.

The second act begins with the chorus, which describes Sanjaya, the rational sculptor of words and his bewilderment in the forest of doubt and confusion. Then Sanjaya himself comes on the stage and expresses his sense of confusion, "I have lost my way on this path of thorns and stones" (p. 47). Although several soldiers have died, Sanjaya has not died. He is very sad to be alive and witness the defeat of the Kauravas by the Pandavas,

> Yes, I am still alive.
> The earth for miles around is strewn
> With the corpses of Kaurava soldiers
> Slaughtered by Arjuna.
> The Kaurava army is scattered;
> All its heroes are dead. (p. 48)

Sanjaya was about to be killed by Satyaki, but Vyasa had told the latter, "Sanjaya cannot die. He is immortal" (p. 49). Sanjaya was cursed by Vyasa, "You will survive disasters, floods, revolutions, and wars of annihilation so that you can tell the truth" (p. 49). Sanjaya is thus destined to tell or report the whole truth of the events like the modern news reporters of the various media. Speaking the bitter truth is indeed a very unpleasant job. He finds it humiliating to tell the whole truth about Duryodhana's death to King Dhritarashtra and his Queen. But Kritavarma exhorts him to be brave enough to tell the truth.

Kritavarma is sad to learn that that Duryodhana is defeated by the Pandavas and that only three of them are alive (i.e. Kritavarma, Kripacharya, and Ahvatthama). Now the scene focuses on Asvatthama and his psychology of revenge. He thinks that his father Dronacharya was cut to pieces by Dhristadyumna when Dronacharya threw down his weapons on the battlefield on hearing Yudhisthira announcing triumphantly the death of Asvatthama, the elephant but giving an impression of the death of Asvatthama, the man (and son of Dronacharya). Thus, according to Asvatthama, his father was killed by the Pandavas immorally and unjustly. Hence, he decides to avenge the death of his father by becoming a metaphorical beast, "I decided to turn myself into a blind, ruthless beast" (p. 52). He wants to be blind and ruthless like a beast and turn his hands into claws, and strangle Yudhisthira for lying and for being responsible for his father's death. In his frenzy he mistakes Sanjaya for a Pandava and wishes to kill him, but Kripacharya prevents him from doing so by clarifying to him, "Sanjaya cannot be killed as he was neutral and took no sides in the war" (p. 55).

Kritavarma says that Duryodhana is still alive and intends to look for him. Sanjaya tells them about the whereabouts of Duryodhana, "With his extraordinary powers he has stilled the waters of a lake. And there unknown to the Pandavas, he sits strangely still in the floor of the enchanted lake" (p. 57).

Meanwhile the Mendicant is rather unhappy to learn that his prediction about the victory of Kauravas over the Pandavas has proved wrong. Asvatthama is also terribly angry with him and finally kills him blindly and indiscriminately. Kripacharya tries to pacify him. Asvatthama confesses how he became a blind medium of revenge and does not know how he killed the Mendicant, "I did not kill him! I was blind with rage. I wanted to annihilate the future, which has been prophesied. Believe me I do not know the old man was killed" (p. 63). Kripacharya suggests to them to sleep and rest for the night.

In the third act, the narrator says that King Dhritarashtra and Queen Gandhari listen to the story of the defeat of Kauravas by the Pandavas narrated by Sanjaya. "His painful story turned Gandhari into stone. Her face pale with sorrow seemed lifeless" (p. 65). The Kaurava soldiers have been limping back to the city in defeat and disgrace. King Dhritarashtra is waiting to hear the news of the last battle between Bhima and Duryodhana. Meanwhile the Guard 1 tells Vidura that an enemy soldier has entered the city with their defeated army and that he is a sorcerer, a shape-changer, who can take any form at will" (p. 69). That soldier is none other than Yuyutsu, the son of Dhritarashtra, who has fought on the side of truth and not on the side of Kauravas, though he belongs to their party. He expresses his views as follows:

> What is my crime?
> That I was on the side of truth?
> No other warrior—
> Neither Drona nor Bhishma—
> dared to oppose Duryodhana.
> Only I had the courage
> To declare:
> I will not fight
> On the side of untruth.
> I may be a Kaurava
> But truth is higher
> Than my clan! (p. 71)

Obviously, Yuyutsu is one of the Kauravas, who retains his moral integrity, loyalty to truth and rational approach to life. He has transcended the selfishness, greed and vengeance indulged in by the Kauravas. He knows that even his mother Gandhari may not like to see him. But Vidura appreciates his position and moral approach to life, "Do not say that. In this evil episode you are the only one of the Kaurava clan, who has held his head high with pride" (p. 72). He asks Yuyutsu further not to bother about the people of the city, who look at him with contempt. When Yuyutsu meets his mother and bows down to her feet, she taunts him about his siding with the enemies and refuses to bless him. Yuyutsu is rather sad about his mother's undignified behaviour. He feels that "It would have been better if I had accepted the untruth" (p. 75). He is so desperate that he thinks his siding with truth has earned his mother's curse and the people's hate and turned out to be a futile act in the final analysis. But Vidura consoles him by advising him, "Great suffering must be endured with grace" (p. 75). Yuyutsu is sad to know that everybody hates him now. He thinks that he is damned but Krishna is victorious wherever he is.

Meanwhile the Guard 1 reports that Sanjaya has brought the news that Duryodhana has been defeated by Bhima in the final battle. The Pandavas are blowing the conch-shells and declaring their victory. But Balarama is enraged with the Pandavas because he thinks that Bhima violated *dharma* in defeating Duryodhana and Bhima's immoral action was abetted by the 'unprincipled rogue' Krishna known for his holiness and cunning.

Kripacharya and Kritavarma also want to take revenge upon the Pandavas, but not through treachery. But Asvatthama is terribly vindictive and wants to be declared as the Commander of the army in Duryodhana's presence. Accordingly, Kripacharya is directed by Duryodhana to anoint Asvatthama as the Senapati of the army. Now Asvatthama decides to wreak vengeance the next morning and orders his soldiers to sleep that night. But he keeps watch by pacing up and down. It is at this time that he happens to see a dance of war between a crow and owl. Then the crow sleeps and the owl watches it nervously. The owl prods him to make sure that he is really asleep and then attacks him. After a ferocious fight between them, the owl kills the crow finally. Asvatthama, who is watching the scene, breaks out of his trance, laughs confidently for having found the truth. He wants to rush to the Pandava camp, where the victorious Pandavas must be unarmed and sleeping and slaughter them mercilessly in the manner in which the owl has killed the crow. He fastens his cummerbund and wants to attack the Pandavas especially when Krishna has gone to Hastinapur to console Gandhari. He says, "Like a beast I will crush Dhristadyumna with my feet—like a mad beast trampling on a lotus-flower. I will not even spare Uttara, who is carrying Abhimanyu's son and the future of the entire Pandava clan in her womb! (p. 88). Kritavarma and Kripacharya try their best to dissuade him from the immoral and treacherous vengeance, but Asvatthama turns a deaf ear to them.

Meanwhile the Mendicant's ghost appears on the stage and deplores the blindness of the people and their inner contradictions. Yuyutsu's spectre deplores his stagnant life symbolized by a firm wheel fixed to a chariot. Sanjaya's spectre laments his uselessness as a decorative wheel. Vidura's spectre laments his faith in the Lord, who is like a useless axle, which has lost its wheels and cannot turn by itself. The spectral vision acts as a commentary on the overall blindness, darkness and meaninglessness of life. The Mendicant's ghost now happens to descry a peacock feather wafting in the air and understands that Lord Krishna is returning from Hastinapur after trying to console Gandhari.

In the fourth act, Asvatthama rushes to the Pandava camp to slaughter them vindictively and mercilessly, but happens to see Lord Shankara, the god of annihilation, standing guard at the gate and challenging him, "Defeat me before you enter" (p. 95). Asvatthama attacks him vehemently but ultimately accepts his defeat and begs the Lord for mercy. Then Lord Shiva blesses him, "Asvatthama, you will be victorious. The Pandavas have lost their sense of righteousness. Because I loved Krishna, I protected them, gave them victory, renewed their confidence. But they have violated the dharma of war and opened the doors for their destruction" (p. 97). Thus blessed by Lord Shiva Asvatthama reaches Dhristadyumna's tent with the speed of lightning and wrings his neck mercilessly. Then he proceeds to kill the Pandava soldiers and Shikhandi also. Likewise Kritavarma and Kripacharya also slaughter the children, old men, and servants heartlessly. Queen Gandhari feels happy to learn about Asvatthama's heroic feat. Duryodhana is still alive and wants to tell something his party men, but cannot. Kripacharya narrates to Duryodhana how Asvatthama has slaughtered the important leaders of Pandava camp. Duryodhana dies after listening to it. Queen Gandhari is so happy about Asvatthama's vindictive heroism that she wants to remove her blindfold, gaze upon Asvatthama and transform his body into a bright diamond. But ironically Sanjaya has lost his vision and therefore cannot show Asvatthama to the Queen. That is because Vyasa has granted him vision only for a limited time of eighteen days.

Now the Kaurava city is desolate and the diamond throne is empty and the people have left to perform the last rites for Gandhari's dead sons. When Yuyutsu meets his father Dhritarashtra, the latter cautions him against Asvatthama's rage and advises him to hide somewhere. But by that time Sanjaya brings the news of the unexpected transformation of Asvatthama from a hero into a fearful coward. He is hit by Arjuna's arrows. Because of his helplessness, Asvatthama releases his Brahmastra at Arjuna, not knowing the dire consequences of it for the earth and mankind. Vyasa explains sadly, "For centuries to come nothing will grow on earth. Newborn children shall be deformed. Men shall become grotesque. All the wisdom men gathered in the *Satya*, *Treta* and *Dwapara Yugs* shall be lost forever. Serpents shall hiss from every ear of corn and rivers shall flow with molten fire" (p. 114). Then Vyasa requests Asvatthama to recall his Brahmastra. But Asvatthama pleads his inability and helplessness, "Vyasa, I am powerless! I only knew how to release the Brahmastra. My father did not teach me how to recall it" (p. 115). Consequently, Asvatthama's Brahmastra is about to destroy the child in Uttara's womb. But again a miracle happens. Krishna saves the child in Uttara's womb by exchanging his life for Uttara's stillborn child. Then Krishna forces Asvatthama to surrender his talismanic gem in exchange for his life, under the shadow of a curse forever. Now Asvatthama bows his head in defeat and leaves the place.

Queen Gandhari removes her blindfold and wants to see Asvatthama, but the latter goes away from there. As his body is covered with boils and open sores, he smells worse than a diseased dog! Vidura tells Gandhari that Krishna has cursed Asvatthama for the sin of infanticide, with immortality and condemned him to live forever and ever. Gandhari mourns the death of her son, Duryodhana and is enraged with Krishna for his incitement of Bhima's *adharma* and his vile curse on Asvatthama. She, therefore, curses him,

> You may be a god
> You may be omnipotent
> Whatever you are
> Whoever you are
> I curse you
> And I curse
> All your friends and kinsmen.
> They shall attack and kill each other.
> They shall eat each other

Like rabid dogs.
And many years later
After you have witnessed
Their destruction
You will return to this forest
Only to be killed
Like a wild animal
By an ordinary hunter! (p. 122)

Krishna accepts Gandhari's curse without any grudge and even explains his divine as well as human aspects,

I may be a god.
I may be omnipotent.
But I am also your son
And you are my mother.
...
If I am life
Then, Mother
I am also death.
I accept your curse, Mother! (p. 123)

The fifth act shows the victory of Pandavas and a series of suicides. Though Yudhisthira has won his throne and his kingdom, he is not really happy. He feels lonely and dejected. He is sad to know that his brothers are either ignorant or foolish; either insolent or weary. He trembles to watch the encroaching darkness and hears the sinister steps of the coming age. Yuyutsu, who upheld *dharma*, is taunted by Bhima and ill-treated by the beggars. He, therefore, commits suicide by plunging a spear into his own heart. Now Yudhisthira's kingdom has grown decadent.

On the contrary, the forest catches fire. Both Gandhari and Dhritarashtra are consumed by the fire. Whereas the Kaurava dynasty is destroyed completely, the Pandava kingdom also comes to an end. Yudhisthira grows increasingly dejected day by day. Slowly, he loses his faith in everything and realizes the hollowness of his victory in the war. He understands that his victory is also a long and slow act of suicide.

The chorus in The Epilogue describes Krishna's death.

He leaned against the tree
Placed his left foot
Shaped like a deer's face
On his right thigh
And with a sigh whispered:
'A strange age has passed'. (p. 148)
...
Mistaking
Krishna's foot for a deer
He draws his bowstring
And takes aim. (p. 150)
...
The stars went out
Darkness covered the earth
And that forest of fear
Became even more terrifying.
The moment Krishna was killed
Dvapara Yug came to an end
And on this god-forsaken earth
Kali Yug took its first step
And that forest of fear
Became even more terrifying. (p. 151)

The death of Krishna represents the beginning of the age of darkness. The chorus strikes an affirmative note that in spite of the overwhelming darkness of Kali Yug, there is a seed of light buried in the human mind and might grow into a big tree of high moral ideals,

And yet it is also true
That like a small seed
Buried somewhere
In the mind of man
There is courage
And longing for freedom
And the imagination to create something new. (p. 161)

The chorus iterates further that the seed, which is buried without exception in each one of us, will grow from day to day in our lives as duty, honour, freedom and virtuous conduct; makes us fear half-truths and great wars and always saves the future of mankind from blind doubt, slavery and defeat.

Presenting even a small chunk of the great epic, the *Mahabharata* in the form of a play is not a joke. It requires a lot of intelligence on the part of the dramatist. He has to present his vision of life through the dramatic medium by showing a few bits of action on the stage, by highlighting the moral ideas through verse, by linking the events on the stage with the off-stage one through choric narration and comments. Thus, the direct (on-stage) and indirect (off-stage) action is linked intelligently and the authorial comment and interpretation is articulated through the chorus. In his note to the directors, Dharmavir Bharati confesses, "The choric songs are arranged between the acts in a style borrowed from the traditions of Indian folk theatre. The chorus is either used to give information about events, which are not shown on stage or to underline the poignancy of the action. Sometimes, it also clarifies the symbolic importance of the events" (p. 19). Although the chorus is borrowed from the Indian folk theatre, it easily resembles the chorus of Greek plays and captures the attention of the spectators.

Dharmavir Bharati has shown his dramatic talent in distributing the theme conveniently into on-stage and off-stage action. For example, Duryodhana and his battle with Bhima or the murder of the Old Mendicant by Asvatthama, or the release of the Brahmastra by Asvatthama, the killing of Krishna by the hunter and such other terrible events are not shown on the stage (or in the form of direct action), but are narrated as happening off-stage (in the form of indirect action). Similarly, the eagle killing the crow and the cloud-like gathering of eagles waiting to devour the dead bodies of Kauravas are shown symbolically on the stage, which holds mirror to Dharmavir Bharati's experimentation with the dramatic technique. *Andha Yug* easily attains the grandeur of a Greek tragedy and succeeds in conveying its universal message. It teaches the modern man the futility of indulging in selfishness, terrorism, fundamentalism and such other evils and suggests an affirmative philosophy of life to be followed for the attainment of true happiness. It offers the moral lesson that Truth will be ultimately victorious, although un-Truth may enjoy some power temporarily. In other words the play is a dramatization of the formula, *satyameva jayate*.

References

1. Lal, Anand, *The Oxford Companion to Indian Theatre*. New Delhi: Oxford University Press. p. 53.
2. Bharati, Dharmavir, *Andha Yug*. Tr. Alok Bhalla. New Delhi: Oxford University Press. p. 27. (All the subsequent page references are to this edition.)

• • • • •

5

Fall of Kalyana: A Historical Play about Religious Revolution

Basaveswara happens to be one of the greatest mystics and social reformers of 12th-century Karnataka and therefore is easily comparable to the other great men of the world like Bhagavan Buddha, Karl Marx, Martin Luther, Mahatma Gandhi, Ambedkar, Nelson Mandela, and so on in different aspects. Mahatma Gandhi said that Basaveswara was one of the earliest free thinkers of India. Basaveswara was so great as a minister, mystic, poet, and social reformer that many Kannada poets like Harihara, Palkurike Somanatha, Bhimakavi have raised him to the level of a legendary figure and glorified his achievements in their short and long narratives. In the twentieth century also many novelists like B. Puttaswamaiah, H. Tipperudraswamy, A. Chandrasekharaiah and dramatists like Yenagi Balappa, Mahadev Banakar, P. Lankesh, Girish Karnad, M.M. Kalburgi, Chandrasekhar Kambar and H.S. Shivaprakash have written their novels and plays dealing with different aspects of Basaveswara's socio-religious revolution in 12th-century Karnataka. Basaveswara's personality is so complex that no writer has so far been able to depict the totality of his life satisfactorily. Every writer has depicted only a couple of aspects of his personality according to his light.

Fall of Kalyana (2003) is the English translation of the original Kannada play, *Kettittu Kalyana* (1996) written by the heavy-weight scholar and Basavologist (and former Vice Chancellor of Kannada University at Hampi), Dr. M.M. Kalburgi (1938-). It is the product and quintessence of his thirty years research in Basava Studies. In fact, it is written as an answer to Girish Karnad's *Tale-Danda*. When Karnad wrote *Tale-Danda* and showed it to Dr. Kalburgi, the latter did not like it and even pointed out its deficiencies. But Karnad, having settled his own pattern of thought, did not and could not revise his play, perhaps because he could not go deep into the vast and complex Basava-lore. Hence, Dr. Kalburgi wrote his play as a corrective to Karnad's play. Obviously, there is a great deal of difference between the two in their treatment of the same theme.

Dr. Kalburgi has chosen for his play the life of Basaveswara, who was a historical personage of 12th-century Karnataka and who consolidated the Virasaiva or Lingayat faith and began a new brand of religion. Naturally, the historical period of Basaveswara shows a transition from Vedic brahmanic orthodoxy to non-Vedic democracy of devotion. Basaveswara may be described as a saint-hero *a la* Carlyle and a world-historical personage in Hegelian parlance. For, he brought in a revolutionary change in the society of Karnataka in social, religious, and literary and linguistic aspects.

One broad difference between the traditional *puranic* poets and the 20th-century writers on Basaveswara is that the formers poetry contains a great deal of mythical, legendary, supernatural, and miraculous elements defying the law of probability, whereas the latter's works are free from these elements and present the life of Basaveswara quite realistically.

Kalburgi's *Fall of Kalyana* belongs to the second group of realistic plays. It is a serious historical play based on the historical characters and events available in historical records. The central conflict in the play is between Basaveswara and the Vedic religion in social, psychological and spiritual aspects. Kalburgi's main intention is to highlight the Virasaiva (or Lingayat) doctrine and therefore he selects only those events in Basaveswara's life which are supportive of such doctrine. Basaveswara'a life, his interaction with people around him is very rich, complex and variegated. But Kalburgi has chosen only the major and representative events of life to highlight the collision between the orthodox Brahmins and the reformist and revolutionary Basaveswara.

The action of the play takes place in three towns, Bagewadi, Kudala-Sangama and Kalyana respectively thereby showing three important phases of Basaveswara's life. Basaveswara is not a mere individual but a representative of a new religion and ideology. Through the depiction of Basaveswara's life, the dramatist suggests the wider panorama of the 12th-century life and the larger ideological collisions. Consequently, he achieves the desired universality of vision through the depiction of historical particularities of 12th-century Karnataka life.

Kalburgi has transformed the selective historical material by following his own method of emplotment, as per the requirements of dramatic technique. As he says in his *Preface*, he was inspired by Attenborough's film, *Gandhi* in mind to write this play, "I had Richard Attenborough's film, *Gandhi* in mind when I wrote this play. Basaveswara's life passed through three stages: one, the *agrahara*-culture of Bagewadi; two, the temple-culture of Kudala-Sangama and three, the palace-culture of Kalyana. All through those stages he grew from the static to the dynamic level and by transforming the former into the latter. He progressed from *karma* to *dharma* in Bagewadi; from the physical to the spiritual in Kudala-Sangama and from the spiritual to the social in Kalyana. Basaveswara, who faced the problems arising in the first two environments, came to the third environment, where he was tortured by the triple force" (*Preface*, p. vii). These three stages of Basaveswara's life have been shown in five acts with varying number of scenes in each act.

The protagonist, Basava's rebellious nature asserts itself at the beginning of the play itself (I. i.). For example, the sacred thread is the great symbol of Vedic Brahmanism. A Brahmin, who is already born physically in the world, becomes twice-born metaphorically when he undergoes the initiation ceremony (*upanayana*) and wears the sacred thread (*janiwara*). It is a compulsory ritual for all Brahmins and others who came under the Brahmanical fold. But Basava, who is a precautious boy with an inborn rebellious spirit in him, refuses to wear the sacred thread in spite of his father, Madarasa's persuasion and is ready even to be excommunicated by the Brahmins of Bagewadi:

BASAVA: No, no. I don't want this sacred thread, which makes me a Brahmin instead of a human being. I would like to follow the path of dharma. I don't want this sacred thread, which pushes me into the swamp of karma. I don't want it. (*The Brahmins of the lane hear these words and rush in.*)

BRAHMINS: What's the matter? Why this crowd? Why so much confusion?

BASAVA: See, today is the Full Moon Day when everybody has put on a new sacred thread. This boy has torn off even the old sacred thread, let alone the new one. (*Addressing Basava*) Basava, please don't protest against the sacred thread, which you have worn for the past six years. Please don't cross the boundary line of tradition. (*They draw him across the threshold.*)

BASAVA: I do cross it. (*He crosses the threshold by dragging both the Brahmins along with him.*) For the past six years I have tried to understand the meaning of the sacred thread. This has been a thread, which simply binds me to *agrahara*-culture. I feel a stifling sensation and have my growth arrested ever since I have worn this thread.

(I. i. pp. 1-2)

But his parents, Madarasa and Madalambika and his maternal uncle, Baladeva, who are traditional Brahmins, are deeply worried about Basava's decision to leave for Kudala-Sangama. Basava refuses to attend the meeting at the *agrahara*-hall where judgment will be given about his sacrilege of abandoning the sacred thread. But his parents forcibly take him to the meeting, where he defies the authority of Vedabhatta, who feels exasperated by Basava's radical views and independent nature, passes judgment on him and excommunicates him and his parents as per *Manusmriti*:

BASAVA: No.

VEDABHATTA: If the boy doesn't wear the sacred thread by tomorrow evening, the whole family would be excommunicated. This is the judgement given by the divine brahmins. Please sound the gong of judgement.

MADARASA: (*Interfering.*) Please wait, Vedabhatta, please wait. Give me a week's time. I shall try to bring the boy round. Kindly give me a week's time.

VEDABHATTA: Impossible! If we yield to you, others also will take advantage of the situation. Consequently the whole brahmanical system would be ruined. At the most.... (*By then, Basava comes there.*)

BASAVA: At the most.... What? Tell me.

VEDABHATTA: At the most, we will not excommunicate your family from the Empire. Instead, we'll restrict it only to the Brahmapuri of Bagewadi.

BASAVA: You excommunicate us from the Brahmapuri? This is, indeed, maladministration in the name of religion. I can live without the help or cooperation of Brahmins. If you have the courage, you may excommunicate us.

MADARASA: (*Embraces his son.*) Please don't, son. Please don't.

VEDABHATTA: I understand. The councilors have resolved to excommunicate the family of Madarasa from the Brahmapuri. Henceforth, the Brahmins of the city should not have any contact with Madarasa's family. This is the judgement given by the divine Brahmins.

PRIEST 1: (*Holding up the Manusmriti.*) This is the judgement of *Manusmriti*. (*The gong of judgement is sounded.*)

BASAVA: I won't accept the *Manusmriti*. On the contrary I defy it. (*He snatches away the book, which falls on the ground and the pages scatter about. Priest I slaps Basava's cheeks. Blood oozes out of his mouth. But he endures the pain of the blow.*) Further, I am leaving for Kudala-Sangama. Kindly bless me. (*He picks up the stick with the bundle of clothes and keeps it on his shoulder and goes away from there without waiting for an answer. People look at his with wonder and sorrow.*)

(I. iii. pp. 9-10)

Basava, thus, rebels against the Vedic way of life so rigidly practiced in the *agrahara* of Bagewadi. He, therefore, leaves for Kudala-Sangama. Being fed up with the meaningless ritualistic *agrahara*-culture of Bagewadi, Basava goes to Kudala-Sangama to pursue his formal education and understand the meaning of life, in the midst of a better environment. The dramatist has shown the conflict between orthodox Brahmanism and the rebellious behaviour of Basava very powerfully in this scene.

After his departure to Kudala-Sangama his father and mother are deeply worried about his absence from home. They sadly remember how Sambhusastri slapped the cheek of their son; and how the orthodox Brahmins cannot tolerate his liberal thinking. They suffer from existential inconvenience caused by the social segregation due to their excommunication. Basava's elder sister, Nagalambika suffers from utter loneliness in his conspicuous absence from home. These events, obviously, show how the orthodox Vedic Brahmanism had a powerful hold on the society and how *Manusmriti* controlled the day-to-day life of people in 12th-century Karnataka (as also in other parts of India).

Basava goes to Kudala-Sangama with a great hope to find an atmosphere which could be congenial to his liberal thinking. But there also he is rather disappointed to see the regular practice of animal sacrifice and rebels against it because of his rational approach to life. When he sits meditation on the istalinga on his palm in the temple of Sangameswara, a few Brahmins bring a sheep and a lamb to sacrifice them there. But Basava, who is horrified to learn about this inhuman practice rebels against it and asks them a few rational questions to which they cannot offer satisfactory answers as they have vested interest in such animal sacrifices.

BASAVA: (*Lifting up the lamb.*) What is this, man?

VIPRA 1: This is the sheep brought for the sacrifice to Lord Varuna. Before we could kill it along with the lamb, it escaped from our hands.

BASAVA: What will you do now?

VIPRA 2: We will take them and sacrifice them. Well gratify Lord Visnu and get rains in return.

BASAVA: All right. Supposing it doesn't rain? (*The Vipras look at each other and disarmed by the question.*) Come on, tell me. What'll you do if it doesn't rain?

VIPRA 1: What does it matter, if it doesn't rain? By killing the sheep we can have bellyful food.

BASAVA: If you need an animal for your food, why this pretext of a sacrifice? Let it be. Why do you need an animal for your food?

VIPRA 2: I don't know. Our High Priest has ordered us. Therefore, we are taking this sheep. (*They try to capture the sheep. But Basava sets down the lamb and catches the sheep to prevent it from being taken by them.*)

BASAVA: I'll not leave this sheep. You ask your High Priest to sacrifice me and release this animal. Lord Varuna might be better pleased with the human sacrifice. Tomorrow's rains might come today itself.

VIPRA 2: We don't want your painted words. If you don't leave this sheep, we will sacrifice it here itself to Lord Sangameswara. (*He sweeps the machete. Basava tries to hold it with his hands. Blood spurts out of his hands. Basava calls Nagalambika and Nandikesa repeatedly. The frightened Vipras throw away the machete and run away. Nagalambika and Nandikesa rush it. Nagalambika screams loudly at the sight of Basava's wound.*)...

BASAVA: (*Lifting the lamb.*) Look at this poor lamb, which is bleating out of fear. (*Sadly.*) O cruelty! O religion devoid of compassion!

(II. i. pp. 23-24)

This scene, obviously, shows Basava's strong opposition to animal sacrifice, which is part of Vedic *karmakanda* and affirms his essential humanism and compassion. Thus all through his life Basava goes on getting into conflict with the orthodox Brahmanism and its inhuman rites, rituals and practices because of his liberal and reformatory thinking and extraordinary courage of conviction. (Such frontal attack on the orthodox Brahmanism by Basava is not at all depicted in the plays of Lankesh, Karnad, and Shivaprakash.)

When he meets Isanyaguru, he is accepted as a student by the latter on account of his liberal thinking and questioning spirit and quest for deep knowledge. Soon his reformist and revolutionary spirit asserts itself. He develops ideological difference with Isanyaguru and the traditional Vedic learning there. But Isanyaguru, being a liberal teacher recognizing the liberal thinking of his disciple, Basava poses a few questions to Basava, who explains the meaning of his new concepts. For example, Basava does not give importance to external worship of the idol. That is why he sits with his back to the idol of Lord Sangameswara and worships the newly discovered (by him) *istalinga*. Isanyaguru remarks ironically that this practice of sitting with one's back to the idol is "like sitting with one's back to the sun and lighting a lamp" (p. 25). But Basava insists on inner purification and replies, "What can I gain by worshipping the exterior,/ When I am not purified inwardly?" (p. 25). He explains further that "Spiritual purity is of utmost importance for man. Meditation is very necessary for that. But nowadays the worship of idols and the spiritual meditation are separate. In order to prevent this rift one should consider one's soul itself as God and worship its symbol, i.e. *istalinga*.... Whereas the sacred thread divides the society, the Siva-string unifies it, and considers its members as believers and the rest as non-believers" (pp. 26-27). He explains further that the worship of the istalinga, the symbol of the inner divinity of man helps a believer to examine his self everyday thereby purifying his soul. One can easily see how the concepts of social and religious reformation are combined in the new concept of *istalinga* and the Siva-string for bearing it on one's body. When Isanyaguru asks him if the sacred thread creates four classes, the Siva-string creates at least two classes in society, Basava replies very clearly, "Not like that Sir. The sacred thread classifies people on the basis of their birth; the *istalinga* does it on the basis of merit. In the former approach, birth is more important whereas in the latter, merit is more important. Not only that. According to Vedic religion not only a *sudra* or *vaisya* but also a *ksatriya* cannot become a Brahmin. He has got to be born a Brahmin to be called a Brahmin. But Lingayat religion is opposed to that. According to it, a man, who is considered as a non-believer on account of his bad conduct, can become a believer in this life itself by virtue of his good conduct" (p. 27). One can easily see in this dialogue how Basava struck at the very root of *Manusmriti*, the basis of Vedic Brahmanism. (This kind of thinking is easily comparable to that of Dr. B.R. Ambedkar, although there may be other differences between the two.)

For some time he undergoes the formality of learning there. But soon he grows dissatisfied and disillusioned with the meaninglessness of the mechanical reading of *rudra* and mantras at the school of Kudala-Sangama. He thinks that the ritualistic education imparted there is good only for a priest and a pedant and not for him. He, therefore, opines that the minds of the Vedic Brahmins and Saivas are blackened by the smoke of sacrificial fire. Isanyaguru detects the liberal thinking of Basava and understands his extraordinariness and therefore decides to guide him properly. Besides he finds fault with the institutional or monastic religion when he observes the rampant corruption corroding the holy place. He does not like the Devadasi system attached to the temple service and the exploitation of the poor devotees. He finds fault with the village temples also where the superstitious folk religion is practiced, "They also cannot uplift us. In such temples, pots and pans, roadside stones and trees enjoy the status of gods. Barking like dogs after worshipping God Mailara, walking about naked after worshipping God Bhairava, walking on cinders, torturing the body, sacrificing the pregnant women and the women in confinement or marriageable girls and such other cruel practices have grown around the village temple. This is the reason why, once the temple is rejected, the negative activities will disappear automatically" (p. 32). He complains to Isanyaguru against the rampant corruption found in the monasteries, "Financial business has grown rampant in this monastery. The people, who have pledged their land to the monastery, have been losing them. As soon as it becomes dark, the monastery becomes a centre of black-marketing.... Sir, if this habit continues, the monasteries, i.e., the public property, which have become the property of one caste, will one day be the property of one family" (pp. 40-41). In Basava's opinion individual spiritual happiness cannot be separated from the social happiness. That is why he articulates his opinion clearly to Isanyaguru, "Sir, universal experience is nothing but socialization of spiritual experience. Every individual should partake of the universal experience. So far I had considered individual purification very important, but how I have realized that the purification of society is equally important. Just as society cannot improve unless the individual improves, so also the individual cannot improve unless society improves. It is, therefore, not possible for people to be happy until and unless they destroy the old order of the society and create a new one" (p. 41). He is unhappy to notice that "These days, Emperors have been exploiting the subjects; priests have been exploiting the devotees and men have been exploiting women. Thus, the society has been divided into two streams i.e., the exploiters and the exploited" (p. 42). One may easily see the seeds of Marxism, communism, democracy and feminism in these sociological views of Basava.

But Basava's dissatisfaction with the ritualistic education continues to grow stronger. He feels great psychological and spiritual restlessness. He articulates his sense of turmoil to his classmate, Nandikesa:

NANDIKESA: O, Basava, it is time we went to the monastery.

BASAVA: (*Coming out.*) Henceforth, I'll not come to any temple or monastery.

NANDIKESA: Basava, the way you were treated by the monastery was indeed very cruel. But why do you dislike the temple?

BASAVA: Being fed up with the *agrahara*-culture, I came down to this temple-culture. But here also is taught that religion is temple and vice versa. The rituals of *agrahara* have entered here also thickly.

NANDIKESA: So what? Is there any religion apart from the temple? Temples are the centres of our uplift.

BASAVA: No, friend. These rich temples and rituals cannot uplift us. The practice of the rich class supporting the rich caste through alms and charity has been going on continuously here. There has arisen a situation wherein the poor have to borrow money from the rich for offering their devotion to the deities....

NANDIKESA: True. If the temples, big and small, are abolished, the gaudy show of devotion and superstition will disappear. Then the field of religion will be purified to a great extent.

BASAVA: Not only that. These priests have brought the evil practices even into the houses, in addition to temples. The meaningless rituals to be observed at birth and death, initiation and marriage have been dragging people astray. By removing these rituals we can reduce the problems of the people by half. I, who have defied the brahmanical *agraharas*, have now to defy the Saiva temples and rituals.

ISANYAGURU: (*Entering.*) Defy the temple also?

BASAVA: Yes, reverend Sir. We must defy the temples, which have become centres of misusing the God. Instead our legs should be pillars, our head, the golden pinnacle and our body, the temple. Every man should be a moving temple. Our personality should be transformed from static to dynamic.

ISANYAGURU: (*With satisfaction.*) Basava, like others you were born as a child of the age, but you have been growing as the father of the age. If your thoughts were translated into action, this age would definitely turn from static to dynamic. Definitely.

(II. iv. pp. 31-33)

He confesses to his friend that he has not been able to sleep and that he has to get used to be awake. He wants to remember his soul rather than his parents. When the two of them are bathing in the river (confluence of River Krisna and River Malapahari):

NANDIKESA: Why friend? I have been watching you from the beginning. You have been so introverted. Is that because you remember your parents?

BASAVA: Bo. For me the remembrance of my soul is more important than remembering my parents. The soul wrapped in my impure mind has to be purified. (*They enter the river and bathe. Basava takes some water in his cupped palms again and again and says happily.*) Yes. The soul has to be purified. The soul has to be purified like this water. The dirty water has the capacity in itself to be purified. If water has to be pure, it should flow on and never be stagnant. The stagnant water is impure and the flowing one is pure. The static perishes whereas the dynamic doesn't. Yes. It flashed across my mind. Yes, it flashed. I understand it now. This is not mere water, but my mentor. (*He dances ecstatically.*)

(I. vii. p. 16)

Basava suddenly realizes the motto of his life. He wants to be dynamic like the flowing water of a river rather than the stagnant water of a pool. Right from this moment his philosophy of dynamism gets consolidated phase by phase. "The static perishes, but the dynamic doesn't" becomes the central tenet of his philosophy of his life. The playwright develops this motto as the leitmotif of the play.

Now eight years have elapsed. Basava has returned home at Bagewadi as his father is sick. Madarasa tells him how they suffered for eight long years because of the latter's sacrilege and how his mother died at her parental home. Madarasa dies before Basava pours some water into his mouth. Then the collision between the orthodox Brahmins and the liberal minded Basava erupts. The Brahmins unwillingly relax their order of ostracism for Madarasa's funeral only. But Basava defies their order and asks them to get out and not to touch the body of his father. The orthodox Brahmins go out cursing him. Basava brings some firewood from his farm to prepare a pyre. Then he carries the dead body of his father to the burning place. Through this scene the playwright shows the extraordinary courage of Basava in defying the order of orthodox Brahmins, who were highly powerful in the religious matters, and in his spirit of independence and self-reliance.

The death of his parents has made him a forlorn. The hostility of orthodox Brahmins has exasperated him beyond measure. These events have rendered him desperate. Consequently, his spiritual inclination is accentuated by these tragic and irritating events. He, therefore, distributes his property and wealth to his domestic servants and decides to go back to Kudala-Sangama to resume his education.

In Kudala-Sangama also Basava's opposition to Vedic *karma-kanda*, especially the animal sacrifice becomes vehement. For example, while he is rapt in the worship of *istalinga* (the symbol of the inner soul of man) two Brahmins come chasing a sheep and a lamb into the temple of Sangameswara and tell him that they are going to sacrifice them to Lord Visnu to induce rains. But Basava holds the lamb in his hands and prevents them from taking it away. Then a Brahmin sweeps his machete, which wounds Basava's hand. Consequently, the Brahmins feel frightened and run away from there. By that time Nagalambika and Nandikesa rush in there and are utterly shocked by the sight. Nagalambika bandages his hand and wonders at the cruelty of Brahmins and the compassion of Basava. Through this scene the playwright shows how the seed of compassion is sown in the soul of Basava. Later it blossoms into his avowed Religion of Compassion.

In the next scene, the playwright shows another event to illustrate Basava's resistance to Vedic symbols, which affirm the *varna*-hierarchy, division, exploitation, suppression of certain classes of people. The scene also shows Basava's proposition of an alternative (non-Vedic) symbol. For example, Basava sits with his back to the idol of Sangameswara in the temple and worships *istalinga*. This reversal of the normal practice surprises Isanyaguru no end. The guru wonders at the strange behaviour of Basava and asks him the meaning of *istalinga* and Siva-string. What is ironical in this scene is that the guru has to be enlightened by the disciple instead of vice versa. The scene easily and clearly brings out the original philosophical thinking of Basava. He explains clearly that the *istalinga* is the symbol of the inner soul of man (and not of any icon or idol in the temple) and that the worship of *istalinga* involves daily self-examination. Likewise he explains that the Siva-string unites people socially whereas the sacred-thread divides the society on the basis of four *varnas*. The allied symbol of *istalinga* and Siva-string are alternative principles or ideas offered by Basava, which hold mirror to his extra-ordinary originality. The playwright has executed his intention of highlighting the tenets of Virasaiva doctrine. (Such much needed doctrinaire element is conspicuously missing in the plays of Lankesh, Karnad, and Shivaprakash.)

Basava does not like the rigid ritual-oriented education at the temple-school of Kudala-Sangama. That is why he begins to absent himself from some of the programmes of the school, like the common service to the idol of Lord Sangameswara. When the news of Basava's defiant behaviour reaches Pasupati, the local chairman, the latter complains to Isanyaguru against the former's liberal thinking and expression; his absence from the common service and his dislike of rituals. Pasupati grows terribly exasperated and sends for Basava to take him to task. Basava comes there and exhibits his extra-ordinary moral courage by complaining against the increase of criminality in the monastery, especially during Pasupati's regime. Angered by the frontal attack, he threatens Basava and orders him to be chucked out of the monastery. But Isanyaguru interferes and promises to mend and train Basava properly.

Basava's dissatisfaction with the Vedic rituals and their reflection in folk culture is articulated clearly in his conversation with his classmate, Nandikesa. Basava tells Nandikesa that he does not like the temple-culture of Kudala-Sangama (and other places by implication) and the attendant evils like Devadasi system, procession of the palanquin, etc. He points out how in the villages petty gods at road-sides are worshipped and how they are meaningless rituals. He dislikes the temple-culture as much as the *agrahara*-culture. He strongly pleads for the abolition of temples and for the transformation of human beings themselves into moving temples. Here the playwright highlights the vaster conflicts between the Saivas and the Virasaivas. During and before the time of Basava the practice of building huge temples for their respective deities like Siva and Visnu as part of their religion was very common. But unfortunately such temples gradually degenerated into centres of corruption, prostitution, priestly exploitation of devotees, etc. Basava wanted to abolish all these evils attendant upon stone-built temples and suggested an alternative plan of transforming the human person itself into a moving temple. The playwright has borrowed the concept of the divinization of the human body intertextually from Basava's mystic utterance or vacana.

Pasupati, the Pontiff of the monastery is sour and angry at Basava's defiant behaviour and fears the exposure of their defects. He, therefore, sends for Basava, who initially refuses to come. But Marjalappa brings him by force. Pasupati asks Basava to confess his guilt in writing. But Basava refuses to do so. Then they make him write his confession by forcibly guiding his hand. In the meanwhile the leaf falls down on the floor. Basava, therefore, bends down to pick up the leaf. But Pasupati puts his foot on Basava's hand thereby wounding it. He, then, orders his people to drive Basava out of the monastery and the town of Kudala-Sangama.

Nagalambika, the elder sister grieves over Basava's wound and remembers her late mother. Basava tries to cheer her up and comments on the evil nature of the pontiff, his monastery and followers. He opines that these orthodox people can kill him but not his ideas. One can easily see Basava's extraordinary courage of conviction here.

By that time Isanyaguru comes there and consoles both the brother and sister. Then he takes Basava out for a stroll. They discuss the rampant corruption, nepotism, exploitation, financial transactions found in the monasteries and the ostentatious life of the pontiffs. They are sad to notice that the monasteries have been slowly degenerating into private family properties. These views of Basava are a strong attack on the evils of the institutionalization of religion in the form of temples and monasteries in Karnataka as well as in South India. That is exactly the reason why Basava struggled hard to abolish the temple-culture and the attendant evils by proposing the concept of *istalinga*. Isanyaguru understands the potential greatness and intellectual acumen of Basava. He, therefore, tells Basava that Kudala-Sangama is too small a place for the growth of his personality and achievement of his goal. He advises Basava to go to the city of Kalyana (the capital of Chalukya kingdom) thereby becoming the light of the world. (This aspect of Basava's personality is not at all covered by the clever playwrights like Lankesh, Karnad, and Shivaprakash.)

A new phase of life begins for Basava when he goes to the city of Kalyana where he comes in contact with King Bijjala, the Emperor of Chalukya Empire. King Bijjala is worried about the lack of tally in the accounts of the royal treasury, which is reported to him by his officers, Mancanna. It is at this opportune time that Baladeva, the maternal uncle of Basava, brings the latter and introduces him to King Bijjala. Basava volunteers to set right the accounts. He states that honesty and hard work are his qualifications. King Bijjala is so impressed by Basava's moral qualities and self-confidence that he appoints him as the Chief Accounts Officer.

Basava's appointment as the Chief Accounts Officer helps him to realize his spiritual potentialities. As the servants of the accounts office discuss between themselves, Basava has brought in a lot of improvement in his office, due to his hard work, efficiency, economy, holiness of financial transactions and the practice of dignity of labour. Servant 1 reports how Basava himself opened the door of the office and swept the floor when the attendant was late in coming to the office:

SERVANT 1: Yesterday Basava said, "Earn money profusely like water, but spend it economically like *tirtha*." Day before yesterday he said, "Why do you extend the Empire? Wars are also redundant. If everyone works hard and practices compassion, even royal administration could be dispensed with."

SERVANT 2: He not only preaches it, but practices it as well. He works hard as he can and receives only a meager salary. That is his ethics of work and salary.

SERVANT 1: Not only that. He never discriminates between the jobs. The other day, for example, his servant had not come to the office on right time. But Basava himself opened the door, swept the floor and busied himself in his work. Such things have become great models for us. (*They go on sweeping the floor and exit.*)

(III. ii. p. 46)

The dramatist has shown in this scene how Basava sets an example of honesty, hard work, regularity, and dignity of labour and holiness of economic dealings thereby offering a utopian vision of life.

King Bijjala wonders at his own destiny. He, who was a mere vassal at Mangalveda, became an Emperor at Kalyana quite unexpectedly. He, therefore, tells his queen, Rambha that he wants to use the influence of a dynamic man like Basava for this purpose. He has already noticed the sterling moral qualities of Basava and been waiting for a chance to make use of him for his own self-aggrandizement.

By that time Baladeva and Basava come there. King Bijjala appreciates Basava's improvement of the Treasury and therefore promotes him to the higher position of the Finance Minister in the post vacated by the death of Siddharasa. He asks Basava to face the fire-ordeal of dealing with the wealth of the kingdom. Basava replies that fire-ordeals are very dear to him and accepts the appointment order from the king.

Basava's philosophy of *kayaka*, which is parallel to Karl Marx's concept of labour, begins to be consolidated after his taking charge of the post of the Finance Minister of the kingdom. His political power as minister helps him to translate his philosophy of *kayaka* into action. '*Kayaka*' means any work or labour—physical or mental—done through the body (*kaya*) dedicated to God. Hance '*kayaka*' becomes the foundation of all human progress, *a la* Karl Marx. (The only difference between Basava and Marx is that whereas Basava believed in God, Marx did not believe in God at all.) Minister Basaveswara invites the poor people to come to the government treasury and collect the necessities of life like clothing and agricultural implements. He draws their attention to the difference between the privileged and the underprivileged; between the rich and the poor—caused by 'religion' and 'labour' respectively. His concern for the poor easily echoes Marx's concern for the proletariat. As he has seen the rampant corruption of various kinds in temples and monasteries, he asks those people to reject the monasteries and temples and to transform themselves into moving temples and worship the symbol (*istalinga*) of their inner soul as well as of social equality, "Since the monasteries have rejected you, you reject the monasteries. Think of your own homes as monasteries. Since the temples have rejected you, you reject the temples. Think of your own persons as temples" (p. 50). The dramatist has borrowed this idea intertextually from Basava's own mystic utterance or *vacana*. Basava continues to teach the citizens that "Labour is the only way essential" (p. 51) for overcoming their poverty. Basava's concept of *kayaka* is easily comparable to Marx's idea of labour which the foundation of all human progress. He tells them further that "it is the moral responsibility of the Empire to provide the basic necessities of your life, as you are its primary citizens. It is, therefore, arranged to supply a house to live in, clothing to cover yourselves and a few other things from the treasury" (p. 51). Basava's democratic view of the government may be seen in his view that "The royal treasury does not belong to the Emperor. It belongs to you. You have contributed to it without knowing it. Please come tomorrow and collect your papers from your houses, lands and the necessary professional tools. Right now, you may take some clothing and money for your immediate use" (p. 52). Obviously, Basaveswara teaches the spiritual democracy here. This scene is brought in by the dramatist to show Basaveswara's defiance of the temple-culture and the attendant priestly corruption and *varna*-hierarchy and social oppression. He teaches them that labour is the only essential way to overcome poverty. It is in line with his famous mystic utterance, *Kayaka* itself is 'Heaven' (parallel to the modern dictum, 'work is worship'). He wants to arrange for their collective work and collective feeding. (His desire echoes the tenets of Russian communism and the ideals of Plato's *Republic*.) He tells them further that the royal treasury belongs to them and not to the king. One may easily see how the image of Basaveswara as a progressive thinker emerges here.

In the next scene the playwright highlights Basaveswara's compassionate nature by depicting the historical event depicted by many *puranic* poets. For example, a cowherd comes in running and tells Basaveswara that some thieves have stolen their cows and that they have to reclaim them by fighting with the thieves. But contrary to their expectation, Basaveswara tells the cowherds to take the calves also to the thieves and hand them over to them. He feels that the calves should not be separated from their mothers. The cowherds are utterly baffled by Basaveswara's unusual and idealistic way of thinking. It holds mirror to his compassionate nature *a la* Buddha.

Basaveswara has great respect for the labourers and therefore upholds the dignity and holiness of work. For example, when a few *jangamas* come to him with their working tools, he bows down to their feet and addresses them as gods. He asks them to practise their respective professions by dedicating themselves to God and considering them as holy and divine so that their labour may turn out to be *kayaka*. He feeds them as part of *dasoha* programme and explains its meaning. Once all the professions are considered as holy, dignified and done in the name of God, the question of inferiority or superiority or *varna*-hierarchy does not arise at all. Basaveswara's philosophy has close parallels in Marxism and modern democracy. Through the philosophy of *kayaka* Basaveswara subverted the age-old *varna*-system. All these new concepts of Virasaivism propounded by Basaveswara are preached and practiced after being discussed and debated in the Socio-Spiritual Academy (*Anubhava Mantapa*):

(*The saranas have gathered in the Socio-Spiritual Academy in the evening.*)

BASAVA: My dear *saranas*, rapid changes have been taking place in Kuntala Empire. Our dreams have been coming true. The saranas, who are the embodiments of the principle, '*Kayaka* itself is Kailasa', have been converting their lanes into veritable heavens.... In *kayaka*, there is nothing superior or inferior. That is why all the *kayakas* are deemed to be respectable now.

NILAMBIKA: True. Lord. All the *saranas* not only continue to do their original *kayakas* with respect, but also believe in the equality of all *kayakas*. Consequently,

> the *saranas*, no matter which professional caste they come from, can choose any *kayaka* with an open mind. Marayya, the King of Kashmir, chose the sale of faggots instead of administration. Because of such a change, *kayakas* are free from the discrimination of purity and pollution.
>
> (IV. vi. pp. 84-85)

Meanwhile, two soldiers fetch a prostitute who was trying to throw away her new born baby into the dark. When Basaveswara comes to know it he asks the prostitute about it. She pleads her helplessness and confesses her economic insecurity and necessity. Basaveswara gets her released from the soldiers and asks her compassionately, "I know. Mother, are you willing to give up this profession if we provide you food, clothing, a job and possibly arrange your marriage?" (p. 86). She exclaims ecstatically, "O God! Is there a better luck than this? I am driven into this profession by the force of circumstances. The more I try to wriggle out of it, the deeper am I pushed into it. Sir, you are a veritable god for me!" (p. 86). Just then a young *sarana* comes forward and volunteers to marry the prostitute. Basaveswara instantly conducts their wedding symbolically. Then the former prostitute, who has become a respectable wife and a *sarane* (female devotee, who has surrendered herself to Lord Siva) now, addresses and thanks Basaveswara whole-heartedly, "Dear brother, is there a better example than this for the conversion of Kalyana into Kailasa? You, who wrought the miracle of converting the impecunious fellows into rich people, have worked the miracle of converting me, a prostitute into a respectable wife. You are the veritable Lord Supreme for me" (p. 87). This scene testifies to Basaveswara's social amelioration, progressive ideology and revolutionary bent of mind.

In the following scene, we get a glimpse into the various reformist activities carried out by Basaveswara and his companion *saranas*. For example, Macideva, Basaveswara, and Madhuvayya discuss their ameliorative agenda, which involves abolition of class and caste-discrimination, gender-inequality and the employment of Kannada language (instead of elitist Sanskrit) in their *vacanas* (mystic utterances) for common people's comprehension and working towards social justice and change. These vaster social missions and issues are shown only by indirect action through discussion among the characters.

Basaveswara's liberal and democratic thought and action are strongly opposed by the orthodox Brahmins. For example, Kesavabhatta and Kriyasakti complain to King Bijjala that Basaveswara has reduced their salaries and grants to the *agraharas* and temples. Further, they try to prejudice the mind of King Bijjala by carrying tales against Basaveswara. They tell him that Basaveswara thinks that the royal treasury belongs to the people and not to the king and that he does not care for the king. This is Basaveswara's economic policy. But this piece of news about Basaveswara's democratic thinking is unpalatable to the king who believes in the tradition of monarchy. He registers the complaint in his mind and tells the orthodox Brahmins that he would take an appropriate decision at the right time.

The political power of a minister has given Basaveswara a great deal of zest to carry out his liberal, democratic, religious policies. In his noble mission, he is supported by the like-minded *saranas* who are his admirers and companions. Basaveswara has been offering free food to all the genuine *jangamas*. But sometimes some fake *jangamas* also try to take advantage of this privilege. For example, once some *jangamas* try to force their way into the house of Basaveswara to have their free meal, but Ghattivalayya, an ardent follower of Basaveswara, prevents them from entering the house on the ground that they are not genuine *jangamas* with noble thoughts. Deeply angered by this insult, the *jangamas* thrash Ghattivalayya, who falls unconscious on the ground.

Basaveswara's social reformist activities may be seen in the next scenes. For example, Basaveswara fights against the terrible and inhuman practices of *velevali* and *sati*. Basaveswara sees a crowd of people consisting of a loyal servant Sankappayya committing *velevali* sacrifice for his master, Marasinga and his wife ready to commit *sati*. Then he sees a scavenger boy of untouchable caste. Basaveswara is shocked beyond his wits by the sight of these monstrous and inhuman practices. Consequently, he exercises his political power as a minister and cancels both *velevali* and *sati* practices in the kingdom, "Enough of argument. Now onwards the practice of *velevali* and *masti* are strictly forbidden in our Empire" (p. 67). Similarly, he orders the untouchable boy scavenger to stop cleaning the private latrines of the upper-caste people.

In the next phase of his visit to the city, Basaveswara sees a skeleton tied to a well. When he asks his subordinate officers about it, they reply that the skeleton tied to a well indicates that it belongs to the untouchables and that it acts as a warning to the upper-caste people to keep away from it to maintain their caste-purity. Basaveswara, who is bent upon eradicating the evil of caste-discrimination, goes to the well and removes the skeleton from there thereby defying the orthodox ways of life, "Why should they identify it at all? Please get it removed.... Oh God! How long should this inhuman practice continuc?" (p. 69).

A little while after this event Basaveswara happens to meet Nagimayya, an untouchable and partakes of food in his house:

BASAVA: Greetings, Sir. (*Basava touches the feet of Nagimayya.*)

NAGIMAYYA: Don't touch me, Lord. You are a great man whereas I am nobody. The ocean should not roll over on a delicate shoot.

BASAVA: That is what I am trying to clarify. You are a great man whereas I am nobody. You are not mere Nagimayya, but Sivanagimayya. I beg your pardon for the society's crime of keeping you away from itself—you, who are like the beclouded sun.

NAGIMAYYA: Let it be, Lord. This practice has come down from time immemorial. And it goes on till the end of time.

BASAVA: I won't allow it to continue. "The earth is common to the temple of Siva as well as to the lanes of untouchables. Water is common to ablution as well as to libation. Caste is common to those who know their selves." This is my view. None is low or high by birth. Low is he, who created this division.

OLD MAN: Then why did they create these castes, lord?

BASAVA: Purely for their selfish ends. "He who melted the metal became a blacksmith; he, who washed the clothes became a washer-man; he, who wove the cloth, became a weaver; and he, who read the Veda, became a haruva." These are all different aspects of labour. This being the truth, how is a mental worker superior to a physical worker? We have got to destroy this evil tradition.

I have got to remove the very concept of the untouchable lane from the map of Kalyana City and Kuntala Empire. I have to remove the difference between highborn and lowborn. (*Basava embraces Naginmayya.*)...

NAGIMAYYA: No. lord. Please do not go that far.

BASAVA: I have got to sanctify myself by feeding on your food. Please give it to me quickly.... Sivanagimayya, where's the difference between the food of your house and that of my house? It is the attitude that is important. Both the meals will be material food if received with a sense of discrimination. They will be consecrated food if received with a sense of Siva-consciousness. You and I are not different from each other. Both of us are *maheswaras*. The food prepared out of the earnings from hard labour is indeed very great food. (*They continue to take their food.*)

(III. x. pp. 69-72)

A Brahmin taking food in the house of an untouchable is something unimaginable not only in the 12th century, but even in the 21st century in India. It is indeed a revolutionary act which requires extraordinary courage of conviction on the part of Basaveswara.

This revolutionary act infuriates the orthodox Brahmins deeply. They feel that the superiority of their caste is threatened by it and fear that the caste-purity of Brahmins may be polluted. They, therefore, oppose it vehemently. Kesavabhatta, therefore, complains to King Bijjala that Basaveswara has violated the *varna-*

system by partaking of food at the untouchable, Nagimayya's house and insists that Basaveswara should be tried for upsetting the social norms. King Bijjala considers it to be his duty to inquire into the matter. He, therefore, orders his soldiers to fetch Basaveswara. By that time Basaveswara himself comes there with a few untouchables with him. Influenced by the purity-mania of orthodox Brahmins, King Bijjala gets his throne from the court to the verandah and conducts the trail of Basaveswara in the open:

BIJJALA: The reason for calling you here is that you went to the lane of untouchables, had your food there and violated the caste-system. It means disobedience of the royal order.

BASAVA: Your Highness, which scripture says that it is the violation of the royal order?

BIJJALA: *The Laws of Manu* says it.

BASAVA: But I don't reckon it.

BIJJALA: Basaveswara, if you say that you don't reckon *The Laws of Manu*, you mean indirectly you don't reckon the royal order also. *The Laws of Manu* is our indirect constitution. Every citizen of our Empire should follow it.

BASAVA: But I beg your pardon, Majesty. It is not acceptable to me. My stand is quite different.

NARANABHATTA: Does it mean that Basaveswara's constitution is different from His Majesty's?

BASAVA: You may think so.

BIJJALA: Impossible! I cannot allow another constitution growing parallel to mine. I'll destroy it if it does. I am the owner of the royal treasury. It is my duty to protect the caste-difference.

BASAVA: I cannot accept both of them. This is my final decision.

BIJJALA: Basaveswara, the severe punishment for disobeying my law is beyond your imagination.

BASAVA: I can imagine it, Your Majesty. These are the hard working labourers. Therefore, these are my people.

> These are the masters not merely of this Empire, but also of the whole world. (*Basaveswara goes away from there. Countless untouchable men and women follow him shouting the slogan, 'Down with the varna-mongers!' Emperor Bijjala goes away in the opposite direction. His officers and priests follow him shouting the slogan, 'Down with the opponents of varna-system.' The motif, 'The static perishes, whereas the dynamic doesn't.' is heard.*)
>
> (IV. i. pp. 76-77)

He charges Basaveswara of violating the *varna*-system, the Laws of Manu; of questioning his ownership of the royal treasury and his authority itself. But Basaveswara is not ready to relent, but willing to get the punishment. Although Emperor Bijjala knows that Basaveswara's liberal thinking is right, he cannot allow it because he knows that tradition cannot be changed so suddenly. He has to maintain a balance between the orthodox Brahmins and the liberal *saranas*. But he cannot punish Basaveswara so abruptly. He waits for some more time to watch the course of events.

Basaveswara's religious activities are continued. In the Socio-Spiritual Academy (*Anubhava Mantapa*) Basaveswara tells his companion *saranas* how it is difficult to survive in the Empire after earning the wrath of the Emperor. Macideva suggests that they should carry out their reformist activities publicly; of reducing the economic inequality, gender-inequality and caste-discrimination. He suggests further that the caste-discrimination can be overcome only by encouraging blood relation between different castes. As though in line with this suggestion, Nilambika, a Ksatriya bride and younger (foster) sister of King Bijjala, volunteers to marry Basaveswara. Basaveswara accepts her as his second wife as it if the will of God. Likewise a few young *saranas* come forward to marry the daughters of slaves and prostitutes. Here Basaveswara has set an example for his followers, in his agenda of social amelioration and abolition of *varna*-hierarchy and discrimination.

Nilambika's marriage with Basaveswara comes as a shock and surprise to King Bijjala. He, therefore, asks her as to why she had to marry a mere minister. But Nilambika replies that she wanted to be an intellectual wife of Basaveswara, who has been struggling to bring some change in the society. King Bijjala becomes helpless as his own younger sister drifts towards the *sarana* philosophy and their reformist movement.

While engaged in a spiritual colloquy in the Socio-Spiritual Academy, Nilambika highlights the principle of *kayaka*, which involves the dignity and holiness of physical labour. She quotes the example of the King of Kashmir who has come all the way to Kalyana and chosen the *kayaka* of collecting and selling the faggots. By then a few soldiers bring in a prostitute who was trying to throw away her baby. Basaveswara and Nilambika enquire the prostitute and advise her to give up the ugly profession. Then a young *sarana* volunteers to marry the prostitute and accept her baby also under his custody. The prostitute reveres Basaveswara as a veritable god. Through this scene the dramatist shows how progressive Basaveswara's sociological ideas were.

Due to the liberal and progressive ideology of Basaveswara, the society has been transiting from the orthodox to the liberal one. As a consequence of the socio-spiritual atmosphere, Madhuvayya (a Brahmin), and Haralayya, (a cobbler) agree to arrange the wedding of their daughter, Nila and son, Silavanta respectively. Now that the Brahmin and the Sudra have become *saranas* and assumed a new identity, they have no caste-differences between them. The marriage is willingly blessed by Basaveswara:

(*The Socio-Spiritual Academy*)

MACIDEVA: Dear *saranas*, our Kuntala Empire has been growing into an ideal one. Because of our reformist movement, a free society without gender or *varna* or class discrimination has been emerging. The people of other provinces, who are fed up with the exploitation by the Emperors and priests, have been rushing in here to lead a free life. That is the reason why the *sarana*-society has been enjoying wide popularity on account of its varied schemes.

NILAMBIKA: Yes, the society has been progressing from diversity to unity. People have already realized that *varna*-discrimination is only a false notion.

MACIDEVA: Why only realization? A marriage, which can be a supreme example of this realization, is going to take place here.

BASAVA: Whose marriage?

MADHUVAYYA: My daughter's marriage. Sir, I have decided to give my daughter in marriage to *Sarana* Haralayya's son.

HARALAYYA: Sir, I have also consented to this proposal.

SARANAS: This is a matter of not only pleasure, but also of pride. It has our whole-hearted support.

BASAVA: If at all the marriage takes place, it is going to be the first example in the history of our land.

SARANAS: Why if at all? Madhuvayya is no longer a Brahmin, nor is Haralayya a *sudra*. Both of them are *saranas* now. What's wrong in the blood relation between the *saranas*?

...

MACIDEVA: The marriage, which is going to take place shortly, happens to be another experiment. By accepting food in Nagimayya's house, you removed his sense of artificial inferiority. Now by arranging the marriage we are going to remove the sense of artificial superiority of Brahmins. And that is just also.

BASAVA: True indeed! This marriage is remarkably different from the earlier ones. It is not a marriage between different high-*varnas*, but is one between high-caste and low-caste people. Brahmins and *Sudras* happen to be two poles of the society. We have to wait and see how the *varna* advocates accept this marriage. The class advocate, Emperor Bijjala has already been seething with intolerance. The *varna*-advocates may join hands with him and brand us as criminals.

MADHUVAYYA: We, the members of two families, have come to the decision only after visualizing all the possible dangers. Principles are for practicing and not for merely preaching. That is what you said. We believe in your words. We don't see any mistake in it. "If the *saranas* ask for a *muhurtam* for a wedding, tell them: this very instant is the right one for it." Let this *vacana* of yours be translated into action. Come Silavanta, come Nila. (*Both of them come and stand in the midst of people.*)

BASAVA: Come on, groom and bride, swear.

SILAVANTA: I swear by my conscience and by the *sarana* society here that I accept Nilavati as my wife.

NILAVATI: I swear by my conscience and by the *sarana* society here that I accept Silavanta as my husband. (*Both of them clasp each other's palms.*)

BASAVA: Dear *sarana* couple, you live the ideal taught by Prabhudeva in his *vacana*, which says, "If husband and wife align their temperaments like two eyes having a single sight, they will be very dear to Lord Guheswara."

SARANAS: May God bless the *sarana* couple. Victory to secular marriage! (*The static perishes, but the dynamic doesn't," is heard again and again.*)

(IV. viii. pp. 90-94)

Another revolutionary act done by Basaveswara is that he and the companion—*saranas* enthrone Allamaprabhu on the *Sunya*-Chair which was lying vacant for the last twelve years. Allamaprabhu, a great mystic and super-*sarana* hails from the subaltern caste of *nattuvanga* or dance-teachers in the temples. Their enthroning a *sudra* on the *Sunya*-Chair is strongly resented by the orthodox Saivas. The Saiva pontiffs like Lakulisapandita and Kriyasakti Sivacarya protest against this revolutionary act of Basaveswara. They think that only the Saiva *jangamas* have a right to occupy that prestigious chair. But Basaveswara defends himself and his philosophy by saying that they believe in knowledge-oriented *jangama*-culture and not in the caste-oriented one:

MACIDEVA: Basaveswara, the Saiva pontiffs like Lakulisapandita and Kriyasakti Sivacarya have gathered outside. You know, yesterday we enthroned Allamaprabhu on the *Sunya*-Chair. These pontiffs have been shouting slogans against it.

BASAVA: Is that so? I had expected it. (*By then Kriyasakti, Lakulisapandita and other pontiffs rush into his house.*) What's this, holy sirs? We proposed the view that the religious institutes should be propagators of progressive ideals. The society accepted our proposal. But it is only you, holy pontiffs, who did not agree with us.

KRIYASAKTI: Who are you to advise our holy institute? Why should we change the tradition of the institute that has come down from a thousand years?

BASAVA: Leave it, Sirs. Keep your holy institute for yourselves. The institute that we have established is not of caste, but of mystic experience. Because of our movement, a comprehensive worldview has emerged. We need an institute to hand over such a worldview from generation to generation. That is why we have established such an institute.

LAKULISA: But your institute comes in the way of our *holy* institute.

MACIDEVA: How is that possible? Where's the similarity between your institute and ours?

KRIYASAKTI: Stop this babbling. We have opposed it for the last twelve years. We oppose it even now. Your institute will be alternative to ours and will certainly be a hindrance to our activities.

BASAVA: If any pro-civilian philosophy acts as a hindrance to your system, what should we do about it? Allamaprabhu is a great scholar and an able proponent of *sarana* philosophy.

LAKULISA: Whether he is able to otherwise is not important for us. We don't know which place he belongs to. But we strongly oppose a *Sudra* occupying the religious Chair.

BASAVA: Dear Lakulisapandita Sir, don't you know that "The *jangama* has no caste as water has no pollution?" There is no connection between caste and knowledge. The *sarana* philosophy believes in the view that a man, no matter whether he is the son of a maid-servant or of a prostitute, will be the veritable Lord Siva once he is spiritually initiated.

KRIYASAKTI: You bring in whatever change you like within the framework of Vedic society. But don't interfere with our religious institute, which will be tantamount to snatching away our authority. We can't tolerate this. We alone, who hail from the Saiva-Jangama family, have the right of managing the religious institute. It's we, who deserve the highest respect.

BASAVA: Sir, I repeat myself. Please listen carefully. 'Jangama' is an indicator of knowledge and not of caste. Our chief motto is to uphold knowledge and defy caste at all levels—be it social or religious. (*Some jangamas shout slogans like "We protest against it," and sit here and there.*)

MACIDEVA: Sir, nothing will come out of your adamancy. Prabhudeva is not an ordinary *jangama*, but a super *jangama*. Who else is able to occupy this spiritual Chair?

LAKULISA: I see! (*Addressing Basava.*) Basaveswara, please think twice. By stretching the concept of '*jangama*' too far, you will be creating a great problem for all....

KRIYASAKTI: This policy of your may pave the way for the fall of Kalyana. Basaveswara, please remember the City of Kalyana may go to rack and ruin on account of your new concept of the 'pride about the *jangama*.'

BASAVA: If the City of Kalyana is ruined, another ten cities like this could be built. But my concern is with the welfare of the people. That is why I would like to end the caste-oriented *jangama* tradition and establish the knowledge-oriented *jangama*-culture.

LAKULISA: Do you think people like Allamaprabhu are available at all times? Power is very subtle. Nobody is free from selfishness. In course of time your own people will develop this institute along a narrow channel.

BASAVA: Sir, I know that. I have already guessed it. It's the property of water to freeze in winter and to flow on in summer. Likewise, it is the nature of society to stagnate on account of karma and to grow dynamic on account of dharma. We cannot prevent the society from being dynamic now with the fear that it may stagnate in future. Our experiments in galvanizing it must continue. We have evolved our philosophy in such a way that it does not allow for any stagnation of the individual or society.

(V. i. pp. 95-98)

All these revolutionary activities of Basaveswara have a cumulative effect on the orthodox Brahmins, who are deeply disturbed and even threatened about their social superiority and privileges. They, therefore, gang up against Basaveswara and decide to nullify his new religion and philosophy. The Vedic Brahmins and the Saiva pontiffs rush to King Bijjala and complain against Basaveswara's violation of *varna*-system, religious system and imperial system. Consequently, King Bijjala, who has been waiting for a golden chance to punish Basaveswara on some pretext or the other, summons him and warns him to mend himself and stop his revolutionary activities. But Basaveswara is not ready for any compromise. Thus, the ideological conflict reaches its climax:

BIJJALA: O Basaveswara, there is a grave charge against you that you have been violating both the social ethic and the royal ethic under the guise of social reform.

BASAVA: Your Majesty, I am not a man to indulge in 'destruction'. On the contrary I believe in 'construction'.

KESAVABHATTA: This man does not seem to have realized his mistake yet from this arrest.

BASAVA: I have not committed any crime. This arrest is an insult not to me but to those, who have arrested me.

BIJJALA: It means insult to me?

BASAVA: Did I say like that, Your Majesty? I mean that those, who insult the Truth in the present, will be permanently insulted in the future.

BIJJALA: Hold your tongue. Who is the person who questioned my authority and insulted me?

BASAVA: Authority, authority, authority. Whose authority of the Empire? Authority rests with those, who love the Empire, and not with those, who love authority.

BIJJALA: So you mean that you love the Empire, whereas I love authority.... Basaveswara, I am giving you the last warning. Think over it once again. Your religious reform has my total approval. But you had better give up both the foolish ideas of 'economic equality' and 'social equality'.

BASAVA: Your Majesty, it is not possible for me to forsake Truth.

BIJJALA: If this is your final decision, I am afraid, you'll have to quit your position of a Minister.

BASAVA: Your Majesty, I am ready to give up even my life, but I cannot leave economic equality, social equality and religious equality and the citizens practicing these ideals.

KESAVABHATTA: Between the Emperor and the citizens, who is greater?

BASAVA: A believer is greater than a non-believer.

LAKULISA: Then, you mean that our Emperor is a non-believer?

BASAVA: I cannot make it explicit. A non-believer, however great he may be, is an individualist, whereas a believer, however small he may be, is a socialist and a humanist.

KESAVABHATTA: You mean then, that your *saranas* are humanists and our Emperor is an individualist? O

Basaveswara, talk carefully lest the City of Kalyana should go to rack and ruin.

BIJJALA: (*Shutting his ears.*) Enough, enough! I cannot hear these ominous words. Don't talk any more. (*Seriously.*) This is the Emperor's decision. Basaveswara, who has violated the royal order and the religious order is terminated from his service as a Minister and banished from the Capital City. The trial of Haralayya and Madhuvayya is adjourned for tomorrow.... (*Emperor Bijjala is about to go.*)

BASAVA: Your Majesty, Your Majesty. (*Emperor Bijjala turns a deaf ear to Basava's words and goes away from there. The soldiers instantly draw their swords and surround Basava. Some soldiers draw Haralayya and Madhuvayya away from there. Contradictory slogans like "Victory to Basaveswara!" "Down with Bijjala!" "Down with Basaveswara" are heard repeatedly. The motif "The static perishes but the dynamic doesn't," is heard again and again and slowly fades out.*)

(V. iii. pp. 107-09)

Then King Bijjala inevitably terminates Basaveswara from the post of Finance Minister and banishes him from the city of Kalyana. He is not willing to listen to Basaveswara's clarification of his stand. The soldiers arrest Basaveswara and lead him away from there. Then the king orders Haralayya and Madhuvayya to be dragged to death by an elephant and *vacana* literature to be banned from the kingdom:

TOWN CRIERS: Hear, gentlemen, hear. His Majesty has ordered that Haralayya and Madhuvayya should be punished by being dragged to death by an elephant on account of their violation of *varna*-system through the marriage of their son and daughter.... Hear gentlemen, hear. His Majesty Bijjala has banned the *vacana* literature, which questions the imperial system and *varna*-system. Ban on *vacana* literature, ban, ban, ban.

(V. iii. p. 109)

Thus, political power crushes the religious activities of Basaveswara. The conflict is mounting up fast. The Vedic brahmins and the Saiva *acharyas* triumph over the protestant religious leader, Basaveswara. Thus, one conflict is resolved in favour of the orthodox Brahmins. But this conflict leads to another conflict. For example, Jagadeva and Mallibomma are enraged by the death-sentence passed by King Bijjala to Haralayya and Madhuvayya; and by the banishment of Basaveswara from the city of Kalyana. Here the dramatist has made some minor changes in the number of characters. (According to historical sources there were three personals, Jagadeva, Mallayya, and Bommayya, who hatched the plan of killing King Bijjala. But the later poets compressed these three characters into two, Jagadeva and Mallibomma. The dramatist has followed the later practice of retaining only two characters, Jagadeva and Mallibomma, who hatch and execute the murder of King Bijjala.) Although Jagadeva and Mallibomma are the apostate *saranas* and staunch followers of Basaveswara, they do not follow Basaveswara's non-violent principles. As they are the zealots of a new religion they want to encounter a sword with a sword. Both of them, therefore, kill King Bijjala when he is going in his palanquin to the court. Thus, they wreak vengeance on the king for his anti-*sarana* stand:

(*The front yard of Emperor Bijjala's palace. Jagadeva and Mallibomma are readying the torches.*)

JAGADEVA: Mallibomma, it is horrible to see or hear about the death-punishment meted out to Haralayya and Madhuvayya.

MALLIBOMMA: Jagadeva, what a cruel punishment this is! The Vedic priests, the Saiva pontiffs and Emperor Bijjala have insulted our saranas in broad daylight. They have done great injustice to our literature.

JAGADEVA: Our organization was weakened by half by the withdrawal of Vedic Brahmins and even more of Saiva *jangamas*. It became a paralyzed body.

MALLIBOMMA: By banning our leader Basaveswara, these fellows have sundered the head from the trunk of that paralyzed body.

JAGADEVA: Yes, basaveswara was driven out of the City of Kalyana yesterday itself....

MALLIBOMMA: Jagadeva, Basaveswara must have gone far away from the City of Kalyana, in Bijjala's view. But he will be alive amidst us and our hearts as his principles are prevalent in our lives. He will propel our movement from century to century.

JAGADEVA: Yes, friend. Truth will not die. Truth will not die at all.

MALLIBOMMA: Jagadeva, we established dharma in place of karma and formulated the body-temple culture in place of stone-temple culture.

JAGADEVA: We established the spiritual-home culture in place of palace-culture and the socio-spiritual culture in place of monastery-culture. But nobody listened to this.

MALLIBOMMA: Dear friend, how could the deaf hear the melody of a fiddle?

JAGADEVA: These are not deaf fellows, but pretenders. Let it be so. What's the next plan of our *saranas*?

MALLIBOMMA: Our *saranas* had gathered yesterday in the Socio-Spiritual Academy. They decided to tackle this violence with our non-violence only because of our basic principle that "compassion is the foundation of religion."

JAGADEVA: What? Should we encounter a sword with a flower? No, no. We must encounter a sword with a sword itself. Because of the death of two *saranas* by being dragged by an elephant yesterday, the City of Kalyana was gored with the blood of *saranas*. The blood of Haralayya and Madhuvayya was spilled on the roads of Kalyana! If we remember it, our blood will boil. (*He draws his sword.*) From today, it is not the *kayaka* of the palace, but the service of the prison.

MALLIBOMMA: (*Drawing his sword.*) Yes, Jagadeva, today should be our last day of torch-bearing service to the Emperor.

JAGADEVA: Yes, friend. The drawn sword must take the life of Bijjala. (*He whispers something in Mallibomma's ears. The court panegyrists utter the eulogy, "Victory to the Emperor Sri Sri Sri Bijjala, the Protector of the whole world; Lord of the earth, Emperor of Emperors; God Supreme among the Emperors, Master of Kalanjarapura, Hearer of the beats of* damaru-*drum and the Owner of the banner bearing the signet of the golden bull!"*) His Majesty must be going to the court now. Let us light the torches. (*They hold the torches in their left hands and swords in their right. Emperor Bijjala comes out seated on the palanquin amidst the sound of pipes and drums. Jagadeva and Mallibomma walk ahead with torches in hand and beckoning to each other. When they reach the vantage point, they throw away the torches, shout the slogan, "Down with the enemy of* saranas! *Down with the non-believer!", drag Emperor Bijjala out of the palanquin and sever his head. People are frightened and scatter away from there. There is great turbulence among the people. Emperor Bijjala's soldiers chase Jagadeva and Mallibomma and kill them.*)

(V. v. pp. 109-12)

But yet the royal soldiers chase and kill them. Then they rush to the Socio-Spiritual Academy and kill several *saranas* there. Jagadeva, Mallibomma and other *saranas* become martyrs of their faith. The conflict between orthodox religion (of Vedic Brahmins and Saiva *acharyas*) is finally resolved in favour of orthodox religion. But still the play ends on a tragic note. One cannot help pitying King Bijjala, who had to sacrifice his life at the hands of two fanatics, i.e. Jagadeva and Mallibomma simply because he had to please the orthodox Brahmins of his kingdom. Actually, being a Kshatriya king, he has no axe to grind with any religion, be it Vedicism or Saivism or Virasaivism. He had to please the orthodox group who were sour about the emergence of a new, liberal and protestant religion of Basaveswara. In the tussle between Brahmanism and Virasaivism in his kingdom,

King Bijjala had to sacrifice his life unnecessarily. Although Basaveswara was unseated from the position of Finance Minister and banished from the city of Kalyana by King Bijjala, Basaveswara's new religion of Virasaivism and its attendant doctrine could not be destroyed. Although Bijjala's orthodox group was triumphant politically Basaveswara's new religion could not be defeated or destroyed in the long run. Whereas King Bijjala's group triumphs over Basaveswara's group politically, Basaveswara's group of *saranas* achieves their own ideological triumph. As the later history of Karnataka shows, Basaveswara's religion, social-spiritual doctrine and liberal humanism have been kept alive all through these centuries. Lingayatism or Virasaivism has been a living religion in Karnataka and the surrounding states in South India. As Sri Kumara Swamiji rightly points out, "It may be stated as a fact that the greater the man, the larger the number of detractors. The time comes when the voices lifted in blame are stilled and the worth of a man is placed beyond criticism. Pilate, priests and the Pharisees have passed away; who now speaks ill of Jesus? Buddha was maligned by Devadatta and others spoke ill of him, but time has silenced those voices. Basava was criticized by the calumniators, but their voices are now drowned. Today Basava is acknowledged as one of the great prophets that the world has ever seen."

Thus, there is a double dimension to the play. *Fall of Kalyana* is thus a solid historical-religious play known for its historical authenticity and accuracy. It highlights Basaveswara's doctrinaire philosophy and practice very convincingly. The playwright has succeeded in representing the historical reality with its ideological backdrop quite successfully by covering all the important aspects of Basaveswara and his movement like the religious, social, and ideological doctrines. The playwright has compressed the vast material of 12th-century Karnataka history in his representation and offered a rich, authentic and panoramic picture of the era, which is not a joke. Such a comprehensive picture of Basaveswara and his *sarana* movement is, unfortunately not offered by the clever playwrights like P. Lankesh, Girish Karnad and H.S. Shivaprakash.

The play has its relevance even today as the problems faced by Basaveswara in the twelfth century are still prevalent in modern India. The similar problems are to be fought against and solved by great social activists like Raja Rammohun Roy, Mahatma Gandhi and Dr. B.R. Ambedkar. Hence, the present-ness of the past is strongly affirmed by this historical and religious play.

Notes

* In the third quarter of the 12th-century Karnataka witnesses a political revolution, which shook the very Chalukya Kingdom. In fact, it sounded the death knell of the Chalukya power. This revolution was spearheaded by a family famous in Karnataka history as that of the Kalachuris. The Kalachuris were the feudatories of the Chalukyas of Kalyana.

The Kalachuris of Karnataka claim to be descendents of the Kalachuris of central India. The latter in turn claim to belong to the lunar race, although some of them, i.e. Kalachuris of Ratanpur claim to belong to the solar race.

They trace their ancestry to puranic origin. Kartavirya is said to be the first ancestor of the family. This king famous in the epics, was the descendent of Pururava, whose grandfather, (Buddha's father) was Soma (Moon). Ila, wife of Soma, was the daughter of Surya (Sun). Hence, the members of the Kartavirya family belonged to the lunar race paternally and to the solar, maternally. Kartavirya's predecessor was a Haihaya and several ruling families came into existence through the king bearing that name. The Kalachuris were one such. Mahishmati, the present Onkar Mandhata was one of their capital cities.

But historically the Kalachuris appear as Katachchuris in the 6th century A.D. Krishnaraya of this family ruled over a vast area comprising Malava, Gujarat, Konkan, Maharashtra and Vidarbha. His son, Sankaragana ably held the kingdom, but the latter's son, Buddharaja was unfortunate and lost the battle against Mangalesa, the Chalukya King of Badami.

Years later, one of the descendents of Buddharaja, by name Vamaraja conquered the fort of Kalanjara, a place in the present Banda district of Madhya Pradesh. Tripuri, modern Tewar, near Jabalpur was their capital. The region over which they ruled was called the Chedi or Dahala-Mandala. These Kalachuris are referred to as the Kalachuris of Tripuri. The territories over which these kings held sway was known as Chedi-mandala or

Dahala-mandal, which included Bundelkhand and Baghelkhand of later days. They were also closely associated with Kalanjara, which was their early stronghold and was regarded as a holy place dedicated to Lord Siva. It is now in Banda District, 90 miles west-south-west of Allahabad. These Kalachuris remained in power roughly from the 6th to the 13th century. Of all the Kalachuri families, the Kalachuris of Tripuri were the most powerful and famous, having the longest record of political power.

A few more Kalachuri families ruled in different regions during the medieval centuries. One was the Kalachuris of Sarayupara, also called the Kalachuris of Gorakhpur. Another family was ruling in south Kosala comprising modern Chhattisgarh in central India and the adjoining tract in the Odisha State up to the Cuttack District. The main line of this dynasty is styled the Kalachuris of Ratnapur or Tumman. It was later split up into a younger offshoot which ruled from Raipur.

As political rivals and rulers of neighbouring kingdoms, the Kalachuris clashed with the kings of Karnataka. Apart from this, the former could also contract matrimonial alliances with the latter.

Forced by adverse circumstances and impelled probably by an ambitious motive to seek fortune elsewhere a member or a family unit of the Kalachuris of Tripuri appears to have migrated to the south, though it is not known precisely when. The Kalachuris of Karnataka were the lineal descendants of the Kalachuris of central India and inherited many traits and traditions of their ancestors. There was a little controversy about their religious faith also. For several years scholars erroneously believed that these Kalachuris were the followers of Jainism, but it has been established now through serious research that they were Saivas.

Being adherents of Siavite Faith they had Nandi, the Divine Bull, the mount of Lord Siva was adopted as their royal emblem by the northern Kalachuris. The southern Kalachuris of Karnataka also the same deity as their royal emblem painted on their banner, which is invariably mentioned as *suvarna-vrisabha-dwaja* in their *prasasti*.

The meaning of 'Kalachuri' is variously understood as 'powerful like the Sun' and 'skilful (clever) like the sword'. This is a controversial issue which has not been resolved yet by the Kannada epigraphists and linguists.

* The city of Mangalaveda or the modern Mangalavedhe (presently in the Solapur District of Maharashtra) played a significant role in the early and later history of the Kalachuris of Karnataka. Bijjala II (1130-68)—the protagonist of the present play, *Fall of Kalyana*—was the son of Permadi (son of Jogamarasa) and Nagaladevi. He had two brothers, namely Rajala and Mailugi (or Mallikarjuna).

He had six sons: (1) Vajradeva, (2) Sovideva, (3) Mailugi (Mallikarjuna), (4) Sankama, (5) Ahavamalla, (6) Singhana, and two daughters, (7) Siriyadevi (who married to Sinda Chavunda), and (8) another daughter (whose name is not known correctly yet married to Barmarasa).

Like his father and grandfather, Bijjala II started his career as a Mahamandaleswara or feudatory chief under the Chalukya Emperors of Kalyana. But he was strong and powerful and wielded considerable influence at the Chalukya court and in their dominions on account of the matrimonial alliance of his house with that of his suzerains.

In 1150 A.D., Jagadekamalla's rule ended and his younger brother Taila III ascended the Chalukya throne. This prince was junior to Bijjala II and in no way superior to the latter. He did not possess any outstanding ability as events show.

The defeat and discomfiture of Taila III at the hands of his Kakatiya feudatory Prola II in 1155 A.D. gave a fillip to the mounting ambition of Bijjala II. Soon Bijjala II decided to set himself free from the state of subordination and behave like a sovereign king, divested of Chalukya suzerainty. He made rapid progress in his plan of usurping the Chalukya throne and finally succeeded in doing so in 1162 A.D. and became the overlord of the Chalukya dominions. Taila III became a victim of evil machinations of the usurper and lost his life.

Bijjala's usurpation of the Chalukya throne by unfair means and the atrocities committed by him to achieve his end, contaminated the entire political and social atmosphere in the country, and its effects were far-reaching.

Mangalivada or the modern Mangalavedhe was the permanent capital and headquarters of all the rulers of the Kalachuri family. His kingdom extended from Mandalavada up to Banavasi in the south Karnataka.

The political situation in his kingdom was far from satisfactory. Bijjala was not destined to enjoy the fruits of his ill-gotten prize long and peacefully. He reigned for a short period of six years at the end of which he seems to have been forced to step down from his office in an adverse condition.

In his palace itself there were parties and factions which were the breeding house of intrigues.

* According to the historian Dr. P.B. Desai, the dates of Emperor Bijjala II's life are as follows:

Birth: 1110 A.D.
Started his career in 1130 A.D. in the reign of Someswara III.
Became the Governor of Karahada-4000 province in 1142A.D. in the reign of Jagadekamalla II.
Became the Governor of Tardavadi-1000 division in 1147 A.D.
Death: 30 April 1196.

* According to the historian Dr. P.B. Desai, the dates of Basaveswara's life are as follows:

Basava's Birth: 21 Jan. 1140 A.D.
Employment: 1157 A.D.
Went to Kalyana: 1160 A.D.
Gave up office: 1168 A.D.
Left Kalyana: 12 Feb. 1196 A.D.
Died: 02 July 1196 A.D.

(For more details, the reader may refer to *Basavesvara and His times*, by Dr. P.B. Desai, Dharwad: KRI, Karnatak University, 1968.)

Basava (later known as Basavswara) was the second son of Madarasa and Madalambike. He had an elder brother, Devaraja and an elder sister, Nagalambike.

Madarasa was a nobleman of *Kamme* community of Brahmins and lord and Mayor of Begewadi *agrahara* consisting of 500 learned counselors or *mahajanas* and it was near another famous village Ingaleswara both in the present Bijapur district. Vedic sacrifices were performed and animals were immolated in Bagewadi as also elsewhere during that time. The boys in the agrahara of Bagewadi were made to learn Sanskrit from the beginning. The lessons and courses taught included less of secular subjects like language and literature, and more of religious lore like the Vedas, Agamas, Epics, Puranas and a few disciples such as lexicon, grammar and logic. While undergoing training, rites, and rituals had to be performed. Thus, even in education, the atmosphere was not free, being rigid with instructions, restrictions and disciples.

Sangama or Kudala-Sangama (also known as Kappadi-Sangama) now a village in the Hungaund taluka of Bijapur district connotes a confluence of River Krishna and River Malaprabha. The Temple of Sangameswara is erected just on the brow of the confluence itself. It is of about the eleventh century and presents an interesting spectacle with its artistic and epigraphical treasures. The site of the confluence below is graced with a modest *mantapa* with a Linga installed in it. Sangama is renowned as a great *tirtha* or sacred place, visited by thousands of pilgrims all-round the year. Its sanctity has been augmented by its later association with Basaveswara who chose this place for his austerities, spiritual elevation and final beatitude. Sangama was an eminent religious centre, a centre of education and a stronghold of the Kalamukha or Pasupata Saiva sect.

At Sangama, Basava had the good fortune of securing his guide and preceptor, Isanyaguru, who was the chief of the township, a divine of deep insight and a well-read scholar of catholic views. This preceptor appears to have been a follower of the Pasupata doctrine. Basava spent about twelve years at Sangama.

Mangalavada (modern Mangalvedhe) which means an 'abode of good' is at present situated in the Pandharapur Taluka of Sholapur District in Maharashtra State. It is about twelve miles from Pandharapur. Mangalavada was a flourishing town where Bijjala ruled with authority and affluence. He had his palace and administrative departments whose officers were engaged in activities like the collection of revenue, accounting, and maintenance of the army. As an apprentice seeking employment, Basava secured entry into the Accounts Branch of the secretariat as a junior accountant on a salary of 101 *hons* (gold coins) per year. Basaveswara lived at Mangalavada for over two decades from 1132 to 1153 A.D.

Kalyana (in the modern Bidar District in north Karnataka) stands out as a great centre of historical importance on account of the fact that it had the privilege of becoming the capital city of the extensive empire of the Chalukya monarchs who are known in history as the Later Chalukyas or the Chalukyas of Kalyana.

Anubhava Mantapa is variously translated as the Mystic Academy, Socio-Spiritual Academy, Mystic Parliament and so on. It easily brings to our mind Plato's Academy. It can also be described as mystic seminary where all the *saranas* gathered and discussed their spiritual experiences and codified them into mystic utterances. The galaxy of enlightened sages, saints, and seekers known as *saranas* came to Kalyana for inspiration from Basaveswara and to be benefited. All of them participated in the discussion or seminar at the *Anubhava Mantapa*, shared and exchanged their views of life and codified them into mystic utterances. The charismatic personality of Basaveswara attracted a number of spiritual seeks from different parts of India. To mention a few of them here: Allamaprabhu, Siddharama, Madivala Machayya, Havinahala Kallayya, Aggavaniya Honnayya, Bahuru Bommayya, etc. (from Karnataka); Urilingadeva, Kumbara Gundayya (from Maharashtra); Bahurupi Chaudayya, Telugesa Masanayya, Sakalesa Madarasa, Sripati Pandita (from Andhra Desa); Madara Chennayya, Meremindadeva (from Tamil Nadu); Bhadragayaka, Cheramaraya (from Kerala); Adayya, Soddala Bacharasa (from Gujarat); Moligeya Marayya and his wife Mahadevi (from Kashmir).

There were many distinguished women too; for instances Mahadevi, Akkamahadevi, Satyakka, Muktayakka, Gundavve, Remmavve, Ammavve, Kalavve, Vaijavve, Annaladevi, Pittavve, Sivapriya Nachi, who came from different parts of the country.

These devotees belonged to all sections of the society, high and low, rich and poor, learned and uneducated. They pursued various avocations and were associated with different skills and crafts. For instance, Marayya and Sakalesa Madarasa belonged to the ruling class; Basava himself was originally a Brahmin; Adayya was a merchant; Madivala Machayya was a washerman; Kumbara Gundayya was a potter; Talavara Ramideva was a village servant; Kinnari Bommayya was a goldsmith; Jodhara Madanna was a soldier; Dohara Kakkayya was a tanner; Madara Chennayya was a cobbler. Besides these, there were devotees who belonged to the other occupations like those of a tailor, weaver, basket-maker, oil-miller, farmer, cowherd, ferryman, barber, hunter, grass-rope maker and prostitute.

In this Anubhava Mantapa Basaveswara and his companion *saranas* discussed their socio-spiritual experiences and endeavoured to envision their Utopian society free from caste, class, and gender-discrimination.

Basaveswara had two wives: (i) Gangambika, daughter of his maternal uncle, Baladeva and (ii) Nilambika (or Nilalochane), daughter of Siddharasa Dannayaka, whom King Bijjala informally gave (as his foster-sister), in marriage to Basava. According to Harihara, the name of Basava's second wife is Mayidevi. There is some critical controversy about the identity of Basava's second wife. Basaveswra had a son named Balasangayya or Chikkasangayya in *vacana* literature. (For further details, see Dr. R.C. Hiremath's biographical essay in the Commemoration Volume.)

The thirty-six years of Basaveswara's temporal and spiritual career can be divided into the following three well-marked stages or periods:

1. Nine years: Commencement and rise to supreme position in his official career; experiments in socio-religious reforms; spiritual advance.

2. Twelve years: Intensive socio-religious reformist activities; spiritual and mystic attainments.

3. Fifteen years: Indifference to secular pursuits; plunge and dedication to serve the devotees and uplift the masses.

The impetuous followers of Basaveswara, who murdered Bijjala, were not two but three, i.e. Jagadeva, Malla and Brahmayya, as named in the original Telugu *Basavapuranamu* (by Palkurike Somanatha) as well as in Kannada *Basavapurana* (by Bhimakavi). But in the later works they become two, the second name, Mollibommanna being the merger of the last two.

Basaveswara has been held in high esteem by the people of all castes, creeds and is regarded as an epoch-making personality. In the words of K.S. Srikantan, "It is no exaggeration to say that the message of Sri Basava is like a reservoir into which all previous thoughts flowed in and from which all later thoughts flowed out. Kind like Buddha, simple like Mahavir, gentle like Jesus, bold like Mohammad, Basava strikes us almost as a wonder of creation. But what attract us most to him are those teachings of his in which he anticipated the greatest of modern thinkers—Karl Marx and Mahatma Gandhi" (*Sri Basaveswara: A Commemoration Volume*, p. vii).

Dasoha: Literally means 'I am the servant of God', but metaphorically indicates total effacement of the ego. In Virasaivism, it has a special meaning according to which man is a servant of God as well as of the society. In empirical terms, it means 'free distribution of food to the believers.'

Istalinga: A tiny black symbol resembling a blueberry or *jamun* fruit, made of the soot of ghee containing within it a tinier icon of Iswara-linga. This icon symbolizes the union of microcosm and macrocosm and is, therefore, worshipped by Lingayata or Virasaivas everyday by being kept on their left palm, decked with vermillion, *vibhuti* and flowers and stared at constantly for a brief or long while (from five minutes to even six hours) simultaneously accompanied by transcendental meditation, i.e. mental repetition of Siva mantra (*Om Namah Sivaya*) with or without the help of a rosary of *rudraksi* beads.

Jangama: Literally 'dynamic, moving, kinetic, flowing, lively, mobile, active', etc. By extension it suggests an itinerant preacher interested in social welfare and fighting vehemently for his faith.

Kalamukha-Jangamas: Also known as Saiva-Jangamas. These people are said to have lived in and around Karnataka from tenth century A.D. to twelfth century A.D. They were closely associated with the temple-culture consisting of Saiva temples and monasteries. They were closely connected with the professions like priesthood, education, medicine, and food. They were like Vedic Brahmins, but slightly different from them.

Karma: Literally 'work or deed.' But in religious field it suggests the rituals preached by the *karma-kanda* section of the Vedas. In twelfth-century Karnataka, such rituals were practiced very rigidly. Basaveswara found them to be meaningless and rebelled against them vehemently.

Kayaka: Any labour, physical or mental done in the name of God. The concept of *kayaka* is easily comparable at least partially to Karl Marx's idea of 'labour'. *Kayaka* may, therefore, be said to be any labour dedicated to God.

Static (*Sthavara*): It means stagnant, still, immobile. It refers to the immovable stone temple built in the name of God. These sacred abodes were desecrated by the priestly exploitation of poor people, animal sacrifice and prostitution (*devadasi* system). Basaveswara, therefore, rebelled against the building of static temples and pleaded for the transformation of human being himself into a mobile temple.

Virasaivism: The new religion propounded by Basaveswara is known as Virasaivism, i.e. Protestant Saivism (or militant/heroic Saivism). Since the Virasaivas wear the symbol, istalinga on their chest or around their neck, they are also called Lingayats (or Bearers of the Linga on their persons). As J.M. Hondius, scholar and philosopher from Amsterdam opines, "Virasaivism is an up to date religion, closer to Christianity, Judaism and Western Gnosticism than any eastern religion I know. In my opinion Western religion and Western philosophy could learn from Virasaivism that you can experience God immanently as Sakti.... In that case you can immanently get in tune with the universe and in harmony with the spiritual growth of mankind.... At the same time you can transcendently meet God as 'The Other One' (Siva). If your experience is genuine the innermost Self as Sakti (Maria-Sophia) and God as the Other One (Siva) go together in full harmony. There is no conflict as there has so often been in the opinion of the Western churches and in Western philosophy. But there is more, the significance and the influence of Basava has not ended yet" (*Sri Basaveswara: A Commemoration Volume*, p. 84).

Sunya-Chair (Sunya-Pitha): Literally means the Chair of Absolute Void or Principle or Abstract Truth. *Sunya* does not mean void as in Buddhism. On the contrary, it bears a special, positive meaning in Virasaiva parlance. Such a Chair had been created and kept vacant for twelve years until an eligible saint or mystic was found. Basaveswara considered Allamaprabhu to be the ideal and worthy saint and therefore, enthroned him as the Chairman of the *Sunya*-Chair.

Vacana: A mystical, metaphysical, and poetic utterance marked by pithiness, concreteness of imagery or philosophical reflectiveness. Normally, it is recited rhythmically, but occasionally it can be sung to the accompaniment of music. The *saranas* (male saints) and the *saranes* (female saints) of twelfth-century Karnataka composed countless *vacanas* impromptu inspired by their experiences and observations of life. For example, Basaveswara himself has composed about 1100 *vacanas* most of which are available in scholarly as well as popular editions in Kannada. Some of them are available in English translation also.

Velevali: 'A loyal servant' of the master, who has taken a vow in his life that he would kill himself by severing his head with a master-sickle whenever his master dies, in order to show or prove his loyalty to him.

Reference

Kalburgi, M.M. *Fall of Kalyana*, Tr. Basavaraj Naikar, New Delhi: Sarup Book Publishers, 2010. All the page references are to this edition.

Works Cited

Bhimakavi, *Basava Purana* (Kannada). Ed. Hiremath. R.C. Dharwad: Murughamath, 2010.

Chidananda Murthy, M., *Basavannanavaru* (Kannada) Bengaluru: Sapna Book House, 2003.

Desai, P.B., *Basavesvara and His Times*, Dharwad: KRI, Karnatak University, 1968.

Gopal, B.R., *The Chalukyas of Kalyana and the Kalachuris*, Dharwad: Karnatak University, 1981.

Hendi, B.B., *Basaveswara*, Tr. Sadanand Kanavalli, Dharwad: Karnatak University, 2010.

Iswaran, K., *Speaking of Basava: Lingayat Religion and Culture in South Asia,* Oxford: Westview Press, 1992.

Jaware Gowda, D., *Basava Samhite*, Mysore: J.S.S. Mahavidyapitha, 2010.

Karmarkar, A.P. *A Cultural History of Karnataka*. Dharwad: Karnataka Vidyavardhaka Sangha, 1947.

Kumara Swamiji, "Sri. Basaveswara: A Prophet," in *Sri. Basaveswara: A Commemoration Volume*, p. 59.

Tipperudraswamy, H., *Basaveswara*, New Delhi: Sahitya Akademy, 2008.

Wodeyar, Sadashiva, *Sri Basaveswara (Eighth Centenary Commemoration Volume)*, Bengaluru: Government of Mysore, 1967.

• • • • •

6

Ramanujar: The Story of a Religious Reformer

Indira Parthasarathy has written three (many) plays on Indian history dealing with South Indian, especially Tamil religious history (like *The Legend of Nandan* and *Ramanujar*) and one dealing with the Mughal history of North India (like *Aurangzeb*). In all these plays Parthasarathy has successfully presented the slices of Indian history in artistic terms in a very convincing manner thereby highlighting their contemporary relevance. These plays show the dramatist's deep historical scholarship, research-oriented approach and a strong dramatic sense which combined together ideally produce a powerful dramatic vision of life.

The present play, *Ramanujar: The Life and Ideas of Ramanuja* was originally written in Tamil and published in 1999 and translated into English by T. Sriraman and published in 2008 by the Oxford University Press, New Delhi. It is due to his solid contribution to the genre of religious drama that Indira Parthasarathy was honoured with the prestigious award of Saraswati Samman in 1999. Although the play apparently deals with a religious theme and a religious hero like Ramanujacharya, it is built on a strong foundation of South Indian history, especially that of Tamil and Kannada countries. The playwright has rightly chosen a transitional phase of medieval South Indian history involving a change of religious philosophy from Saivism and Jainism to Vaishnavism. Ramanujacharya is a hero as a religious saint in the Carlylean phraseology who consolidated his distinctive philosophy called Qualified Monism (*Visistadvaita*) declared the supremacy of Lord Narayana and organized and regulated the monastic institution of Vaishnavism.

Although the life and history of Ramanujacharya is wide, lengthy, complicated, complex, and even contradictory according to the hagiographical sources, Parthasarathy, like a typical experienced dramatist, has selected a few important external facts of his life found in historical sources like epigraphs and hagiographic and poetic narratives and successfully offered a coherent and convincing picture of Ramanuja's life and mission. In this sense, his play has the ideal qualities of historical authenticity and accuracy to a great extent. He has taken liberty only with a few minor details, but on the whole his play and vision of life is in conformity with the historical reality of 11th century Tamil and Kannada countries.

All the major characters of his play are borrowed from the matrix of South Indian history—like Alavandar (Yamunacharya), Ramanujar (the eponymous hero), Tanjamma, Tirukkachi Nambi (Kanchi Purna), Kuresar, Andal Amma, Mudaliyandan, Yadava Prakasar, Araiyar, Amudanar, Periya Nambi, Maraner Nambi, Attuzhay, Urangavilli, Ponnachi, Tirumangai Ashwar, Kidambi Achan, Govindaperumal, Yagnesan, Varadan, Puruttikkollai and Naluram. These historical personages are accompanied by other typical characters like disciples, visitors, alms-seekers, brahmins, young women and so forth. The interaction of all these characters (with proper names and general, typical names) contribute a great deal to the dramatic vision of life projected by Indira Parthasarathy.

The external facts about Ramanujacharya's life and philosophy are available in the discursive and desiccated form. But the dramatist has organized them in a coherent dramatic art-form and fleshed them out with the immediacy of experience impregnated with the inner thought process, ideology or philosophy. In other words, he has given the characters and their mutual interactions a psychological and ideological structure and dimension enlivened with sense-perceptions and emotions. The dramatic experience presented through a variety of such characters generally conforms to the law of probability and historical authenticity. Hence, it easily appeals to the spectators, captures their attention and offers them the much coveted aesthetic delectation or *rasananda*.

The dramatist's achievement may be said to be twofold: one, the judicious selection of historical events and personages and two, the transformation of this historical reality into art, especially dramatic art through the employment of a distinct technique. A detailed analysis of his thematic concerns and the dramatic technique may be seen in the following paragraphs.

The dramatist's intention is to show Ramanujar's sincere and serious attempt to synthesize the Tamil spirituality and Sanskrit spirituality and to perceive the deeper unity in them. This attempt at synthesizing the pan-Indian great tradition and the local, Tamil, little tradition may be exemplified by his extension of recognition for both the Azhwars and the Acharyas. For example, the tradition of Azhwars is represented by the three historical personages like Poykai, Bhootama, and Pey, whereas the tradition of Acharyas is represented by Nathamuni, Uyyakondar, Manakkal Nambi, Alavandar, and Ramanujar. In order to show this synthesis of two traditions, the playwright employs the technique of a prologue. Obviously, the prologue sets the scene several centuries before Ramanuja by dramatizing a very famous legend about the three primal Azhwars in Tamil country known as Pei, Poigai, and Bhootam.

As the prologue begins, three persons drenched in rain come one after another and seek shelter. Then they see the fourth person, who is said to be God. Then all the three of them sings songs (*pasurams*) about the earth as lamp—lamp of supreme knowledge and Goddess Lakshmi.

Then a Voice announces that Poykai, Bhootama, and Pey are the first three Azhwars who taught the humanitarian religion. This is illustrated by the three persons seeking shelter from rain. After the Azhwars comes the Acharyas like Nathamuni, Uyyakondar, Manakkal Nambi, Alavandar, and Ramanujar. Thus, the historical tradition of the Azhwars and the Acharyas is shown symbolically through the technique of the employment of a prologue and preparing the proper ground for dramatic action. "Indira Parthasarathy's purpose in beginning his play on Ramanuja with this episode seems to be twofold: (i) The origins of Vaishnavism lie in the mystical experiences of the Azhwars of the supremacy of Lord Narayana; (ii) humanism and empathy are the indisputable paths to the Divine. The playwright hence uses the hymns of the three Azhwars intertextually to reiterate that the acharyas (preceptors) of Vaishnavism, including Ramanuja, derive their humane spirituality from the tradition of the Azhwars.... Thus the hovel in which they are forced to huddle together becomes the site of manifestation of Divine light. Hence in each hymn, the dominant image and image clusters have to do with the lamp, wick, ghee, light, and finally, enlightenment and vision. Enlightenment comes only in a moment when one realizes, 'Thy need is greater than mine.' When such a realization dawns on the soul the Lord reveals Himself in all splendour. Hence the third song uses the phrase 'I have seen' in a reiterative manner. The Prologue thus serves the purpose of highlighting the humanist spiritual tradition from which Ramanuja descends. It also prepares the reader for a redefinition of the term 'Vaishnava' which occurs as a leitmotif throughout the play" (Indra, C.T., Commentary on the Play, *Ramanujar*, pp. 103-04).

The first scene of the first Act begins with Alavandar's[1] immersion in the devotional music. A great and revolutionary preceptor of Vaishnavism, Alavandar believes in the immateriality of Vishnavism. After getting out of the rapture of singing the *pasuram*, he announces that the Vaishnavite never dies spiritually. He has cherished three dreams in his life: (i) to establish a casteless society thereby making spiritual salvation possible even for the lowliest man; (ii) to expand the boundaries of Vaishnava dharma; and (iii) to write a Commentary of the *Brahmasutras*. He is happy to know that his first mission is done, as the slum-dweller Tambi Maraner has become his disciple. But the other two dreams are not fulfilled yet. He believes hopefully that his mission will be continued by his disciple, Ramanujar. He has, therefore, sent Periya Nambi (or Mahapurna) to fetch Ramanujar from Kanchi as he believes in the view that continuity is the principle of life. But he is dead before Periya Nambi brings Ramanujar there. Ramanujar observes the three fingers of Alavandar's right hand folded up and therefore asks the disciples for the reason. They explain that the three-folded fingers symbolize the three unfulfilled desires of Alavandar. Ramanujar now realizes his responsibility as a disciple of Alavandar and therefore decides to fulfil all the three desires of his Guru through the grace of God and practice of *bhakti*.

In this scene, the dramatist seems to have taken some minor liberties with the historical details. According to historical sources, the disciples of Alavandar did not know the three dreams or desires of their Guru. It is the bystanders who give a vague picture of the three likely desires of Alavandar. The three desires are (i) gratitude must be shown to the memory of Krishnavyyasa and Parasara; (ii) a tribute should be paid to Nommalwar; and (iii) Vyasasutras or Brahmasutras must be commented on from the point of view of Visistadvaita. But the playwright has changed at least two of the three desires to suit the requirements of modern times like caste-equality and gender-equality *a la* Ambedkar. This is an attempt on the part of the dramatist to interpret history from the modern standpoint or to contemporize history. The playwright seems to offer a revisionist historiography to satisfy the psychology of the modern man. Indira Parthasarathy states in his Preface to the play that he deliberately gave an ideological underpinning to the first two wishes because in his opinion such a far-sighted acharya, who wanted to spread an enlightened doctrine, could not have conceived of naïve desires as having far-reaching consequences for the society. As C.T. Indra rightly opines, "As a modern playwright with a revisionist sense of history Indira Parthasarathy thinks that the first two wishes must be in consonance with the third wish. He finds it somewhat ridiculous to reduce the stature of Alavandar by interpreting his wishes so literally. Hence the first wish of Alavandar in this play is to uplift the outcaste and the oppressed and establish a casteless society. The second wish metamorphoses into a desire to see the expansion of an enlightened Vaishnavism. Thus Indira Parthasarathy alters the text and textuality of hagiographic writings along the lines of the thinking of Vaishnava acharya. His justification for this rewriting is the fact that Alavandar was the progenitor of Ramanuja in social reform and that social reform is not separate from spiritual reform" (C.T. Indra, p. 103).

The dramatist wants to highlight Ramanujar's philosophy and practice of caste-equality, which were really revolutionary adventures viewed against the 11th century Indian context. That is why he makes Ramanujar prostrate at the feet of Tirukkachi Nambi, who stops the former on the ground that he is Vaisya and not a Brahmin. [The Tamil biographer, Kalyanarama Iyengar points out that Tirukkachi Nambi's caste is now known as Bel Chettis (Kalyanarama Iyngar 1978:166)]. The dramatist has not merely presented the South Indian religious history here, but also evaluated it through the important characters. For example, Tirukkachi Nambi comments that caste has not disappeared even with the efforts of Alavandar and that a Chetty has to stand at a distance from a Brahmin. But Ramanujar promises to eradicate the caste-difference among the Vaishnavites. In order to prove his liberal outlook on life, he invites Tirukkachi Nambi to partake of food (*amudu*) at his house the next day. Though Tirukkachi Nambi considers it as a great occasion, he expresses his doubt about Ramanujar's wife's purity-mania. But still he agrees to go to Ramanujar's house for food. In the Tamil biographies, there are two separate events that are collapsed here into one scene by Indira Parthasarathy. One takes place before Ramanujar's marriage when he meets Tirukkachi Nambi and offers to prostrate before him. The other takes place after his marriage to Tanjamma when he invites Tirukkachi Nambi for a meal. One may easily see how Indira Parthasarathy has compressed the two historical events into one for the artistic purpose of focusing and concentrating on the caste-hierarchy and caste psychology of the people in the mediaeval age.

The playwright has depicted the character of Tanjamma very realistically and convincingly. She is a beautiful lady but yet does not know how to smile. She is an embodiment of rigid brahmanical orthodoxy. When Ramanujar tells her to prepare lunch for the guest, she remains rather indifferent to his request. She grows angry and sarcastically points out the caste-difference between the two, i.e. Ramanujar and his Guru, Tirukkachi Nambi. She reminds her husband that he belongs to Somayaji family and that he should not forget the superiority of his caste. But Ramanujar clarifies that Kanchi Purna happens to be his Guru, who is equal to one's father. But Tanjamma being a rigid lady does not wish to entertain a guest of Chetty or Vaisya caste, which is one step below the Brahmin caste in the *varna*-hierarchy. But Ramanujar, who is quite liberal in his outlook on life, orders her to prepare the food as he, a Vaishnavite cannot go back on his words:

RAMANUJAR: Tirukkachi Nambi comes to our house tomorrow to have food.

(*Tanjamma, startled, looks up at him.*)

RAMANUJAR: Why, isn't that good news?

(*Tanjamma doesn't reply but continues to cut vegetables.*)

RAMANUJAR: Why this silence?

TANJAMMA (*looking down*): Tomorrow is a *Purattasi* Saturday.

RAMANUJAR: Yes, I know. We are truly blessed that Kanchi Purna comes to visit us tomorrow.

(*Tanjamma looks up at him quickly but bends her head immediately to resume cutting vegetables. Her indifference annoys him.*)

RAMANUJAR: I don't understand your silence.

TANJAMMA (*sarcastic*): Nice guest to have on an auspicious day!

RAMANUJAR (*pretending not to have caught her sarcasm*): Nice words!

TANJAMMA (*angry*): You belong to a Somayagi family, let not the thought slip your mind.

RAMANUJAR: Kanchi Purna is my guru. Isn't a guru the same as one's father?

(*Tanjamma attempts a smile. The smile doesn't look natural on her hard countenance.*)

RAMANUJAR (*smiling*): You had forgotten how to smile, and now you do. Isn't that a good outcome of the coming visit?

TANJAMMA (*angrily*): The son of a Chetty is my father-in-law. That is a nice outcome?

(*Anger shows on Ramanujar's face, but he contains it. He rises and paces for a while. He had not expected that Tanjamma would take the news in this way. There is now more pain than anger on his face.*)

RAMANUJAR (*suddenly, turning towards Tanjamma and in a firm voice*): There will be a feast for him tomorrow at our house. The Vaishnavite does not go back on his word.

(*He exits from the forestage L, with a pained look. Tanjamma stands like a statue. Darkness.*)

(I. ii. pp. 14-15)

Next day when Tirukkachi Nambi goes to Ramanujar's house, Ramanujar has already gone to the former's cottage to invite him for the lunch. This event is historically true, but the dramatist has taken minor liberty with the details. According to historical sources, Tirukkachi Nambi asks Ramanujar's wife to serve him food as he is in a hurry to attend to some holy service somewhere. But the playwright has made Ramanujar's wife ask the guest to have his lunch without waiting for her husband. Tirukkachi Nambi is quite confused and does not know what to do. She tells him to have his food and serves his food on the pial outside her house and does not reveal the fact that her husband has actually gone to the guest's house to fetch him there. By doing so she exhibits her purity-mania, brahmanical arrogance and contempt for the so-called shudra guest. Helpless as he is, Tirukkachi Nambi partakes of his food on the pial and goes away from there to attend to some urgent ritual elsewhere. He swallows the insult stoically and takes it his stride magnanimously. Here the dramatist's intention is, obviously, to highlight the caste-consciousness, superiority-complex, purity-mania, and arrogance of Tanjamma:

TIRUKKACHI NAMBI: It is my humble self...

(*He stops and stands a few steps before the entrance to the house, which is at the C of the rear stage. Silence for a while.*)

TIRUKKACHI NAMBI (*a little loudly*): It is my humble self...

(*Tanjamma enters from the opening in the rear stage.*)

TANJAMMA (*in a voice showing no emotion*): He is not at home. You can eat and go.

(*Nambi is a little shocked at this.*)

NAMBI: I will come later.

TANJAMMA: It is his order and it is my duty to carry it out.

(*Nambi does not know what he should do. He wonders whether Ramanujar would have asked her to serve him even he himself was not at home. He stands silent.*)

TANJAMMA: Please sit on the pial. I will serve you food.

(*This is another shock for Nambi. He is also worried that Ramanujar might feel unhappy if he went away without eating. He stands, confused.*)

TANJAMMA: Please sit.

(*She goes in, without waiting for his reply. Darkness. When the lights come on, Tanjamma is seen washing the pial. As she is doing so, Ramanujar enters from L forestage. He goes towards the rear stage. She continues washing the pial pretending that she had not noticed his coming. Ramanujar is puzzled.*)

RAMANUJAR: What are you doing? Why wash the pial at this time?

TANJAMMA (*Without looking at him*): *Atithi puja* is over.

RAMANUJAR: I don't understand.

TANJAMMA: That Vaisya came. Hospitality was shown to him.

RAMANUJAR: Even before I returned? I went to his house, he wasn't there.

TANJAMMA: It seems he had some urgent work. I served him food. He has left.

(*As if suddenly remembering, Ramanujar looks at the pial that she has just washed clean. There is anger on his face.*)

RAMANUJAR: You served him food on the pial, isn't that so?

(*She is silent.*)

RAMANUJAR: The place has been defiled by the Vaisya's sitting there, so you are cleansing it, isn't that so?

(*She is silent.*)

RAMANUJAR: So you didn't tell him that I had actually gone to fetch him?

(*She is silent.*

Extremely pained, he looks at her. She stands motionless, like a statue.)

RAMANUJAR: Does orthodoxy consist in crushing the *aniccha* flower?

(*Seeing that she has not answered any of his questions, he exits, disappointment reflected on his face.*)

(I. iii. pp. 15-16)

When Ramanujar returns home, he is surprised to observe that his wife is washing the pial. On enquiring her about it, he is shocked and disappointed to know that she has already served the food to the guest on the pial in an insulting manner and that she has not told the truth to the guest that her husband had actually gone out to fetch him. Ramanujar is very angry and helpless about his wife's arrogant behaviour. She has violated all the three Upanishadic commands: *Pitru devo-bhava, acharya devo-bhava, atithi devo-bhava.* He tells her that orthodoxy does not consist in crushing the *aniccha* flower. The scene ends with an intertextual use of a verse from Tirukkurul in which a guest is compared to an aniccha flower. Ramanuja uses this image to refer to Tirukkachi Nambi's sensitive being which Tanjamma has hurt by her acharam. The dramatist has, thus, highlighted the contrast between Ramanujar's liberalism and Tanjamma's rigid orthodoxy and the inevitable conflict between these contradictory approaches to life. This microscopic domestic conflict easily symptomizes the macroscopic social conflict among the castes. As Carmen remarks, "Ramanuja's wife had the usual Brahmin attitude towards those of all lower castes and even towards other Brahmins of sub castes considered inferior to one's own. And this attitude is typically expressed as a fear of ritual pollution" (Carmen, 1974:32). In fact, the act is described in the biographical/historical sources graphically. There she uses a stick to remove the plantain leaf on which food was served to Tirukkachi Nambi and then cleans the place with cowdung mixed with water and begins to cook afresh after bathing again.

The dramatist brings in one more episode to intensify the temperamental incompatibility between husband and wife. For example, one day Ramanujar is waiting for a masseur, who comes a bit late and looks rather pale and tired. When Ramanujar asked for the reason the masseur confesses to his hunger. Then Ramanujar asks Tanjamma to bring some food from the kitchen, but she lies that there is no food in the kitchen as she has not started cooking yet. Being suspicious of his wife's nature, Ramanujar goes into the kitchen and brings out a vessel of cooked rice. But he is surprised to notice that by that time the masseur has already left the place with a sense of humiliation. Ramanujar scolds his wife angrily and says that the Merciful God will not forgive her for denying the food to the hungry. But Tanjamma, due to her arrogance, does not care for his words. This episode reinforces the contrast between the liberal husband and the callous and rigid wife. In this episode, the playwright thus made minor alterations to the historical details. According to the historical sources, "on a certain morning some poor people came to Ramanuja and asked for food as they were hungry. Ramanuja inquired of his wife if she had any food left. 'No, not so much as a grain of it,' she said. Ramanuja suspected her sincerity, entered the kitchen and examined the vessels and lo! He found food hidden away. He called his wife, and angrily spoke to her thus: '/art thou capable of this, that when hungry men are waiting at the door, thou shouldst lie? Is there worse manners than this vice, refusing food to those who come in dire need of it and a lie is added to the meanness? O what a sin'" (Yamunacharya, M. *Ramanuja's Teachings in His Own Words*,

Bombay: Bharatiya Vidya Bhavan, 1970, pp. 13-14). Instead of making a few people asking for food, the playwright has made a masseur ask for food. In other words, he has compressed the number of people from many to one, i.e. masseur. This is quite in conformity with the dramatic principle of achieving the effect of concentration. He has followed the *Guruparampara* sources fairly closely even in the style of the dialogue in this scene.

A slow change has been taking place in the life of Ramanujar over the years. Periya Nambi has come to Kanchi in order to take Ramanujar to Tiruvarangam. Ramanujar acknowledges the knowledge that he has earned from Periya Nambi and the later Alavandar. But Periya Nambi replies humbly that he is only a formal teacher of Ramanujar, as Santipani was the formal teacher of Krishna, though the latter was a god. Here, Indira Parthasarathy echoes verbatim Ghoshti Purna in the sources but transfers the context from Maladhara (one of the five disciples of Alavandar mentioned in *Life of Ramanuja*) to Maha Purna.

He tells Ramanujar further that the latter is going to ascend the throne of Alavandar very soon when the Lord of Kanchi ordains it. The dramatist has maintained close proximity to historical sources which testify to the fact that Ramanujar kept Periya Nambi (Mahapurna) in his own house for six months and learnt the Tamil scriptures: "Ramanuja led his Guru Mahapurna and his consort to his house and accommodated them, providing them every comfort. For six months, Ramanuja sat at the feet of his Guru, and received from him important lessons on the Dravida scriptures and other mystery lore (*rahasya*) of the Sri Vaishnava faith" (Yamunacharya, p. 13).

The playwright brings in a third episode at this juncture. Tanjamma once gets irritated and complains that Periya Nambi's wife's pot touched her own pot while they were drawing water from a well and defiled her caste, because, she argues, the south is below the north and that Tiruvarangam is below Kanchi. Periya Nambi's wife cautions her to think before speaking cantankerously and compliments Ramanujar for putting them at his house. But Tanjamma wants to protect the purity of her caste (of Asoori family) from now onwards:

TANJAMMA (*irritated*): Defiled.

NAMBI'S WIFE (*shocked*): Defiled?

TANJAMMA: Yes...it is defilement. The Asoori family is known for its *acharam*.

NAMBI'S WIFE: What are you saying?

TANJAMMA: The south if below the north. Tiruvarangam is below Kanchi. Don't you understand?

NAMBI'S WIFE: Please think before you speak.

TANJAMMA: I am not in the habit of thinking before speaking. I am a fool. Will that do for you?

NAMBI'S WIFE: Did I say you were a fool? It was your husband who put us up in your home. What a noble soul he is!

TANJAMMA: Lots of people have said that and spoilt him. We have had enough of that. The reputation of the Asoori family has been sullied because of him. Hereafter it is my responsibility to protect our caste.

(I. v. pp. 18-19)

There is a social dimension to the sense of superiority that Tanjamma feels towards Maha Purna's wife. As Carmen points out, Maha Purna belonged to a slightly lower sub-sect of 'forelock Brahmins', also called *brahacharanam* who wore their sacred tuft further forward on their heads and with whom the higher *vedama* sub-sect did not have marriage alliances (1974:32).

By that time Ramanujar has returned home and overheard their conversation. Being exasperated beyond measure by his wife's arrogant behaviour he points out the three insults that he has done to people: (i) by serving food to Tirukkachi Nambi on the pial outside the house; (ii) by denying food to the hungry masseur; and (iii) by humiliating Periya Nambi's wife. These three episodes highlight the incompatibility of temperaments, philosophies, and outlooks between the couple. Whereas Ramanujar is spiritually oriented and transcendental in his approach to life, his wife is materially oriented and restricted by the rigid caste superiority and exclusivism. Hence, the twain cannot meet. These events spark off his latent spirituality and awaken his sense of renunciation. He, therefore, renounces the life of a married man or of a householder and orders her to go her own way. Thus, there is a major change in his life from worldliness to spirituality:

TANJAMMA (*guardedly*): She was the one...

RAMANUJAR (*steadily*): I have not asked you anything.

TANJAMMA: Is it wrong to be concerned about defilement?

RAMANUJAR: Nothing is wrong. It is only our conjugal life that is wrong.

TANJAMMA: What wrong did I do?

RAMANUJAR: What wrong you didn't do? You cast Kanchi Nambi aside, as though he were a scum. Where was the defilement? In your mind or in his caste? You denied food to someone who came hungry... was it *ahankaram* or *acharam* that made you do that? Today, you have insulted Peroya Nambi's wife. What wrong haven't you done? (*Silence for a few seconds.*) No, the mistake is mine.... There should be compatibility of hearts for conjugal union. If that is missing...

(*Silence for a while.*)

RAMANUJAR (*suddenly, turning towards her*): Why this façade of husband and wife?

(*Tanjamma looks at him, shocked. He paces for a while.*)

RAMANUJAR: Our paths are different. They can never meet. It is wise for us to live apart. Here and now. I renounce the life of a married man. I shall hereafter live for society.

TANJAMMA (*shocked*): What is this? I did wrong...

(*She makes to prostrate before him.*)

RAMANUJAR (*stopping her and picking her up*): No... Let me go my way. All my things will be yours from now. There is nothing that I shall call my own hereafter.

You go your way. I shall not interfere. That is best for both of us.

(I. v. pp. 19-20)

Thus, Ramanuja asks his pointblank that he wants to go his way and asks his wife to go her own way. This is the change that Parthasarathy has made in his play. But some of historical/biographical sources say that Ramanuja asked his wife to go to her family for a wedding and in her absence he went to Lord Varadaraja's sanctum and took the triple staff called *tridanda* to distinguish himself from the *advaitins* who hold a single staff or *eka danda* and who also cast off the sacred thread. He became Ramanuja Muni: 'He took ochre robes and triple staff'.

Now a new phase, of asceticism, begins in Ramanujar's life. He prays to the Merciful Lord to bless him with the courage of conviction to serve the society and bring equal justice to all, which is the life-breath of his Vaishnavism. (Here he sounds like our beloved Ambedkar.) He has become a full time sanyasi and resides at the monastery at Kanchi. His ascetic career is congenial for the fulfillment of his dreams. In this spiritual venture, he is assisted by Mudaliyandan, who is his sister's son. Parthasarathy compresses various historical events and episodes in Ramanuja's life into dramatically significant scenes. Thus, Act I foregrounds Ramanuja's youth and his householder life after renouncing which he spends time as an ascetic serving the Lord at the Kanchi temple. Eventually, he becomes the pontiff of the Srirangam monastery. This also entails a shift from the northern town of Kanchipuram to the southern town of Srirangam, which is the heart of Chola kingdom. He assumes leadership of the developing Vaishnava community, attracting intelligent and dedicated youngsters to the service of the new faith. Parthasarathy, once again, fuses the various episodes relating to Ramanuja's life between Kanchipuram and Srirangam to bring focus to bear on his progressive thinking and humane responses to the world. At this juncture a few like-minded people flock to him and add strength to his reformatory mission. For example, Kuresar and his wife, Andal Amma, go to the monastery at Kanchi and meet Ramanujar who welcomes them with great warmth. Now he has two great assistants in his spiritual mission. He considers Mudaliyandan and Kuresar as his staff (*tridandam*) and pennant (*pavitram*), and therefore two pillars of the edifice of Vaishnava community. Ramanujar defies the patriarchal norms of the society and believes in and practices gender-equality. That is why he welcomes Andal Amma also and declares that man and woman are equal in their community.

The dramatist has been true to historical sources which show clearly that Kuresar belonged to a rich family and well known for his munificence and charity and fed and clothed all the needy visitors to his house. As he was deeply impressed by Ramanujar's teaching, he gifted away his riches to the other people of his village and joined Ramanujar's company for the spiritual accomplishment. The dramatist has shown this briefly. For example, Kuresar has abandoned his riches before coming to see Ramanujar. While trudging the path in the thick forest Andal Amma feels apprehensive about the possibility of attack on them by robbers. But Kuresar attributes this fear to her possession of a golden cup in her bag. He, therefore, takes it out and throws it away. Thus, both husband and wife have overcome their worldliness before joining Ramanujar's spiritual mission.

There has been a philosophical conflict between Ramanujar and his guru, Yadava Prakasar. Whereas Ramanujar is a proponent of *Saguna Brahma* (Concrete Reality or Reality with Attributes), Yadava Prakasar is a proponent of *Nirguna Brahma* (Abstract Reality or Attribute-less Reality). Due to this scholastic disagreement between the two, Yadava Prakasar had caused a lot of hardship for Ramanujar in the past. But Ramanujar has taken everything in the right spirit. That is why he wants to take his *gurunathar* to Srirangam. But Mudaliyandan expresses his sense of surprise at Ramanujar's readiness to take with his *gurunathar*, who caused a lot of hardship in the earlier days. But Ramanujar says magnanimously that Yadava Prakasar did not act with any personal animosity towards him. Similarly, Yadava Prakasar introspects himself and feels guilty and restless for ill-treating his own disciple. When Ramanujar enters Yadava Prakasar's house to take him away, the latter seeks his disciple's forgiveness. Ramanujar pacifies his guru and takes him with him to Srirangam. The historical sources point out that Yadava's conversion was the result of his mother's admiration for Ramanuja. Parthasarathy has ignored this domestic detail in his play and instead made Yadava Prakasar repentant and given it a psychological dimension.

In this scene, the older generation of preceptors is represented not only by Tirukkachi Nambi but also Tiruvaranga Perumal Araiyar, the Cantor in Srirangam Temple. The latter comes to Kanchi to call upon Ramanuja to take up Alavandar's seat at the Srirangam monastery. Parthasarathy employs the *deus ex machina* as it is used in the biographical sources when the Cantor asks Lord Varadaraja for a boon which turns out to be Ramanujar himself. In the sources, the voice of the Lord is heard by everyone, and Ramanuja has to leave Kanchi.

The Second Act shows the next phase of Ramanujar's life busy with religious and social reformation. Ramanujar is middle-aged now and sufficiently experienced. His main target is to fortify the temple administration at Srirangam, because he believes that a culture built around the temple is the creed of the Vaishnavite religion and social justice is its very foundation and that it will be possible only if the temple administration comes into their hands. Kuresar intuitively prophesies that that day is coming soon.

As though in conformity with this expectation Amudanar, a Vaishnavite comes and meets Ramanujar, confesses to his old age and inability to control the selfish people and hands over the keys of the temple of Srirangam to Ramanujar who accepts them reverentially. He introduces Govindaperumal, Kidambi Achan and Mudaliyandan to Amudanar who wants to stay in their company in the temple itself as his home. In the play, surprisingly, Parthasarathy eulogizes the encounter between Ramanujar and the Chief Priest. It is made out in the scene as though the Chief Priest willingly surrendered the keys. However, there is no doubt that Ramanujar was a reformer who wanted to redefine the temple-centered life which was the axle of the wheel of Hindu society. Ramanujar wanted to follow an assimilationist policy by bringing about a friendly interaction between the various castes of society.

Ramanujar knows that his acceptance of the reins of administration of the temple will provoke resistance from many quarters, but he resolves to swim against the current courageously. By possessing the power of temple administration he thinks he can bring all his liberal policies into force. He has an impressive organizing ability. Parthasarathy has shown the various reforms that Ramanujar brought into effect in a brief manner without going into the details which may mar the concision of the dramatic form.

(But it is interesting to note these historical details as a contrast to Parthasarathy's compressed dramatization of them. The Tamil biographer, S. Kalyanarama Iyengar (1978: Ch. 17) gives some details about Ramanujar's reformist acts. We learn some interesting features in Ramanujar's distribution of work. For example, the administration of the inner shrine had ten divisions (*kothu*) which were entrusted to Brahmins. The outer administration of the rest of the temple too had ten divisions which were managed by Sudras or non-Brahmins. Iyengar lists the officials put in charge. Various non-Brahmins and subcastes were each assigned a temple task, be it the agrarian Vellala community or the blacksmiths, the carpenters, or the weavers who had to make fresh cloth for cooking, even the dhobis or laundering community, the rowers who had to cross over to the other side of river Kaveri during floods to bring provisions for the temple, etc. According to his order, the tenfold Sudra officials, as well as other upper-caste non-Brahmin merchants, in fact every group, had a designated privilege of serving the temple.)

Ramanujar wants to reform the function of the temple by admitting the devotees of all castes including women and allowing the Tamil hymns of Azhwars as well as Sanskrit Vedantis thus encouraging *Ubhava Vedantis*. The term *Ubhaya Vedanti* indicates a scholar who is equally proficient and knowledgeable in Sanskrit and Tamil. Ramanujar himself was such *Ubhayavedanti*. The truth of this scene is confirmed by the epigraphic evidence offered by the epigraphist, B.R. Gopal. Culturally speaking, Ramanujar's praise of Tamil also throws light on the tension between the two linguistic groups in South India—the hegemonic Sanskrit tradition and the Dravidian tradition led by Tamil. However, there is no recorded evidence that Ramanujar wrote anything in Tamil, although a number of statements are attributed to him in the oral tradition. Indira Parthasarathy's *Ramanujar* throws the privilege of reading the scripture open to all.

He intends to practice caste and gender-equality which is a revolutionary reformation in the caste-ridden patriarchal society of 11th-century India. As part of this liberalist agenda, he wants to allow the interpretation of the Tamil Veda by everyone and anyone (not necessarily by Brahmins) who is competent to do it. Further he pleads that aesthetics and spirituality are not different from each other. Being a liberal thinker he recognizes the unity and universality of spiritual or mystic experience cutting across the barriers of caste and language. He recognizes that Tamil, the language of common people can be as powerful a vehicle of articulating the mystic experience as Sanskrit, the elitist language (or the so-called divine language) can be. In other words, he wants to synthesize the Aryan and the Dravidian languages; the great tradition and the little tradition. That is why he easily yields to Amudanar's suggestion that they should learn the secret knowledge of Vaishnavism couched in Tamil language from the famous but tight-lipped scholar, Ghoshtipurna Nambi.

In those days, the spiritual or esoteric knowledge was couched in the form of philosophical poetry and kept in the custody of religious monks, saints, and scholars, especially Brahmins but occasionally and exceptionally non-Brahmins. It is against such background that Ramanujar takes his disciple Kuresar to Ghoshtiyar Nambi's house for the eighteenth time and requests him to reveal the secret knowledge of Tamil Vedas so that he may fulfil an unfulfilled wish of Alavandar. But Ghoshtiyar Nambi cold-shoulders them. When Ramanujar calls on him again, for the nineteenth time, the latter reminds him of coming alone with his *tridandam* and *pavitram*. Ramanujar explains that his two disciples, Kuresar and Mudaliyandan are his staff (*tridandam*) and pennant (*pavitram*), respectively. But Ghoshtipurna dismisses Ramanujar's explanation as a clever answer. However, he conveys the secret meaning of the Tamil Veda, especially the secret formula or mantra to Ramanujar privately and asks him not to reveal it to others and even threatens that he would go to hell if he did so:

NAMBI: This Rahasyartham is conveyed only to you. If you communicate it to anyone else, it will be betrayal of the guru and you will go to hell. This is my warning to you. Do you understand?

(II. ii. p. 31)

Ghoshtipurna's revelation of the secret knowledge of Tamil Vedas and its symbolic formula to Ramanujar is quite in keeping with the general practice of religious monks during the medieval age of India. But Ramanujar wants to revolutionize the whole thing and subvert the caste hierarchy and the closed system. That is why he violates his guru's instruction and warning quite boldly. He stands on the top of the temple wall and declares the Narayana mantra openly to the public. He declares further that the four-caste system is an injustice to Narayanan and that service to society is their supreme mission:

(*Ramanujar stands silent. Darkness. After a while, the stage is flooded with light. At C is a structure which looks like a temple wall. Ramanujar climbs on to it and stands there. He is flanked by Kurattazhwar and Mudaliyandan. In front of him stand together people of all castes.*)

RAMANUJAR: My purpose is to share my bliss with you. The one who has put on the universe as his body and who permeates the universe is Narayanan. There is no place where God dwells not. If we see Vikuntam everywhere, there is no high or low in what we see. The four-caste division is an injustice we do to Narayanan. He is *Bhuvanasundaram*, one who has put on the universe as his beautiful form. He is the land that we should reach and He is also the Guide who will take us there. He is our sole heaven and refuse. It is our duty to walk the path He shows. Action! Action! Action! That is our *tarakamanatram*. That is the essence of the fruit of what the *Gita* teaches us. Let us lean on Him and march on, with service to society as our supreme mission. Om namo Narayanaya!

(*When he articulates the Narayana mantra aloud, the crowd echoes it. At this moment, Tirukkhoshtiyur*

Nambi enters from L and rushes towards Ramanujar angrily.)

NAMBI (*aloud*): This is betrayal of the guru, Ramanujar.

(II. ii. p. 31)

Shocked by Ramanujar's promulgation of the Narayana mantra, Ghoshtiyar Nambi accuses the latter of betrayal of him, his Guru. But Ramanujar gives a clever and ingenious answer that there are so many who have listened to the Rahasyartham and will attain Vaikuntham and that there is no loss if he alone goes to hell. Ghoshtiyar Nambi seems to be released from his secretive shell of orthodoxy and suddenly appreciates Ramanujar's interpretation and asks him to sing the song of the Azhwar in full. When Ramanujar sings it the crowd roars in ecstatic joy. Therefore, Ghoshtiyar Nambi describes Ramanujar as *Emberumanar* (meaning our leader):

RAMANUJAR (*With a smile*): Please come, gurunatha.

(*He climbs down from the wall and bows to Nambi. Nambi moves a few steps away.*)

NAMBI: What did I say before teaching you the lesson?

RAMANUJAR (*Smiling*): You said I was not to communicate the Rahasyartham to anyone else. You also said that if I did, I would go to hell.

NAMBI: And still...?

RAMANUJAR (*Smiling*): See, gurunatha! There are so many here who have listened to the Rahasyartham and will attain Vaikuntam. Is it a big loss if I alone go to Hell? Should we not rejoice and sing, 'Hail! Hail! Hail! Gone is the curse of existence.'

(*Nambi is silent for a while.*)

NAMBI: You are right. Let us indeed rejoice. Please sing it in full, the song that the Azhwar has composed and left for us, out of his infinite grace.

(*After a few seconds.*)

RAMANUJAR (*sings*):

Pasuram

Hail! Hail! Hail! Gone is the curse of existence. Hell has declined, receded, withdrawn, relented. Yama has no work here anymore, even Kali (Yuga) shall end. Behold, the ocean-hued Lord's spirits have descended on Earth in a host. We have seen them singing and dancing everywhere.

(*The crowd cries out in unison, Om Namo Narayanaya. Nambi embraces Ramanujar tightly.*)

NAMBI: May your name henceforth be *Emberumanar*.

(II. ii. p. 32)

In this scene, Parthasarathy makes Ramanujar a modern-day Ambedkar-like leader who has a social goal to achieve, namely dissolving caste distinctions and opening up scriptural learning to all. Even his preceptor Ghoshti Purna recognizes the large-heartedness of the young Ramanujar.

Nowadays Ramanujar has been growing stronger in his conviction and liberalism and more powerful in executing his liberal policies. He has to wage a war with traditional Brahmins. For example, four Brahmins complain that they were betrayed by Alavandar whose gurus were Tirukkachi Nambi and Maraner Nambi. They observe with terrible anger and wonder Periya Nambi feeding Maraner Nambi with food. They attribute the desecration of their caste to Ramanujar and accuse him for that and even threaten to excommunicate Periya Nambi. But Ramanujar is so firm and strong in his secularist conviction that he asks the Brahmins to go ahead with their task. The angry Brahmins warn him that he would have to pay for it. But Ramanujar turns a deaf ear to their words of threat. On the contrary, he tries to put in more confidence in Maraner Nambi by advising him that they should shun the disease called low self-esteem and try their best to remove the unwanted and unhealthy caste-consciousness. As part of his reformatory mission he asks Maraner Nambi to make everyone a Vaishnavite to do away with caste and to teach everyone in the slum to sing the *prabandham* so that Lord Ranganathan may dwell with them. Thus, social reformation paving the way for caste-equality and gender-equality becomes an important agenda of new religion of Vaishnavism. His conflict with the orthodox Brahmins and proponents of *varnasrama dharma* continues. The enormity of his struggle with the patriarchal system with its inbuilt caste-hierarchy and gender-inequality may be understood only after one studies seriously the multiple checks, restrictions, and rigidities of the eleventh-century South India.

Another deliberate departure that the play makes is, in the prominence given to Maha Purna's daughter Attuzhay. In the source, she is a timid and weak girl who could not face her mother-in-law's taunts. Ramanujar had to send his nephew and prime disciple Dasarathi as a domestic help to help her. But in this dramatic version there is a fresh textual moment created by Parthasarathy when as a young woman, Attuzhay dares to confront the orthodox Brahmins and even halt the procession of the deity. Parthasarathy is at his theatrical best in such scenes which dismantle received social structures. Not only are the orthodox Brahmins and their ugly intrigues exposed by the young woman, but they are also driven into a corner when she appeals directly to Lord Ranganatha Himself to expose the villainy of his so-called pious priests. Using the time-tested theatrical technique of the *deus ex machina* the playwright makes the Lord Himself indict the wicked Brahmins. However, Parthasarathy follows the sources closely in the employment of this device because in the sources the Lord speaks through the priest. The term used for this mode is *Archaka Mukhena*, meaning, as Carmen points out, 'through the priest'.

The violation of caste-purity of Brahmins by non-Brahmins, especially the low-caste people or *dalits* provokes the terrible anger of Brahmins. Hence, they try to harass their enemies in different ways. For example, they have thrown the thorny weeds in the path of the young women, Attuzhay just to harass her. But she does not know who has scattered them on her path. She, therefore, prays to Lord Ranga to help her out of the difficulty.

Then four Brahmins complain to her that her father (Periya Nambi) will have his food only in Maraner Nambi's house as he has turned the slum folk into his kinsmen and that the Brahmins of the *agraharam* will not so much as look at them and she cannot, therefore, enter the temple anymore.

But Attuzhay is not cowed down by the threats of excommunication. She tells them rightly that Lord Ranga dwells not merely inside the temple, but everywhere in the world. She does not want any contact with Brahmins, but wants to demand justice of Ranga. She lays a condition that the processional idol will not move a step ahead next day unless she gets justice. The Brahmins are dumbstruck by her courage.

As the nadaswara music is heard and comes near, Attuzhay stretches out her arms and blocks the path of the processional idol of Lord Ranga and prays to Him to answer her about the Brahmins who insult her father. The Brahmins do not like the *prasadam* to be given to the man of the lowest caste. But Attuzhay believes that there is no caste for the Vaishnavites. The Brahmins believe that one attains caste by virtue of one's *karma*.

The question of whether a Brahmin or a man with spiritual education gets his Brahmin-hood by birth (by virtue of his *karma*) or by virtue of his moral conduct has been a perennial one in the history of Hinduism. Lord Krishna himself declares in His *Song Divine* (*Bhagavad Gita*) that a man can become a Brahmin by virtue of his moral qualities, though he may be accidentally born as a *sudra*. The same argument is put forth by Attuzhay here. She confronts the Brahmins and asks them if their idea of *karma* is supported by the knowledge of the *prabandhas*; and if they have in their community a man like Maraner/Periya Nambi. She asks Lord Ranga if the caste inequality is acceptable.

By that time three men come there and accuse the Brahmins that they have excommunicated Periya Nambi just because he took his food from Maraner Nambi. Then Ramanujar comes there and announces that the devotees of Lord Visnu have a right to speak out and defy arrogance. Man 3 says that the deity will return to the temple only if the thorny weeds are removed from the front of Periya Nambi's house. Attuzhay opines that Lord Ranga is speaking through these people. Then Priests 1 and 2 pretend to compliment Attuzhay and Periya Nambi and comment on the four Brahmins. Now the Brahmins retaliate against the priests for violating the code of their community and ironically ask them to go and build a temple for Ranganatha in the *cheri*. They are angry with Alavandar for betraying them and enabling all the pariahs to become Brahmins. Then the priests confess that they deliberately put on that play-acting the previous day just to wriggle out of the difficulty. Now the Brahmins are happy to see that the laws of Manu will be kept alive. Thus, the civil war between the orthodox Brahmins and the liberal Vaishnavites continues endlessly. This scene shows that Parthasarathy is highly skilled in dramatizing the power motivation in human beings and its subtle as well as crude manifestations in specific social milieus. There are several aspects of inter-caste and intra-caste encounter which the scene brilliantly captures. As for the Brahmins, there is, among those from the southern district of Tamil country. There is also contempt for his idea of Vaishnavism because he sought instruction from a non-Brahmin teacher. Appropriating the legend that the illustrious Brahmin Acharya Alavandar took an outcaste Maranar Nambi as his disciple, the playwright forges an eloquent scene involving Periya Nambi, Maraner Nambi, Ramanujar and the Brahmins. In the source narrative, Maraner Nambi was stricken with an incurable disease and was nursed by Periya Nambi. This is briefly mimed in the scene. In the source when Maraner Nambi died Periya Nambi decided to accord him the funeral rites which are normally performed for only a dead Brahmin. There is a profoundly interesting exchange between Ramanuja and Periya Nambi in the source at this point. Ramanujar is startled by the radicalism of Maha Purna's thinking and action. He fears that such a subversive move might destroy the very fabric of Hindu society. He tells his teacher that while he was doing everything to keep the fence intact, Maha Purna was doing away with it. To this Maha Purna gives an eloquent reply. In a virtual peroration, he recalls all the great sages, seers, kings, and ministers in Indian tradition who had not been Brahmins, for example, Veda Vyasa, the sage and Vidura the wise minister of the Kauravas in the *Mahabharata*. But in the play all the enlightened ideas and utterances of Maha Purna are virtually transferred to Ramanujar. Ramanujar supports Maha Purna's efforts to protect Maraner Nambi from the wrath of the Brahmins and even challenges them. Thus, the play reverses the roles of Ramanujar and Maha Purna as we find them in the hagiographies. In this scene, Maraner Nambi is alive and

Ramanujar proclaims the universality of his Vaishnava *dharma*. Whereas the sources project Ramanujar as one who does not engage in violent subversion but aims at persuading people to think with sweetness and enlightenment, Parthasarathy gives a subversive and iconoclastic edge to everything that Ramanujar says and does.

The orthodox Brahmins consider Ramanujar as a constant threat to their *varnasrama* system and to their own survival and security. Hence, they hatch a plan of getting rid of Ramanujar by poisoning his food. For a couple of days, they arrange for serving poisoned rice in his alms-bowl. But luckily Ramanujar detects the fact and throws away the rice. He tells the Araiyar of the temple that God did not want to take him back from the mortal world. Similarly, he tells Periya Nambi that there another plot by the temple priests to kill him, but that he does not want to die so easily. It is very ironical that the non-religious evils like poisoning a reformist zealot like Ramanujar and misappropriation of the temple property have been happening right at the temple, which should be a controller of the morals of humanity.

The dramatist shows Ramanujar's ability to transform people from worldliness to spirituality. This scene virtually repeats the source narratives in their details. It underscores Ramanujar's openness of mind with regard to people, their caste, their complexion, their social position. For example, a dark complexioned man called Urangavilli has a fair-complexioned wife called Ponnachi and he always protects her beauty from the hot sun by holding an umbrella on her head. When Ramanujar's disciples joke about this strange habit, Ramanujar scolds them and explains that Urangavilli worships the beauty of his wife—both inner and outer and that there is no difference between the beauty of a wife and that of Ranga. Urangavilli's aesthetic appreciation is confined only to the uxorious beauty, but Ramanujar shows him the divine beauty of the idol of Ranganatha. Consequently, Urangavilli is deeply impressed by the Lord's beauty and sheds tears of mystic joy and sings a *pasuram*. Ramanujar complements it with a description that the Lord permeates the universe and manifests Himself as the universe which is large and wide. Thus, Ramanujar has extended Urangavilli's aesthetic sensibility from the appreciation of the human, feminine and uxorious beauty to that of the Divine Beauty. He has also expanded his vision from the ritualistic and theological to the cosmic and transcendentalist one. Deeply impressed by Ramanujar's indoctrination Urangavilli bows down to Ramanujar's feet reverentially. Thus, Ramanujar transforms the hearts of sensitive people from stark worldliness to pure spirituality.

The collision between Ramanujar's liberalism and the traditional Brahmins' orthodoxy continues. For example, Ramanujar violates the normal puritanical code of Brahmanical behaviour by touching the body of a warrior of low-caste after having a bath and by placing his hand on the shoulder of a Marava. The two disciples who observe this strange behaviour of Ramanujar question him about it. Then Ramanujar tells them that they have not understood the Vaishnavite philosophy and the relation between life and philosophy.

Ramanujar wants to teach a practical lesson to his disciples and enable them to overcome their caste arrogance and purity mania. He, therefore, asks them to go to Urangavilli's house and steal Ponnachi's ornaments. Although they are shocked by his suggestion, they agree to carry it out. Accordingly, they go to Ponnachi's house and steal the bangles from her right/left hand and report it to Ramanujar. But Ramanujar asks them to go again to her house and watch what is happening there. So they go there and overhear the conversation between Urangavilli and Ponnachi in which Urangavilli accuses his wife of the pride of possession and arrogance:

> *When dim light returns, we see the two disciples at the back of L corner and Urangavilli and Ponnachi at C. Urangavilli appears angry.*

URANGAVILLI: And you turned to the other side?

PONNACHI: Only in order that they might take the bangles from the other hand too. Poor wretches...

URANGAVILLI (*Interrupting her*): You told yourself, 'These are *my* bangles. *I* will give them to another.' And this pride of possession, this arrogance, scared them off.

PONNACHI: What are you saying?

URANGAVILLI: Your pride drove them away.

PONNACHI (resentful): The fault was mine, Swami. Humility cannot be taught. It has to develop spontaneously.

(II. iv. p. 46)

Then the disciples come back and report it to Ramanujar, who reasons with them about who has realized the Brahman and teaches them that there is no caste difference between a Brahmin and a Marava in the community of Vaishnavites. Having thus realized the essential unity of humanity and equality of castes, the two disciples of Ramanujar prostrate at the feet of Urangavilli, who is taken aback by this act. Ramanujar, thus, engages himself in fighting against the Brahmanical purity mania, superiority complex, arrogance and exclusivism.

The playwright shows another incident to illustrate Ramanujar's ability to transform the people around him from stark materialism and sensuality to flawless spirituality. For example, once Ramanujar and Kidambi Achan go in search of the house of his disciple, Varadan in Ashtasahasram village and finally locate it. Varadan and his wife suffer from crushing poverty and undergo an ordeal as it were. When Ramanujar and Kidambi Achan go to their house, Varadan is not at home, but his wife, Paruttikkollai welcomes them. As she hesitates to see Ramanujar with her torn upper clothes, Ramanujar throws in his *parivattam* for her to cover her chest. Covering herself with that parivattam, she bows down to Ramanujar. She is an extremely beautiful woman. But her moral beauty turns out to be greater than her physical beauty. Ramanujar tells his disciples that Varadan and Paruttikkollai are a Brahmin and a non-Brahmin respectively and theirs is an inter-caste marriage. Ramanujar is so affectionate towards them that he along with his disciples wants to have his lunch in their house, after having a bath elsewhere. But Paruttikkollai worries deeply about the lack of rice grains in her house and does not know how to treat Ramanujar and his companions.

The playwright has taken some minor liberty with the historical details here in the presentation of the relationship between the merchant and Paruttikkollai. In the historical sources, the merchant is not related to her in any way. But in the present play, the dramatist has made her a relative of the merchant, i.e. she is the younger sister of the merchant's wife. The merchant is sad to know that all his wealth is useless, especially when he could not marry the beautiful girl that he wanted to, but had to marry her elder sister. But the beautiful girl, Paruttikkollai married the emaciated parpan, Varadan. When the merchant is thus pondering about his so-called bad-luck, Paruttikkollai comes to him and begs him to give some grocery to enable to treat some unexpected guests at home. This is a golden opportunity for the merchant to exploit her. He promises to give her the necessary items of grocery, but demands a price (of sexual pleasure) for that. Obviously, Paruttikkollai is thrown into a great moral dilemma, but yet she solves it quite boldly. She promises to pay his price by offering the pleasure of sex after treating her honorable guests. He asks her not to deceive him. She promises to keep her word. Consequently, the merchant sends all the necessary items of grocery to her house. Paruttikkollai treats her guests with great reverence. Ramanujar and his disciples are fully satisfied with the feast, thank Varadan profusely for that and return to Srirangam.

After the departure of the guests, Varadan asks his wife as to how she managed to cook such excellent food when there was not even a grain of rice at home. She then takes him inside the house and reveals the secret. Varadan is such a great man that he does not find fault with his wife, but understands the pressure of the circumstances and even concedes to his wife's emergency decision (*Apat-dharma*). Meanwhile the merchant is eagerly waiting for the fulfillment of his sexual desire.

Now both Varadan and his wife go to the merchant to pay the price of the grocery bought on credit. Obviously, the merchant is embarrassed by the presence of Varadan with his wife. Varadan asks the merchant to copulate only with the body of his wife, Paruttikkollai as her heart already belongs to him (her husband). They thank the merchant for supplying the grocery in a critical moment for the treatment of the holy man like Ramanujar and ask him to take his price. The merchant had never expected that his secret condition would be made so public. Consequently, he is utterly embarrassed by this situation and therefore, asks Varadan to take back his wife. The moral behaviour of Varadan and his wife is simply superb and marvelous. When Ramanujar learns from one of his disciples the strange behaviour of the merchant, he sends for the merchant, who has not lost his basic decency and whom he wants to make a true Vaishnavite. The whole episode testifies to Ramanujar's and his disciples' moral height and ability to transform even the sensual people into spiritual ones. This is, obviously, one of the most powerful scenes in the play. Indira Parthasarathy uses this scene to underscore the point that one need not be a Brahmin or be 'chaste' in a conventional sense to be a Vaishnavaite. Ramanujar has no sense of false propriety either. Even the lascivious merchant who tries to blackmail Paruttikkollai is reformed by her inner sense of chastity and her dedication to higher truths. At the end of the scene Ramanujar praises the merchant for his fairness and decency, which has prompted him to act according to his *dharma* as a Vaisya (belonging to the merchant class) whereas Ramanujar's own disciples have no such credentials. Mere caste superiority in social organization cannot be used to claim superiority for the upper castes. This is certainly crucial to Ramanujar's reinterpretation of *Varnasrama dharma*.

The third and last dream of Ramanujar is to write a Commentary on the *Brahmasutras* as per the desire of the late monk Alavandar. The playwright shows this scene very convincingly. This scene holds mirror to Ramanujar's recognition of gender equality. Here we have Andal Amma, wife of Kuresa, who is as well read and of as high intellectual caliber as her husband. That is the reason why she is sitting with him in compliance with Ramanujar's instruction when the *acharya* is dictating his magnum opus *Sri Bhashyam* on Vyasa's *Brahmasutra*. In fact, Indira Parthasarathy makes a departure here from the sources. In the sources Andal Amma is merely present during this dictation. But in the play and in this scene, she is actively involved in the philosophical discussion regarding the nature of consciousness. In fact, none of the so-called disciples of Ramanujar is given such recognition by the guru. Two disciples discuss that Ramanujar is dictating his commentary on the *Brahmansutras* without even bothering about his food; that Andal Amma is sitting with them at the time of writing; and that Kuresar has said that he would stop the writing if the views are not acceptable to him. But the disciples know the limits of their own knowledge and therefore keep quiet.

Now Ramanujar dictates that both *chit* and *achit* (soul and body) are attributes of God, just as a flower possesses both fragrance and colour; and that the concepts of *Nirguna Brahman* (Abstract Reality) and *Maya* (illusory nature of the world) are not acceptable to him. By now Kuresar has stopped writing. Ramanujar, therefore, gets slightly angry and gets up and calls them for food. But Kuresar does not want to have his food until he completes the writing. Kuresar tells Ramanujar that his view on the independence of consciousness is not acceptable to him, because soul is not independent of God. Then Ramanujar realizes his mistake and corrects himself and thanks Kuresar for drawing his attention to it:

RAMANUJAR: Chit. That is, the soul. Achit. That is, the body. Both are the attributes of God. Just as a flower possesses both fragrance and colour. Just as the sea consists of both waves and the waterdrops that make up the waves. When the Upanishads say, 'No it isn't, it isn't, it isn't', what they mean is 'It is not as these attributes alone that Brahman exists'; they do not mean that Brahman has no attributes. Therefore, *Nirguna Brahman* is not an acceptable concept. If you say that a clay pot is an illusory manifestation of clay, it can only mean that the pot cannot exist without clay. If you say that the entire universe is an illusion, it can only mean that the universe cannot exist without God. Therefore, the doctrine of *maya* is not acceptable. Even though chit, achit, and God are all basically one, chit and achit have existence in so far as they are God's attributes. They are not merely illusory appearances. God represents the frontiers of all meaning. And our life is a journey towards that end. Chit, that is the soul, can know everything. The soul is consciousness turned wholly on itself.

(*When Ramanujar says this, Kuresar stops writing. Andal sees this and smiles, but does not say anything.*

Ramanujar has not noticed that Kuresar has stopped writing and continues to dictate.)

RAMANUJAR: The body is mere lifeless matter. When I say, 'I see this', the object that is seen acquires the special marked attribute of 'what is seen'. But what 'sees' is not the body; 'seeing' is merely the consequence of the existence of the body in accord with the soul. Wisdom lies in assimilating objects in the outer world to one's own experience. It is by means of wisdom, which mediates between the inner consciousness and the outer world, that we see objects, feel them, experience them.

(*It is only at this point that Ramanujar notices Kuresar is not writing.*)

RAMANUJAR (*a little surprised*): Why aren't you writing?

ANDAL: In accordance with our agreement.

RAMANUJAR: What agreement?

ANDAL: Your view is not acceptable to him.

RAMANUJAR (*appearing slightly annoyed*): Which view?...

KURESAR: You will understand that the view that you expressed after that point is not acceptable to me.

(II. vi. pp. 56-57)

Ramanujar gets angry and calls them to have their lunch, but Kuresar refuses to join for the lunch until he has completed the writing. Then Ramanujar comes round and gets ready to dictate the commentary further. It is at this time that Andal draws Ramanujar's attention to his mistake:

RAMANUJAR (*With a smile*): Andal Amma, you please tell me. What mistake did I make?

ANDAL: Do I have to say it as a riddle?

RAMANUJAR: Please do.

ANDAL: If the small one is born in the womb of the dead one, what will it feed on and where will it dwell?

(*Ramanujar contemplates this. After a few minutes, his face brightens. He gets up, raises Kuresar, and embraces him.*)

RAMANUJAR: The mistake was mine. Please forgive me.

KURESAR: You must forgive me too. I spoke harshly.

RAMANUJAR: It was indeed wrong of me to say, 'The soul has the attribute of knowing everything. The soul is consciousness centred on itself'. When the soul has no existence independent of the Divine, it was indeed a mistake for me talk of 'consciousness centred on itself'. It was a contradiction in terms. Is that right, Andal Amma?

(*She smiles.*)

RAMANUJAR: All right... What next...

ANDAL: Food for the stomach. We shouldn't incur the sin of having starved Udaiyavar.

RAMANUJAR: Well, I shouldn't incur the sin of having starved you.

(II. vi. p. 58)

It is likely that Ramanujar was automatically explaining the Brahman/the self as contentless consciousness. It is only logical that Kuresar should register his protest at the conception of the human soul as self-existing, because such an idea is anathema to a Vaishnava. If granted, it will negate the value of surrender to the Divine which has been conceptualized at various levels as *prapatti*, *saranagati* and in general called *bhakti*. Ramanujar comes to realize the grave error that he has committed and steers himself back onto the right path of interpretation. This is interestingly dramatized in this scene, with Ramanujar asking Andal Amma to indicate where he went wrong. It shows his respect for her intellectual acumen and power of discrimination. In his characteristic intertextual style, Indira Parthasarathy makes Andal Amma quote, by way of answer, the verse which is part of a similar colloquy between Madhurakavi Azhwar and Nammazhwar about Brahman (Reality). This verse, which is in the form of a riddle, makes Ramanujar realize where he has gone wrong. It is this humility, which has been remarked on by all biographers, that makes Ramanujar seek forgiveness of Kuresar. Ramanujar continues the commentary consulting Andal Amma in between. In the source, it is mentioned that when Kuresar did not budge, Ramanujar kicked him. Indira Parthasarathy omits this very human detail because it may be embarrassing, given the status of Ramanujar as an *acharya*.

Now that Ramanujar has fulfilled all the three desires of his guru, Alavandar, he has been expanding the scope of his reformative activities and magnetically attracting innumerable disciples and devotees towards him. His democratic agenda has turned out to be a great threat to the hegemony of Brahmins in the society. They are very unhappy with him and wish to wage war against him. For example, four orthodox Brahmins discuss Ramanujar's radical activities of equalizing all the castes and communities and the threatening possibility of gradual disappearance of all the Brahmins. They are sore about the fact that Ramanujar made even the Panchamas wear the sacred threat; that he has even prostrated himself at the feet of a Panchama woman who quotes lines from Thiruvaimozhi. This scene is testimony to Indira Parthasarathy's brilliant dramatic powers. As a playwright and theatre artist, his forte is pungent satire and cryptic stichomythic dialogue, invariably employed in situations of intrigue and cunning. In *Nandan Kathai* (*Legend of Nandan*), the playwright provides many such instances where he exposes the lust for power in human nature which conceals itself under the garb of religious piety and orthodoxy. The Vaishnavites are those whose interests have in some way been injured by Ramanujar's temple reforms. They are willing to join hands with their arch-enemies the Saivites and incite the Chola King against Ramanujar. Here the playwright has created a brilliant 'writerly' text out of the sources.

Like the Brahmins, some four Saivites also come and meet the former (Brahmins) and repeat the same complaint. The Brahmins complain that they are not allowed to enter the temple of Ranganatha, according to Ramanujar's decree. The conflict between the liberal Ramanujar and the orthodox groups (of Brahmins and Saivites) has been leading to a climax. Both the

Brahmins and Saivites gang up together against Ramanujar and want to suppress Ramanujar politically by appealing to the Chola King through the official influence of his minister, Naluram (who was himself betrayed like them). But the persecution of Ramanujar by a Chola King is still a controversial issue and has provoked a lot of historical debate as recently as 2002. The biographies and Vaishnvaite sectarian accounts mention the Chola King, but nowhere is it clear who that king was.

In response to the appeal of these two groups of orthodox Brahmins and Saivites, Minister Naluram requests the Chola King (Kulottunga I) to enquire into Ramanujar's disconcerting activities. He complains that both Saivites and Vaishnavites oppose Ramanujar; that all Siva temples will be transformed into Vishnu temples if Ramanujar is allowed to grow powerful. Minister Naluram suggests to the king that Ramanujar should declare that no God is greater than Siva, so that the commoners may believe the same; and that Ramanujar should be banished if he does not oblige the king. Indira Parthasarathy presents the king as a neutral, impartial, and balanced man who has to give his judgment on the so-called accused man, i.e. Ramanujar. The king, therefore, orders the guards to summon Ramanujar. Taking the clue from the king, Minister Naluram asks the Army Chief to arrest Ramanujar and bring him to the court. Indira Parthasarathy makes a nuanced presentation of the scene here in which the Army Chief hesitates for a moment to carry out the order. In this scene, Indira Parthasarathy brings out the political dimensions of religion. Religion, power and politics have been located in the same grid, in earlier epochs too as in our times. The playwright wants to demystify the hagiographic image of religion which tends to dissemble the political.

The Army Chief is secretly in sympathy with Ramanujar and therefore sends a secret message to Kuresar that Naluram has betrayed him (Kuresar) and that the palace guards are coming to arrest Ramanujar and take him to the palace and that Kuresar should ask Ramanujar to flee. All of them realize the emergency and begin to act quickly. Kuresar asks Periya Nambi to convey the message to Ramanujar. Accordingly, Periya Nambi orders his disciples to convey the message that Ramanujar should put on the white clothes and escape. By that time three guards from the palace come to arrest Ramanujar. Kuresar has put on the saffron robes and impersonated Ramanujar. So the soldiers take Ramanujar (i.e. Kuresar in disguise) and Periya Nambi in a palanquin.

When Ramanujar returns from his bath and searches for his saffron robes, a disciple tells him that Kuresar has impersonated Ramanujar by wearing his saffron robes and being arrested and taken to the court for trial and that Ramanujar should escape through the secret passage and leave the Chola country. Actually, Ramanujar is not willing to escape, but Kidambi Achan persuades him to do so in the interest of Vaishnva religion. Mudaliyandan hasten the escape of Ramanujar. Ramanujar is presented in a very human light when confronted by this unexpected turn of events. He is indeed upset by Kuresar's suggestion. But Andal Amma reminds Ramanujar that he is not an individual but an institution and has a responsibility to society. Indira Parthasarathy thus makes Andal Amma a strong woman in the face of danger to her own husband in this politically unsettling situation. In the hurry, Ramanujar requests Andal Amma to take care of the monastery (temple) and leaves the place as he thinks that it is also a command of Ranganatha. He suspects that it must be a conspiracy hatched by the Vaishnavite Brahmins who hate him. He wants to move westwards to the Nilgiris, where his friend, Nallan Chakravarthi lives. Nallan Chakravarthi was also excommunicated once for performing the funeral rites of a Panchama. But the Lord Himself praised him declaring, "In the eyes of the world you are a bad man; but to me you are a good man" (*AKVG* 1906 (2004): 152). Indira Parthasarathy follows the source in this as it serves the purpose of highlighting the values of the new Vaishnavism, which is emerging, effacing the stigma of caste from Hinduism.

The religious system is controlled by the political system, which creates its own adverse effect on the former. For example, when Kuresar in the guise of Ramanujar is produced before the king, he is identified correctly as not Ramanujar but as someone else and cross-questioned by the king and the minister about the whereabouts of Ramanujar. This court scene does not seem to have any recorded historical source, although all the hagiographic narratives make a dramatic situation out of the Chola presentation of Kuresa and Maha Purna. The important departure from all such sources is that he does not present the king as a wicked, rabid, and religious fundamentalist. In Indira Parthasarathy's view, the king is neutral like Pontius Pilate who was compelled by the Jews to persecute Jesus Christ. Naluram is the Judas who betrays Ramanujar. Then Kuresar reveals his true identity and tells them that Ramanujar has left the Chola country. Minister Naluram brings to the attention of the king the double offence of Kuresar in (i) helping Ramanujar to escape and (ii) impersonating Ramanujar and insulting the king. He, therefore, recommends that Kuresar should be punished for both. Further, they want to take a declaration from Kuresar (as a proxy for Ramanujar) that no God is greater than Siva, but Kuresar writes on the palm leaf that *dronam* is greater than *sivam*, thus playing upon the words connected with weights and measures. Consequently, the Brahmins, especially Saivites feel insulted by this insolence.

Minister Naluram vents out his hatred of Ramanujar for having wrested the village temple from him in the past and he, therefore, wanted to take revenge upon Ramanujar. He callously orders that the eyes of the two persons (Kuresar and Periya Nambi) should be plucked out. Obviously, Naluram has employed his political power to counter and suppress the religious power of Ramanujar and his disciples.

Accordingly, two soldiers with burning torches move towards Kuresar and Peroya Nambi, but they snatch the torches away from the soldiers and burn their eyes by themselves. Then both of them are dragged away. Both of them sit on the ground at Pasupati Kayil. Periya Nambi places his head on the lap of Kuresar and dies. By that time the soldiers sent secretly by the Army Chief comes there and arrange the last rites for the swami, Periya Nambi and escort Kuresar to Srirangam. Kuresar admires the humanitarianism of the Army Chief, who in spite of being a Saivite, has helped the Vaishnavites.

Now that Ramanujar is forced by the political circumstances to flee the Chola country, a new phase begins in his life wherein he is able to exercise his liberal and secular policies and extend the frontiers of Vaishnavism. For example, when Ramanujar, Kidambi Achan, Mudaliyandan and other disciples move about in a forest, they are met by a few hunters who happen to be the followers of Nallan Chakravarthi. The Indian social organization had kept tribals and forest dwellers outside its pale. But there was interaction between the various groups depending upon the circumstances. In this scene, we have a reference to one Nallan Chakravarthy who was a devotee of Ramanujar and who took kindly to the hunters and initiated them into Vaishnavism. Although there is no specific historical record for it, the Vaishnava hagiographic literature describes such legends. Vaishnavism today is widespread even among tribals, besides upper and lower caste Hindus. In the play, Ramanujar actually embraces one of the hunters notwithstanding the fact that physical touching of a lower caste Hindu was considered polluting. In the sources, hunters bring fruit and honey to Ramanujar, but no cooked food, as noted earlier. They prostrate at Ramanujar and request him to have his food with them. Ramanujar hugs them and agrees to have food with them, although they are Panchamas. Ramanujar, thus, practices his liberal and secular policies sincerely, a fact that is almost revolutionary when viewed against the rigid caste-hierarchy and discrimination in 11th century India.

The hunters are so happy with Ramanujar that they suggest that he should go to Melukote near Tondanur, meet King Bittaladevan and his queen, Chandala Devi and spread the name of Narayana there. Historically speaking, Ramanujar's moving towards Tondanur in the Karnataka region is socially and religiously significant. B.R. Gopal, the editor of *Epigraphia Carnatica* provides epigraphical confirmation of Ramanujar's sojourn in Karnataka and his effort to spread the Sri Vaishnava faith in Mysore region. In his later book, *Sri Ramanuja in Karnataka* (1983), Gopal points out that Tondanur, also called Tonnur, has a Narasimha temple which is an old one and Ramanujar must have stayed there. It was a capital outpost of the Hoysalas. He notes that 'Tondanur' is a Dravidian, specifically Tamil word and etymologically derived from the root *tondu*, meaning 'service to the Lord by a devotee who is a *dasan*, that is, slave'. Its original name was Yadavapura, capital of Vishnuvardhana in 1129. Now the whole atmosphere turns out to be favourable to Ramanujar. By that time Tondanur Nambi meets Ramanujar and suggests to him to see the Jain king by driving out the spirit possessing his 18-year-old daughter. The hunters also request Ramanujar to accomplish the task.

Ramanujar is taken by Tondanur Nambi to King Bittaladevan, who after clarifying his doubts, requests Ramanujar to cure his daughter of the possession by a spirit for the last three years. Ramanujar invokes the name of Narayana and highlights the importance of *prapatti* and plays down the effect of *karma*. King Bittaladevan confesses that he has lost one finger to preserve his country and rule from the enemies and as an acknowledgement of the enemy's sovereignty. He tells Ramanujar the name of his daughter as Neela Devi whom he has imprisoned in a small room. Ramanujar asks the king to take her out of the room and leave her in the garden where he can control her.

Princess Neela Devi, who is brought in front of Ramanujar, confesses that she is Goddess Kali. Ramanujar talks to the spirit inside the princess and says that the varied beauty of the garden is the expression of God. He asks her to smell a jasmine so that she may be all right. He sings a *pasuram* about the transformation of a flower-garden into the celestial Brindavan. The exorcism proper takes place in this scene. But far from using traditional methods of uttering some esoteric mantras and waving a bunch of Margossa leaves, or throwing sacred ash over the possessed person, Ramanujar speaks to her in a kind and sweet manner and evokes in her a sense of beauty by talking about various flowers in the garden and using music therapy, so to say, by singing a Tamil hymn from Periyazhwar. This method of exorcism looks rather goody-goody and sleek and does not convince the modern reader.

Princess Neela Devi seems to be deeply influenced by Ramanujar and asks him reverentially who he is. Ramanujar claims to be a saviour and guide to the pathway of knowledge. King Bittaladevan marvels at the occult powers of Ramanujar and the efficacy of the *Ashtakshari mantra, Om Namo Narayanaya*. Princess Neela Devi also confesses that she was possessed by the spirit of fear and that she is completely cured now. Queen Chandala Devi is also very happy about her daughter's recovery.

But Ramanujar's successful exorcism of the princess and the deep impression it creates on King Bittaladevan arouses the ire of the Jain scholars of the king's court. They look at Ramanujar with deep distrust. The Jain Chief talks sarcastically to Ramanujar, but Ramanujar gives a philosophical explanation of Lord Narayanan, who is easily accessible to man (*saulabhyam*) in the form of Rama and Krishna. But the Jain Chief calls the whole thing a clever trick. This opposition between Ramanujar and the Jain Chief is indicative of the larger conflict between Brahmanism and Jainism in Karnataka (also possibly in the whole of India).

Profusely pleased by Ramanujar's curing of his daughter, King Bittaladevan requests Ramanujar to ask for something so that he may give it. But Ramanujar does not ask for anything for himself. On the contrary, he asks the king to provide a feast to the people of his country. But the Jain Chief does not wish to partake of the feast, because the feast would be hosted by a king with a deformity (one finger missing). That is the common belief. (Here the dramatist seems to have taken the common legendary belief that King Bittaladevan was a Jain by birth.) But B.R. Gopal (1983:15) categorically affirms that "there is nothing to show barring traditional, legendary accounts, that Vishnuvardhana was a Jaina by faith. But various epigraphic and historical details show that he was already called Vishnuvardhana, followed a liberal policy in religious matters, and that Bittaladevan is a Kannada derivation of the Sanskrit 'Vishnu'. But the sources as well as the play show that the chief purpose of Ramanujar was not to convert anybody, but that he was pressurized by some of his devotees to go to Melukote to meet the king and seek his patronage. Parthasarathy follows the legends about Ramanujar exorcising the spirit possessing the king's daughter, which was one of the reasons cited for the king's turning a devotee of Ramanujar and his conversion to Sri Vaishnava faith" (C.T. Indra, *Commentary on the Play*, p. 128).

But Ramanujar explains that in Vaishnava religion there is room for everybody—Brahmins, *panchamas*, the deformed—as all are the children of God:

RAMANUJAR: In the Vaishnava religion there is room for everyone. Brahmins, Panchamas, the deformed—all are God's creation. Please arrange for the feast. We will all take part.

JAIN CHIEF: The king cannot do anything in violation of our religious decree.

BITTALADEVAN: I will. Tomorrow is the feast.

JAIN CHIEF (*furious*): We will excommunicate you from our religion.

BITTALADEVAN: Do. I will be only too happy. I am a Vaishnavite from today. Oh Ramanujar, bless me.

(*Exit the Jain Chief in rage. Bittaladevan and Chandala Devi rise, go to Ramanujar, and prostrate themselves before him. He blesses them.*)

RAMANUJAR: From today your name will be Vishnuvardhana Rajar. Om Namo Narayanaya.

(III. vii. p. 81)

Thus, Ramanujar philosophically overriding the Jain Chief, asks the king to arrange for the feast. But the Jain Chief objects to it strongly and threatens to excommunicate the king if he violates the religious decree. The king, Bittaladevan asks him to excommunicate him as he has accepted Vaishnavism from that day and seeks the blessings of Ramanujar, who re-christens him as Vishnuvardhana Rajar. Thus, Ramanujar emerges as a religious hero by winning the heart of the king, following his exorcism of the spirit from the person of the princess. Ramanujar's religious, especially occult power has won and subordinated the political power to it. In this scene, the playwright foregrounds the leitmotif that religion controls power and that no king can afford to antagonize the majority religious community, here the Jains.

While Ramanujar enjoys the confidence of King Vishnuvardhana an unexpected thing happens, which helps Ramanujar to consolidate his religious mission. For example, when six labourers of Panchama caste clear the thick growth of the Yadugiri forest, they find a gold ornament and show it to Ramanujar, who is happy to see it and guesses that they would get hold of the original idol also of Lord Narayanan. A little later the labourers find the original idol also. Ramanujar is very happy about this find. Then, in conformity with his liberal policy, Ramanujar tells the labourers that they are not Panchamas, but noble people, who should be called Tirukkulattar and prostrates before them. They are simply shocked by Ramanujar's gesture of magnanimity. Ramanujar announces that Melukote should be known as Tirunarayanapuram and wants to speak to King Vishnuvardhana to raise a temple for Lord Narayanan where the so-called Panchamas will have the first honour. In this scene, Parthasarathy dramatically presents Ramanujar's search for the old temple. All the sources narrate how the Lord appeared in his dream and directed him to find the temple. But B.R. Gopal is of the opinion that these writings are a mixture of fact and fiction. Parthasarathy is interested in showing how Ramanujar won over the fifth caste of Hindu society whose members enthusiastically come forward to clear the forests known as the forests of Yadugiri. When the Panchamas discover some ornaments and eventually the idol, Ramanujar rechristens them as 'Tirukkulattar', that is the clan of Sri or Lakshmi. But B.R. Gopal does not find any historical records for this event. But S. Kalyanarama Iyengar cites the historical record of Mysore Gazetteer (1978:325). According to the legend, the outcastes had for centuries enjoyed certain privileges in these temple in Karnataka. Govindacharya cites certain other sources to attest Ramanujar's historical recognition of the untouchables (*AKVG* 1906 (2004: 165)). It is even pointed out that Mahatma Gandhi was inspired by Ramanujar's egalitarianism when he named the pariahs 'Harijans', children of Hari or Vishnu.

But Ramanujar develops a doubt before thinking of raising a temple, i.e. they have found the original stable idol but not the processional idol (*utsava murti*). When Ramanujar consults King Vishnuvardhana about the missing idol, the latter replies that it was taken away by the Turkish king, and that he has given it to his daughter to play with as if it is a doll. Then Ramanujar wants to go meet the Turkish king and try to bring it back. The king is utterly shocked by the suggestion, but finally yields to the saintly pressure. Ramanujar, who is not afraid of any one, goes and meets the Turkish king (who is not named properly, nor is his place or city is mentioned), introduces himself as a Vaishnavite and speaks about the unity of all religions. Then he asks the young Turkish king for the processional idol possessed by a girl in the ladies chamber of the palace. The young king, even breaking the protocol, takes Ramanujar to the ladies chamber, where the eight year girl is playing with the idol and, talking of marrying it and never wanting to part with it. The girl's name is revealed as Raziya. Now Ramanujar wants to take Razia along with the idol to his place, Melukote. Luckily, Raziya agrees to go with Ramanujar. The young king explains that Raziya is the daughter of his father's third wife (hence his step-sister). He sends Raziya with Ramanujar on one condition that she should not be converted into Hinduism. Ramanujar promises not to convert her but announces her name as Turukka Nachiyar and that there will be a shrine for her in all their temples, thereby showing the divine Vaishnavite-Muslim connection. But there is some historical controversy about Ramanujar's journey to Delhi to meet the Turkish king. Alkondavilli Govindacharya has extensively argued by citing semi-historical sources that Ramanujar could not have gone all the way to Delhi to retrieve the idol of Sampat Kumara, for in those days any Turkish ruler of the north was referred to as 'Delhi Sultan'. It is probable that Ramanujar went to the court of some Muslim chieftain or even a king who ruled north of the Hoysala region (*AKVG* 1906 (2004: n 5, pp. 163-65)). Some historians wonder whether Ramanujar was acquainted with Islam as a religion. However, he does not seem to have shown any hostility or ill-will towards the Turkish ruler. But the meeting with the Muslim girl who is infatuated with the image of Sampat Kumara, is somewhat filmy in dialogue, lacking in spiritual as well as political pressure. The sociologically interesting detail in this otherwise sentimental scene is the appellation '*Turukka Nachiyar*' given to the young Muslim girl by Ramanujar in analogy with Tamil women devotees in the Hindu bhakti tradition. In several Vaishnava temples, even today, there is a shrine for a Muslim lady. Therefore, what Ramanujar prophesies in this scene is attested by later developments in Vaishnavism. The playwright himself says in his Preface that the Lord in Srirangam when he pays an annual visit to the shrine of Bibi Nachiyar (Turukka Nachiyar) wear a lungi like a Muslim youth. S. Kalyanarama Iyengar refers to the folk memory and tradition regarding the Turkish girl. She is also known as Varanandini. However, the encounter with the Turkish sultan, at any rate, confirms that Ramanujar was conciliator par excellence in all his activities.

Having accomplished the difficult task of getting the processional idol from the Turkish king, Ramanujar installs the stable statue at the temple of Melukote and calls it a golden day on which his guru's dream has come true. There is a sense of carnivalesque in this scene located at Melukote after the Sampat Kumara idol has been installed and festivals initiated. He considers the eight-year-old girl, Turukka Nachiyar as a mother to all of them as she has given them the *sampathkumaram*. The Panchamas get the honour of carrying the Lord. There is a lot of music and dancing. Here, popular culture and art forms are given free play by royal and religious authorities. Indira Parthasarathy compacts twelve years of Ramanujar's stay in Karnataka region into a couple of prominent scenes. Scene 10 is a kind of epilogue to the Karnataka period. He has achieved a sense of fulfillment after raising a temple at Melukote, as per God's will. He is grateful to King Vishnuvardhana. Now he wants to return to Srirangam. Historically speaking, Ramanujar returned to Srirangam after his Karnataka mission was accomplished. But legend claims that he received a message from Srirangam that the dogmatic Chola king had died of a carbuncle in his neck. Hence, he was known as Krimikantha Cholan, 'worm-necked Chola'. His death pleased Ramanujar no end, according to some of the sources.

But before going to Srirangam he wants to see Kuresar. Ramanujar meets Kuresar, who is blinded by the Chola king's order instigated by Minister Naluram, is led by his two sons, Parasara Pillai and Srirampillai. Though shocked by Kuresar's loss of sight, he admires the latter's sacrifice, but Kuresar says with all his humility that he did his little service to Vaishnavism and that although his physical eyes are blinded, he can still see the Lord Ranga, with his inner eye. He does not even want to go to Kanchi because he can see Lord Varadan even in Ranga's shrine. He has achieved such height of nobility that he prays to

Lord Varadan to grant His grace to Naluram too, in spite of the fact that Naluram was responsible for his loss of sight. Far from growing vindictive about his betrayer and harasser, Kuresar reaches his moral altitude when he prays to the Lord to grant His grace even to Naluram, who has turned out to be his enemy. His sublime act easily testifies to the truth that there is greater heroism in forgiveness than in revenge. He has proved to be the great and exemplary disciple of Ramanujar. Ramanujar admires Kuresar who has gone above the contradictions of life like love and hatred. Ramanujar says that a thousand Ramanujars will be equal to one Kuresar. As a mark of his appreciation and admiration for Kuresar's ethical sublimity Ramanujar prostrates at the latter's feet:

RAMANUJAR: Kuresar now stands in the blessed state which is beyond the petty existence susceptible to things such as friendship and enmity. The state he dwells in now is the ultimate ideal of Vishnavism. Do you remember what Guhan said in the Ramayana? 'A thousand Ramas cannot equal one Bharata'? In the same way, a thousand Ramanujars cannot equal one Kuresar. O, Kuresar, I pay you obeisance.

(*He once again prostrates himself before Kuresar. That Kuresar doesn't stop him is a little surprising to the others.*)

(IV. p. 93)

Ramanujar is happy to have fulfilled the three wishes of his guru, Alavandar: (i) establishment of a caste-less society, (ii) expansion of Vaishnava religion, and (iii) completion of a comprehensive commentary on the Brahmasutras. He declares Parasaran, the son of Kuresar, as his heir to continue the rich tradition of Vaishnavism for ever.

Note

1. Yamunacharya, the grandson of Nathamuni, is known as Alavandar, which means 'one who has come to rule', and which is the honorific name given to him as he defeated a well-known pandit, Akki Azhwar. As J.B. Carmen observes, "Nathamuni was a Brahmin from a family with a tradition of

Sanskrit scholarship". Yamuna was called back to scriptural study and initiation into Yoga by his grandfather's disciple, Rama Mishra or Manakkal Nambi. Yamuna renounced secular powers to become a spiritual leader of the small Vaishnava community that had formed around Nathamuni. He composed great works like *Siddhatraya* and *Stotratraya* in Sanskrit and *Divya Prabandham*. He is known for his spiritual egalitarianism.

Reference

Parthasarathy, Indira, *Ramanujar: The Life and Ideas of Ramanuja*, Tr. from Tamil by T. Sriraman, New Delhi: Oxford University Press, 2008. (All the page references are to this edition.)

• • • • •

7

The Legend of Nandan: A Tragedy of Gullibility

Indira Parthasarathy (pen name of Ranganathan Parthasarathy, b. 1930-) is a multifaceted personality. He is a scholar, creative writer, literary critic, cultural historian, and thinker all rolled into one. As a creative writer, he has made a name for himself in Tamil drama and fiction. So far he has written nine plays: *Pasi* (*Hunger*, 1977), *Mazhai* (*Rain*, 1977), *Kala Iyanthirankal* (*Time Machines*, 1977), *Nandan Kathai* (*The Legend of Nandan*, 1978), *Koil* (*Temple*), *Porvari Porthiya Udalkal* (*People with Hidden Selves*, 1978), *Aurangzeb* (1978), and *Kongai Thee* (*The Breast Fire*, 1990). Most of his plays expose, with Marxian and Freudian overtones, the existential dilemma of the modern man.

He founded the Sankardas Swamigal School of Performing Arts, Pondicherry University and became its Director, resuscitating the moribund Tamil theatre with adaptations of the *Cilappadikaram* and Shakespeare's *King Lear*. He then composed the highly acclaimed drama *Ramanujar* (1996) on the eleventh-century reformer, philosopher and founder of the Vaishnava school of *Visistadvaitism* (Qualified Monism). *Nandan Kathai*, directed by R. Raja in 1997, was perhaps the best production of any of his plays. Some of his works have been staged in Hindi by troupes in Delhi and Lucknow.

Indira Parthasarathy has picked up the story of Nandan from the earlier Tamil Saivite saints like Sundarar (8th century), Nambi Andar Nambi (10th century), Sekkizhar (12th century) and Gopala Krishna Bharati (19th century). This story was treated by the earlier poets in the poetic form. But Indira Parthasarathy's originality lies in giving a dramatic form to the theme—a process that involves elimination of unnecessary descriptions, stress on historically presentable action, accentuation of certain aspects like caste, superstition, knavery, and gullibility, etc., and contemporization and relevantization of the historical theme. Basically, a man of the theatre, Indira Parthasarathy has dramatized the theme of Nandan's martyrdom by highlighting the conflict between the high-caste and the low-caste people. The theme presupposes the *varna*-system and stratification of the Hindu society. As per the Aryan myth the Brahmins come from the mouth, the Kshatriyas, from the arms, the Vaishyas, from the thighs and the Sudras, from the feet of the *Virat Purusha*. The people belonging to the four *varnas* (i.e. colours) were assigned different jobs or tasks, which were to be inherited by the next generations. It was a social system, which had to be maintained by the mutual complementarity of castes, hence professions. A man's merit was decided by his birth rather than by his individual accomplishment. Hence, the social system remained rather static and never encouraged, mobility or crossing over. Thus, caste remained part of the fatalistic or deterministic force. And the law of *karma* was linked with caste system in the sense that man's birth in a particular caste was determined by his good or bad deeds in his previous life. Within the four *varnas*, the contrast and the distance between Brahmins and Sudras were very conspicuous. In a way, Brahmins and Sudras come to be binary opposites within the caste-system. Although political (and military) power rested with Kshatriyas, religious power was invested with the Brahmins, who considered themselves to be the sole agents and distributors of gods. The Law of Inheritance helped them a lot to enjoy the religious power permanently thereby denying the people of other *varnas*, especially Sudras such privileges. The *varna*-system worked smoothly as long as the non-Brahmins remained complicitous with them. The high-caste people felt threatened whenever complicity was transformed into protest or resistance due to their awakening in general.

In the Tamilian context, devotional religion (or *bhakti* cult) was very powerful around the 10th-12th centuries. But the *varna*-system prevented the non-Brahmins, especially Sudras from competing with the Brahmins because of their belief in the heritage of merit by birth and not by individual accomplishment. It is this conflict between Brahmins and the progressive Sudras, which is depicted in *The Legend of Nandan*. Whereas Vediyars represent brahmanical strata with their sense of superiority, authority, and exclusiveness, Nandan represents the Sudras or *dalits* with their desire for religious awakening and union with God. The conflict between these two binary opposites is confined to the religious dimension to the exclusion of other dimensions like social and political, etc.

The play begins with the awakening of Nandan's aesthetic and religious sensibility, which is exceptional. Nandan, who is a Sudra by caste, perceives this awakening in himself alone, but not in all the Sudras. Thus, he happens to be alone in his awakening. The other Sudras continue to live in the age-old manner with habits like alcoholism. Thus, there is a conspicuous contrast between Nandan and other Sudras. He is very unhappy to note that the other Sudras have not awakened unlike him. He says, "Look! Sir! This is our *paraiyan* hamlet. These are fellows, who think toddy is heaven" (p. 3). The Sudras consider toddy as their God and Heaven. That's why they sing:

Toddy in my hand
Song on my tongue
There's bounce in my feet!
Ah, what a beat!
Isn't all this God?
...
If we perform pooja, offering pongal
And worship with love
Veeran Irulan Katteri
Verim Nondi Chamundi
Thoori Thoondi Nallannan
Thottiyac Chinnan Peddhannan
Arrack in the hand

Songs on the lips
Jig in the legs
Say, this is your god.... (pp. 5-6)

These Sudras worship their own brand of gods, who are folksy and quite different from the standard Vedic or Brahmanical gods. In anthropological terms, the gods of Sudras belong to the 'little tradition', whereas the brahmanical gods belong to the 'great tradition'. Whereas the brahmanical religion is the standard religion, the Sudras' religion is folk-religion, which is different from the former.

But Nandan, who has woken up from his spiritual slumber, has developed a sense of beauty, which does not generally go with a Sudra's existence. He sees a contradiction in his very being, "The god, who made me a *paraiyan* committed a mistake in also giving me eyes to see" (p. 3). According to traditional belief, a *paraiyan* is supposed to be a mindless creature, almost equal to an animal. When Nandan notices that his mind has started working, he thinks that he has become human (instead of remaining a mindless animal) and attributes it to God's grace. He says, "It's the mind, which makes a *paraiyan* human; the one, who opened up the mind is God..." (p. 3).

Nandan is awakened from his mindless animalism and wants to worship the God of Brahmins through the devotional path. But the other people of his caste are not awakened yet. On the contrary, they wallow in their own filthy habits and are quite satisfied with them. Nandan, therefore, feels very unhappy about them and wants to uplift them also. Thus, there is in him a desire not only to worship God with deep devotion, but also to elevate the other *paraiahs* from the low level. Thus, his desire is both religious and social at the same time.

Nandan's desire to leave his caste habits and gods and preference for Brahminical religious habits and gods indicate the broader process of Aryanization or Sanskritization in the Indian history. According to this process, man's highest aim in life is to give up his little tradition and follow the great tradition, to give up the Sudra style of life and follow the brahmanical style of life.

But Brahmins cannot tolerate the awakening and elevation of Sudras to their level because of the fear of loss of their own authority and privileges and contamination. They feel that the security of their caste is threatened. That is why they want to suppress it at the beginning itself. For example, the Vediyars are unhappy to learn that Nandan has been turning the *paracheri* into an *agraharam*; that he talks of Sivapuja and Chidambaram; and that he wants to have the *darshan* of Nataraja in the month of Aani; that he would flaunt a sacred thread. They, therefore, want to nip it in the bud. "We are finished if this is allowed to go on" (p. 6). The Vediyars fear that the Sudras are encroaching upon their own exclusive territory thereby upsetting the existing social system based on division of labour. They are disturbed to know that the *paraiahs* want to give up their own God and worship the *paarpaara* God, who is a beautiful God of the town. If the *paraiyan* follows the path of *paarpaans*, then the division of labour will be violated and create problems for the Brahmins. Their problem is "Who will remover the weeds from the fields?" (p. 7). And their fear is, "We'll have to do it" (p. 7). If is the *jati dharma* is violated, "We will all be orphaned" (p. 7). Thus, the Brahmins' privileges, superiority and security are threatened by the awakening of the Sudras symbolized by Nandan. They, therefore, decide to finish Nandan in a very clever and systematic way.

But Nandan's awareness of beauty has been deepening day by day. "The other day in Thiruppunkur when that wench danced, any man, who didn't realize how beautiful she was, was a fool; her dance was 'an interest' earned for realizing that it was beautiful! Ah, what a beauty! What a beauty!" (p. 4). The intensification of Nandan's aesthetic sensibility has brought him to Thiruppunkur to meet the *dasi*. He has to temporarily overcome the restrictions imposed upon his low caste, "I must don this dress to be able to see that woman. (*He points to his upper cloth across the shoulder.*) Or else, can a *paraiyan* enter the town? (*The sound of dogs barking.*) Dogs may enter, a *paraiyan* may not. Dog is Bhairava. A *paraiyan* is meaner than a dog" (p. 8). After overcoming the initial hindrances, Nandan manages to enter the town and meet the dancer. He introduces himself as

Nandan, the slave of Beauty, who was impressed by the beauty of her dance in which she had become Nataraja Himself. For him beauty is not different from Truth or Goodness (or God). He tells her, "It's your beauty that has made me speak" (p. 9). The dancer wants to know if he refers to the objective beauty of her body. But Nandan refers to the subjective beauty and says, "Beauty is not in the body but lies in the mind of those who experience.... It was your dance, which made me talk like this; it was your God, who made me sing" (p. 9). As Abhirami, the dancer moves closer to him, he hesitates and requests her, "Please don't come near me.... I'm a *paraiyan* by caste" (p. 9). Then she teases him, "You said just now, the body is low born, but for the mind there's no caste.... Why? You have gone back to thoughts about the body so soon...! (*She smiles.*)" (p. 9). Then he clarifies that he saw Lord Nataraja Himself in Abhirami. Abhirami explains further that beauty has no meaning in the absence of appreciators of the same, "Be it a *paraiyan* or a Brahmin, beauty has meaning only when there are people who perceive beauty" (p. 10).

After having acquainted himself with Abhirami, Nandan broaches the secret desire of his heart to her, "I have a longing.... I must go into Thiruppunkur temple and worship the deity. Can you help me in this?... I am bringing around the folks in my *cheri* to my way of thinking. I shall bring a few of them... those who wallow in squalor worshipping the *palla* deity, should know what a *paarpaara* deity is like" (p. 10). When Abhirami asks him back as to how she can take him into the temple, he pleads ignorance and expresses his helplessness and difficulty in having the *darshan* of God, "I don't know. It is my wish that I should go into the temple. The bull blocks the view. So that the *paraiyan* can't have *darshan* of the Lord.... It is the *jati dharma* sitting there in the form of the bull, literally take it that way, if you please. The bull must move away and we must have *darshan* of the Lord. That is my wish" (p. 10).

Whereas Vediyars are unhappy about Nandan's spiritual awakening, Nandan is unhappy about the low and animalistic kind of life led by *paraiyans*. Since they are connected with menial job, especially the agricultural labour, they are satisfied with non-vegetarian food, liquor, and engagement in labour. Their philosophy of life is articulated in their song:

Crab is what we catch,
Meat is what we eat,
Toddy is what we drink.
...
Toddy pot in our hands,
Clay between our feet.
And areca nut! A good chew in the bag.
...
Offering cooked rice to the gods
We beat the freshly-ploughed earth with long canes
Rolling it and leveling it
We cast the seed and watch
We pluck the seedlings and plant them again
We open the bunds to let the water out
Weed the field and watch and wait
We reap when ripe and thresh
We tie up the grain in sheaves
And we blow the horn and keep watch. (p. 11)

Apart from agricultural labour, they spend their time in worshipping the stone god. For them rice for the belly is god. They believe that for the *paraiyan* the belly is the mind, and that the bullock and the *paraiyan* are one. Thus, the *paraiyans* believe in leading a physical hence animalistic life and not a mental life that characterizes the human life.

Nandan, who is concerned with the welfare of the people of his caste, wants to change them. He, therefore, advises them to worship Beauty so that they themselves may become Beauty, which is another word for becoming human (as contradistinguished from being animals). He tells them emphatically, "No...we are beasts, we must become human" (p. 12). He suggests to them, "Let's go to *paarpaara* temple" (p. 12) to worship Beauty. He does not like the *paraiyans*' complicity and reminds them that they should be slaves of God and not of men. He says, "I am a slave of the Lord of the Lords, but I'm no slave of any overlord"

(p. 13). He asks them to forget the Lord of the belly and follow him to Thiruppunkur temple so that they may know what Beauty means. Thus, Nandan has a noble cause of awakening and uplifting the people of his caste by introducing them to the cultivation of devotion (*bhakti*) to the standard God of the Saivas, i.e. Siva or Nataraja.

But this awakening of the Sudras shocks and threatens the Brahmins, who are afraid of losing their age-old importance and authority and security. They believe that they are the sole agents and distributors of God and have their own right on their God. Thus, the Brahmin establishment is threatened by the slow awakening of the masses. Their fear and anger are vented out by people like Mudaliyar, Vediyar, and Udaiyar. They are very angry to know that the new awareness of the masses is "all the handiwork of Nandan" (p. 14) and that the *paraiyans* have started ruling the roost. The fear of insecurity and loss of privileges stimulate the Brahmins to destroy the leader of the untouchables, Nandan, not openly but cunningly. They hatch clever plans of destroying him. Vediyar says, "The *bhajan* that Nandan sings will be his own undoing. Wait and see" (p. 14). They decide to destroy him not by beating him black and blue or by breaking his legs, but by a cunning method. "No, not by the stick, but by a trick alone can we win" (p. 14). That is the *tantram* that they wish to follow. Their modus operandi of destroying Nandan is to allow him a long rope to hang himself. Vediyar cleverly suggests, "The *paraiyan* is trying to become a Brahmin. All that we need to do is to make him don the sacred thread.... It'll become his noose" (p. 14). They want to make Nandan feel that he has been blessed with god's grace and therefore become a *bhakta*. Finally, they want to see that Nandan's *bhakti* will pave the way for his *mukti*, which is a euphemism for death. Thus, the orthodox Brahmins prepare a master plan of cunningly and systematically destroying the innocent Nandan. The contrast between the Brahmins and Nandan is the one between knaves and a gull.

But Nandan's religious hunger for God and conviction grow stronger as days go by. His admiration for Lord Siva both in concrete (*saguna*) and abstract (*nirguna*) aspects is articulated in the passionately devotional song that he sings. He longs to be a slave of God instead of being a slave of a landlord.

Nandan's concept of God includes both the transcendent and the immanent aspects of Him, as expressed in the following lines:

Either a name or a form,
To Him, who has none of these,
Let us (give and chant) a thousand names
And acclaim our clear conviction.
(that He is no other than Civan.)

For Nandan, God is Light Supreme (*Mahajyoti*) hence transcendent as well as concrete in the form of Lord Nataraja dancing on the Kailasa Mountain—He, who wears the swaying snake round his waist, who has swallowed the poison and kept it in his throat—consisting of beauty, grandeur, terror, sublimity, and serenity, etc.

Nandan's intense devotion to the Lord has helped him sever his attachment to the worldly life. It easily signifies his spiritual growth:

I became dead to my surroundings,
How the kinsfolk
Called *karma* of rare might fell away,
How my infatuation with the world died away,
And how moreover,
I lost also the powers of speech and action,
Which were left to me. (p. 16)

Nandan is immersed in the sea of devotion and achieves union with God when all duality is gone:

I lost my body and soul,
Lost my sense of perception
And lost my mind and ego too. (p. 17)

Having overcome the sense of difference between I and Thou, Nandan dwells in yogic trance, wherein there is no distinction between subject and object, but a state of pure joy or bliss. Thus, Nandan becomes the highest kind of *bhakti yogi*.

As a contrast to Nandan's awakening, the people of his caste are happy with their own *paraiyan* way of life and do not want to change it. The Old Man happens to be a spokesman of the old way of life. He asks them to leave chanting Sankara and go to the fields and attend to plucking out seedlings and plant them in neat rows. He advises them to make an offering to the *paraiyan* God Karuppanan and pray. He asks them to keep their stick handy, to beat the *parai* and sing a *pallu*. He advises them to drink toddy and get rid of shame and guilt. He says that for *paraiyans* the field is God. He has his own reservations about finding God in the temple and achieving *mukti* (liberation) through *bhakti* (devotion). He believes in the view that one can see God by having a taste of the toddy. Finally, he declares, "We don't want *darshan* of the Lord, the *darshan* of the earth is enough" (p. 19). He drinks toddy and joins four men of his caste and dances while singing. Their song iterates their alcoholism, their caste-gods, their profession, their entertainments, their enjoyments and their contentment. They sing as follows:

A delicious fowl and a fine juicy cockerel
And the bewitching brew
These are what we give our God.
This our heaven, this *cheri.*
This village pond for us is the sacred lake, our Kailasa!
And rain, our God!
...
We shall plough the field golden
We know no guile, so we feel no guilt
What else do we need, *paraiyan* girl?
In my hand, I have a pot of toddy!
Knee-deep in slush, in the field of paddy!
On the tip of my tongue is a song, already! (p. 20)

Thus, Nandan has to fight a two-fold war, one with Brahmins and the other with the people of his own caste. Therefore, the chances of success are very bleak. The Brahmins feel that their security, privileges, and superiority are threatened by Nandan's awakening. But they cannot argue or discuss with him their private problems. Hence, they hatch a cunning plan of destroying him by giving him a false recognition of his great devotion and flattering him. It is said that tiger is cruel, but it is not so systematically cruel as man. There is a proverb in Kannada that a Brahmin will cut your throat not with a knife, but with a thin cotton thread. The same technique of knavery is employed by the Vedic Brahmins here. Vediyar 1 flatters Nandan hypocritically, "This is where Nandan lives. How can you call it *paraccheri*? This is indeed the temple, I say" (p. 20). Nandan is a bit confused by this flattery. But Vediyar continues his hypocritical rhetoric and flatters him more. He says, "The Lord whom we see in the temple appeared in my dream and told me.... Nandan is the dear devotee of the Lord, he is a liberated soul, who has come to redeem our birth.... Nandan's birth was a marvel; our eyes were fortunate to behold him" (p. 21). Hearing these words Nandan cannot believe his own ears. He, therefore, asks Vediyars, "Sir, did you say that the Lord appeared in your dream?" (p. 21). The Brahmin cunningly counter-questions him, "Don't you have faith in my word, Nandan?" (p. 21). Nandan, who believes in the so-called moral uprightness of Brahmins, trusts the words of the Vediyar. Nandan's trust in the Brahmins testifies to the totality of his belief (in the higher values of life) on a higher plane and to his foolish gullibility on the practical level. The Brahmins have been deceiving him systematically by using the language of the higher plane for accomplishing their mean task on the practical level. For example, Vediyar 1 bloats Nandan's ego further by praising him, "Look, how fortunate Nandan is! He has received a blessing, which even the Rishis haven't got! It is certain that he's going to perform miracles, he'll ever shine as a realized soul" (p. 21). He removes the Old Man's doubt by certifying further, "The word emanating from Nandan's lips is verily the light held up for you by the Lord. Nandan will perform the miracle. You are the oyster, which has yielded this pearl" (p. 21). It is said that a lie becomes a truth if it is repeated several times. Vediyar 1 employs this technique of brainwashing the innocent Nandan and the men of his caste. Consequently, both the leader (i.e. Nandan) and his followers (i.e. caste-men) are psychologically forced to believe the lie masquerading as Truth. The Old Man is inspired to say, "Is that true? Come, let's worship Nandan! What the Brahmins say will surely come true" (p. 21).

The Brahmins' strategy to destroy Nandan is systematically organized. When the *dasi*, i.e. Abhirami, the temple dancer at Thiruppunkur pressurizes the priest to allow Nandan into the temple, the priest goes to Nandan's place to 'put sense into the *paraiyan*' (p. 22), but Vediyar replies that Nandan won't listen to his advice and opines that "No use rapping him. One must win by craft.... If you put down one Nandan, half a dozen of them will rear their heads" (p. 22). So he suggests to the priest, "Let Nandan have his way. We will make him a *bhakta* and thereby destroy him" (p. 22). The priest from Thiruppunkur fails to understand the paradox. Then Vediyar 1 offers the example of the Buddha, who founded his religion, which died along with him due to the Hindus' strategy of assimilation of the Buddha as one of the avatars in Hinduism. "Do you know, which is the enemy's enemy?... The strategy of assimilation, which accepts the enemy.... We made Buddha an avatar, along with him died his thought" (p. 23).

Thus, all the Brahmins have been systematically brainwashing and fooling Nandan to perform the miraculous feat. Unable to penetrate the organized knavery of Brahmins, Nandan continues his gullible behaviour along with his quest for spiritual ecstasy. At the temple at Thiruppunkur, he dances ecstatically singing. His ecstasy is characterized by intense devotion to God, his sense of gratitude to Him and his desire for union with Him.

> Of virtue void, of penitential grace
> Devoid, undisciplined, untaught—
> As a leathern puppet dancing about, giddy,
> I whirling fall, lay prostate there!
> He showed me wondrous things; He showed the way
> To pass to worlds not reached before;
> The raft He show'd; when shall I come, a wretch,
> To Him, who made me His? (p. 23)

Thus, Nandan has his mystic experience, which is devotionally charged. The cunning Brahmins, who know his innocence and gullibility hatch a further plan of deceiving him. All of them join their palms together and pretend to respect him, while one Brahmin hides behind the icon of Lord Nataraja and speaks as though an astral voice is speaking. God seems to be speaking in His astral voice, "Nanda! You are my devotee. There is nothing that you cannot accomplish. Performing wonders you shall attain to my feet" (p. 23). When Nandan hears this voice, he mistakes it to be really the divine voice and feels ecstatic. Tears of joy trickle down from his eyes. Again in that ecstatic frenzy he sings a song articulating his sense of gratitude, good luck and fulfillment:'

To me, who toiled and moiled 'mid fools, that
Know not the WAY of final peace,
He taught the WAY of pious love; and that 'old deeds'
Might cease and flee.
Purging the foulness of will, made no pure bliss, took
For His own—
'Twas thus the Father gave me grace: O RAPTURE!
WHO IS SO BLEST AS I?
A way that was no rightful WAY I followed,
Deeming it the WAY,
That I might seek no meaner way, but only seek
His sacred grace
To gain—He, whom no signs describe, His mystic
DANCE has given to know!
'Twas thus the great DANCER gave me grace: O
RAPTURE!
WHO IS SO BLEST AS I? (p. 24)

Nandan, thus, sings ecstatically about the grace of God that he has been endowed with. Abhirami is also deeply moved by his ecstatic singing and dance. The Brahmins' knavery and strategy have been so systematic and impressive that Nandan is easily deceived by the appearances. He feels confused also. He says, "I don't seem to understand anything. Vediyar said the Lord appeared in his dream...then the priest had the same dream. Now the astral voice speaks. Am I really such a great devotee?" (p. 24). His illusion is accentuated further by the astral voice, "Don't you believe it Nanda?... Do you think I have no other business but to appear in everyone's dream?" (p. 24). Nandan is cowed into acceptance of the divine injunction. The astral voice orders him, "All right...Listen to me.... Do accept Abhirami....

Yes. She is also my devotee. You have to receive the *prasadam* I offer" (p. 24). Nandan has no choice but to accept Abhirami. As she kneels at his feet, he raises her up. Then she leans against his shoulder. He gets into the trap set up by the cunning Brahmins because of his gullibility.

The Brahmins discuss the details of their conspiracy among themselves. Since the arrival of the *dasi* girl, Nandan has a new problem to tackle. Some people have become envious that such a beautiful girl has stuck to such a swarthy fellow. Mudaliyar asks Vediyar 1, "As though it were not enough that you made him don the sacred thread, tell me, why have you also allowed him to have this girl?" (p. 25). Then Vediyar explains his vulpine plan, "If I don't adopt this strategy how else will Nandan confront fresh problems?" (p. 25). One of the problems posed to Brahmins by the awakening of *paraiyans* is that the latter wish to be engaged in "Three times a day worship of Siva, farm work only in the remaining time" (p. 25). This new habit of *paraiyans* would upset the division of labour between Brahmins and *paraiyans*. If the *paraiyans* refuse to do the menial work especially agricultural labour, the Brahmins will be forced to it by themselves and put to a lot of inconvenience. It is this fear that goads them to suppress the *paraiyans* and destroy their leader, Nandan.

Another Brahmanical strategy is to cleverly create infighting among the lower caste people. "If there is infighting among the lower caste, isn't it like a shower of rain in the field for the upper caste?" (p. 26). They are happy to know that a new chap has arrived on the scene as an enemy opposing Nandan. Vediyar 1 says, "Lamenting that the *paraiyan* tradition was lost, some of the old fashioned people have joined hands with the new fellow and are baying for his blood" (p. 26). They are waiting for a continuation of Nandan's gullibility. "If we wait for some more time we can finish Nandan" (p. 26). They hope that the internal fight of the low caste people will weaken them finally. Vediyar is aware of this socio-psychological truth and explains it to his friends, "If a man fights against the system, let the system just accept him. The party opposing him will splinter into two. Damning him as the stooge of the system, new fellows will rise opposing his leadership. Now this is what's happening. Just wait for some more time, you may take it from me that Nandan's story is as good as over!" (p. 26).

Now the opposition has come from the people of Nandan's own caste. This internal fight turns out to be very advantageous to the Brahmins. The *paraiyans* do not like Nandan's so-called progressive ideas and they want to stand by their own tradition. They go to the extent of complaining to the Brahmins like Vediyar 1, Mudaliyar, and Udaiyar against Nandan's offbeat activities. They complain that Nandan is an owl that has come to ruin the clan; that he cries aloud 'Siva, Siva'; that he keeps harping on the temple, clanks the *kinnaram*; that he smears holy ash all over himself; that he has a female whom he considers as a goddess and she considers him as a Brahmin. They wish to break Nandan's legs, gag him, and pluck his eyes if the Brahmins give them the green signal. But Vediyar 1 wants to use this situation to his advantage. He, therefore, suggests that there should be a contest between the two traditions, i.e. *paarpaara* and *paraiyan* so that Nandan's so-called enemies (from within his own caste) may be weakened and Nandan's position strengthened. Vediyar 1 says, "If we set up a contest and decide, those, who are against you will become weak.... This is a contest between two traditions. You contend that the *paraiyans* need a new *dharma*? That'll be accepted only if *Bharatam* wins over the ancient *Koothu*. You are the Lord's blessed devotee. Why should you be plagued by doubts?" (p. 29). Vediyar's ulterior motive is to bloat Nandan's illusion further so that finally he may puncture it. Thus, pressurized by the Brahmanical machination, Nandan yields to their suggestion. He even justifies this contest by aligning himself with the Brahmins' rationalization of it, "Iyer said the other day...the contest that is going to take place now is a contest between two traditions. It is a contest between knowledge and ignorance.... It is my contention that the *paraiyans* should not perpetually remain slaves and barbarians. If you kindle the fire of knowledge you will see for yourself how the demon of ignorance will meet with a grueling death. That's what Abhirami's dance will show you" (p. 30).

So the competition begins. Abhirami mimes both the sages and the demons and shows how the latter fall into the fire of *yajna* set up by the sages. The miming concludes with the sages offering their reverence to the sacrificial fire:

> Dawn has come, the Muse has come
> And so has the sun!
> Haven't we been blessed by
> The blazing fire that we built—right now?
> Hail the celestials! Hail the sacrifice
> Long live Humanity! Forever.
> Long live the Earth! Long live the Vedas.
> Long live the Fire! Fire! Fire! (p. 32)

After the Bharatanatyam is over, seven *paraiyans* dance their folk dance to the accompaniment of drums, while singing the glory of their alcoholism and *pallaccheri*. After the competition is over, Vediyar 1 announces the judgment, "*Bharatam* was good. The *paraiyans* too danced well. It's very difficult to say which one is superior, which lowly. However taking into account the way people were enjoying it, Mudaliyar and Udaiyar have come to the conclusion that *Bharatam* has won.... You must all keep quiet. From this it is clear that the *bhakta* chosen by the Lord is none but Nandan. That the Lord came in my dream is true. That the Lord spoke with Nandan in astral manner is also true" (p. 35). It is obvious that the judgment given by Vediyar 1 is prejudiced and has the ulterior aim of deceiving Nandan. They give Nandan a beautiful illusion that he has developed miraculous powers. As though to reinforce this illusion, some four men (of his caste) approach Nandan and thank him for his so-called miraculous deeds. One man says, "You gave us some holy ash/ Our stomach ache was cured" (p. 35). The second man confesses, "You touched me with your hand/ The pain in my hand is gone" (p. 35). The third man acknowledges, "Nataraja you said/ I who was maimed/ am on my feet" (p. 35). The fourth man confesses, "A single glance from you/ The pain in my eye disappeared" (p. 35). When people attribute miraculous powers to Nandan, he wonders at his own self and tries to understand the strange phenomenon, "Is it Nandan who does the healing?/ Who even can understand the Lord? Is it Nandan who performs the miracles? Rather it is the essence of devotion" (p. 35). The four admirers praise the radiance in his face, compassion in his eyes, charity in his words and concern in his actions.

But in spite of all this admiration of his miraculous powers, Nandan is rather unhappy to know that there is so much opposition to him, his devotional practice and reformative action. He says, "I am disturbed by the hostility" (p. 36) and that "They don't like Abhirami at all.... They keep talking recklessly. This slander is painful to Abhirami" (p. 36). But Vediyar 1 hypocritically suggests that Nandan should go to Chidambaram. But Nandan is apprehensive that his master may not allow him to leave until after the harvest is over. Then Vediyar gives him more interesting ideas. He says, "Nanda, I have an idea.... This is going to be an achievement of yours.... You and your people start the *bhajans*.... You will see for yourself the harvesting of devotion manifest in the field!... You continue singing *bhajans* at home. The fields will be harvested by a miracle. This is my advice" (p. 37). Although Nandan is not willing for that, Vediyar, like a knave, pressurizes him with false promises, "I will inform your Master of this news—it will indeed be a harvest of piety. The Master also will come to realize your worth. Your enemies too will understand your greatness.... Perform it, I suggest, all through the night tomorrow. The very next day the whole place will fall at your feet" (p. 37). Gullible as Nandan is, he believes the words of Vediyar and gets ready for the all-through-the-night *puja*.

Just as Vediyar 1 prepares the mind of Nandan for the all-night *puja* and *bhajan*, he also prepares the mind of New Vediyar, who is the master of Nandan, by explaining his cunning plan to him. He says, "Nandan will be performing *bhajans* in his house.... During that time the harvest can be completed employing other people" (pp. 38-39). Mudaliyar considers Vediyar 1 a new version of the great Chanakya. Vediyar then explains his conspiratorial plan to the *paraiyans*, who are a few less than a hundred, to harvest four veils in Iyer's field. He tells them, "Nandan would be doing the *bhajans* in his home" (p. 40). Mudaliyar says, "He will think that it was the fruit of devotion" (p. 40). So all of them get ready to accomplish the task of harvesting the field at night and give a grand illusion to Nandan that his devotion to God has wrought a great miracle.

Nandan and Abhirami sing the praise of Lord Siva, who is ageless, birthless and deathless and controls the whole world. At the same time the *paraiyans* appointed by Vediyar 1 harvest Iyer's field. Nandan reaches the mystic height in his devotional singing. It is at this juncture that the cunning Brahmins use the trick of the astral voice to deceive Nandan further by taking advantage of unalloyed faith and gullibility:

> Nanda...
> The fields you ought to have sown I have had sown
> So that the owner may be gratified
> Without being disappointed.
> I, the Lord of Thillai, proclaim
> That there is in all of mankind
> To equal you in devotion.
> May you be filled with bliss
> Your body pulsating
> Your mind in glee
> Because of your faith
> That there is no prop but Sankaran. (p. 45)

After using the trick of the astral voice, the Brahmins praise him as the noblest of souls and fall at his feet hypocritically just to bloat his ego. New Vediyar requests him, "Please come and look at the fields. The miracle accomplished by *bhakti*!" (p. 45). Nandan is surprised by these happenings and believes them to be true. Now Vediyar 1 nudges the New Vediyar and they continues their conspiracy against Nandan. They ask him to leave for Thillai next morning itself as the same command is given by God in their dream. Although Nandan is not inclined to go there, they pressurize him to go there. Vediyar 1 tells him, "There will be a huge fire opposite the temple.... The great sin of being born a *paraiyan* will be wiped out if you take a dip in the fire" (p. 47). Nandan is really frightened by the suggestion. But Mudaliyar tries to misguide him, "Fire, which consumes sinners, will be like a cool stream for the *bhakta*" (p. 47). They convince him that a dip in the fire will miraculously turn a *paraiyan* into a *paarpaan*. "It is by the fruit of previous birth that one is born a *paarpaan*. It is by God's blessing that man is transformed into the divine" (p. 47). They promise him that "On all the *paraiyans* there will appear the sacred thread" (p. 47) and that everyone including Abhirami will attain to Kailasam. But Nandan asks them, "Isn't it enough if one is a Brahmin in mind? Why should he become one in body too?" (p. 47). They clinch the argument by declaring that "This is the command of the Lord" (p. 47). Cleverly misled and systematically misguided by the Brahmins, Nandan yields to their suggestion and says, "All right, sirs. I shall go to Thillai tomorrow" (p. 47).

Accordingly, Nandan goes to Thillai ready to have a fire bath. The Brahmins cheer him, "Long live the devotee Nandan/ Long live the devotee Nandan" (p. 47). Both Nandan and Abhirami walk towards the fire with folded hands. Nandan sings ecstatically before entering the fire:

> No more am I a wretched dog reeling
> Beaten up by the rod of caste, clan and birth.
> The knot of suffering out,
> Redeemed, my separateness transformed,
> Dying to my ignorant nature, 'I' and 'my',
> Becoming blemish less and nectar-like—
> I had *darshan* of the beloved Thillai. (p. 48)

Like Nandan, others also sing the praise of Lord Siva. Then there is a rain of flowers on Nandan and Abhirami. The Brahmins use the trick of the astral voice as their final stroke. The astral voice declares, "Nanda! My Devotee, come!... You are the true Brahmin! Abhirami, do come, both of you, bathe in the fire and come back with brahmanical resplendence" (p. 48). Then the Brahmins shout cheerfully, "Hail Nandanar, hail Abhirami" (p. 48).

As both Nandan and Abhirami enter the fire (which is shown off stage) they are burnt alive. A non-human wail of a man-beast frightening and chilling to the spectators is heard. Now that both the devotees are systematically and cunningly destroyed, the Brahmins become very happy. Vediyar 1 says, "Ah... What a wonder! Nandanar and Abhirami have become fused with the ether of Thillai! They have become fused with the ether of Thillai! *Om Namasivaya Namaha*" (p. 49). Vediyar 1's explanation is very hypocritical. Then Udaiyar reveals his beastly nature by asking the *paraiyans* gathered there, "Are there any more *paraiyans*, who desire to become *paarpaans*?... Come, come! If you take a dip in the fire..." (p. 49). The frightened *paraiyans* run away for their dear lives. Now the conspiracy of the knavish Brahmins comes full circle. Nandan's gullibility has cost him his precious life. Thus the game of the knaves with the gull is complete.

Although the legend of Nandan has been depicted by the earlier poets like Sundarar (8th century), Nambi Andar Nambi (10th century), Sekkizhar (12th century) and Gopala Krishna Bharati (19th century), Indira Parthasarathy has rehistoricized the story of Nandan once again. His originality and novelty lie not only in giving a twenty-first century angle to the original legend but also in shifting the story from the poetic medium to the dramatic (theatrical) medium. One may notice how the focus of the earlier writers changed from one aspect to the other of the legend of Nandan according to their subjective vision as well as the ethos of their age. Whereas Nambi Andar Nambi and Sekkizhar highlights Nandan's getting rid of his lower-caste identity through self-immolation and becoming a Brahmin reaching the Lord's feet, Gopala Krishna Bharati highlights the caste conflict and the Divine Grace operating through the supernatural medium.

But Indira Parthasarathy tries to present and interpret the legend of Nandan from the twentieth century point of view. He, therefore, makes some major and minor changes in the plot and philosophy. "The play *Nandan Kathai* does not exactly present the Brahmin or the highest castes in an edifying light. Indira Parthasarathy's Brahmin has none of the ancient hallowed sacred qualities. M. Uthirapathi...regards the play as centred in class conflict. However, the work predicates its action on power and its play and foregrounds the question of how 'to translate power into authority'. Power is coveted and resented in some, while with others, authority is feared and respected. In this sense, this play critiques the institution of religion in unsparing terms because religion is put to the service of power instead of to the service of the soul and God" (Introduction, xviii). In the original myth of Nandan, the element of self-realization and inner purity and genuine devotion (*bhakti*) are stressed, but Parthasarathy foregrounds the caste-conflict between *paarpaans* (Brahmins) and *paraiahs* (untouchables) and the systematic and organized cruelty of Brahmins towards Nandan, the *paraiah*. He also ignores Nandan's achievement of true salvation through God's grace and becoming a Brahmin with a sacred thread on his body—which are found in the original legends. But Parthasarathy takes only first half of the legendary story and presents it on a realistic level by removing the mythical, i.e. supernatural dimension from it. He has cast it in the Foucauldian and Althusserian mould. "He is interested in a deconstructive use of the Nandan story and hence sees himself as extending the scope of Gopala Krishna Bharati's use of the same legend to offer a trenchant critique of social iniquity. Indira Parthasarathy introduces the characters of the Brahmin (Vediyar 1) and the other upper caste Hindus, the Mudaliyar, and the Udaiyar as a departure from Gopala Krishna Bharati's musical narrative. The intention is to show how vested interest brings them all together to halt the social mobility of the untouchables. All the upper castes whose interests are jeopardized by the rise of new leadership like Nandan's are denoted by the author as Brahmins. He also presents the Master of Nandan as a degenerate feudal landowner so familiar in colonial India, whereas in Gopala Krishna Bharati's version he is an honourable gentleman" (p. xix). The intention of Indira Parthasarathy is quite clear. He "re-reads the story of Nandan through the already intertextualized quilt of Gopala Krishna Bharati's opera on the same tale. He makes his historicism more radical than even Bharati's in as much as he presents the supernatural—the astral voice believed to have been heard by Nandan as well as the priests of the Nataraja temple—as a contrived ploy, part of the stratagem. There is reason to believe that all this was deceit. In fact, Nandan is hailed as a true devotee. Even Gopala Krishna Bharati (also used as a subtext by the playwright), who spends his energy in condemning the caste system and its evils, does not question the authenticity of the supernatural. But the playwright presents it as a device to secure legitimization of upper caste hegemony. His play is an expose of the subtle collusions in the cultural struggle for power..." (p. 81).

Reference

Parthasarathy, Indira. *The Legend of Nandan*. Tr. C.T. Indra (New Delhi: Oxford University Press, 2003). (All the page references are to this edition.)

• • • • •

8

Duality of Experience in *Sirisampige*

Chandrashekhar Kambar (1937-) has been one of the popular writers of Karnataka and a practitioner of a variety of literary forms like poetry, fiction, and drama. Academically, a folklorist, he is deeply rooted in the native folk tradition of North Karnataka. Unlike the modernist writers of Karnataka, who cleverly copy or imitate the Western writers, Kambar does not fall a prey to this slavish habit as he is deeply rooted in the native tradition of North Karnataka. As he says in his interview with Kirtinath Kurtkoti, "As you know, I belong to Belgaum district, which was under British rule. Belgaum was the center of a British regiment. The atmosphere was oppressive and filled with suspicion. Right from my childhood I began to suspect anything that was foreign, alien to our native sensibility."[1] His lack of knowledge of English language has saved him from the undesirable pseudo-Westernization. His collaboration with A.K. Ramanujan in collecting the folk tales of North Karnataka has given him an additional advantage of understanding the rich texture of folk-culture of North Karnataka. Folk mythology has wielded a deep influence on him, which is why many of his plays like *Jokumaraswamy*, *Huliya Neralu* (*Tiger's Shadow*) have folk-mythical dimensions. Happily free from the disease of Westernization or Anglicization, Kambar has not only internalized the folk culture, language, literature, and mythology of North Karnataka, but also creatively deployed them as vehicles of his literary vision. In this sense, Kambar may be compared with the African dramatist, Wole Soyinka, who deliberately defied the Euro-centric concepts of drama and experimented with the revival of native (including folk) tradition of drama, although he employed the colonially handed English language. But the difference between Wole Soyinka and Kambar is that the latter is as powerful in his virile Kannada as poor in English. But as far as the imaginative reconstruction of folk-myths is concerned Kambar has no parallel in Karnataka. As U.R. Anantamurthy says, Kambar has no parallel not only in India but also in the contemporary West. Obviously, Anantamurthy's opinion is not an exaggeration. As far as the depiction of mythological themes is concerned Kambar may be easily compared to W.B. Yeats, who deliberately avoided the classical mythology and chose to dramatize the Celtic myths. A striking difference between Kambar and Girish Karnad is that the former is rooted in North Karnataka, whereas the latter is not rooted at all in Karnataka; the former is deeply steeped in the rich, virile, and poetic Kannada, whereas the latter being educated in English cannot think in Kannada. (Incidentally, it may be pointed out that Karnad thinks in English, writes in colourless Kannada, which is improved by his editors and then he translates the Kannada plays into English.) But Kambar's forte happens to be his deep-rooted-ness in the specific folk culture of North Karnataka, which is distinct from that of southern Karnataka. That is why his plays are culture-specific and do not deal with the pan-Hindu mythology as do those of Karnad. *Sirisampige* is a fine example of dramatization of a typical folk-myth of North Karnataka, although written in the *yaksagana* technique of coastal Karnataka. (By the way, there is an interesting background to the composition of this play. Once K.V. Subbanna or somebody expressed a strong doubt about the possibility of writing a play with a North Karnataka theme in a technique of coastal Karnataka, i.e. of *yaksagana*. Then Chandrashekhar Kambar accepted the challenge and composed *Sirisampige* dealing with a folk-mythical theme of North Karnataka objectified in the technique of *yaksagana*.)

There is a tradition of mythological drama in Kannada. Kuvempu, Pu Ti Na, T.P. Kailasam (only in his English plays), Masti and Girish Karnad have dealt with mythological themes borrowed from Hindus epics and *puranas* like the *Ramayana*, the *Mahabbharata* and the *Bhagavata*, etc., which belong to the great tradition of pan-Hindu/brahmanical culture. But Buddanna Hingamire, Chandrashekhar Kambar and H.S. Shiva Prakash stand apart from these playwrights as they deal with folk-mythical themes belonging to the little traditions of Karnataka or India. Hence, their plays have a peculiar ethnic beauty in them. As Milton Singer points out, the little traditions are not in any way inferior to the great tradition, but different from it. Thus, Hingamire, Kambar, and Shiva Prakash have de-centred the great tradition by moving the folk-mythical and ethnic culture from the margin to the centre, which is a very happy sign in the Indian context.

Chandrashekhar Kambar was not only deeply rooted in the rural, native, and folk-mythical tradition, but also was deeply influenced by the folk-dramatic form of *bayalata* (open air play) of North Karnataka with its subcategories like *doddata* (big play) and *sannata* (small play). Incidentally, it may be pointed out here that the topic of his doctoral thesis also happened to be the folk drama of North Karnataka. Thus, his critical knowledge of folk theatre reinforced his creative practice of play writing. Kambar explains the impulses behind his dramatic sensibility as follows, "I was searching for a form of drama, which would adequately express the sensibility to which I was born. *Bayalata* not only gave me necessary format but also the language. The language of *bayalata* is an odd mixture of pedantry and slang, which I use for the expression of a complex of emotions, which is serious and also ridiculous. My *Rishyashringa* is in that form...I continued my search for a theatre, which would be effective and could communicate immediately. And that is how I wrote *Jokumaraswamy*. Kannada theatre had developed and also had gone away from our native theatre."[2]

Kannada amateur (as different from the professional drama or Company Natak) drama has gone through the three historical stages, i.e. *navodaya* (renascent), *pragatisila* (progressive), and *navya* (modernist) movements. The Kannada poets and dramatists, who were educated in English but not deeply rooted in their native culture, were easily attracted to the *navya* style of writing. But Chandrashekhar Kambar, while living right in the midst of these movements, did not allow himself to be swept over by them due to his deep-rooted-ness in native culture and folk-mythical sensibility. What Kirtinath Kurtkoti says about Chandrashekhar Kambar's mythopoeic sensibility in general and *Chakori* in particular is particularly relevant to *Sirisampige*, "Kambar's poem once again take up the story of genesis and it is rather unusual in modern times. Modernity rejects the past and goes forward. Most of our national amnesia is deliberate in the sense that we have forgotten the past for the sake of modernity. But there is another form of modernity, which goes back, in order to go forward. Although it is a paradoxical situation, it is true of poets like Kambar. Kambar started writing poetry at a very early age and he was exposed to the world of folk poetry. He used the folklore as a language, a kind of meta-language for his poetry. Kambar knows that he is and he is not a folk poet. Folk-lore for him is the 'supreme fiction', which he has to create and which is efficacious in interpreting the world."[3] While identifying the structural principle of the folk-drama in India, Kambar says in *The Tradition of Kannada Theatre* that "The concept of '*lila*' or divine sport has been the structuring principle" and that "The folk drama sometimes consciously and sometimes unconsciously imitates the process of incarnation of god."[4]

The play dramatizes a folk-myth of North Karnataka dealing with the duality between the material and the spiritual, between the body and the mind. Folk literature is generally connected with oral transmission of the community, collective or group ethos from generation to generation. The concept of the folk is described by Alan Dundes as follows:

> The folk were contrasted on the one hand with 'civilization' —they were the uncivilized elements in a civilized society, on the other hand, the folk were contrasted with the so-called savages or primitive society, which was considered even lower on the evolutionary ladder. In terms of the assumed unilineary cultural evolutionary sequence of savagery, barbarism and civilization through which all peoples were believed to pass, the folk were more or less considered as barbarians. More civilized than savages, the folk had not yet attained civilization. Moreover the folk

> were believed to have retained survivals of savagery. Since the elite (which included anthropologists and folklorists) was vitally interested in its own origins, it sought to collect the traditions of its adjacent folk. These traditions could then be compared with the supposedly fuller versions to be found among savage societies.[5]

Folk literature is, thus, associated with the 'unlettered,' 'pre-literate,' 'illiterate,' 'peasants,' 'primitives,' 'uncivilized,' 'savage,' 'backward,' 'people of lower stratum' of society or 'vulgar' people. Such people cannot think in rational or conceptual or abstract terms, but are used to think in terms of imaginative and concrete entities. Such folk literature is generally transmitted orally from person to person and from generation to generation. Because of the orality of transmission the folk tales were improvised and sometimes varied in minor details according to the local background of the tellers of tales.

Now we let us have a brief view of the myth in general. According to William Troy, myth is a mode of cognition and "like science at once a method and a body of ordered experience."[6] Malinovsky says in his *Myth in Primitive Psychology*, "Myth is a narrative resurrection of primeval reality."[7]

According to Levi-Strauss, myth is the common language used by the primitive or savage man, who had an imaginative mind, instead of a rational or scientific mind. As Jung says, "We see the antique spirit creates not science but mythology."[8] Myth was a *bricolage* of understanding the world. One may ask the fundamental question as to why the primitive man used the myth for understanding and expressing his view of life. The commonly accepted view is that myth is the universal language of the primitive man to express the general or universal truths of life. "Like *bricolage* on the technical level, mythical reflection can attain brilliant and unforeseen results on the intellectual level."[9] Another feature of the myth, according to Levi-Straus is that it is structured on the basis of binary opposites, which has to be x-rayed by the critic intelligently. Myth has to convey a moral lesson or message to mankind. That is why some scholars consider myth as 'picturesque metaphysics'[10] or philosophy. Joseph Campbell supposes that myth is a system of metaphysics;

it is a "revelation of transcendental mysteries"; it is "symbolic of the spiritual norm for Man the Microcosm."[11] Many scholars assume implicitly or explicitly that "myth is philosophy, that it is a system of metaphysics or symbolic thought, that it is a theology, a body of dogma, or a world view, that is in direct opposition to science."[12]

T.S. Eliot says that myth is 'emotional equivalent of philosophy.'

As Susanne Langer opines, "Myth...whether literally believed or not, is a taken with religious seriousness, either as historic fact or as a 'mystic' truth. Its typical theme is tragic, not utopian; and its personages tend to fuse into stable *personalities* of supernatural character."[13] Mythical discourse does not teach the moral lesson directly but indirectly in a disguised fashion.

The sophists of the Greek enlightenment interpreted myths as "allegories revealing naturalistic and moral truths."[14]

Mircea Eliade considers myth as "sacred history" and "sacred narrative."[15]

Schelling defines myth as "theogonic process."[16]

Giovanni Battista Vico interpreted myth as "allegorical Euhemerism."[17]

As Wole Soyinka explains, "...myths arise from man's attempt to externalize and communicate his inner intuitions."[18]

Another important feature of myth is that it is closely associated with belief, religious or secular. Most of the times, myths are closed related to rituals. As Radcliff Browne says, "In the case of both ritual and myth the sentiments expressed are those that are essential to the society."[19] There is no ritual without a myth, but yet there are myths without ritual. Myth is thus both a model and a justification for ritual.

The psychoanalytical school of Freud and Jung considers myth as basically an expression, not of the external world but of the collective or individual unconscious. The repressed dreams, desires, hopes, and fears and so on stored in the unconscious mind of man will be waiting for a chance to express themselves in a disguised fashion so that they may be accepted by the society. Freud says, "The investigation of this folk-psychologic formation, myths, etc., is by no means finished at present. To take an example of this, however, it is probable that the myths correspond to the distorted residue of wish phantasies of whole nations, the secularized dreams of young humanity."[20]

Whether myth is a collective and universal in its vision, or inspired by the external world or by the unconscious mind of man, it has one conspicuous feature, i.e. its symbolism. Myth invariably uses the symbolic language, because it deals with higher truths of life not to be easily portrayed by the realistic or empirical details. Hence, it may be said that myth becomes mythopoeic in the sense that the underlying truth is expressed in terms of some images, similes and metaphors and so on. There is thus a close connection between the mythical symbols and archetypes, which are quite common to the entire humanity. As Northrop Frye says, "The myth is the central informing power that gives archetypal significance to the ritual and archetypal narrative to the oracle. Hence the myth *is* the archetype, though it might be convenient to say myth only when referring to narrative, and archetype when speaking of significance."[21] The binary opposite like God and devil, light and darkness, mother and child, storm, sea and ship, etc. are found in the myths of the world, of course, with local variations. Frye offers a beautiful insight when he says that the quest-myth is the central myth of literature.

There is a general impression among people that myth is antagonistic to history. They believe that whereas myth is a bundle of beautiful lies, history deals with hard facts and hence very reliable. This notion is questioned by a few scholars, who opine that though myth deals with improbable events, it becomes part of parahistory. Michael Grant considers myth as 'parahistory.'[22] According to him, parahistory is a record of the beliefs of the people with which they have led their lives and viewed different life-situations. Such a parahistory is incorporated within the myths of those communities. Thus, the combined knowledge of both history and parahistory of a particular culture helps scholars to have a comprehensive and holistic picture of their past.

***

The setting and the characters are mythical in that they are timeless, universal, and symbolic and not rooted in history. Kambar has combined two Kannada folk tales of two motifs, i.e. split and double and woven them into an interesting play. It is interesting to note that both Chandrashekhar Kambar and Girish Karnad have borrowed their themes from the same source, i.e. a folk tale entitled *The Serpent Lover* narrated to them by A.K. Ramanujan.[23] But there is a conspicuous difference between the dramatic treatment of the theme by the two playwrights. Whereas Karnad's *Nagamandala* is more intellectual and confined only to the Freudian overtones of woman's sexuality, Kambar's treatment is more metaphorical or symbolic and reaching the higher realms of human quest. Kambar has intelligently woven other two folk tales entitled, *The Prince who Married His Own Left Half* and *The Lampstand Woman*.[24] Not only that, Kambar has added the split motif to the double-motif, which is missing in Karnad's *Nagamandala*. In *Nagamandala*, the characters act within the framework of the folk-tale on the axis of Freudian sexuality alone, but in *Sirisampige* the characters are elevated to the metaphysical height. The dialectical relationship between the images of split and wholeness, integration, and disintegration, unnatural authority and natural ways of the primordial freedom has been the playwright's preoccupation from the beginning. As he confesses, "It is not unusual that I wrote this play. Right from the beginning I was concerned with the problem of double-ness, the difference between what we are and what we become.... My father was a blacksmith, a village saint. Once he told a story to a small audience in his smithy. The story of a prince, who was very handsome. The prince used to go to a lake and look into the still water. A dead body would come to the surface and the prince would eat it up. When hunger was satisfied he used to throw the dead body again into the water. This, I think, is our version of the Narcissus myth. Somehow, this myth has entered into my consciousness and I have been writing about it continuously, up to my recent play, *Sirisampige*, where it has its final expression."[25]

The concept of division and integration is symbolized by Lord Siva in the Hindu classical mythology. Lord Siva is known as *Ardhanariswara*, which means he is split into masculine and feminine principles and yet he is integrated. Lord Siva, thus, simultaneously symbolizes the duality and unity, *dvaita* and *advaita*. This classical mythology acts as the back up for Kambar's folk-tale that he has chosen to dramatize in *Sirisampige*. As pointed out by K.R. Nagaraj in his introduction to the Kannada version of the play, "The conflict between body and soul is a dominant major thematic concern of Kambar in his poetry. There is a substantial structure of the same in his play, *Sirisampige*."[26]

It should be remembered that although Kambar has borrowed these folk tales and combined them in his play, he has not done so mechanically. On the contrary, he has modified them creatively by reducing, displacing, eliminating, and enlarging some of the aspects of the original folk tales. Consequently, what emerges from this creative permutation and combination is Kambar's own dramatic vision transcending the limits of the primary sources.

One is struck by the names of major characters in the play. For example, Sirisampige indicates screw-pine, which is known for its strong smell and snakes are said to be residing in it. She is the daughter of Pushparaja, the king of flowers. The king belongs to Sevantipura, the City of Chrysanthemums. Similarly, Kamala suggests the lotus, which is again a flower. According to Sigmund Freud, flowers suggest the genital organs of the female species. Hence, by implication flowers symbolize sexuality and woman, the seat of sexuality. Somehow there is a close connection between flowers including their fragrance and beauty and snakes including their sexual magnetism and dynamism. In the world mythology, the snake symbolizes the earth-consciousness and the nether world. Thus, there is a combination of the floral symbolism and serpentine symbolism in the play. The prince's palace is called Indrabhavana, which easily signifies riches and happiness, but ironically it does not offer any happiness to the prince. His mother is called Queen Mayavati. Her name contains the word *maya* in it. One might interpret it as follows. The prince wants to escape from the *maya* or illusion of this mundane/mortal world by seeking the transcendental truth.

Prince Sivanaga, the protagonist of the play, becomes the site for the manifestation of human destiny and man's vain attempt to fight it. This folk-myth of North Karnataka easily brings the Greek myths to our mind. (The folk-myth has natural association with the classical Hindu mythology. For the name of the protagonist, Sivanaga contains references to Lord Siva, who is known for his split and wholeness simultaneously. Lord Siva wears the serpent as his necklace. Thus, Sivanaga means a divine serpent.) Human life seems to be controlled by the invisible Destiny. The appeal and interest of the play is to be seen in man's constant struggle with his fate or destiny and the consequent self-realization. In this play, the motives of characters and their action are all oriented to the mythical world thereby violating the laws of probability of the real world. Hence, the reader has to achieve 'the willing suspension of disbelief' *a la* Coleridge. In this play, Queen Mayavati has been taking care of her prince-ling Sivanaga after the death of her husband, King Nagara Raya. (Incidentally, it may be pointed out that it is the father, who worries about the prince's marriage in the original folk-tale in Kannada, but Kambar has changed the parent of the protagonist from the father to the mother.) When the prince attains the age of sixteen, the negative path of his destiny is revealed to his mother through an oracle. The Bhagavata articulates it as follows:

> Our family god spoke through an oracle, and foretold his future. See! Two dangers threaten: When his voice breaks he may become a monk, when his brother dies, he also dies.[27]

The oracle reveals in a seminal form his spiritual orientation or tendency of the protagonist and his congenital connection with his brother. After hearing the divine oracle, Queen Mayavati is deeply worried about the future of Prince Sivanaga. At the request of the Queen, the family suggests a way out, "When your son's voice breaks, arrange without delay for his marriage. Make sure he does not see his own image in water!" (p. 2). Being thus alerted by the family god, Queen Mayavati wants to expedite the prince's marriage,

> The Mother said, "My son, your voice
> Has broken so this is the right
> Time to marry. Hear me now—
> Wed a woman and rule the world,
> Please your mother and live long!" (p. 3)

(This warning by the oracle easily reminds us of the astrologer's warning about Siddartha's future life.) She tries to reason with Prince Sivanaga, "I'm only a woman and becoming old, and I can no longer bear the responsibility of the kingdom, so I desire to celebrate your marriage in a way acceptable to you, witness your coronation and spend the rest of my life in peace. The Elders of the family have, therefore, been sent to Sevantipura to see King Pushparaja's daughter, Sirisampige and have approved her as a bride for you. Now you must accept" (p. 3).

The initial problem goes on snowballing as the play progresses. A painful aspect of human suffering is the state of disintegration. Many tragic heroes like Oedipus, Orestes, Hamlet, and Macbeth are made to suffer due to the rift between their thought and action, a clash between the individual and the external world and confusion between appearance and reality. Sivanaga easily belongs to their tribe. He hurts the feelings of the Elders and the well-wishers of his family by forcing them to split his body. The courtiers worry about his fate and fear the wrath of the family deity also. The mother's desire to get her son married is frustrated by the son's unwillingness to get married. Hence, the dramatic conflict asserts itself. He objects, "Why do you want me to marry straightaway, tying a grinding stone round the neck of a child at play? Why should responsibility fall on me while there are Elders living? Please don't make me unhappy, Mother, by constantly telling me such cruel things" (p. 3). But when the Mother persuades the Prince, the latter expresses his private problem, "Only because the maidens you chose all had some defect or other. I have refused to marry. For no other reason" (p. 4). The Prince's idea of a bride is a Platonic in that he has an inner picture of an ideal bride because of which all the real brides of the world fall short. But still he keeps on searching for an ideal bride, "I have faith that a flawless one must exist, Mother. From the day my voice broke, I have felt that she is hiding somewhere, like butter in milk. She is also trying to come out of her hiding place somewhere. Give me time to show her to you" (p. 4). Thus, the Prince lives at an ideal level whereas his Mother lives at a very practical level. As there is no meeting point between the two, the problem continues. The Mother asks him for the ulterior reason, asserts her maternal power and orders him to marry the bride selected by her, if he cannot get his ideal bride, "Do you need time to tell me the name of the maiden you admire? Or is it just another excuse to postpone the marriage? That's enough. You shall have one week's time to say who the maiden is. If you give me her name, well and good. If not, you will marry Sirisampige. Is that understood?" (p. 4).

In the meanwhile something marvelous happens in the palace, which is described by the Bhagavata,

> Thus the Prince in Indrabhavana Palace
> Having laid down full of worries
> —how can I believe my eyes?—
> saw the carved lamp-stand come to life,
> saying 'Beloved,' becoming,
> inviting intimacy? Was that the wonder?
> From the scabbard came the sword
> Came alive between the thighs. (p. 9)

When the Prince is sleeping in his palace, he sees a dream in which a lamp-maid comes alive, dances and finally dissolves into his body. The marvelous experience is possible only in the mythical world and not probable in the real world. The marvelous experience is vividly described by the Prince, "Oh! What a marvel! Could it be some goddess under a curse, turned to stone all this time, who has now rid herself of the curse and come to life again? Or some nymph, who fell in love with me and hid in the stone waiting for me, and has now come out of her stone-hiding place and bloomed into life? That creature, who kept the burning lamp in her palm and leapt like flashing lightning, has dissolved into my body! Is she suggesting that this is how I should get married? Yes, she must be the woman that satisfies all desires, who I have been longing for these many days. If that is so, I have found my bride" (p. 9). Having seen the ideal bride and dream girl, the Prince confesses the secret to Jawali and agrees to marry her. In a way, his search for the ideal has been fulfilled. Later he tells his Mother and Elders of his palace that he is willing to marry the girl provided they agree to the condition to be laid down by him. The Queen and the Elders, who are eager to arrange his marriage, agree to his terms by swearing by the feet of the family god. They promise to arrange his marriage with the ideal bride of his choice. The Prince reminds them that their promise is irrevocable and binding on their part, "You have sworn. Your words are not different from the prophesies of gods. Do not ignore my words, thinking me only a boy..." (p. 11). The Queen Mother and the Elders, who are very practical in their approach, wish to know his desire. He expresses his desire as follows:

> Split, split my body into two equal halves,
> Chop, chop it into even pieces.
> Place at once those pieces into two pots!

That's not all. After I have been cut into two, each piece should be stuffed into a pot. Both pots should be buried among flowers. On the next full-moon day, when you open the two pots, you will see come out of one a Prince of matchless charm, that's myself. From the other will come the palace lamp-maiden, a woman of statue-like beauty holding a light in her hand. Then you should get the two of us married. If this is agreed, there will be a marriage. If not, no" (p. 12). Both laying down a condition and laying down an impossible condition are possible only in the folk-mythical world and not probable in the real world. The desire of the Prince Sivanaga to be split into two indicates a universal type of personality in psychology, i.e. schizophrenic personality or a divided soul in philosophy/spirituality. The psycho-spiritual truth has been mythically presented in the play in the character of Sivanaga. On hearing the Prince's conditions, the Queen Mother and the Elders are simply shocked and attribute it to madness and possession by a spirit. But the Prince denies their charge, affirms the truth of his own dream experience and even threatens to become a monk if they failed to keep their word, "If the Elders act according to the word they have given, they are the equals of god and the fates. If they do not, they are the equals of human worms. If mother consents to this, she is the equal of the goddess of creation, if not she is the equal of the black goddess. If you agree to what I say, there will be a marriage. If not, you will see leave here as a wandering monk" (p. 12). This strange and negative development of the Prince causes great anxiety to the members of the royal family. They suspect that the human destiny is unwinding itself and the family curse, coming true. "Is the curse coming true, is our family's sin overflowing? Is our acquired merit wasted, has this lineage begun to burn?" (p. 12). Deeply disturbed by the strange development in the family, the Queen Mother implores the Elders to solve the problem of the Prince's marriage without tarnishing the prestige of the lineage. All of them helplessly agree to fulfill the Prince's desire to be split into two. The desire to be split into two and its execution by the members of the royal family are indeed absurd and improbable on realistic level in medical terms, but the same may be accepted by the reader/spectator on the mythical/symbolic level for enjoying the aesthetic beauty of the play.

Accordingly, the Queen Mother and all the Elders gather at the shrine of the family god and split his body into two and bury the two halves into two pots. But when they open the pots after a month, they are shocked to learn that a snake and a prince came out of the two pots, but not any lamp-maid as the Prince had prophesied:

> In flowing light the Elders gathered,
> The feet of all the gods were worshipped,
> The Prince's body split and buried then opened.
> See, what is this like the sun burning,
> A precious gem its hood adorning,
> Lifting its hood like a big basket as it moves?
> Saying 'Careful!' tittering, scattering,
> Saying 'Hit it!' 'Kill it!' they attacked it.
> Alas! They saw it disappearing into the forest.
> Anxiously, the pot remaining
> They raised and opened, calling on Siva.
> The smiling Prince, the best of men came out. (p. 13)

They are all disappointed to know that no lamp-maiden has come out of the pot. The Prince's hope has misfired. The Queen Mother attributes it to the curse on their family, "What is this madness, Son? Listening to the words of your youthful rashness, we have done many things that we ought not to have done. All this comes from the curse on our lineage. Why else should it happen? By the blessings of the family god, you have come through to a new birth, at least. That's enough" (p. 13). His rebirth has unfortunately nullified his expectations. After reborn from the pot, the Prince asks the Elders about where the Lamp-maid is. They reveal the harsh truth to him by saying that what came from the other pot was a 'hideous, horrible demon,' 'an evil creature,' or a 'ghost.' The Prince feels furious to know that he is cheated. But the Elders tell him that it is they, who are cheated and not he. Thus, things have gone awry due to the family curse and they have to continue according to the dictates of Destiny.

Since the Prince's hop of marrying his dream girl, the Lamp-maid is shattered, he has to yield to the pressure of the Queen Mother and Elders and marry Sirisampige ultimately. Although Queen Sirisampige is a good wife, Prince Sivanaga does not find her satisfactory. He, therefore, goes in search of the Lamp-maiden.

> Sirisampige he married
> but she could not satisfy him,
> Everywhere he went searching only for the Lamp-maiden.
> The Prince's ever-growing madness
> Made his ageing Mother worry,
> "What god, what angel can protect our family?
> Who'll guard our lineage in the future?
> Lovely Queen Sampige Devi's
> Lotus face? How can I bear to look at?" (p. 16)

The Prince's search for the Lamp-maiden is a mythical expression of the symbolic truth. It symbolizes his search for the transcendental truth or ideal image or spiritual light. The image of lamp easily connotes spiritual light in addition to signifying the physical light. His dissatisfaction with his neogamist Queen Sirisampige, who is liked by one and all in the royal family, suggests that the Prince is not an ordinary person of the mundane world, but an extraordinary one with a hunger for the higher truth of life. He thus provides a sharp contrast to his Mother and Elders, who belong to the mundane world and live their life on a very practical level. Viewed from the perspective of the mundane world, Prince Sivanaga's behaviour appears to be very peculiar and even absurd. The Mother's words amply bear it out, "So much we possessed, Elders and what has become of it? I had hoped to spend the last days of my life gazing on my son as King and head of a family, playing with my grandchildren. How can Siva punish me so? They say that after marriage a son leaves the mother that bore him and falls under the spell of his bedfellow. No such thing happened here. I have not seen husband and wife laughing together even once. From the first day of their marriage, he would disappear at any time. Come back at any time. He goes off as if searching for something he has lost and returns as if hopeless at not finding what he seeks. He does not talk to anyone. When the family god was consulted, he sobbed and did not open his mouth to say anything. I cannot bear to see the face of my daughter-in-law, who is weeping all the time. My son's face I do not see. Tell me, Elders, what is to be done now?" (p. 16). Obviously, there is no meeting ground between the two planes of life, i.e. transcendental and mundane; spiritual and material.

The Queen Mother and the Elders do not and cannot understand the meaning of the Prince's search for the Lamp-maiden. The Lamp-maiden may easily be accepted as symbolic of light, especially spiritual light. But they want to ascertain where he goes repeatedly and what he does there. They, therefore, order Jawali to spy of the Prince by following him and watching his activities secretly. Accordingly, Jawali follows the Prince secretly and observes what the latter does there. He returns and reports to the Queen Mother that the Prince used to look at his own reflection in the water of the pond and cry for the joy of seeing the Lamp-maiden in it. The Queen Mother grows deeply worried, "What should not have happened, what I was guarding against for sixteen years, has happened now out of my sight. The only difference is that he, who should have become a monk on seeing his reflection, is now thinking of the Lamp-maiden" (p. 18). She does not understand why the Prince prefers the Lamp-maiden to her daughter-in-law, who is a thousand times prettier than the former. She attributes the Prince's abnormal behaviour to some kind of madness. When Jawali accuses the Prince of madness, the latter denies the charge and describes his vision of the Lamp-maiden in the pond, which is nothing but the mystic experience of the union with the transcendental Reality, "Today I was beside a pond. She was inside it. She was swimming in the waves and ripples, glittering like a fish. Moving her tiny arms. 'I must catch her,' I thought. 'No,' I thought. 'I can catch her in my hand,' and I stretched out my cupped hands. When my breath touched the water in my hands—do you know?—she trembled for love? Slowly she dripped down again between my fingers. Saying 'silly girl' I pinched her cheek. She laughed—do you know?—like lines running in the waves. Seeing her I laughed too, and I spoke. She also spoke as I did. Everything I did she did too, or everything she did I did too, there was so much harmony between the two of us that like two halves coming together we had become one. Gradually we became, both together, an indivisible zero transcending form, becoming the Sivalinga, becoming God. Nor did the shadow of imperfect sorrow linger around this new god—ah—it was like air, it was like light, it was like the blue of the sky, it was like empty space—it seemed it was impossible for anything physical to touch him. After seeing that god, I realized what beauty is and what ugliness is. Suddenly I felt that there is something lacking in this world we live in. Ah, God! It is a puzzle how we go on living with so much lacking in this world" (p. 20). Jawali, the materially oriented person, cannot understand the higher spiritual experience of the Prince and therefore accuses him, "What you saw was your own reflection" (p. 20). But the Prince, who knows the low and mundane level of Jawali, expresses his anger at the impossibility of communication between the two levels of experience, i.e. sense-experience and transcendental experience, "Ay! Blast my foolishness in arguing with an ignorant person like you. Seeing one's reflection and becoming one with it means seeing the shape of the soul. But you cannot understand all this. You are stuck to the body. People, who refuse to see any further than the body, cannot understand such things" (p. 20). The Prince's description of his experience of the pond makes explicit the multiple aspects of mystic or transcendental experience as codified in all the organized religions of the world. Man-God relationship is always a mutual affair. God will not descend to Man until and unless Man ascends to God. There is thus always a balance between desire and satisfaction or quest and fulfillment. Man's life will be complete only when he attains the divine consciousness or spiritual harmony with the Absolute. The union between Man and God has been described by all religions of the world as *yoga samadhi*. The Prince has achieved such a mystical union at the pond. The numerical metaphor of 'zero' easily brings to our mind the Virasaiva concept of 'Sunya,' which, far from meaning the Buddhist 'void', symbolizes wholeness or plenum or awareness of the Formless God. The Prince has divinized himself and become a new god. This mystic union of the Prince is indeed indescribable and intangible. That is why it is compared to air (which is vital and universal, suggested by the concept of *pranalinga* in Virasaivism and by the concept of spirit in Christianity); to light (of spirituality or *Jyoti* or *Paranjyoti* in pan-Hinduism); to sky (symbolizing Infinity) and to empty space (or '*bayalu*' in Virasaiva parlance). The Prince easily stands for Everyman, who is mortal and finite, but who longs for the immortality and merger into Infinity. He stands for the individual soul eager to merge into the Oversoul. The Prince, unlike the other mortals of the palace, is elevated to the spiritual level. Hence, he cannot be understood by the ordinary run of people around him.

Whereas Prince Sivanaga represents the luminous side of human life, Kalinga represents the dark side of the same, as his very name indicates. He is obviously a dark god of the nether world. (Incidentally, he brings to our mind the Lawrentian concept of dark gods.) He easily symbolizes the sexual urge in human beings *a la* Sigmund Freud. In the present play, he provides a binary contrast to the Prince. Whereas the Prince represents the angelic aspect of human life, Kalinga represents the devilish aspect of the same. The battle between the two aspects happens in the life of Sirisampige. It must be specially remembered that both 'Sivanaga' and 'Kalinga' are variant names of the reptile, i.e. the snake. But whereas 'Sivanaga' suggests the serpent serving as an ornament of Lord Siva, 'Kalinga' suggests a black-skinned snake and has a devilish, animalistic and instinctive quality about it. Whereas Sivanaga belongs to the upper world (i.e. Kailasa of Lord Siva), Kalinga belongs to the nether world. Sivanaga is caught in a conflict between light (symbolized by the Lamp-maid) and darkness (symbolized by Kalinga) or between conscious mind and unconscious mind respectively.

When Prince Sivanaga fails to pay attention to his wife, Sirisampige because of his obsession with the Lamp-maid, Kalinga wakes up and listens to Sirisampige's voice. Being a symbol of sexual instinct, Kalinga begins to long for her. Instinct, which represents Nature, cannot be subject to the restrictions and prohibitions of culture. Although not legally married to Sirisampige, Kalinga begins to lust for her, "Aahaaah! We the traveler and acclaimed great hero of the eight directions and the fourteen worlds were resting once after our daily duties in our palace in the nether world, when a girl's voice appeared to be calling us. While we were wondering how a woman's voice could be making itself heard in a bachelor's palace, as if descending to plunder our world she appeared before us. Loosing all sense of ourselves, we knelt before her. Was it a dream or was it real? Such a thing might perhaps occur once in a while, but that was not the case here; every day we saw the same vision. Why should we be thinking about a woman, who belongs to someone else? But that also did not seem to be the case. She seemed to be our rightful wife, known to us for a long time. From the day we saw her, the desire to possess her stirred in us. Very well. We decided to go in search of her" (p. 21). When he goes round searching every region of the earth, he finds her in the backyard of Indranivasa Palace in Sivapura. Just as Kalinga symbolically hears the cry of sexually starved woman (in this case, Sirisampige), the woman (in this case Sirisampige) also feels tempted by the vision of a sexually virile man (in this case Kalinga, the black snake symbolizing the dark instinct and sexual urge). The woman, in spite of the restrictions of culture, feels an inward temptation for a sexually satisfying man:

Who is this comes riding up
My body, who is he that I
Don't know, but yet upon my mind
Is printed?

Wherever I go I see arise
And stand by me his handsome shape
And longings of desire are born
To trouble me. (p. 22)

Sirisampige, thus, feels an uncontrollable sexual urge for the stranger secretly, although she does not know him. Obviously, this shows the primal biological urge in woman for man and vice versa. The urge in both for each other goes on intensifying. For example, Kalinga fantasizes about Sirisampige's lush beauty, "Aha! Her body is like a festival for my aroused senses. It seems to be beckoning. Big buttocks, big, big breasts! Small waist, pool of pleasure! Eyes trained in hunting. Whether she's maid or wife, even if my life is lost in the attempt, it doesn't matter. Unless I bed her, my life has been wasted" (p. 22). Like Kalinga, Sirisampige, in spite of being a married woman, feels the sexual urge and attraction for a non-husband inwardly. She says, "I have become like a boat caught in a storm and overturned. Someone is opening the doors of my youthful breast, and shaking all my desires to awaken them. No. I must not sacrifice my judgment to such base desires. I will talk with that man, who is coming to seduce a woman belonging to another, scold him and send him away" (p. 23). What is to be noticed is that there is a great sexual awakening in both Kalinga and Sirisampige, although the latter can control it (at least initially). Kalinga declares his love and persuades Sirisampige like any adamant lover. He changes his guise to that of Prince Sivanaga, when the Queen Mother enters Sirisampige's chamber. When Kalinga in the guise of the Prince, rests his arms on Sirisampige's shoulders, she is sexually electrified and wonders at his magnetic quality, "So much joy wells up in me at his touch. Who is this wizard, who has come to plunder me?" (p. 24). But still she is not able to understand his exact identity, as she has noticed his ability to change his guise at will. She, therefore, asks him, "Before madness overcomes me, please tell me who you are. You were like a hissing snake, and now you are like the Prince. How many existences do you have?" (p. 24). Kalinga answers her, "As many as you want" (p. 24). Kalinga's double identity helps him deceive Queen Sirisampige and helps the dramatist to prove her ignorance and innocence, although it is quite natural for her to be sexually aroused by a powerful man, as she happens to be in the prime of her youth. Again the disguised identity is in tune with the mythical world and cannot happen in the real world. Kalinga may be looked upon as the alter ego of Prince Sivanaga. Together they are complementary to each other and constitute the whole reality. But Sirisampige is not able to understand it completely.

Sirisampige knows that Kalinga looks like the Prince, but she has also noticed that the latter is a little effeminate to look at and that was because the Prince split himself to search for the Lamp-maid. Kalinga asks her, "In that case, now tell me—am I a stranger?" (p. 24). Kalinga answers her symbolically that he is the later ego (or the other half) of the Prince. He symbolizes the unconscious level of human mind (psychologically), the nether world in the depth of the palace and the world (mythically): "While you were in bed with your husband, who was lying there like a piece of wood, was there not in the nether region of your mind a king kneeling before you, begging for your love?... That was me. Did you recognize me as King Kalinga, ruler of the nether world in the depth of the Prince's palace?" (p. 24). But Sirisampige is not clear about it as she is confused. Since Kalinga symbolizes the unconscious level of human mind, he has an intimate knowledge of dreams, which are a manifestation of the Unconscious. He, therefore, tells her, "But I know you. I can even tell you what dreams you dream. And I will teach the dreams that you shall have from today on" (p. 25). When Sirisampige's latent dreams (of her unconscious mind) are made manifest to her, she really enjoys seeing them. In those dreams she sees a forest in which there are fruit trees, fresh sunlight and a golden river. When she enters the burrow near the river she sees the concretization of a variety of joys. "Aah! How fine this world is. How many coffers of gold there are in the nether regions! In every corner so many nameless joys are sleeping freely" (p. 25). Sirisampige realizes the latent dreams of her own unconscious mind and beauty and sweetness symbolized by the nether world of Kalinga.

Prince Sivanaga's transcendental experience at the pond does not last long. The God, who showed smiling in the water dripping from his cupped hands, has gone back to the depths. He feels he is cheated by his God. His faith in his God is shaken because of his wife's secret (but innocent) adultery with Kalinga. This experience shows that man cannot be happy when he is divided. He can achieve real happiness only when he can harmonize the two aspects of his personality like the physical and the spiritual. Although Queen Sirisampige welcomes the Prince with open arms, he seems to detect her sin of adultery. He says, "The body is pure, my Lady, but the soul is dirty. Sins are visible to the soul" (p. 30). He accuses her, "In reality you are a Queen and in dreams you are a lover. You can handle the selves of two worlds. But the day I was deceived by the god, I lost my dreams too, Lady" (p. 30). The Prince has realized the tragedy of imbalance between body and spirit. In fact, body serves as a medium of the spirit. Too much of spiritual obsession or renunciation will not help man to lead a normal worldly life. One should not run away from this worldly life to become otherworldly. The worldly life itself should be converted into Heaven. Neither extremity (i.e. physical or spiritual) is desirable in life. Prince Sivanaga seems to have realized this truth rather late. He tells his Queen, "Rejecting my body, leaving it with you, I went to the pond to see the god. What came floating in the water neither the Lamp-maiden nor a god. It was not even my reflection, Lady, it was my corpse. And that was what I held daily on my lap and ate of. The more I ate, the hunger I felt. I ate more and more of it, and by the time I realized it was a corpse, it was too late. When I repented and came back, my body itself had vanished. In the meantime someone had entered it and gone off with it. Now I am almost air, Lady. I cannot even make your skin feel my touch; I don't exist except as air that speaks. I need a body to show myself in. My hunger for life is growing. Lady, I need a body. Please help me" (p. 31). He suspects that his body has been stolen by Kalinga and therefore wants to test his wife through a public trial. Sirisampige is really puzzled by his behaviour and asks him why she should undergo the trial. He answers her that it is meant for the revelation of the truth of her illicit pregnancy. His Queen Mother is also shocked by the words of the Prince and tries to defend her daughter-in-law. But he clarifies his motive, "Please forgive my irreverence,

Mother. That foetus in her womb is not mine. To whom does that poison belong? That is the truth that must come out" (p. 32). The Mother attributes the Prince's strange behaviour to insanity and lack of judgment. But the Prince confesses to her his split nature and the duality of his experience. Even his hatred of his so-called cuckolder is not unalloyed. But he wants to know him whether he be his elder brother or enemy, "Even my hatred is split in two, Mother. I cannot wholly hate the Queen. And he, who in my absence illicitly was joined with her, who brought a treasure without anyone knowing and hid it in her womb—I have no wholehearted hatred for him either, Mother. Admiration and jealousy, yes, but I need him. That is why tomorrow morning the Queen's deception must be exposed" (p. 32).

Intent on exposing his wife's sin, the Prince calls a meeting of the Elders and the Queen Mother at the Nagalinga temple and cleverly asks them, "What should be the punishment for a woman, who has abandoned her husband, has illicitly joined with another, and has become pregnant?" (p. 33). The Elders suggest that the question should be solved by the inmost conscience of husband and wife or by an ordeal. Then the Prince tells the Elders, "The woman, who has committed a crime here and is illicitly pregnant, is the Queen of the country, and the one, who is asking for justice is the King" (p. 33). The Elders and the Mother are, obviously, shocked by the Prince's request (which is equivalent to a command). All of them become helpless and agree to arrange a divine ordeal. Princess Sirisampige agrees to prove her chastity by undergoing the ordeal publicly, "Look, that snake, which is crawling there on the Nagalinga—I will let it climb on my body. If I am a pure and virtuous wife, it will move over my body without stinging me and go away. Otherwise it will use its poison and sting. By this trial the truth can be tested and punishment be given at the same time" (p. 35). Everybody accepts the condition and watch the divine ordeal curiously:

> With hands joined above her head
> She came before the snake-linga
> Bowed and trod devoutly round the idol.
> Abandoning fear she stretched out her arms;
> Saying 'snake, protect the truth.

Come to me,' she took the snake upon her body.
Were they friends, she and the snake?
Did the dumb creature know the truth?
Showering the Queen with kisses, charming
Opening its hood it played on her,
The light in its hood-jewels gleaming,
Happily twined with her plait, her womb caressing
Turned its hood-light to the front
Slipped down the slope of her thighs
And seeking its linga master moved away.
All the people stood like painted beings.
'A strange thing we saw,' they said,
'truth depicted by the Queen's grace for us all.
Hail, oh hail, to our godlike Queen!
Hail to a mother's faithful womb!
Hail to the lineage!'
All bowed to Sampige. (pp. 35-36)

The ordeal of the divine snake (Nagalinga) happens to be far from trustworthy. The irony of the Prince's life is that there is an element of deception and corruption even in the so-called divine ordeal (like deception and corruption to be seen at the heart of modern judiciary, bureaucracy, and anti-corruption agendas). The snake, which is taken by the Princess in her arms, does not seem to be the real divine snake of the temple, but her lover Kalinga himself in the guise of a snake. The situation is as ironical as the one described by Rabindranath Tagore in some other context. When somebody is haunted by a ghost, you search for an exorcist. But what will you do if the ghost itself comes in the guise of an exorcist? Far from biting the Princess for her sin of adultery, the snake moves quite affectionately on the Princess's body and slithers away from there thereby hiding her sin and proving her so-called chastity. Although the Elders and the Mother are taken in by the so-called divine ordeal, the Prince is not convinced by it as he inwardly questions its veracity. That's why he shouts with frustration, "This is cheating, cheating!" (p. 36). The Prince is not convinced by the ordeal at all. His suspicion of a rival, who has been sleeping with his wife, continues to harass him mentally. He shares his confidential problem with Awali, "You are fortunate, at least you are alone. Look at me. Even when I am sitting alone, I feel there is someone like me sitting next to me, wandering around in my body, talking in my voice, stealing me. I thought it was not a man, but a mirror, but he is not a mirror, because a mirror cannot talk, and he talks. A mirror will not move by itself, but he wanders all through the palace, not caring about me. I will tell you a secret, don't tell anybody. He has stolen my wife also, and slipped into her bed" (p. 39). The Prince has realized that somebody has been acting as his other half and stealing his wife. He, therefore, wants to detect and catch him.

The adulterous relationship between Queen Sirisampige and Kalinga has continued. Consequently, Sirisampige has given birth to a child. Kalinga wants to see his child and continue his flirtation with Sirisampige, but she reminds him, "I also have my responsibilities and my honour, Kalinga" (p. 39) and asks him to go away from her. But Kalinga, who has cleverly and cunningly saved her in the ordeal, taunts her and accuses her of utilitarian approach, "Remember, my goddess. Remember the dark boy, who played with your hair. Sometimes you would say, 'Kalinga, dear snake!' and sometimes you wanted me to become the Prince. Using both of us you set your womb alight. Wooing my mind with smooth talk you won your trial. Now after using me, do you want to throw me away like a spent firebrand?" (p. 40). Like a typical adamant lover, Kalinga wants to haunt her, but she being a Queen has her honour and dignity to maintain. That's why she explains to him rather sadly, "My body is not a commodity, Kalinga. For you that child may be an extension of your pride in yourself, but for me it is a wound you have given me" (p. 40). Queen Sirisampige asks him to escape from there, but Kalinga tells her that he is not angry with the Prince, although he has cuckolded him. His attitude to and relationship with the Prince seems to be ambivalent. He says, "When I see him I don't feel angry at all. I don't know why. May be my own entrails continue in him. May be we were brothers in a previous birth" (p. 40). Kalinga's sympathetic attitude towards the Prince is paralleled by the Prince's similar attitude to Kalinga at the last moment of his life.

Just as Prince Sivanaga had realized the inadequacy of exclusive spiritual experience of life, Kalinga also has realized the inadequacy of exclusive physical, especially sexual experience of life. Kalinga says, "Listen Sampige, I am surprised at how I have spent so many days with you. I started feeling that I was desiring some shadow beyond you, or that I had caused it some pain. Whenever I lay with you that shadow beyond came to tease me. All these days I forgot it only in the momentary happiness of the body. I mean to embrace you in such a way that not even air can slip between us, but between us there remains a huge empty space. And in that space the dark shadow appears, beckoning to me. Before, I saw your body. Now I see nothing but the shadow. That shadow is the truth between us, I feel" (p. 40). After revealing his realization to Queen Sirisampige, he assumes the form of a seven-hooded snake and escapes through the gutter.

Prince Sivanaga, who suspects his wife has a regular love affair with a lover, wants to catch the culprit. He has appointed Awali to guard the harem and capture the culprit, who might be escaping from there. Awali obeys him, but regrets his inability to capture anyone. He also tells the Prince that a snake escaped by the gutter-drain and disappeared inside a darkness-filled anthill. Now the Prince's anger and suspicion are raised further. He tallies Awali's description of the snake with his own memory of the snake that had participated in the trial of Queen Sirisampige at the Nagalinga temple and concludes that both are the same. "Its royal poise proves that it is the same snake as the one, which was there on the day of the trial. And if it is definitely the snake of the trial, then it is also definitely my enemy. He can take on any form he wills, and now, scared, he has run away as a snake. Go! If he enters an anthill, set fire to the anthill; if he enters the forest, set fire to that too. Even if you have to mix poison with the air we breathe, he must be caught and killed" (p. 42). The Prince's anger and vindictiveness are quite natural and obvious.

The Prince's suspicion about his wife's secret adultery is confirmed by now. She describes Sirisampige as a "lover inside and Queen outside." He asks her about the escape of the snake from her chamber; the sameness of the two snakes, i.e. one from the anthill and the other from the Nagalinga temple; the secret and immoral love between her and the snake. Now the final moment of reckoning has come. She confesses her sin rather desperately and helplessly, "At last you have come to know of it. I am glad. I was wondering all the time how I could reveal it to you" (p. 42). The Prince is very angry with her for her betrayal of faith, "You cheated the Elders, you cheated everyone. You wounded them in their faith in you, didn't you? Your name, which has been that of a goddess of town and temple will become a term of abuse for the whole country, do you know that?" (p. 43). Sirisampige's answer to her husband's question brings out the matrimonial truth on a practical level and the philosophical truth on a cosmic level simultaneously. It provides a contrast to his experience from a woman's point of view and makes him aware of the other side of truth. It also makes explicit the central problematic of the play. She says, "That is your ill fortune. My immorality started, my Lord, when you forgot the body and began craving for the god and slipped away from our bed. I, who was lying on the bed, counting rafters in the roof and sighing never notice when you slipped away. I searched for you, but wherever I searched, in the palace garden, or in the words you spoke, you were not to be found. In the end you saw the god by taking handfuls of water from the pond. I too took a handful of water and there was a god in my handful too, but if he turned out not to be the same god as yours is it my fault?" (p. 43). Her answer confirms the universal truth about matrimonial disharmony. Their marriage has been rendered meaningless on account of their temperamental incompatibility. As a normal wife, she needs sexual satisfaction from her husband and therefore wants to possess his body. She is, naturally, frustrated when her desire is frustrated when the husband fails in his duty to satisfy her biological urge. Sirisampige, who wants to construct her sexual identity as a woman, easily yields to the earliest temptation by Kalinga and makes the best use of the golden opportunity secretly without violating the outward rules of family life in the patriarchal society. Her frustration with her husband is caused by his negligence of the physical or sexual aspect of marriage and his going away to the pond in his search for a god or transcendental experience. It only proves that generally no normal wife would go in for a lover unless she is frustrated with her husband for some reason or the other. Similarly, the Prince was also frustrated with Sirisampige, as he could not see the Lamp-maiden in her. Thus, both of them are frustrated as they suffer from half-ness or incompleteness. Theirs is a tragedy of half-ness, incompleteness and imbalance. It is exactly this tragic suffering, which Sirisampige has undergone and which she articulates, “I am half widow, my Lord. You can’t understand the grief of one, who is always half a widow! When you split yourself you split me also. When you are before me, my body is widowed, when I am with him, lying with him, my mind is widowed. Thus I am always half widow. There is nothing to equal such a torture. My sorrow is that no one understands me. I am alone. Afraid of loneliness, I search for a companion. But all the companions to be had are half men. Was I born for half men? I was born for and I am seeking the wholeness of the *linga* of the god Siva. But what fell to my lot was a child born illicitly to an incomplete being. A child born to a widow. You have come here to kill the women, who gave birth to an illegitimate child? Look, I am ready!” (p. 43).

The Prince wants to take his wife to task after killing his rival and cuckolder, Kalinga. He roars, “You, who lay with my woman,/ You, who polluted my lineage,/ till I kill you I will not cease” (p. 44). He accuses Kalinga of taking any form that suits him. He compares himself to Kalinga’s destiny’s eagle. He provokes and challenges Kalinga for a fight. Both of them fight bravely initially but Kalinga opposes the Prince less strongly because he considers the latter to be his own kith. The Bhagavata describes it,

> Enraging each other, fighting
> With roars their bravery flaunting
> Both fought mightily their awful battle.
> At last the snake king’s entrails aching
> He opposed his foe less strongly;
> The Prince like thunder felled him
> Stamping on his body.

Gazing at sky's distance
Life flew from the Snake Spirit;
In his open eyes the Prince
Saw a wonder unforgettable.
Looking there—ah ha—himself
He felt his spine's knot slipping;
'My entrails have gone cold' he said
coming to the palace. (p. 45)

Although both fight with each other under the illusion that they are rivals, they seem to be bound to each other emotionally (i.e. through the entrails) because they were separated from each other only after the Prince had split himself into two. That is exactly the reason why he feels that his entrails have gone cold after the death of Kalinga. The Mother and other royal members of the Palace are happy about the Prince's victory over Kalinga. But the Prince does not feel happy because "My navel is growing cold. My spine is loosening" (p. 47). So far the Prince does not know that Kalinga came out of the pot as his other half when the former had split himself into two. The Mother and the Elders had hidden the fact from the Prince. But blood is thicker than water. The Prince and Kalinga have experienced mutual love and sympathy for each other in spite of their so-called rivalry and hatred. Thus, their experience of duality or separateness was a consequence of ignorance about each other. But the right knowledge of reality helps them to experience the unity of being and harmony of life. The Prince has an epiphany of the unity of being after killing Kalinga. His description of his experience to the Mother amply bears it out, "In his eyes the lovely blue sky was reflected. I saw in the sky an eagle and a snake flying together. The snake, which had within it all the dark black secrets of the nether world, was not in the claws of the eagle, but was wound around its neck and body in friendship. The duality of the snake and the eagle had been erased and they had become one. The mercy of Siva's divine eyes was falling on them in the form of the sun's golden rays. What I saw now was like a snake playing in the sky, opening its hood. Only the snake was visible, having completely taken over the eagle, and it looked as if the snake with its open hood had sprouted wings and was flying. Then that eagle, with its forehead set to the streaming sun, climbed fearlessly into the eternity of the sky" (p. 48). The Prince, obviously, has had a vision of the unity of being, which is the result of the right knowledge. This vision helps him understand his wife Sirisampige from a new perspective. He, who had considered Sirisampige as an adulteress, has now realized that she is a chaste wife. He, who considered Kalinga as a cuckolder and rival, has now realized that he is the other half of his own being. He, who considered his child as an illegitimate one, has now realized that it is his own legitimate child. His crisis of identity is finally resolved. He explains the meaning of his vision to his Mother, "The Queen would have understood all these things. Sirisampige has not committed any wrong, Mother. When I split myself, we got separated into body and mind. Kalinga became my body, I became his mind. Sirisampige became pregnant by my body" (p. 49). The Prince's realization of the complementarity of Kalinga and himself coincides with his own death necessitated by the killing of Kalinga. The mythical event, obviously, shows the philosophical truth that killing one half of one's being involves killing the other half also. Accordingly, having killed Kalinga, the Prince realizes that he has killed himself and therefore is going to die. But before his death, he warns his Queen Sirisampige not to allow his son to split himself. Sirisampige, who was a half widow, has become a complete widow now. The Prince has suffered the tragedy of divided self or split personality. His realization of the dilemma of half-ness or completeness comes at the last stage of life, when he has no time to rectify his past. It is this irreversibility of events or action that is really tragic. The Prince becomes a tragic figure because of his belated realization of his flaw and the inevitability of accepting the consequences of his action. He has no choice except to die. In this sense, he is easily comparable to the tragic hero of the Greek tragedy as he is fated to be a divided soul. But his realization of his tragic flaw is achieved through his individual experience, which makes him a Shakespearean tragic hero. Thus, the tragedy of fate and the tragedy of character are beautifully combined in this play. He is negated by the moral order of life as a result of his negation of the holistic principle of life. Thus, the play affirms and upholds the principle of unity, wholeness and harmony by showing the negation of the Prince and his division of personality. The question as to why Prince Sivanaga has to suffer this tragedy invites varied answers. T.G. Vaidyanathan cleverly interprets that Sivanaga suffers because he disobeyed his mother and the Elders of the palace. Vaidyanathan offers a Freudian interpretation when he says that Sivanaga wanted to escape from the crippling influence of his mother. Although such interpretation is supported by the Freudian theory, it cannot be applied to *Sirisampige* totally because there is no internal evidence in the play to bear it out.

Whereas the tragedy is division and half-ness forms the main theme of the play, that of twin or double-ness forms the subsidiary but contrastive theme of the play. As already observed, the playwright has grafted the folk motif of the split with that of the double. The folktales dealing with twins (either brothers or sisters) are found all over the world. The concept of twins is internally connected with that of the split of the whole personality. A brief look at Levi-Strauss's explanation of the concept of twins in the context of South and North America will throw some light on the topic:

> In other words, the elder sister starts to split the body of the animal (hare); if this split were carried out to the end—if it did not stop at the nose but continued through the body and to the tail—she would turn an individual into twins, that is, two individuals, which are exactly similar or identical because they are both a part of a whole. In this respect it is very important to find out what conception the American Indians all over America entertained about the origin of twins. And what we find is a general belief that twins result from an internal splitting of the body fluids, which will later solidify and become the child.[28]

The twin brothers have a love-hate relationship with each other until they realize their one-ness through experience. The similarity of their looks, behaviour and tendencies add to the confusion, which may be sometimes tragic and sometimes comic. Kambar has grafted this story to that of the split personality and achieved a peculiar beauty in the play.

The story of the twin brothers, Awali and Jawali forms the sub-plot of the play reflecting the theme of the main plot in a minor key. The twin brothers, Awali and Jawali represent the peculiar problems indigenous to them. Their physical resemblance to each other adds to the confusion of their identities. Similarly, their hierarchy also cannot easily be ascertained. For example, Awali and Jawali do not know and cannot decide who is elder and who is younger between them. In spite of their physical separateness, there is a resemblance between the two as far as their constitutional tendencies are concerned. Their relationship with each other is characterized by ambivalence. There is a love-hate relation between the two. For example, both of them look, think and talk alike thereby adding to the confusion of identities. When the Bhagavata asks them, "Oh, so you are the twins! Between you two who is the elder brother and who is the younger one?" (p. 5). Jawali replies, "I am the elder brother and he is the younger one" (p. 5). Thus, there is no agreement between the two. Their relationship is marked by a deeper similarity and apparent dissimilarity. For example, both of them want to get married, but unfortunately there is only one girl available. Their love as well as jealousy towards each other is parallel. When Awali suggests to Jawali to marry the only available girl, Jawali replies, "Well, say I got married. Since you resemble me so much, my wife may go to bed with you mistaking you for me" (p. 5). This reply easily shows how love is combined with jealousy. It is indeed ironical that they love as much as hate each other. For example, Awali says angrily, "If I had a couple of fangs, I would have sucked your blood. I have spared you because I don't have them" (p. 5). Jawali replies, "If I had a couple of horns, I would have run them through your belly. I have spared you because I don't have them" (p. 5). When they happen to meet a young lady, Kamala, both of them long to marry her and plead for themselves forcefully. But Kamala suggests that they should fight a duel and that she would marry the winner. Accordingly, both of them fight with each other. As Jawali wins the duel, Kamala accepts him as her husband. But Awali wants to take revenge against his own brother and his wife in his own way. He says, "I will go to the forest, do penance and return a God to bestow the boon of death on both of them. Look, I am going to the forest" (p. 8).

Awali and Jawali are like an object and its image or shadow. They cannot be separated. Awali has returned from the forest after having a sort of enlightenment. By this time Kamala has realized that her husband does not love her. She has a great anxiety about her inability to have a child. But her anxiety is alleviated a bit when she is directed in her dream by her family god to go to the anthill under the banyan tree outside the city, pluck the jasmines, make a garland and put it around her husband's neck so that he might transform himself into a snake and unite with her. The god has promised her that she would have children if she follows his directions. Here the snake is obviously a symbol of sexuality. So when Kamala is preparing to go for worship, she experiences the truth that both Awali and Jawali are like an object and its image or shadow. As Awali says, "Apart we two may be/ Yet, down below the tree's root is one" (p. 28). Kamala is indeed confused by their resemblance and inseparability. Whatever happens to one must necessarily happen to the other. Although Jawali does not like his brother Awali taking interest in his own wife, Kamala, Awali makes it clear, "I have as much of a right as you have to both this house and Kamala" (p. 28). But Awali does not have the courage to fight another duel with his brother to win Kamala. Jawali and Kamala go to the anthill to offer worship. Awali also follows them secretly with a pot of milk.

After the worship of the *linga* near the anthill Kamala takes the jasmine garland on the *linga* and puts it around her husband's neck. No sooner does she garland him than he becomes a snake and begins his amative play with her. Awali feels deep jealousy at the sight of their sexual play. "As soon as he became a serpent, he began the love-play with Kamala. Later he even proceeded to do things, which, out of shame, I can't mention. Gradually, with accelerated pleasure, they both began to pant like flood-water rushing down into a valley. To cater to the fatigued and hungry ones, I made a small fire and put the milk on to boil. The milk got heated and started to boil. The boiled milk began to overflow. The smell of the overflowing milk reached the serpent inside Kamala. The serpent came out. Since he was hungry, he spread his food and dipped his mouth right into the pot. His mouth was burnt and he died writhing badly" (p. 37). Awali feels the deep pangs of jealousy and kills the serpent with an axe. Kamala, who is lying speechless in her intoxicated sexual pleasure, is not aware of the murder of her husband by Awali. When Awali asks her gently to go home, she mistakes him for Jawali and follows him slowly. On the way, she sits and lays three eggs consecutively, but Awali crushes them between his hands because they are the serpent progeny. When Kamala discovers his mischief, she grows terribly angry, curses him and disappears into the forest. Although Awali has killed Jawali out of jealousy, he now realizes that he is incomplete without the latter. He begins to suffer from a great sense of loneliness, "As long as he was here, behind or in front of me, near or far from me. But now without him I have become half myself. That's why I feel I too should die. I am alone" (p. 38). The relation between the twin brothers is like that between an object and its image of shadow. The removal of the object involves the concurrent removal of the image. When Awali has killed Jawali, he also has got to die somehow or the other. He kills himself by trying to kill Jawali, whose reflection he sees in the water of the pond. The whole event is reported by the servant, "Awali had already begun to climb the tree on the bank that bends over the water. The tree's reflection was in the water. Awali's reflection had appeared too. Suddenly, he remembered Jawali and the quarrel and he thought that the one in the water was Jawali. Seeing Jawali he grinned at him menacingly. In the water, Jawali too laughed to show that he was not afraid. He too laughed and raised his arm, threatening to strike. The other did the same. He clenched his teeth and indicated that he would strangle the other. The other did the same. He became extremely angry and determined to kill, he jumped right into the lake. I watched all this, standing on the bank. I thought that he was probably miming your fight. But he drowned after having drunk so much water. He did not come up at all, my Lord" (p. 46). Awali has, obviously, died because he has killed his twin brother Jawali thereby affirming the truth that the twins have common thoughts, feelings, and desires in spite of minor dissimilarities. They are double in appearance, i.e. they have two separate bodies, but are one psychologically or spiritually. Together they form a whole. They suffer the tragedy of murder and suicide when they are separated from each other. The cause of division between the two is a young lady Kamala, who chooses the stronger one between the two. The sub-plot of Awali and Jawali provides a good contrast to the main plot of Prince Sivanaga and Kalinga. But in both the cases the duality of being or experience has to be overcome and converted into unity of being. In a way the life of Sivanaga and that of Jawali run almost parallel. The similarities between Sivanaga and Jawali include many dissimilar aspects in their life situations and deaths also. Whereas Sivanaga dies by mistaking reality for falsehood, Jawali meets his death by mistaking falsehood for reality.

Kambar's idea of the 'total theatre' has inspired him to adopt the theatrical conventions and features of *yaksagana* in writing *Sirisampige*. The folk theatre whether it is *yaksagana* or *bayalata*, may be described as total theatre as it contains dialogues, songs, and dance. Bertolt Brecht borrowed his idea of the total theatre from the Indian Sanskrit Drama. The Indian folk theatre shares the same quality with the classical Sanskrit drama. As Kambar explains in his note to the play, "This play is written in the form of *yaksagana*. Narration is the soul of this form and it makes extensive use of song, mime and dance to create a total theatrical experience. The Bhagavata (narrator) tells the story in third person and other characters dramatize in the first person what he narrates. In the beginning, the characters have no independent existence; they are just a passive part of the narrative. Later they become full-blooded characters. While the Bhagavata is singing the story the characters interpret it through mime and dance. Later, they transform the same song into a dramatic event" (p. xi). The stylized dialogues, songs, and the solo voice of the omnipotent Bhagavata add to the theatrical beauty of the play. A spectacular design of tragedy of destiny and tragedy of character reveals itself through the song of the Bhagavata. The dramatist attempts to understand the interplay as well as the reversal of the abstract and concrete principles and the visible and the invisible existence of these forces in the important stages of the human affairs of the dramatic characters. T.G. Vaidyanathan is right when he observes, "In achieving these larger truths through the use of indigenous myth, *Sirisampige* goes way beyond traditional *yaksagana*" (p. x). Kambar's greatness lies not only in using the *yaksagana* style and technique, but also in transcending it.

Sirisampige, which is translated into English by Rowena Hill, K.P. Vasudevan and N.S. Ramaswamy is quite satisfactory on the whole. But there are a few minor errors, which need to be corrected in future. One wonders how these errors have crept into the translation in spite of the language editor of the prestigious publishing firm like Seagull Publishers. It may not be inappropriate to point out a few samples of these errors of literal translation. The Mother says, "My son, your voice has broken" (p. 3). It should have been, "your voice has cracked." In the same scene, the Mother asks her son, "'Is that understood?" (p. 4). It should have been, "Do you understand?" In scene Eight, the Bhagavata asks Kalinga, "For what reason do we suddenly see you here?" (p. 21). It should have been, "Why did you come here?" In the same scene, Kalinga says, "She's the one who stole my mind away!" (p. 22). It should have been, "She's the one, who stole my heart." In the Kannada language '*manassu*' means mind, but in this context it is used to suggest heart rather than mind. In scene Thirteen, Kalinga says, "My eyes have had no sleep" (p. 39). This is a literal translation of the Kannada sentence and hence looks un-English and outlandish. It should have been, "I couldn't sleep at all" or something like that. In the same scene, Kalinga says, "Now my mind is lighter" (p. 41). This sentence repeats the earlier mistake. It should have been, "Now my heart is lighter" or "Now I feel relieved." In scene Sixteen, the Mother says, "Should you look at her evil face at such a time of gladness like this, child?" (p. 45). It should have been, "at such a happy time or moment." Such translation may not be grammatically wrong, but it is stylistically inappropriate. These errors go to prove that translation is a risky job and that one has to be extra careful. Especially, the language editor of any publishing firm should be very alert.

But in all fairness, it must be said that the English translation of *Sirisampige* is a valuable addition to the corpus of Indian

Literature in English translation as it certainly extends the boundaries of Indian literature and releases the text from the regional orbit to the international circle.

Notes

1. Kambar, Chandrashekhar, "Interview with Kirtinath Kurtkoti," *Contemporary Indian Theatre*, Ed. Paul Jacob. New Delhi: Sangeet Natak Akademi, 1989, p. 22.
2. *Ibid*., p. 22.
3. Kurtkoti, Kirtinath, "Creative Time in Kambar's *Chakori*," *Sirisampige Kambara*, 60. Ed. H.S. Shiva Prakash, Bangalore: Ranga Nirantara, 1997, p. 51.
4. Kambar, Chandrashekhar, "Folk Drama: Its History and Hopes of Survival," *The Tradition of Kannada Theatre*, Ed. K.D. Kurtkoti. Bangalore: IBH Prakashan, 1986, p. 105.
5. Dundes, Alan. *Essays in Folkloristics*, Meerut: Folklore Institute, 1978, pp. 2-3.
6. Quoted by Richard Chase, "Notes on the Study of Myth," *Twentieth Century Criticism*, Eds. William J. Handy and Max Westbrook, New Delhi: Light & Life Publishers, p. 244.
7. *Ibid.*
8. Jung, C.G. *Psychology of the Unconscious*, London, Kegan Paul, Trench, Trubner & Co. Ltd. Fifth Impression, 1946, p. 12.
9. Quoted by Derrida, Jacques. "Structure, Sign and Play", *Contemporary Criticism: An Anthology*, Ed. V.S. Sethuraman. Chennai: Macmillan Company of India, Reprint 1998, p. 304.
10. *Ibid*., p. 310.
11. Quoted by Richard Chase. "Notes on the Study of Myth", *Twentieth Century Criticism*, Eds. William J. Handy and Max Westbrook. New Delhi: Light & Life Publishers. 1976, p. 245.
12. *Ibid.*
13. Langer, Susanne K., *Philosophy in a New Key*, New York: Mentor Book, 1952, p. 142.
14. Quoted by Lalita Handoo, *Folk and Myth*, Mysore: Central Institute of Indian Languages, 1988, p. 35.
15. *Ibid*., p. 33.
16. *Ibid.*

17. *Ibid.*
18. Soyinka, Wole, *Myth, Literature and the African World.* Cambridge: Cambridge University Press, 1999, p. 3.
19. Quoted by Lalita Handoo, *Folk and Myth*, Mysore: Central Institute of Indian Languages, 1988, p. 35.
20. Quoted by Jung, C.G. *Psychology of the Unconscious*, p. 15.
21. Frye, Northrop, "The Archetypes of Literature," *Twentieth Century Criticism*, Eds. William J. Handy and Max Westbrook. New Delhi: Light & Life Publishers, 1976, p. 240.
22. Quoted by K.L. Gopalakrishnaiah, *Purana (Myth)*, Bangalore: Karnataka Sahitya Academy, 1990, p. 31.
23. Ramanujan, A.K. *A Flowering Tree and Other Oral Tales from India*. New Delhi: Penguin Books India (P.) Ltd., 1997, p. 155.
24. *Ibid.*, p. 142.
25. Kambar, Chandrashekhar. *Contemporary Indian Theatre*, Ed. Paul Jacob, p. 23.
26. Nagaraj, K.R. Introduction, *Sirisampige* (Kannada version). Heggodu: Akshara Prakashan, 1998, p. 5.
27. Kambar, Chandraskekhar, *Sirisampige*, Calcutta: Seagull Books, 1992, pp. 1-2. (All the subsequent page references are to this edition.)
28. Levi-Strauss, Claude, *Myth and Meaning*, London & New York: Routledge, 2003, p. 25.

• • • • •

9

Quest for Completeness in *Hayavadana*

Girish Karnad (1938-2019) has been an important Kannada dramatist, in addition to being an actor and a film director. By now he has written nine plays in Kannada and translated them into English. Out of nine plays only three happen to be historical (like *Tughlaq*, *Tale-Danda*, and *The Dreams of Tipu*) whereas the other six are mythical or folk-mythical and only two are social. Karnad is very fond of going back to standard Hindu myths or folk-myths for treatment in his plays and for reinterpreting them in the light of contemporary events or situations. In many interviews, Karnad has honestly confessed that he does not like to take up the contemporary themes and treat them realistically but prefers to go back to myths and history and invest them with contemporary relevance. Hence, there is no quarrelling with his taste and temperament. But Vijay Tendulkar provides a sharp contrast to Girish Karnad in choosing the contemporary themes of Indian, especially Marathi themes and treating them in a very realistic style.

Although Karnad is considered as a Kannada playwright, Kannada does not happen to be his mother tongue. On the contrary, Konkani is his mother tongue. Nor does Kannada happen to be the medium of his education. Being a convent product, he thinks in English, but writes in Kannada, gets it edited or corrected by somebody and then again translates it into English. Though a Kannada playwright, he does not choose a typically Kannada theme. On the contrary, he chooses a pan-Indian mythical or epical or historical (except *Tale-Danda*) theme for dramatic treatment, which in turn, ensures him a pan-Indian appreciation.

The theme of *Hayavadana* is borrowed from *Kathasaritsagara* (an ancient collection of stories in Sanskrit) via Mann's retold story, "The Transposed Heads." Obviously, *Hayavadana* is a mythological play catering to the Indians generally brought up on myths and legends (or even living in the prison-house of myths). It is commonplace truth to say that mythology is nothing but a universal language to express the general truths of life. Myths deal with higher truths of life and therefore, are not anchored in reality and do not follow the laws of probability. In other words, myths deal with and present ideologies or philosophies disguised in stories that violate the unities of time, place, and action and the laws of Nature. They deal with supernatural characters or events to present the higher truths, which cannot be articulated in terms of realism or naturalism. To put it in a different manner, myths are disguised ideologies or philosophies. From this point of view, *Hayavadana* may be described as an ideological play. Then what are the central ideas presented in it? Obviously, the body-mind dichotomy and man's search for completeness and man-woman relationship happen to be the philosophical concerns in the play. Within the story of search for completeness, that of *Hayavadana* also is dovetailed.

Nature (or reality) is characterized by the inseparable togetherness of mind or body. But it is only in theory or speculation that we tend to think of mind and body as two separate or independent entities. In the empirical world, mind and body are inseparable, although they may not be equal to each other in proportion or measure. In some people, the mental (i.e. intellectual or imaginative) qualities may dominate over physical (manual and adventurous) qualities. And in some other people it may be vice versa. Hence, they are taxonomically divided into mental type and physical type. This body-mind schism presented in *Hayavadana* from the point of view of a woman. Whether a woman wants or likes the body or the mind in a man (or husband)—that is the central question posed in the play. It is this ideological/theoretical question that has to be answered through the mythical apparatus.

The scene is set in a mythical place called Dharmapura, which means a City of Virtue and therefore has an allegorical significance. But it cannot be pinpointed geographically. Similarly, Dharmasheela, the King of the City is named allegorically and it means a Righteous Man. The dichotomy between mind and body is presented through two characters, Devadatta and Kapila, who are a pair of binary opposites. Whereas Devadatta is a man of intellect, Kapila is a 'man of the body,' with all the respective and attendant features. For example, Devadatta is comely in appearance, fair in colour, and unrivalled in intelligence. He is the only son the revered Brahmin Vidyasagara (again an allegorical name meaning 'Ocean of Learning') and an expert on logic, love, and in poetry. His talents seem to be gifted by God to him. Hence, the allegorical name Devadatta. Kapila provides a good contrast to the brainy Devadatta. The word Kapila has about four contrastive meanings, but the nearest meaning in the present context is 'monkey' or 'apish.' He is a brawny man, who has all the attendant features. "He is the only son of the iron-smith Lohita, who is to the King's armoury as an axle is to the chariot wheel. He is dark and plain to look at, yet in deeds, which require drive and daring, in dancing, in strength and in physical skills he has no equal".[1] Thus, there is a clear contrast between brain and brawn. Although they are a pair of contrastive characters, they are close and complementary to each other. As the play proceeds, we learn that Devadatta has sighted a girl and fallen in love with her and pines for her. He wants to marry her and takes a dangerous vow of sacrificing his limbs to Goddess Kali and Lord Rudra, "I know this girl is beyond my wildest dreams. But still—I can't help wanting her—I can't help it. I swear, Kapila, with you as my witness I swear, if ever I get her as my wife, I'll sacrifice my two arms to the goddess Kali, I'll sacrifice my head to Lord Rudra..." (p. 14). Kapila being a close friend of Devadatta wants to help the latter by locating the girl's house and winning her over to his friend. Finally, he succeeds in bringing the lovers together into matrimonial bondage. "Padmini is the daughter of the leading merchant in Dharmapura. In her house, the very floor is swept by the Goddess of Wealth. In Devadatta's house, they've the Goddess of Learning for a maid. What could then possibly stand in the way of bringing the families together? (*Marriage music.*) Padmini became the better half of Devadatta and settled in his house. Nor did Devadatta forget his debt to Kapila. The old friendship flourished as before. Devadatta—Padmini—Kapila! To the admiring citizens of Dharmapura, Rama—Sita—Lakshmana" (p. 19). The name, 'Padmini' creates some problem to the reader. According to Vatsayana's taxonomy, Padmini or Lotus-Woman is known for her sexuality and artistic nature and fickle-mindedness. But the Padmini of the present play is not of Vatsayana's type.

After marriage, Devadatta and Kapila live like friends and brothers for some time. Devadatta is a married man now whereas Kapila continues to be a bachelor. But as days go by, Devadatta develops subtle kind of jealousy for Kapila as he notices Kapila's attraction for Padmini, "Does she really not see? Or is she deliberately playing the game with him? Kapila was never the sort to blush. But now, he only has to see her and he begins to wag his tail. Sits up on his hind legs as though he were afraid to let her words fall to the ground. And that pleading in his eyes—can't she really see that?" (p. 22). Padmini is pregnant now. She insists on going to the Ujjain fair. But Devadatta does not approve of it, as he is concerned about her safety. Padmini blows hot and cold alternately and finally forces Devadatta to go to Ujjain fair with Kapila as their cart man.

On the way, Padmini notices Kapila's physical prowess and beauty and appreciates it openly, "How beautifully you drive the cart, Kapila. Your hands don't even move, but the oxen seem to know exactly where to go" (p. 25). She also knows how by contrast her husband Devadatta was an utter failure as a cart man in an earlier trip. As they proceed further, Padmini wants to know why a particular flower is called the Fortunate Lady's flower, Kapila climbs the tree to bring the flower to her. Again Padmini appreciates his physical beauty and agility, "How he climbs—like an ape. Before I could even say 'yes', he had taken off his shirt, pulled his *dhoti* up and swung up the branch. And what an ethereal shape! Such a broad back—like an ocean with muscles rippling across it—and then that small, feminine waist, which looks so helpless" (p. 26). She admires him further inwardly, "He is like a Celestial Being reborn as a hunter. How his body sways, his limbs curve—it's a dance almost.... No woman could resist him" (p. 26). Devadatta notices Padmini's deeper feelings now. Although she is a married woman, she cannot help appreciating the handsomeness of a man other than her husband. Devadatta realizes the true and deeper nature of a woman (in this case, wife), "Only now—I see the depths—now I see these flames leaping up from those depths" (p. 26). Padmini finds it difficult to keep her adulterous feelings secret, she asks herself inwardly, "How long can one go on like this? How long? How long? If Devadatta notices..." (p. 26). At the same time she notices that Devadatta has already begun to suspect her psychological loyalty to him.

As all the three sight a temple of Rudra on the way, they break their journey for a while. Kapila and Padmini walk to the temple of Rudra, whereas Devadatta stays back with some pretext and wishes them, "Good-bye Kapila. Good-bye, Padmini. May the Lord Rudra bless you! You are two pieces of my heart—live happily together. I shall find happiness in that" (p. 28). After the departure of Kapila and Padmini, Devadatta walks to the temple of Kali, remembers his promise to the goddess and severs his head, "Take it, Mother, accept this little offering of my head" (p. 28).

But when Kapila and Padmini return from the temple of Rudra, they do not find Devadatta there. Kapila leaves Padmini there and goes to the temple of Kali where he is shocked to find him dead. He is unable to bear the sorrow, "You spurned me in this world. Accept me as your brother at least in the next. Here friend here I come. As always, I follow in your path" (p. 30). With these words he cuts off his head.

After waiting for long Padmini goes to the Kali temple wherein she stumbles over the dead bodies and feels heart-broken. When she also tries desperately to sever her head, the Goddess's voice is heard. Then the Goddess appears in her terrific aspect, but yet in sleepy mood. As Padmini requests her to save her by reviving the two dead bodies, the Goddess orders her, "Now do as I tell you. Put these heads back properly. Attach them to their bodies and then press that sword on their necks. They'll come up alive. Is that enough?" (p. 32). The Goddess says, "The rascals! They were lying to their last breaths" (p. 33). That is why she allowed them to die. But she appreciates Padmini's honesty, "Only you spoke the truth" (p. 33). As directed by the Goddess, Padmini puts the heads back to the bodies, but in her excitement she mixes them up so that Devadatta's head goes to Kapila's body and vice versa.

The appearance of Goddess Kali and the rejuvenation of the dead persons are, of course, acceptable only on the mythical level. But the mythical event is used to symbolize the psychological truth. A bit of Freudian psychology helps us understand it clearly. Although Padmini is married to the intellectual Devadatta, she secretly admires and longs for the physical prowess and beauty of Kapila. She wants to have the cake and eat it too. (She is like the modern feminist, who wants to have a rich husband and yet wishes to have the freedom to have a couple of lovers on the sly or openly.) But so far she has had no courage to express it due to the fear of society or morality. But when a chance is given to her to express her innermost desires or subconscious desires (in Freudian terms) she makes her choice by selecting Devadatta's head and Kapila's body, which will perhaps give her a sense of fulfillment.

Now that Devadatta and Kapila are revived with exchanged heads, Padmini realizes her folly and tells them what has actually happened. The situation is comic and absurd at the same time. After the exchange of heads a new confusion of identities is created. A theoretical question about whether a man is his body or his mind is posed here. Old friendship between Devadatta and Kapila is replaced by a kind of blood relationship now. The question whether Padmini has married Devadatta's head or his body (now attached to Kapila's body) crops up. Thus, a dichotomy between mind and body is created. Kapila claims Padmini as his wife because she has married his body. Similarly, Devadatta claims her as his wife as she has married his head, as head is the topmost in position as well as in importance. But Kapila does not accept this argument.

But at last they approach a *rishi* for a solution. The *rishi* offers the following solution, "As the heavenly Kalpa Vriksha is supreme among trees, so is the head among human limbs. Therefore the man with Devadatta's head is indeed Devadatta and he is the rightful husband of Padmini" (p. 40). Consequently, Devadatta (with Kapila's body) and Padmini are reunited. Kapila desperately goes to the forest. Before he leaves Padmini, she tells him, "It's my duty to go with Devadatta. But remember I'm going with your body. Let that cheer you up" (p. 41). Padmini's viewpoint represents feminine psychology in general and the feminist stand in particular. She wants to have the cake and eat it too. She wants to have the security of a husband and a secret lover too. Anyway Devadatta and Padmini return to Dharmapura and plunge into the joys of married life.

Now that Devadatta's head is combined with Kapila's body, some changes are seen in his behaviour. The physical features of Kapila assert themselves in Devadatta. He feels inspired to fight and defeat wrestlers and never feels tired. His hands have become rough like a labourer's. For a while his body overshadows his mind. Meanwhile, the couple gets a baby boy.

Similarly, Kapila with Devadatta's body feels a change in his life. With a brahmin's body attached to his head, Kapila feels weak, "When this body came to me, it was like a corpse hanging by my head. It was a brahmin's body after all—not made for the woods. I couldn't lift an axe without my elbows moaning. Couldn't run a length without my knees howling. I had no use for it. The moment it came to me, a war started between us" (p. 55).

But this change does not continue for long perhaps due to the effect of Time as well as to the principle of irreversibility of things in God's design. For example, Devadatta wants to return to his brahmanical duties after a brief spell of bodily prowess and accomplishments. "It was fun the first few days because it was new. All that muscle and strength. But how long one can go on like that? I have the family tradition to maintain—the daily reading, writing and studies" (p. 46). His palms have become soft again as they were earlier. He cannot enjoy going to the gymnasium any more. Thus, Devadatta has returned to his usual self. Padmini consoles him, "What does it matter that you are going soft again, that you are losing your muscles? I am not going to be stupid again. Kapila has gone out of my life—forever. I won't let him come back again" (p. 49).

Although Padmini is apparently happy with her husband, she loves Kapila unconsciously. In her dream, she sees a man, but not her husband. He has a labourer's face, but a nice body. Similarly, she is obsessed with Kapila during her waking hours also. Even when Devadatta asks her to keep some sweets and lime-juice ready for a Sanskrit pundit, who is coming to meet him, Padmini is obsessed with Kapila and his mother's death. One may easily see a dichotomy between her inner feelings and outer profession.

When Devadatta goes to Ujjain fair to buy new dolls for his baby, Padmini goes out with her child and happens to meet Kapila. She shows him the child and confesses that he is Kapila's son, "Your body gave him to me" (p. 54) and looks exactly like Kapila and "He has the same mole on his shoulder" (p. 54). Kapila is happy to have recovered his old self and black body and spends his time in hard labour in the forest. He asks Padmini as to why she has come there. She confesses, "I had to see you" (p. 56). But Kapila wants to uproot all the memories and continue to be rough and violent. He does not like to have a crack between his head and his shoulders. He asks her to go back to her husband. But she wants to sit there for some time and look at him and have her fill for the rest of her life. Kapila's memories of his enjoyment with Padmini are awakened. He, therefore, lifts Padmini and takes her into his hut. It is quite obvious that Padmini has committed adultery with Kapila without her husband's knowledge.

Devadatta returns from the Ujjain fair and goes straight to Kapila's hut in the forest. After exchanging their disconcerting memories of partially changed identities, they come to the brass tacks. Devadatta asks Kapila, "Do you really love Padmini?" (p. 60). Kapila answers in the affirmative. Both of them love Padmini. Kapila therefore asks him, "Devadatta, couldn't we all three live together—like the Pandavas and Draupadi?" (p. 60). But he knows that it cannot be done. They think that the only solution to the problem is that "We must both die.... We must fight like lions and kill like cobras" (p. 61). Accordingly, they kill each other.

After their death Padmini asks the Bhagavata to hand over her son to hunters in the forest until he is five year old and then to revered Brahmin Vidyasagara of Dharmapura. Then she commits *sati*. When the child grows into a boy of five years, he happens to meet Hayavadana and is puzzled to hear the human voice from a horse. Hayavadana tells his story of how he requested the Goddess to make him and how he became a complete horse instead of becoming a complete man, but yet cursed with human voice. But after talking a few sentences with the Bhagavata and boy, his human voice changes into neighing thereby making him a complete horse in all respects.

The central message of the play seems to be that man searches for completeness but unfortunately it is not possible. The arbitrary completeness that Devadatta and Kapila achieve does not remain for long as everything is subject to the effect of Time. So the quest for completeness remains only a wishful desire rather than a permanent possibility. In the case of Hayavadana, there is an achievement of completeness of the wrong kind—complete horse-hood rather than man-hood. There is a triumph of the animal body over the human head. The whole play may be understood on the mythological or fantastical or ideological level by achieving the willing suspension of disbelief. Otherwise the absurdity of the whole situation—including the characters, their motives and action—makes no sense to the modern reader. As the Western critics have pointed out, Ibsen's *Ghosts* has to be understood against the nineteenth century background when science had not yet made its strides. Syphilis was a deadly disease paving the way for human tragedy then. But after the inventions of new medicines, syphilis was no longer deadly but easily curable. Thus, tragedy ceased to be tragic. Similarly, the central question of the dichotomy between body and mind posed in Karnad's play may be accepted only at the mythological and ideological level, but it cannot be borne out by the medical truth. Medically speaking, it is impossible to differentiate between body and mind; to sever them from each other; and to exchange and rejoin them. Such medical and empirical impossibilities are possible only in the mythical world. Similarly the story of Hayavadana bracketing that of the trinity of Devadatta, Kapila and Padmini seems to have no direct connection with it and therefore looks rather arbitrary.

Besides, the story of Hayavadana, which forms the subplot of the play, is highlighted in the title thereby misleading the reader and obscuring the main story of Padmini. The title *Hayavadana* gives an impression that Hayavadana is an eponymous hero, but as the play proceeds, he recedes into the margin much to the chagrin of the reader. It would have been better to entitle the play as *Padmini* rather than as *Hayavadana*. Such themes of mythological fantasy are more appealing to the children and orthodox people rather than to rational readers and spectators.

Perhaps the modern relevance of the play may be seen in the man-woman relationship and caste difference. It is the woman, who occupies the center stage in the play—a fact, which may give immense pleasure and satisfaction to modern Indian feminists. Padmini belongs to a merchant's family, but her caste is not clearly known. But Devadatta and Kapila represent the Brahmin and the Sudra—two opposite poles of the *Varna* hierarchy. It is possible to consider Padmini as a representative of modern woman, who wants to have a brainy husband and a brawny lover too, secretly. But unlike Padmini, the modern woman cannot commit *sati*, but she would rather go in for new lovers.

As for Hayavadana's references to modern life, national Congress, politicians, sentimentality, theatre critics, one feels that they are not called for. Although such comments may titillate the modern spectators temporarily, they do not really belong to the fantastic or mythical world and look rather absurd, incoherent, jarring, and anachronistic. References to contemporary life brought into the mythical play are a negative feature of folk plays and Company Nataks. Though Karnad claims to have been influenced and inspired by the Company Natak, the clubbing together of the mythical theme and contemporary allusions is not a welcome feature, as it discounts the dignity and purity of the mythical play. Such contemporary and satirical references may be conceded in the folk plays and Company Nataks in view of the fact that the spectators are mostly illiterate and folksy and therefore are not bothered about the relevance or otherwise of such element in the play. But it cannot be tolerated by the elitist spectators, who are educated and enlightened. Even if the playwright wants to write an absurd play, it (i.e. the absurdity) should be only on one level, i.e. either mythological or realistic, or allegorical or symbolic. One level cannot intersect another level. Similarly, the use of dolls in the play is very unconvincing. The dolls may be considered as external (Freudian, if you like) symbols of woman's unconscious or deeper inner feelings. They show Padmini's attraction for a non-husband or in other words her adulterous feelings. But her innermost of secret feelings are not borne out by any action by Padmini for their fulfillment. Nor does she articulate them clearly to her husband. Nor does she have the courage of a modern feminist to assert her identity by having both the husband and the lover at the same time. On the contrary, she commits *sati* like a *pativrita* in spite of having adulterous leanings—a fact that is least convincing. Her recourse to *sati* runs contrary to Freudian or feminist expectations. The playwright has not succeeded in giving a coherent and consistent motivation to the character of Padmini.

All the characters in the play behave on the allegorical lever and therefore, remain one dimensional like those of John Bunyan's *The Pilgrim's Progress*. They do not have the flesh and blood of their own. They are automatons moving along the allegorical axis. They are not anchored in reality. On the contrary, they stand for certain fixed ideas. *Hayavadana* may, therefore, be called an ideological or thesis-play in spite of having a mythical facade.

There are also a couple of minor errors, which have crept into the play because even Aristotle nods sometimes. For example, soon after Devadatta marries Padmini, Padmini insists on going on a trip to some place in a cart. But Devadatta does not like it because it is dangerous for her to do so in that condition, i.e. pregnancy. Padmini replies, "My condition! What's happened to me? To listen to you, one would think I was the first woman in this world to become pregnant" (p. 20). So the idea is very clear here that she is pregnant by her husband even before Kapila has grown close to them. But after the exchange of heads followed by the arbitration by a rishi, Kapila has to leave them and go away from to a forest. Again when Padmini meets Kapila in the woods in the absence of her husband, she tells him (Kapila) that her child is his, "And yours.... Your body gave him to me.... He has the same mole on his shoulder" (p. 55). If Padmini has become pregnant by her husband before the exchange of heads takes place, how can the child be fathered by Kapila and have the mole on his shoulder? This is an error of anachronism even on mythological level, let alone on medical or empirical level. It is really a matter of surprise that many critics have not noticed it.

There are also a few minor inconsistencies in the play. For example, the Bhagavata's comic or satirical references to contemporary life may be accepted by way of concession. But Hayavadana, who has a mythical lineage and network of Hindu mythology, is expected to keep to his own realm. But he refers not merely to Hindu myths, holy shrines/places/things, but also to non-Hindu ones like the Muslim, the Christian and the Buddhist ones, "So I took interest in the social life of the Nation—Civics, Politics, Patriotism, Nationalism, Indianization, the Socialist Pattern of Society.... I have tried everything..." (p. 9). He continues to say that he has visited "Banaras, Rameshwar, Gokarna, Haridwar, Gaya, Kedarnath, the Grotto of the Virgin Mary—I have tried them all..." (p. 9). At the end of the play, Hayavadana wants to sing the National Anthem to get rid of his human voice, "That's why I sing all these patriotic songs—and the National Anthem! That particularly! I have noticed that the people singing the National Anthem always seem to have ruined their voices..." (p. 69). Similarly, he comments on Indians' sentimentality, "I believe—that it's this sort of sentimentality which has been the bane of our literature and national life. It has kept us from accepting Reality and encouraged escapism" (p. 70). Although such comments and remarks titillate the audience, strictly speaking, they are not concordant with the serious mythical context of the play. Such admixture of myth and contemporaneity adds to the discordant hybridity rather than contributing to its eclecticism.

A similar but minor mistake may be seen in the doll's comment on Padmini's son. The son says, "And then comes this son of Satan..." (p. 45). Again the reference to the Christian character, i.e. Satan in a Hindu mythical story is a bit jarring to the sensitive minds.

M.K. Naik says rightly, "Karnad does not succeed fully in investing the basic conflict in the play with the required intensity, but his technical experiment with an indigenous dramatic form here is a triumph, which has opened up fresh lines of fruitful exploration for the Indian English playwright."[2] L.S. Seshagiri Rao also feels that Devadatta's so-called intellectuality is not convincing. Hayavadana's becoming a complete horse finally appears rather arbitrary and fails to convince us. *Hayavadana* cannot rise to the level of *Tughlaq* according to Seshagiri Rao.

But in spite of all these ideological aberrations and absurdities, the play is admirable in its theatrical effect and experimentation. The use of folk technique like Bhagavata arbitrating and linking the characters and action, the chorus and the dolls speaking like live children and the supernatural element in the form of Goddess Kali and masques, etc. add a lot to the theatrical effect of the play. This sort of technical experimentation is quite new to the Indian English Drama.

Notes

1. Karnad, Girish, *Hayavadana*, New Delhi: Oxford University Press, p. 2. (All the subsequent page references are to this edition.)
2. Naik, M.K. and Mokashi-Punekar, S. *Perspectives on Indian Drama in English*, Madras: Oxford University Press, 1977, p. 75.

• • • • •

10

The Collision between Religious Fanaticism and Eclecticism in *Aurangzeb*

Aurangzeb happens to be one of the famous historical personages of India who has attracted the attention of not only a few Indian playwrights but even of the British dramatists like Dryden. He is a 'world-historical figure' in Hegelian parlance and one of the negative heroes of Indian history *a la* Carlyle. In fact, he is at once famous and notorious for different reasons from different perspectives. He played an important role in the Mughal history of India and is known for his distinctive personality, exercise of political power and ideology. He fought not against the external enemies, but against his own brothers for the attainment of political power. This domestic fight is described by historians as a war of succession. As far as his political ambition is concerned he is easily comparable to Macbeth.

Indira Parthasarathy has borrowed this historical theme and tried to present it in the dramatic form. He has taken the important external facts of history connected with Aurangzeb's domestic war of succession and tried to fill them with flesh and blood of experience including sensation, and ideology thereby presenting a clear picture of Aurangzeb's struggle for political power and of the transition of Mughal rule from religious liberalism and aestheticism to religious fundamentalism and ethical rigidity. Parthasarathy has achieved historical authenticity and accuracy with regard to the names of characters, events, and their mutual relationships. He has followed the traditional dramatic technique of presented a chronological picture of the events of Aurangzeb's life and highlighted the thought processes and ideologies of all the main characters and the conflicts among them by achieving the clarity of motivation, which adds to our clear understanding of the drama of history.

The play depicts the central conflict between two sets of characters symbolizing two forces and ideologies. Whereas Dara Shikoh and Jahanara represent the offensive force, Aurangzeb and Roshanara represent the defensive force. Shahjahan tries to hover between the two forces, although initially he belongs to Dara's party. This basic conflict goes on growing stronger and stronger as the play progresses, until it reaches its climax.

Dara, the eldest son of Emperor Shahjahan, is known for his liberal view of religion. In fact, his vision of religion is eclectic due to his comprehension of the deeper unity and universality of all religions of the world. This is borne out by the conversation between two soldiers at the beginning of the play. They discuss Dara's broad perspective on religion and his special liking for Hinduism. Dara asks why a man cannot be a Christian, a Hindu and a Mussalman at the same time! He has written a book entitled *Sir-ul Asrar*, a translation of Hindu scriptures. He wears rings on his fingers engraved with Sanskrit mantras. He questions the relevance of five-times *namaz* per day. He feasts during the Ramzan period and hobnobs with Sufis. In other words, he has accepted the validity of the positive and universal qualities of Hinduism and questions some of the so-called negative features of Islam. He has adopted a rational approach to religion and understands the essence behind all the apparent diversity of religions. It is because of his ecstatic view of religion that Dara has become very popular as the darling of the nation. He enjoys the support of Rajputs. Being the eldest son of Shahjahan he is naturally entitled to the throne of the Mughal Empire.

The dramatist has created the right kind of historical atmosphere of the Mughal Empire by showing the state machinery of espionage and counter-espionage, which is quite common in most of the kingdoms of the world. Two soldiers discuss the widespread espionage and counter-espionage in the Empire.

Soldier 1 confesses that he has been spying on Khalilullah Khan and Soldier 2 confesses that he has been spying on Asghar Khan.

Aurangzeb, the eponymous hero, provides a sharp contrast to Dara in his temperament, attitude, and behaviour. In Dara's opinion, Aurangzeb is a very suspicious man and won't trust his own hand and fears that the Rajputs and the Shia Muslims would rebel against them if Aurangzeb harassed them in the Deccan. Dara's opinion is corroborated by Jahanara's. She tells Dara that when he built the new palace and invited his father and brothers to look at it, everybody went into it except Aurangzeb who suspected that Dara would kill him.

Dara is rather sad to learn that even his brothers like Shuja and Murad dislike him and that Aurangzeb has weaned Murad to his side and promised to make him king. Jahanara tells him that Murad wants nothing but wine and women and that Shuja is preparing for a battle. Dara thinks that he belongs to Akbar's time and does not believe in theocracy. But Jahanara reminds him that he has not even become a king and asks him how he can be an Akbar. Dara thinks that the people love him deeply and show it in their behaviour, but Jahanara opines that people's love does not count when men in power clash with each other. She tells him further that Aurangzeb complains against Dara's so-called anti-Muslim thinking.

Shahjahan is known for his extraordinary love for his late wife, Mumtaz and for the Taj Mahal, which is a constant reminder of his beloved wife. He is known for his aesthetic and highly poetic approach. That is why he begins to look at the Taj Mahal built in white marble bathed in the red light of the evening sun. Like a poet he compares the Taj Mahal to a white flower and to frozen milk. He happens to be a great dreamer of beauty. He wants his Mumtaz in the Taj Mahal of white marble to look at him in the Taj Mahal of black marble on the other side of the River Yamuna. He tells his son, Dara that he is going to build another Taj Mahal in black marble to be a replica of the Taj Mahal of white marble. He considers Taj Mahal a 'poem of death' and an 'elegy in stone.' He dreams of beauty which cannot be measured in terms of price and wants to fulfil his dream at any cost.

But Jahanara tries to convince him about the undesirability of wasting people's money on such a tomb—not to be forgotten in history. Jahanara's practical suggestion is simply ignored by Shahjahan, the dreamer. He wants people after 300 years to be impressed by the two elegies in stone and that those people do not bother to know how many people died of hunger now. She compares this tendency to Hinduism (quote, p. 433).

Shahjahan wants one of his sons, especially Dara, to fulfil his dream. Although Dara does not approve of his father's plan of a new *mahal*, Shahjahan asks him to fulfil his dream as he is his true heir. As Jahanara says, Aurangzeb abuses his father as a spendthrift wasting crores of rupees on another tomb. She asks Dara to be practical as he is going to be the king.

Shahjahan knows the contrast between Dara and Aurangzeb. He comments on Aurangzeb as the one who has made a religion of his hatred of beauty and is devoid of any aesthetic sense. He himself enjoyed the music of Tansen which inspired him to build the Taj Mahal. As Dara knows that his father has pinned his hope on him, he promises Shahjahan that he would make the latter's dream come true and enable him to see the mahal of black marble in his life-time. Shahjahan seems to be satisfied by the promise. He feels sleepy and wants to see his Mumtaz in his dream.

As Dara has internalized the Upanishadic philosophy he believes in the concept that everyone should realize the full limits of his potential and discern the divinity in oneself. This principle of immanence of God has infuriated the Muslim fanatics, especially the Imam. That is why a Moulvi rushes in and tells Dara how the Imam is furious with him for claiming himself to be the God. Then Dara explains the meaning of the Vedantic formula, *aham brahmasmi* as everybody has a spark of divinity in him (i.e. 'I am myself Brahman'). He does not want to be a slave of God as it implies the difference between man and God and that man has no existence without God. He claims to be quite humble and says that he is quoting from Jalaluddin Rumi and not from Hindu scriptures. Then the Moulvi, who is obviously bound by his professional fanaticism, comments that there is no difference between Sufis and *Kafirs* (i.e. Hindus). He repeats his warning to Dara by bringing to his notice the fact that their religious leaders are furious with him and have been sending secret information about it to Aurangzeb, who is the grand fanatic. He warns Dara that he and his father, Shahjahan may come to harm and asks him to keep down his views until he is crowned as king. He tells him that the basic truth that all ideology (or philosophy) becomes valid only if and when it is supported by (political) power. Then Dara remembers Jahanara's words and rightly realizes the truth that "Only power can ensure that my doctrine ascend the throne with me" (p. 436).

Shahjahan's aesthetic dream of having another mausoleum of black marble is not approved by anyone on the grounds of economic difficulties. When Dara consults the Moulvi about Shahjahan's obstinate dream, the Moulvi advises him to stop this plan involving the wastage of huge amount of money. Otherwise, the Moulvi warns, things will be easier for Aurangzeb.

After the exit of the Moulvi, Dara introspects about his ability to tackle Aurangzeb, who is his ideological enemy. He knows that Aurangzeb has the support of his other brothers like Shuja and Murad, but those two brothers are mere idiots in his opinion. He decides to nip Aurangzeb in the bud and destroy him so that things may be easy for him for the establishment of a secular State in Hindustan.

There is a basic temperamental difference between Dara and Aurangzeb. Whereas Dara is an idealist and liberalist, Aurangzeb is a pragmatist and orthodox believer in Islam. Whereas Dara is an inclusive thinker, Aurangzeb is an exclusivist. It is this fundamental difference between the two brothers which is pointed out by Jahanara. When Shahjahan discusses with her about whether Dara can deal with Aurangzeb, she highlights the fact that Aurangzeb is a great warrior and tricky and that he along with Murad, has been preparing for a battle.

Realizing the unhealthy rivalry and competition among his sons for political power Shahjahan thinks of giving all of them the power of ruling over their respective provinces of which they are now in charge. He suggests to Jahanara that Aurangzeb should rule the Deccan and Dara and Shuja should rule their respective provinces like Delhi and Agra. He especially wants Dara to be the ruler of Agra so that he can fulfil his father's dream of building another mausoleum of black marble. But Jahanara tries to make him aware of the harsh reality of life. She draws his attention to the fact that Shuja, Murad, and Aurangzeb may get together and attack Agra and that they need huge amount of money for another mausoleum. But Shahjahan's aesthetics refuses to take economic problems into consideration. He suggests that the money required for the construction of the mausoleum may be collected from levying more taxes on the people. He is so deeply immersed in his dream that his indifference to the common man's economic burden appears to be tantamount to callousness. His senility forces him to dream of the elegy in black marble, which is a combination of beauty and sadness, in his opinion.

It is ironical that in the same royal family of Shahjahan there are two groups of contradictory ideologies. Whereas Jahanara belongs to Dara's group and Shahjahan sympathizes with Dara's ideology, Roshanara belongs to Aurangzeb's group and always supports his thinking and behaviour. She defends Aurangzeb's Muslim piety, recitation of the Holy Quran, offering namaz for five times per day, keeping away from wine and women and worship of the Prophet (quote, p. 339). She complains that the Emperor and Dara have treated Aurangzeb badly, that the Emperor has called Aurangzeb a spendthrift and accused him of misappropriating the State's money for strengthening his own political position. She opines that Shahjahan cannot understand Aurangzeb's affection for him. She supports Aurangzeb's point of view and comments on her father's impractical dream of building another mahal of black marble. She complains that the people of the country have been paying heavy taxes to meet the cost of the Taj Mahal. She thinks that only Aurangzeb can stop the foolish and criminal wastage of money. She defends that although a practical man, Aurangzeb has his own dream of building one country, one language and one religion in Hindustan (quote, p. 441). When Jahanara repeats Shahjahan's suggestion that the four brothers may rule the four parts or provinces of India,

Roshanara replies that Aurangzeb will never agree for the partition of the country as he wants to rule it as a whole.

The ideological conflict has, obviously, resulted in a physical war of succession in which Dara has been defeated by Aurangzeb. Consequently, Dara's liberalism and eclecticism is vanquished by Aurangzeb's religious patriotism, fanaticism, and fundamentalism. It is reported by a soldier that Dara has lost the battle mainly because of Khalilullah Khan's treachery. But Roshanara is not ready to call it treachery thereby implying that it is nothing but religious pride. Anyway, there has been a reversal of the political situation in the country. Aurangzeb has attained political power and ascended the throne and Dara has lost the battle and fled to Lahore.

Shahjahan is deeply frustrated and exasperated by this new situation. He is unhappy about Aurangzeb's victory as well as Dara's defeat in the battle. He feels that the black flower of his dream is trodden underfoot and destroyed by Aurangzeb. He taunts Roshanara to celebrate Aurangzeb's victory. He comments further that Aurangzeb's dream is only to kill his brothers, father and their friends and grab the throne by bloodshed. But Roshanara complains that Shahjahan has not understood Aurangzeb properly.

Then Shahjahan grows angry and shouts that he has not understood Dara and the Rajput scoundrels who betrayed him (Dara); that there was a competition between Hindus and Muslims to stab Dara in the back; that the *dharma* of the Hindus leans to the winning side; that Dara does not know the ABC of politics and is shameless enough to run away from the battlefield. He wishes Dara to die. At the same time he seems to be apprehensive of some kind of insecurity for him under the rule of his fanatic son, Aurangzeb.

The relationship between father (Shahjahan) and son (Aurangzeb) is characterized by a combination of love and hate. Roshanara assures Shahjahan that no harm will come to him from Aurangzeb. But Shahjahan fears that Aurangzeb will bury his dreams, hence him. In his opinion, a man cannot be separated from his dream and that man without a dream cannot be different from a beast. He thinks that it is unfortunate that Hindustan's fate is to be ruled by a beast like Aurangzeb, who has no noble ideals. But Roshanara reminds him that Aurangzeb has a political dream of one country, one language and one religion contrary to Shahjahan's private dream of a black mausoleum.

Now that things have gone beyond his control, Shahjahan helplessly wants to welcome Aurangzeb and expects him to fulfill his dream. But Roshanara assures him that Aurangzeb will not harm him in any way, although he may not fulfill his dream. She tells him further that Aurangzeb will hunt Dara and kill him and that otherwise he will cease to be Aurangzeb.

Shahjahan feels repentant of having allowed Aurangzeb to grow so powerful. Now he does not want to allow Aurangzeb to enter the Agra fort. He feels that he should have plucked the weed so that the crop would not have been destroyed. He feels that Shuja should not have saved Aurangzeb from the attack by the mad elephant in the past.

Shahjahan orders the Commander of the Fort to bar the gates of the fort and fight with Aurangzeb to the finish. But the Commander tells the Emperor that more than half the people of the fort are waiting to welcome Aurangzeb. Then Shahjahan gets up angrily and shouts at the Commander ironically to open the gates of the fort, kneel down before Aurangzeb when he (Aurangzeb) sits on the throne. He calls Aurangzeb an ungrateful wretch. He wishes that nothing of him should be left. He angrily asks his Commander to demolish the Red Fort, set fire to the Peacock Throne, blast the Taj Mahal by the cannon; pour molten lead down the throats of musicians like Jagannath, Ramdas, and Lalkhan; tear up all books of poetry and turn the rose gardens into graveyards.

Jahanara asks the Commander to obey the order of the Emperor and bar the fort gates. But the Commander replies that they cannot hold out against a siege for more than a week. Jahanara silences him with the gesture of her fingers on her lips.

But contrary to their expectation, Dara barges into the hall by that time and wants to see the Emperor, but a soldier bars his path. Then Dara pushes aside the soldier. Jahanara tells him that the Emperor does not want to see him as he is disappointed by Dara's defeat in the battle. Dara sadly expresses his feeling about how he was betrayed by his own people. He thinks that the people of Hindustan will rise in support of him. But Jahanara taunts that the people of Hindustan are philosophers who will accept the winner in the battle. Dara insists on seeing the Emperor, but Jahanara cautions him that the meeting will only increase the grief of the Emperor. She conveys the Emperor's order to him to go to Delhi where he would get help and tells him that the Emperor will tackle Aurangzeb at Agra. But Dara wants to fight from inside the fort and die as he is not afraid of death. He tells Jahanara that he must fight Aurangzeb who is a visionless mediocrity and that the Hindustan of his dreams will not be built if Aurangzeb ascends the throne and that the Mughal rule will come to an end. He claims that his ideals are high and noble and that victory and defeat in war are only ephemeral. But Jahanara tells him that the world is only for mediocrities, who decide the conventions and rules of life; and that Dara's philosophical learning did not help him on the battlefield of Samugarh; and that Aurangzeb is not going to have a philosophical battle with him. She asks him to go away to Delhi and fight. Dara says that he may not be able to see them again if he dies in the battle and requests them to remember him as a brother who loved her dearly.

After the departure of Dara, Shahjahan worries about Dara's ability to bring an army from Delhi and defeat Aurangzeb and fulfil his (Shahjahan's) dream of a black mausoleum. He complains that everybody is conspiring against him. But Jahanara refutes the charge and says that she desires Aurangzeb's fall, although she admires his practical preoccupation with the present. By that time a soldier rushes in and conveys the shocking news that Shahjahan's grandson, Muhammad from one side and Aurangzeb from another side are approaching the fort entrance with their troops. But Shahjahan begins to dream of the Taj Mahal and Mumtaz almost in a senile fashion. He seems to have a streak of King Lear in him. The Commander comes and tells him that he has sealed all the doors, but the Emperor does not listen to him. The Commander is, therefore, puzzled by his strange behaviour. But Jahanara asks the Commander to resist the enemies as far as possible without bloodshed. Shahjahan in his dreamy mood apologizes to Mumtaz for killing her by subjecting her to too frequent (as many as sixteen) childbirths. The Commander reveals the news that Roshanara has gone away from the palace to her brother, Aurangzeb. This comes as an additional shock to the Emperor, who curses everybody to go away. He wants to fight alone with Aurangzeb and kill him or get killed by him.

Having defeated Dara and taken charge of Agra, Aurangzeb has accomplished his task and fulfilled his ambition. Ascending the throne he has assumed the much coveted political power. In order to make his power absolute and unrivalled, he has got rid of his own brother, Murad. As Muhammad Sultan tells Khalilullah Khan that Uncle Murad has been killed while drunk, Aurangzeb defends his action by pointing our Murad's crime. He opines that Murad was a drunkard and a womanizer and was not fit to ascend the throne.

Now that Aurangzeb has achieved political power, he is able to bring his philosophy of life or ideology into force. According to his strong belief only a government based on religion, laying down right and wrong, can lead them as a shepherd leads his flock. He, therefore, wants to close all wine-shops and brothels in Hindustan and ban dance and music from the country (quote, pp. 452-53).

When Khalilullah Khan says that the king should not interfere with the personal likes and dislikes of the people, Aurangzeb tells him to change his own lifestyle from that of profligacy to that of self-control. He asks Khalilullah Khan to send away all the women except those, whom he has married, from his harem (quote, p. 453).

Now Shahjahan seems to be reconciled to the change in the circumstances involving the assumption of power by Aurangzeb. He, therefore, sends a letter to Aurangzeb to go and see him and informs him that he has no objection to the latter's becoming the king. Aurangzeb, therefore, wants to go and meet his father. But Bahadur Khan alerts him about there being some possibility of conspiracy. Aurangzeb is confident that no conspiracy is possible when everyone has surrendered and Dara has fled to Delhi. He, therefore, tells the soldier to convey the message that he is going to meet Shah-in-Shah, but does not want to waste huge money on the latter's crazy dream of a black mausoleum. He wants to be very firm about it. He remembers how he was an unwanted son for his father. The frustration of his childhood has, perhaps, made him hate his father. He has, thus, a love-hate relationship with his father.

When Aurangzeb is about to go and meet his father, his sister Roshanara alerts him about the conspiracy against him by their father, Shah-in-Shah. She tells him that there is a plan to kill him. Then Aurangzeb suddenly gets angry and wants to arrest his father and keep him in Agra. He says, he has sent a large army to Delhi to arrest Dara. Not only that. He himself wants to go to Delhi.

Aurangzeb orders Khalilullah Khan and Islam Khan to arrest his own father, Shahjahan and see to it that nobody shall communicate with him without his (Aurangzeb's) permission; but that there should be no reduction in the normal privileges and honours due to him; and that whoever transgresses these orders will be sentenced to death. He orders further that Jahanara should be allowed to stay with the Shah-in-Shah if the latter wants her.

Just as he exercises his power to punish his own father and sister, Jahanara, he uses the same power to elevate the position of another sister, Roshanara to a higher level. He announces that Roshanara Begum will be the first lady of this Islamic Empire. He swears by Allah that he wants to consult Roshanara before taking any decision. Roshanara is very happy to know that Jahanara's dominance in the harm has come to an end.

Dara has been desperate after the defeat in the war. His wife Nadira Banu is dead. She used to accompany him to all the battles just to look after him. Dara wants her tomb near the tomb of Mian Mir in Lahore. He asks his aide-de-camp, Muhammad to take her body to Lahore. He says rather desperately that his struggle is over, and his dreams are buried and that he has lost everything in the game of chess of life.

Muhammad wants to cheer him up by asking him to follow the model of his grandfather's grandfather, Humayun. But Dara says that Humayun was fortunate because Sher Shah Suri died young. Dara has realized that he is not equal to Aurangzeb either in battle or in politics. He has grown humble and acknowledges Aurangzeb's achievements.

Muhammad draws Dara's attention to how Aurangzeb forged a letter to falsely prove Nawaz Khan's betrayal to him (Dara) and admires Dara's magnanimity in allowing Nawaz Khan to serve Aurangzeb.

Dara confesses that he is not fit to rule a kingdom. He is sad to know that his father Shahjahan and his dear sister, Jahanara are in prison and that Shah Nawaz Khan has lost his life in the battle and that they have killed the guru Sarmod also.

Dara seems to be disillusioned by the people of India who are a flock of sheep. In his opinion they are selfish people who are ready to betray anybody for a few crumbs. The people of this country have killed truth and buried it on the banks of the Jamuna River. They deserve only a few Aurangzebs. Even the brave Rajputs have only betrayers like Jaswant Singh and Jai Singh who have changed sides four times. The European merchants who seek permission to trade in India may buy up this country later. Deeply frustrated and disillusioned as he is, he does not want to return to Hindustan. He asks Muhammad to go and join Aurangzeb while he himself wants to spend some days with Jeevan Malik whom he had got released from the Shah-in-Shah in the past.

He says desperately and philosophically that he is an emperor hereafter only of six feet of earth and an uncrowned king. After the departure of Muhammad with the body of Nadira Banu for burial in Lahore, Dara begins to feel utterly lonely and undergoes a crisis of identity. He asks himself the fundamental questions about the origin, the destination, the purpose of his life and his own role in it.

Dara is a believer in the plain truth of life. He thinks that all that is white is milk. But in the political situation it is very difficult to decide who is a friend and who is a foe. Nobody can forecast when a friend turns out to be a foe or a betrayer. Dara thinks that Jeevan Malik will give him shelter for a few days as a mark of his gratitude to the former. When Jeevan Malik meets him, he pretends to be grateful to Dara and calls himself a slave of Dara. Dara requests him not to address him as Shah-in-Shah and to arrange for his getting out of Hindustan. Jeevan Malik pretends to be loyal, friendly, and grateful. But suddenly he reveals his true colour as a treacherous betrayer. He claps his hands and gets him bound in chains by his soldiers. He shamelessly tells Dara that he would get a reward from Aurangzeb for handing him (Dara) over to Aurangzeb. He accuses Dara of being a traitor to Islam and trying to leave Hindustan, go to Persia and seek the help of the King of Persia. He says that he has sent word to Jai Singh to take him (Dara) to Aurangzeb. Dara is really stunned by this betrayal and calls Jaswant Singh, Jai Singh, and Khalilullah Khan as traitors. Unable to swallow the insult Jeevan Malik angrily spits on Dara and kicks him in the stomach. Malik boasts that he is ready to sacrifice himself for Islam. Then Dara asks him if Jai Singh and Jaswant Singh are also ready to sacrifice themselves for Islam. Then Jai Singh comes there and is ordered by Jeevan Malik to drag Dara away (quote, p. 463).

Now the defeated Dara is brought before the victorious Aurangzeb. Both Aurangzeb and Roshanara taunt and accuse him of being a pro-Hindu and anti-Muslim in his belief. They mock at his eclectic secularism and not having an exclusive belief in the Prophet or Islam. Aurangzeb says mockingly that the *kafirs* (i.e. Hindus) have realized the truth and calls Dara a *Mulhid*. One may easily see how the political collision between secularism and fundamentalism or in other words between multi-religionist and mono-religionist. To this is added a psychological dimension also. For example, Aurangzeb confesses that he hated Dara because everyone was charmed by his (Dara's) looks and nobody looked at him (Aurangzeb). He confesses that he felt he was an orphan then just as Dara feels he is an orphan now.

Then Dara accuses Aurangzeb of lacking in aesthetic sense and therefore not willing to fulfil his father's dream. But Aurangzeb replies that he does not wish to waste a huge amount of money on a black mausoleum. He confesses further that he has a love-hate relationship with his father and that is why he has not killed him but only imprisoned him in the palace.

Aurangzeb is so angry that he orders his soldiers to kill Dara and bring his head. But Roshanara suggests that Dara should be tried before being hanged to death. Dara, now certain of dying, asks Aurangzeb not to destroy what Akbar has built. But Aurangzeb brands Dara as a traitor to Islam and promises to save his life and grant him the grace of life-imprisonment if he apologizes for his anti-Muslim views. By that time Jeevan Malik comes there and tells Aurangzeb that the crowd of people attacked him for betraying Dara. Irritated by Dara's popularity Aurangzeb asks his soldiers to drag Dara away for executing him.

Shahjahan seems to have reached the height of senility and has been still dreaming of a black mausoleum and his late wife, Mumtaz. He is not aware of his own present condition. Jahanara tells him that Aurangzeb is the Emperor now and he (Shahjahan) a prisoner; that Dara has been hunted down, arrested and is going to be beheaded. She gets irritated by her father's senile repetition of the same old questions. Finally, she accuses him that he liked her (Jahanara) because she looks like her mother, Mumtaz and not because she is his daughter; and that it created a wall between Roshanara and her (Jahanara). She charges him further that he liked Dara for his selfish purpose of having a black mahal, which created a rivalry and hatred between Dara and Aurangzeb.

The last scene of the play shows Aurangzeb in his old age. The playwright employs a supernatural technique here by using a feminine voice and commenting upon his policy and cruelties and weaknesses of his personality. Aurangzeb hears a feminine voice which accuses him of having murdered so many people, especially brothers and close relatives like Dara, Murad, Shuja, Suleiman, Shah Nawaz Khan, Sultan Muhammad and of creating a myth about religion and thrusting it on the people of the Empire.

Aurangzeb calls the voice a ghost, although as a Musalman he does not believe in spirits. The feminine voice replies that it is the spirit of Nature, of the Universe. (This technique of using the voice of Nature easily brings to our mind similar practice by Wole Soyinka in his plays, especially in *A Dance of the Forests*.) Aurangzeb wants to talk to the voice and asks it to assume a form and come before him. Then a young girl stands before him. The girl accuses him of murdering music and poetry and hence living alone with his sorrow. The playwright has employed the character of this girl, an embodiment of the spirit of Nature and Universe, to lead Aurangzeb to the day of reckoning or self-examination. Like a tragic figure he has achieved what he wanted to but he has paid the price for it. That price is nothing but terrible loneliness. He confesses that he knows no love as nobody has taught it to him; that he has no companion as he trusts none (in line with the lesson of the *Bhagavad Gita* that *samsayatma vinasyati*, i.e. he who doubts gets destroyed); and that his own son has become his enemy (history repeating itself in that just as he hated his father, he is now hated by his own son). In a way history has repeated itself in his own family. His dream of one country, one religion, and one language is shattered now. He is led to the moment of great disillusionment and self-examination and self-realization, but it is too late for him to rectify his life now. He orders the girl to go away and not to confuse him. But he introspects himself and realizes that he came to the mortal world empty handed but is going back carrying a heavy burden of sin; that the waters of the Jamuna will not be enough to wash his hands of its bloodstains. He is not sure whether he is a religious fanatic or an orphan. But he certainly knows that he himself has become a part of history.

Reference

Parthasarathy, Indira, *Aurangzeb*. Tr. K.V. Ramanathan, *Modern Indian Drama: An Anthology*. Ed. G.P. Deshpande. New Delhi: Sahitya Akademi. Reprint: 2004. (All the page references are to this edition.)

• • • • •

11

Political Hostility and Emotional Attachment in the Historical Play, *Fall of Mevar*

Dwijendra Lal Roy (1863-1913), born in Krishnanagar of Nadia district in the present West Bengal, a Master of Arts in English from the University of Calcutta, was an important Bangla poet, essayist, and playwright in addition to being a Civil Servant. He wrote many social plays like *Parapaare* and *Banganari* and historical plays like *Tarabai*, *Rana Pratap*, *Durgadas*, *Nurjahan*, *Shahjahan*, *Chandragupta*, and *Mevar Patan* in addition to a few mythological plays. Most of his plays have been translated into many Indian languages and staged also successfully. He is ranked as next only to Rabindranath Tagore. Tagore himself has said about him, "I have always taken deep delight in the poetical gifts of Dwijendra Lal Roy, even when he was comparatively little known to the literary public of Bengal.... The only thing worthy of note, so far as my relationship with him was concerned, is that I have always felt the profoundest admiration for his lofty genius" (quoted in *Introduction*, p. 8). It is unfortunate that such a brilliant writer died at the age of forty-nine.

His *Fall of Mevar* (*Mevar Patan*) happens to be his most famous play among his entire dramatic oeuvre. Bryan Rhys rightly describes the play, "It is the epic of the downfall of Mevar conceived in all its solemnity and grandeur, which forms the subject of this drama" (*Introduction*, p. 9).

It deals with the transitional period of Indian history around the beginning of the seventeenth century showing the conflict between the Rana Amar Singh of Mewar and the Moghul Emperor, Jehangir. Thus, it may be described as a historical-political play depicting the inter-religious, inter-racial, and political conflict in Hindustan. Broadly speaking, there is a conflict between two groups: one of Rajput kings and officers like Rana Amar Singh (son of the heroic Rana Pratap Singh), Rani Rukmini, Princess Manasi, Commander Govind Singh, Ajay Singh, Satyavati, Arun, and Kalyani. The other and opposite group consists of Emperor Jehangir, Sagar Singh, Commander Mohabat Khan, Hidayat Ali, and Shahzada Khurram and other officers.

The play begins with the meeting of Govind Singh, the Commander of the Rana's armies and his son Ajay Singh. Like an epic it plunges into the middle of action. The Moghul king has already declared war on Mevar and therefore the Rana has called an assembly meeting of his ministers and courtiers to discuss the emergency and the possibility of having a peace treaty with the Moghul king. He has invited Commander Govind Singh also to participate in the discussion. But Govind Singh is not for a peace treaty as he is a born fighter, who knows how to kill his enemies and obey the orders of his king. He says, "On that day when the great Rana Pratap died, I felt within me that the hour of Mevar's downfall had struck. Did not that mighty ruler prophesy with his dying breath that the jewels of Mevar would be sold at auction at the feet of the Moghuls, during his own son's reign? And the Moghuls are drunk with the dark wine of power. In the fever of their blood, they will destroy us utterly. All will be lost" (p. 18). Govind Singh is not for a peace treaty with the Moghul Emperor Jehangir. He remembers his heroic days of his youth and tries to lift his sword patriotically but he realizes that he has grown too old now to wield it heroically. Though physically weak, he has not lost his patriotic fervor, zest, and heroism.

Rana Amar Singh himself is in favour of a peace treaty with the powerful enemy as he does not want to lose his precious kingdom and cause widespread and avoidable bloodshed. When Jaya Singh pleads for a war with the enemy, Rana Amar Singh reasons with him, "Jaya Singh, is it not utter folly for us to attempt to oppose the mighty forces of Jehangir, the acknowledged Emperor of all Hindustan?" (p. 17). Keshav reminds him that the courage of a Kshatriya king never calculates and suggests going in for war with the enemy without bothering about the consequences. Krishnadas reminds the Rana that the latter's father Rana Pratap Singh fought for the liberty of his Mevar kingdom by all means and suggests that they should follow the example of the heroic father. Shankar refuges to recognize the greatness of the enemy when he says, "Tribute to the enemy? Who is this Moghul? Whence comes he? By what right does he claim tribute from the descendants of Lord Shree Ramachandra?" (p. 18). But Rana Amar Singh thinks practically and is inclined to sign a peace treaty with Emperor Jehangir. Then he seeks the opinion of his Commander Govind Singh who refuses to give his consent for a peace treaty. On the contrary, he speaks romantically and nostalgically about his heroism and ability to bear all sorrow stoically and heroically, "I only know what sorrow means. From my childhood up, I have been the friend of sorrow. I was brought up in the school of risks and dangers. Rana, for twenty-five years I wandered with your father Pratap Singh through forest and desert land. I have scaled countless mountains without food, without sleep. Seated at his feet, I learned to live a life of denial. I have learned the deep sweetness of sorrow" (p. 18).

By that time an envoy from the Moghul Emperor Jehangir comes and conveys his message asking them whether they are ready for war or for peace. Initially, Rana Amar Singh is inclined towards a peace treaty and therefore he expresses his opinion before the envoy, but Govind Singh does not like it. But when Satyavati, a peasant woman comes there unexpectedly and declares that she is ready to lead the Rajput army if the Rana is not willing to send his Commander to the battlefield. "If the Rana will not lead you, I will be your General" (p. 19). Then she reveals her identity as a patriotic lady, "I am only a peasant woman. From village to village, throughout the Kingdom of Mevar I go, singing praises of the Motherland. That is all you need to know" (p. 19). She talks rather insultingly about the Rana when she says, "Noble chiefs, let the Rana be. Leave him to dream his dreams of pleasure in the palace bowers of Udainagar. I will lead you to the battlefield" (p. 19). Commander Govind Singh approves of war and wants to save the son of Rana Pratap Singh from the deep disgrace and supports Satyavati's suggestion. Then Rana Amar Singh seems to feel ashamed of his earlier decision in favour of peace and finally sends words through the Moghul envoy that they are ready for war. He asks his Commander to bid his servants to bridle his stallion.

Meanwhile the Moghul Emperor Jehangir has appointed his nephew, Hidayat Ali as the Commander of his army to fight with the soldiers of Mevar. But Mohabat Khan does not like this nepotistic decision of the Emperor as he knows that Hidayat Ali is a coward. He expresses his disappointment, "Real merit, in these times is accounted but little men despise it. There are mushrooms in plenty to be found springing out of every dung-heap" (p. 20). Abdulla the Moghul General explains that "Hidayat Khan became Khan Khanan Bahadur just because he happened to be the Emperor's nephew" (p. 20). Mohabat Khan speaks ironically about Hidayat Ali's confirmed cowardice, when he says, "This is great news indeed! Out Hidayat Ali the Commander of an army! You might as well lay hold of a tottering hunchback and force him to mount a horse saddled in gold!" (p. 20).

The war between the Moghuls and Rajputs has already started. Hidayat Ali, Commander of the Moghul army is sitting in his tent outside the battlefield discussing the military matters with his attendant, Hussain. Hidayat Ali goes on boasting about his own heroism and the so-called cowardice of the Rajputs by calling them a flock of sheep. Hussain reminds Hidayat Ali about how the war has started and the sound of gun fire and flashing of swords is heard from the battlefield and asks the Commander to go to the spot and see it personally. He wants to conquer those unbelievers, i.e. Rajputs. "Why a couple of gunshots and we shall scatter them helter-skelter, like goats. It is almost beneath my dignity to go and fight with them at all!" (p. 22).

On the Rajput side, Ajay the prince of Rana Amar Singh has already left for the battlefield. Now Manasi, the princess also wants to go to the battlefield and serve the wounded soldiers and is not bothered about her marriage at all. But her mother

Rani Rukmini insists on her getting married at the earliest. Thus, the Queen's priorities are quite different from the King's and the Prince's. Manasi wants to go to the battlefield, "I...I too will go to help the sufferers. The dead I cannot save, but the wounded at least I may tend and comfort" (p. 24). The Queen reminds her daughter, Manasi that there will be many deaths on the battlefield and advises her to better remain at the palace comfortably. But Manasi is firm in her decision and expresses her priorities in a clear fashion, "My mind is bent on something far more important than marriage...I can do nothing for those who die, but surely I can serve the wounded, in love and humility?" (p. 25). Thus, she wants to lead a life of dedication. Consequently, the Queen grows helpless and remains silent.

Meanwhile the war has already started and been progressing. But Commander Hidayat Ali is sitting in his tent without having a glance at the battlefield. He expresses his cowardice by saying "But there is really not the slightest need for me to leave this tent. My brother-in-law Inayat Khan is quite capable of fighting the whole pack of them and putting them to rout singlehanded. Why should I fight then, Hissain?" (p. 26). He does not allow Hussain to leave him alone in his tent nor is he willing to go to the spot of fighting and see what is happening there. By that time a soldier comes and conveys the sad news that Shamsher Khan has fallen. After a little more time another soldier comes and conveys the message that their soldiers are breaking rank and taking to flight. But Hidayat Ali does not budge at all. Again after a little gap of time another soldier comes and conveys the news that Inayat Khan has been killed in action and that their soldiers have all left the battlefield and been running away from there. Obviously, the Moghul army has been successfully defeated by the Rajput army. Therefore, the Rajputs shout the slogans of victory. When Ajay comes to the tent and finds the chicken-hearted Commander Hidayat Ali and wants to kill him, Hidayat Ali begs him to spare his life. He has proved his cowardice without any sense of shame. On the contrary, he begs for some water as he is thirsty.

Then Princess Manasi observes the horrors of the battle like bloodshed, wounded and dying soldiers and exclaims about the futility of war. When she goes on locating the wounded soldiers, she offers water to Hidayat Ali, who is thirsty and begs for some water. So Hidayat Ali thanks Allah. Manasi goes on attending to the wounded soldiers by getting them shifted to her tent.

Later Hidayat Ali boasts of his so-called heroism; that his soldiers carried the sheaths instead of swords to the battlefield due to hurry and confusion and that their defeat at the hands of the soldiers of Mevar was due to ill-fate and how he had spent a fortune to learn the art and science of war. Thus, he makes a fool of himself in the presence of his General Abdulla and assistant like, Hussain.

In the next phase, we see Sagar Singh, the uncle of Rana Amar Singh talking with his grandson, Arun. He does not know anything about Rama and *Ramayana* or *Mahabharata* as he has spent his entire life in fighting. He defends himself that he joined the Moghul side against the Rajputs because a snake can never win the battle against a mongoose. He suggests that the Moghul ruler is more powerful than the Rajputs and he sided with the stronger party. He tells him further how his son, Mohabat Khan, uncle of Arun was converted to Islam. He indirectly attacks Hindus who do not allow conversion and admires Muslims for their practical sense in allowing conversion of others into their religion thereby swelling their number.

Meanwhile Abdulla Saheb, the Moghul General comes and conveys the Emperor's message to him that he has to assume the position of Rana of Chittor, the capital city and the Emperor has deposed Rana Amar Singh. But Sagar Singh does not wish to be the Rana.

In the meanwhile Princess Manasi is singing a song to Lord Krishna in her apartment at the palace of Udaipur at dawn. As she is a young lady she is full of concealed amorous feelings expressed in her song to Lord Krishna. By that time Prince Ajay, son of Govind Singh comes there accidentally and begins to talk with her. When their mutual admiration for each other is being expressed by the two, Rani Rukmini, mother of Princess Manasi comes there and rebukes Ajay for seeing her daughter secretly and warns him never to repeat the mistake. At the same time she reminds Manasi that she is no longer a small child but a young lady and should remain in the palace and not to see Ajay. But Princess Manasi being oversensitive begins to cry. Rana Amar Singh notices it and warns his Rani Rukmini not to chide their daughter who is like an angel. "I want you to promise me that you will never scold Manasi again. Remember that she is a ray of celestial light come down to us in a human form to show us what light is. If you offend this radiance it will return to its home leaving our house a legacy of darkness" (p. 87).

By then Commander Govind Singh comes and tells Rana Amar Singh how again the Moghul forces are marching to besiege Mevar for the second time. Rana Amar Singh knows that the Moghuls will not rest until they have laid waste the whole of Rajputana. Commander Govind Singh requests the Rana to make preparations for the second war with the Moghuls and save the honour of Rajputs. But the Rana brings to his notice that the first war against the Moghuls was won at great cost of countless lives of his soldiers; that now their military strength has been reduced by half and there can be no new recruitment of soldiers to fortify their forces. Thus, Rana Amar Singh expresses his practical wisdom by telling him the actual problems. "But what do we gain by these efforts? Set our hands to whatever we may, I know that our labours henceforth will be spent in vain; nay, rather, we shall bring down ruin—incalculable disaster, upon our heads. Half our Rajput army fell in the last war; where, then, are we to find the men for the next?" (p. 38).

Just at that time Satyavati comes and meets Rana Amar Singh and persuades him to go ahead with the war and not to stake his honour unnecessarily. She taunts him provocatively and goads him to face the situation bravely, "Or does the Rana fondly imagine that he will buy eternal life by selling his honour? Rana, this is not time for dreaming. Awake and play your part—that of a great leader, a Man of Destiny" (p. 39). When the Rana suspects that she may not be an ordinary peasant woman, she reveals her identity by declaring that she is Satyavati, the daughter of Rana Sagar Singh and confesses that she expiates the sins of her father, who joined the opposite side of the Moghul Emperor, Jehangir in the past. She tells him further how the Emperor has made her father the puppet Rana of Mevar. She expresses her patriotism when she says that she has renounced palaces, pleasures, father, and son and wandered in the shadow of those mountains singing the glory of Motherland. Then Rana Amar Singh recognizes her as his cousin and changes his decision of signing a treaty of peace with the Moghul Emperor and decides to fight with the enemy. He asks his Commander Govind Singh to prepare for the battle and muster the army.

Meanwhile although Sagar Singh has been made the Rana of Chittor and posted there by Emperor Jahangir, Rana Sagar Singh feels guilty of his betrayal of Rajputs and Mevar Kingdom. Like Macbeth he suffers from deep guilt consciousness. That is why he cannot sleep well and peacefully in his fort. He seems to hear the strange sound of enemy soldiers marching to attack him. The sentry clarifies to him that it is not the sound of the enemy soldiers but that of a storm razing at night. But Sagar Singh is not pacified by that answer. He seems to have a strange hallucination and sleep-talks, "I never wanted to come here. They forced me to come. I am no Rana. Amar Singh is the real Rana.... Don't kill me! Don't kill me!... Who are these? The Ranas of the past...Bheem Singh, Pratap Singh, Jayamal...no... no...I'll leave this fort tomorrow and go away. No...No... Don't look at me like that! Don't... Who are you? Don't kill me!" (p. 44). Overwhelmed by his fears Sagar Singh falls to the ground in a swoon. His grandson, Arun attends to him.

Princess Manasi has opened a refugee camp for lepers in Udaipur and takes delight in serving them on humanitarian grounds. When she is relaxing in her apartment at the fort of Udaipur Kalyani meets her and tells her how her brother, Ajay Singh worships Princess Manasi. By then a picture-vendor comes there to sell some pictures of big men. Princess Manasi buys three pictures: one, of Akbar, another of Jehangir and yet another of Mohabat Khan, as she appreciates their heroism. She expresses her idealistic philosophy of life and enheartens Kalyani for her loving her husband Mohabat Khan, although the latter has left the Rajput religion and embraced Islam. Although Kalyani hates her husband for his conversion into a Muslim and betrayal of his native kingdom, she is advised by Princess Manasi not to hate him but to accept him as the lord of her heart: "As for Mohabat

Khan, Kalyani, he is certainly not an unbeliever. He may not be a Hindu, but he is a Moslem. How can the Creator of All be concerned to know whether He is worshipped under the name of Brahma or Allah? Does man become a sinner because he calls a thing by one of its two names?... In the kingdom of love there are no castes, no warring religions.... Love's magic mansion is built in the rose-red light of the morning sky" (p. 46). Princess Manasi is not bothered about her marriage, though her mother is worried about it to a great extent.

Commander Govind Singh does not approve of his daughter Kalyani staring at the picture of her husband, Mohabat Khan as the latter has betrayed his Rajput religion and converted himself to a Moslem because of his greed for the crumbs thrown to him by the Moghul Emperor. He considers Kalyani as a metaphorical widow now, but Kalyani, perhaps being influenced by Manasi's idealistic philosophy, considers her husband as sacred to her and even sends a letter to him declaring her renewed love and attachment for him. But Ajay Singh returns and tells her that Mohabat Khan has refused to accept her and tells his father that the Moghul army, twenty thousand strong, has been marching towards Mevar to attack it and that it is headed by Commander Shahzada Parvez. So Commander Govind Singh despairs that everything of Mevar will be lost now. Kalyani insists on her loyalty to her husband, though he has turned a Moslem, "Yes, father, I am your daughter and I will protect your honour. But even as you have dedicated your life to your country, I have dedicated mine to my husband. Who can hold me back?" (p. 50). So Govind Singh gets irritated by his daughter's intransigence and disowns her and asks her to leave his house. So Kalyani leaves the house, but Ajay Sigh also joins her.

There is an emotional and ideological conflict between Sagar Singh on the one hand and his daughter, Satyavati and his grandson Arun Singh on the other. Whereas Sagar Singh has sold out his soul to the Moghul Emperor, Satyavati and her son Arun Singh are very patriotic about their native kingdom of Mevar. When Sagar Singh admires the seventy-eight glimmering mosques in Agra, Arun Singh counters it by showing his patriotism, "To me one broken temple in my own country is dearer than a hundred mosques carved out of solid gold.... Grandfather, believe me, the simple smile of a brother is richer than a treasure-house choked with gold received as a gift from the hands of foreigners" (p. 53). Satyavati embraces her son Ajay Singh and displays her maternal affection to him and also tells her father and her son how she had taken the garb of a beggar and wandered through the kingdom and observed the atrocities of the Moghul rulers over the people of Mevar and accuses her father, Sagar Singh in a very deeply touching manner: "What sin? You do not know? You deserted your motherland, most precious of all jewels, and ran to the Moghul to gather crumbs at his feet. You became a bond slave to him...to him who has dared to come and tear our country ruthlessly away from us.... To him who has destroyed our temples, polluted our shrines, soiled the purity of our sisters and crushed the manhood of our brothers.... And you have striven, in a slave-like emulation, to rob your brother's son, the son of Pratap Singh, of his throne. Yet you ask what sin you have committed!... Come my son, you are the only fellow-traveller left to me in this dark wilderness" (p. 54). Satyavati argues so strongly in favour of her native country that her father Sagar Singh feels terribly guilty and repents over his crime. There is a sudden transformation of his heart towards his motherland. He declares it, "Wait, wait, wait a little, don't leave me and go! Your words have opened by eyes at last. The sacred Motherland stands revealed to me in awful purity. I will return to the Motherland and uphold her in poverty and in affliction" (p. 54). He embraces his daughter affectionately after changing his decision in favour of his Motherland.

When Rana Amar Singh has achieved success in his first war with the Moghul Emperor the courtiers like Jaya Singh and Keshav are celebrating it joyously, Rana Amar Singh is not happy inwardly as he seems to telepathically see the fall of Mevar in future. By then Satyavati meets the Rana and tells him that her father Sagar Singh has left the fort of Chittor and made it over to him (Rana Amar Singh) as it legally belongs to him.

Arun Singh goes as an envoy to Maharaj Gaza Singh, ruler of Jodhpur from Rana Amar Singh and asks him to join the kingdom of Mevar to fight against the Moghul Emperor, but

Gaza Singh refuses to accept the alliance. He tells Arun Singh, "Return to your Rana and tell him that I will not accept such an alliance" (p. 59). A little later Commander Mohabat Khan conveys Emperor Jehangir's order by telling Maharaj Gaza Singh to lead the Moghul army against Mevar and defeat Rana Amar Singh and wipe out the entire Rajput race. Mohabat Khan has refused to attack Mevar because it happens to be his birthplace.

Meanwhile Sagar Singh, the father of Mohabat Khan meets him in the guise of a *fakir* and tells him that he is expiating his sin of having abandoned his beloved Mevar kingdom, which is his Motherland. He accuses Mohabat Khan of betraying not only his country but also his religion. Also he repents of having driven out his daughter, Kalyani and son, Ajay Singh from home by disowning both of them. But Mohabat Khan persists in his Moslem identity by fanatically defending it, which is his new faith. Mohabat Khan's opportunistic behavior really puzzles the reader. He swears before his father, "I will go to annihilate the Hindus. I go to cast the whole Rajput tribe into the flaming pit. I go to wipe their very name out of the future history of Hinduism. Go, tell this to your Emperor" (p. 63).

Emperor Jehangir is very angry with Commander Shahzada Parvez for losing the battle at the war with Mevar and dying as he considers it as a great humiliation to the Moghul Empire. He considers Hidayat Ali as worse than worthless for losing the battle earlier. Then Rana Sagar Singh meets Emperor Jehangir, who is terribly angry with him for having gifted away the Fort of Chittor back to Rana Amar Singh without consulting him or seeking his permission. But Sagar Singh tells him that he did not feel the necessity of seeking anybody's permission and asserts quite boldly, "I knew that Chittor was Rana Amar Singh's by right.... I learned that the Emperor Akbar did not come into possession of Chittor by fair conquest. It was by treacherous means that Jayamal was killed.... A dark curtain has suddenly lifted and revealed to me the ancient glory of Mevar from the age of *Ramayana*.... And suddenly a resplendent gleam lit up the mists of the past and out of it flashed the glittering sword of my brother Pratap Singh. That visionary sword pierced through me, and I bled for very shame.... I handed over the Fort of Chittor to my brother's son" (pp. 64-65). Emperor Jehangir is so angry with Sagar Singh that he asks the latter if he has come prepared for his death and calls his sentry in order to issue his death sentence for him. But Sagar Singh heroically says that there is no necessity of calling a soldier to kill him as he is ready to kill himself, "Why need you call the entry? I have courage enough to be my own executioner" (p. 65). He stabs himself and falls to the ground. He holds out his blood-stained hands and says, "May my sins be atoned for in this blood!" (p. 65) and dies heroically and patriotically.

Rana Amar Singh, being deeply disappointed by the defeat in the first war with the Moghul army, feels rather disillusioned with life and even thinks of renouncing the life that has turned out to be meaningless to him. But his Rani is still worried about the marriage of her daughter, Princess Manasi, who is not bothered about her marriage but on the contrary, thinks romantically about the beauty of life in general. Rana Amar Singh's thinking is described as simply madness by his Rani and others.

Maharaj Gaza Singh, although a Rajput, is in favour of the Moghul Emperor, perhaps for opportunistic reasons or because of his helplessness. Rana Amar Singh is both unhappy about this stance taken by the Rajput King Gaza Singh and helpless in the current political context where loyalties are changed for various reasons. Sometimes their political opportunism makes them change their religions as in the case of Mohabat Khan or their political loyalty only as in the case of Sagar Singh (father of Mohabat Khan) and Maharaj Gaza Singh. All this is ascribable to the mystery of human nature.

Now the second war with the Moghul army is about to begin. Rana Amar Singh knows that he is going to lose the battle but yet he cannot back out from fighting as he happens to be a heroic Rajput king. Mohabat Khan has refused to participate directly in the attack on Mevar because of his emotional attachment to the land which happens to be his birthplace. He has at least that much of humanity left in him. But he orders Commander Shahzada Pervez to attack Mevar, "Go and besiege the fort of Chittor (part of Rajput Kingdom). Take ten thousand men with you" (p. 71). Likewise he instructs Maharaj Gaza Singh, "And you Maharaj, see that the villages are burnt down from one end to the other. If anybody crosses your path, cut him down. But no one woman must be touched; bear that carefully in mind" (p. 71). One may easily see how the political rivalry is intertwined with religious rivalry in this situation as depicted in the play. Mohabat Khan explains it quite clearly in his aside, "Beware Hindus and Rajputs, beware Mevar! This time it is not a battle between nations; it is a struggle for life and death between two religions. We shall see who wins" (p. 71).

When Commander Govind Singh suggests to Rana Amar Singh to proceed to the battlefield, the latter tells him how they have to send their limited number of five thousand soldiers into the jaws of death while fighting with the almost twenty times larger army of the Moghuls. Both of them embrace each other for the last time as they are not sure of returning alive from the battlefield.

When the war begins, the Moghul soldiers burn the villages of Mevar kingdom indiscriminately thereby killing the innocent civilians. Then the Moghul soldiers follow them with guns in hands and shoot the people of Mevar. When Ajay Singh is trying to protect his sister, Kalyani and fighting with the enemies, he is shot dead by the Moghul soldier. He therefore dies a heroic death. Kalyani mourns the death of her brother, praises his heroism and wants to go to meet their Commander on her own responsibility. Hence, the Moghul soldiers take her to their Commander. When they take her to their Commander, that person happens to be her husband Mohabat Khan who tells her how he ordered his soldiers to wipe out the entire race of Rajputs ruthlessly in order to wreak vengeance on Mevar. He does not have any qualms of conscience to have ordered the mass massacre of Rajputs, although he himself has the blood of a Rajput in him. Kalyani is very angry with him for having abandoned his faith and embraced Islam rather opportunistically. "Like a dog, you have licked up the crumbs of another faith; you exult aloud in your devilish cruelty" (p. 80). Finally, she says goodbye to Mohabat Khan for betraying the faith of Rajputs as she is deeply disillusioned by his lack of respect for his original Hindu faith.

Mohabat Khan has defeated the Mevar kingdom completely. The Rana, Amar Singh is naturally depressed by the unexpected and harsh reality of life. Commander Govind Singh is sad to have lost his son, Ajay Singh. Kalyani is grief stricken to lose her dear brother. And Princess Manasi is aggrieved to lose her husband, Ajay Singh whom she had married secretly.

Mevar has been devastated completely by Mohabat Khan, but the women warriors of Mevar have been getting ready to fight the Muslim army. Commander Shahzada is coming with a new force there to counteract them. Commander Govind Singh is so heroic and patriotic in his attitude to life that he meets the Moghul Commander Mohabat Khan and asks him to kill him, "You shall not enter Udaipur unless you pass over my dead body. Take up this weapon" (p. 89). But Mohabat Khan does not wish to kill him nor does he want to enter the fort of Mevar. Govind Singh persuades him to kill him because of his strong love for Mevar. "I am not here to listen to what you wish to say. My heart lost my daughter...and now I want to end my life. I want to die before these eyes see my beloved Mevar trodden under the foot of the enemy. I want to die before I see the son of Rana Pratap Singh become a slave of the Moghuls. And I want to die at the hands of one who is a slave of another though a child of my country, who, though born a Hindu, is a Moslem by conversion, who is an enemy of his own brother.... Come, no more delay. Where is your sword? (p. 89). Although Mohabat Khan says that he has renounced the sword Govind Singh persuades him to kill him by inviting him for a dual. But when both of them are preparing to fight with each other, Maharaj Gaza Singh comes there and shoots Govind Singh and calls him a thief. But Commander Govind Singh dies heroically by answering them properly, "I am no thief, Maharaj. You are the thieves. I never wanted to loot another's kingdom. You have come and looted another's kingdom. Mohabat Khan, go now to Udaipur. Nobody will now defy you. Go seize your own mother and consign her to slavery. (*He dies.*)" (p. 90). Thus, Commander Govind Singh has proved that honour, patriotism, and heroic death are more important to him than defeat at the hands of the army.

Then Satyavati and her son Arun happen to meet Commander Mohabat Khan and discover that he is none other than her own brother. Again the motifs of political hostility and emotional attachment are pitted against each other here. Arun is surprised to learn that the Moghul Commander Mohabat Khan is his maternal uncle (Mama). Mohabat Khan boldly confesses his sin of conversion, but at the same time recognizes the emotional bondage with his sister. "Perhaps, you mean, that I sinner when I embraced Islam? But there I do not hold with you. Each one of us has a right to his own beliefs.... And even if it was sin, was it one which can wipe out all the tender feelings and noble qualities in the human heart? Sister, I know that a woman's heart is pure as a lake of evening time, as sweet as a garden of roses; her soul is the mirror of the sky.... Pray, forget for one moment that you are a Hindu and I a Muslim, that you are the oppressed and I the oppressor.... Remember that I am the brother and you are the sister.... Remember that we are two motherless children, sister and brother" (p. 95).

By that time Hidayat Ali comes and tells Mohabat Khan that he is no longer the Moghul Commander but that Shahzada Khurram has taken over the charge of the kingdom of Mevar. Meanwhile Rana Amar Singh meets Mohabat Khan on the bank of Udaisagar and asks him to kill him and offers him his sword. For him death is always preferable to defeat and loss of his kingdom. Mohabat Khan refuses to oblige him by clarifying that he is a warrior and not a murderer. But Rana Amar Singh taunts and persuades him to fight with him. When both of them (cousins) inevitably take up swords in their hands and prepare to fight, Princess Manasi comes there and prevents it by saying, "Father, have done. The tale of the havoc wrought is already dark enough. You shall not add to the sum of horror with this unbrotherly strife. How can murder and revenge help us to heal the wounds and console us in this fearful tragedy? All that we hope to do is to forget the wrong and rise above ourselves once more" (p. 98). Thus, Princess Manasi speaks in her typical idealistic manner and prevents their fraternal fight and further tragedy.

Fall of Mevar is thus a serious historical play dealing with the political conflict between Rajput King Rana Amar Singh and the Moghul Emperor Jehangir thereby showing the transitional period of Indian history in the seventeenth century. In it are intertwined the political hostility and emotional bondage in a paradoxical way, both caused by the political ambition of conquest of the new land or territory involving acquisition of great wealth belonging to others. Politics and religion are intertwined in the play in an interesting manner. Whereas Sagar Singh has changed his loyalty from native Rajput King to the Moghul Emperor, but his son Mohabat Khan has gone a step ahead of his father by changing not only his political loyalty from the Rajput King to the Moghul Emperor but also his religion from Hinduism to Islam, which is not depicted convincingly and satisfactorily by the playwright. Hence, it is irritating as it appears to be quite irrational and absurd. That is why Mohabat Khan's sister, Satyavati does not like his conversion. Similarly, his Hindu wife, Kalyani also does not like him but abandons him for good. Thus, Mohabat Khan's stand remains enigmatic, whereas his father, Sagar Singh's behavior looks convincing as he realizes, though belatedly his mistake of changing his political loyalty and repenting for it by committing suicide by stabbing himself in the presence of Emperor Jehangir.

This historical play could have achieved a ferocious atmosphere if the playwright had not toned it down with a romantic element of bringing frequent songs into it and an idealistic character of Princess Manasi, who always speaks idealistically like a philosopher thereby reducing the terroristic atmosphere of the play. For example, Satyavati and Manasi frequently sing songs about the beauty of Mevar hills, Nature, Sri Krisna and so on thereby giving a romantic aura to the play. Thus, Dwijendra Lal Roy romanticizes history, although it is very terroristic and ferocious at its bottom. Generally, his characters speak in a poetic, romantic or paradoxical style and easily remind us of the language of Rabindranath Tagore used in his plays.

The patriotism and heroism of Rana Amar Singh, Ajay Singh, Commander Govind Singh, Satyavati, and Kalyani are more than admirable. Likewise the atonement of Sagar Singh for betraying his own Rajput kingdom and his heroic death by stabbing himself is also an admirable act on his part. Govind Singh asking Mohabat Khan to kill him shows his high integrity and uncompromising patriotism and self-respect, but his murder by Maharaj Gaza Singh is rather treacherous and unpardonable. Similarly, Rana Amar Singh, after having lost Mevar to the Moghul Emperor, asks Mohabat Khan to kill him in a duel, which testifies his uncompromising patriotism, heroism, and self-respect, which are typical of the Rajput blood. Satyavati's admiration for the mother, Mevar, and Kalyani's abandonment of her husband, Mohabat Khan for his betrayal of Hindu faith are as appreciable as admirable. Princess Manasi's idealistic and poetic speeches help to tone down the ferocity of the historical hostility between the two kingdoms. But Mohabat Khan's fanatic adherence to his new Muslim faith defies our understanding as it looks rather irrational and arbitrary. Hidayat Ali's cowardice and empty boasting are as interesting as comic.

Although Harindranath Chattopadhyaya had hastily translated this play from the Bangla, Dilip Kumar Roy was not satisfied with it and therefore improved upon it by meticulously correcting it and got it further scrutinized by the British scholar, Bryan Rhys. Therefore, the final version of translation has become an excellent one, which is standard and chaste English with a poetic grace about it. It reads as though it was originally written in English. It creates the aura of the old world and the nostalgic beauty of Mevar and its landscape studded with Blue Mountains.

In spite of all these peculiarities, *Fall of Mevar* is an interesting and a significant historical play in the rare genre of Indian English Historical Drama. It needs to be reprinted by the national level publishers of India for a greater circulation and publicity. At the same time it needs to be studied seriously by the students of Indian English Literature.

Reference

Dwijendra Lal Roy, *Fall of Mevar* (*Mevar Patan*). Tr. Harindranath Chattopadhyaya and Dilip Kumar Roy, Bombay: Nalanda Publications, 1946. (All the page references are to this edition.)

• • • • •

12

Artistic Liberty and the Slavery of Authority in *One Day in Ashadha*

Mohan Rakesh (1925-72) happens to be one of the important dramatists in Hindi. He is a short story writer, who started the movement called *Nayi Kahani*. He was born in Amritsar, Punjab. After earning his Master's degree in English Literature, he taught for some time and then moved to Bombay as the editor of *Sarika*. Soon he resigned from there, did some freelance writing sand entered the literary scene with short story writing as his chosen genre thereby starting the *Nayi Kahani* Movement. His complete short stories are available in four volumes. He died young at the age of 47, leaving incomplete his research project on dramatic diction for which he had a Nehru fellowship.

He is well known for his plays like *One Day in Ashadha* (*Ashad Ka Ek Din*, 1958), *Half-Way House* (*Aadhe Adhure*, 1959), *The Great Swans of Waves* (*Leheronke Rajhamsa*, 1963). Almost all of his plays have been successful on the stage. The great feature about Mohan Rakesh is that he can write plays about old or classical themes as well as about new or modern themes with equal ease, confidence, and mastery.

"The author's grasp of the contemporary situation is equally sharp in his novel, *Andhere Bund Kamare*, wherein he tries to depict the alienation of modern man living a life of indecision and rootless-ness. Over-mechanization in the post-war period and the existentialist agony that followed have eroded the simple piety of Indian society. According to Rakesh there is no permanent value called love, as personal ambition invariably overrides all romantic considerations. His other novel, *Na Aanewala Kal* also touches the pulse of contemporary life."[1]

The present play, *One Day in Ashadha*[2] depicts the anxieties and dilemmas of the famous Sanskrit poet and dramatist, Kalidasa. Hence, it may be described as a meta-literary play. In other words, it is a work of art dealing with the life of an artist, or a play delineating the life of a dramatist. Kalidasa, who happens to be the protagonist of the play, was closely connected with Nature like landscape, sky, clouds, animals and stars, etc. and their beauty, glory, and terror. In other words, he was a child of Nature. The month of *Ashadha* is known for its dark clouds and heavy rain. Mohan Rakesh has tried to problematize the poetic career of Kalidasa in the play and indirectly shows it relevance even to the present-day society.

The play begins with a domestic scene wherein we are shown Ambika and Mallika, mother and daughter respectively who have different approaches to life. Whereas Ambika is practical and down-to-earth, Mallika is romantic and idealistic in her outlook on life. This contrast may be seen in the first scene itself wherein Mallika returns home drenched in the rain of the first day of *Ashadha* month and tells her mother how she had a thrilling experience of beauty in the pouring rain. But the mother ignores her fussing about the rain as she minds her own business of attending to the household chores like winnowing the paddy.

Like a typical mother, Ambika is worried about her daughter's marriage. She, therefore, tells Mallika that Agnimitra has returned from the place where she had sent him and suggests to her to get married to him. But Mallika does not want to be married so soon. But Ambika is worried about the gossip in the village about Mallika and Kalidasa. She accuses Mallika that she is losing control over herself these days. But Mallika does not feel guilty about her feeling which is pure, tender, and immoral. But Ambika interprets Mallika's purity of feeling as a mere illusion or self-deception, because she believes in the material values of life and not in aesthetic values. She makes it clear that she hates the lover of Mallika, i.e. Kalidasa who has ruined her house. She suspects that Mallika was with Kalidasa during the rain and worries about the gossip about them in the village.

By then Kalidasa comes there with a little fawn wounded by an arrow shot by somebody. He wants to save it by applying ghee to its wound and feeding it with some milk. By then Dantul, a gentleman from the royal family comes there in search of the fawn that he has shot by tracing the marks of blood drops up to their house. He does not know the poetic identity of Kalidasa but takes him to be just a villager. He, therefore, accosts Kalidasa and asks him to return the fawn to him as it belongs to him as he has shot it. But Kalidasa refuses to part with the tender creature. Thus, there is a simple contrast between Kalidasa as a humanitarian and saviour and Dantul as a callous hunter and destroyer. (This episode easily brings to our mind a similar episode of the encounter between Siddhartha and Devadatta in Buddha's life.)

When Ambika rebukes him and refuses to provide a bed for the fawn, Kalidasa starts going away from the house along with the fawn, without caring for Dantul's demand. Both of them are ignorant of each other's identity and importance. Then Dantul angrily draws his sword and wants to follow Kalidasa, but then Mallika prevents Dantul from chasing Kalidasa and tells him that Kalidasa's sensitivity is not frightened by Dantul's authority. At the mention of the name, 'Kalidasa' Dantul is deeply surprised and tells Mallika that Kalidasa is the author of *Ritusamhar*; that the court of Ujjayini wants to honour him and appoint him to the position of Poet Laureate and that Acharya Vasumitra came that day for that very purpose. He, therefore, wants to go and apologize to Kalidasa.

Recognition has come to Kalidasa's door without his having to manipulate for it. His beloved Mallika naturally feels proud of him who is going to be honoured at the court of Ujjayini and tells her mother about it. But Ambika, with her robust sense of reality, does not show any response to the news as it is not important or relevant to her. Being a practical lady, she does not want to imagine things unnecessarily. She even complains that Kalidasa is self-centred and cares for nobody in the world.

There is a contrast between Ambika and Mallika. Whereas Ambika is a down-to-earth, practical lady, Mallika is aesthetic, emotional and romantic in her temperament. That is why there is a difference between them in their assessment of the character and behaviour of Kalidasa. Ambika, for example, cannot understand Mallika's so-called emotional or aesthetic relationship with Kalidasa or the reason why Kalidasa is not willing to marry Mallika. But Mallika understands the economic crisis and psychological problem of Kalidasa and hence sympathizes with his present helpless condition. For example, she explains to her mother that Kalidasa has been crushed by poverty and been ill-treated by his uncle at home, which is the reason for his not thinking about the marriage. Ambika is worried about Mallika's livelihood and security in future when she is dead and gone. But Mallika, who is sympathetic about Kalidasa's condition, does not want to pester him for marriage when life is about to take a new direction.

Though the government officials have come to the village to take Kalidasa to the capital city of Ujjayini for honouring him as the Poet Laureate of the Gupta court, Kalidasa is not willing to receive the honour for fear of being bought by the government and losing his identity as well as liberty as a poet.

Ambika and Matul do not have good opinion about Kalidasa due to their own personal reasons like distrust and jealousy respectively. But Mallika always wishes Kalidasa well in his future career.

Kalidasa goes to the Jagadamba temple just to avoid the government officials who want to take him to the capital city of Ujjayini. He is so much attached to his land that he does not wish to leave it. But Ambika in her distrustful way opines that Kalidasa is merely play-acting indifference to the State honour and that nobody is going to persuade him to go to the capital city. Vilom, the family friend, also thinks along the line of Ambika. He thinks that Mallika is very young and innocent and therefore knows nothing about the ways of the world; and that she does not like him (Vilom) to come to her house because Kalidasa does not like it and that he can easily see through Kalidasa's hypocrisy. There is a streak of hidden sexual jealousy between Vilom and

Kalidasa. Vilom knows that Ambika has suffered a lot in her life and alerts her to see that Mallika is married to Kalidasa before the latter leaves for Ujjayini.

Nikeshep and Mallika hold opposite views as they happen to be sympathizers and well-wishers of Kalidasa. For example, Nikshep opines that Kalidasa will lose a great opportunity in his life if he does not go to Ujjayini; and that talent constitutes only one quarter of a man but recognition constitutes the remainder (what he says about Kalidasa holds good in modern times also. That is why many modern Indian writers pull all kinds of wires—communal, regional, linguistic and gender—to get prestigious awards like Jnanpith and Sahitya Akademi, etc.) and that Kalidasa must go to the capital.

Mallika, the beloved of Kalidasa, naturally wants to persuade Kalidasa to go to the capital to receive the honour. Otherwise, she thinks, he will miss a great chance. She, therefore, goes to the temple of Jagadamba along with Nikeshep, in spite of her mother's disapproval and returns home along with Kalidasa. By that time Vilom is already present there. So both Mallika and Kalidasa are angry with Vilom and ask him to leave the house. But in spite of this insult, Vilom expresses his own sincere feelings. He tells Kalidasa that he is rather sad to be separated from Kalidasa if the latter goes away to the capital, become preoccupied and be among so many attractions like theatres, taverns and other things.

But Kalidasa asks Vilom not to interfere with his private life. He refuses to go to the capital because he does not want to part from Mallika and be separated from his native village, land, and mountains. But Mallika, like a true beloved, encourages him to go to the capital in order to grab the opportunity, although his absence may cause suffering to her in the form of loneliness, pangs of separation and emptiness. In order to overcome that loneliness she wants to wander through the countryside and watch the sunset from the temple. After the departure of Kalidasa from her house, she begins to sob and shed tears of joy.

The Second Act shows the next phase of Mallika's and Kalidasa's life. Now Ambika is sick, perhaps due to old age and Mallika prepares a medicine by pounding a few herbs and administers it to her mother, who has been suffering from fever for the last two years. Besides, she, being careless about her health, does not take the medicine regularly.

Mallika is not disheartened by the ill-health of her old mother. She seems to have only positive thinking and optimistic outlook on life. For example, when Nikshep tells her that Kalidasa has settled down in Ujjayini permanently, she feels proud of him because he wrote only *Ritusamhar* when he was in the village, but now after settling down in the capital he has written many plays and poems like *Kumarasambhavam* and *Meghadutam* and one more poem which is widely discussed.

Nikshep tells Mallika another news, i.e. that Kalidasa has married the Gupta princess, who is educated and learned in many *sastras*. Instead of feeling shocked and insecure, she justifies that also by saying that a great genius should marry an extraordinary lady like the princess and that she herself is very ordinary. She knows the limitations of her life, i.e. her poverty, her humble domestic background, and her illiteracy. Nikshep points out that there is a great change in her household, but Mallika replies that there is no change except the fact that she has to do the domestic work which her mother used to do earlier. Nikshep tells her one more thing that he has seen the government officers coming to the village and also Kalidasa in royal robes riding towards the mountain-top. Even then Mallika does not complain against Kalidasa for having not visited her before riding towards the mountain-top. But still she collects blank pages and keeps them bound so that Kalidasa may write his poetry in them whenever he likes. Thus, Mallika happens to be an embodiment of acceptance of the harsh reality of life and her love for Kalidasa is strong that she is not ready to find fault with any acts of Kalidasa. Her love for him is too pure to be tarnished by any doubt about his integrity. She is ready to sacrifice her personal happiness for the sake of his love. She does not rave and rant like a modern feminist girl who is interested in asserting her identity and seeking her own fulfillment. In fact, she is too good for a selfish lover like Kalidasa.

The playwright highlights the yawning gap between reality and imaginative poetry through the scene in which the art-students visit Mallika. Rangini and Sangini are the art-students learning dance, vocal, and instrumental music at the Centre for Dance and Drama at Ujjayini. They meet Mallika at her house and tell her that they have come to study the background of Kalidasa. They ask her about the herbs that give off light, but they feel utterly disappointed when Mallika gives them a negative answer. They find nothing romantic there in the village unlike the picture painted by Kalidasa in his poetry. Hence, they excuse themselves and go away from there. They want to know if Kalidasa has written false. Obviously, these art-students fail to understand that beauty lies in the beholder's eyes. They are not able to distinguish between photographic beauty and poetic or imaginative beauty. They are incapable of discriminating between *laukik* reality (of the mundane world) and *lokottara* (or artistic/poetic) truth. Their entire attempt is ironical. The playwright's depiction of this scene is obviously satirical and universally relevant.

By now conspicuous changes have happened in Kalidasa's life. He has not remained a mere Poet Laureate of the Gupta court but has been promoted as the King of Kashmir. The details of these remarkable changes are offered by two characters, Anuswar and Anunasik. They come and knock at the door of Mallika and introduce themselves as the servants of Lord Matrugupta, the author of *Ritusamhar* and other poems; that his queen, Priyangumanjari is going to visit her house; that Matrugupta is the new name of Kalidasa, who is going to rule over the Kingdom of Kashmir. Mallika is really surprised to hear this news but she never shows any psychological perturbance over that. She seems to have remarkable self-control.

As part of the protocol of the royal visit to Mallika's house Anuswar and Anunasik want to rearrange the things and pieces of furniture of her house systematically to receive the royal guest and make her comfortable. But after a lot of experimenting with the rearrangement, they revert to the old arrangement itself. After they ascertain that everything is arranged properly in Mallika's house, Matul ushers Queen Priyangumanjari into the house. The

Queen reciprocates Mallika's greeting. It is very strange that Mallika never shows her jealous or anger at the Queen who has snatched her own (Mallika's) place in Kalidasa's heart. She asks Matul to go and rest as she has already tired him. But Matul replies that he is not tired at all and flatters her unnecessarily. Matul easily represents the servile behaviour, sycophancy and flatter of the subordinate workers in the presence of the higher officers in the bureaucratic set-up of India.

The Queen, Priyangumanjari does not seem to know Kalidasa's pre-marital love affair with Mallika. Hence, she cannot understand how much Mallika would be disturbed by her own presence. She talks amicably with Mallika that her lord, Matrugupta (erstwhile Kalidasa) is always reminded of this place and that that is why she wanted to see the place and brought him here while he was on his way to Kashmir. She wants to take some of the atmosphere of this place.

The Queen explains the difficulty of being the ruler of any province as it involves so much responsibility, alertness, tension, and restlessness. She says that the political life in Kashmir is so unstable.

The Queen compliments Mallika for her love of poetry and sees Kalidasa's books on her laps. She does not like King Matrugupta to feel the absence of this place. So she wants to take some fawns, local herbs, etc. to her place so that Kalidasa may feel happy.

She is so generous that she offers to get Mallika's old house demolished and rebuilt. She even volunteers to take Mallika and her mother, Ambika to Kashmir to live with her as her companions and arrange the marriage of Mallika with some official of her choice. Mallika is so gentle and sensitive that she does not want to hurt the Queen, who has come to visit her as a guest.

But by that time Ambika comes out and tells the Queen that her daughter has no desire for material comforts as she dwells in her life of feelings. The Queen volunteers to help them in some way or other, if they want. She tells them that Kalidasa went to the mountain and in the meanwhile she came to visit Mallika here. After the departure of the Queen, Ambika taunts Mallika and asks her to accept the help and payment from Kalidasa for her life of feelings.

Then Vilom comes and tells Mallika how the entire village is excited by the royal visit and how the officials are collecting stones and fawns and drawing pictures of everything—trees and mountain, etc.—in sight, which is so unusual to them. He says that they want to take these things and show them to others.

The main point that the dramatist wants to highlight here is that Kalidasa, who was not willing to part from Mallika once, has not bothered to come to her house to meet her, perhaps because of his superior political status now. The dramatist has shown how power of any kind, especially the political one, makes a man conceited. Ambika and Vilom seem to be quite right in their assessment of Kalidasa's character, his selfishness, and egotism. For example, Vilom waits for some time in Mallika's house thinking that Kalidasa might come there, but the hoof beats of the horses come near and fade out gradually. Now it becomes clear to Vilom that Kalidasa does not want to come there. But Ambika is not surprised by Kalidasa's behaviour as she knows his selfish nature and egoism instinctively. Vilom is also disappointed to learn that Kalidasa did not come to meet him as a friend, perhaps because the latter does not consider the former worth his friendship. Obviously, the new status of a king with political power has brought in a conspicuous change in his behaviour. Ambika, who had expected this kind of reaction from Kalidasa, hugs Mallika and asks her not to cry for Kalidasa even now. Mallika bears the shock stoically and silently.

In the Third Act, the playwright shows many conspicuous changes in the life of many characters. Incidentally, he highlights the contrast between the rural life and the urban life; between the life of poverty and the life of luxury and power. Indirectly, he shows the eternal flux of life and rotation of the wheel of fate.

Matul, for example, symbolizes the truth that a life of luxury demands its own discipline and adjustment and that political power demands the exercise of one's public self and suppression of one's private self. Matul, who is drenched in the rain, comes leaning on his crutches to Mallika's house. His experience testifies to his peculiar suffering in the midst of luxury. He tells Mallika how he broke his leg on the marble floor of the palace in Ujjayini; how his old house in the village is also reconstructed and covered with marble flooring and how he cannot live in it comfortably. He confesses that he prefers the old type of mud flooring for his house.

Matul tells her further that his life in the palace was most uncomfortable because wherever he went, he was followed or preceded by guards and that everybody used to bow down to him in deference to him and that even his discarded clothing was to be honoured by them. But he confesses that he is happy to be back in this village, but he finds that only the rain is unbearable. The contrast between the country and the city is presented effectively by the dramatist here. Matul has paid the price for living in the palace by getting his leg broken.

A slight difference may be seen between Matul and Mallika. Whereas Matul is disillusioned after going through the experience of living in the luxury of palace life, Mallika is never tempted by the desire for riches, comforts or luxuries of the palace life. She seems to be content with her given situation of poverty, insecurity, and helplessness. She has the existential courage to be herself. Even after the death of her mother, she does not feel disheartened. When Matul asks her if it was correct for her to return the gifts and the gold sent by the Queen, she replies that she did not need them and that she did not allow her rural house to be remodeled by the Queen's architects. She is admirable for her non-possessiveness, absence of attraction for gold and her strong sense of self-respect and dignity as a human being.

Before returning to his own house, Matul tells Mallika a shocking rumour that he has heard. According to this rumour, there was a rebellion in Kashmir, as a consequence of which Kalidasa left Kashmir, has taken the vows of a *sanyasi* and gone to Banaras, but not to Ujjayini. But Mallika does not believe this rumour.

Mallika's deep love for Kalidasa has not diminished at all in spite of all the vicissitudes of her life. That is why, after the departure of Matul, she looks at Kalidasa's book and addresses it as though it is the author himself. She introspects herself and realizes that he is present in her life, but she is not present in his life. In other words, their love affair has been a one-way traffic. She understands that her life has been utterly meaningless now; that she has suffered a lot; that she has a child of her destitution and that she has lost her name and become a mere adjective. She is unhappy to hear the rumours that Kalidasa spends much of his time with prostitutes in Ujjayini; that he has become a *sanyasi* and that she has suffered so much pain of destitution due to his indifference to her.

But when Mallika is brooding about her bad luck, Kalidasa has already returned to the village and meets her, who cannot believe her eyes. Kalidasa tells her that everything in the village has changed or perhaps his own vision has changed. He tells her that he left Kashmir as he wanted to be free from his love of power and authority and because of his attachment and bondage to his homeland.

He explains his own behaviour further. Initially, he hesitated to accept the honour due to his lack of self-confidence and fear that it may change the direction of his life. He confesses that he accepted the responsibility of ruling over Kashmir because of his dire poverty and humiliation here. But in course of time, he says, he realized his shortcomings and could not change his nature. He says that his poetic career conflicted with his administrative duties; that he felt disgusted with himself and disliked those who celebrated his coming as a festival and that his mind longed for freedom.

He tells her further that although he wrote many plays and poems in Ujjayini, he wrote them only by recollecting his own experiences in the village and his separation from Mallika.

But Mallika is such a good girl that she does not complain against or shout at Kalidasa like a modern young lady. She has borne her suffering silently and stoically. She shows him all the copies of his poems that she has bought from the traders. Kalidasa takes a book from Mallika and finds it blank, but stained with her tears. She wanted him to write his greatest epic in that book. But instead of Kalidasa writing his epic on these pages, it is Mallika who seems to have written her epic of suffering by staining them with her tears. Had she been a modern feminist girl she would have asserted her identity by choosing another man and married him as soon as Kalidasa left for Ujjayini. But Mallika is cast in the traditional mould. She has a lot of self-control and contains a lot of sorrow within her. That is why she has sacrificed her life, her personal pleasures and comforts because of her good wishes for Kalidasa. She stands for pure and complete love, whereas Kalidasa stands for false and incomplete love. That is why he could marry Queen Priyangumanjari in spite of his so-called love for Mallika. In a way, Ambika's assessment of Kalidasa as a selfish and egoistic and hypocritical man has come true, but Mallika is not willing to complain against him as she loves too deeply, but not wisely.

At this time, Kalidasa hears the cry of a baby inside the house. Mallika tells him that it is her gift to him. By that time Vilom comes in fully drunk and is surprised to find Kalidasa there and asks him to embrace him and tells him the philosophical truth that times does not wait for anyone and that it creates privileges and opportunities for others also. He asks Kalidasa to look at Mallika's child whose eyes are as beautiful as a fawn's. When Mallika goes inside to bring the crying baby, Kalidasa leaves her house without even telling her because he has realized that time does not wait for anyone. He has no moral courage to see the child of another man, i.e. Vilom and becomes speechless with a deep sense of shame and embarrassment. But Mallika cannot follow Kalidasa as there is thunder and lightning. It is very ironical that Mallika, who used to dislike and avoid the company of Vilom in the past, has now been forced by the circumstances to marry him only, as she has no choice. She has accepted the harsh reality of life and realized that love and marriage do not always go together.

Vilom provides a sharp contrast to Kalidasa. Whereas Kalidasa is a poet, Vilom is a non-poet and a very practical man. He frequently intermeddles and interferes with the daily life of Mallika and her mother Ambika. He is a bitter critic of Kalidasa's selfish nature and egotism. As some Hindi critics have suggested, Vilom is an alter ego of Kalidasa. Whereas Mallika, with a poetic heart and romantic temperament is unlucky to marry a drunkard like Vilom, Vilom is lucky to marry Mallika who is far above him in cultural aspect. The main factors that have brought these two individuals of unequal cultural levels and equalized them are the economic condition of poverty and the pressures of circumstances.

The play may be described as a satire on a great poet's life. While the playwright highlights the purity of Mallika's love for Kalidasa, he concurrently satirizes Kalidasa's callous indifference to her love. Similarly, the dramatist foregrounds the conflict between the artistic liberty and the administrative responsibility and bondage in the life of a poet and shows that the two cannot go together and that one of them has to be forfeited for the accomplishment of the other. This universal truth is applicable not only to Kalidasa's life but also to the life of modern writers and artists as well.

It is said that Mohan Rakesh did some historical research in order to write this play, but there are a few unconvincing things in the play, which leave the modern reader rather disappointed. For example, he has kept the village anonymous. One wonders why he has not mentioned the actual name of the village. The mention of the proper name of the village would have added to the geographical particularity and historical authenticity. Mentioning an anonymous village would be preferable in an allegorical work rather than a historically realistic play such as this.

Another disappointing deficiency in the play is the blatant lack of clarity of motivation or logical continuity of events. One may detect a few contradictions in the presentation of characters and dialogues. For example, how can Kalidasa visit the prostitutes and yet become a *sanyasi*? Another major lacuna in the logical development of the plot is about Kalidasa's marriage. For example, the reader wants to know what happened to Kalidasa's marriage with Queen Priyangumanjari when he left Kashmir and went to Banaras to become a *sanyasi*? If he did so without telling the queen about it, is it not tantamount to cheating her also in addition to already cheated Mallika? If the play happens to be a product of historical research, these logical gaps should not be there.

One more problem in the play is that the character of Vilom and his behaviour are not sufficiently convincing. The reason why Mallika had to marry Vilom in spite of her earlier dislike for him is not examined or presented convincingly. Most of the collusive action and tension is presented either prospectively or retrospectively through indirect action (or off stage) and never through direct action. The silence of Mallika about Kalidasa's betrayal of love and Kalidasa's silent departure after hearing the cry of Mallika's baby is not in keeping with the articulate aspect of drama.

Yet another disconcerting thing about the play is the lack of consistency in the choice of characters and their proper names. The character of Vilom is said to be an invented or imaginary one. The characters like Anuswar and Anunasik happen to be allegorical and borrowed from the field of linguistics. One wonders why they should have linguistic terms for their names, if at all the play is based on historical research and evidence? Similarly, the characters of Rangini and Sangini seem to be just imaginary characters. Why should there be imaginary characters in a historical play?

References

1. Lal, Moham. Chief Editor, *Encyclopaedia of Indian Literature*, Vol. IV, New Delhi: Sahitya Akademi, Reprint. 2007, p. 3526.
2. Rakesh, Mohan, *One Day in Ashadha*, Tr. Sarah K. Ensley, in *Modern Indian Drama: An Anthology*, Ed. G.P. Deshpande, New Delhi: Sahitya Akademi, Reprint, 2004. (All the page references are to this edition.)

• • • • •

13

Kanyasulkam: A Satirical Comedy

Gurajada Venkata Appa Rao Pantulu (1862-1915) was a harbinger of new poetry, the short story and social drama in modern Telugu literature. Along with his lifelong friend Gidugu Venkta Rama Murthy, he propagated the need for harnessing the power inherent in the spoken dialect and put his persuasive arguments into practice through his few but trend setting creative works. "Appa Rao is mainly remembered for his classic *Kanyasulkam* (*Bride Price*: performed 1892, published 1897), a timeless play that not only reflects the Telugu character but his own personality. He made fun of people's shortcomings and eccentricities but hailed the human spirit found in the lowest strata. He appreciated Kandakuri Veereshlingam's attempts to correct social ills, acknowledging his indebtedness to Kandakuri's *Brahma Vivaham* (*Brahman Marriage*). However, he found Kandakuri's work bordering on comedy of manners, whereas *Kanyasulkam*, on the same subject, is a full-fledged comedy with a complex plot."[1] Appa Rao started two other plays that remained unfinished. *Kondubhattiyum* (*Kondubhatta's Tale*) extends *Kanyasulkam*, discussing broader ethical issues. *Bilhaniyam* (*Bilhana's Tale*) has a mythological plot that he ridiculed as irrelevant but, as he himself indicated, he composed it to show that even such drama could be written in the spoken dialect.

Gurajada Appa Rao was an Epigraphist to the Maharaja of Vizianagaram, H.H. Ananda Gajapathi Raju and enjoyed the special favour of the royal household and frequented the Durbar of the Maharajah. He was deeply influenced by the progressive ideologies of his employer. Ananda Gajapathi Raju, who has a special place in the colonial administration of the time, used his influence with the government to bring in social reforms, especially concerning the amelioration of women. As a member of the Madras Legislative Council he proposed the Kanyasulkam Bill—"a Bill to discontinue the sordid practice of selling girls in marriages among the Brahmins under the guise of religion"[2] (Sharma and Prasad, 799). But the colonial government cautiously ignored it because of their unwillingness to interfere with the private matters of the natives. Ananda Gajapathi's proposal was referred to a council of experts and promptly dropped.

But the Maharaja was not discouraged by the political decision of the colonial government. On the contrary, he successfully consolidated public opinion in favour of his cause. Gurajada Appa Rao, who believed in the nobility of his master's cause, wrote *Kanyasulkam* to extend his patron's movement for social reform and dedicated it to him. Since his purpose was to reach out to the masses, he chose the colloquial Telugu idiom as a medium accessible to the common people. Until then he had written his poems only in English. He successfully proved that colloquial Telugu was not unsuitable to drama. He was a revolutionary in the sense that he gave up both Sanskrit and English and undertook to write in Telugu because of his strong conviction. "I view the Telugu literary dialect as a great disability imposed by tradition upon the Telugus. Let those who love letters, venerate it. My own vernacular for me, the living Telugu, the Italian of the East in which none of us is ashamed to express our joys and sorrows, but which some of us are ashamed to write well. Literature in the vernacular will knock at the door of the peasant and it will knock at the door of the Englishman in India. Its possibilities are immense."[3]

Kanyasulkam (*Bride Price*) happens to be a big and robust comedy written more than a hundred years ago (1897) by Gurajada Appa Rao. The dramatist has tried his best to hold mirror to the contemporary nineteenth-century Telugu society (in South India) and to expose the social evils like child marriage, widow marriage, bride price, prostitution, and English education thereby curing them. In the process of exposing these events, the dramatist has also critiqued so many other aspects of the Telugu society, the details of which are discussed in the later part of this article.

Gurajada Appa Rao is a master comedian, who has a clear vision of what he wants to expose and satirize in his play and who has an in-depth insider's knowledge of Hindu, especially brahmanical society of Telugu area (the present Andhra Pradesh). Perhaps in the whole of modern Indian languages there is no comedian, who can be compared to Gurajada Appa Rao in the robust comic sense and knowledge of contemporary society. Perhaps the only other dramatist, who may be compared with Gurajada Appa Rao in quality if not in quantity, is T.P. Kailasam, the Kannada comedian from Karnataka. It is said by many foreigners that Indian writers generally lack a sense of humour and hence have not produced memorable comedies. The truth of this observation cannot be denied. Indians are known for their serious temperament accentuated further by the survivalist problems. They, therefore, tend to write tragic or melodramatic or sentimental works. Viewed from this perspective Gurajada Appa Rao occupies a very significant position in the Indian dramatic literature. One is easily reminded of Ben Jonson and Christopher Marlow (to some extent) as far as their comic sensibility is concerned.

Though *Kanyasulkam* has been a very popular play in Telugu and performed in that area regularly for the last hundred years or so, it was not known to non-Telugu Indians (let alone foreigners) because of the absence of its translation in English by a big publisher. But now luckily this play has been made available in English translation by C. Vijayasree and T. Vijayakumar. These translators have to be congratulated for liberating the text from the local Telugu boundary and introducing it into the global realm of English letters. Although Gurajada Appa Rao has written about the Telugu social problems, his play easily achieves the universal appeal. That is why it can be enjoyed and appreciated by non-Telugu readers and spectators also. "*Kanyasulkam* enjoys several distinctions; it was the first social play in Telugu, the first full length play in prose, the first to employ colloquial Telugu, and the first to use 'local' actors. But for Telugu readers, *Kanyasulkam* is not an archival document—words and phrases from the play have now become part of their language, and characters and their mannerisms become familiar points of reference" (Foreword, p. xi).

"*Kanyasulkam* offers a picture of Telugu society in the later nineteenth century—the twilight period between the certain collapse of an old cultural order and the uncertain emergence of a new one" (Afterword, p. 266). The play is set in different cities or villages of Telugu area like Vizianagaram, Ramachandrapuram and Krishnarayapuram in the latter part of nineteenth century. The characters are drawn from brahmanical as well as non-brahmanical culture. Although brahmanical culture is very strong in the society as well as in the play, there is also a colonial element in it represented by British administration, judicial system, constabulary system, and educational system. Both brahmanical culture and anglicized culture are critiqued and exposed from each other's point of view.

The central thematic concern of the play is the widow-marriage with its own advantages and disadvantages. Obviously, widow marriage and child marriage are among the greatest evils of the Hindu society. The Indian social reformers like Raja Ram Mohan Roy and the Arya Samajists in Bengal tried to remove such evil practices and tried to reform the Indian society by suggesting practical solutions to such problems. Likewise the British Government also tried to reform the Indian society by introducing new laws banning child marriages, bride price and recommending widow-remarriages. It is this socio-cultural background, which is presented in the play. There is thus a conflict in the play between traditional Brahmins and the progressive people represented by two sets of characters.

In the depiction of some characters, Gurajada Appa Rao easily resembles Ben Jonson. For example, the two characters like Girisam and Venkatesam, though representing the teacher-disciple or *guru-shishya* relationship of the Indian mode, it also corresponds to the knave and gull relationship so common in Elizabethan comedy, especially in Jonsonian comedy.

When the play opens, Girisam enters and gives a hint about his typical nature and specific problems. For example, he is a young man suffering from biological urges, who has been visiting dancing girls or prostitutes. He has stolen some money from the boarding house woman and spent it on dancing girls. He has also written a love letter to a married lady. He is very garrulous, boasting about himself and showing off his so-called English learning. The following part of the dialogue amply testifies to his profligate nature:

> It is evening now. I took twenty rupees a month ago from the boarding house woman promising to buy her groceries from the fair and spent it on dancing girls. The boarding house woman and I had a big fight this morning. I got so angry that I could have broken her head. But as Poor Richard said, you cannot go on in the world without patience. Has she not kept quiet many times in the past, when I filched money from her like this? Now she seems to have got wind of the dancing girls. Some jealous idiot must have carried tales to her. Going by this morning's episode, it doesn't look like she will feed me any longer. My tricks don't seem to work any more in this town. There are debts all around. One of these days for writing a love letter to the daughter-in-law of Venku family, they will give me a good thrashing. (p. 3)

Girisam, who is a first-class knave, easily succeeds in trapping a perfect gull Venkatesam, a dull student and son of Venkamma and Agnihotravadhanlu. As Girisam wants to escape from Vijayanagarm, he wants to go to Venkatesam's place, i.e. Krishnarayapuram *agraharam* with the pretext of teaching him in the vacation. As Venkatesam has failed in his examination, he is afraid of facing his parents. But Girisam wants to save Venkatesam from the wrath of his parents by his beautiful lies and false promises. When Venkatesam complains that he has learnt nothing useful except smoking and gossiping, Girisam defends himself and gives him a new plan:

> Then listen to my plan. I'll also come with you to your village and tell your people that you have passed your exam. You tell them that I have come to teach you. At

> the end of the holidays, I'll admit you in the higher class in the town school. (p. 5)

He, then, gives his disciple a list of books to be purchased for his education. He makes tall promises to him, "If you listen to me and do what I say, I will make you as great a man as Surendranath Bannerjee. But don't let even a bird know of my coming with you" (p. 6).

Before leaving for Venkatesam's place, Girisam meets his keep, Madhuravani for the last time and feels embarrassed by the unexpected arrival of the boarding house woman there and therefore cleverly escapes from there.

When Girisam goes to Krishnarayapuram agraharam along with Venkatesam, Agnihotravadhanlu asks his son, "You idiot, have you cleared the exams this time at least?" (p. 18). Girisam replies, "He has passed, sir, in first class. I have taken great pains to coach him" (p. 18). As the play realistically depicts the nineteenth-colonial Indian society, we may easily see a sort of cultural war between traditional brahmanical Sanskrit learning and English learning. Agnihotravadhanlu, who is a scholar in Sanskrit, does not have any respect for English learning. But Venkamma, the mother of Venkatesam, is keen on giving English education to her son. Like in the twenty-first century, even in the nineteenth-century India, English was the language of both fashion and power. Banking on her craze for English, Girisam makes tall promises, "...if you leave your boy under my care for just three years, I will see to it that he will pass the exam in criminal law and become a police man" (p. 19). Venkamma requests Girisam, "Will you please converse once with our boy in English, babu? I wish to listen to that" (p. 22). Then Girisam bamboozles them by reciting the nursery rhyme, "twinkle twinkle, little star/ How I wonder what you are!" (p. 22). Girisam, who represents English language and anglicized Indian culture, delights in highlighting the usefulness of English learning, "In white man's school, they don't pay much attention to Telugu poetry. They bombard the students all the time with geography, arithmetic, algebra, mathematics" (p. 23). By contrast, he plays down the importance of Sanskrit learning. When Mahesam reads a line from Kalidasa's *Kumarasambhavam*, Girisam tries to point out the utter uselessness of the sentence, "I vaguely remember having read this. It means the deer are running, doesn't it? Is it such a great thing for a poet to talk about? Who cares whether the deer run or don't. Don't the dogs run? Don't foxes run? What about cats? Not one useful word in this book. What does Kalidasa know about comparing figures or calculating interest rates? There lies the genius of the white man. Ask Girisamgaru which town is situated where, or which mountain is located where, and he will tell you in a jiffy" (p. 28). The contrast between the so-called uselessness of Sanskrit learning and the usefulness of English learning continues throughout the play.

Girisam, who considers himself a social reformer, pleads for widow-marriages and abolition of child marriages and bride-price. When he goes to Venkatesam's house, it is a pleasant surprise for him to find a beautiful young widow, i.e. Butchamma there. He, who has been teaching his disciple about the enormous importance of widow-marriage, finds a golden opportunity to convert his theory into practice. As Venkatesam introduces his sister, Butchamma to Girisam, he feels quite elated.

> To have one's hair uncared for means widowhood. Oil or geeyil—forget it. I've been lecturing to you on widow marriage all along, but you never mentioned this story at all? So, there is an unfortunate beautiful young widow in your own house. What a pity! My heart melts. If I were her father, I would have arranged widow marriage for this girl and earned eternal fame (*To himself*). What a beauty! Never seen such grace anywhere. I thought I might get bored in this village, but it's my good fortune that I found a chance for a big campaign here also! (p. 27)

Girisam gets a chance to realize his mission of widow-marriage here. Likewise he also has another chance of fighting against the marriage between young girls and old men, especially widowers for the sake of relatively higher bride price that the parents can earn from their prospective sons-in-law. For example, Venkatesam has another, younger sister Subbamma. His father, Agnihotravadhanlu intends to give her in marriage to a middle-aged man, Lubdhavadhanlu, who is past fifty and a widower with a widowed daughter, Meenakshi, with the sole intention of getting the high bride price of ₹ 1800. Agnihotravadhanlu, who strongly believes in the patriarchal system, wants to sell his daughter to Lubdhavadhanlu. He says,

> He is a lakhiere. He has offered to pay eighteen hundred rupees for my daughter Subbi. He will bear all expenses and arrange a grand wedding. All that we have to do is to take our girl to their house and perform the marriage. We will have no hassles. I shall use those eighteen hundred for Venkudu's marriage. (p. 24)

In the traditional Hindu society, the young girls have no freedom of choosing their husbands, as their identity is suppressed by the family concerns. It is the father, who decides the fate of his daughters. Many times marriages become basically economic arrangements rather than psychological or spiritual alignments. Young girls are commodified as it were in the marriage market. Agnihotravadhanlu is an excellent example of the patriarchal Hindu society. He takes a high-handed decision to arrange Subbi's marriage with an aged man. He does not want to consult his wife Venkamma in this case. He declares arrogantly, "Deliberation with wretched females? If I don't finalize this alliance, I will change my name and caste" (p. 25). Girisam tries to convince Agnihotravadhanlu that *kanyasulkam* or bride price is an evil practice tantamount to selling the girls. But he turns a deaf ear to Girisam's advice.

But Venkamma, who is concerned about the happiness of her daughter Subbamma, does not approve of the marriage decided by her husband. For her marital happiness is more important than the bride price. She, therefore, requests her brother Karataka Sastrulu to avoid the marriage somehow or the other, "Brother, if he finalizes this alliance for my girl, I will jump into a well. The elder girl is a burden on us, as it is. This man has grown in years and not in sense. He has brought this miserable alliance for the younger one to wreck her life. If you don't want to see me dead, do something to abort this match" (p. 25). Girisam opines that it is inhuman to marry a young girl to an old man for the sake of money (p. 25) and promises that "I will bring a change of heart in him" (p. 25). Venkamma implores Girisam, "Babu! If the bridegroom is your cousin, try and change *his* mind. I will fall at your feet. I shall get *chappals* stitched for you with my skin" (p. 25). Thus, both Girisam and Karataka Sastrulu try to avoid the marriage of Subbi with the middle-aged Lubdhavadhanlu.

After some deliberation Karataka Sastrulu hits upon a clever plan of avoiding Subbi's marriage. He asks his disciple Mahesam to impersonate a bride for ten days, "Yes, this particular problem can be solved only by you and no one else. You must become a girl for ten days.... You don't need any jewellery. If your hair is done up properly and you are dressed in a sari, you will look a virgin of twelve. I will then take you along and get you married to Lubdhavadhanlu. You conduct yourself tactfully in his house for a couple of days, and then you throw away your make-up and take to heels" (p. 30). He promises Mahesam, "If you come through the ordeal successfully, I will give you my daughter in marriage and keep you with us" (p. 31). By resorting to this clever trick Karataka Sastrulu can help his sister Venkamma a sense of satisfaction and prevent her from jumping into the well and avoid the tragic marriage of young Subbi with the aged widower, Lubdhavadhanlu. But he keeps Agnihotravadhanlu in the dark about his entire plan.

On the other hand, Ramappantulu, the *niyogi* and current lover of Madhuravani, has been encouraging Lubdhavadhanlu to go in for the second marriage. Knowing fully well the miserly nature of Lubdhavadhanlu, he wants to bank on it and goad the miserly fellow to get married for the second time with the intention of growing more prosperous by the support of the second wife's stars as promised in her horoscope. As Ramappantulu explains his intriguing plan of fooling Lubdhavadhanlu to Madhuravani, "Lubdhavadhanlu is a damn miser...I tempted him with the belief that he will come into a lot of money through marriage.... You know what our *siddhanti* did after some cajoling? He took a good look at Lubdhavadhanlu's horoscope and declared that a second marriage is on the cards for him very soon. And that wealth will accrue through marriage. With that, the old man began to waver between the greed for money and the reluctance to spend on marriage. Meanwhile the panda-guru arrived, and I managed him also. When Lubdhavadhanlu showed him the horoscope to clear his doubt, what did the panda say? He said, 'there are strong indications of marriage and wealth. But you are an elderly person, who will give you their girl in marriage? How will the marriage come about? These are great but impossible boons. If they figure in the horoscopes, they cause more harm than good. That is, either death or loss of wealth will occur to you. So appease the planets and feed the Brahmins generously. Your luck will end with some minor indisposition. Find and auspicious day and start sun-worship.' Avadhanlu's heart sank at this and he began looking for alliances. This is the story" (p. 43). Although Madhuravani requests Ramappantulu to stop this marriage he tries to silence her with his promise that "I'll arrange for your performance in this marriage and get you some money, keep quiet" (p. 45). She, therefore, remains silent for the time being.

Karataka Sastrulu has already started executing his plan of avoiding Subbi's marriage with Lubdhavadhanlu and arranging a fake marriage for him with a dummy bride (i.e. Mahesam in disguise). He, therefore, takes the bride (Mahesam) to Madhuravani's house and seeks her help. He tells her his plan, "I'll wash off this false mustache and cropped beard and go my way. Leaving this saree with you, my disciple will go his way. After that, like other women in the neighbourhood, you also express your wonder at what has happened. Recommend this plan to your Pantulu and work out a fool-proof way of executing it" (p. 52). Madhuravani opines that the task cannot be done by Pantulu alone. On the contrary, she suggests a plan of involving Meenakshi and Siddhanti to cheat Lubdhavadhanlu in a systematic manner. She tells Karataka Sastrulu, "After you talk to our Pantulu, go and meet Avadhanlu's daughter, my good friend, Meenakshi without the knowledge of her father and offer her two sovereigns. After that, meet the Siddhanti and make him a similar offer. In this plan, Siddhanti is the key person. I'll give my support from behind the screen, according to the situation" (p. 52). Karataka Sastrulu agrees with her plan and promises to pay some money to her by way of remuneration. But she expresses her nobility of character in spite of being a prostitute, "I am disappointed that you even mentioned it. Because I'm a prostitute by profession, I make money where I have to. But you thought Madhuravani has no kindness at all? When your own sister's life is in trouble, will I aspire for money? But let's tell the Head Conishteebu some truth; whatever happens, he'll save us. He will come here now, and I'll speak with him, you wait here" (p. 53). Because she is a prostitute, she has her customers from all walks of life, who can oblige her due to her charisma and sexual power. She, therefore, marshals all her energy in roping in the services of her customers in trapping Lubdhavadhanlu into a fake marriage.

After having persuaded Madhuravani to extend her help in arranging a fake marriage of Lubdhavadhanlu with a dummy bride, Karataka Sastrulu wants to make use of *niyogi* Ramappantulu's services. He knows that Ramappantulu is a very practical administrator in the area and knows how to achieve worldly success. Besides, Ramappantulu is a close friend of Lubdhavadhanlu. Karataka Sastrulu wants to capitalize on this friendship between the two and requests for his help in the matter. He explains his motives to Ramappantulu as follows, "I'm heavily in debt. If I don't redeem a bond by next full-moon, I'll lose my petition. After it was decided to sell this girl to Venkata Dikshitalu of Nallabilli for sixteen hundred, when we actually arrived, they said they can give the money only a month after the marriage and not now. That's why I gave up that alliance, and hearing that Lubdhavadhanlu is making marriage trials, I came to see you. If you can arrange this, I'll submit ten gold coins" (p. 57).

Ramappantulu wants to facilitate the fake marriage by forging a horoscope with the help of the siddhanti. He tells Karataka Sastrulu, "To forge a new horoscope is a five minute job. Long live our siddhanti! I've an attic full of old Palmyra leaves and pens. I've thirty-year old paper and a variety of inks. Pay me a hundred as my fee and bear the expenses. I'll run the show" (p. 59). After some negotiation, Karataka Sastrulu agrees to pay one-fifth portion of the bride-price to Ramappantulu as his fee (or bribe). Then Ramappantulu examines the bride's (i.e. Mahesam in disguise) left palm and appreciates the wealth line.

Ramappantulu has persuaded Lubdhavadhanlu to go in for a marriage with a cheaper bride-price than the earlier one. But

Girisam, who is ignorant of the new alliance, has been trying his best to avoid Subbi's (i.e. Agnihotravadhanlu's daughter) marriage with Lubdhavadhanlu. He has, therefore, written a letter to Lubdhavadhanlu apparently praising him but ironically denigrating him and frightening him about Agnihotravadhanlu's avarice and short temper. The letter is very interesting and reads as follows:

> Your servant and your dearest brother Girisam offers obeisance to you and submits the following. I heard that you have decided to remarry in your ripe old age and my heart is filled with boundless joy.... That your prospective wife is my dear student Venkateswarulu's sister fills me with great pleasure. I am taking care of the wedding arrangements at Agnihotravadhanlu's place. He looks after me like his own son. He certainly is a very noble man. But just as the moon has its dark spots too he has his own drawbacks—avarice and short temper.
>
> Note—If you manage to avoid him when he is in that fit of temper you will keep your bones intact, and your life safe. Therefore, there is nothing to worry about his temper. Now for his greed. Let me tell you it helps neither of you. Some mischievous fellow from your village informed him that you are very affluent and would arrange for a grand style wedding with a lot of fanfare. On hearing this Avadhanlugaru is arranging to transport the whole of his village in fifty carts to your place. In addition, he is also borrowing an elephant, three camels and five horses from the Diwanjee saheb for this occasion. He will also bring a golden palanquin to add to grandeur of the procession.
>
> It would be a feast to my eyes to see you so in this magnificent marriage procession seated in the palanquin, but as one close to you, I am worried about the wasteful expense involved. "The bull's wound offers a feast to a crow," as the saying goes. The expense is yours, what does Ramappantulu lose?...
>
> There's an important secret in this. This Ramappantulu is a jackal in trickery and a big ass in intelligence...Jackal in English means a cunning fox. (p. 95)

When Ramappantulu himself reads this letter shown to him by Lubdhavadhanlu, he feels deeply insulted and angry. Lubdhavadhanlu is so upset by the letter that he wants to file a defamation case against Girisam. However, Ramappantulu continues to read the letter, which contains more damaging statements about Subbi:

> P.S.—the young one is no doubt a pretty maiden but shows signs of balding on account of dandruff. Elders consider that a sign of impending widowhood. This is simply supe... super...sti...tion, i.e. stupid belief. Cultured men like us need not take it into reckoning.
>
> Note One: There's a home remedy for this. If you pull out the affected hair and apply powder...that is medicinal ointment...dandruff may be cured. However, in the meantime, by god's grace, if she becomes a widow, she will have to get her head shaved regularly and dandruff will no longer bother her.
>
> Note Two: If my sister-in-law decides to keep her hair even after widowhood, neither you nor I can do anything about it....
>
> Note Three: As you are aware, widow marriage is a big issue these days. When you are in heaven enjoying the celestial bliss, she may think of remarriage. You may kindly note that I cannot stop her, and do you know why? Suppose, she turns round and asks me: "Your brother is enjoying great pleasures in heaven in the company of Rambha, what about me?" I will have no answer to give her.
>
> Note Four: All the remaining factors are very much favourable. You must certainly accept this alliance. Your mother-in-law is a gem of a lady, like Arundhati herself. But between you and me, I must confess to you that she does not approve of this alliance at all. She has been telling her neighbours that she would commit suicide by jumping into the well in your compound at the time of wedding. Never mind. We shall tie up her hands and legs for those couple of minutes until you tie the wedding knot. Let her

> jump into the well after the wedding is over, who cares? To avoid trouble from the police we will have to bribe them, of course. I hope you appreciate that I have written all this to you, only in your own interest. Please don't let anyone here know about it. There's another thing that I forgot to mention: the girl's horoscope I believe is flawless. That is also manipulated by Rama.... (pp. 99-100)

Lubdhavadhanlu is extremely hurt and shocked by the contents of Girisam's letter. He begins to suspect a rat in it. He tells Ramappantulu, "There might be some truth in all this. Polisetty said that, the mother-in-law is against this alliance. I don't want this alliance, under any circumstances.... That's all" (p. 100).

By that time the postman comes and delivers another letter from Agnihotravadhanlu addressed to Lubdhavadhanlu. Ramappantulu reads the letter and tells him the contents of the letter that "He doesn't want your alliance at all" (p. 101), that "Someone has told him that you are a miser" (p. 101) and that "you are old and suffer from tuberculosis" (p. 102). After experiencing this kind of insult Lubdhavadhanlu decides to cancel the marriage and file a suit against Agnihotravadhanlu.

But the clever Ramappantulu advises Lubdhavadhanlu to go in for another alliance, for keeping the family line alive. "If you marry and raise a family, your house will grow into ten houses. If you die without a spouse or an offspring, who will inherit all this hard earned money?" (p. 107) Besides the importance of inheritance there will be other practical advantages also resulting from this marriage, according to Ramappantulu. He advises him, "Try for another alliance, and get married. Your wife's presence will be a check on Meenakshi's moves. Meenakshi's presence in turn will keep your wife under check. Am I right or not?" (p. 107). Then he threatens him further, "Have you forgotten that as per your horoscope you will not live long unless you remarry?" (p. 108). He suggests that there is a Brahmin from Guntur, who has been looking for an alliance for his daughter and that Lubdhavadhanlu should go in for that match. "If we finalize that match, it will be a slap in the face for Agnihotravadhanlu" (p. 108).

Ramappantulu further tempts Lubdhavadhanlu that the Brahmin from Guntur would be able to sell his daughter for only ₹ 1200, as he is in a hurry to solve his financial problem. Then he describes the bride's buxom beauty, signs of prosperity on her face and wealth line on her palms. Thus, Ramappantulu persuades Lubdhavadhanlu to accept the new alliance, whereas Madhuravani is, obviously, buffeted between the opposite pressures.

Ramappantulu promises that "I shall get Madhuravani's necklace, give it to the bride on the occasion and take it back" (p. 113), and suggests that they should finish off the wedding with minimum expenses.

Later Lubdhavadhanlu tells his would be father-in-law to go in for one-day wedding unlike the earlier three-day wedding. In turn Karataka Sastrulu tells his prospective son-in-law to keep the wedding a secret, "Till you tie the sacred thread around the bride's neck, don't mention anything to anyone" (p. 114). Lubdhavadhanlu agrees to it rather unwillingly.

A little later Karataka Sastrulu pretends to be sad of parting from his daughter and requests Meenakshi, daughter of Lubdhavadhanlu to take care of her new stepmother. "Parental bond, amma! That's why I am telling you again and again. From today, you are her mother and father as well. (*Feigns sadness*) (p. 115). He asks her to collect a gold coin from her new mother, "Amma, I have given a gold coin to my daughter to be passed on to you. Please take it" (p. 115).

While everybody is under the impression that the wedding is to be celebrated four hours after sunrise, Siddhanti shocks a surprises them cleverly that the wedding has to be celebrated four hours before sunrise. Since the Hindus set great store by the astrologers, they cannot oppose his commands.

Ramappantulu manages to show the bride (i.e. Mahesam in disguise) to Lubdhavadhanlu. Then he utilizes the services of Siddhanti to impress the gullible groom further. In the Indian context people have a lot of faith in astrological predictions. Siddhanti, who is secretly bribed and forced by Ramappantulu, offers a very impressive prediction about the marriage. He says,

> If you are thinking of marriage, I assure you, you won't find a girl with better prospects. Look at this fate line, this wealth line! Pantulu, order a couple of trunks right away to store the wealth you are going to get on account of her good luck. Turn you palm...Children—one, two, three.... (p. 112)

Ramappantulu persuades Lubdhavadhanlu to fix the *muhurtam* at the earliest, because they say *subhasya sighram*. By then Karataka Sastrulu comes there. On Lubdhavadhanlu's request, Ramappantulu negotiates with Karataka Sastrulu and conveys the result to Lubdhavadhanlu, "I got him to agree to twelve hundred. But he insists that we give the girl some gold ornament. What do you say?" (p. 113). Lubdhavadhanlu agrees for the payment of ₹ 1200, but expresses his inability to give the gold ornament. But Siddhanti forces Meenakshi to give the bride a sacred bath. When Lubdhavadhanlu worries about the possibility of Ramappantulu's late arrival, Siddhanti snubs and silences him, "Who's getting married, you or Pantulu? Take bath without any further ado" (p. 117).

The unexpected advancement of the wedding from four hours after sunrise to four hours before it creates many problems for the people concerned, especially Ramappantulu, who has been fooling Lubdhavadhanlu systematically. When Ramappantulu comes to the wedding according to the earlier announcement, Lubdhavadhanlu apologizes to him, "I feel sorry that you missed our wedding *muhurtam*.... The siddhanti looked at the planetary positions, calculated the time and got the ritual performed exactly at the time of the *muhurat*" (p. 117). After listening to the details, Ramappantulu feels that Siddhanti has duped him. He learns from the priest that Madhuravani refused to sing at the odd hour of the wedding. "And Madhuravani? She stood there stunned like a gold statue in the pandal. The entire Brahmin lot pleaded with her, but she wouldn't sing" (p. 118). Ramappantulu is surprised to learn that the wedding is not a five-day affair, but a one-night affair and that Guntur Sastrulu has already left for his place after collecting the bride price of ₹ 1200 from Lubdhavadhanlu. Ramappantulu is so angry with

Guntur Sastrulu that he wants to call a couple of policemen and ask them to chase him.

Ramappantulu wants to clarify some of his doubts. He asks Kondibhatlu whether Madhuravani performed her musical recital in the wedding or not and whether she was chatting with some men. Kondibhatlu answers that she did not sing in the wedding, but chatted with men like Bhukthagaru, Siddhanti and Head Conishteebu, etc.

Lubdhavadhanlu has been systematically cheated by Ramappantulu. But after the marriage, Lubdhavadhanlu begins to suffer from some delusion and brahmanical superstition. He thinks that his wife Subbi's first husband has become a ghost and is trying to kill him. He screams, "Asiri! Asiri! Asiri! He has killed me! *Ramanama tarakam, Ramanama tarakam, Ramanama tarakam.* She is definitely a second-marriage slut. Her husband has become a ghost, and will strangle me to death. What's the way out?" (p. 140). He considers himself as a fool to have married a widow-whore and fears that he may not remain alive. He curses her father, "Useless father, worthless father! Son of an ass! Tying a second-marriage slut to my neck, he has destroyed me completely. I won't live any more, I won't" (p. 141). Although his daughter Meenakshi tries to reason with him, he does not listen to her, but persists in his superstitious belief. "That slut's first husband! Just before you came, as he climbed on to my chest and squeezed my neck, I thought life had gone out of me" (p. 143). Lubdhavadhanlu thinks that the ghost said, "Fool, you married my wife. I'll kill you" (p. 143) and that it looked exactly like Girisam. Lubdhavadhanlu is in a dilemma as to what to do. "Should I read a chapter from the Veda, or chant the Gayatri? These ghosts care a feather for Vedas and mantras. I could use demonic rites, but they may boomerang. That's another worry. What's the way out? *Ramanama Tarakam*.... If this slut remains in this house, I won't live. *Ramanama Tarakam*.... Where is the rosary?" (p. 144). He then squats on the floor and asks his daughter Meenakshi to enquire his 'new' wife Subbi if her late husband appears to her in her dream. Meanwhile he curses Ramappantulu, "Ayyo, ayyo! May Ramappantulu's house turn into a graveyard! How he duped me into this bogus marriage!

Let cats be fed at his funeral! What does the widow's husband look like?" (p. 144). Meenakshi falsely confirms that "He appears to her every day, it seems. Apparently a mustache and long hair. And is dark skinned" (p. 145). Lubdhavadhanlu wants to keep the *Bhagavatam* under his pillow when he goes to sleep.

Meanwhile there happens some misunderstanding between Meenakshi and her new mother (i.e. Mahesam in disguise). Meenakshi has given the gold coin sent to her by Karataka Sastrulu to her mother to be kept in Meenakshi's trunk. The 'mother' has kept it in the trunk but lost the key. Angered by this Meenakshi pulls the arms of the mother and pinches her cheeks. But the 'mother' bites Meenakshi's hand and runs away. Meenakshi, therefore, wants to mash her brains.

Now both Lubdhavadhanlu and Meenakshi dislike the bride for different reasons. So Lubdhavadhanlu takes the final decision, "Now my nagging doubt is cleared. Either her husband's ghost will kill me by throttling my neck, or this woman will bite me to death. Death is inevitable in the hands of one of them. And I spent so much to buy this fatal marriage! Ayyo, Ayyo! If I can drive the bride away, I can get rid of that ghost" (p. 146). He thinks for a while and decides to send her away to Ramappantulu, "After all, it is Ramappantulu, who tied this whore to my neck. I'll send her back to him.... Along with that saani, he can keep this girl also as a mistress. I'll even make an offering of ten rupees to him" (p. 147). But he and his daughter are surprised to discover that the bride is absconding. The absence of the bride creates another crisis for Lubdhavadhanlu.

The bride (Mahesam in disguise) goes straight to Madhuravani's house and places the necklace on her neck. Madhuravani is happily surprised by the re-possession of her necklace and thanks him with a kiss. She then assigns a new role to Mahesam of being a mendicant for some time. Although she has recovered her necklace stealthily from Mahesam, she does not allow Ramappantulu to step into the house until and unless he returns her necklace, which she had lent him. Thus, she mischievously makes Ramappantulu also helpless.

Now Lubdhavadhanlu has to worry about another problem, i.e. the absence of his new bride Subbi. He thinks about the pros and cons of her absence. He also realizes his folly of marrying a young girl with dubious credentials. In a way he wants to repent for his folly by going to Kasi to have a dip in the Ganga.

> (*Walking up and down*) If she is not found anywhere, what could have happened to her? Has she jumped into the well? If she has, the police will loot my house. If she hasn't, then where has she disappeared? She may have gone to Ramappantulu's house. That must be it.... She was such a beautiful girl! It is my misfortune that I lost her. How soon the moonlight has turned into darkness! I was happy that she would come of age soon. Perhaps, she has matured already. Why doubt that? How could such a big girl have not matured? Wonder how many such marriages she has gone through and how many husbands she has seen the end of. Your rotten corpse! What happened to your eyes? How did you marry a matured slut with your eyes wide open? There is no salvation for you. You have joined the ranks of those, who married widow-sluts in Rajamahendravaram. Ayyo! Ayyo! There is no penance for this sin. If I want some remedial rituals to be done, the Sankaracarya will demand an offering, and the brahmins will eat away all my property. The police people are better. If I quietly put twenty-five rupees in the Head's hand and leave for Kasi tomorrow night, and take a dip in the Ganga there, all my sins will get washed away. Yes, I'll set out for Kasi. God has made me learn a lesson. Otherwise, why this fatal desire for a second marriage in this old age? This Ramappantulu has destroyed me in every way. (p. 158)

Lubdhavadhanlu is very angry with Ramappantulu for having trapped him into this dubious marriage. When Ramappantulu demands the necklace that he has presented to Lubdhavadhanlu's bride, Lubdhavadhanlu denies having presented it. He angrily charges Ramappantulu of having deceived him, "The marriage was a conspiracy you and that Guntur Sastrulu hatched together. Now I know the truth. That slut must have gone to your house. Along with Madhuravani, keep her also as a mistress. Don't bother me. I beg of you" (p. 159).

Now both Lubdhavadhanlu and Ramappantulu are shocked to learn that the bride is missing. Meenakshi reports that her stepmother has thrown the book into the well before absconding. Then Gavaraiah brings a bottle and tells that the bride is a kamini ghost and that he has put her along with her former husband into the bottle. Naturally, Lubdhavadhanlu and Ramappantulu are scared by it. Gavaraiah has played a trick on them successfully. Now Lubdhavadhanlu is utterly confused. But Ramappantulu's practical sense makes him cast aspersions on Lubdhavadhanlu's character. He accuses Lubdhavadhanlu, "Gavaraiah said your wife has become a ghost! You and your daughter perhaps killed her" (p. 162).

Then Lubdhavadhanlu gets into another problem. Apart from the sorrow of losing his new (i.e. second wife), he has to face some serious legal problems. For example, Ramappantulu is worried about the necklace that he has borrowed from Madhuravani and lent it to the new wife of Lubdhavadhanlu. He, therefore, complains to the Head Constable, "The wench that Lubdhavadhanlu married ran away with Madhuravani's necklace" (p. 172). He gives some advice to the Head Constable as to how to tackle him, "If you threaten him with a murder case, he will give back my necklace, and in the process your palm will be greased" (p. 173). But the Head Constable is not willing to threaten Lubdhavadhanlu with a murder case unnecessarily. Instead he advises Ramappantulu to get back to Lubdhavadhanlu and pressurize him to return the necklace. Ramappantulu does not know what exactly has happened to the necklace. After a lot of cogitation he meets Meenakshi, daughter of Lubdhavadhanlu (by his first wife) and kisses her and expresses his desire to marry her. He learns from Meenakshi that his keep (Madhuravani) is not loyal to him. He cleverly asks Meenakshi about the necklace. She replies that her stepmother (Subbi) has kept it in the trunk but misplaced the keys. When Ramappantulu embraces Meenakshi in the dark, he is seen by Lubdhavadhanlu, who strikes him on the legs with a stick. In his fit of anger, Lubdhavadhanlu drives his daughter out of home. Now Meenakshi, being utterly helpless, suggests to Ramappantulu that they may elope and get married. But Ramappantulu is too clever to agree to that. He avoids Meenakshi cleverly and rushes to the tank to complete his morning ablutions. He feels the dilemma acutely and says, "On that side of the door, the saani bitch and on this side the family bitch. Together, they are preventing me from getting in" (p. 188).

Agnihotravadhanlu is completely ignorant about the fake marriage of Lubdhavadhanlu with Subbi (i.e. Mahesam in disguise). According to the original agreement of marriage of his second daughter (and minor girl Subbamma) with Lubdhavadhanlu, he comes to Ramachandrapauram agraharam with two carts of marriage party. He expects to be received ceremonially by his would-be relatives. But he is utterly disappointed and exasperated when Ramappantulu tells him, that "But Lubdhavadhanlu's marriage is already over" (p. 187) and that "It is you, who must be joking, sir. It's ten days since he was married. I heard you had written to him that you were not interested in his match. That is why he paid twelve hundred rupees and married the daughter of some Sastrulu from Guntur" (p. 190). Now Agnihotravadhanlu grows so exasperated that he bursts out, "Ayyo! Ayyo! What courage. Come let's go and break the bones of that donkey's son" (p. 190). He starts searching for the house of Lubhdavadhanlu. On the way, Mahesam in the guise of a mendicant meets him and teases and irritates him by his lousy and inauspicious song.

Agnihotravadhanlu returns from Lubdhavadhanlu's house and announces, "I have given that son of an ass a sound thrashing. I have brought elephants and horses—for his funeral! He says he won't give me a single paisa even to meet the travel expenses" (p. 193). Besides being shocked by Lubdhavadhanlu's cheating, he feels an acute financial problem. He contemplates to file a suit against Lubdhavadhanlu and claim damages. He requests Ramappantulu for some money, but the latter pleads his inability to lend him the money. On the contrary, Ramappantulu suggests to Agnihotravadhanlu to pawn some ornament to get some money. Agnihotravadhanlu, therefore, sends his wife Venkamma to call Butchamma and bring her ornament.

Now another shock is awaiting Agnihotravadhanlu. He learns to his dismay that Butchamma is not in the cart at all and that she has eloped with Girisam. Venkamma is deeply shocked by her daughter's elopement. He had trusted Girisam as a reliable young man and a good teacher of Venkatesam, but is shocked and hurt by Girisam's behaviour. He tells Ramappantulu, "With your funeral—he eloped with that wretch. My stupid son's English education is responsible for all this" (p. 196). But he has to find a way out of the financial problem. Unable to get his daughter's ornament, Agnihotravadhanlu worries about how to get some money. But persuaded by Ramappantulu to pawn his bracelet to the prostitute (Madhuravani), he offers his bracelet to Ramappantulu to be pawned by him. Agnihotravadhanlu is now cured of his greed for money and his folly of giving his child-daughter to a middle-aged bridegroom. He is taught a good lesson by the circumstances themselves.

Like Agnihotravadhanlu, Lubdhavadhanlu also has learnt a lesson of his life and been suffering the consequences of his greed for money and indifference to the age factor in matrimonial alliances like those of his daughter (Meenakshi) and of his own self. Because of this evil quality of greed he has entered an arena of endless and unexpected troubles. Now he attributes all his problems to the malefic effect of Saturn. His condition is really pitiable. The moment of his repentance is conspicuous:

> What a miserable situation! There can't be anyone in this world more unfortunate than me. I should have left for Kasi as soon as my seven-and-a-half-year Saturn-period commenced. I have done an unwise thing. Well, if my fate is so destined, how could I have escaped it? Saujanyarao Pantulu is god-incarnate. Nature is still kind to us humans only because good people like him still exist. As he said, I shouldn't blame others when the entire fault lies with me. Although I am fairly well off, I sold my only daughter out of greed to an old man. Out of frustration, if she goes astray now, is she to blame? Foolish man that I am, why should I think of marriage in my old age? Why should I believe that Ramappantulu, knowing fully well what a horrible crook he is? Where did that cunning wench disappear? What's all this nuisance about the necklace? Why should that Inspector harass us on a charge of murder? It's the iron age of Kali! Kali is at large. Saujanyarao appears to be the

> only truthful person around. The rest of them—lawyers and police—are all cheats. If Saujanyarao intervenes and saves me from the trouble, I shall go off to Kasi immediately after that. What strange things are happening these days! There are monasteries for widows now, I believe. I have asked my daughter to look up one of them. If she likes it there, I'll give her the required money, she will go and stay there. Otherwise she'll go to Kasi with me. (p. 199)

It is ironical that Lubdhavadhanlu has not only lost his money in the form of bride price and his new wife, but also has to face the charge of murder. Once he gets involved in the criminal case, there is no knowing how far he will go on suffering. Ramappantulu promises to hush up the murder case if Lubdhavadhanlu gives him two thousand rupees. He suggests to the latter to sign a promissory note if he has no ready cash with him. He wants to bribe the Deputy Collector and the Inspector to hush up the case.

Lubdhavadhanlu does not know how to wriggle out of the situation. He, therefore, approaches Lawyer Saujanyarao Pantulu to seek his help. Saujanyarao Pantulu is a man of integrity and high morality. He dismisses the scoundrel Ramappantulu within a few seconds. He seems to be a mouthpiece of the playwright. First of all he begins to doubt the veracity of the man called Guntur Sastrulu. He tells Lubdhavadhanlu, "From the description you have, I sent a profile of the man to a friend of mine in Guntur. But I got the reply that there is no one of that description there" (p. 202). Lubdhavadhanlu promises to leave all his assets at the Lawyer's feet and go off to Kasi. But Saujnayarao advises him properly. His advice seems to come straight from the author's mouth. He says, "I have already told you that I am not interested in your money. If you are convinced of my argument that old men shouldn't marry young girls and that Kanyasulkam is an offence, donate whatever you can to the association in Rajamahendravaram, which fights such social evils. I earnestly advise you to send your daughter to a widow's home" (p. 202). Now there is perfect alignment between Lubdhavadhanlu's repentance and Saujanyarao's advice. He, therefore, confesses,

"As you order, sir. The blunders I have committed have ruined me. I have learnt a lesson, sir" (p. 202).

Lawyer Saujanyarao Pantulu represents the moral order of life. He easily brings Dharmaraja to our minds. Everybody seems to be afraid of him due to his high morality and truthfulness. Lubdhavadhanlu is driven by despair to come under the moral protection of Saujanyarao. It is a well-known truth that evil destroys itself by its very weight. This principle is operative in the play. For example, Karataka Sastrulu, who has played a trick upon Lubdhavadhanlu by arranging a marriage with a fake bride just to cure him of his greed for money, has now realized how his comic trick has landed Lubdhavadhanlu in a criminal case, which is very tragic. He has realized that the situation has gone beyond his control and expectation. He, therefore, relents and wants to restore justice to the poor Lubhdavadhanlu. He tells Mahesam, "I love comedy, but this murder issue has killed my sense of humour. So no jokes now. I am thinking of returning to Lubdhavadhanlu the twelve hundred rupees I have taken from him, anyway I never intended stealing that money. If we could somehow manipulate Madhuravani and borrow her necklace, we can send the ornament and the money together by post to Avadhanlu. Everyone will then see that the murder case is a bogus one. I'll also be spared of the sin of harming a Brahmin" (p. 203). He tells his plan to Madhuravani and wants to borrow her necklace for that purpose. He assures her that she would get her necklace back safely after the problem is solved. He tells her that Saujanyarao Pantulu is making a hectic effort to save Lubdhavadhanlu because of his selfless nature. Madhuravani is so much impressed by Karataka Sastrulu's praise of Saujanyarao Pantulu's goodness that she wants to see him, but Karataka Sastrulu tells, "He doesn't allow saani women into his presence" (p. 208). Finally, Madhuravani lends her necklace to Karataka Sastrulu out of friendship, Karataka Sastrulu wants to use the necklace to help Lubdhavadhanlu to wriggle out of the criminal case.

Just as Saujanyarao Pantulu tries to advise Lubdhavadhanlu against his greed, he advises Agnihotravadhanlu also against giving young girls in marriage to aged men, "If you give away young girls in marriage to aged men, how can they escape widowhood? Please think coolly about the whole thing" (p. 216). When Agnihotravadhanlu tries to defend his action in terms of fate, Saujanyarao Pantulu asks him as to why he has come to him, i.e. lawyer instead of leaving everything to his fate? He reasons with him, "Is selling girls not against our scriptures? Out of sheer avarice, you sell girls to old men and call it fate! Is that fair? Please reply?" (p. 216). Agnihotravadhanlu counter questions the lawyer, "People of your class—aren't they collecting a thousand or two as dowry from the bride's parents? As Girisamgaru, damn that scoundrel, put it, is it not an accepted practice among you to insist that the bride be given a certain amount of gold and silver as per the demands of the bridegroom's family? Is that not a kind of kanyasulkam?" (p. 216). Saujanyarao Pantulu replies honestly, "I don't support that either" (p. 216). Then he advises Agnihotravadhanlu as a well-wisher, "Accept me as your friend, don't consider me an outsider. Please listen to my advice. Find a good boy from a respectable family for your younger daughter. The elder one can join the widow rehabilitation society; they will educate her.... Some property of hers is in your custody, I heard. My friend and secretary of the widow marriage association has sent me a letter asking me to appeal to you to transfer that property to her without any ado" (p. 217). When Agnihotravadhanlu refuses to transfer the daughter's property, Saujanyarao threatens to file a suit against him. On the contrary, he would make Lubdhavadhanlu withdraw his case against Agnihotravadhanlu if the latter agrees to transfer the property of the daughter. Being a hard-boiled traditionalist, Agnihotravadhanlu accuses the lawyer of taking side with the parties. But Saujanyarao Pantulu warns him clearly, "I'll be pleading the case against you on behalf of Lubdhavadhanlu. You will not only lose money and reputation but also face penal action" (p. 218).

The false murder case filed against the old Lubdhavadhanlu has recoiled upon the Head Constable himself. When the veracity of the case is to be proved, the Head Constable runs the risk of being exposed. He, therefore, seeks the spiritual help of a Bairagi, who is said to have come from Kasi. He requests the

Bairagi, "Guruji! The murder case is now on my head. Though there was no case at all, we concocted a story about murder case and implicated that innocent old man to extract some money from him. Then the Tahsildar came and made a lot of noise and extracted some money for himself. Since he didn't get back his necklace, Ramappantulu shot off petitions to the Inspector and the Police Superintendent. Now the Tahsildar and I are being accused of hushing up a real murder case" (p. 222). All of them can wriggle out of the murder case if they can locate the father of the missing girl, Guntur Sastrulu. The Head Constable implores the Bairagi further, "Until my job is done, I shall not leave your feet. If you help me get out of this problem, I will donate one hundred and sixteen rupees to the monastery you are building in Haridwar" (p. 223).

When Agnihoravadhanlu attends the court case filed against him by Lubdhavadhanlu, he disturbs the staff there by his loud talk. The Collector is irritated by the disturbance and asks about who the man is. Then Naidu offers a brief history of Agnihotravadhanlu thereby throwing light on his evil habits like avarice and opportunism, etc. His evil habits are, of course, symptomatic of the larger social evils of Hindu society, "He is a resident of Krishnarayapuram agraharam and is called Nulaka Agnihotravadhanlu. He is a highly (ig)noble Brahmin. A reputed Vedic scholar. He is the one, who had agreed to sell his daughter to Lubdhavadhanlu for eighteen hundred rupees and then flogged his would-have-been son-in-law. That's why Lubdhavadhanlu filed a petition in this Honorable Court. This great man is the accused in that case. For two hundred rupees, he has given his daughter in marriage to a thousand-month-old Brahmin from Mallaram. And the bridegroom died even before the wedding ceremonies could be completed. Later he filed a suit claiming all the property of the diseased on behalf of his widowed daughter" (p. 224).

Agnihotravadhanlu is easily exposed by the Collector when he fails to give the correct year of his daughter's birth. Agnihotravadhanlu mentions the year of his daughter's birth as 'Angirasa', but the Collector knows that it is 'Bhava'. So he animadverts Agnihotravadhanlu rather angrily, "The horoscope says Bhava! You have brought disrepute to the Brahmin caste. Out of greed, you've sold your daughter for a price. On top of it you forge horoscopes too? The fraud and meanness you find among Brahmins is indeed unparalleled" (p. 227). When the Collector glances at the case papers and asks the lawyer about the nature of the case, Bheemrao Pantulu replies, "Yes, Your Honour. Mr. Girisam, engaged as a tutor to coach this gentleman's son, eloped with his widowed daughter taking away her jewellery and other valuables" (p. 225). When the Collector wants to know the address of Girisam, Agnihotravadhanlu pleads his ignorance about it thereby making himself a laughing stock.

Just as Saujanyarao Pantulu advises and threatens Agnihotravadhanlu, he tries to help Lubdhavadhanlu also purely on humanitarian grounds. He, therefore, tries to collect evidence from eye-witnesses. He tells Polisetty, "See, if you give evidence, you can save the man from peril. Otherwise if he is presented, the sin of suppressing the truth will be on your head" (p. 229). Initially, Polisetty is inclined to speak the truth of the case, but later he grows nervous and upset and tells the lawyer to get the evidence from some Brahmins, "These Brahmins, I tell you sir, are real crooks; if you grease their palm a little, they give any evidence you want" (p. 230).

Like Polisetty, Girisam, the Head Constable, and Asiri also refuse to give evidence in the court. When Girisam meets the lawyer, Saujanyarao Pantulu tells him, "There's only one way out. If you can get hold of that Guntur Sastrulu, we'll not require any other evidence" (p. 246). But unfortunately nobody is able to locate Guntur Sastrulu. And without him the murder case on Lubdhavadhanlu cannot be disproved or dismissed. Saujanyarao Pantulu is also helpless without sufficient evidence or witnesses. It is at this juncture that a stranger comes to meet him alone at night without prior permission or intimation. Before telling the lawyer his errand, the stranger engages him in conversation about virtue or vice, widow marriage, anti-nautch question and finally about prostitution. He asks some direct, fundamental and embarrassing questions to the lawyer Saujanyarao Pantulu, "If prostitutes are not invited to perform, what about their livelihood?" (p. 252). Pantulu replies, "They should get married"

(p. 252). Then the stranger counter-questions him, "In that case how will prostitutes, who want to marry, find eligible grooms, sir? Or do you suppose any groom is good enough for them?" (p. 252). Then Pantulu suggests that the prostitutes may acquire other skills and lead better lives through other professions. Then the stranger embarrasses Pantulu by asking him, "If they do that, will a gentleman like you marry them?" (p. 252). The stranger sounds the lawyer by his fundamental but embarrassing questions. He confirms the fact that the lawyer is highly puritanical in his approach to life and rather blind to the socio-economic necessity of prostitutes.

Then the stranger tells Saujanyarao Pantulu that he knows somebody, who can be of great help in Lubdhavadhanlu's case and that that somebody happens to be a prostitute. The lawyer suggests that the prostitute may be given some money for her service as a witness in the case. The stranger tells him that the prostitute does not care for money, but wants to be either kept as a mistress or be married by the lawyer. Now Saujanyarao Pantulu is completely nonplussed and does not know how to answer the stranger. Then the stranger removes his disguise and reveals his real self, "You want to know my name and address? I come from Vizianagaram. My name is Madhuravani" (p. 256). Saujanyarao Pantulu is angry with Madhuravani for her so-called fraud and for violating his vow. Madhuravani teases him a lot by asking him to kiss her. Finally, when Saujanyarao asks her about how to save Lubdhavadhanlu from the murder case, she reveals the top secret, "It is very simple—the girl Lubdhavadhanlu married is not a girl at all.... Now I tell you. Karataka Sastrulugaru dressed his disciple as a girl and performed the marriage" (p. 259). She tells him further that Guntur Sastrulu is none other than Karataka Sastrulu. She explains the noble motive of Karataka Sastrulu to Saujanyarao Pantulu, "He is not at fault, sir. Agnihotravadhanlu's daughter is his niece. You know that she was to be given in marriage to Lubdhavadhanlu. Karataka Sastrulugaru thought of this strategy only to foil that marriage. Please make sure he is not penalized for this" (p. 259).

Madhuravani's revelation of the truth about the deceptive and illusionary nature of Lubdhavadhanlu's marriage helps

Saujanyarao Pantulu to exonerate Lubdhavadhanlu from the false murder case. After revealing the truth, Madhuravani mischievously asks Saujanyarao Pantulu for her fee in the form of a kiss. When he reluctantly gets ready to kiss her, she refuses to accept his kiss because she says she has to follow her own principles. She tells him, "My mother has asked me not to corrupt the innocent.... So I won't let you kiss me" (p. 260). Saujanyarao Pantulu is relieved of his puritanical tension.

Although Madhuravani has mischievously teased the lawyer, she is deeply influenced by his virtue. She wants to read the *Bhagavadgita* and become a good person. There is, thus, a sudden transformation in her. Saujanyarao Pantulu sees an element of virtue even in vice. He, therefore, takes the liberty of making an observation on her, "You are a good woman. You must be the offspring of a virtuous man's moral lapse. Can't you give up this profession? Are you hard of living?" (p. 261). Then she promises to give up her profession and lead a respectable life. She replies, "I am not, by god's grace. I am quite aware of the heinous nature of my profession. Now that I am blessed with the kindness of a virtuous man like you, why will I continue in that wretched profession?" (p. 261). She wants to see him now and then after leaving her heinous profession.

Saujanyarao Pantulu does not know the hypocritical nature of Girisam, who has eloped with Butchamma. He asks Madhuravani about Girisam, "You are concerned about his life. But if he is not a man of character, Butchamma's life will be ruined. You haven't probably thought of that" (p. 262). Madhuravani reveals Girisam's secret by confessing, "Yes, he taught me English for some time. He also kept me as his mistress for some time" (p. 262). Girisam is completely exposed by Madhuravani. Now that Saujanyarao Pantulu learns about the unreliable nature of Girisam, he admonishes him and advises him to send Butchamma (with whom he has eloped) to the widows' home and to pursue higher education. He pays high compliments to Madhuravani for helping the poor Lubdhavadhanlu out of the murder case and saving the innocent Butchamma from a man of dubious character, "She has saved the life of an honest Brahmin and rescued Butchamma from falling into the clutches of a villain like you. She had done me a great favour too. Therefore, to expresses my happiness, here I am shaking hands with her" (p. 263). He, then, orders Girisam, "Napoleon. Get out of my house at once" (p. 263).

Once Saujanyarao Pantulu is convinced about the falsity of the murder case charged against Lubdhavadhanlu, the case is as good as dismissed. The playwright does not show the actual hearing of the case in the court and the final dismissal of it. He only hints at that.

Thus, at the end of the comedy, the follies of major characters are exposed and cured. These follies are expressions of the social evils of Hindu society prevalent in the latter part of the nineteenth century. For example, Agnihotravadhanlu is exposed for his practice of giving his minor daughter Butchamma in marriage to an old man who died exactly at the time of tying the sacramental *tali* around the neck of the girl-bride's neck. Likewise he is also exposed for his greed for money. Because of his avarice, he has sold his second daughter Subbamma (Subbi, for short) for ₹ 1800 to a bridegroom of fifty plus called Lubdhavadhanlu, who has a widowed daughter, Meenakshi at home. Like Agnihotravadhanlu, Lubdhavadhanlu also has a flaw in him. Though past fifty, he wants to marry a young (minor) girl, instead of being reconciled to his widower's condition. Ramappantulu, who is a cunning and mischievous administrator (*niyogi*), abets Lubdhavadhanlu to get married so that he may come into fortune. On the other hand, Venkamma, wife of Agnihotravadhanlu and mother of Subbamma, is dead set against the marriage of her minor daughter to an old man, Lubdhavadhanlu. Agnihotravadhanlu, because of his greed for money and belief in the orthodox brahmanical ways of life, wants to push his innocent daughter into the uneven marriage. But Karataka Sastrulu, the brother of Venkamma, wants to cancel this marriage and avoid the social evil by a comic trick. He manages to arrange the wedding of Lubdhavadhanlu with the daughter (also called Subbi) of Guntur Sastrulu. The bride is not a real girl but a young man called Mahesam in disguise. After the wedding the bride is found missing. By that time Agnihotravadhanlu comes to Lubdhavadhanlu's place and is shocked to learn about the wedding having been over. He feels cheated by Lubdhavadhanlu and goes to his house and thrashes him. Thus, Karataka Sastrulu's trick has succeeded in avoiding his sister's (Venkamma's) daughter's (Subbamma's) marriage with the widower Lubdhavadhanlu. Agnihotravadhanlu's folly is automatically cured by this. The false murder case, charged against Lubdhavadhanlu cures him also of his folly of marrying a young girl after his fiftieth year.

By exposing and curing the follies of these characters, the playwright satirizes the social evils like child-marriage; uneven marriage and bide-price or *kanyasulkam* and shows how these evils create many legal, economic and emotional problems in society. Gurajada Appa Rao's comedy is aimed at the social reformation in India especially in South India, where Brahmins indulge in these unscientific orthodox practices.

Another evil connected with these is prostitution, which is the oldest profession in the world. Prostitution was recognized in Hindu society as a safety valve to receive the excess energy of the society. It also provided a means of livelihood for women, who had no economic security. Thus, both sexual needs of men and economic needs of women were combined to fulfill them mutually. Madhuravani, who is a singer, dancing girl and prostitute rolled into one, easily represents a part of Hindu society. Because of her financial insecurity Madhuravani (which means melodious voice) has to entertain the customers, who can maintain her financially. The character of Madhuravani is brought in by the playwright to problematize the *nautchi* or dancing girl question. He has also created other characters some of whom are pro and some others are anti-prostitution. Through this debate the playwright not only creates an intellectual awareness about this social evil, but also attacks the hypocrisy and double-dealing of the people in connection with it. Initially, Madhuravani is kept by Girisam, but later she becomes the keep of Ramappantulu and is shifted to his village. One of the admirable qualities of this character is her extra-ordinary liveliness, naughtiness, wit, and humorous sense. She teases and tantalizes all men in general and never remains loyal to any one of them. She books all sorts of men from peons to officers, from young to old and gets her work done by bribing them with stealthy kisses. At the same time she has the nobility of Vasantasena (of Sudraka's *Mricchakatika*) to help people in dire need by lending her necklace to them temporarily. Just as there is virtue in vice, although she is a prostitute by profession and therefore, sexually loose, she has the moral integrity that overshadows her heinous profession. She easily brings to our mind Shen Te, the Good Woman of Setzuan depicted by Bertolt Brecht. According to him, the three gods, who descend to the earth, finally declare that it is the prostitute, who is the only good woman on the earth. Madhuravani happens to be such a good woman.

There is an element of nobility in her in spite of her heinous profession, which is thrust upon her by the financial pressures and contingencies of her life. She convinces even the puritanical lawyer Saujanyarao Pantulu about the inevitability of this social evil. She tells him further that no respectable man would come forward to marry her even if she is ready to give up her profession. Saujanyarao Pantulu is awakened from his puritanical ignorance of this social evil and cannot answer her satisfactorily. Although she teases Saujanyarao, she is convinced about his puritanical piety and moral uprightness. That is why she promises to read the *Bhagavadgita* and become a good person. The transformation of Madhuravani from a prostitute to a respectable woman is as unexpected as admirable and forms part of the affirmative vision of Gurajada Appa Rao.

We have already seen in brief the unfolding of the comedy leading to the fake marriage and finally unraveling the illusory nature of it. Through this comic process the characters are cured of their follies. Thus, the comedy serves a psychological and therapeutic purpose. In this sense, Gurajada Appa Rao resembles Ben Jonson.

But apart from this comic element in it, the play has also a strong dose of social criticism and offers a dense picture of the cultural ethos of South Indian society. Many characters argue vehemently for and against the social problems like child marriage, widow marriage, bride-price (*kanyasulkam*) and prostitution. Obviously, their ideas hold mirror to the conflict between tradition and modernity; orthodoxy and liberalism; Sanskrit learning and English learning and so on.

Some of these ideological conflicts may be seen in the following paragraphs. For example, Girisam comments on child marriage and widow marriage from a commercial and yet comic point of view. He tells his disciple Venkatesam, "Unless there are infant marriages, there won't be any young widows. Unless there are young widows, there is no scope for a widow marriage reform right? When the essence of civilization is widow marriage, civilization comes to a halt in the absence of infant marriages. There won't be any progress. Therefore infant marriages must be encouraged. This is a new discovery" (p. 34). Then Girisam enumerates the advantages of child marriage and advises his disciple Venkatesam, "So, you marry a small girl to an old man and when he dies, to another and then, to yet another and so on. Collect a thousand or so from each of the grooms, and like a *roti* on ghee and ghee on *roti*, you extract multiple *kanyasulkam* and finally marry the girl to a gentleman like me" (p. 34). Girisam's commercial philosophy is as comic as impractical. He considers child marriage as a child's play without reference to reality.

When Venkatesam's sister Subbi is betrothed to an old man, Girisam comments on the advantages of such marriages, "Lubdhavadhanlu is an old man and affluent one too. In another two or three years, he will kick the bucket. Your sister will then become a rich widow. When you grow up you can arrange widow marriage for her and earn eternal fame" (p. 35). Girisam's commercial idealism is as absurd as ridiculous.

Because of his passionate approach to widow marriage, he has written a poem on 'widow' and recites it before his disciple. Although Girisam has come to Krishnarayapuram with the intention of coaching his disciple Venkatesam, and his secret desire to enjoy life. After coming to Venkatesam's house he is happily surprised to learn that Venkatesam has a sister Butchamma, who is a young and beautiful widow. He, therefore, instantly falls in love with her. He confesses, "This widow's beauty has completely unsettled me. But she is not the kind to fall prey easily" (p. 62). He thinks comparatively that his marriage with the boarding house woman will be a stupid slut-marriage. He considers Butchamma as a "personification of the purest widow with gilt letters" (p. 63). But yet he feels a Hamletian dilemma,

"To marry a widow or not to marry, that is the question!" (p. 63). Then he thinks of the advantages and the disadvantages of the widow marriage. Finally, he overcomes the Hamletian dilemma and decides to win the heart of Butchamma by narrating to her the tales of the *Arabian Nights*, Kasi Majili stories and Madana Kama Raju stories. He wants to persuade her by teaching her that "widow marriage is good. If the plan works, Ramavaram *chalo*, widow marriage *karo*!" (p. 64).

Girisam's discourse on widows is at once realistic, reformative, and comic. He teaches his disciple, "Among all the things in the world, the widows are the most important" (p. 67), "The real duty—that is the ordained task—of a bachelor is to marry widows" (p. 68). He is clever enough to give a philosophical interpretation of a woman's cosmic duty. He teaches that God created women "To marry and to give birth to children. Therefore, widows, who remain unmarried are committing the sin of defying god's command" (p. 68). He enlightens Venktesam that "A widow marriage association in Ramavaram, which gives hundred rupees a month to support all those, who go in for widow marriage. So far, five hundred widows got married and attained marital bliss" (p. 68).

Backed up by his discourse on widow-marriage, Girisam tries to win the heart of Butchamma, who is a highly puritanical, innocent and ignorant girl. He tries to brainwash her cleverly and orientate her towards his goal of widow marriage. Butchamma is so traditional and foolish that she cannot easily understand his innuendos and love-signals. He tells her, "I'll marry only when someone like you with divine beauty and character decides to ignore what others say and chooses her own happiness, and taking pity on me says, 'Girisamgaru, marry me'. Otherwise do you think I'll give up my ideal brahmacharya and social service and burden myself with Atchamma and Pitchamma?" (pp. 79-80). When Butchamma requests Girisam to avoid the marriage of her younger sister Subbi with the old man, Lubdhavadhanlu, who is related to Girisam, Girisam cleverly uses the occasion to declare his own love to Butchamma, "I haven't been able to stop this marriage. Nor could I make beautiful Butchamma, when I have more than my life, a housewife. In utter despair and self-contempt

I decide to leave, and even act out, but my heart pulls me back. I know I can't live without seeing my Butchamma. She may not be kind to me, but I must stay here so that I will at least have a glimpse of her now and then and be happy" (p. 133). Thus, he tries slowly to brainwash Butchamma in his favour.

At the same time he points out the nature of traditional Hindu (in this case brahmanical) marriage and the role of a wife in it. "In Africa they have a system called slavery. That means they sell human beings like cattle in the market. A slave has to render life-long service to his owner. In the same way my brother is buying your sister to be a slave, under the respectable name of marriage. He hopes she would slave for him as an unpaid servant during all the household chores" (p. 133). This is important practical reason for Lubdhavadhanlu's marriage with Subbamma. Another important reason is to check the biological urges of the widowed daughter of Lubdhavadhanlu (i.e. Meenakshi). Girisam explains it after some hesitation, "I shouldn't be letting our shameful family secrets. Yet I can't hide anything from you. Meenakshi has been getting pregnant almost every year after her husband's death; each time there is a scandal over the issue and sometimes she even runs the risk of losing her life in aborting her pregnancy" (p. 134).

Girisam uses the technique of indirect suggestion and persuasion to win the heart of Butchamma. He says he cannot live without marrying her. He cannot be even in Heaven without her. Finally, he suggests to her to elope with him, so that her sister's marriage could be averted. Butchamma is mentally ready to elope with him.

When Agnihotravadhanlu goes to Lubdhavadhanlu's place, he is shocked to discover that his eldest daughter Butchamma has eloped with Girisam. The whole family feels betrayed by the young man and the young woman. Later when Girisam meets Lubdhavadhanlu, he tries to show sympathy for the latter, "I heard that you got implicated in a murder case. I rushed here at once forsaking food and sleep" (p. 234). Then Lubdhavadhanlu is happy to know that Girisam has taught Agnihotravadhanlu a good lesson by eloping with her, "Look, boy, I heard that you had eloped with Agnihotravadhanlu's daughter. You've taught him a good lesson. But, I hope you haven't married her" (p. 234). Girisam gives him a satisfactory answer, "Do you think I will do such a senseless thing?" (p. 235).

Girisam has an axe to grind with Lubdhavadhanlu. He, therefore, asks Lubdhavadhanlu to adopt him as his son, "Brother, all my people are hoping that you would adopt me and get me married" (p. 235). He tries to persuade Lubdhavadhanlu, "So, please listen to my words for your own good. Write an adoption deed—you don't have a son of your own, should you think of your future or not?" (p. 235). If Lubdhavadhanlu is not willing to adopt him, Girisam suggests the alternative of giving the attorney-power at least. His reasons are very clever, "Suppose you are sentenced to imprisonment, don't you need someone to manage your affairs on your behalf? Among your relatives I am the only one who knows English and is worldly-wise. Scribble a power of attorney in my name" (p. 236). But Lubdhavadhanlu does not oblige him at all.

Later Girisam meets Saujanyarao Pantulu and confesses, "With a resolve that I should dedicate my life to social reform, I decided to remain unmarried and joined as a lieutenant to my guru. I was touched by Butchamma's pure heart and her present predicament. Besides my love for my *shishya* evoked in me love for his sister as well. That's why I have agreed to marry her sir, but not out of any desire for sensual pleasures. She, too, has fallen in love with me, and having been convinced of the sanctity of widow marriage, agreed to marry me. Therefore our marriage, sir, is a true love marriage and not a common widow marriage" (p. 246).

Girisam's hypocrisy, tall talk and false reformist zeal are all exposed finally when Madhuravani tells Saujanyarao Pantulu that he (i.e. Girisam) taught her English for some time and also kept her as his mistress for some time. Saujanyarao Pantulu can easily see through the cunning and double-dealing of Girisam and asks him about his behaviour. Now Girisam cannot fool the virtuous lawyer and therefore confesses that he committed a sin by keeping Madhuravani as a mistress, that he has reformed himself through penitence and craves the lawyer's mercy. But Saujanyarao Pantulu gives his moral judgment after animadverting him thoroughly,

> How dare you! How easily friends like you could cheat people including the likes of your guru and myself! I shall send a telegram to your guru asking him not to entertain you any more, and to send Butchamma to the widow's home in Poona. She will study, come up in life and marry whomever she likes or remain unmarried. You say that you are reformed: all right, join a real college and pursue higher education. As long as your conduct is good, I shall extend monetary help to you. Try to lead a sensible life. You call Madhuravani a devil! You are the Devil. She didn't even mention your duplicity until she was pressed to reveal facts. She has saved the life of an honest Brahmin, and reserved Butchamma from falling into the clutches of a villain like you... Napoleon! Get out of my house at once. (p. 263)

Girisam's hypocrisy being exposed, he is cut to his real size and put in the proper place by Saujanyarao Pantulu, who happens to be the conscience keeper and moral referee in the dramatic world of *Kanyasulkam*.

Girisam's character is characterized by glaring contradictions and therefore hypocrisy and double-dealing are the hallmarks of his behaviour. Although unmarried, he has kept a boarding house woman and stolen her money. After leaving her, he has kept the prostitute Madhuravani as his mistress until she is weaned away from him by Ramappantulu. Although he has kept her as a mistress for some time, he boasts of being anti-nautch. His attitude shows the irony of Hindu social life, where the so-called respectable people condemn prostitution and prostitutes publicly, but visit them secretly. Prostitution is a socially recognized institution in India as elsewhere in the world. In fact, it is the oldest profession in the world. It serves as a safety valve to receive and regulate the excess of sexual energy of the society, and maintain the health of the society. Prostitutes were not only recognized, but also respected in the Indian society. But it is only recently in the nineteenth and the twentieth centuries, perhaps due to the British influence, especially Victorian morality and monogamy, that Indians have started looking down upon prostitutes publicly, though they need them privately.

The so-called anti-nautch movement to be launched by Girisam and the like gas an element of hypocrisy about it. Though apparently it has the dignity of social reformation, it has an element of complicity in it. It is this contradiction in the behaviour of people like Girisam, which is pointed out by Karataka Sastrulu to Madhuravani. Showing the contrast between a righteous man like Lawyer Saujanyarao Pantulu and others, Karataka Sastrulu says, "What comparison? One is a cur and the other a milch cow. Saujanyarao is anti-nautch in thought, word and deed. If you just utter the word 'prostitute' in his presence, he would warn you to mind your language. Gentlemen like him are rare. The others are anti-nautch when it is convenient. Most members of the anti-nautch brigade are heroes in words alone, and Girisam is foremost among them. Some of them are anti-nautch in the morning, pro-nautch in the night. Some are anti-nautch in the hometown, and pro-nautch outside it. Some are pro-nautch as long as they are fit and anti-nautch once they get old. Some are pro-nautch as long as they are alive and anti-nautch after death. Some lucky men are pro-nautch even after death. That means they perform rituals here in this world so that they can book their ticket to pleasure in the other world. Smaller fry like me, however, are anti-nautch whenever they have no access to dancing girls" (p. 208). Karataka Sastrulu's comment on the anti-nautch question is self-critical as well as critical of the Hindu society. It is satirical as well as comic at the same time.

The nautchy question is one of the thematic concerns of the play. We have already seen some people defend this practice, whereas some others oppose it vehemently. Whether we like it or not, the dancers-cum-prostitutes have been recognized in the Hindu society from the earliest days. These prostitutes provide an outlet for the regulation of sexual energy, which has no legal channel for its flow. For example, a prostitute will be necessary for the unmarried young men, widowers, divorcees and married men with frigid wives. Some of these aspects are revealed in the play in the life of Madhuravani. We have already seen how Girisam, an unmarried young man, had kept her for his sexual satisfaction. Later his contract with Madhuravani expired when Ramappantulu began his own contract with her.

Ramappantulu happens to be a *niyogi* or administrator and not a Vaidiki. As an administrator he is very practical in his approach to life. He offers two hundred rupees to Madhuravani so that she may sever her relation with Girisam. But when Girisam comes to Madhuravani's house unexpectedly, Ramappantulu hides himself beneath a cot. But when the boarding house woman comes there, Girisam also hides himself beneath the same cot and Ramappantulu comes out. Hence, the boarding house woman beats Ramappantulu with a broomstick mistaking him for Girisam.

Finally, Ramappantulu has brought Madhuravani to his village Ramachandrapuram agraharam. She has surrendered her life and honour to him because of her trust in him. She asks him not to ditch her. Then she requests Ramappantulu to avert Lubdhavadhanlu's marriage with Subbamma, the daughter of Agnihotravadhanlu. But Ramappantulu is a clever man, who does not want to avert it, but on the contrary expedite it. He knows that Lubdhavadhanlu is miserly by nature and therefore he wants to teach the latter a good lesson by his clever-trick. He tells Madhuravani, "I tempted him with the belief that he will come into a lot of money through marriage" (p. 42). Ramappantulu resembles a Jonsonian character in his mischief and trickery. He explains his stand as follows, "That is diplomacy! To make the impossible possible and possible impossible!" (p. 42). He employs all the cunning ways to deceive Lubdhavadhanlu. He proudly narrates the Machieavellian plan that he adopted, "You know what our siddhanti did after some cajoling? He took a good look at Lubdhavadhanlu's horoscope and declared that a second marriage is on the cards for him very soon. And that wealth will accrue through that marriage. With that the old man began to waver between the greed for money and the reluctance to spend on marriage. Meanwhile, the panda-guru arrived, and I managed him also. When Lubdhavadhanlu showed him the horoscope to clear his doubt, what did the panda says? He said, 'there are strong indications of marriage and wealth. But you are an elderly person, who will give you their girl in marriage? How will the marriage come about? These are great but impossible boons. If they figure in the horoscopes, they cause more harm than good.

That is, either death or loss of wealth will occur to you. So appease the planets and feed the Brahmins generously. Your ill luck will end with some minor indisposition. Find an auspicious day and start sun-worship.' Avadhanlu's hear sank at this and he began looking for alliances. This is the story" (pp. 42-43).

Just as Ramappantulu has hoodwinked Lubdhavadhanlu with a false horoscope, Agnihotravadhanlu also has got a false horoscope of his daughter. Ramappantulu knows the secret, "It is said that the wealth of the house she steps into will multiply tenfold, and everything she touches will turn into gold" (p. 43). Thus, there is perfect alignment between two falsities. Ramappantulu honestly and shamelessly confesses about the manipulation of horoscopes, "This is common among us Brahmins. Not one horoscope sent for marriage alliances is ever genuine" (p. 43).

There is another reason for Ramappantulu's support for Lubdhavadhanlu's marriage, i.e. Meenakshi's character. Although it is a delicate matter, he explains it to Madhuravani, "Lubdhavadhanlu's widowed daughter Meenakshi's conduct is not good, that's all. Every once in a while she creates a crisis and the police use it as a pretext to extract money. And for the old man, spending money is like giving up life. He also thinks Meenakshi swindles money in running the household. Her game will be up once this marriage takes place" (p. 45).

In spite of all the justification of the marriage between Agnihotravadhanlu's daughter and Lubdhavadhanlu put forth by Ramappantulu, Madhuravani asks him to avert it. She says, "I don't know these tangles. I just want you to stop this marriage, somehow" (p. 45). But Ramappantulu ignores her request and promises to get some money for her, "I'll arrange for your performance in this marriage and get you some money, keep quiet" (p. 45).

Ramappantulu's attitude to life is generally commercial and opportunistic. He has no stable morals. For example, when Karataka Sastrulu brings his daughter (i.e. Mahesam in disguise) and seeks his help, Ramappantulu agrees to help and cooperate with him for one-fifth share of the bride price. But the same man writes letters in the name of Agnihotravadhanlu to Lubdhavadhanlu complaining against his age. Lubdhavadhanlu wants to go to Agnihotravadhanlu directly and tackle him. Now Ramappantulu is scared of being exposed and dragged into legal trouble. He tells Madhuravani, "If this rogue shows that letter to Agnihotravadhanlu, he will file a forgery case against you. My head will be cut off. What's the way out?... The only course left for me is to fall at the feet of Meenakshi, his daughter" (p. 92).

At the same time Lubdhavadhanlu has received a letter signed by Girisam. In that letter Girisam has written that Agnihotravadhanlu is going to bring fifty carts, three camels and five horses and a golden palanquin to his daughter's wedding and to add to the grandeur. He has also mentioned that the pretty maiden (Subbi) shows signs of balding on account of dandruff, which forebode the impending widowhood. He has mentioned further that Venkamma does not approve of this marriage and threatens to commit suicide by jumping into the well. Just then Lubdhavadhanlu receives another letter. This time it is from his would-have-been father-in-law Agnihotravadhanlu. Ramappantulu reads the letter and tells Lubdhavadhanlu that "Someone has told him that you are a miser" (p. 101) and that "There is a strong rumour that you have been excommunicated on account of your widowed daughter's misconduct" (p. 101). Lubdhavadhanlu is so irritated and angry with these letters that he wants to cancel the alliance with Agnihotravadhanlu's daughter. Now Ramappantulu cleverly suggests to Lubdhavadhanlu to go in for another alliance, "Try for another alliance and get married. Your wife's presence will be a check on Meenakshi's moves. Meenakshi's presence in turn will keep your wife under check. Am I right or not?" (p. 107). He suggests to him to marry the daughter of Guntur Sastrulu at a lower bride price of ₹ 1200. Thus, Ramappantulu persuades Lubdhavadhanlu to agree to the new alliance. He has an axe to grind in the wedding. He has arranged a performance of music by Madhuravani so that she may earn some money from it.

But ironically enough Ramappantulu is himself deceived by the trickery of the siddhanti, who has advanced the wedding from four hours after dawn to four hours before dawn. Ramappantulu is rather disappointed to know that Mahuravani refused to sing at that odd hour of the wedding and that Guntur Sastrulu has collected the cash and absconded without returning ₹ 100 to him. Ramappantulu suffers from sexual jealousy about his keep, Madhuravani. He inquires Kondibhatlu about how Madhuravani behaved with the men folk in the wedding. Madhuravani is smarter than Ramappantulu thinks her to be. She has a knack of winning every man by her stealthy kisses. Also she teases Ramappantulu about the necklace that she has lent to the bride, Subbi (i.e. Mahesam in disguise). He goes to Lubdhavadhanlu's house and asks for it. But when Lubdhavadhanlu pleads his ignorance about the whereabouts of the necklace he threatens to file a suit against him. Thus, Ramappantulu suffers a lot when he fails to get back the necklace and is therefore not allowed by Madhuravani to enter the house. Then Ramappantulu bribes the servant, Asiri and stealthily sneaks into Lubdhavadhanlu's house and kisses Meenakshi. He even wants to marry her by eloping with her. When Ramappantulu's intimacy with Meenakshi at night is accidentally seen by Lubdhavadhanlu, he is struck by a stick on the leg by the latter. Lubdhavadhanlu instantly drives his daughter Meenakshi out of his home. Now Meenakshi really wants to go away with Ramappantulu, but Ramappantulu does not have the courage to elope with her. Leaving Meenakshi there, he runs away from there, to his own house, where Madhuravani pesters him for her necklace. Again Meenakshi rushes in there and publicizes her affair with Ramappantulu. Obviously, Ramappantulu is deeply embarrassed.

When Agnihotravadhanlu comes to Ramachandrapuram with the carts of the marriage party to celebrate his daughter's wedding with Lubdhavadhanlu, Ramappantulu surprises and shocks him by saying that Lubdhavadhanlu's wedding with another girl is already over. As Agnihotravadhanlu has no money with him, he asks Ramappantulu to help him out. Ramappantulu suggests to him to pawn his bracelet with Madhuravani. Agnihotravadhanlu gives the bracelet to Ramappantulu rather unwillingly and asks him to pawn it with the prostitute.

When Lubdhavadhanlu is anxious about the false charge of murder case against him, Ramappantulu advises him to wriggle out of the case by bribing two thousand rupees to the officers concerned, "With just two thousand rupees, the entire murder case will melt away like snow" (p. 200). Further he threatens Lubdhavadhanlu about the serious consequences of the possible adverse judgment against him, "If this verdict goes against you, just imagine what's going to happen to you.... The Deputy Collector is no friend of Brahmins, mind you. The Tahsildar will be sacked first, and then the gallows will be ready for you and Meenakshi. Because of my friendship with the Inspector, I have been able to get him to agree to this settlement. Please pay heed to my advice and save yourself" (p. 200). He even meets the noble lawyer Saujanyarao Pantulu and promises to bring a strong 'defence' witness. But Saujanyarao Pantulu cuts him to his size and dismisses him, "I know all about you, clear out... get out" (p. 201). He chides even Lubdhavadhanlu, "Why did you let this scoundrel in?" (p. 201).

Ramappantulu is thus a worldly wise man and unscrupulous opportunist. A *niyogi* or administrator he knows how to deal with people, misleading them and encouraging them to make mistakes and again pretending to help them out. He takes advantage of the helplessness of people and tries to extract some money from them. There is an element of irony in his very name. Although he bears the name of the epic hero, Rama, who is known for upholding *dharma* and who is a monogamist, Ramappantulu does not have any of these qualities in him. Far from being a monogamist, Ramappantulu has kept a prostitute Madhuravani openly by maintaining her in a separate house. He is not ashamed of it, but even proud of it. Not only that. He even tries to tempt Meenakshi, the daughter of Lubdhavadhanlu to elope with him and marry him. Far from being a truthful man, he is a liar, tempter, misleader, and exploiter of helpless people. The ideals of Rama (the epic hero) are totally subverted in Ramappantulu. It is a matter of satisfaction to know that such a desecrator of ideal values is finally exposed and dismissed by the god-like figure, Saujanyarao Pantulu.

As has already been mentioned, prostitution or the nautchy question is one of the important thematic concerns of the play. Whether this oldest profession of the world can be totally abolished, remains very problematic. But it is quite clear from the play that music, dance, and prostitution were closely connected with one another and that prostitutes were recognized and respected as part of the Hindu society until very recently. Madhuravani, who represents the institution of prostitution in this play, happens to be a very interesting person. It is quite clear from the beginning of the play that she is compelled to follow her profession due to dire economic necessity. She is very helpless about it and does not feel ashamed of it at all. As the common proverb goes, poverty has no sense of shame. Initially, Girisam kept her by giving her the regular maintenance allowance. But when he can no longer afford to pay her, she accepts Ramappantulu as her master, who gives her ₹ 200. So Madhuravani closes her contract with Girisam and begins afresh with Ramappantulu.

The first thing that impresses us about her is her strong sense of professional ethics. Although she is about to change her master from Girisam to Ramappantulu, she does not show any disregard for Girisam. On the contrary, she has respect for and loyalty to Girisam and blind to his faults. Her question to Ramappantulu, "You think a saani has no morals?" (p. 40) testifies to her integrity.

Madhuravani knows the dignity of her profession in the patriarchal society. Though she needs money, she knows that there are higher things in life than money. As she tells Ramappantulu, "Perhaps it appears to you that only money is important for me. I care a straw for money. If I know that your lands are under mortgage, would I have taken the two hundred from you? If you don't cut down your wasteful spending and put your house in order, I will not agree. I feel honoured only when people say that such and such a Pantulugaru prospered after keeping that particular saani. Moreover this is our family tradition, Pantulugaru. So, please don't imagine the saanis as a blot on the world" (p. 40).

Although she is a saani, Madhuravani is against the middle-aged Lubdhavadhanlu marrying a very young girl, Subbi, the daughter of Agnihotravadhanlu. Her concern for another woman and her opposition to the mismatch are really admirable. That is why she pressurizes Ramappantulu to avoid the said marriage, "Unless you avert Lubdhavadhanlu's marriage, I'll not let you kiss me" (p. 41).

Madhuravani is very intelligent and exposes Ramappantulu's double-dealing and hypocrisy in a humorous fashion. For example, when Ramappantulu says that Meenakshi's conduct is not good, she taunts him, "After all, which woman's conduct can remain good after she is sighted by you?" (p. 45). There are several instances like this in the play, which testify to her sharp intelligence, worldly wisdom and practical approach to life. She is open-hearted and very articulate and therefore able to wean all kinds of men to her side or point of view.

Her sense of humour may be seen in several instances. For example, when Karataka Sastrulu introduces his so-called daughter (i.e. Mahesam in disguise), Madhuravani is so willing to marry the person, "If so, I'm ready! I'll dress up as a man and marry this girl! What a chance to get a wife like this, and become the son-in-law of the world renowned Karataka Satrulu!" (p. 50). She even kisses the bride and says, "Innocent! He can spoil a hundred like me. He is after all you disciple. This maiden's mouth is smelling of cigar" (p. 51).

Madhuravani, though a prostitute by profession, has innate nobility in her, which easily resembles the nobility of Vasantasena, the courtesan in Sudraka's *Mricchakatika*. There are several instances wherein her sublime ethics is revealed. For example Karataka Sastrulu wants to give her some money for her cooperation in arranging a fake marriage between his daughter (i.e. Mahesam in disguise) and Lubdhavadhanlu, but Madhuravani refuses to take the money, "I am disappointed that you even mentioned it. Because I'm a prostitute by profession, I make money where I have to. But you thought Madhuravani has no kindness at all? When your own sister's life is in trouble, will I aspire for money?" (p. 53).

Madhuravani is a clever psychologist and knows how to compliment men and bloat their egos. When Lubdhavadhanlu is sad to be called an old man, she tries to console him cleverly, "You...old? Who says so?... Have you lost a single tooth? Is your eyesight any poorer? Look at your muscles—strong like those of a wrestler.... What a wide chest!" (p. 103).

She is very sociable with men of all sorts due to her professional habit, though she is currently kept by Ramappantulu. She achieves instant friendship with men by her clever talk and bribe of kisses and makes use of them for her clever intrigues. Many times she evokes sexual jealousy in Ramappantulu, who cannot do anything about it. She lends her necklace to Ramappantulu to facilitate Lubdhavadhanlu's marriage with Subbi (i.e. Mahesam in disguise) but later she tantalizes Ramappantulu when the latter fails to return it to her, although she has secretly received it from Mahesam himself. That shows her cleverness and trickery.

Madhuravani warns Karataka Sastrulu and Mahesam, "Head Conishteebu is looking for both of you. The moment he finds you, he'll put you behind bars. That I am quite certain of" (p. 205). Now there is a perfect coincidence between moral awakening and legal threat. On the moral level, Karataka Sastrulu has repented over his cheating of Lubdhavadhanlu with a fake wife and taking ₹ 1200 from a Brahmin. On the legal level, the police people have been searching for Guntur Sastrulu (i.e. Karataka Sastrulu) and his so-called daughter (Mahesam in disguise). Karataka Sastrulu wants to return ₹ 1200 and the necklace to Lubdhavadhanlu by registered post. But the necklace is with Madhuravani. Karataka Sastrulu requests her to lend it to him and not to think only of profit. It is again at this juncture that Madhuravani's nobility is revealed, "My friendship is only with people like you. Well, it's out of friendship that I am lending my necklace to you. If my mother gets to know of this, she'll kill me. As for love—if there is life, love adds to its charm. Have you not heard the saying, 'A sweet vendor's desire for sweets and a dancing girl's love should always remain suppressed?' Our life depends on youth, which is transient, and so our love is fixed on one thing alone.... Gold. When beauty wanes, gold is necessary to make up for it. Even then I am parting with gold for your sake" (p. 211).

Madhuravani's words testify not only to her nobility but also to her alertness about the risk involved in her profession. She is perfectly right when she says that gold is necessary for her in her old age when she may not have any customer to look after her.

She is rightly taught by her mother to be provident and wary of the flattery of men.

Madhuravani further expresses her views about her predicament. She has become a prostitute simply because she belongs to a family of professional prostitutes. She has no other choice, which is her predicament. As a prostitute she has no financial and emotional security enjoyed by a married woman. She expresses her wish for a secure life, "I would have been better off if I were born in a farmer's family. I would have worked in my husband's brinjal or chilli field and felt secure in the company of someone I could call my own" (p. 211). Nobody can fail to commiserate with her plight. What is admirable about her is that in spite of this deeper frustration in her heart, she keeps up a cheerful face and has not lost her gusto for life.

Madhuravani's goodness may be seen in her warning to Karataka Sastrulu, not to spoil the innocent boy, Mahesam, "From now on don't spoil him by making him take part in plays or taking him with you to whorehouses" (p. 214). Also she attacks Karataka Sastrulu by a generalized comment on Brahmins, which is born out of her first-hand experience with them, "Brahmins preach a lot and practice little.... You may be a Brahmin, but can't throw dust in god's eyes, I suppose.... Can you bribe Chitragupta? You can't send Madhuravani to him and get your sins wiped out, perhaps" (p. 215).

Although a prostitute by profession, Madhuravani never suffers from any inferiority complex. In fact, she has accepted her 'heinous' profession as part of the patriarchal society. And she has the existential courage to be what she is. She shocks and embarrasses Saujanyarao Pantulu by her direct questions about her profession. She wants to know if the society is ready to accept her as a wife if she leaves her 'heinous' profession; if any man would come forward to marry her. Saujanyarao Pantulu has no satisfactory answer for that. In spite of silencing Saujanyarao Pantulu, she takes a clue from his advice and decides to leave her profession and lead a good and respectable life. Thus, in spite of all her mischievous nature, she decides to be a good woman, which testifies to her innate nobility. She easily resembles Vasantasena of *Mricchakatika* in her nobility but the conspicuous difference between the two is that whereas Vasantasena is married by Charudatta, Madhuravani is not married by anyone. Although there is a great difference between the conditions of Vasantasena and Madhuravani, yet Madhuravani remains as a lovable woman in our memory.

Apart from the major social evils like child marriage, widow marriage, bride price, and prostitution presented by the dramatist, there are also other lesser problems, which are exposed and satirized by him. For example, using religion—with all its attendant superstitions—for cheating the illiterate and unenlightened people is beautifully presented and indirectly criticized by Gurajada Appa Rao. The activities going on in the garden behind the arrack shop in Ramachandrapuram agraharam throw ample light on the desecration of religion for sensuous purposes. The wine shop or tavern is the place where all sorts of people gather to have spirituous enjoyment. The shopkeeper's ironical comments provide a lot of humour in addition to stating the facts of sensuous life. When the drunkards quarrel about their gods like Rama, Brahma, and Shiva, the shopkeeper explains the unity of life, "Why do you quarrel? Your Shiva is true—there he is shining in that bottle. Your Rama is also true—there he is that in the other one" (p. 164). He explains further to the Bairagi (of dubious integrity), "Guruji, you know everything. The body is a glass bowl. What lies in the body is the soul. What lies in the glass bowl is the essence of food. Unless this essence goes into the body, the soul doesn't burn brightly" (p. 165). The shopkeeper equates arrack with nectar and says that it is essential to grasp the ultimate Brahman.

The two characters, i.e. Bairagi and Yogini provide a satirical picture of religious hypocrisy so common among Hindus. Bairagi, for example, claims that he has come from Haridwar aerially, "Two days ago. We were in Prayag the day before yesterday, and in Jagannath yesterday. While traveling in the sky, my ethereal flight came to a halt at the garden of your village deity. Wondering why I looked with my yogic vision and found a great mystic diagram lying buried, six lengths deep under the deity's idol. Then I descended to the earth, prayed to the deity and even as I was leaving unobtrusively this devotee—the shopkeeper—

recognized me and held me back" (p. 166). The Bairagi boasts of his occult powers and generally speaks the philosophical language. For example, when the Head Constable asks him his age, he replies, "Why calculate that which has neither beginning nor end, brother? I am as old as the Paramatma" (p. 167). He boasts further about his occult powers to impress upon the Head Constable and the shopkeeper, "Two hundred and fifty years ago, in Kasi, during the regime of Almgir Padishah, a merchant invited all the *siddhas* like us to his abode. In the middle of the Ganga, aboard a boat he filled the bottles with liquor and served it in gold tumbler. By the second half of the night, the drums were empty and everyone was out.... I and a Nepali Brahmin were the only ones left standing. That Brahmin kept on asking for more and more liquor. 'Bring more liquor, or I shall curse you' threatened the Brahmin. Poor merchant from where can he bring more? He fell at my feet, and I told him not to worry. I took a tumbler and blessed it, and when it is filled with the water from the Ganga, the water turned into wine. The Brahmin drank a thousand tumblers and belched with satisfaction. There are such great souls even among Brahmins. For a wise man, who can discover the truth, isn't the entire water of Ganga liquor?" (p. 167). What is ironical and humorous about this situation is that there is an equation and interchangeability between sensuality and spirituality. For example, there is a *yogini*, who is closely connected with the liquor shop. She has to serve the customers with liquor or hookah. Whenever the customers find her in the vicinity, they snatch the opportunity of kissing her stealthily. When somebody is kissing her, it is euphemistically described as 'somebody is giving her a private lesson.' The irony here is that *yoga* and *bhoga* or self-continence and indulgence are interchanged and equated very conveniently. Their hedonistic philosophy is summed up by the shopkeeper, "All these are secrets of wisdom. What is ultimate happiness? Stomach full of liquor, nose full of smoke, and a beautiful young girl—isn't it?" (p. 171). This philosophy easily brings to our mind the *Rubaiyats* of Omar Khayyam. Behind the verbal irony one may see the situational irony too. For example, the people belonging to the constabulary and judiciary ironically believe in the so-called occult powers of the Bairagi, however fake they may be. Similarly, the Bairagi, who ought to be in a secluded monastery or a distant forest, is found in the vicinity of the liquor shop. And the bar-girl is ironically named as yogini. These ironical situations help the dramatist not only to provide robust humour, but also to satirize the hypocrisy and inner contradictions of Hindus' behaviour.

The Bairagi's boastfulness is revealed further when he talks to the Sudra men in Visakhapatnam. He tells them that he came from Kasi, "Left this morning after worshipping River Ganga in Kasi.... Held my breath and traveled at the speed of the air" (p. 219). He bamboozles the illiterate fools further with his so-called miraculous powers, "Four days ago, a gold plate fell from the sky in Viswanath Temple. The script written on it was not intelligible to any Brahmin. I have deciphered it. In the language of *siddhas*, two formulas were written on it: one for making gold and the other for eternal life" (p. 220). He tells them further that he eats fruits for fifteen days and lives on air for the next fifteen days, "Milk, sugar, bananas—this regimen for fifteen days and just air for the next fortnight" (p. 220). After hearing some news of some unpleasant events in the town, he comments with his superior airs, "This town seems to be full of sin. I shall not stay here.... It looks like alcoholism is rampant here. I don't talk to drunkards. Before that shopkeeper comes here, let's turn into this by-lane" (p. 220). The Bairagi's hypocrisy is exposed by the shopkeeper, who snaps at Ramanna thus, "Shut up your mouth. Is this fellow a guru? He has polished off all the liquor in my shop and disappeared without paying for it" (p. 221). The shopkeeper asks the Bairagi to pay the bill, "Cash before you talk" (p. 221). The Bairagi continues his game, "If what you want is money, bring a *tola* of copper; I shall turn it into gold" (p. 221) and asks him not to reveal the secrets of a yogi to the illiterate. Then the shopkeeper tells him pointblank, "The yoga of deceit doesn't work with me. What's the big secret about it, anyway? Everybody is a guru in that art" (p. 222).

It is ironical that the Head Constable, who has involved himself in concocting a false murder case against Lubdhavadhanlu, is now forced to seek the help of the Bairagi in locating Guntur Sastrulu so that he may be extricated from the professional hazard. The Head Constable has, therefore, been hectically searching for the Bairagi. But Gavaraiah wants to fool him by capitalizing on his helplessness. He tells the Head Constable that the guruji is sitting right in front of him invisibly and converses with him, "Why do you ask like that? Here he is, right in front of you! (*Points to an empty space*) Can't you see him? (*Looking at the empty space*) What, guruji, have you again taken to your vanishing tricks? Oho, you are obeying your guru's directions? Then how is it I am able to see you? Oho, is it because I am initiated into the power of *mantras*? Then how long will you remain invisible? Fifteen days? (*To Head Constable*) That's what the guruji says" (p. 242). Gavaraiah tells the Head Constable further that the guruji will locate Guntur Sastrulu with the help of his magic balm. But when the Head Constable is unable to see the (invisible) guruji, Asiri pretends to see him. Hence, Gavaraiah generalizes, "Godmen and ghosts are visible to miracle men like us, and to those blindly devoted like him. They are also visible to innocent children but not to the rest" (p. 243). Such events, obviously, throw light on the superstitions and belief in occult powers rampant in the Indian society of nineteenth century and provide robust humour to the audience.

An important aspect of the play happens to be its satire on the judiciary. Although judiciary is meant to uphold truth and justice, it unfortunately vitiated by corrupt and illegal practices. Most of the lawyers are more interested in making money than in fighting for justice. The lawyers like Bhimarao Pantulu and Naidu represent such lawyers. But Saujanyarao Pantulu is an ideal lawyer, who is interested in nothing but truth and justice. That is why people resort to him, as though he is a god for them. He commands respect from not only his clients, but also from the members of his own fraternity. He is very unhappy about the element of corruption in the judiciary. He tells Girisam, "Even the leading lawyers shamelessly teach their clients to give false evidence. Some moderate ones ask that the evidence be manipulated. Some old-fashioned ones like me refrain from such sinful practices, but keep discreetly quiet even when we know our parties are producing false witnesses. It is on account of this moral compromise that I am slowly cutting down my practice. I intend giving up this profession eventually" (p. 245). Commenting on the inevitability of corruption, he tells Girisam further, "It is not just untruth, there are many bad practices in this profession. I think that soon there will be a need to start an anti-lawyer movement along the lines of the anti-nautch movement in our country. You really can't blame the Head Conishteebu. Unless false witnesses are produced, one can't win cases these days. Since you are trained in the ways of truth, you find the conduct of cases today abhorrent" (p. 245).

Although Gurjada Appa Rao has satirized the judiciary system of colonial India in the nineteenth century, it is easily applicable even to the postcolonial India of twenty-first century. His courage, honesty and candour in depicting the corruption of the judiciary system are indeed admirable.

One of the conspicuous aspects of the social theme of the play is the contrast between tradition and modernity represented by Sanskrit learning and English learning respectively during the colonial period of nineteenth-century India. Language being the vehicle of a culture and an approach it enters into conflictive relation with another language of another culture. During the colonial period, English happened to grow as a strong rival to Sanskrit, the divine language of India. Whereas Sanskrit represents tradition, Hinduism (especially Brahmanism), English represents modernity, Christianity and European values of life. The colonial encounter between Sanskrit and English is beautifully portrayed by Gurajada Appa Rao in the present play. Whereas Sanskrit is represented by Agnihotravadhanlu and other Brahmins, English is represented by Girisam. In this linguistic and cultural encounter each party defends its own virtues and points out the negative aspects of the other. It is a very interesting debate. It redounds to the credit of Gurjada Appa Rao that perhaps no other play in India (either in regional language or in Indian English) has recorded such a beautiful dialogue between two linguistic cultures.

In the twenty-first century, Indians have a good deal of craze for English language, which can open the window on the world. English is not only a language of fashion, but also one of power. A similar craze for English language was there in the nineteenth-century India also. Many parents wanted their children to be educated in English. To learn English was to be modern and up-to-date. It is because of such craze for English language that Venkatesam's parents, especially the mother, want their son to be tutored in English by Girisam. Girisam, who has a good knowledge of English language, makes use of their craze for his own advantage. Venkamma wants to hear her son talk in English, which is conspicuously different from Sanskrit and Telugu in pronunciation and vocabulary. She asks Girisam, "Will you please converse once with our boy in English, babu? I wish to listen to that" (p. 22). Girisam obliges her deferentially, "Sure, amma. My dear Venkatesam—Twinkle, twinkle, little star/ How I wonder what you are!" (p. 22).

English language is closely connected with English educational system as contradistinguished from Sanskrit (or Telugu) educational system, which is very traditional. Girisam echoes this view in his answer to Karataka Sastrulu, "For the present, students learn poems by rote like people learn the Vedas. In white man's school, they don't pay much attention to Telugu poetry. They bombard the students all the time with geography, arithmetic, algebra, mathematics" (p. 23). According to the general belief, English education including its language is more useful than traditional education comprising Sanskrit or Telugu. When Mahesam reads a line from Kalidasa's *Kumarasambhavam*, he shows his contempt for and indifference to the imaginative beauty of the verse by contrasting it with the usefulness of English (i.e. Western) education, "I vaguely remember having read this. It means the deer are running, doesn't it? Is it such a great thing for a poet to talk about? Who cares whether the deer run or don't. Don't the dogs run? Don't foxes run? What about cats? Not one useful word in this book. What does Kalidasa know about comparing figures or calculating interest rates? There lies the genius of the white man" (p. 22). Mahesam's underrating of Kalidasa is obviously influenced by his exaggerated respect for Western/English education. That is why he decides, "I shall stop this study here and learn a few English words from Girisamgaru. Venkudu is so proud that he has learnt to prattle a few English words!" (p. 28). Karataka Sastrulu wants to pay for Mahesam's English education provided the latter obliges him to go through the ordeal of a fake marriage by disguising himself as a bride. Mahesam has lost his faith in Sanskrit books and hence takes an oath on an English book. Thus, both Mahaesam and Girisam believe in the usefulness of English education.

On the contrary, Agnihotravadhanlu is a staunch supporter of traditional Sanskrit education. He tells Girisam once, "This useless English education has ruined Brahmanism. They gibber in English even at dinner time as if it were the language of the gods. All the rituals have anyway been burnt to ashes!" (pp. 31-32). Although Agnihotravadhanlu is a strong advocate of Sanskrit education, he has allowed his son Venkatesam to be tutored in English by Girisam. Girisam initiates his disciple Mahesam into English through a sort of ritual, i.e. smoking. Girisam shows utter irreverence to things of Hindu culture. He takes Venkatesam to a temple for smoking. When Venkatesam queries him if it is not a sin to do so, Girisam tries to convince him, "Temple is the best place for smoking, man. What's incense compared to tobacco smoke? Best tobacco, best curds, good ghee—that's why poets crave for country life" (p. 36). Girisam finds Indian life rather dull as compared to Western life, which he has come to know through the English language. He claims to be a poet, "I too am fond of country life, but here you don't have beautiful shepherdesses and love making like in the West. Well, there are some grass girls, but they smell awful. Besides, in our country you don't get maidens to indulge in love making, you must be content with widows. There is no other way" (p. 36). He thus delights in referring to the English life expressed through English literature and language. He exhibits his admiration for the widow by writing a poem on her in English. He even boasts, "When I published this in *The Reformer*, Tennyson read it and was stunned" (p. 37).

When Agnihotravadhanlu sees his son Venkatesam climb the guava tree, he scolds him. But Girisam tries to convince him about the necessity of physical labour and the interconnection between English language and culture, education, and philosophy, "There is nothing like work in this world. I get bored sitting idle. This way, I can water the plants and exercise my body. The Governor works in the garden, the English queen stitches clothes to give to the poor and the needy—the English fellow doesn't tolerate idleness. You know what their greatest poet Shakespeare said? He said, 'dignity of labour', which means that neither the Collector nor the judge but only the man who does physical labour is a great man. That is why all these whites do gardener's work to earn reputation. Climbing trees is considered a great skill among them. The whites don't do anything unless there is gain in it. Suppose, when a white officer is traveling from place to place, he feels thirsty, and sees fruits on the trees. But if he hasn't learnt to climb trees, he would have no alternative but to die of thirst in the middle of nowhere. Or imagine when he is commanding the 'agency', he encounters a tiger. If the white man is capable of climbing trees, he'll save himself. That is why they also learn tree climbing as a part of their education" (p. 81). Girisam's views are comic as well as serious at the same time. He goes to the extent of warning Agnihotravadhanlu, "If you opt for white man's education you can't escape white man's training. If you shout like this, he'll get scared and fall down. If you don't like these things, stop his English education and teach him the Veda" (p. 82). Girisam argues with Agnihotravadhanlu so persuasively that the latter repents of his ignorance of English, "My ignorance of English has become a big problem" (p. 82). Agnihotravadhanlu cannot understand the legal papers as they are in English.

English acts a means of access to all the privileges and opportunities of life. Ramappantulu, for example, repents of not knowing English and hence missing the golden opportunities. He tells Madhuravani, "If only I could speak English, the white ladies would be running after me" (p. 85). Madhuravani also has some attraction for English. She tells Ramappantulu, "Yes, when you mention English, I remembered something. I believe Girisamgaru speaks English as stylishly as the whites" (p. 85). That is why she had made Girisam teach her English for some time when he kept her as a mistress.

Thus, Girisam teases and tantalizes everyone with his knowledge of English, which is easily the vehicle of English education, culture, and philosophy. Although his bandying of English has apparently a comic touch about it, it has a deeper significance in the context of colonial encounter between two cultures, i.e. Brahmanism and Christianity. Girisam's boasting and his missionary zeal about English in the nineteenth-century South India resemble similar behaviour of modern English teachers of India, who return from British Universities and exhibit their King's or Queen's English and the Received Pronunciation, which is not understood easily by Indians. English, obviously, has a snob value. Gurjada Appa Rao laughs at the conceit of the speakers of English. His satire has not dated so far as it is still relevant in the twenty-first century India.

Apart from situational humour, the play has a lot of verbal humour too. Girisam provides an abundance of such humour by his exaggerated speech and fanciful ideas. A few examples will suffice to prove it. He instigates his student Venkatesam to steal tobacco from his father and justifies it. His rationalization about stealing is very comic and provides good humour to the audience, "When I was young, my uncle used to be hot tempered, just like your father. He used to twist my ear and make me learn the Upanishads by heart. I don't remember the name, but in some Upanishad the disciple keeps shooting questions and the teacher replies. You are much like that disciple, and I that teacher. If someone records our questions and answers on palm leaves, in two hundred years from now it would become known as the *Tobacco Upanishad*. Why do you think stealing tobacco is sinful? After all, you don't keep it; you just smoke it away to ashes. Stealing tobacco from those, who crush it into snuff is indeed a great service to humanity, believe me" (p. 129). In case God decides to send Girisam to hell to spend a stint, he would like to argue with God as follows, "O God Almighty! Please tell me whether you have created me a dependent being or an entirely independent one. If you have created me to be independent, I have the right to do what I like. Who are you to ask me for an explanation? If you interfere in my affairs and make trouble for me, I shall start a small National Congress in heaven. On the other hand, if you have created me to be dependent, you should take the responsibility for my sins. So you should take the punishment. Therefore, *chalo*, off you go to hell. And if you let me have your authority in your brief absence, I shall set right certain anomalies in your creation" (p. 130).

Girisam highlights some of the anomalies in God's creation. Much of creation is ineffectual according to him. Out of seven oceans "many among them are superfluous! When you have the milk sea why do you need a curd-sea and a ghee sea? This is what is called Pleonasm. Mere duplication. Have you noticed another instance of God's foolishness? The utterly useless salt sea is dumped here for us, while curd, milk, ghee, sugarcane juice seas are all placed beyond our access. If God takes me into his ministry for a year, I shall get milk sea for Bheemunipatnam, fresh water sea for Visakhapatnam and sugarcane juice sea for Kalingapatnam. I shall turn the Eastern ghats into a forest of tobacco. When I make god see all these possibilities, do you know what he would say? He would realize that he has an extraordinary human being to deal with, and will order his assistants to take me round Heaven in his golden chariot to look at all the palaces and gardens there, and let me have whatever I fancy. I shall tell these demigods that I would get bored unless I have the company of my dear student, Venkatesam. Then they will fetch you in an aeroplane. Two of us can have great fun in heaven" (p. 131). Such boasting and impractical wishful thinking easily reminds us of Dr. Faustus of Marlow and Bobadil of Ben Jonson and provides a good deal of humour and entertainment to the reader and spectator.

***

We have already seen how Gurjada Appa Rao rejected Sanskrit and standard (i.e. bookish) Telugu and chose to write his *magnum opus* in the colloquial Telugu, which is ideally suited to drama, especially realistic and satirical comedy. Not all the nuances of colloquial language can be brought out in English translation. But the two translators have intelligently retained certain linguistic practices, i.e. use of double-words or reduplications in which the second word serves only as a rhythmic and rhyming counterpart, but has no meaning at all. Such twin words are quite common in Indian languages, especially Dravidian languages. The use of twin words like romance-*broomance*, marbles-*geerbles*, shastra-*geestra*, letter or *gitter*, *madhuram-gidhuram*, oil-*geeyil*, and drama-*geema*, etc. gives a local flavour of the language and culture and tickles the totally anglicized Indians and the English-speaking readers and spectators of the world.

On the whole, Kanyasulkam is an extraordinarily interesting satirical comedy of epic proportions. It holds mirror to a number of cultural details of nineteenth-century South India. Not only literary critics, but even the sociologists can benefit from a study of it. It deals with a number of social evils like child-marriage, widow-marriage, bride-price, prostitution, Sanskrit education, English education, constabulary system, and corruption in judiciary, belief in ghosts and religious superstitions, etc. The play is known not only for its satirical element but also for its robust humour. "The playwright's intent is serious, but his essential dramatic mode is comedy. In creating both sentimental and verbal humour, the writer traverses the whole gamut—farce, slapstick, burlesque, parody—and employs a range of comic devices—disguise, mimicry, and charade. Through humour and levity Gurjada foregrounds an encounter between tradition and modernity that has not lost its relevance" (Foreword, p. XI). It is therefore a remarkable contribution to the realm of Tamil Drama as well as Indian Drama in English Translation, thanks to the masterly translators, C. Vijayasree and T. Vijayakumar.

*****

References

1. Lal, Ananda, Ed. *The Oxford Companion to Indian Theatre*, New Delhi: Oxford University Press, 2004, p. 15.
2. Appa Rao, Gurjada Venkata, *Kanyasulkam*, Tr. Vijayasree, C. and Vijayakumar, T. New Delhi: The Book Review, *Literary Review*, 2002. p. 265. (All the subsequent page references are to this edition.)
3. Preface to the Second Edition, *Kanyasulkam*. p. ix.

• • • • •

14

The Conflict between Bondage and Liberation in *Mukta-dhara*

Mukta-dhara happens to be one of several plays written by Rabindranath Tagore. Like most of his plays, it is at once lyrical and symbolic dealing with particularities as well as universalities of life. Mukta-dhara, which happens to be the name of a river, is also symbolic of the human quest for freedom. The setting of the play is Bengali. The place names like Uttarakut and Shivtarai easily bear it out. As the play advances, these place names take on symbolic, hence universal significance also. The central conflict in the play has been created between two binary opposite forces, i.e. the natives of Uttarakut and those of Shivtarai. Although the action of the play cannot be located factually in any particular year or decade of Indian history, it easily suggests the period of colonial India, foreshadowing the subsequent nationalism, freedom struggle, and the tension between religion and science. Tagore has symbolically captured the broad trends of social, economic, political, emotional, and spiritual aspects of Indian life. A born poet and a symbolist by temperament, Tagore has not cluttered the play with drab and mundane details of life. On the contrary, he presents the characters and situations in the symbolic mode thereby disguising his ideology.

The central conflict in the play emerges between the offensive force of Uttarakut and the defensive force of Shiv-tarayans. Mukta-dhara happens to be the bone of contention between these parties. The water of this river assumes many layers of significance in the play. The river runs in both their villages and therefore belongs to both of them. Water, a precious gift of God to man cannot be hoarded by any one party. It is one of the basic necessities of life. It is absolutely necessary for agriculture, which is again a sustainer of human life. Like air, water also belongs to one and all. The main conflict between the natives of Uttarakut and those of Shivtarai begins when the former hoard the water of the river by building a huge dam across it thereby preventing free flow of the water to the region of Shivtarai. King Ranajit of Uttarakut, who symbolizes the feudal type of government, is very selfish in that he thinks of the welfare of only his people and does not even bother about the welfare of the Shiv-tarayans. Far from accepting the fact of the universal ownership of the water by humanity, he delights in his selfish possessiveness and therefore wants to hoard the water for his own kingdom. King Ranajit's political power combined with selfishness is further assisted by science (and technology). He has encouraged Bibhuti, the royal engineer of his kingdom to build a huge dam across the river. Through this situation Tagore brings in his favourite theme of the conflict between science and religion. In the early decades of twentieth century, the Indians had been torn by the dilemma between science and religion. All through the ages, India has been a very religious country. In fact, it has been known as a land of several major and minor religions. But science, which had made great strides in the West, had inevitably entered India and disturbed the religious attitude of Indians. Originally, science had been invented and pursued in the West for the advancement and expansion of human happiness by offering him maximum material comforts. But ironically enough, the same science subjected to political order of selfishness was employed for the destruction of happiness of its so-called enemies. It is this universal story of science becoming a handmaid of selfish politics, which has been symbolically presented by Tagore in *Mukta-dhara*. Thus, the emotional conflict between Uttarakut and Shivtarai and the ideological conflict between science and religion overlap each other.

The dramatist shows the intersection between religion with science in the first act itself. When a procession of devotees passes across the stage singing the glory of Lord Sankara and when a pilgrim from a foreign land enquires a citizen of Uttarakut about a fearsome sight in the sky. The citizen of Uttarakut describes it as a Machine and explains, "Our royal engineer Bibhuti has been working at it for twenty five years. It's just finished, so today is a festival" (p. 10). He further explains quite proudly, "It stops up the springs of Mukta-dhara" (p. 10). The two characters express the diametrically opposed attitudes to science. The pilgrim from the foreign land points out the destructive, deforming and desecrating nature of science: "Ugh! It looks like a demon's head, a grinning skeleton head, lying in wait to devour your city in its sleep. To have it before your eyes night and day will dry up your souls like dead wood.... It seems to irritate the whole sky.... It seems like a blasphemy that it should soar so high above the temple tower" (p. 10).

Throughout the play, the contrast between science and religion is kept up. Whereas religion recognizes the presence of God and the meaning, beauty and purpose of his creation, science tries to challenge it and even compete with it. Scientific knowledge and achievement are no joke either. Science holds a mirror to human intelligence. Bibhuti, the royal engineer is very proud of his intelligence and its successful application. "The purpose of my dam was that human intelligence should win through to its goal through sand and stone and water all conspired to block its path.... My thoughts are full of the splendour of the power of the Machine" (p. 12). He is proud of having completed the Machine and blocked the flow of water.

Although science is a testimony to the enormity of human intelligence, it is employed by the King of Uttarakut for the benefit of his own people and to the disadvantage of Shiv-tarayan. Though science may achieve something great and remarkable, it involves the sacrifice of many lives for its sustenance and growth. Bibhuti, the royal engineer knows the truth, but does not bother about it. He says, "I had no time to think of whether some farmer's paltry maize crop would die" (p. 12). "See here, at one time there were no labourers to be had in Uttarakut. We went at the king's command to every house in Chandapattana. We seized every boy of eighteen years upwards. Most of them never returned. All mothers cursed me, yet my Machine has triumphed.

When a man fights the power of gods, does he care for the curses of men?" (p. 13). Several young men have been sacrificed to the Machine in the process of its construction. Amba, a village old woman who has lost her son Suman, has been waiting for him for long in vain. But Bibhuti does not bother about such sacrifices. The friends and classmates of Bibhuti admire him whole-heartedly and feel proud of him. They not only wish to garland him, but even lift him on their shoulders. They sing the glory of the Machine:

> All hail, Machine, we worship thee,
> We bow to thee, we honour thee,
> Machine, O Lord Machine....

Though the Machine is a proud manifestation of Bibhuti's engineering expertise and achievement, it is used by the king, Ranajit, symbolic of political power to control and suppress his enemy. Scientific knowledge has become a handmaid of selfish politics. The king says, "You have never been able to manage those Shiv-tarayan at all. Now that Bibhuti has Mukta-dhara under control at last, we have a way of making them submit" (p. 16). The Machine (i.e. science and technology by implication) becomes a means of suppression of the alien Shiv-tarayan, by blocking the waters of Mukta-dhara River, which belong to everybody by the divine rule. Thus, science has become a competitor for religion or divine order of life.

The river, which is a symbol of free flow or liberation or dynamic principle, is linked up with Abhijit, the present Yuvaraja of Uttarakut. Whereas King Ranajit stands for the feudal order of life, Prince Abhijit symbolizes the democratic order of life. Though staying in the palace, he does not identify himself with the royal life, but remembers his low birth and therefore longs to belong to the river and practice liberal principles of life. As the Minister explains it to King Ranajit, "Maharaja, you are forgetting our real reason for sending the Yuvaraja to Shivtarai. He seemed so unsettled in mind and we suspected, you know, that he had somehow got a hint of the truth that he is not of royal birth, but was picked up below the falls of Mukta-dhara" (p. 17). Abhijit who has acquired the knowledge of his low birth (perhaps also illegitimate) by the side of the river seems to have developed a filial affinity with the place of his birth. King Ranajit is rather puzzled by the 'strange' behaviour of Abhijit. "Every night he used to go and sleep below the falls when I heard them about it. I went to him there one night and asked him straight, "What's the matter, Abhijit, why are you here? And he replied, 'In the sound of this water I hear my mother's voice'" (p. 18). There is thus a contiguous connection between Abhijit and Mukta-dhara. Being a forlorn child, he identifies himself with the common people, especially the oppressed people and being a child born near the river, he identifies himself with the spirit of freedom. Whereas the river stands for dynamism and free flow, the palace made of rocks stands for sterility and heartlessness.

When Abhijit is posted as the prince and officer of Shivtarai, he takes decisions and acts in favour of Shiv-tarayan thereby ignoring the economic interests of Uttarakut people. That is the reason why King Ranajit has begun to lose his faith in Abhijit's imperial destiny. He says, "I've had nothing but loss from this lad. Ever since my grandfather's time the road over the Nandi Pass has been blocked, to prevent the wool trade of Shivtarai going to foreign markets. Now Abhijit has thrown open that road and here in Uttarakut the price of food and clothing will go up" (p. 18). Abhijit's identification with Shivtarai people is interpreted by King Ranajit as 'treachery'. He bursts out, "Treachery against his own people, I call it" (p. 18).

Prince Abhijit's broader, humanistic and truly religious approach is supported by King Viswajit, uncle of King Ranajit. He does not approve of the religious celebration of inhuman scientific and technological achievement in the form of a dam across the river. He says, "I have come to tell you that Bhairava will not accept today's worship" (p. 19). He questions King Ranajit's parochial intention and plan; "God pours out his water freely for all, for every thirsty soul on earth. Why have you blocked the streams?" But Ranajit tries to defend his own parochial and shortsighted viewpoint, "Bhairava is Uttarakut's own god. Our victories are His. So Bhairava takes our side and takes back his gift. He will pierce Shivtarai with his thirst-spear and fling it before the throne of Uttarakut" (p. 20). Ranajit wants to hoard the waters of Mukta-dhara with the political intention of harassing the people of Shivtarai. In this sense he becomes a symbol of selfishness and possessiveness. His very name suggests that he is interested in quarrelling or battling.

Like the river Mukta-dhara, the road is also an important symbol of liberty. Prince Abhijit is very closely connected with the road that leads him to the final destination of freedom. King Viswajit explains Prince Abhijit's major mission in life, "He was a guest in our palace for the Diwali festival. In the sunset light, I found him standing on the terrace, gazing towards Gouri's Peak. 'What do you see, brother?' I asked. 'I see roads', he said, 'roads that are not yet made, the roads of the future across those forbidding passes, roads that will bring the distant near.' And as I listened I thought, 'Some vagrant mother bore him by the springs of Mukta-dhara and who can keep him bound?' I could no longer keep silent. 'Brother,' I said, 'from the moment of birth the Lord of the Hills gave you welcome to the road. No conch-shell called you within doors'" (p. 21). Prince Abhijit who is attached to the river and road cannot be restricted to any narrow space. That is the reason why he feels alienated from the royal palace of Uttarakut. He is more interested in opening the road than in blocking it because "A road once opened is a road for all, for Uttarakut and Shivtarai alike" (p. 21).

Tagore's attack on the negative aspect of scientific achievement is very strong. The so-called achievement of the scientist, i.e. Engineer Bibhuti seems to have bloated his ego beyond limits and made him forget his humble past. The first citizen expresses it very clearly, "You saw how Bibhuti avoids us nowadays. He would like to rub his upbringing out of his skin altogether. One day he'll find out that it's not good for the sword to get too big for its sheath" (p. 25). The final achievement in science is preceded by man failures. The first citizen voices it, "You fellows make far too much of him. That dam of his nearly finished him, and it has given way at least ten times" (p. 25). The dam has fallen down many times before it is finally constructed and there is no guarantee that it will not fall down again in future. The Machine, an embodiment of scientific achievement has not only claimed many lives of young men in the past, but requires human sacrifice even in the present i.e. on the day of its celebration.

Batuk says, "There will be sacrifice, human sacrifice. They took away my two lusty grandsons by force; they have not come back" (p. 27). The Machine, the demon of Thirst, "The more he gets, the more he wants. His dry tongue grows longer and longer, like a flame fed with ghee" (p. 27). Batuk says further "Bhairava is being turned out of his temple today—Thirst demon will sit on the altar instead" (p. 27).

Prince Abhijit has felt an inner urge to identify himself with the river and follow his own path of life in tune with the Vedantic philosophy, "Somewhere or other in the external world, God writes for us the secret mystery of each man's spirit. Mukta-dhara is His word to me bearing the secret of my inner being when her feet were bound in the iron fetters. I was startled out of a dream. I realized the truth—the throne of Uttarakut is the dam, which binds my spirit. I have taken the road in order to set it free" (p. 29). Prince Abhijit has discovered his own spiritual path. Vedantic philosophy teaches that every man should discover his own path of life and not imitate others blindly. Abhijit, therefore, asks Sanjaya not to follow him, but to find his own path. Abhijit, like a mystic, hears the transcendental music in all the microscopic and variegated beauty of the earth. He, therefore, decides to offer his reverence to all the things of life. "To each smallest thing that has sweetened my life, I offer my reverence tonight" (p. 30).

Prince Abhijit has opened the Nandi Pass road, but his noble act is resented by King Ranajit and his group. But Abhijit clarifies his intention when he says that he has opened the road "To save the people of Shivtarai from continual famine" (p. 31). Abhijit thinks of the well-being of both Uttarakut and Shivtarai people, but his broad-minded attitude is not liked by the partisan King Ranajit. He, therefore, orders the Commander-in-Chief Vijayapal to arrest Abhijit. Abhijit is now kept in the tent as a prisoner. King Ranajit has recalled the Yuvaraja from Shivtarai and decided not to reappoint him. The people of Shivtarai led by Dhananjaya meet the king and request him to reappoint Abhijit as the administrator of Shivtarai. Further, they refuse to pay taxes to King Ranajit due to their poverty and poor harvest.

King Ranajit is very angry with Dhananjaya for his leadership and defense of Shivtarai people and orders him to be arrested.

Different people attribute different motives to Prince Abhijit. They offer contradictory opinions and misinterpretations about his philosophy of life. People who are angry at the king's imprisonment of the prince in a tent set fire to it. King Viswajit orders Uddhav to release both the prisoners, i.e. Abhijit and Dhananjaya. King Viswajit wants to take Abhijit to Mohangarh, but Abhijit has decided to release the waters of Mukta-dhara from the demonic dam. "I must pay my debt, the debt of my birth. Mukta-dhara was my nurse. I must set her free" (p. 57). Meanwhile Dhananjaya begins to tell the people of Uttarakut that Lord Bhairava is awakened by now and that He would do justice to the world. The people of Uttarakut, unable to relish his prophetic words arrest him for a brief while and then release him. But Dhananjaya refuses to return to Shivtarai as he wants to attend Lord Bhairava's festival. "It is Bhairava's festival. Only the evening lamps of Shivtarai remain to be offered" (p. 63).

Meanwhile the so-called damage done by Prince Abhijit has been ordered by King Ranajit to be repaired instantly. The soldiers, therefore, catch hold of all the civilians available and force them to rebuild the Nandi Pass fort overnight. The soldiers exhibit their usual callousness and inhumanity in dealing with the poor and innocent people. But the bold people like Banwari refuse to oblige the soldiers.

The rebuilding of the Nandi Pass fort exactly on the day of celebrating the dam is taken by Bibhuti as a deliberate insult to him. He thinks that some rival is cleverly frustrating his plans. But nonetheless he decides to face the situation boldly. King Ranajit is ignorant about the escape of Prince Abhijit from the prison-tent. The people of Shivtarai who are still under the impression that Prince Abhijit is kept in prison rush to Uttarakut to release him and make him king of Shivtarai.

Meanwhile Prince Abhijit has accomplished his task of breaking the dam. Bibhuti is surprised by the sound of rushing water. "There is no mistaking it. The sound of running water.... My God, it is—it is Mukta-dhara! The water is rushing out. The dam, the dam, who has broken the dam? No chance for him now! (pp. 74-75). King Ranajit, although shocked by the sound of the rushing water, worries about the safety of Prince Abhijit. But Sanjaya comes and tells them "The Yuvaraja has broken the bonds of Mukta-dhara" (p. 76) and that "He had somehow found a weak spot—there he struck. The monster machine struck him back. Then Mukta-dhara, like a mother, took up his wounded body in her arms and carried him away" (p. 76). Dhananjaya sings, "Fetters fall and bondage ends" (p. 76). Abhijit, thus, sacrifices his life for liberating the water of the river from the bondage of the dam and concurrently achieves his fulfillment in *videha mukti* (posthumous liberation of his soul).

The tension between science and religion; parochialism and humanism; feudalism and democracy and between bondage and freedom is finally resolved by the triumph of the latter over the former. Abhijit who symbolizes religion, broad humanism, spiritual democracy, and liberation triumphs over King Ranajit who stands for science, parochialism, feudalism, short sightedness, exploitation, suppression, and bondage. Prince Abhijit becomes a martyr in the cause of empirical freedom as well as spiritual freedom.

He characters and situations in the play are not rooted in the geography and history of India, especially Bengal from which Tagore hails. On the contrary, they are either allegorical or symbolic. The names of places like Uttarakut and Shivtarai sound Bangla, but it is not certain if such places exist in reality. But Uttarakut and Shivtarai being an elevated mountainous place and a lower plain respectively provide the symbolic contrast between the powerful and the powerless people respectively. Likewise the names of characters are allegorical if not symbolic. King Ranajit indicates a fighter or warrior or conqueror. Prince Abhijit indicates victorious man. King Viswajit indicates a conqueror of the world, hence endowed with a cosmic vision. Dhananjaya indicates a conqueror of desire for money. He is also a prophetic man and a Gandhian figure. Bibhuti indicates a seer as well as a prophetic man but ironically, he is power-hungry and money-hungry man. Their actions either intensify the meaning of their names or set up an ironic contrast to their names.

Although the central theme of the play happens to be the conflict between science and religion, feudalism and democracy, parochialism and humanism, bondage and freedom, there is also a good deal of satirical element in it which has a contemporary relevance. Tagore satirizes the master or teachers brainwashing their students in favour of their own kingdom and prejudicing them against the others. When King Ranajit is to confer honour upon the royal engineer Bibhuti, the master wants to take his boys there to share the rejoicings. The boys are made to believe that the Shivtarai people and their religion are very bad and that they do not have high-ridged noses. The Masters teaching such parochial ideas to their students helps the politicians or rulers to run their administration very smoothly. When King Ranajit comments upon the schoolmaster's ignorance, the Minister highlights the positive aspects of such brainless people, "But Maharaja, fellows of this kind have their uses. Day after day they repeat, mechanically, exactly what they have been told. Things wouldn't run so smoothly if they had more sense" (p. 24). Tagore's satire on how the rulers thrive on the ignorance of their subjects is quite obvious here. His satirical vision is relevant to India even today as the modern politicians bank upon the illiterate, ignorant, and misguided voters for their survival.

Tagore's satirical exposure of stealing of ideas from others may be seen in the case of the royal engineer Bibhuti. Although Bibhuti enjoys the high reputation of having made a great intellectual (i.e. scientific) achievement in building a dam across the river, at least some of the citizens know the secret of his theft. "I know myself he stole it all from Benkot Varma. Now he was really a clever chap. What a head! My word! Yet Bibhuti gets a feather in his cap, while he, poor fellow, died from want of food" (p. 26). It is very clear from this that Bibhuti has stolen his insights from an earlier scientist, Benkot Varma who was a talented person but who died of starvation. Bibhuti has made the best use of this golden opportunity of misappropriating the intellectual property of another man and getting undeserved recognition for the same. The biographies of many great scientists of the world reveal many such examples of misappropriation and exploitation by clever people. This holds well not only in scientific research but in all other kinds of research all over the world. Tagore's satire attains a universal dimension in this case.

We have already discussed the allegorical and symbolic significance of the characters and situations in the play. That seems to be the reason why there is a preponderance of poetic and dialogistic element, which is not supported by physical action, which is very essential for the success of drama. In other words, all the important physical action happens to be indirect or offstage and the direct or onstage action happens to be very little. Since Tagore's dramatic vision is controlled by his ideology. The characters and situations are governed more by concepts than by the laws of probability. That is the reason why they fail to convince us. Many times the units of action appear to be arbitrary and artificial and not the logical result of preceding events. For example, the causes for the rivalry between Uttarakut and Shivtarai have not been clearly established in the play. If the Shivtarai people are foreigners, why should they be ruled over by the King of Uttarakut or his deputy, Abhijit? This question is not answered in the play. Similarly, the most important aspect of the play, i.e. the discovery by Prince Abhijit of his low birth is not very convincing. The question as to why a boy of low birth should be in a palace is never answered in the play. Likewise, the psychological identification of Prince Abhijit with Mukta-dhara is not established in a convincing manner. We learn it more through reportage than through the characters own words. His crisis of identity could have been explored minutely by Tagore in order to give an in-depth picture of man's inner world. But the playwright seems to have taken it for granted. The arrival of Maharaja Viswajit of Mohangarh to Uttarakut, his support of Prince Abhijit's cause is not convincing at all, as it seems to be so arbitrary and unexpected. The flower girl sending a white lotus as a gift to a sadhu is very arbitrary and unconvincing. Similarly, Bhairagi Dhananjaya's behaviour is not convincing as he, like many other characters, talks in paradoxical terms, which is not understood by the simple folks of Shivtarai who have accepted him as their leader. Likewise, Sanjaya claims to be a close friend of Abhijit, but the closeness of their friendship is not established properly through action. We have to believe him only on the face of his words. The second arrival of Maharaja Viswajit to arrest and take away Abhijit is not logically satisfying. Prince Abhijit's identification with the river and his effort to break the dam all by himself violate the law of probability. Although Tagore wants to project Abhijit as a martyr, he has not established the nature of his martyrdom in a sufficiently convincing manner. The king's order to rebuild the Nandi Pass fort reported by the sergeant comes rather abruptly without preparing the audience to receive it. King Ranajit's crass ignorance about the burning of the prison-tent where Abhijit is kept is unconvincing as it is not in accordance with the administrative alertness of a royal personage. Prince Abhijit's so-called self-sacrifice makes him more a religious figure than a political ruler. His basic protest against the construction of the dam across the river is caused by his knowledge of injustice done to Shivtarai people. But his intimacy with Shiv-tarayan is never shown or established in the play. Had he really cared for the Shiv-tarayan he would have taken a more practical course of action. Thus, there are many links in feeling, thought and action missing in the play. The entire play is infused with an aura of vagueness.

The play, though written in prose, contains many songs and poetic passages. Tagore being a poet at heart expresses his poetic attitude to life even in his prose. *Mukta-dhara*, therefore, contains many similes and metaphors thereby giving expression to Tagore's poetic vision of life. Tagore's disapproval of the negative aspect of scientific achievement is articulated in his simile of a demon's head. As the pilgrim says, the Machine "looks like a demon's head, a grinning skeleton head lying in wait to devour your city in its sleep" (p. 10). It seems to irritate the whole sky and be soaring so high above the temple tower. Whereas science is symbolized by the Machine, religion is symbolized by the temple. The Machine is further metaphorised as a vulture, a grim magician, the menacing fist of a demon, an arrow, thirst demon, and a monster. The river Mukta-dhara remains as an extended symbol throughout the play.

Although the play is not very clear about the historical period of Indian life, critics have inferred the background to be of colonial India. The rivalry between Uttarakut and Shivtarai people for the exclusive possession of water has a great contemporary relevance to post-colonial India also. The people of Karnataka and Tamil Nadu quarrelling over the Kaveri water or those of Karnataka and Maharashtra quarrelling over the river water can learn a good lesson from Tagore's play. Since water is a gift of God for the entire humanity, no State should fight with another to possess it exclusively.

Reference

Tagore, Rabindranath, *Mukta-dhara,* in *Three Plays*. Seventh Impression. Tr. Marjorie Sykes. Madras: Oxford University Press, 1969. (All the page references to the text are from this edition.)

• • • • •

15

Tughlaq: A Tale of the Failure of Idealism

Tughlaq happens to be the first historical play written by Girish Karnad (1938-2019). Later he wrote his second and third historical plays like *Tale-Danda* and *The Dreams of Tipu Sultan* respectively. Muhammad bin Tughlaq is such an enigmatic figure in Indian history that it is difficult to classify him in any neat category of kings or rulers. Many historians, Indian as well as foreign, have expressed their own contradictory assessment of his character. For example, Tughlaq is known for his 'unusual originality of mind,' 'high ambition,' 'exalted aspirations,' 'visions of universal conquest,' 'great love of honour,' 'extra-ordinary sense of prestige,' 'visionary qualities,' 'scholarship,' 'rich imagination,' 'poetic appreciation,' 'philosophical speculation,' 'knowledge of various subjects like metaphysics, medicine, astrology, poetry, etc.,' 'rationalism', 'indomitable will,' 'prodigious memory,' 'knowledge of Koran by heart,' 'broad and dynamic political vision,' 'dogged tenacity of purpose,' 'liberality and kindness,' 'brilliant calligraphy,' 'extension of agriculture,' and 'his desire to be not only an Alexander (the Great) but also a Solomon.' These extraordinary qualities have compelled the historians to consider him as 'a wonder of creation.'

But ironically the same historians have pointed out the negative qualities also of his personality. For example, Tughlaq was notorious for his 'insanity' or 'madness,' 'inordinate pride,' 'over-ambition,' 'lack of practical judgement, commonsense, sense of proportion, balance and patience,' 'lack of the power of discrimination between offences,' 'headstrong temper,' 'barbarity,' 'blood-thirstiness,' 'a second Yezid,' 'a tyrant,' and 'a heretic.'

All these contradictory qualities are found together in Tughlaq. That is why he is variously known as 'a freak of nature,' 'a nightmare,' 'a mixture of opposites,' and 'a compound of contradictions.' Hence, it is rather difficult to understand his personality completely and satisfactorily.

Girish Karnad (1938-2019) happens to be the first playwright who tried to dramatize the life of such a king. This play was a theatrical success in India during 1970s, perhaps because of the enigmatic personality of the Emperor, which accorded well with the short-lived tradition of Absurd Drama in Kannada.

Girish Karnad has borrowed the character of Muhammad bin Tughlaq from the history of medieval India because Tughlaq happens to be an important historical personage who played a significant role in the drama of Indian history. He may be called a hero as king *a la* Carlyle and represents a transitional period in Indian history. Along with the characters of the eponymous hero, i.e. Tughlaq the playwright has borrowed other historical characters also like Barani, Najib, Ainul Mulk, Ghiyasuddin Abbasid, Sheikh Imamuddin and so on thereby achieving historical authenticity (and accuracy). To the galaxy of these historical personages he had added some imaginary characters also like Aziz and Aazam just to accentuate his own distinctive vision of life. He has borrowed the external facts of history like Tughlaq's transfer of his capital from Delhi to Daulatabad, introduction of copper currency and his attempt to maintain a balance between Hindus and Muslims in his empire. He has transformed this historical raw material into art, especially drama in his own manner. In writing this historical play the playwright is interested in interpreting history not from the point of view of the past but from that of the present. In other words, he is more interested in the present-ness of the past than in the past-ness of the past. His play may, therefore, be said to be attempt at the contemporization of history. He sees a similarity between Tughlaq's era and Nehru's era in several details. As U.R. Anantamurthy rightly says, "it is a play of the sixties, and reflects as no other play does the political mood of disillusionment which followed the Nehru era of idealism in the country" (*Introduction*, p. viii). Karnad himself comments on the need for writing such a historical play, which has a contemporary relevance now:

> What struck me absolutely about Tughlaq's history was that it was contemporary. The fact that here was the most idealistic, the most intelligent king ever to come on the throne of Delhi...and one of the greatest failures also. And within a span of twenty years this tremendously capable man had gone to pieces. This seemed to be both due to his idealism as well as the shortcomings within him, such as his impatience, his cruelty, his feeling that he had the only correct answer. And I felt in the early sixties India had also come very far in the same direction—the twenty-year period seemed to me very much a striking parallel. (Quoted, p. viii)

Muhammad bin Tughlaq strikes us as a man cursed with several inner contradictions of his personality and ideology and the external, socio-political contradictions of his empire. His tragic problem consisted in his ceaseless to reconcile the opposites in empirical terms.

The political life of Tughlaq is very rich and complex, consisting of several battles, victories, achievements, and failures. But Girish Karnad, like a typical historical playwright, selects only a few well-known external facts of Tughlaq's life, fleshes them out with experiential and ideological details, thereby offering a consistent and coherent picture of his life and making it more intelligible and appealing then the dry, discursive historical narratives. He succeeds in making the historical characters come alive on the stage and touch the chords of the spectators. In other words, he transforms the historical reality into an artistic vision through his animated reconstruction. Through the artistic presentation the playwright evaluates history and articulates his ideological stand and satirical dimension. Having chosen a crucial period of medieval Indian history involving multiple socio-political collisions, the playwright highlights the psychological crisis of Muhammad Tughlaq.

The play begins at a moment when the eponymous hero has already grabbed the throne of Delhi, the seat of political power and has been consequently trying to retain it and build a Utopian kingdom. But the path of progress is beset with a number of hindrances and encumbrances. The main intention of Tughlaq is to be impartial to both Hindus and Muslims and project an image of himself as a man of divine protection to one and all. But his special love for Hindus is not liked by his own co-religionists, i.e. Muslims. It is expressed in the first scene wherein a young man and an old man discuss Tughlaq's administration, his special love for Hindus, their exemption from the payment of jiziya tax and Tughlaq's so-called insult to Islam. The Hindu feels safe only when he is kicked to pay up the jiziya tax. The old man comments that the Hindu may turn Islam into another caste and the Prophet an incarnation of his god. The dialogue between the young man and the old man obviously expresses the anti-Hindu opinion of the Muslim population and their dislike of Tughlaq for that very reason.

Since Tughlaq happens to be an idealist and impartial ruler, he wants to be kind and fair to the Hindus, who form nearly half of the population of his kingdom. He does not wish to be a religious fanatic like Aurangzeb. He wants his impartiality to be known to the public of his kingdom. That is why an announcer announces that Rishnu Prasad, a Brahmin of Shikaner filed a suit against His Merciful Majesty with the Kazi-i-Mumalik and won the case and got a compensation of 500 dinars and even a post in the Civil Service to ensure him a regular income.

Then Tughlaq addresses the people of his kingdom and draws their attention to how justice works in his kingdom. He makes a shocking announcement that he wants to shift his capital from Delhi to Daulatabad in order to make life more purposeful. He explains that his empire has become larger than earlier due to his imperialist expansion of territory and embraces the South and therefore he is justified in having a capital in the South, which consists of huge Hindu population. Tughlaq, thus wants to achieve a geographical balance between north and south and a communal balance between Hindus and Muslims and project his image as an ideal king recognizing all the sections of Indian society.

The playwright has rather simplified the intention of Tughlaq in moving his capital from Delhi to Daulatabad. According to historical sources, Tughlaq's decision to shift the capital from Delhi to Deogiri or Daulatabad was motivated by the political pressure and contingency. His empire had expanded from north to south and from east to west and therefore he wanted to have his capital in central India and to be equidistant to all the four directions of the frontiers of his empire, especially to be at a safe distance from Mongolia and Persia (whose rulers might attack Delhi at any time). Another reason for his shifting the Muslim population consisting of Amirs, Sayyids and Ulemas to Daulatabad was to break the dominance of Hindus there by implanting Islamic culture there. These historical details are not mentioned by Girish Karnad in his play. Tughlaq is a far-sighted Emperor much ahead of his time. But the Muslim officials and leaders could not understand the political problem from the Emperor's point of view. On the contrary, they dreaded the inconvenience of displacement and exile as they were deeply entangled to their original land of birth, i.e. Delhi. They, therefore, consider their Sultan as a mad man incapable of understanding the practical problems of life.

Another complaint that the people make against the Sultan in the play is that the Sultan killed his father at the prayer time (quoted, p. 5). This event is corroborated by the historical sources, which offer a detailed picture of how Tughlaq cleverly got a wooden structure constructed and saw to it that it collapsed the moment the elephant touched it thereby killing his father and brother. This interesting historical detail is missing in Karnad's play.

There is obviously a conflict between the Sultan and his Muslim subjects. The people know that the Sheikh in his public speech has accused Tughlaq of murdering his father and brother. They see that Tughlaq's power as a king is rooted in his moral corruption, although he pretends to be a pious Muslim and venerating the holy man, Sheikh Imamuddin. The contradiction between his sinful parricide and fratricide and his pretension of religiosity, especially his disciplinarian adherence to prayer is too conspicuous to be ignored. When Najib and Barani tell the Sultan about the Sheikh's public comment on him as incompetent, a disgrace to Islam and a murderer of his own father and brother, the Sultan does not take the accusation seriously. On the contrary, he wants to project himself as a broad-minded and liberal ruler who can tolerate the religious man's comments on him.

He, therefore, fixes a programme in the evening after the prayer in which Sheikh Imamuddin will address the gathering and analyze the behaviour and action of Tughlaq and show where he has gone wrong in taking wrong measures harmful to the country and the Faith. But when the holy man comes to address the gathering nobody has come to listen to him. Then the Sultan wants to call his officers and courtiers to listen to the speech, but Sheikh Imamuddin is not willing to address a gang of bootlickers. He would like to go to the marketplace next day and speak out his mind there. The Sultan is so clever and cunning that he has ordered his soldiers to prevent the civilians from attending the public speech by the holy man, although he pretends to respect him as a representative of Islamic Faith. This may be described as the political strategy that he employs for the maintenance of law and order in his kingdom.

The dialogues between the Sultan and the holy man bring out the interconnection between politics and religion. The Sultan defends himself by saying that he has never gone against the tenets of Islam. But Sheikh Imamuddin accuses Tughlaq of indulging in so many transgressions, due to ignorance or deliberate design—like putting the Sayyids and Ulema behind bars. Then Tughlaq defends himself by replying that he had to imprison them because they indulged in politics, contrary to their religious profession. He confesses that there is dirt and sickness in his kingdom but that he does not want to call on God to clean it. But Sheikh Imamuddin advises the Sultan to listen to the voice of God and spread the kingdom of God on earth and repay His debt. He further asks the Sultan not to be another God, as slaves have often tried to replace their masters. Tughlaq understands the irony of the holy man's statement as he very well knows that his grandfather was a slave who became a king.

Tughlaq's reply to Sheikh Imamuddin brings out his liberal thought and eclectic philosophy of life. Although he is born a Muslim and venerates his religion, i.e. Islam, he is not satisfied by its narrow thinking and fanatical rigidities and restrictions. His reading of Plato and Socrates has given him a vision of Utopia or Platonic world which is governed by the laws of ideal life. He tells the holy man that he read the Greek philosophers like Socrates and Plato who gave the world their vision of Truth and found a new world in them not found in Arabia and even in the Koran. Obviously, Tughlaq seems to believe in an eclectic vision of life and not restricted or shackled by the fundamentalist vision of Islam. He knows that he and his kingdom are torn into pieces now and therefore he wants to maintain a balance within himself (between apparently contradictory ideologies) and outside in the kingdom (between Hindus and Muslims).

The internal conflict may be seen between Tughlaq the clever administrator and Tughlaq the philosopher-poet. Tughlaq, for example, is an idealist, who is influenced by the Greek philosophers like Plato and Socrates and therefore wants to achieve a balance between opposite principles:

TUGHLAQ: I still remember the days when I read the Greeks—Sukrat who took poison so he could give the world the drink of gods, Aflatoon who condemned poets and wrote incomparably beautiful poetry himself—and I can still feel the thrill with which I found a new world, a world I had not found in the Arabs or even the Koran. They tore me into shreds. And to be whole now, I shall have to kill the part of me which sang to them. And my kingdom too is what I am—torn into pieces by visions whose validity I can't deny. You are asking me to make myself complete by killing the Greek in me and you propose to unify my people by denying the visions which led Zarathustra or the Buddha. (Smiles) I'm sorry. But it can't be done. (p. 21)

But Sheikh Imamuddin points out how it is almost impossible to achieve this balance of which Tughlaq dreams:

IMAMUDDIN: You are a learned man. You may be able to manage this delicate balance within yourself. But a kingdom

> needs not one king but a line of rulers. Will they manage this balance? Where are these brilliant successors of yours? Where are these guarantors of your balanced future? (p. 21)

He tells Sheikh Imamuddin that the people did not come to listen to his speech because they suspected a trap. But Sheikh Imamuddin, who can see through the Sultan's acts, congratulates him for his clever trick.

Tughlaq is so clever that he wants to exploit even the holy man for his political purposes. One may see here how religion becoming a handmaid of politics instead of politics becoming a handmaid of religion. Tughlaq tells the holy man that Ainul Mulk is marching on Delhi and therefore requests Sheikh Imamuddin to go meet him and dissuade him from pursuing his folly. He offers the robes of honour to the Sheikh and asks him to meet Ainul Mulk near the plains of Kanauj. The Sheikh tells him that he is the cleverest man in the world. In spite of knowing the Sultan's cleverness he yields to the latter's request and goes to meet Ainul Mulk on the battlefield of Kanauj and loses his life in a most unexpected manner, due to Tughlaq's clever military strategy of facing the enemy. This is reported by rattan Singh to Shihabuddin (who has accepted him as his adopted brother) in detail. Ratan Singh describes how Tughlaq trickily made Sheikh Imamuddin clad in royal robes sit on a royal elephant; that Sheikh Imamuddin stood up on his elephant to plead for peace with the enemy (i.e. Ainul Mulk); that a small platform stood 100 metres behind the Sheikh; that Tughlaq himself camped there with his large army behind a mountain; that when Sheikh Imamuddin stood up on his elephant, Tughlaq's own soldiers sounded off a bugle and started shooting the arrows and consequently Sheikh Imamuddin was killed within no time; that then the enemies marched towards the mountain and were trapped cleverly and gored to death. Ratan Singh replies that luckily he escaped death, although he was posted in the front of the army. All these events testify to Tughlaq's ability and cleverness to exploit even the religious leaders or holy men like Sheikh Imamuddin for his political safety and advancement. In a way, Tughlaq has wreaked vengeance on the holy man for criticizing and incriminating him publicly.

Tughlaq's idealism of maintaining a balance between Hindus and Muslims, his desire to project an image of himself as an impartial ruler and his special love and concessions shown to the Hindus is not appreciated by the Muslim population of his empire due to their fanaticism and parochialism. Instead, some Muslims like Aziz want to trap the Sultan in his own virtue and exploit the situation to their own advantage. We have already seen how Aziz impersonated a Hindu farmer called Vishnu Prasad, filed a suit to the Kazi against the Sultan and won the case and even a government job in the Emperor's service.

The Muslim Amirs and Sayyids fail to understand the Sultan's ulterior motives or hidden agenda of breaking the dominance of Hindus in Daulatabad by populating the southern capital with Muslim noblemen and introducing the Islamic culture there. On the contrary, they are worried about their own cultural roots, land-entanglement, security and physical comforts. Besides they are unhappy about the Sultan's imposition of various taxes (instead of only four, as per the Koran's dictum) and his love for Hindus as brothers. Thus, there is an ideological conflict between the Sultan and his own courtiers. Since Tughlaq has a dictatorial temperament, he is not in a position to listen to them and change his decision. Intransigence may be said to be his flaw. Hence, they are compelled by the peculiar circumstances to hatch a conspiracy against them. They, therefore, consult one another and request Shihabuddin to plead their case to the Sultan. But they know it for certain that the Sultan will not yield to their request. Hence, they are compelled by the dire circumstances to resort to a negative way of dealing with Tughlaq. In this conspiracy, they seek the help of Shihabuddin. After mutual consultation, Ratan Singh suggests that they should murder Tughlaq at the prayer time because, he argues, the Sultan is a fanatic of prayer and the whole palace is unarmed at the time of prayer. He justifies his view by saying that Tughlaq should be killed at that time itself as the Sultan himself had killed his own father and brother at the prayer time. The conspiracy is quite systematic and shows how even religion is made part of their politics of survival.

Accordingly, they attend the meeting with the Sultan in his durbar. Tughlaq tells them that Abbasid Ghiyasuddin Muhammad has accepted his invitation to come to the new capital, Daulatabad, and that the holy man is a member of the hallowed family of the Abbasid Khalifs. At that opportune time Shihabuddin requests the Sultan not to shift the capital from Delhi to Daulatabad, but Tughlaq replies that his kingdom cannot flourish with Delhi as its capital and that he has explained everything to his Amirs; and that he is going to introduce copper currency instead of silver currency because it is a question of trust and acceptance. He wants to enjoy the trust of his Amirs. He even requests them and wants to kneel before them thereby embarrassing them utterly. He takes up a copy of the *Koran* from the throne and asks them to take an oath on the holy book to support him in his measures. But they say that he should not distrust them so much as to make them take an oath on the *Koran*.

The whole situation is ironical. By that time the muezzin's voice is heard, calling the faithful to the prayer. Tughlaq, therefore, unbuckles his sword, places it on the throne. The servants bring water and mats for the Amirs. All of them sit for prayer. Muhammad Tughlaq leads the prayer. But half way through the prayer there is a commotion in the Durbar Hall. As the Amirs pull out their daggers and rush towards the throne, suddenly some twenty Hindu soldiers rush towards the Amirs and prevent them from murdering the sultan. Instantly, all the Amirs are dragged away except Shihabuddin. Tughlaq gets up only after completing his prayer. Such conspiracies and intrigues are quite common in the Indian as also in world history. The conspiracy of the Amirs has recoiled upon themselves. Tughlaq has outsmarted the smart Amirs.

Now Shihabuddin asks the Sultan how he could guess at their conspiracy against him. Tughlaq replies that he found a letter from Ratan Singh offering intelligence about the conspiracy. Here one may see how conspiracy is intertwined with betrayal. Ratan Singh has acted doubly treacherously by betraying both the parties mutually. Shihabuddin is really frightened by the betrayal by Ratan Singh. He learns that Ratan Singh has got his deserts, i.e. he is already killed by the Sultan's order. Shihabuddin is shocked to learn from the Sultan that his letters addressed to his father have been sent by Ratan Singh to Tughlaq treacherously.

As Muhammad Tughlaq happens to be a man of quick action, he stabs Shihabuddin mercilessly. He wonders why all those he trusted in life have turned out to be traitors. He orders Najib to see that everyone involved in the conspiracy is caught and beheaded. But Najib opines that Shihabuddin's father is a powerful man who cannot swallow the bitter truth—of the murder of his son. But Tughlaq is so clever that he orders that a public announcement should be made that Shihabuddin died a martyr's death in defending the Sultan when the court tried to murder him (the Sultan) during the prayer. The Sultan knows how to hoodwink the people by his beautiful, but probable and hence credible lies with the help of his dictatorial power.

Tughlaq hoped that every act in his kingdom would become a prayer and leading a step further to knowledge and nearer to God. Since their prayers are ridden with disease, he orders a ban on prayers in his kingdom. But he revises his decision in the light of Najib's suggestion that prayers should be banned till Ghiyasuddin Abbasid, the descendant of Khalif visits them. Yet he issues an ordinance that all the citizens of Delhi should leave Delhi and proceed to Daulatabad and that the State will take care of their comforts like food, clothing and medicine, etc.

Now five years have elapsed after the Sultan has moved to the new capital in the south, Daulatabad. He has built a magnificent fort and the widest, but serpentine road to connect Delhi with Daulatabad. As an able and ambitious and dynamic ruler he has done his best to improve the material conditions of life. His imperialist ambition is combined with his dreaming tendency. His dream almost borders on the mystic experience. One day the Sultan remembers his younger days when he was just twenty-one when he came to Daulatabad and built the grand fort. At that time he had a semi-mystic experience of the darkness of night entering his blood stream. But his present experiences have reversed all that hope. He has been searching for the lost moment in vain. He feels that everything is ugly. He cannot sleep now due to his frustration and restlessness like a Macbeth-figure. He wants to go to Mecca in search of peace. The reasons for his frustration are many. His idealism is not appreciated by his noblemen. Likewise he is not able to understand the human nature and yield to their practical suggestions, their land-entanglement and bondage of blood. They feel deeply disturbed, displaced, and disconcerted. On the way to Daulatabad many common people have perished due to starvation, illness, and fatigue. Consequently, the new capital, Daulatabad has turned out to be a great Muslim graveyard. Thus, Tughlaq's high and noble intentions have misfired.

The economic condition of his Empire is in shambles. People are starved to death and forced to eat the barks of trees. So they do not want prayer, but long for food for the belly. In spite of this economic crisis of the Empire, the Sultan welcomes H.H. Ghiyasuddin Abbasid for the joyful function and requests him to make his kingdom holy again by re-starting the prayer that was cancelled earlier and prostrates at the holy man.

As Ghiyasuddin Abbasid (Aziz in disguise) comes to the spot the Sultan bows down to him and tells him about Aazam's murder, but His Holiness pretends to be surprised. Tughlaq has already identified Aziz impersonating the holy man. He, therefore, stares into the eyes of His Holiness and asks him, 'who are you?' and 'how long have you been fooling me?' Then Aziz gets frightened and confesses that he is a dhobi from Shikaner; that he murdered Ghiyasuddin Abbasid; that he won the case against the Sultan by impersonating Vishnu Prasad; and that he indulged in minting the counterfeit copper currency. When Tughlaq asks him as to what punishment he should be given, Aziz shamelessly replies that he should be made an officer in his government. Then Tughlaq gives him a letter of recommendation to Khussau Malik to make him an officer in the army in the Deccan. But still he orders Aziz to playact his role as H.H. Ghiyasuddin and re-start the prayer. Barani repeatedly asks Tughlaq to punish the scoundrel Aziz severely, but Tughlaq refuses to do so. He says he has pardoned even Ainul Mulk in the past. Thus, Tughlaq's treatment of Aziz is enigmatic. The playwright fails to give a clue to understand the behaviour of Muhammad Tughlaq.

Aziz and Aazam are an interesting comic pair in the play. (But there is no historical evidence to show that they are drawn from historical sources. They seem to be imaginary characters invented by Girish Karnad just to highlight Tughlaq's special love for Hindus and subvert all the noble plans of the Sultan.) Aziz wears the guise of Vishnu Prasad and tricks the Sultan cleverly and gets justice from him by buying the land from Vishnu Prasad retrospectively by back-dating the deed. He tells Aazam that he is going to join the civil service next day and that the Sultan will like the friendship between a Hindu and a Muslim. Thus, Aziz has trapped the Sultan in his own idealism and democratic justice to one and all. He has capitalized on the Sultan's greatness and trust for his selfish purpose.

Aziz and Aazam resume their trickery and fraud during the process of migration of common people from Delhi to Daulatabad. Especially, Aziz employs the communal psychology and politics to his advantage very successfully. He assumes the guise of a Brahmin and does not allow a Hindu woman to take her sick child to a doctor, as it is against the rules. He demands a bribe from her callously, but the lady has no money on her. He does not grant her request simply because she is unable to bribe him. Then Aazam asks Aziz why he did not allow her, Aziz replies heartlessly that the child is too sick to survive and hence no use wasting money on the doctor. His callousness prevents him from understanding the maternal concerns of a woman. After a little while the Hindu woman's child dies. Aazam, therefore, asks Aziz what if the woman complains to the Sultan, Aziz replies that a Hindu woman never complains against a Brahmin because Aziz is in the guise of a Brahmin.

Aziz confesses that he has come to Delhi recently and discovered politics to be very useful and profitable. He suggests to Aazam that they can mint counterfeit copper coins as the Sultan is going to introduce them.

After the lapse of five years Aziz and Aazam have turned out to be robbers and been living in the hide-out in the hills. Aazam confesses that he is tired of the life of stealing and hiding himself. Between the pair, Aazam seems to be more sensitive than Aziz who is a hard-boiled scoundrel. He justifies his scoundrelly against the backdrop of moral degeneration of his contemporary society. He therefore opines that man should never be good, but should commit some crime or the other so that people may praise them; and that a man is called a saint if he rapes a woman.

By that time Karim has brought a man bound. Aziz gives money to Karim for this task. After untying the man Aziz discovers that it is not the Turk merchant but the wrong man. The man reveals his identity as Ghiyasuddin Abbasid, the descendent of the Khalif and that he is going to meet the Sultan at Daulatabad. Realizing this mistake both of them prostrate at the holy man and wish to act as his slaves up to Daulatabad to make up for the sacrilege. Then Aziz frightens Ghiyasuddin about the Sultan's suspicious frame of mind. Aziz suddenly changes his mind and wants to kill Ghiyasuddin Abbasid and go in the latter's guise to meet the Sultan. Aazam kills the holy man offstage and feels guilty, but Aziz tries to cheer him up. Aziz brings the turban of Ghiyasuddin to impersonate him.

Now Aziz (in the guise of Ghiyasuddin Abbasid) and Aazam are in the palace and discuss how the city of Daulatabad is filled with corpses, flies and stinking smell. He says he has discovered it by going out of the palace through the secret passage. Both of them are quite conscious of how they have been frustrating the Sultan's socio-political and economic policies. For example, Aazam tells Aziz how the Sultan suffers from insomnia and visits the rose-garden and examines the counterfeit coins (manufactured by Aziz and Aazam and other goldsmiths of the kingdom.) Aazam feels that he is not safe and happy in the palace and wants to escape from there. He invites Aziz also, but Aziz replies that the palace is the safest place for them and dissuades Aazam from leaving the palace. But Aazam finally says good bye to Aziz and leaves. He wants to forget all this wealth and these courts, but he gets killed at the gate of the secret passage mysteriously.

Girish Karnad's *Tughlaq* depicts the life of the eponymous hero in relation to his subjects in his kingdom. It is true that he is a very wise man whose way of thinking appears to be foolish to the average man. The problems in Tughlaq's kingdom are caused as much by the peculiarities of his personality as by the unusualness of circumstances involving two contradictory cultures or religions. There are, therefore, two kinds of conflict affecting each other adversely.

IMAMUDDIN: You are a learned man. You may be able to manage this delicate balance within yourself. But a kingdom needs not one king but a line of rulers. Will they manage this balance? Where are these brilliant successors of yours? Where are these guarantors of your balanced future? (p. 21)

Besides, he suffers from the delusion of grandeur and acts the role of a god like Lord Krishna or that of a prophet like Jesus, without unfortunately having the omniscience or omnipotence of God:

TUGHLAQ: .... Then again I want to climb up, up to the top of the tallest tree in the world, and call out to my people: "Come, my people, I am waiting for you. Confide in me your worries. Let me share your joys. Let's laugh and cry together and then, let's pray. Let's pray till our bodies melt and flow and our blood turns into air. (Scene ii, p. 10)

It is indeed paradoxical that he has not been able to achieve a balance within himself between his dream and his practical duty as an administrator, although he tom-toms about his desire to bring about a balance in all the walks of life. Most of the problems encountered by Tughlaq are the result of his inability to reconcile the opposite poles of dream and reality.

Had the population of his kingdom been of a homogeneous culture, Tughlaq would, perhaps, not have faced as many difficulties as he does now. The vertical schism in his self is unfortunately crossed and therefore worsened by the horizontal schism in the population of his kingdom itself. Tughlaq, for instance, would have fewer problems had the population of his kingdom been made up of only Muslims or only Hindus. But the exigencies of his life are such that he has to rule over a society which contains bi-cultural values, altitudes, and expectations. What is most conspicuous about such a heterogeneous society is that one culture is diametrically opposed to the other, in this case, Hinduism is pitted against Islam in many a details. It is the antagonistic nature of these two major cultures (or religious) that makes the Sultan suffer alternately at the hands of Hindus and Muslims. Tughlaq's foolishness lies precisely in his attempt to achieve a balance between these irreconcilable cultures. Hence, the external conflict between the protagonist and the antagonist, i.e. the population of his kingdom as a whole.

A few details of the external conflict between the Sultan and his people are necessary to show how he suffers continuously at the hands of people belonging to mutually exclusive cultures. Although the idealistic emperor wants to achieve a balance between Hindus and Muslims, he fails to realize that it is not wanted by his own co-religionists. The Muslims of his kingdom, for instance, are fundamentalists, who do not like the Hindus being exempted from the payment of *jizya* tax. Further, they do not like the emperor showing special kindness and concessions to the Hindus. (In this case, Tughlaq looks like Mahatma Gandhi who fought for the Hindu-Muslim unity in modern India.) But when the emperor continues to maintain an image of impartiality for himself, the Muslims would like to exploit the opportunity by trapping him in his own virtue. Aziz is an incarnation of this exploitative mischief. He takes the guise of a brahmin called Vishnu Prasad and wins a case against the Sultan himself thereby achieving two things simultaneously, i.e. getting a personal profit at the Sultan's cost and giving the Sultan a sense of satisfaction of being lenient towards Hindus:

AZIZ: You know, the one on the second anniversary of his coronation. (*Mimicking a public announcer.*) "Henceforth people may file a suit against the Sultan himself for the misbehaviour of his officers.... No one need have any fear.... Justice will be done...." Et cetera. Well, I was at the end of my tether then. There's no future in being a dhobi these days. So I did a bit of thinking. There's a Brahmin called Vishnu Prasad whose land had been confiscated recently. I shaved my head and went to him. I said I would buy the land.

AAZAM: Please a little slowly. I—you know I'm not very bright. But what's the point? I mean the land was confiscated, wasn't it?

AZIZ: Exactly, that's what he said too. But I said, "Never mind about that." So he sold me the land—back-dating the contract. And I filed my suit. Well, here I am. Five hundred *dinars* for nothing, and a job in His Merciful Majesty's own civil service.

AAZAM: But what if he had cut off your head instead?

AZIZ *laughs*.

Any way, why did you have to dress up in these ungodly clothes? Couldn't you have come like a proper Muslim?

AZIZ (*scandalized*): But then what would happen to the Muslim king's impartial justice? A Muslim plaintiff against a Muslim king? I mean, where's the question of justice there? Where's the equality between Hindus and Muslims? If on the other hand the plaintiff's a Hindu...well, you saw the crowds.

AAZAM: Complicated!

AZIZ: It's a bit subtle for you. Anyway here's my offer. From tomorrow I join the Civil Service. Why don't you come along too? I'll get you a job under me. You know, a Brahmin with a Muslim friend—the Sultan will like that. (Scene 1, p. 8)

Similarly, the Sultan's decision to transfer the kingdom from Delhi to Daulatabad is motivated by his desire to bring about a balance between the Delhi-based Muslims and the Daulatabad-based Hindus and is therefore strongly resented by the Muslims:

AMIR I: Just consider this. Why is he taking us to Daulatabad? Have you wondered about that? I'll tell you. He wants to weaken the Amirs. You see, we are strong in Delhi. This is where we belong. But Daulatabad is a Hindu city and we'll be helpless there. We'll have to lick his feet.

AMIR III: And it's no use his saying stay behind if you like. We have to be in the capital!

AMIR II: Look at what's happening in Delhi. Just look at it! You can't take a step without paying some tax or another. There's even a tax on gambling. How are we to live? You can't even cheat without having to pay tax for it.

SHIHABUDDIN: But he has done a lot of good work. Built schools, roads, hospitals. He has made good use of the money.

SAYYID: Then why can't he get it the right way? The Koran sanctions only four taxes, but... (*Looks at* RATANSINGH *and stops*.)

RATANSINGH (*smiles*): Carry on, sir. Don't mind me. I'm here because Shihab's here; otherwise I am invisible!

SAYYID: Well...uhm, he could tax the Hindus. The jiziya tax is sanctioned by the Koran. All infidels should pay it. Instead he says the infidels are our brothers...

SHIHABUDDIN (*getting up in disgust*) Come, Ratansingh, let's go. This is worse than I thought. They don't deserve to kiss the hem of the Sultan's dress.

The others are offended and retreat. (Scene 5, pp. 31-32)

That the Sultan is a clever administrator is indubitable indeed. He knows the art of projecting an image of impartial picture in the public. He wants not only to be good to the people, but also to be widely known to be good to them. That is why he orders his announcers to declare to the people how Vishnu Prasad, a Brahmin of Bikaner won a suit against himself (Sultan). Likewise he invites the holy man Sheikh Imamuddin and allows him to criticize himself (Sultan) publicly. He is so clever that he traps the Sheikh Imamuddin himself in his fundamentalism and succeeds in persuading him to act as his royal envoy to Ainul Mulk. The Sultan has made prayer compulsory in his kingdom, but when the Muslim Amirs try to murder him at prayer time, he cancels prayers in his kingdom until Abbasid Khalif comes to Daulatabad and starts it once again. The Sultan, who asked Shihabuddin to take care of his kingdom in his absence, does not hesitate to stab him to death when he discovers that the latter had conspired against him. Later when Aziz impersonates the holy man, Abbasid Khalif after murdering the latter, the Sultan is smart enough to expose him, but yet like a director of drama, orders him to playact the role of the holy man before the public and to re-start the prayers:

MUHAMMAD: Who are you?

Silence. For a moment no one speaks. AZIZ *is obviously frightened.*

Who are you? How long did you hope to go on fooling us with your masquerade?

BARANI: But your Majesty—

MUHAMMAD: Answer me. Don't make me lose my temper.

AZIZ: I am a dhobi from Shiknar. My first name was Aziz. There have been many others since then.

BARANI: But what about His Holiness?

MUHAMMAD: Do you know the punishment for killing a saint like Ghiyasuddin Abbasid? And for deceiving me and my subjects?

AZIZ (*bolder*): No, Your Majesty, though I have never underestimated Your Majesty's powers of imagination. But it would be a grave injustice if I were punished, Your Majesty.

...

MUHAMMAD: What do you want to say?

AZIZ: I was a poor starving dhobi, when Your Majesty came to the throne and declared the brotherhood of all religions. Does the Sultan remember the Brahmin who brought a case against him and won? I was that Brahmin.

MUHAMMAD: Was the disguise necessary?

AZIZ: I think so. (*Pause*) Soon after that Your Majesty introduced the new copper currency. I succumbed to its temptation.

BARANI: God...God...

AZIZ: There was enough money in that business, but too much competition. Soon it became unprofitable, so we took the silver dinars and went to Doab and bought some land there for farming.... One day I heard about a beggar who claimed to be Ghiyasuddin Abbasid and was on his way to the capital—I couldn't resist the temptation of seeing my master in person. I admit I killed Ghiyasuddin and cheated you. Yet I am Your Majesty's true disciple.

...

MUHAMMAD: Don't overdo it. It's time for the prayer. Remember, you are still His Holiness Ghiyasuddin Abbasid and you have to be there to lead the prayer. Be off now. (Scene 13, pp. 82-83)

Likewise, he prescribes death by stone-pelting to his stepmother, who has had Najib murdered. In all these situations, the Sultan acts very quickly like an able administrator and resembles Macbeth. He never Hamletizes over any situation.

But the clever administrator in Tughlaq is not reconciled to the poet-philosopher in him. The two talents in him remain absurdly apart. His desire to immerse in the study of heavenly stars and great poetry has, perhaps, made him blind to the human nature. Although he tries to create a balance between Hindus and Muslims, it never occurs to him that a Muslim like Aziz could deceive him mischievously and hypocritically. His desire to introduce copper currency on par with silver dinars is, of course, evidence of advanced economic arrangement. But the fault lies in his inability to see the possibility of misuse of the new currency. Nor has he taken precaution to prevent such corruption in the kingdom. Aziz and Aazam, therefore, take advantage of the situation to paralyze the economic order. History, thus, goes out of the Sultan's control thereby making him aware of his follies. He learns a belated lesson of his life. His impractical idealism is defeated by the ugly reality. But the defeat of Tughlaq or his idealism does not raise him to the height of a tragic hero, as it does not involve any self-sacrifice (unlike the other tragic figures like Macbeth or Agamemnon). One reason for this could, perhaps, be that he never had a selfish motive in his desire to convert his kingdom into a Utopia. One may easily describe him as an experimenter, who revises his philosophy, however idealistic it may be, in the light of the practical knowledge of reality. When he realizes his folly, he has the open-mindedness to transfer his capital back from Daulatabad to Delhi without having any sense of shame or humiliation. That several families were sacrificed in the process of his experimentation is, perhaps, inevitable. It is, therefore, not proper for us to describe him as a tragic hero. In spite of his absurd behaviour, he has the liberal attitude towards life which enables him to give up the *a priori* knowledge in favour of the *a posteriori* one. He has nothing to lose personally as he has nothing to gain either. The internal conflict is resolved finally when his addiction to stars is cured by the practical administrative alertness. Similarly, the external conflict between the Sultan and the population of the kingdom is resolved when the latter are defeated by him thereby awakening his sense of reality. It is, therefore, better to call Teghlaq an experimenter than a tragic hero. As the population of his kingdom, however large in quantity, is not equal to him in power and therefore becomes an easy victim of his political experimentation.

Work Cited

*Karnad, Girish *Tughlaq*, Delhi: Oxford University Press, 1986. (All the page references are to this edition.)

• • • • •

16

Science, Religion, Truth and Falsehood in *Hunting the Sun*

Utpal Dutt (1929-93) was a versatile genius as he was an Indian actor, director of plays and films, playwright, translator, and critic all rolled into one. But he was primarily an actor in the Bengali theatre, where he became a pioneering figure in Modern Indian theatre, when he founded the 'Little Theater group' in 1947, which enacted many English, Shakespearean and Brecht plays, in a period known as the 'Epic Theater' period, before immersing itself completely in highly political and radical theatre. His plays became apt vehicle of the expression for his Marxist ideologies, visible in socio-political plays like *Kallol* (*Sound of the Waves*, 1965), *Manusher Adhikare* (*Of People's Rights*), *Louha Manob* (*Iron Man*, 1964), *Tiner Toloar* (*The Tin Sword*), *Surya Shikar* (*Hunting the Sun*, 1978), and *Maha-Bidroha* (*The Great Rebellion*, 1989). He also acted over 100 Bangla and Hindi films in his career spanning 40 years, and remains most known for his roles in films like Mrinal Sen's *Bhuvan Shome* (1969), Satyajit Ray's *Agantuk* (1991), Gautam Ghose's *Padma Nadir Majhi* (1993), and Hrishikesh Mukherjee's breezy comedies such as *Gol Maal* (1979) and *Rang Birangi* (1983). In all he wrote twenty-two full-length plays, fifteen poster plays, nineteen Jatra scripts, acted in thousands of shows and directed more than sixty productions, apart from writing serious studies of Shakespeare, Girish Ghosh, Stanislavsky, Brecht and revolutionary theatre, and translating Shakespeare and Brecht.

He received National Film Award for Best Actor in 1970 and three Filmfare Best Comedian Awards. In 1990, the Sangeet Natak Akademi, India's National Academy of Music, Dance and Theatre, awarded him its highest award, the Sangeet Natak Akademi Fellowship for lifetime contribution to theatre.

Utpal Dutt's *Hunting the Sun* (*Surya Shikar*, 1978) may be described as a historical-political play dealing with the life of Emperor Samudragupta, his courtiers and other subjects of his Empire. It deals with a chunk of Indian history of the fourth century A.D. Samudragupta, the Emperor of Gupta dynasty happens to be the protagonist of the play, which is set in the fourth century A.D. North India, with Ayodhya as its focal point. All the important characters like Samudragupta, Urmila, Shishumara Pallava, Mahasveta, Hayagreeva, Basubandhu, Gohil, Suryavarma, Indrani, Virupaksha, Kalhan, Malavika, Madhukarika and Veerak and so on seem to be or sound like authentic historical figures, although no definite information about them except Samudragupta is available in written histories of India. Nor has the playwright suggested any sources for them. Emperor Samudragupta himself may be said to be a hero as king *a la* Carlyle and a world-historical personage *a la* Hegel. Along with the historical figures, the playwright has created a few imaginary characters also like the Vidusaka (Dardura) and the chorus, etc. to support them for the presentation of a coherent picture of Indian society.

Like all the historical playwrights, Utpal Dutt has not tried to present the entire life of Samudragupta and his imperial conquests, but has focused on only a couple of problems encountered by the Emperor as can be presented within the limited framework of a stage-worthy play. Again like a responsible historical playwright, he has chosen the transitional period of Indian history, especially of the Gupta period when there was an ideological conflict between caste-system and secularism and between traditional religion (Hinduism) and the emerging science (Buddhism). Through the judicious selection of a chunk of Indian history he has tried to present the collision of ideologies specific to that period but which are relevant even to the 21st century Indian life. By borrowing the external facts of history he has endeavoured to present them artistically and coherently in the form of a play, which is written in the mode of a traditional Sanskrit play. He has filled the dry facts of history with the immediacy of experience and offered an animated picture of the past life and enables the modern reader and spectator to re-live the past and experience the present-ness of the past (*a la* T.S. Eliot).

As usual in any drama there is a conflict between two forces or groups of characters. Whereas Samudragupta, Urmila, Shishumara, Mahasveta, Hayagreeva, Basubandhu, Virupaksha and Suryavarma belong to the protagonist's group, Kalhan, Indrani, Gohil, Madhukarika, and Veerak belong to the opposite group. Whereas the first group stands for the traditional Hindu religion, mythology, caste-hierarchy and superstition, the opposite group stands for science, atheism, secularism, and rationalism allied with Buddhism. This variegated conflict is presented by the playwright with an extraordinary conceptual clarity so rare in modern Indian drama. The play has solid historical authenticity about it as it deals with another important theme of slave-trade and prostitution that were so common in India at that time. All these social, religious, and biological problems are directly or indirectly connected with the political power of the Emperor. The broader conflicts are intersected with internal conflicts thereby complicating the issues further.

Slavery and slave-trade seem to have been quite common during the Gupta period. The play begins with a scene introducing the slave trade and the oldest profession, i.e. prostitution. In the very first scene Shishumara Pallava, the Nagarakotala comes to a street of Ayodhya to sell two slaves. After some time Suryavarma comes there to sell his slaves like Gohil, Madhukarika and her ten-year-old son, Veerak. It is unfortunate that these slaves are treated with utter contempt and disrespect, though they are absolutely necessary for doing the menial jobs including agricultural labour. Besides, they are not bound by sexual morality as they were treated as goods and chattels of rich people. For example, the slave Madhukarika does not know the name of her son's father as many males in Suryavarma's house have slept with her. When Basubandhu wants to buy her, he wants to see her naked in order to calculate the number of years she will be fit for work as a slave. Though a slave, Madhukarika does not want to show her nakedness in public due to her womanly modesty. She, therefore, appeals to general Hayagreeva to save her the embarrassment of being stripped naked in public, but Hayagreeva, who is a shameless womanizer, does not show any courtesy as he has no respect for woman's modesty or honour. Suryavarma and Shishumara forcibly undress her. On scrutinizing her naked body Basubandhu calculates that she is fit for ten years labour and buys her by paying her price as he learns that she is an expert in bath and massage.

Then General Hayagreeva buys Gohil, a *shudra* slave for 700 dinars, as he knows that the latter is an expert in agriculture and works twice as hard. Hayagreeva exhibits his inhumanity and cruelty in his desire to tie him (Gohil) to his chariot to test how fast he can run.

By then Indrani, a *shudra* young girl comes there and introduces herself to General Hayagreeva, as the disciple of Acharya Kalhan. She talks quite boldly with him and asks him to set Gohil free, but he refuses to release him as the *Narada Samhita* does not allow it. But Indrani quotes from the same book that a slave can redeem his liberty by offering the price of two cows to his master. She wants to offer her savings to Hayagreeva as the price of Gohil. As the Indian society was divided into four groups according to *varna*-system, people happen to be over-sensitive to the caste identities. Hayagreeva, therefore, complains that Gohil is a *shudra* and calls himself a *kshatriya*. This question about the slave's caste-identity recoils upon General Hayagreeva himself. For example, Indrani asks him to prove it. Hayagreeva tries to prove his caste-superiority by boasting that he is the son of his father, the warrior Maudgalya. But Indrani disturbs him by asking him about the identity of his mother, but he does not know it for certain. He believes that he is born of a tree. But Indrani tries to expose the falsity of the myth thereby making him aware of the disconcerting truth. She tells him that it is just a fairy tale and that he must have been found under a tree and therefore he must be a foundling. She accuses him of turning lies into truth with his sword and that he is either a foundling or born of a *shudra* woman. Further she ventures to say that the slave, Gohil and Hayagreeva must have been born in the womb of the same *shudra* woman. In other words, she implies that Hayagreeva is a bastard. She offers him money and asks him to release Gohil as she loves the latter and sympathizes with his condition. Indrani's bold argument has shaken Hayagreeva deeply and disarmed him completely. He, therefore, sets Gohil free.

That slaves are treated inhumanly is evidenced by another event. For example, when Basubandhu and Virupaksha present the newly brought slaves like Madhukarika and her son, Veerak to the Empress Urmila, she orders that they should be branded with hot iron, without feeling any mercy for them. Although Madhukarika requests the man concerned to spare her son from the painful treatment, he does not oblige her, but brands both of them with hot iron. Consequently, they cry piteously but are led away indifferently.

The problem of lust versus love has been highlighted in the character of General Hayagreeva. He is a shameless womanizer, who is exclusively interested in woman's body, that too not permanently but only for a single night. Every night he wants to enjoy a new woman's body. This is perhaps the military psychology everywhere in the world. For example, when he returns from the battlefield after a conquest, he and his companions are greeted with garlands and flowers by the dancers. As usual General Hayagreeva instantly likes the prostitute, Mahasveta and wants her to be sent to his house in the evening for his sexual enjoyment. He declares shamelessly that he enjoys a woman at night and throws her out and that he does not believe in love. He confesses that he killed his chariot-driver the previous day because the latter had looked at Sangarika carnally, before he (Hayagreeva) had enjoyed her. He has returned to Ayodhya after eleven year war after vanquishing Ugrasen, the King of Palakhas and Kuver, the King of Devarashtra. He asks Mahasveta to sing, to eat a betel leaf and hugs her forcibly. Then he orders her to go to him at night for a rendezvous.

General Hayagreeva expresses his mean mentality when he comes in contact with Indrani. For example, he suspects of some sexual relation between Indrani and her guru, Acharya Kalhan and as usual, invites her to his bed. Indrani, in a characteristically candid manner, calls him a dirty womanizer interested only in animal coitus. But Hayagreeva shamelessly confesses that he is interested only in women's body and in outraging it. When Indrani gets into serious trouble about her belief in science and is likely to be arrested, Hayagreeva saves her by taking her to his palace. This is reported to Emperor Samudragupta. Virupaksha tells the Emperor that Indrani cannot be arrested or executed as she enjoys the protection by Hayagreeva and that Hayagreeva has banished all the harlots from his house after possessing Indrani. Though initially Hayagreeva is interested in Indrani as a sex-object, he has gradually developed some kind of love for her without his knowing it. For example, when he comes back to his room in the palace to see if she has escaped from there, Indrani expresses her gratitude to him for saving her life. He seems to have understood his own nature by now. That is why he confesses to his high-handed approach and wants to know if she loves him. She calls him a common rapist and seducer. But Hayagreeva begs her for love, in spite of his inborn arrogance. But Indrani confesses that she is too poor a woman to return his love. Hayagreeva seems to be impressed by her candour and honesty. He, therefore, releases her and lets her go free in a most unexpected manner. He asks her to go to Gohil and find happiness.

It is a matter of great irony Empress Urmila is clandestinely in love with General Hayagreeva. As Vidushaka, Dardura puts it frankly, Empress Urmila is an embodiment of shamelessness, and along with other wives of ministers and officers, who seek men other than their husbands, she lusts after General Hayagreeva. When she asks him why he did not meet her by the Moon Lake the previous night in the garden, he replies that he was busy with his official responsibility. She threatens to kill all his bedmates. She wants to spend at least one night with him, but he loathes her and calls her a prostitute. Though angered by his words, she requests him not to reveal her adultery to others. Then the Vidushaka tells the Empress that General Hayagreeva now owns a *shudra* woman called Indrani; that she is Acharya Kalhan's disciple and that she is more beautiful than the Empress. On hearing this Empress Urmila whips the Vidushaka and begins to feel the pangs of jealousy for Indrani. That is why she sends her slave, Madhukarika to insult and ridicule Indrani before the latter is to be trampled to death by an elephant. She enjoys the sight of Indrani being trampled by the elephant, but feels horrified when General Hayagreeva also is trampled to death by the same elephant, simply because she is in love with him secretly. The playwright has brought out Urmila's sexual jealousy for Indrani and her clandestine adulterous love for the subordinate officer of the Empire very clearly. As she expresses her sense of shock at the unexpected sight, Emperor Samudragupta taunts her for her secret love of General Hayagreeva and calls her a whore. But yet he orders her to pretend to be happy as an Empress to keep the honour of the Gupta dynasty. Empress Urmila grieves that Indrani has taken away her lover, Hayagreeva. It is a matter of great irony that Empress Urmila should long for the clandestine sexual company of General Hayagreeva. In spite having an Emperor for a husband, she longs for a lover and her love remains unrequited. But it is also strange that General Hayagreeva, who fornicates with a new woman every night, does not feel attracted towards the Empress. But his sending away all the harlots from his palace after getting hold of Indrani and releasing her unconditionally and even dying with her after her declaration of love for him—all these events testify to his dramatic transformation. The playwright has tried to show how his shameless lust has been slowly transformed into love and how he has grown so mature as to sacrifice his own life for his beloved. Thus, finally, love is affirmed whereas lust is rightly negated, although rather a bit belatedly.

Indrani is disliked by the Emperor and the Empress for two different reasons, i.e. caste reason and sexual jealousy respectively. For example, Emperor Samudragupta does not like her because of her being a *shudra* woman and for the violation of the orthodox norms by reading the Vedas and by declaring the earth to be round, not flat. Thus, the Emperor's dislike of her is ideological. But Empress Urmila's dislike for her is caused by her sexual jealousy for Indrani to whom General Hayagreeva has taken a fancy and rejected her, i.e. even the Empress's love for him. The political power aligned to the traditional brahmanical

Hinduism cannot tolerate the hard realities of life discovered by new experiences and experiments in science. Hence, it tries to kill the speaker of truth, not knowing that truth cannot be killed at all.

The playwright has problematized the caste-hierarchy and related it to the conflict between science and religion. For example, the Hindus believe that no non-brahmin has the right to study the Vedas and question the veracity of Vedic mythology, religion, and belief. But Indrani, who happens to be a *shudra* girl, has defied this rigid rule and studied the Vedas thoroughly. This looks like a crime to the age-old traditionalists. For example, Virupaksha tells the Empress that Indrani, the daughter of a *shudra*, has defied the Great Books (Vedas) by reading them and been teaching science. When the Empress asks Virupaksha about Indrani's crime, he replies that she has declared that the earth is round and read the Vedas, although she is a *shudra*. When Emperor Samudragupta happens to see Indrani in the house of General Hayagreeva and asks her a number of questions, she answers quite boldly that she is a *shudra* girl; that she has read the Vedas; that there has been an interpolation in the *Ramayana* against the *shudras*, etc. The Emperor is convinced that she is not only pretty, but a scholar and philosopher as well. Indrani tells him that she has been a disciple of Acharya Kalhan for the last eight years and is like his daughter; and that she can prove that the earth is round.

The Emperor knows that Indrani has been repeating her guru's lessons. He, therefore, asks Kalhan to prove that the earth is round. Kalhan demonstrates the scientific truth with the help of a ball and a lamp. His disciples, Sayan and Bibhu assist him. He explains the idea of gravitation and how the scientific facts have been allegorized and mythicized in the *puranas*. But the Hindu traditionalists like Virupaksha and Basubandhu refuse to believe him and accuse him of desecrating their sacred religion and disproving all the *puranas*, gods and goddesses and affirming only matter. They fail to understand how the scientific truth is allegorized and mythologized by the Hindu philosophers. This conflict between the scientific approach and the religious/mythological approach is brought out very clearly and interestingly by the playwright. It shows that Hindustan of the 4th century A.D. was not advanced enough to accept the scientific approach and digest the scientific truth as it ran counter to their rigid, childlike, and traditional beliefs. The basic doctrinal conflict happens to be between the Hindu spirituality and the Buddhist belief in the materiality of the whole universe and lack of soul or spirit. The traditional Hindus cannot accept the scientific and Buddhist thought which they consider nihilistic and atheistic and hence unpalatable. Therefore, Virupaksha and Basubandhu advise the Emperor not merely to arrest but even kill Acharya Kalhan. The Emperor thinks that only he can hunt the sun and not the Buddhist mendicant. Virupaksha says that they need faith and not reason.

The Emperor, who learns that Indrani is a disciple of such a Buddhist monk propagating her guru's ideas, asks Indrani to testify that Kalhan is a hypocrite, charlatan, and seducer. But she, being a lady with a strong conviction, refuses to do so. He, therefore, wants to assert his political power by telling her how it is essential for the State, religion and king. On her refusal to do so, the Emperor orders her to be sent to the dungeon. There is a perfect alignment between political power and the traditional Hindu religion and mythology, which is disturbed by the scientific discoveries.

There is even attempt on the part of the establishment to tempt Kalhan to win him over to the Emperor's side. But Kalhan cannot be won over so easily because of his sterling morality. He provides a sharp contrast to General Hayagreeva, who is a shameless womanizer in his early phase of life. For example, Mahasveta, a prostitute wants to tempt Acharya Kalhan by curling around him, but the Acharya silences her by addressing her as 'Mother.' The State apparatus is trying to malign Acharya Kalhan systematically. Mahasveta then relents and seeks shelter at his feet and confides to him how Shishumara, the Police Chief, has been urging people to slander him. She relents and seeks the life of a Buddhist Parivrajaka and seeks shelter at his ashram. Acharya Kalhan munificently grants her wish by allowing her to stay in his ashram.

Acharya Kalhan is very unhappy about the imprisonment of Indrani by the Emperor, Samudragupta. He tells Gohil about it and that in Ayodhya alone they have kept in chains hundred thousand slaves. He suggests that these slaves should break their chains, stand up and bring down the State erected on sin. Finally, he suggests to Gohil to meet the slave, Girishtha and join his band for rebellion against the Emperor. Just as Acharya Kalhan is interested in liberating the slaves from their physical slavery and bondage, he is also interested in liberating the orthodox Hindus from their mental slavery and bondage to mythology and superstition. He continues his scientific study of the cosmos. When Sayan and Bibhu bring in the telescope, Acharya Kalhan asks them to take down what he declares after looking through the telescope. He sees a parallel between the mythological/*puranic* accounts like Kaliyanaga and the astronomical facts and opines that the *puranas* contain the symbolic truth hiding beneath them hard core empirical facts.

But his scientific approach and interpretation of cosmic facts and events are thoroughly misunderstood and misinterpreted by the traditionalists supported by political power. For example, General Hayagreeva complains that the formers telescope is a weapon made by the Buddhist Tantriks to kill the king; that his ashram is a secret place for Buddhist rebels. Obviously, this is a thorough misinterpretation of Acharya Kalhan's approach to truth. General Hayagreeva asks Kalhan to save Indrani by publicly confessing that his ideas are false and that the earth is not round. But Kalhan does not agree to do so in spite of Hayagreeva's threats. Due to Kalhan's non-compromise and non-complicity General Hayagreeva orders his soldiers to destroy Kalhan's telescope and science books. Kalhan is very sad about this unfortunate event. But Sayan consoles him by saying that truth cannot be imprisoned or destroyed.

The State power wants falsehood masked as truth. For example, when the sentries bring in Indrani almost unconscious on a wheel, the Emperor asks her if she is raped by Kalhan. But she replies that Kalhan is reverend like a father to her. Thus angered by her answer and unwillingness to twist the truth or propagate a falsehood, the Emperor orders that she should be trampled to death by the mad elephant, Jambuka, the next morning.

Then Acharya Kalhan is brought in as a prisoner. The Emperor asks him to face a public trial and declare that he is a liar; that the earth is flat and the moon is a god; that *puranas* are true and *brahmanya* is true. But Acharya Kalhan refuses to oblige him by subscribing to the mythical, religious, and superstitious ideology. He even curses him with the destruction of his Empire.

The Emperor and his State apparatus want to suppress Acharya Kalhan's discovery of scientific truth by artificially producing false witnesses against the so-called crime of Kalhan. For example, Mahasveta, a prostitute is pressurized by the pro-establishment forces to give false evidence against Kalhan in the public trial. She is more afraid of the king than of the sin. She, therefore, confesses before the Emperor that she is ready to declare publicly that she has been raped by Acharya Kalhan.

But certain things have gone out of their control. For example, Mahasveta, the prostitute is poisoned prior to Acharya's Kalhan's trial. Then the political power embodied in the Emperor thinks of an alternative plan of suppressing the speaker of truth and project the falsehood. That is convenient to the smooth functioning of the statecraft. For example, Acharya Kalhan is brought before the Emperor, but he cannot speak as his tongue is cut by the authorities. The Emperor has to impress the public in a manner that is convenient to him. He, therefore, produces a letter of confession from Kalhan (cooked up by themselves) to the effect that the moon is a god; that the Rigveda is true; that the earth is flat; that science is false and that he (Kalhan) has taken the vow of silence (*Mouna Vrita*) now. Now Basubandhu and Virupaksha come to know that Kalhan's tongue is cut and that he is drugged also. In the administrative system, certain things happen secretly and not known to everybody.

Emperor Samudragupta has succeeded in suppressing Acharya Kalhan by getting a fake statement by him against his own convictions. But it is very ironical that he orders Acharya Kalhan to be released and declares him as the Royal Astrologer to be resident in the palace as a counsellor and friend. He even declares him as an incarnation of God. Though Kalhan has rejected God, faith and superstition, the Emperor wants to make him a god and build a temple for him for the propagation of faith, just as they have turned the Buddha, the enemy of Vishnu into the tenth incarnation of Vishnu. The Emperor has thus played his excellent political game of inclusivism whereby even an enemy could be transformed into a kin. Acharya Kalhan is physically helpless now against the political power. But Mahasveta consoles him by saying that his ideas live permanently and cannot be destroyed, as her son, Veerak has the books of Indrani and that the world will find out the truth later. But within the framework of the play the conflict between truth and falsehood is resolved by the triumph of the latter over the former. Thus, the play projects an ironical vision.

The play is historical in its setting, events, and characters. The historical characters like Emperor Samudragupta and his family and retinue lends historical authenticity to the play. The ideological conflict between Hinduism and Buddhism intersected by the conflict between Brahmins and *shudras*, the rampant inhuman slave-trade, prostitution, adultery and the palace intrigue—all these factors create the historical milieu very interestingly. By borrowing the external facts of remote Indian history, the playwright has presented an animated picture of the socio-politico-religious problems of the age. He has been able to make the whole historical conspectus come alive on the stage by creating the immediacy of experience so essential for the dramatic genre.

One of the remarkable qualities of the play happens to be the extraordinary clarity of motivation given to the characters and their thoughts and actions. Hence, the vision of the play is etched clearly. The employment of the character of Vidushaka, namely Dardura and the chorus give it an atmosphere of Sanskrit Drama and historical antiquity. The collision between the political power and the forces of socio-political change has been highlighted in an interesting manner. But one thing missing in this historical play is the court manners of panegyrists announcing the arrival of the Emperor with their stereotypical slogans of glorification. The absence of such court manners impoverishes the historical atmosphere. But the picture of the triumph of reactionary powers over the progressive ones is conspicuously ironical and satirical.

We read history because it repeats itself in the modern form. All history has the seeds of the future hidden in it. This is what T.S. Eliot means when he says that the poet (or the playwright in this context) is interested not only in the pastness of the past but in the presentness of the past. As Utpal Dutt has captured the poetry of history and universalized its message, the play resonates with contemporary relevance. For example, belief in Hinduism, especially its caste-system and mythology being aligned to the ruling party of India and resistance to scientific truth, especially Buddhist thought are still practiced in India on the sly, but under the cover of so-called secularism. The government rendering the speakers of truth speechless and getting the convenient confessions from them in the written form, punishing the culprits who have fought for truth, adultery practiced in the high aristocratic families, clandestine or open practice of prostitution in contemporary India—all these elements of the play testify to the presentness of the past and the play's relevance to the modern age.

Reference

Dutt, Utpal, *Hunting the Sun* (*Surya Shikar*) in *Modern Indian Drama*. Ed. G.P. Deshpande, Sahitya Akademi, New Delhi, Reprint 2004. (All page references are to this edition.)

• • • • •

17

Ghashiram Kotwal: A Tragedy of Power

Vijay Tendulkar is one of the most prolific Indian playwrights who have enriched the Indian drama and theatre by picturizing the varied problems of native life in Maharashtra. The main reason for the attraction for him is that he does not copy from or imitate the Western dramatists and thrust it on the native audience. On the other hand, he takes up typically Indian, especially Hindu problems which are deeply rooted in the Indian culture which include music, theatre, religion, and philosophy. *Ghashiram Kotwal* is not an exception to this general truth about Tendulkar.

The native significance of *Ghashiram Kotwal* begins with the title itself. The story of the eponymous hero belongs to the history of Peshwas and hence has the authenticity of nativity about it. The characters of Nanasaheb, Phadnavis, Ghashiram, Gauri and their situations are all historical. But Tendulkar has tried to make the play not a piece of antique history, but a reflection of ever-operative mystery of life.

The play dramatizes the conflict between Ghashiram Kotwal, the eponymous hero and Nanasaheb Phadnavis, the Chief Minister of the Peshwa or Pune in the nineteenth century. The play may be described as a tragedy of power as there is a conflict between power and powerlessness behind the manifestation of historical characters and events. As Samik Bandyopadhyaya rightly says, "Tendulkar, in his social criticism, is more concerned with the mechanism of power, operating within the society than with the economic and political implications and sources of that power." Ghashiram, a Brahman from Kanauj comes to Pune for making his fortune, but he suffers from an unexpected humiliation at Pune when he is wrongly accused of thievery and therefore arrested and imprisoned. Nobody listens to his honest explanation and clarification. Ghashiram is deeply worried about the loss of his reputation, "but I didn't steal. I swear to god I didn't. I'm not a thief. I'm from Kanauj. I'm a Brahman. I've been here two weeks. I came here to find my fortune—and lost my reputation. How did it happen? What will happen to my wife? To my daughter? What will they say when they hear of this?" (16). He is imprisoned for a few days and released later with a warning to go away from Pune. The soldiers order him, "get lost. Hey! thief, monkey. If you so much as put a foot in the holy city of Pune, you'll lose your head. Go away. Take your ugly face and go far away. Don't come back to Pune. Not even your shadow should fall on the city of Pune. Get lost, go" (17).

The utter humiliation suffered by Ghashiram awakens in him the powerful emotion of revenge. He therefore takes a firm decision to stay in Pune and pay the people of Pune in their own coin: "but I'll come back. I'll come back to Pune. I'll show my strength. It will cost you! Your good days are gone! I am Kanauj Brahman, but I've become a shudra, a criminal, a useless animal. There is no one to stop me now, to mock me, to make me bend to cheat me. Now I am devil. You've made me an animal, I'll be a devil inside. I'll come back like a boar and I'll stay as devil. I'll make pigs of all of you. I'll make this Pune a kingdom of pigs. Then I'll be Ghashiram again, the son of Savaldas once more" (17). Thus, motivated by powerful vindictive desire, Ghashiram thinks of ways and means of achieving his goal without bothering about any moral principles. In other words, far from being an idealist, he becomes an opportunist and exploits the situation to the best possible advantage.

Ghashiram knows that Nanasaheb, the Chief Minister of the Peshwa King, has a notorious weakness for women. Ghashiram, who has a beautiful daughter called Lalita Gauri, wants to use her as a bait to attract Nanasaheb and get some power. In this hurry to achieve his goal, he never thinks of the consequences of his action. It is this indiscriminate opportunism which may be said to be the tragic flaw of Ghashiram. When a haridasa is singing a religious song called abhang, Nanasaheb sits silently ogling at the beautiful women in the audience; when the haridasa changes from abhang to lavani, the mood also changes from the religious to the erotic. Ghashiram's daughter has caught the fancy of Nanasaheb. Ghashiram is in the guise of a servant watching the reactions of Nanasaheb. A womaniser as Nana is, he accosts the sixteen-year young girl Gauri when she is bowing down to the idol of Ganapati. He pats her shoulder. But the innocent Gauri is shocked and embarrassed by his behaviour and tells him that Lord Ganapati is watching his pranks. But Nana talks indifferently about this religious figure, "That idol of holiness? That all holy Ganapati? The maker of good? Look, he has two wives. One on this side, one on that side. If you sit on our lap, he won't say anything about that" (19). When it becomes clear to Gauri that Nana is making advances on her, she tries to dissuade him from the erotic venture by calling him equivalent to a father. But Nana, being utterly shameless, continues his erotic argument: "Only by age. But our devotion is—only to this graceful image.... Don't lose any more time. Youth will not come again; the bloom will not last. (He comes close and tries to put an arm around her.) My dear, you are like a daughter to us-someone else's" (19). When Nanasaheb continues his erotic persuasion, Gauri feels scared and runs away from him like a frightened deer and escapes from there. Ghashiram has stood guard there in the guise of a servant. Nana, who is erotically frustrated by the escape of the girl, grabs the servant in his blind lust. The servant alerts Nanasaheb by saying that the girl has escaped and that the latter has robbed a man-servant. Nana feels utterly frustrated and exasperated. He even wants to get the servant killed. But Ghashiram replies that there is no other servant there to oblige him. On understanding the intensity of Nana's desire for a woman, Ghashiram exercises his opportunistic will to satisfy Nana's need and consequently gets a great reward for it. He commits the tragic crime of sacrificing his own daughter's virginity for attaining some kind of deputation power from Nana. He wants to exploit Nana's sexual weakness to his advantage.

He, therefore, promises Nana that "if the hunter is ready, the prey will be found" (19).

And that "whoever she is, if the order is given, this servant will bring her" (20). It is a matter of prestige for Nana to possess the girl of his choice. Otherwise he will lose his grandeur as also his power. He says: "if she is not found, no one will keep his head! Our grandeur's gone if she's not had. We tell you, if she is found then this nine court Nana will conquer Hindustan! What a bosom! Buds just blossoming we'll squeeze them like this" (20). Thus, Nana wants to buy sex through his political (and special) power as a minister. Ghashiram has a sex object, i.e. his daughter through which he wants to attain some kind of power. Accordingly, he brings his daughter and offers her to Nana. Nana dances with her sensuously and gets amorously entangled with her. Ghashiram watches it from a little distance and feels happy to note that he has succeeded in trapping Nana through sex. Though Ghashiram feels guilty of misusing his daughter, he compromises with his conscience as he is goaded by the powerful emotion of revenge, against the people of Pune. He says, "now he's in my hands.... Oh my daughter...the beast.... (*then yells at the audience.*) Oh you people. Look! I've given my beloved daughter into the jaws of that wolf! Look, look at this father? Putting his heart's child up for sale. Look at him, eating her like a peach.... Spit on me, Shove me. Look, look. But I will not quit. I'll make this Pune a kingdom of pigs" (22).

Having trapped Nana sexually, Ghashiram wants to have a proper reward for his submission of a daughter. He wants to whet Nana's sexual appetite by refusing to send her on the pretext of getting her married off. Nana feels momentarily frustrated and wants to offer anything demanded by Ghashiram. Ghashiram wants to put an end to all wagging tongues in Pune. He, therefore, asks him, "All right sir, to shut people's mouth, make me the Kotwal of Pune" (24). Nana feels disconcerted by Ghashiram's suggestion and grows helpless.

Nana: No! send her. I'll make you the Kotwal. When will you send her?

Ghashiram: After I have the order, signed and sealed, my hand.

Nana: Bastard. You've got me in a narrow pass.

Ghashiram: Yes, the narrow pass of my only daughter. (24)

Nana yields to Ghashiram's terms and gives him a signed order of appointment as Kotwal of Pune. Ghashiram feels that he has succeeded in his clever plan, but like a tragic hero, he does not foresee the future trap into which he is entering. Nana has double advantage in appointing Ghashiram as Kotwal: one, sexual, and two political. He can enjoy his daughter as well as use him as thorn to remove the thorns or control the Brahmans of Pune. Though Ghashiram thinks himself to be very smart, he fails to understand that Nana can be far smarter than he. Nana explains his inner motive as follows: "Go Ghasya, old bastard. We made you. We made you Kotwal. Raise hell if you wish. But you don't know the ways of this Nana. This time, there are two bullets in this gun. With the first one we'll fell your luscious daughter. But with the second we will make the city of Pune dance. Ghasya, child, you're a foreigner. I have put you on Pune's back. Why? As a countercheck to all those conspirators. You'll not be able to join them, they'll never trust you even if you do. Because you're a stranger, you're an outsider. We just raised a dog at our door to the Kotwali. We are sole support. Oh, you're a bastard, Ghasya. Your manner will be more arrogant than that of chitpavan Brahmans. You'll manage the deference nicely. You'll create a court—and a half! No worry about that. What'll happen is that our misdeeds will be credited to your account. We do; our Kotwal pays. (*He claps his hands.*) The opportunity comes in the shape of Ghashiram. And that luscious peach is at hand to be bitten by Nana. Excellent! Yes Ghasya, be Kotwal. This Nana blesses you" (25).

Like a typical tragic hero, Ghashiram suffers from shortsightedness and fails to look at the truth from a larger perspective. Having bought power through sex, he grows intoxicated with it, thereby metaphorically blinding himself further. He grows arrogant and high-handed and tries to impose very strict, but sometimes, very absurd rules according to which no whoring, cremation or intercaste dining can be done without permit. The men and women have to stay at home at night and are not supposed to have extra-marital relationship. As a result of the strict imposition of his rules, "Prostitutes' lane was desolate! The chasing of women was halted! Pimps turned into beggars! Counterfeit coins were worthless" (27). His imposition of rules on the behaviour of the people reaches the height of absurdity.

He imprisons an innocent man returning home at night on the suspicion that he is going to a whore. Similarly, he orders that "if anyone is seen throwing powder at anyone but his wife, bind his hands. Morality must be protected. Take away the Brahmans who are having too good a time" (31). When Ghashiram suspects even a real permit to be a counterfeit one, a woman goes straight to Nana and complains, "My husband and his brother have been arrested by the Kotwal's soldiers. My father-in-law died. They won't let them hold the funeral. The permit is real, but they call it counterfeit. Sir the corpse has been lying in the cremation ground since morning. The dogs are gathering. Sir, please give us justice" (32). But Nana is too busy with his fun with girls to care for the woman's complaint. Similarly, Ghashiram arrests a Brahman priest. Ghashiram's order to test the Brahman priest by putting hot iron bails on his palms is indicative of his callousness, high-handedness, and sadism. When the Brahman priest is scared of the burning iron balls being placed on his palms for the second time, he wriggles out of the situation by falsely confessing his crime of thieving. Thus, Ghashiram's inhuman approach is very disconcerting to the citizens of Pune. The Brahman priest, therefore, curses Ghashiram, "I did not steal, I did not steal I did not steal, O Ghashiram. You have tormented a poor innocent Brahman. You'll die without children. You yourself will endure torment greater than mine. You'll die a dog's death, grinding your heels in the dirt" (36). Ghashiram has been digging his own grave inch by inch by following the path of the heartless callousness and vindictiveness like a tragic hero. The moral law that he has been violating will one day assert itself and crush him properly. His crimes border on sins and will be balanced by retribution. The Brahman's curse gives expression to that law of sin and retribution.

After partially fulfilling his vindictive impulse through power, Ghashiram dreams of finding a good bridegroom for his daughter and celebrate her wedding with great pomp and ostentation. One can see how pregnant his dream is with power. "I've got the Kotwali and I'll have Pune straightened out. All these hard, proud Brahmans are soft as cotton now. No one dares to look at Ghashiram straight in the eye! Now once I find a fitting husband for my darling daughter—that piece of my heart named Lalita Gauri—and get her married, then everything will be the way I want it. I'll make such a show of the wedding that no one's tongue will move to utter one bad word about my daughter. And if some tongue starts wagging, it's easy to cut it Now-first-I'll look for a bridegroom. It's easy to find a bridegroom when one has money, jewels, and respect. And my daughter is beautiful one in a million! I'll send my men right out to look for a husband and I'll arrange everything" (37).

Meanwhile, Nana marries the seventh bride even at his advanced age. Ghashiram is surprised to learn that his daughter is not seen for quite a few days. He threatens Nana and asks him for his daughter. But Nana replies that Gauri has been sent to Chandra, the midwife in Kasba Peth. When Ghashiram enquires of Chandra, she replies that Gauri is buried and that she was pregnant before marriage. Terribly exasperated by the news of his daughter's unexpected death, Ghashiram kills Chandra, the midwife, instantly by throttling her. In his terrific anger, he goes straight to Nana and asks him about the daughter, without bowing to him. Nana reminds him of the protocol to be followed in the presence of power. "Ghasya, how much more will you grieve? Now be calm. Whatever happened, protocol should not be forgotten. Don't you forget that. Whom do you stand before? First you must bow. Now-bow-That's right. Good. We acknowledge your loyalty. By our favour, you have become 'Kotwal'. We are pleased with that" (44). Ghashiram helplessly follows the protocol by bowing to Nana and contains his query about his daughter. But Nana replies to him in very philosophical terms about the temporality and illusionary nature of this life. "It is a misapprehension to think that she was here. It was illusion. The body will burn. It is misapprehension to think that she is no longer here. Death is without meaning, Ghasya. Life too is without meaning. No one belongs to anyone. No one is anyone's daughter. No one is anyone's father. In the end, only oneself belongs to oneself. Life is like a dance of four days' charm. One must do one's duty. That is enough. I am the Chief Minister. You are the Kotwal. These are our duties. So go, go to your duty" (45). Although Nana tries to deceive Ghashiram with the Vedantic philosophy, Ghashiram is not convinced by the answer. But it can easily be understood within the context of the play that he has paid a price greater than his crime deserved. By surrendering his daughter to Nana for the attainment of power, Ghashiram has violated the moral law as well as his paternal duty. Now his daughter has died on account of her premarital pregnancy as well as the possible abortion forced upon her. The very power with which he wanted to enhance the happiness of his daughter has made him impotent. Not only that. As he has violated the holy institution of marriage by surrendering the unmarried daughter to an old man, he has to face the unforeseen consequences of his action. Moral law in the form of nature has taken away the life of his beloved daughter and given him a foretaste of retribution. But far from becoming wiser and mellower, Ghashiram grows more and more vindictive in his actions. He has to plunge further into the path of doom. Ghashiram easily brings to our mind Macbeth who continues to follow the wrong path even after losing Lady Macbeth. He was so much intoxicated with his power and ambition that he could not leave in the middle of the course. In a similar manner, Ghashiram, far from resigning from the post of Kotwal, continues in the same position to take further revenge upon the citizens of Pune. The climax of his high-handed behaviour may be seen in his treatment of south-Indian Brahmans who come to Pune to seek their fortune and enjoy the munificence of the Peshwa. When they pluck some fruits in the garden belonging to Ghashiram, without knowing anything about him, he orders them to be arrested and imprisoned in a small unventilated cell without showing an iota of pity or understanding. As a result of suffocation in the dungeon, some twenty-two Brahmans die. When the news circulates in the city, Sardar Phakade, the enemy of Ghashiram, breaks open the doors of the cell and brings out the dead and the dying Brahmans. Now Ghashiram has to bear the burden of the crime of having murdered twenty-two Brahmans. The law of retribution starts working through the angry Brahmans of Pune who in thousands rush into Nana's chamber and demand justice. Nana has no patience to go into the details of the crime, although he senses the enormity of it all. They demand that Ghashiram should be beheaded. Nana has no choice at all. He, therefore, takes up the pen and paper and writes out the order for beheading Ghashiram. Nana has acted according to his Machiavellian or Chanakyan philosophy. He says, "Use a thorn to take out a thorn. That's great. The disease has been stopped. Any way, there was no use for him any more" (52). Unaware of all these happenings Ghashiram goes to the cell to show them what is justice. But, ironically, he himself is surrounded by angry Brahmans and beaten severely. Like a tragic hero, Ghashiram has a belated realization of his sin and repentance. He is now reconciled to his lot: "I danced on your chests but I wasted the life of my little daughter. I should be punished for the death of daughter. Beat me. Beat me. Hit me" (54). Ghashiram's awareness of his sin is awakened and he is reconciled to his punishment as there is no escape from it. He, like a tragic hero, realizes the irreversibility of his action and the unavoidability of the consequences of his action. Finally, he is murdered by the angry Brahmans. The retribution meted out to Ghashiram proves—the formula that he who negates the moral order of the universe gets negated by it ultimately. It is this law of retribution which is expressed in the callous words of Nana, "Ladies and gentlemen. Citizens of Pune. A threat to the great city of Pune has been ended today. (*The crowd cheers.*) A disease has been controlled. The demon Ghasya Kotwal, who plagued all of us, has met his death.... Everything has happened according to the wishes of the gods. We have commanded that there be festivities for three days to mark this happy occasion." Finally, the demand for moral justice is fulfilled and the circle of action and reaction is complete. Ghashiram rightly deserves our pity for the punishment greater than he deserved. There is a tragic sense of waste illustrated through the death of Ghashiram. Vijay Tendulkar has presented a very striking picture of a tragic figure like Ghashiram.

The history of the performances of the play in Maharashtra shows that it was banned by the Progressive Dramatic Association of Pune on the grounds that the character of Nana Phadnavis as presented by the playwright was historically not correct. Such an objection to the play is based upon a lack of knowledge of the difference between art and life or reality. All art involves the principles of reduction or enlargement; understatement or exaggeration to some extent. Especially in a romantic tragedy, which the play incidentally is, the facts of life or history are bloated to some extent to drive home the higher truth of life. In this play, Nana's callous behaviour is exaggerated to match Ghashiram's callousness and vindictiveness in terms of art. It is, in a way, necessary to show how evil destroys itself out of its own abundance. In other words, a lesser evil has to be defeated by a greater evil as vouchsafed by Hegel, the German aesthetician and philosopher.

It is a strange but happy fact that Vijay Tendulkar has produced a good romantic tragedy in *Ghashiram Kotwal* in spite of the fact that the traditional Indian literary theory does not assign a separate position to tragedy as a form of literature. The tragic vision ingrained in *Ghashiram Kotwal* easily provides a parallel to Shakespeare's tragic vision. Although tragic vision is part of the dynamics of the play, it has been expressed through the mechanics of dramaturgy indigenous to Hindu culture. The role of Sutradhara coordinating the action of the play, sometimes as a commentator and sometimes as a participant; the human wall or curtain of characters occasionally participating in the action of the play and withdrawing themselves; the choric singing and commentary; miming and dancing; the transformation of *abhanga* into *lavani* and such other theatrical devices provide a rich Indian, Sanskrit and Marathi folk element to the play, thereby making it a very enjoyable artistic experience.

Reference

Vijay Tendulker, *Ghashiram Kotwal*. Oxford University Press, New Delhi, 1980.

• • • • •

18

Satirical Vision in *Silence! The Court is in Session*

Vijay Tendulkar (1928-) is one of the very significant playwrights of Maharashtra and India. He is known for his stark social realism, bitter satire, bold presentation and technical experimentation. The characters and situations in his plays are directly lifted from the contemporary society and boldly transformed into dramatic vision. In this respect, he is easily comparable to Ben Jonson, Galsworthy from England, Arthur Miller from America, and Chekhov from Russia. Because of his deep involvement with the Maharashtrian society, he has been able to contribute a variety of new character-types to modern Indian literature. By contrast, Girish Karnad, who is not deeply rooted in Kannada culture, resorts to historical and mythological themes as he has confessed that he cannot invent a story. Besides, Karnad being a convent product does not have the necessary mastery over the natural Kannada. But Vijay Tendulkar is deeply steeped in Marathi language and culture. That is why his characters have a strong Marathi flavour and his situations have a fast local colour. Generally, Tendulkar selects very unusual, hence, original and shocking situations and characters from contemporary Maharashtrian society and presents them in a very bold and uninhibited manner. His famous plays like *Sakharam Binder*, *Vultures*, *Ghashiram Kotwal*, *Kanyadaan*, *Kamala*, and *Mitrachi Goshta*, etc. hold a mirror to his bold vision of life.

"*Shantata! Court Chalu Ahe* (*Silence! The Court is in Session*, 1967, filmed by Satyadev Dubey in 1971 and translated into many Indian languages) revealed through the device of a play within a play the latent human cruelty against the vulnerable."[1] *Silence! The Court is in Session* translated from Marathi into English by Priya Adarkar happens to be an unusual play, which created a controversy among the members of the jury. But in spite of the controversy, the play had an impact on the audience. It was adjudged 'The Play of the Year' and translated into several Indian languages. It was also made into a film by Satyadev Dubey. It was broadcast in English from BBC, London in 1971. Vijay Tendulkar won the Sangeet Natak Akademi Award for playwriting.

The play focuses on a middle-class working woman, Leela Benare and her relationship with a number of men, which is exposed by the co-artists through a mock trial in a court of law. The play, obviously, holds mirror to the contemporary Indian (in this case Maharashtrian) society, which is undergoing some sort of transition from tradition to modernity thereby creating some fluctuation in the valuation of life. The playwright problematizes the issue of feminine identity against the background of Indian patriarchy. The exposure of the contradictions of Leela Benare's life by the male members apparently provides comedy while at the deeper level it reveals the tragedy of a passionate woman. Leela Benare easily brings to our mind similar characters from world literature like Madam Bovary, Renevskaya (*Cherry Orchard*), Nana and Laura (*Streetcar Named Desire*). Along with her, many men are also exposed.

The play begins in a light-hearted manner. It revolves round the idea of a game. Leela Benare, the protagonist is on the offensive in the beginning. The first act begins with the arrival of Samant and Miss Leela Benare. In this act, the playwright offers us a general picture of Leela Benare, the protagonist's personality. She happens to be a young schoolteacher, who is very jovial, humorous, childish, and mischievous. She seems to have a lot of gusto for life and is, therefore, over-enthusiastic. Although she has hurt her finger while putting the bolt, she is not depressed by it at all. She sucks her finger for a little while. She is not worried about it. On the contrary, she says, "But I *am* feeling marvelous. I got down at the station with all the others and suddenly, after many days, I felt wonderful!"[2] (p. 1). She is also a good flirtatious lady, who wants to attract the attention of young men like Samant. She tells him, "And I felt even more wonderful coming here with you. I'm so glad the others fell behind.... Let's leave everyone behind, I thought, and go somewhere far, far away—with you!" (p. 2). Samant is embarrassed by her suggestion. But she continues to flatter him, "Yes, I like you very much.... You're very nice indeed.... You are a very pure and good person, I like you" (p. 2). One may easily see how Leela Benare is a very amiable lady, who establishes instant friendship with menfolk. After learning from Samant that he is not married yet, Leela Benare tries to be physically intimate with him. But Samant being innocent does not reciprocate her silent invitation. Apart from being a sociable lady, Benare is a talkative lady as well. She proudly tells Samant about her punctuality, love of discipline, her devotion to teaching and love of children, etc. "In school, when the first bell rings, my foot's already on the threshold. I haven't heard a single reproach for not being on time these past years. Nor about my teaching. I'm *never* behindhand with my lessons! Exercises corrected on time, too! I am used to standing while teaching. In class, I never sit when teaching. That's how I keep my eye on the whole class. No one has a chance to play up. My class is scared stiff of me! And they adore me too. My children will do anything for me. For I'd give the last drop of my blood to teach them. [*In a different tone*] That's why people are jealous. Specially the other teachers and the management.... But my teaching's perfect. I've put my whole life into it—I've worn myself to a shadow in this job! Just because of one bit of slander, what can they do to me? Throw me out? Let them! I haven't hurt anyone. Anyone at all! If I've hurt anybody, it's been myself. But is that any kind of reason for throwing me out? Who are these people to say what I can or can't do? My life is my own—I haven't sold it to anyone for a job! My will is my own. My wishes are my own. No one can kill those—no one! I'll do what I like with myself and my life!"

(pp. 4-5). These words easily testify to her independent nature, gusto for life and liveliness of spirit.

Leela Benare likes the male company. She tells Samant, "I feel scared when I am alone, you know" (p. 5). She knows how to hide her personal problems and keeps on talking and singing. They discuss the programme of the day. They have to participate in a mock trial in a mock court. Hence, different actors have to assume different roles and conduct the programme by way of a 'game' purely for the fun of it. The other actors have not come yet. But Miss Leela Benare comments humorously about their characteristic features. She comments about Mr. Kashikar's serious concern for the Prime Objective and Mrs. Kashikar's childlessness as follows: "Fun. But Samant, 'spreading enlightenment is also one of the Prime Objectives behind our programme.' So our chairman Kashikar will tell you. Kashikar can't take a step without a Prime Objective! Besides him, there is Mrs. Hand-that-Rocks-the-Cradle. I mean Mrs. Kashikar. What an excellent housewife the poor woman is! A real Hand-that-Rocks-the-Cradle type! But what's the use? Mr. Prime Objective is tied with uplifting the masses. And poor Hand-that-Rocks-the-Cradle has no cradle to rock!" (p. 6). Similarly, she combines humour and irony in her description of people, who are going to participate in the mock trial. For example, she comments upon how Mr. and Mrs. Kashikar have given shelter and educated Balu Rokde and also made a slave of him. Similarly, she describes Balu Rokde as an Expert on Law. "He's such an authority on the subject, even a desperate client won't go anywhere near him! He just sits alone in the barrister's room at court, swatting flies with legal precedents! And in his tenements, he sits alone killing houseflies! But for today's mock trial, he's a very great barrister. You'll see the wonders he performs!" (p. 6). Likewise, she describes Sukhatme as follows: "And we have an Intellectual too. That means someone who prides himself on his book learning. But when there's a real-life problem, away he runs! Hides his head" (p. 6).

In addition to being humorous and ironical, Miss Leela Benare is mischievous also like a child. When Sukhatme, Ponkshe, and Balu Rokde enter the hall, Benare, who is hiding behind the door, frightens them by shouting 'Boo' in a tremendous voice. Consequently, all the three of them start for a moment and then recover their poise. Benare laughs to her heart's content and enjoys the fun. Sukhatme admonishes her, "Miss Benare, whatever happens, you don't want to grow up, do you? Eh?" (p. 7). But Leela Benare says that she knows when to be serious and when to be light-hearted. "Why, in the class room, I'm the soul of seriousness! But I don't see why one should go around all the time with a long face. Or a square face! Like that Ponkshe!" (p. 8). Leela Benare believes in the philosophy of enjoyment of life. "We should laugh, we should play, we should sing! If we can and if they'll let us, we should dance too. Shouldn't have any false modesty or dignity" (p. 8). She also believes in the inalienability of one's life and the importance of making the best of it. "Forget about the sage Tukaram. I say it—I, Leela Benare a lining woman. I say it from my own experience. Life is not meant for anyone else. It's your own life. It must be. It's a very, very important thing. Every moment, every bit of it is precious..." (p. 8). In conformity with her philosophy of enjoyment, she recites a poem and sings a song.

When all the actors gather, they decide to have a rehearsal of an imaginary legal case. It is just a game played for fun. Miss Benare, who professes to be a lover of fun and enjoyment, is easily trapped in it. Benare readily agrees to participate in the game. "I'm even willing to play hopscotch, if you're talking of games. Games are very good for you. I often play quite happily with the children at school. It's fun" (p. 20). Different roles are assigned to different actors. Miss Benare is given the role of the prime accused. Ponkshe says, "Miss Leela Benare, you have been arrested on suspicion of a crime of an extremely grave nature, and brought as a prisoner before the bar of this court" (p. 23). Kashikar, who assumes the role of a judge, states the crime of the prisoner, "Prisoner Miss Benare, under Section No. 302 of the Indian Penal Code you are accused of the crime of infanticide. Are you guilty of the aforementioned crime?" (p. 24). Leela Benare is suddenly shocked by the accusation and looks serious. Sukhatme, therefore, asks her, "Why are you so grave all of a sudden? After all, it's a game. Just a game, that's all. Why are you so serious?" (p. 25). But Leela Benare wants to hide her anxiety by pretending to be lighthearted. "Who's serious? I am absolutely—lighthearted. I just got a bit serious to create the right atmosphere. For the court, that's all. Why should I be afraid of a trial like this?" (p. 25).

Having been trapped in her own words, Leela Benare accepts her role as a criminal guilty of killing a newborn baby. As the judge, Kashikar explains, "The question of infanticide is one of great social significance. That's why I deliberately picked it. We consider society's best interests in all we do" (p. 26). When he asks Leela Benare if she pleads guilty or not, she avoids answering the question by cracking jokes and diverting the attention of the court. Sukhatme, therefore, suggests that "We need seriousness" (p. 29). "Otherwise this game becomes really childish" (p. 29). In spite of the court's demand for seriousness, Leela Benare continues her mischievous behaviour. For example, she says, "Now back to infanticide. I was wrong. Milord. But there's no reason for the prisoner to show such respect for the judge. I plead not guilty. I couldn't even kill a common cockroach. I'm scared to do it. How could I kill a newborn child?" (p. 30). The judge reprimands her for obstructing the work of the court. Sukhatme, the lawyer explains the gravity of accusation made against the criminal Leela Benare, "Milord, the nature of the charge brought against the accused is a most terrible one. Motherhood is a sacred thing.... Motherhood is pure. Moreover, there is a great—er—a great nobility in our concept of motherhood. We have acknowledged woman as the mother of mankind. Our culture enjoins us to perpetual worship of her. 'Be thy mother as a god' is what we teach our children from infancy. There is great responsibility devolving upon a mother. She weaves a magic circle with her whole existence in order to protect and preserve her little one..." (p. 30). Viewed against the elevated Indian concept of motherhood, Leela Benare's crime seems to be really heinous. Woman's role as a mother is greater than that as a wife. Sukhatme, the lawyer, therefore, iterates that "Woman is a wife for a moment, but mother forever" (p. 31). He highlights the gravity of her crime, "Considering this, what would we respectable citizens say if any woman were to take the life of the delicate bundle of joy she has borne? We would say, there could be no baser or more devilish thing on earth. I intend to establish by means of evidence that the prisoner has done this same vile deed" (p. 31). Ponkshe (the world famous scientist) swears by the *Oxford Dictionary* that he speaks nothing but truth. He clarifies that the accused is a schoolteacher, who is unmarried to the public eye and that she runs after men too much. Initially, Benare does not suspect that she is the target of the whole trial. But slowly she realizes that it is targeting her own self. Thus, what started as a comedy begins to assume the gravity of a tragedy. Balu Rokde gives evidence of Benare's intimacy with Prof. Damle. "Yes, I went there in the evening. As night was falling. And there—*she* was! Miss Benare" (p. 38). Now that Miss Leela Benare is directly involved in the scandal, she feels nettled and reacts strongly, "there is no need at all to drag my private life into this. I can visit whom I like. Damle wasn't eating me up" (p. 39). Then Sukhatme tries to pacify her by reminding her that it is just a game and that she need not take it seriously. Then Rokde continues his evidence. As he saw Miss Benare along with Prof. Damle in his room when night was falling and as he was dismissed by Prof. Damle in haste, he concludes that Miss Benare's behaviour is certainly suspicious. But Miss Benare questions the validity of the charge. "If you like. I'll give you the names and address of twenty-five more people with whom I am alone at times. Holding a trial, are you? Suspicious indeed. You don't even understand the meaning of simple words!" (p. 40).

Now there is further accumulation of evidence against Miss Benare. For example, Samant adds a bit of further information to the evidence by stating that Miss Benare was not only alone with Prof. Damle, but both of them were inside the room, which was locked from inside, "Yes. The door was locked. Not from outside. From inside. And I banged on the door. No, that's wrong. I rang the bell. The door opened. An unknown man stood before me. Guess who it was. Professor Damle! I was seeing him for the first time. So he'd be unknown to me, wouldn't he?" (p. 44). He states further that Prof. Damle refused to talk with him (Samant) and slammed the door shut. Since Samant wanted to invite him for a lecture, he stood there, but to his surprise, he heard a woman crying softly inside the room and asking Prof. Damle, "If you abandon me in this condition, where shall I go?" (p. 45). Then Samant heard Prof. Damle's callous answer, "Where you should go is entirely your problem. I feel great sympathy for you. But I can do nothing. I must protect my reputation" (p. 45). Samant heard Miss Benare saying, "If you abandon me, I shall have no choice but to take my life.... Bear it in mind that you will not escape the guilt of murdering two...living beings" (p. 45). When the harshest possible accusation is made against Miss Benare by way of fun and game, she grows terribly angry. Mrs. Kashikar tries to pacify her, "But my dear Benare, as your conscience is clear, why are you flying into such a violent rage?" (p. 46). Miss Benare reacts to it very strongly, "You've all deliberately ganged up on me! You've plotted against me!" (p. 46). She breaks down and even tries to go away from there by opening the door. But again she feels trapped, as the bolt is too tight to be turned or pulled down. Miss Benare has, obviously, become a trapped animal. One may easily see how tragedy creeps into the apparent comedy here.

As the mock-court proceeding continues, Miss Benare is led to the witness box. Her face reveals the terror of a trapped animal. She is asked to swear by the *Oxford Dictionary* to tell the whole truth and nothing but the truth. But she remains silent. Hence, she is warned not to behave in a manner, which amounts to the contempt of court. Then Sukhatme points his finger at Benare and says, "Your name is Leela Damle" (p. 51). She remains silent. Then he asks her about her age. Miss Benare does not answer. Mr. Kashikar offers his opinion about the advantages of child marriages and early marriages. "All right. She's not less than thirty-four. I'll give it to you in writing! What I say is, our society should revive the old custom of child marriage. Marry off the girls before puberty. All this promiscuity will come to a full stop. If anyone has ruined our society, it's Agarkar and Dhondo Keshav Kharve. That's my frank opinion, Sukhatme, my frank opinion" (p. 52). Against this background Sukhatme asks Miss Benare, "Can you tell the court how you came to stay unmarried to such a mature—such an advanced age? (*Waits*, *then*) Let me frame my question somewhat differently. How many chances of marriage have you had so far in your life? And how did you miss them? Tell the court" (p. 52). Now Mrs. Kashikar enters the witness box and explains that anyone who really wants to can get married in a flash and that Miss Benare is unmarried still simply because she didn't want to get married. "What else? That's what happens these days when you get everything without marrying. They just want comfort. They couldn't care less about responsibility! Let me tell you—in my time, even if a girl was snub nosed, sallow, hunchbacked or anything whatever, she—could—still—get—married! It's the sly new fashion of women earning that makes everything go wrong. That's how promiscuity has spread throughout our society" (p. 54). After generalizing about the modern employed woman, who have both economic and sexual liberties, she focuses on Miss Benare and vents out her disapproval of the formers liberal behaviour with men, "What better proof? Just look at the way she behaves. I don't like to say anything since she's one of us. Should there be no limit to how freely a woman can behave with a man? An unmarried woman? No matter how well she knows him? Look how loudly she laughs! How she sings, dances, cracks jokes! And wandering alone with how many men, day in and day out!" (p. 54). As the proceeding continues, we learn that Miss Benare needs Prof. Damle to see her home after the performance and that Prof. Damle is a father of five children—with whom she has a love affair. In fact, Prof. Damle is not the only man with whom she is in love, but there are a few others also whom she has been trying to hook. For example, Balu Rokde confesses that Miss Benare held his hand when she was alone with him at Dombivli and that "I freed my hand. She moved away. She said, Don't tell anyone what happened" (p. 57). Benare denies it briefly. But Lawyer Sukhatme interprets it legally, "Milord, this means that the accused committed an outrage in a lonely spot, on a boy like Rokde, much younger than her—almost like her younger brother. Not only that, but she threatened him with consequences if the matter came to light. She tried to cover up her sinful deed!" (p. 57).

Ponkshe enters the witness box and reveals a bit more shocking information about Miss Benare. He wants the court to know why she keeps a bottle of TIK-20 in her purse. He further informs the court how she sent him a chit sealed in an envelope inviting him to wait for her in the Udupi restaurant just behind the school. He says that he went to the restaurant just to see what her game was. When he sat with her in the 'family room', she opened her purse to take out her handkerchief and a bottle of TIK-20 fell down from her purse. Ponkshe tells the court that she made known her desire to marry him not because she was in love with him, but because she was pregnant. "Miss Benare made me promise never to tell anyone the name of the man, who—so she said—had made her pregnant. So far I've kept my word" (p. 60). The judge Mr. Kashikar is surprised by the unusualness of the proposal, "But what I don't understand, Ponkshe, is why, if Miss Benare was pregnant by one man, she expressed a desire to marry another—I mean, to marry you!" (p. 60). The lawyer Sukhatme is curious to know Ponkshe's answer, "What was your answer, Mr. Ponkshe? Were you prepared to take a broad view of things for the sake of humanity and accept the child along with the mother?" (p. 60). Obviously, Ponkshe says that he was not prepared to accept a pre-maritally pregnant woman. Ponkshe offers further details of how Miss Benare broached the subject of marriage slowly and indirectly, "She asked jokingly: 'Well, are you fixed up somewhere?' So I said, 'Unless I find someone just to my taste, I'm not interested in marrying.' So she asked, 'What exactly do you mean by 'to your taste?' What do you look for?' I replied, 'On the whole, girls are silly and frivolous—that's my opinion. I want a mature partner.' Then she asked, 'Don't you think that maturity—that is, a fully developed understanding—comes to a person only with experience?' 'I don't know,' I replied. She then said, 'And experience comes with age, with a slightly unusual way of life. And this sort of experience is never happy or pleasing. It gives pain to the person, who gains it. And it's usually intolerable to others. But will you bear with it? I mean, supposing it is a really mature person. Older than you and more educated?' 'I haven't yet thought seriously about it.' 'Then you should,' she replied. So I asked whether she had some promising bride in mind. She said, 'Yes. I feel she' the kind you want. 'You just have to understand her unusualness." I couldn't' see why she was making this great effort to get me married. I asked casually, 'What sort of unusualness do you mean?' She replied, 'The girl's just gone through a shattering heartbreak, and—wait I'll think of exact words—yes—'the fruit of that love'—here she stumbled a little—'is in her womb. Actually it is no fault of hers. But her situation's very serious indeed. She wants to bring up the child. In fact it's only for the child she wants to go on living and get married.' She spoke some more in the same vein. I grew suspicious. So in order to get the truth out of her, I said, 'Oh! Poor girl! Her luck seems really bad. Who is the scoundrel responsible?'" (pp. 62-63). When Ponkshe wants to know the name of the scoundrel, Miss Benare reveals that it is Prof. Damle and requests him not to call Prof. Damle a scoundrel. "He may be a good man. He may be very great and wise. She may have fallen short. She may not have been able to convince him how deeply she feels for him. The woman is not the crucial factor. It's the baby that comes first.... She worshipped that man's intellect. But all he understood was her body" (p. 63). Ponkshe reveals further that Miss Benare has been carrying Prof. Damle's child in her womb and how she fell at his (Ponkshe's) feet and how she finally pretended that it was all a joke.

After Ponkshe has finished his statement, Karnik enters the witness box and reveals more interesting information about Miss Benare and Rokde. According to his version, Miss Benare had asked Rokde to marry her, so that she could support him and that he could be free from Mrs. Kashikar. But Rokde did not have the courage to marry her without Mrs. Kashikar's permission. He refused to marry her on the grounds of social respectability. "And if I marry you when you're in this condition, the whole world'll sling mud at me. No one in my family's done a thing like that. Don't depend on me. Or else I'll have to tell Mrs. Kashikar" (p. 65). Karnik reveals further that he learnt from a common friend about how the accused (Miss Benare) had attempted suicide once before. "My information is that the accused attempted suicide because of a disappointment in love. She fell in love at the age of fifteen, with her own maternal uncle! That's what ended in disappointment" (p. 66). Hearing this piece of information, the judge (Mr. Kashikar) and the lawyer (Mr. Sukhatme) express their sense of shock and surprise at the immorality, depravity and licentiousness of the accused.

Now the tradition of the court is broken when the judge, Mr. Kashikar is requested by the lawyer Mr. Sukhatme to enter the witness box and give his witness. Accordingly, Mr. Kashikar enters the witness box and tells the court that he knows the accused too well. "Only too well! A sinful canker on the body of society—that's my honest opinion of these grown-up unmarried girls" (p. 67). He tells the court further that he had met Mr. Nanasaheb Shindhe of Bombay, the Chairman of the Education Society and learnt from him that a schoolmistress from their Education Society's High School had been continually requesting him to drop an enquiry against her. When Mr. Kashikar took a garland of flowers to Nanasaheb's house on the latter's birthday, he heard the latter talking angrily to someone on phone, "It is a sin to be pregnant before marriage. It would be still more immoral to let such a woman teach, in such a condition! There is no alternative—this woman must be dismissed! He was saying. Finally he instructed, 'send the order for my signature this very day!'" (p. 69). Mr. Kashikar guesses the lady to be none other than Miss Benare. Deeply shocked by this piece of news Miss Benare tries to drink the deadly poison TIK-20, but is prevented by Karnik from doing so.

Now Sukhatme is called upon to offer his counsel for the prosecution. His views, obviously, hold a mirror to patriarchal point of view and the social dimension of a woman's sexual freedom. His words offer a critique of women's liberation against the backdrop of traditional Indian society. He says, "Milord, the nature of the charge against the accused, Miss Benare, is truly dreadful. The woman, who is an accused, has made a heinous blot on the sacred brow of motherhood—which is purer than heaven itself. For that, any punishment, however great, that the law may give her, will be too mild by far. The character of the accused is appalling. It is bankrupt of morality. Not only that. Her conduct has blackened all social and moral values. The accused is a public enemy number one. If such socially destructive tendencies are encouraged to flourish, this country and its culture will be totally destroyed. Therefore, I say the court must take a very stern, inexorable view of the prisoner's crime, without being trapped in any sentiment. The charge against the accused is one of infanticide. But the accused has committed a far more serious crime. I mean unmarried motherhood. Motherhood without marriage has always been considered a very great sin by our religion and our traditions. Moreover, if the accused's intention of bringing up the offspring of this unlawful maternity is carried to completion, I have a dreadful fear that the very existence of society will be in danger. There will be no such thing as moral values left. Milord, infanticide is a dreadful act. But bringing up the child of an illegal union is certainly more horrifying. If it is encouraged, there will be no such thing as the institution of marriage left. Immorality will flourish. Before our eyes, our beautiful dream of a society governed by tradition will crumble into dust. The accused has plotted to dynamite the very roots of our tradition, our pride in ourselves, our culture and our religion. It is the sacred and imperative duty of your Lordship and every wise and thoughtful citizen amongst us to destroy that plot at once. No allowance must be made because the accused is a woman. Woman bears the grave responsibility of building up the high values of society. '*Na stri swatantryamarhati.*' 'Miss Benare is not fit for independence.' With the urgent plea that the court should show no mercy to the accused, but give her the greatest and severest punishment for her terrible crime. I close the argument for the prosecution" (pp. 70-71).

Sukhatme's counsel apparently problematizes the unmarried motherhood of woman, but at a deeper level, it affirms the patriarchal framework of values upheld by the Hindu society. Woman's total liberation of the Western kind becomes irrelevant in the Indian contest. The traditional Hindu society upholds the holy institution of marriage, affirms the highest virtue of virginity and chastity and recommends conformity to the ideals of family and society involving the practice of self-control and sacrifice. Too much of freedom to man, especially to woman is too bad as it leads him or her to total ruin. Since woman is biologically at a disadvantage, her freedom will hasten her to ruin earlier than a man's freedom can do.

Before the sentence is pronounced, Miss Benare is asked to say something about the charge made against her. Now that Miss Benare is cleverly exposed by the trial, she has grown desperate. Having overcome her sense of embarrassment, she vents out her stifled feelings very frankly and boldly—which is really admirable. She confesses her difficulties, frustration, dilemmas, biological urges, dreams, and despairs. She articulates her philosophy of life born out of her own experience. She confesses how she found death to be better than life, although she had a lot of gusto for life; how people around her have failed to understand her inner feelings and dilemmas and how her desires of the body remained unfulfilled. She narrates the emotional accidents of her childhood leading to frustration and suicidal thoughts; affirms the importance of the body and expresses her desire for a son, though to be born outside of wedlock. She expresses almost a Lawrentian philosophy of blood consciousness. Her words act as a voice of Nature against the restrictions of culture. Her argument foreshadows the modern Western feminist thought. "It's true, I did commit a sin. I was in love with my mother's brother. But in our strict house, in the prime of my unfolding youth, he was the one, who came close to me. He praised my bloom every day. He gave me love.... How was I to know that if you felt like breaking yourself into bits and melting into one with someone—if you felt that just being with him gave a whole meaning to life—and if he was your uncle, it was a sin! Why, I was hardly fourteen! I didn't even know what sin was—I swear by my mother. I didn't. (*She sobs loudly like a little girl.*) I insisted on marriage. So I could live my beautiful lovely dream openly. Like everyone else! But all of them—my mother too—were against it. And my brave man turned tail and ran. Such a rage—I felt such a rage against him then—I felt like smashing his face in public and spitting on it! But I was ignorant. Instead, I threw myself off a parapet of our house—to embrace death. But I didn't die. My body didn't die! I felt as if feelings were dead—but they hadn't died either then. Again I fell in love. As a grown woman. I threw all my heart into it: I thought, this would be different. This love is intelligent. It is love for an unusual intellect. It isn't love at all—it is worship! But it was the same mistake. I offered up my body on the altar of my worship. And my intellectual god took the offering—and went his way. He didn't want my mind or my devotion—he didn't care about them! (*Feebly*) He wasn't a god. He was a man. For whom everything was of the body, for the body! That's all! Again, the body! (*Screaming*) This body is a traitor! (*She is writhing with pain.*) I despise this body—and I love it! I hate it—but it's all you have, in the end, isn't it? It will be there. It will be yours. Where will it go without you? And where will you go if reject it? Don't be ungrateful. It was your body that once burnt and gave you a moment so beautiful, so blissful, so near to heaven! Have you forgotten? It took you high, high, and high above yourself into a place like paradise. Will you deny it? And now it carries within it the witness of that time—a tender little bud—of what will be a lisping, laughing, dancing little life—my son—my whole existence! I want my body now for him—for him alone. (*Shuts her eyes and mutters a mortal pain.*) He must have a mother…a father to call his own—a house—to be looked after—he must have a good name!" (pp. 74-75). Miss Benare has ultimately revealed her inner dilemma born out of her zest for life, intense feeling of love and the accidental pregnancy. She has defied the patriarchal values and the institution of marriage without knowing it, by her pursuit of love and sexual ecstasy. Happily free from hypocrisy, she has admitted her weakness and tragic dilemma very boldly.

The members of the court—lawyers, witnesses and the judge—have succeeded in exposing Miss Benare through the clever technique of the mock trial. Truly speaking, these men have no business to pry into Miss Benare's personal life. They derive a bit of sadistic pleasure in unraveling her private sexual life. They are also disarmed by Miss Benare's honest confession of her personal secrets. But these men are also motivated by the higher, i.e. social concern. According to them, an unmarried mother is not acceptable to the patriarchal Hindu society, as she sets a wrong model for the future. (On the contrary, the modern feminists of the world may give her a gold medal to her for her achievement!) The patriarchal social philosophy is clearly articulated by the judge, Mr. Kashikar, "Prisoner Miss Benare, pay the closest attention. The crimes you have committed are most terrible. There is no forgiveness for them. Your sin must be expiated. Irresponsibility must be chained down. Social customs, after all, are of supreme importance. Marriage is the very foundation of our society's stability. Motherhood must be sacred and pure. This court takes a serious view of your attempt to dynamite all this. It is the firm opinion of this court that your behaviour puts you beyond mercy. And, what is more, the arrogance with which you conducted yourself in society, having done all these things that arrogance is the most unforgivable thing of all. Criminals and sinners should know their place. You have conducted yourself above your station. The court expresses its indignation at your presumptuousness. Moreover, the future of posterity was entrusted to you. This is a very dreadful thing. The morality, which you have shown through your conduct, was the morality you were planning to impart to the youth of tomorrow. This court has not an iota of doubt about it. Hence, not only today's but also tomorrow's society would have been endangered by your misconduct. It must be said that the school officials have done a work of merit in deciding to remove you from your job. By the grace of God, it has all been stopped in time. Neither you nor anyone else should ever do anything like this again. No memento of your sin should remain for future generations. Therefore, this court hereby sentences that you shall live. But the child in your womb shall be destroyed" (pp. 75-76). The final judgement given by the judge, obviously, upholds the patriarchal philosophy, affirms the institution of marriage and disapproves the unmarried motherhood. Thus, there is a triumph of patriarchy with its moral framework and discipline over the so-called emancipation of woman, which involves economic and sexual freedom. When the judgement is given, Miss Benare is so deeply shaken that she begins to sob and collapse. The trick of the mock trial employed by the members of the troupe has succeeded amply in exposing the inner secrets of Miss Benare's sexual and emotional tragedy. It has also concurrently given expression to its affirmation of the institution of marriage in the Indian society. After the whole thing is over, the members of the troupe try to console Miss Benare that it is, after all, only a game and that she need not take it to heart. Then all of them get ready for the regular show.

The play is very important in the Indian context as it holds a mirror to the changing values of the Indian society. Vijay Tendulkar, who is a keen observer of life around him, has captured the spirit of the time very sensitively in the play. The play shows how in the latter part of the twentieth century Indian society women are liberated psychologically through education. Education, in turn, leads to employment, i.e. economic security and freedom. Psychological emancipation and economic freedom pave the way for sexual freedom. But unfortunately for women, the patriarchal society of India does not change as fast as the educated employed women. Hence, the strong opposition to the promiscuity of emancipated women. A young lady like Miss Leela Benare, who is satirized and attacked by the Indian patriarchal society, would not have suffered like this in a promiscuous society of England or America. On the contrary, she would have been awarded a gold medal by the Women Libbers, for the assertion of her sexual identity and courageous acceptance of unmarried motherhood.

What is interesting in *Silence! The Court is in Session* is that both tragedy and comedy take place here concurrently. Whereas the exposure of Miss Leela Benare is tragic, the conduct of mock trial by the members of the amateur troupe is comic and satiric. Just as Vijay Tendulkar has brought down the sledgehammer on the issue of women's sexual liberation, he has also indirectly exposed the male hypocrisy, double standards and complicity of the members of the patriarchal society. The court, which accuses Miss Leela Benare for her pre-marital pregnancy, does not go to the extent of accusing or punishing Prof. Damle, who has been the cause of her pregnancy and suffering. Similarly, the Management, which insists on terminating her services as a teacher in the school, does not take similar action against Prof. Damle as it connives at male crime. What is most ironical about the mock trial is that even a woman like Mrs. Kashikar behaves rather callously in exposing another woman, i.e. Miss Benare thereby proving the harsh truth that woman can be the worst enemy of woman. But again the difference between the two women should be noted. Whereas Mrs. Kashikar is an uneducated and unemployed woman, Miss Benare happens to be an educated and employed woman. Whereas Mrs. Kashikar enjoys sexual, emotional, hence matrimonial security, Miss Benare is in search of it. Although both of them belong to the same, i.e. female gender, there is a great deal of difference in their personalities in terms of attitude and temperament. Mrs. Kashikar happens to be a staunch believer in the patriarchal values of chastity, sanctity of marriage and motherhood.

Notes

1. Lal, Anand, *The Oxford Companion to Indian Theatre*, New Delhi: University Press, 2004, p. 483.
2. Tendulkar, Vijay, *Silence! The Court is in Session*, in *Three Modern Indian Plays*. Delhi: Oxford University Press, 1996. (All the page references are to this edition.)

• • • • •

19

Immortalization of the Common Man in *Agra Bazaar*

Agra Bazaar is an interesting and at the same time a puzzling play written (rather improvised over the years) by Habib Tanvir in Urdu. As the playwright says in his Preface, he went on adding characters and situations to the original plot until it reached the present shape. There is no story of a single man or family in the play. Hence, it is rather difficult to locate the protagonist of the play who may be said to be the central character around which other characters revolve according to the law of probability.

But the playwright claims that he wanted to celebrate Nazir's poetry, humanism, concern for the common man through his dramatic presentation without bringing him on the stage directly. He therefore picked these ordinary characters of the market as found in Nazir's poetry and tried to reconstruct a picture pay compliments to the poet who preceded the famous Mirza Ghalib. "Nazir was witness to the entire period from Khan Arzoo Shah Hatim, Sanda and Mir to Ghalib. With Mir, an important period of Urdu poetry ends. He died in 1810 when Ghalib was 14 years old. I had wanted to discuss Nazir in relation to the poetry of a major Urdu poet like Mir. The aim was also to indicate that it was this period that witnessed the birth of Urdu's most popular poet, later to be known as Ghalib" (p. 5).

It is difficult to decide as to who is the protagonist of the play. Nazir never comes on the stage. But there are so many ordinary men who populate the market. According to Habib

Tanvir, the characters drawn from the market show a range of people from one extreme to another. "I wanted to highlight the fact that Nazir's love of the ordinary people has immortalized him and that he continues to be popular with the *fakirs* and dervishes of this country even today. Thus, his own poetry gave me the idea of a chorus of *fakirs* which became the plays' main structural component. I also wanted to show that in contrast to the plebeian sections, the educated elite of Nazir's time praised him as a person but totally ignored him as a poet. This gave me the idea of the book-seller and the kite-seller who help the play move forward and whose shops become the two opposing poles of the marketplace. I had read that Nazir would create poetry almost spontaneously at the request of small traders, vendors and beggars. Whether this was true or not, I liked the idea as it was helpful in the development of the play. After reading his works I was quite ready to believe it too. Thus emerged the character of Kakri-seller. It also provided the basic plot of the play, its *mise-en-scene* and the title" (pp. 3-4). The playwright therefore uses the situation of a marketplace of Agra to give expression to his disjointed views about Indian history, Urdu poetry of Nazir and the survival strategies of the vendors of various things. In a way, market itself may be said to the central image of the play where none is important and at the same time everyone is important. In Hindu philosophy, the mortal life itself is compared to a 'three days' market', thereby suggesting the temporariness and the struggle for survival and success. In *Agra Bazaar*, the discordant voices of a marketplace are heard. Through these polyphonic utterances the playwright seems to comment on the past and the present of India, satirize the modern society for its lack of ideals and resort to compromise.

There is no logical development of any particular theme in the play as the market happens to be the central locale here. Hence, the arbitrary logic of the unexpected happenings in the market form part of the logic and development of the play.

In this market all sorts of petty vendors are selling their goods and doing their business. For example, there is a *laddoo*-seller, ice-seller, *kakri*-seller, *paan*-seller or even an ear-cleaner in this market trying to attract the customers to their shops. Obviously, there struggle for survival in the cut-throat market competition may be seen here. Each seller tries to attract the customers to his shop and feels irritated to learn that the other sellers are snatching away his customers to their side or ruining his business. Hence, they start quarelling among themselves for these so-called petty reasons, which are really serious reasons from their point of view and use abusive and uncultured language.

Then a monkey-trainer (*madari*) comes there and addresses and commands his monkey to perform certain feats and the monkey successfully mimes the actions of politicians thereby providing good entertainment to the watching public. Not merely that, the playwright indirectly as well as the monkey-trainer directly reveal the history of North India thereby throwing light upon the colonial attacks on different parts of India by Muslim rulers as well as the British rulers. By asking a few questions to the monkey, the trainer reveals the history of Delhi like Nadir Shah's attack on Delhi; Ahmed Shah Abdali's invasion of Delhi, Surajmal Jat's attack on Agra, the Laat Sahib's firing in the Battle of Plassey and the famine in Bengal. Through these examples, the playwright reveals the details of imperial wars that took place in North India thereby revealing man's inhumanity of man, violence, and cruelty.

The market seems to be rather dull and the sellers have been desperately trying to attack the customers. Thus, the monkey-trainer picks a quarrel with the *kakri*-seller for being responsible for the loss of a customer for himself. After the quarrel, the monkey-trainer leaves the market by cursing the other sellers.

A group of *fakirs* enters and sing their philosophical song in which they highlight the extraordinary importance of bread or food in human (and animal) life. They suggest that even poetry (about moons and stars) and religion (like worship of gods) cannot thrive in the absence of food. (As Sarvajna, the 17th century Kannada poet says, there is no god greater than the food-god.) The chorus of *fakirs* indirectly throws light on the struggle for survival displayed by the various vendors in the market.

The sellers employ the oral and poetic method of advertisement of their goods and often display their poetic talent. (Nowadays it is the other way round—poetry needs advertisement for its sale.) They quarrel among themselves over silly problems and finally come to blows. It aggravates the situation as a consequence of which all the shopkeepers close their shops. Then the *fakirs* sing their song about the pain of poverty, hunger and the insult that go with them. The chorus of *fakirs* plays the same role as the chorus plays in Greek tragedies. As a result of the fight, the potter's pots are broken. The rain has spoiled all the *kakris* of the seller. The *kakri*-seller asks a passerby if he writes poetry. The latter says 'no'. Then a poet comes there. The *kakri*-seller requests him to write a few verses on his *kakri*, but the poet replies that he being a novice, cannot do justice to the subject, but that he would convey the request to Zauq, the famous court poet, who is tutor to His Majesty, the Emperor. Somebody jokes that if *kakri* could be sold with singing poetry, they should better be poets. Likewise the poets should better sell *kakris* along with their singing.

The book-seller refers to Mir Sahib (the great poet of 80 plus) years and his present insanity. The companion narrates how Mir Sahib left home and Delhi, after seeing the unfaithfulness of his own dear ones and witnessing the bloodshed caused by the attacks by the Persians, Turks, Afghans, Rahelas, Rajputs, Jats, Marathas—which formed part of the bloody history. Now Mir Sahib lives in Lucknow and sees the havoc caused by the English. Thus, both the Muslim and the English colonization and the consequent violence and atrocities are revealed through Mir Sahib's memory. The book-seller compares the Mughal Empire to a lion attacked by several cats and dogs. "You are right, these are turbulent times. When I look at it, what I see is not the Mughal Empire but a big, powerful lion being attacked by hundreds of cats and dogs. Seeing it wounded and helpless, vultures and other birds of prey have also gathered to tear it to pieces. And the lion has neither the leisure nor the luxury to die" (p. 42).

The poet requests the book-seller to publish his collection of poems and the book-seller wants to publish it.

Then the *fakirs* sing a song about flattery—that one should flatter everyone including God, saints and prophets—to serve their selfish interests:

All the world loves a flatterer
God loves one too.
Flatter to serve your own interest.
Flatter even if you have none.
Flatter God, saints and prophets.
In short flatter everyone.
Flatterers get whatever they want.
Those who can't, live in poverty and want.
Flattery brings house, land and crown.
Turns white to black, black to brown.... (p. 43)

The book-seller tells the *fakirs* that there was a big quarrel and dispute among some low class persons, but no damage happened to his bookshop because luckily there is no great demand for books in the world. The playwright indirectly satirizes the unwantedness of knowledge and especially poetry in a country where everyone is worried about his food. The poet and his companion discuss the beauty (merits) and limited scope (demerits) of Ghazal form practiced by Mir Sahib. Mir Sahib did not want to pollute his language by talking to the ordinary people in his journey on a horse-carriage from Delhi to Lucknow.

There comes a Tazkiranawis (biographer, who is intended by the playwright to be a typical name rather than a proper name) who refuses to write verses for the riff-raff like the *kakri*-seller. He narrates how Mir was disappointed and disillusioned by his birthplace, Delhi when he returned there from Lucknow after some thirty years gap, because none of the early great poets, scholars and *munshis* and intellectuals remained alive there now. He indirectly throws light on the contrast between the past glory and the present emptiness. He deplores further the depression of the present times when Persian books are not available in bookstores. The poet wants to publish his collection of poetry. The book-seller opines that nobody wants to read Nazir's poetry these days. The poet opines that people's literary taste has degenerated these days and that the poets who write cheap verses or rhymes on Holi and Diwali are considered as great. In other words, great poetry has given place to cheap and populist poetry, an evidence of degeneration of literary taste in India. When the poet requests the book-seller to publish his book of poems, the latter confesses that he has no money to publish it. But the poet suggests to the book-seller to borrow some money from Ganga Prasad, but the latter refuses to do so. So the chorus of *fakirs* sings a song highlighting the importance of money for every transaction in life.

Tazkiranwis opines that although Nazir was a good-natured and soft-spoken man, his poetry is rather cheap and vulgar and nonsensical verse and that he is a versifier rather than a poet and the poet discusses Nazir by saying that as a young man Nazir spent the life of a kite-flier, roaming the streets, playing the Holi and visiting brothels, but that in old age he has become very pious. Tazkiranwis comments on Nazir's visit to the Swimming Pool in order to observe half-naked mermaids and derive vicarious pleasure even in his old age. When Hamid, a small boy sings a song of Nazir on the Swimming Fair, many people listen to it admiringly. Thus, the playwright reveals the contradictory qualities (both positive and negative) of Nazir's personality indirectly without bringing him on the stage.

The book-seller comments upon the changing times as a result of colonial conquest of India by the Englishmen. He says that new translations of the *Quran* and the *Bible*, new printing presses, establishment of the Fort William College at Calcutta by an Englishman, teaching of Indian languages, establishment of new colleges at Delhi, the age of atheism, lack of a crusader spirit, new system of education, new jobs for the educated and lack of jobs for all the educated, the beginning of a new publication house at Delhi. The book-seller wants to stop publishing books and start publishing the newspapers.

We learn further from the dialogues of the book-seller and the customers that Delhi and Agra are known for the rapacity of the people dwelling therein; that *Nadirnama* is not available in the market. We learn that people of different faiths practice their own religions by singing the songs pertaining to their gods or god-men. For example, the Sikh devotees sing about Guru Nanak, whereas the Hindu devotees sing about Baldev's fair. Thus, the multi-religious atmosphere is prevalent in Delhi.

***

Manzoor Hussain, a horse trader has returned from Hyderabad to Agra, taken a vow of silence, as he is deeply in love with a courtesan. Beniprasad explains that Manzoor Hussain was robbed of all his horses and possessions near Jhansi and out of shock he has become a mad *fakir* now. The chorus of *fakirs* describing the emptiness and ephemerality of life helps us to interpret Manzoor Hussain's life of disillusionment and despair.

Beniprasad narrates how Nazir became a friend of Manzoor Hussain and praises his essential goodness and Nazir's indifference to money. By then Nazir's granddaughter comes there unexpectedly and tells the *kakri*-seller how her grandfather never touches money as it is dirty. The kite-seller tells the *kakri*-seller that Nazir's house is located at Tajganj area. The *kakri*-seller wants to approach him and request him to write a few verses on his *kakri* so that he may sell them better with the help of the verses describing their merits.

Ganga Prasad wants to go to Delhi and start publishing journals in English and asks the book-seller to stop publishing the Urdu books of poetry, as there is no market for them in Agra. All these dialogues reveal the change of times and change of interests from one colonial literature (i.e. Urdu) to another (i.e. English) in India.

***

Another important feature revealed in the play is the presence of courtesans and the prevalence of brothels in the Muslim rule. Nobody thought it to be a sin to visit a courtesan (or prostitute) as it was deemed to be evidence of one's good taste and appreciation of art. Once a Rake visits the brothel, meets the courtesan Benazir and requests her to sing a song. As a professional singer she does her duty by singing a song by Nazir, which expresses her own experiences. Then a Police Constable comes there and is greeted by Benazir. He, like all men, wants to spend some happy time with her, but she gently asks him to come the next day as she is busy with some other customer during the present night. He is well behaved enough to understand her problem and therefore obliges her. Then she welcomes the Rake and tells the latter that the poet, Nazir also visits her regularly. Thus, the courtesan happens to be quite democratic in her welcome and treatment of customers from poets to Rake to police constables. The brothel-culture encouraged during the Muslim rule is part of the social structure wherein the surplus energy of the male members of the society has to be channelized, their pent up emotions, to be released.

Another feature revealed in the play happens to be the life of a Police Constable. A Police Constable like all the members of the constabulary is not very intelligent, but high-handed in his approach to the social evils. For example, a Police Constable comes to the market and enquires Maulana about the riot of the previous day. Maulana replies that it was a fight among the low-class street-vendors, especially started by a *kakri*-seller. But the Police Constable, without examining the case minutely, threatens to levy a fine of one rupee per head on all the shopkeepers. He asks the *kakri*-seller to deposit the fine, but the *kakri*-seller replies that he has not sold anything since the morning and has to starve. The constable arrests the Rake coming out of the brothel by falsely charging him of causing the riots in the market the previous day.

As the playwright explains his intention, "What helped was the scene that I had written as the culmination of the story of the rivalry between the Police Constable and the Rake, which shows how through duplicity, falsehood, brute force and misuse of his position the Police Constable has the Rake arrested on trumped -up charges and thus achieves a victory over him" (p. 18).

The next day the Police Constable visits Benazir in the brothel, where Manzoor Hussain, who is reduced to the level of a pauper now, takes money from her and brings betel-leaf from a nearby shop. He does not mind serving her as he happens to be her old lover.

Habib Tanvir ends concludes the play with a chorus of *fakirs* which contains a philosophical speculation about the human life made up of contradictory natures, qualities, faiths, functions, and duties:

Man is the king, who rules over the rest,
Man the one clad in rags or richly dressed,
He also is man, who dines on the best,
And the one who lives on crumbs too is man.
They are men, who build temples and mosques,
Men are also those who perform religious tasks,
Men also those who pray and recite holy texts,
Men steal devotees' shoes and indulge in other thefts.
And the one who catches the thief too is man.
...
The noble, ignoble, the king and his slave,
Respectable wise man to contemptible knave,
He who sought knowledge and he knowledge gave,
Man is the best that we have,
And the worst and the meanest too is man. (pp. 88-89)

This chorus of *fakirs* helps understand the overall human nature, life and history in India in particular and in the world in general.

Certain other events in the play like Potter Ramu becoming the father of a baby-boy and his friends singing a song about him are not really organically connected with the logic of events in the play. They are just disconnected parts in the absurd assemblage of events taking place in a market. One is easily tempted to describe the play as partially absurd, because the dialogues are quite rational, but the link between the events happens to be arbitrary, unexpected and hence absurd. But in spite of this partial absurdity, one may derive a lesson about the contrast between the past glory and the present desolation; between the history and the present situation in North India. The chorus of *fakirs* reminds us of similar choruses in Greek tragedies and provides philosophical and polyphonic comments upon the events happening in the play.

Javed Malick has to be congratulated for releasing this interesting play by Habib Tanvir to the wider market of English speaking world. The translation is masterly for its modern idiom and readability, which is the test of any good and successful translation. The English translation is a welcome addition to the realm of Indian Drama in English Translation.

Reference

Tanvir, Habib, *Agra Bazaar*. Tr. from the Urdu by Javed Malick. Calcutta: Seagull, 2006. (All the page numbers are from this edition.)

• • • • •

20

The Drama of P. Lankesh

P. Lankesh (1935-2000) is a very significant writer of Karnataka. He has a multifaceted personality, and therefore, expressed his talent in a variety of literary forms like fiction, short story, drama, and criticism. Besides, he is a translator and journalist also. His novels like *Biruku* and *Mussanjeya Kathaprasanga*, short story collections like *Umapathiya Scholarship Yatre* and *Nanalla* and his translations of Greek plays like *Antigone* and *Oedipus Rex* and French poems like *Papada Huvugalu* have been acclaimed as very significant contributions to Kannada literature. Like many modernist (*navya*) writers of Karnataka, Lankesh happened to be a Lecturer in English (at Bangalore University) before launching upon his very popular Kannada weekly *Lankesh Patrike* with a large circulation of more than two lakh copies. All his works are an evidence of his sharp intelligence, minute observation, and contemporary consciousness. An attempt has been made in this article only to highlight his dramatic output which can easily be compared with that of other Indian dramatists like Mohan Rakesh and Vijay Tendulkar.

The drama of Lankesh can be described as Drama of Revolt with an absurd element in it. In spite of the rebellious and satirical element in his plays they cannot be said to form part of Bandaya Literature which is generally known for protest and propagandistic element. They hold a mirror to the dramatist's contemporary consciousness and linguistic experimentation. The total dramatic bulk of Lankesh consists of eight plays which may be examined in the following paragraphs.

Giliyu Panjaradolilla (*The Parrot is not in the Cage*) may be described as an absurd play which depicts the theme of middle-class dilemma between the willingness to help the poor and the financial inability to do so. Set in the city of Bangalore, it consists of only four characters: Husband, wife, Gayatri their daughter and the barber Muniswami. When the husband goes to the station, he is accosted by the barber for the first time in four years. The barber asks him whether the latter has his parents and children. The latter answers in the affirmative. After he returns home he finds the barber approach him and ask for ₹ 30 towards the expenditure of his father's funeral. The husband asks him to see the former after two hours and collect the money, when the barber sees him for the second time the husband has changed his mind and scolds him for depending upon others, for financial help. He asks him to collect ₹ 20 after another hour. But when the barber sees him for the third time, the husband asks his wife to tell the barber that he is not at home. The change of the husband's decision is not only absurd but throws light upon the middle class dilemmas dissolving into a compromise involving lack of courage and engendering hypocrisy.

Siddhate (*Preparation*) delineates the theme of frustration in an artist's life. Ranganna, the protagonist of the play is a sixty-year-old man who is celebrating his son Ramu's birthday and waiting for his daughter Jaya. His wife Lalita teases him about his past affairs. Ranganna is not really happy. All his life seems to be an epitome of dreams and desires. His ambition of becoming a great dancer was never realised. His marriage has been a great hindrance to his artistic achievements. His life is a bundle of broken dreams. His office life is also not congenial to his artistic adventures. At last Ranganna dies rather unexpectedly. Thus, his whole life seems to be a preparation for death. The play is infused with the contemporary consciousness of modern Indian society which is characterised by frustration of artistic dreams. The theme of the play amply illustrates what Mr. Nirad Chaudhuri says about an Indian wife who is like a harpy "who looks upon any activity in the husband other than earning money and eyer more money as a sin against marriage vow" (*The Intellectual in India*, 71). The play obviously shows the triumph of humdrum life over artistic pursuit and the martial incompatibility of temperaments. While the play testifies to the dramatist's keen observation of life around him, it is not without echoes from T.S. Eliot's *The Family Reunion* like frustration, death-in-life and death on the birthday, etc.

A similar theme of frustration resulting in persecution-mania is portrayed in *Polisariddare Echcharike* (*Beware the Police*). Although accidentally based upon the personal life of a Kannada dramatist, namely Samsa, the playwright gives universal touch to it. The apparent comedy of the play serves only to heighten the deeper tragedy in it. Rudramurti, the protagonist of the play is a playwright who is frustrated because of the rejection of his manuscript by the publisher. Ranganna who has brought Chandrasekhar, elder brother of Rudramurti tries to please the latter by offering to publish his play. Rudramurti's refusal to recognise his own elder brother is really very comic and absurd. Likewise he refuses to accept from Ranganna an advance of ₹ 20 towards the royalty of his book to be published. The peculiarity of his behaviour lies in his demand of a receipt from Ranganna for the amount he has received from the latter. He is constantly under the impression that he is chased by policemen because he has "no job, no money, and no relatives". When his brother tries to console him, he accuses the former of persecuting him. He calls everybody a policeman, wears the *khaki* uniform and behaves like a policeman. When Ranganna and Chandrasekhar suggest that Rudramurti should get married and then write works of art in keeping with his stature, he refuses to write that which is agreeable to society; to obey friends and government. When they tell him that his early attempts at suicide are a crime and that they would get a 'no doubt' certificate from the police. Rudramurti refuses to accept their accusation. The next day when Ranganna tries to understand Rudramurti's problem, the latter confesses that he is a coward and has led his life in the worship-room and on the battlefield rather mechanically and that he is dubbed as a coward for that. They advise him to live and produce good literature. They accuse him of being off his mind. Finally, Rudramurti dies because he protests against all kinds of rules, regulations, restrictions, government, elders, and marriage, etc. Thus, *Beware the Police* is a satire as much about the protagonist as about the society of Karnataka (i.e. of India as well). The dramatist employs the absurd technique in order to lay bare the nature of society which kills the true spirit of man. Lankesh uses the satirical device to show how society exercises every kind of restriction upon the individual and allows him neither to live nor to die. Rudramurti's final suicide is the culmination of his revolt against the society. He becomes a representative of all those who want to have the highest freedom of spirit. The dramatist knowingly or otherwise preaches that man's willingness to revolt against the society is proportionate to his helplessness to do so.

The problem of matrimonial maladjustment caused by extreme boredom is depicted in *T. Prasannana Grihasthasrama* (*T. Prasanna's Household Life*). The playwright shows the two families in connection with each other for their stealthy compensations. T. Prasanna finds that his wife Laxmi is bored with him and that she has been writing love letters to innumerable lovers and receiving a number of letters from them. She has developed a special liking for Dr. Sivasankar. Prasanna contrives the situation in such a way that the affair between Laxmi and Dr. Sivasankar is found out by Sulochana, wife of Dr. Sivasankar. Laxmi hates her husband because he does not love or understand her heart. Prasanna is so liberal in his attitude to his wife that he does not object to her love affairs which are secret or otherwise. She is fed up with her husband so much that she protests against him openly. The play shows the inevitability of matrimonial discord caused by woman's assertion of her true identity. Nobody is singly responsible for this maladjustment. Prasanna continues to be in his bachelorhood in spite of his marriage with Laxmi because of the lack of true emotional companionship. The playwright wants to show the cat-and-dog life of the middle-class couple of Karnataka. The play holds a mirror to the crumbling institution of marriage and the concurrent relaxation of the values of life like fidelity, chastity, and decency. Such a relaxation is really a shocking phenomenon in the puritanical middle-class society of Karnataka.

Teregalu (*Waves*) delineates the theme of crime and punishment through the absurd technique. The play consists of only four characters like man, Kanti, Kitti, and Vitti. The man has been living in a house which does not belong to him. He has left the earlier job of a teacher in a college and entered into politics because of his ambition. He is said to have murdered his master in whose house he has been living now and amassed a lot of money. The three fellows Kanti, Kitti, and Vitti who come to his house ask him as to the whereabouts of the master of his house and charge him with the crime of murder and hang him. The play is, obviously, an attack upon political overambition, opportunism, and cupidity so rampant in the modern society of Karnataka. The play, in spite of its political theme, attains symbolic height. The house in which the man is living now does not belong to him. The play, on the whole, assumes the nature of an extended image, the dialogues border on the absurd though the underlying theme is a fine political satire.

The compulsion to revolt against the society and the paradoxical helplessness of the rebel has been beautifully presented in *Nanna Tangigondu Gandu Kodi* (*Give a Bridegroom for My Sister*). The problem of marriage comes as incidental to the theme of social revolt. Jagannath and Kamala are son and daughter of a Minister. Saraswatamma is the Minister's wife. All of them stay at Shimoga only because of their attachment to home. Ramanna who is a confidant of the Minister enjoys free access to the latter's family. He is also a special friend of Saraswatamma. The Minister is always at Bangalore, and therefore, cannot take care of his family. Ramanna wants to bring a bridegroom for the Minister's daughter Kamala. But Jagannath opposes Ramanna's plan as he thinks that the bridegrooms want to marry his sister only on account of her father's money, position, and influence. Jagannath wants to marry off his sister to a poor young man called Ranganna who has been dismissed from service by the Minister. They are waiting for the arrival of the Minister from Bangalore to settle the matter, but finally they are all shocked by the news of the unexpected demise of the Minister. Jagannath realises the harsh reality that his house has been sold to Ranganna who asks them to vacate it overnight.

The play is, obviously, a fine satire on the modern society which is marked by mammon-worship, opportunism, political ambition destroying the family happiness. Jagannath acts as the mouthpiece of the dramatist. But the irony is that he, in spite of his protest, is compelled to accept his defeat caused by the quirks of Fate. Lankesh wants to show the victimisation of the rebel in the Indian context.

A similar problem is treated in its political aspect in *Kranti Bantu Kranti* (*Here Comes Revolution*). That no revolution of any kind is possible in India is a commonplace truth which assumes a special significance in the case of Karnataka. That the Indians are heroes only in words and action of any kind is irrelevant to them is depicted in the present play. Bhagavan is a college teacher who gives frequent lectures on revolution from public platforms. He feels elated by the audience's cheers and claps. He has two student-*chelas*, Lalita and Malati who go on feeding his ego by their flattery. His colleagues Sankara and Ramadasa ridicule him for his instigation of students to indulge in revolutionary activities. Dinakara is a Naxalite and student of Bhagavan who is being chased by the police. Sudha, wife of Bhagavan is a very practical lady and is, therefore, indifferent to her husband's ideal of revolution. One day Bhagavan returns home after delivering a lecture on revolution. On the way, he is followed by the Naxalite Dinakara who wants a night's shelter in the former's house. Bhagavan, in spite of his wife's opposition, offers him shelter but has no courage to face the police. He, therefore, hits upon an ingenious plan of locking Dinakara in his house and goes to a movie. When Dinakara is alone in the house, he sees a thief bend the bars of the window and enter into the house. There takes place a heated argument between the thief and the Naxalite. The thief laughs at Dinakara's communism, collects the valuable items and even offers half the share to Dinakara who refuses to accept it. At last the thief wants to make away with all the booty but Dinakara tries to prevent it. However, the thief escapes from there on hearing the footsteps of the master and mistress. Sudha and Bhagavan are really puzzled at the sight of Dinakara and think him responsible for the whole thing. Dinakara tries in vain to convince them about the thief's arrival and departure.

Finally, Sudha asks him to quit the house and shoots him dead when he refuses to. Bhagavan sits helplessly. Then the Police Inspector who is informed by Sarikara and Ramadasa about the death of the Naxalite, goes to the spot and even coaxes the couple to give a false statement. Later on Bhagavan delivers a grand speech about revolution and becomes a hero for having murdered a Naxalite. He is cheered and lifted on hands by the enthusiastic audience.

The play is, evidently, a fine satire on the Indian ado about revolution. The playwright wants to show the irony of the Indian profession of revolution. Revolution, far from being a matter of active participation, has become a matter of mere preachification and platform promulgation in India. The most vehement proponent of revolution has, paradoxically enough, not an iota of courage to face the reality. He is an arm-chair revolutionary who has got by heart the jargon redolent of Marxism, Socialism, and Communism with which he can exhort the audience. But he betrays his cowardice whenever there is a need for actual action. The play, thus, lays bare the essential impotence of the rebel who dreams of destroying the old order by creating the new.

The playwright employs the technique of contrast in his depiction of characters. Sankara and Ramadasa provide a good contrast to Bhagavan on account of their philosophy of compromise. They also act as critics of fake revolution. The wife of Professor Bhagavan is again dead set against his obsession with revolution and the concomitant indifference to the family. Again there is a fine contrast between Sudha and Professor Bhagavan's sycophantic students like Lalita and Malati who, probably because of their innocence, impracticable ideals and feminine naivete, are not able to see the discordance between the Professor's speeches and his empirical behaviour. Dinakara the Naxalite also provides a good contrast to Professor Bhagavan because of his radical ideology and action. Bhagavan's lukewarm revolutionism cannot cope with Dinakara's conviction. The thief's opportunism again provides a sharp contrast to the Naxalite's intransigent idealism. In this play, Lankesh exhibits his awareness of contemporary life by showing the unsuitability of revolution to a country like India where there are innumerable institutions which are perpetually trying to negate and neutralise the revolutionary action.

A similar theme of social protest is depicted in *Sankranti* (*Transition*), a play based upon the great social-economic-political revolution wrought by Basaveswara at Kalyana (Bidar district of north Karnataka) in the twelfth century. It is a well-known fact of history that Basava, the Minister at King Bijjala's court was a Brahmin by birth, but rebelled against the Brahmanical caste-discrimination and ritualistic obsession. But Lankesh in his typical modernist fashion, selects the life of an untouchable young man called Rudra, son of Ujja and makes him a mirror of Basava's protestant philosophy and action. The dramatist shows how Rudra's love for a Brahmin girl Usha costs him his life: One might say that Basava acts like a catalytic agent in the play as he is the direct and indirect cause of the social disturbance in the Kingdom of Kalyana. Lankesh shows how Rudra, the protagonist has come under the spell of Basava and is out to improve the lot of his untouchable community by advising them to give up the bad habits of drinking, hunting, and womanising. In spite of his son's injunctions, Ujja continues to indulge in these old habits. Rudra has gained new confidence as he has been converted into a *Sarana* under the influence of Basava. He has been able to win the heart of a Brahmin girl, Usha. In response to Basava's call, all the downtrodden people have to adopt the *Sarana* way of life. But the unconventional event of Rudra's love marriage with Usha has deeply upset the traditional Brahmins who lodge repeated complaints to King Bijjala against Basava. King Bijjala is in a pretty pass indeed. He does not know how to control his Kingdom seething with perpetual war between Brahmins and *Saranas*. He has to punish either of these groups to please the other. He has no moral courage to punish Minister Basava as he knows that the latter is an extraordinarily dynamic leader. He therefore devises an ingenious plan. He visits Rudra's village and asks the Brahmin girl, Usha whether her love for Rudra is natural or forced upon her. She says that it was 'forced' upon her. When asked how, she clarifies her point of view by explaining that she had fallen in love with Rudra the untouchable who had become a *Sarana* without her knowledge thereby transforming her love into a rape. King Bijjala revokes his remorseless administrative logic and orders for the execution of Rudra as a punishment for his *Sarana* style of life. Rudra's revolt against the conventional society becomes meaningless at last. The play shows the ultimate helplessness of the rebel in a society controlled by conventional laws. Lankesh's characterisation of King Bijjala is subtle and sophisticated. King Bijjala is made to look like a modern diplomat. The main conflict in the play is between Brahmins and *Saranas* rather than between Brahmins and *Shudras*. That is the herself why the Brahmin girl Usha who does not mind yielding herself to an untouchable complains against him when she comes to know his conversion into a *Sarana*.

The language employed by Lankesh in this play is the dialect southern Karnataka, which can be used successfully only by the southern Karnatakians, although geographically it is not suited to the southern play.

Alienation, boredom, loneliness, frustration, corruption, ambition, revolution and victimisation of the rebel are some of the major thematic concerns of Lankesh and hold a mirror to his keen observation of the contemporary society of Karnataka. In all these plays, he achieves a sophistication that is typical of all the modernist works of art. In spite of the Western influence upon the dramatist, Lankesh has the nativity that is enviable and rarely to be found among the other modernist writers of Karnataka like Girish Karnad, for example. Being a poet at heart, Lankesh is naturally able to graft the poetic symbols into his dramatic structure. The house and the owner (borrowed from the *vachana* of Sri Basaveswara) and the cage and the parrot (borrowed from the song of Purandaradasa) symbolise the human body and the soul respectively.

As for the language employed by Lankesh in his drama, it may be said that it is deeply steeped in the southern Karnataka dialect. Sometimes we feel that his drama is burdened with a linguistic abundance which again reminds us of the garrulity of the drama of Sriranga and Kailasam. Most of the theatrical attraction of Lankesh's drama lies in dialogues. The other theatrical aspects like songs, dance and music are conspicuous by their absence. His drama may be designated as Drama of Ideas which appeals to the amateur actors and educated audience and tends to bore and even irritate the professional actors and uneducated spectators. Nevertheless, it invites comparison with the Indian drama of other regional languages.

Reference

Lankeshara Samagra Natakagalu, Bengaluru: Patrike Prakashana, 1978.

•••••

21

The Kannada Comedies of Chandrashekhar Patil

Chandrashekhar Patil (1939-2022), an important playwright of north Karnataka, has written several stage plays and street plays in Kannada, which have been staged or performed successfully and appreciated by connoisseurs of Karnataka. Besides being a poet and journalist, he is an activist, who identifies himself with the *Bandaya* (Protest) Movement, which has been gaining momentum in the Karnataka State in recent years. He edits a Kannada monthly called *Sankramana*, which provides an expression to many a rebellious voice of Karnataka. Because of his active participation in the J.P. Movement, he was jailed in 1975 during the Emergency. He also took a very active part in the Gokak Movement in Karnataka in 1982 and fought for the primacy of Kannada in the primary and secondary educational system in Karnataka.

His plays are generally known for their wit, humour, and satire. Basically, a man of satirical temperament, Chandrashekhar Patil looks around the society and ridicules men and manners with a view to awakening them to their own deficiencies and deviations. Like all satirists, he is not happy with the world around him as it is. He wants to see a better future world. His satire of the present society is part of his idealism though of a negative kind. But in Patil, satire does not become bitter as it does in Jonathan Swift, but is tinctured with brilliant wit and humour, which takes away the sting from it. A significant aspect of all his writing is the contemporary consciousness, which supplies the foundation to the psychological and mythical themes of his drama. His early plays belong to the Theatre of the Absurd, whereas the later ones are social and satirical in tone.

Appa (*Father*, 1971) is a very interesting play of the early period. The theme is inspired by a line in Basaveswara's *vacana*. The title of the play easily brings to our mind a similar play, *Father* by Strindberg. It deals with the identity crisis of a boy of six called Basava, son of a prostitute. The boy's experience of the absurdity of life is caused by the taunts and innuendos hurled at him by his friends and classmates in the village. He is puzzled by the concern shown to him by Paramesi and Kulkarni-Master. He wants to know why he does not have a father when every other boy in the village has one. Embarrassed by his questions the mother tries to divert his attention by narrating a story of a king and a princess. But when Basava pesters her further for an answer, she is unable to satisfy him. She cannot name the father of the child, as she herself cannot fix him properly. She puzzles the boy resorting to metaphorical language. She says that there is a flower with innumerable petals, which is a product of innumerable seeds. Is it, in that case, possible to trace back the exact seed, which has produced a particular petal? She asks. The boy is confused rather than satisfied by the interrogative answer. When he looks around, he finds that his mother has gone away from there to receive her customer.

The absurdity of the dramatic technique lies in the boy's point of view, which is a combination of curiosity and innocence. Official prostitution is an accepted part of the Indian social system. There is nothing absurd about it. Had the boy been an adult, perhaps he would not have taken it so seriously as he would know and accept the inevitability and normality of his fatherless ness. (In other words, the anonymity of his father in the institution of prostitution.) The same problem of the boy's identity would have degenerated into the banal if the playwright had not resorted to the metaphorical language of the Kannada folk-tradition. The mother evades the boy's question by asking him counter questions about the princess, seeds, and flowers. The question of identity posed by the dramatist here is not related to the wider truths of life like the social and the religious. But the beauty of the play lies in lyricizing the problem. It may, therefore, be described as a lyrical absurd play, which is marked by simplicity and directness.

Patil's *Gurtinavaru (Acquaintances*, 1971) shows the paradoxical truth of how in life acquaintances turn out to be strangers and *vice versa.* Set in a non-local area, the play has four anonymous but typical characters: Guest, husband, wife and a person. The guest goes to the protagonist's house and introduces himself as a person who had proposed a flattering vote of thanks when the protagonist had delivered a grand lecture on Life and Literature in a village a few years ago. The guest wants a character-certificate for his son from the protagonist. It is the strange behavior of the protagonist, which converts the normal situation into an absurd one. After being requested by the guest, the protagonist dictates a letter of recommendation in which he absurdly says that his acquaintance with the boy (guest's son) dates back to previous lives and that he deserves the job of either a peon or a President of a nation. Similarly, he seems to grow a stranger to his own wife with whom he has lived for the past so many years. In keeping with the absurd behavior of the husband, the language is full of farfetched associations and marked by a mixture of the realistic and the metaphorical.

Kodegalu (*Umbrellas*, 1971) is a short, beautiful, lyrical absurd play, which depicts the difficulty of disowning or exchanging one's identity with others'. Umbrellas symbolize the identities of the characters in the play. The anonymous characters like X and Y are shown to be moving about in an anonymous atmosphere. Both of them hold an umbrella each in hand. Whereas X keeps his umbrella shut, Y keeps it open, no matter whether there is rain or sun. Both of them are reluctant to change their habits. After some discussion, they agree to exchange their umbrellas, but only to feel that they cannot do it for long. They feel utterly miserable when they part with their own umbrella and hold the other's. Finally, they exchange them once again thereby re-possessing their original ones.

The absurdity of the play is to be seen in the coming together of two characters of opposite natures and their laughing at each other. The playwright, obviously, shows the bio-psychological truth that a man cannot change his nature or identity however much he may try to do so; that there is no greater satisfaction in the world than being one's own self. The play may also be seen as a lyrical illustration of the Hegelian philosophy, which states that the world is a reconciliation of opposites. That the opposites may be seen in the same family, society or nation is depicted symbolically and lyrically in the play.

Kunta Kunta Kuravatti (*The Lame Man of Kuravatti*, 1970) is a short absurd comedy in which the playwright tries to show how every man wants to possess that which he lacks. There are three anonymous but typical characters, namely the Blind, the Lame and the Deaf. All the three are brought together and are made to interact with each other. The Blind wants to depend upon the Lame for sight and the Lame, upon the Blind for movement. Each one is obsessed with one's own deficiency and tries to compensate for it by resorting to dreams or wishful thinking. The Lame wants to wear Bata shoes and walk about in style; the Blind wishes to see the beauty of Lalbagh at Bengaluru and the Deaf longs to enjoy the melody of classical music. Of course, they do not succeed in their efforts. Since each one is obsessed with one's own deficiency, he cannot understand the other one's problems. Hence, there is a lack of communication among the three, which adds to the absurd humour of the play. The playwright tries to show the psychological reality in a little exaggerated fashion. It has been very successful on the stage. The folk idiom and songs of north Karnataka intensify the element of humour in it.

Tingara Buddanna (*The Dwarf*, 1971), another short absurd play, recreates the mythical story of Bhasmasura in terms of a modern folk play. It shows the ironical reversal of power of destroying others into self-destruction. The play delineates the theme of self-destructiveness of evil through the absurd technique, which violates the rules of probability. The protagonist of the play is a boy who, when insulted by a squirrel, a butterfly and a few villagers, tells his grandmother that he would not go to school the next day. The grandmother, who has great affection for her grandson, teaches him a spell (*hram, hrim, hrum*, etc.) and asks him to utter it whenever somebody calls him a dwarf (*budda*). Armed with the spell, the boy goes around in the village and takes revenge upon all those like the squirrel, the butterfly, Ningi, Gangi and the school-teacher, who had insulted him in the past. On the way, when he is hungry, he kills a banana-vendor and swallows the whole bunch of bananas and brings home one in his pocket. He exultantly tells his grandmother how he took revenge upon all the insulters. He asks her to prepare his meal, as he is very hungry. But he cannot wait until she cooks his food. He recites his spell when he is asked by her to wait. Consequently, the grandmother falls dead on the floor. The boy pushes the dead body under the cot. He kills the grandfather also when the latter scolds him for having killed his dear old wife. The boy does not remember that he has thrown the banana skin thereabout. He begins to dance there, but slips upon the banana skin. He grows angry with the fellow, who has thrown the banana skin there and recites his destructive spell. Not knowing what is happening, he sags on the floor and dies.

The play may be called an allegorical drama. It is absurd in so far as it violates the law of probability. It is didactic in so far as it offers a message to mankind. The anonymity and typicality of characters and the removal of the scene from the limits of time and space contribute to the universality of theme. The poetic language employed in the play has a strong flavour of the north Karnataka non-Brahmanical dialect.

In *Gokarnada Goudasani* (*The Duchess of Gokarna*, 1974) which won the Karnataka State Sahitya Academy Award of the year, the playwright shows two themes parallel to each other. One is that of Ravana and Lord Siva and the other of a Gowda and Sivakka. Both of these themes go on alternating, of course, occasionally linked by the Bhagavata, who engages in meta-dramatic discussion about technique, use of language and audience response, etc., thereby providing a good deal of humour.

The playwright has mischievously combined the spiritual theme with the sexual one. Ravana, who earns the grace of Lord Siva through hard penance, gets the much-coveted boon, i.e., *sivalinga*, but is unfortunately unable to possess it permanently. As he has drunk a lot of nectar in Heaven, he wants to ease himself on the way when his bladder is full. He, therefore, entrusts the *sivalinga* to the care of Ganapati and sits for making water. But Ganapati places the *sivalinga* upon the earth when Ravana fails to return from his nature call even after the third call from Ganapati. The *sivalinga* is thus finally established by Ganapati at Gokarna. The story is drawn from mythical *Ramayana*. The playwright cleverly weaves a modern story, which runs parallel to the mythical one. The Gowda (i.e. village chief) has taken a fancy to a maid called Sivakka and gets her to his residence through his confidant-servant, Basya. But when the maid is waiting for the rendezvous, the Gowda starts suffering from indigestion and stomachache. Consequently, he goes away from there to relieve himself. In the absence of the Gowda, Basya seduces Sivakka. Basya's sexual achievement parallels Ganapati's spiritual one. Similarly, Ravana's failure parallels the Gowda's. Finally, when Sivakka is rejected by Basya and neglected by her parents, she goes mad. The plot of the play goes on alternating between the two stories thereby showing the parallel between the contrastive themes.

The play is known for the meta-dramatic element in it. The playwright ridicules the functions of the dramatist as well as of the director through the character of Bhagavata. One wonders whether Chandrashekhar Patil was not influenced by Pirandello's *Six Characters in Search of an Author.* Patil uses Bhagavata to link up the two parallel themes and to make occasional comments upon the free pass holders and the querulous nature of legislators, etc. But at the same time he makes Bhagavata an egoistic director, who is not bothered about the dramatist's intentions, but directs the play according to his own fastidious taste. He is also used, as in Sanskrit Drama, to act as a bridge between life and art, now addressing the audience, now animadverting the actors and actresses, now explaining the difficulties of coping with dramatic technique. The play has thus a double plot (Ravana, Lord Siva, and Ganapati; the Gowda, Sivakka, and Basya) and double dimension (dramatic and meta-dramatic). The play was said to be a grand success when it was first staged at Dharwad in 1973. It is a comedy, which satirizes the impotence of the village chief, who wants to be a great lover.

Chandrashekhar Patil is thus a very significant dramatist of Karnataka known for the delineation of lyrical, allegorical, symbolic and folk-mythological themes and experimentation with dramatic technique. His plays stand out for the strong element of nativity expressed both in theme and in technique. His language is characterized by the vigour of north Karnataka dialect attaining lyrical height and beauty at the same time. Let us wait for many more plays from his fertile pen.

Reference

Patil, Chandrashekhar, *Champa Natakagalu*, Bengaluru: Sankramana Prakasana, 2008.

• • • • •

22

Mother-Son Relationship in *Mother of 1082*

Mahasweta Devi (1926-2016) has been a Jnanapith Awardee known for her social activism and literary treatment of the burning problems of contemporary Indian, especially Bengali society. As she has stated in many if her interviews that in her early life she never thought of becoming a writer, but she immersed herself in understanding and solving the problems of the subaltern classes of society. Far from living in her ivory tower and thinking of mythical issues drawn from the *Vedas*, the *Ramayana*, and the *Mahabharata*—a disease common to many Hindu writers—she actually lives among the untouchables, the tribal and the lower-class people. Her first experience of the harsh and bitter social reality has enabled her to convert it into literature. It was only when her soul was filled with authentic experience that she thought of articulating it in words thereby becoming a writer. She decided to be a writer only after she had crossed her forty-fifth year or so. Her first publication was *Jhansi Rani* (1956), which was based on her deep study of Indian history and meticulous fieldwork carried out in and around Jhansi. Being a woman, she is naturally interested in the gender issues along with the wider social problems. She is a short story writer, novelist and playwright. *Amruta Sanchay* (1964), *Andharmanik* (1967), *Aranyer Adhikar* (1977), *Chotti Munda O Tar Teer* (1979), *Beast Stories, Bitter Soil, The Armenian Champa Tree, Rudali and Old Woman, Our Non-Vegetarian Cow and Other Stories*, etc., are some of her important works. She is generally interested in historical, social, and folk life and writers about them in a realistic style rather than in a romantic or sentimental mode. She does not believe in art for art's sake, but strongly pleads for the ameliorative function of literature. As she has declared in her interview with Samik Bandyopadhay, "Once I became a professional writer, I felt increasingly that a writer should document his own time and history. The socio-economic history of human development has always fascinated me. But some of the greatest political happenings of my times like the Tebhaga revolt of the Bengal peasants or the Partition and its aftermath had passed me by before I had become a writer. So I chose to resurrect older periods in history in their immediate physicality, as if they were nothing less than contemporary. The Naxalite movement between the late sixties and early seventies, with its urban phase climaxing in 1970-71 was the major event after I had become a writer that I felt an urge and an obligation to document" (pp. vii-viii).

The social problems that form part of her major thematic concerns in her works are poverty, hunger, bonded labour, landlessness, indebtedness, class struggle, caste discrimination, gender inequality, injustice, and exploitation and so on. As a realistic writer, she wants to look into the face of the society and write about it with a view to transform it. Far from simplifying the problems of life, she recognizes the complexity of life and writes about it in a frank and bold manner. As she says, "Life is not arithmetic, and man is not made for the game of political programmes and creeds should aim at the realization of the claims of man to survival and justice. I desire a transformation of the present social system. I do not believe in narrow party politics. After thirty-one years of Independence, I find my people still groaning under hunger, landlessness, indebtedness and bonded labour. An anger, luminous, burning and passionate, directed against a system that has failed to liberate my people from these horrible constraints, is the only source of inspiration for all my writing.... Hence I go on writing to the best of my abilities about the people, so that I can face myself without any sense of guilt or shame. For a writer faces his judgement in his lifetime and remains answerable" (pp. viii-ix).

The *Mother of 1082* is written by Mahasweta Devi against the background of Naxalite movement in West Bengal. Although the play is a short one containing only twelve scenes, it succeeds in presenting the mother-son relationship against the socio-political atmosphere of West Bengal. Also it throws light on the working of the constabulary, an instrument of the government. The title itself of the play indicates the impersonal and inhuman working of the police department in giving numbers to the dead bodies of people, who were killed or burnt in the clashes between Naxalites and others. For the police records, Sujata happens to be just the mother of the dead body No. 1082 and nothing else.

The play deals with the important Naxalite movement, which germinated in Bengal and spread to all parts of India gradually. Many people, especially young men and women were attracted to this movement, which offers a satisfying theoretical solution to the problems of Indian society. In the present play, the young boys like Brati, Somu, Bijit and others belong to such a group of hot headed and over-enthusiastic youth. It shows the clash between the Naxalites and the Police Department, the internal schism among its own members involving betrayal, and the agony of a mother in losing her darling son and trying to understand him and his noble cause retrospectively.

When the play opens, Sujata gets a phone call from the Police Station in the early morning. She is told to go over to the Police Station at Kantapukur and identify (the dead body of) her son, Brati Chatterjee. She is surprised and shocked so much that she does not know what to do or how to react. She is so innocent that she does not understand or even guess what must have happened to her son. Even when the officer-in-charge asks her for some identification marks on her son's person, she cannot understand why they need those details. But when she goes to the Police Station, she realizes that her son is dead. She wants to see his face, but the Dome responds, "What's there to see, Mother? There's nothing left of the face!" (p. 6). When she wants to take his body home, the officer-in-charge says, "No. You won't get the body" (p. 6).

It is only the mother, who can feel the loss of her son and remember him. Her filial attachment to her son is too deep to be explained. But somehow the other members of the family like Tuli (Sujata's youngest daughter), Jyoti, and Dibyanath Chatterjee (Sujata's husband) are not bothered about Brati as deeply as Sujata is. On the contrary, they are busy with their personal dreams and desires. For example, Tuli's engagement is scheduled on Brati's birthday itself, which is also his death anniversary day. Naturally, Sujata as the mother of Brati does not like this arrangement. That is why she tells Tuli that she returns home in the evening (after visiting Somu's mother) to be present at the engagement ceremony, "Why not? It's Brati's birthday today, if that didn't matter to you when you chose the day, I think I have to be there" (p. 8). But Tuli escapes from the embarrassment by attributing it to the Swami, "It was the Swami's decision" (p. 8). Sujata's love for her late son is so deep that she does not like any member of her family to talk negatively about him. She complains to Tuli, "To Tony and his crowd, to the others, you, your father, Jyoti, Neepa, the way you speak his name, as if Brati was a criminal" (p. 8). She does not like her husband's practical (almost callous) approach to the problem of preventing the news from getting into the newspaper. When Tuli justifies it by saying that it is natural to try to hush it up when something like this happens, Sujata vents out her maternal agony and anger, "But so soon? Even before the body's been identified? A father gets the news on the telephone and doesn't even think of rushing to have a look? All he can think of is that he'd be compromised if his car went to Kantapukur?... Brati was dead to all of you long before, isn't that so?" (p. 9). As a mother she always sympathizes with her son and his noble political cause and puts up with all the weaknesses of the other members of the family, "With Brati, they've cast me too in the opposite camp. If Brati had been like Jyoti, or a drunkard like Neepa's husband, Amit, or a hardened fraud like Tony, or had run after the typists like his father, he'd have belonged to their camp" (p. 9).

Although Sujata has a big heart and therefore deeply attached to her son Brati, she seems to be rather a brainless woman, who is unaware of what has been happening around her socially and politically. That is why she is called an apolitical mother. It is indeed puzzling that in spite of being a working-woman, she has very little socio-political awareness. She seems to have loved her son too deeply to love him wisely. It is a big irony that she has never tried to 'understand' her son when he was alive, but on the contrary others have understood him better than she did. She confesses, "I didn't know Brati well enough, Somu's mother knew him better" (p. 9). After a lapse of two years after Brati's death, Sujata has been trying to understand her son by piecing together the bits of information gathered from his friends and their parents. It is an epistemological question for her. In human life, as also in the modern existential world, although people live together physically, there is no guarantee that they understand one another automatically. Not only should they be interested in understanding another human being—be it parents, or children or brothers or sisters—but also make a conscious effort to understand them. For example, Sujata never attempted to 'understand' her son when he was alive. She was content only in loving him cordially. But she makes an attempt to understand him retrospectively after his death, through other's memories about him. For example, she gathers a number of details about her son's Naxalite activities from Somu's mother when she meets the latter in her house. Somu's mother grieves over the loss of her own son along with other four young boys involved in Naxalite activities. But she reveals a lot of information about Brati and his friends. She tells Sujata, "Your son, sister, gifted his life away. He had come to warn Somu and his group. They had got wind that the four of them were there in the colony, there was the fear that they wouldn't survive the night. When Brati came and asked, where's Somu, Mashima, I asked why? He said, I've a message for Somu, I'll leave right now" (p. 10). Somu had gone out to call Bijit when Brati had gone to Somu's house. That night Somu's mother had prepared *chapattis* for all the boys. Somu and his friends asked Brati to stay with them in Somu's house. "Somu asked why? Are you dying to get killed? Stay here. I too joined in. Don't go, dear, stay here for the night. They were killing the young men of the locality itself, a stranger would be a surer target. Who knows, sister? If we had let him go that night, he might have escaped death" (p. 10).

Somu's mother tells Sujata a few more details about Brati and his group of friends. For example, she says that her own son Somu was rough and that "Laltu was the best of them. It was he, who drew them into this, and he died for it" (p. 11). Somu's mother is really puzzled by Sujata's lack of understanding of her own son Brati's social activities. She says to Sujata, "You're a working woman, you've a rich home, I wonder why Brati chose such a course! Didn't you ever realize what your son was up to?" (p. 11). But Sujata' confesses, "I didn't know" (p. 11). But she has learnt retrospectively that it was Anindya, who had betrayed Brati and his group by not warning them and by informing the police department about the burning of the house because of his selfish motives.

Sujata remembers her playing ludo with her son Brati on that evening, reminding him of his birthday next morning, and his demand for some money from her and his hurried exit from home. Then Sujata learns the other side of the story from Somu's mother. It was all unexpected. Somu's mother says sadly, "One can't send one's son to his death knowingly.... It was still a while to midnight. A nightmare.... Still seems like a nightmare. It was not midnight yet. They had surrounded our house already" (p. 15).

The remaining part of the retrospective story is learnt by Sujata from Nandini, who was a beloved of Brati. According to Nandini, Brati and his friends were betrayed by Anindya. She therefore curses herself and her group for not judging the people (like Anindya) properly. She says, "It was Anindya, who betrayed us" (p. 18). Sujata, the innocent and foolish mother confesses, "I don't know everything, Nandini" (p. 18). Nandini offers a few more details about the betrayal, "And yet Brati, like a fool, trusted Anindya. Do you know why he trusted him?... Because it was Nitu, who had introduced Anindya. Nitu had been in many actions. And Nitu had been killed. It was simple arithmetic. Nitu had introduced Anindya plus Nitu was dead plus Nitu's death itself was proof of his integrity. Therefore, Anindya, who was Nitu's recruit, must be dependable. That's how we argued. We never judged, never made enquiries, and yet we should've known.... We should have known that they too had their programme, just as we had ours. We had a cause. They too had one.... A programme of betrayal" (p. 19).

Just as Nandini helps Sujata understand her son Brati retrospectively, she also understands the limitations of their group. She explains to Sujata how betrayal by Anindya was caused by temptations about material gains, "Money, job and power didn't mean a thing to us. But these were the temptations that seduced those, who had joined us only to betray us. You shouldn't underestimate the power of those temptations" (p. 19). Nandini understands the deficiencies of her youthful group. She attributes it not merely to their youth, but also their idealism and romanticism, "No, no, it was an overdose of romanticism. We didn't have a clue to the reality. These were among the major failings of that time" (p. 19).

Nandini extends her personal experience of being betrayed to the national level and deplores it. Mahasweta Devi's criticism of the moral degeneration of Indian society is articulated through the words of Nandini. She says, "Failings, mistakes, deviations. I still wonder how we could afford not to know that with all that has happened since 1947, all human loyalties had dissolved by 1970. I wonder how we could be unaware that they could betray us to kill us. I wonder how we could be shocked whenever we heard that behind an assassination there was someone closely related to the victim—a father, a brother, a relations, a friend or an acquaintance" (p. 19). Thus, betrayal was rampant but they had not been taught to be suspicious.

Nandini remembers her past days of youthful zest, delight and wonder smacking of romantic idealism and paradisal state, "We thought we were bringing in a new era. I (*pause*) and Brati walked from College Street to Bhowanipur day in and day out, talking, just talking. Those days there was sheer delight in talking, in looking at the streets, in the processions, in people, in the red roses at a street crossing, in the neon lamps, in watching, in Hindi songs on the radio. We could burst with delight" (p. 20).

But Nandini laments the loss of that paradise, when she says, "I'm not the same person any more. An era's gone by. What I had been those days is dead forever" (p. 20). She is so sad to know that the Naxalite movement in spite of its basic noble cause, is either misinterpreted or shown only lip-sympathy by the government due to its self-interest. Nandini deplores the rhythm and ubiquity of betrayal in West Bengal with poetic intensity. Betrayal. The prison walls rise higher, new watch towers shoot up, there are so many young men still in the prisons, and yet a political party will not take a stand until it has been able to determine how it'll serve its own interest and affect its standing with the Centre. Betrayal. The worst reactionaries make avowals of their sympathy for us and in the process they spoil our image in the public eye. Betrayal. We are not allowed the use of the press, paper, type-lead to explain our views. And yet there are all those journals that claim to be sympathetic to our cause. Betrayal. Every supposedly sympathetic piece tries shrewdly and skillfully to prove us adventurist-romantics. Betrayal. Even when we were being killed, all the writers and all the periodicals were crying over Bangladesh, they had nothing to say about West Bengal. And the same ones now write lamentations about us. Betrayal. And...within the prisons... (p. 21).

Likewise, Nandini is unhappy about the clever and deliberate silence of the media, the organs of the government about the suppression and torture of the Naxalites. She says, "Do you think, they've stopped only because the newspapers don't report them? Arrests? Tortures? Murders in the name of encounters? A whole generation between sixteen and forty is being wiped out" (p. 21).

Nandini is right when she accuses Sujata of ignorance and lack of a noble cause, "You...my mother,...you all speak the same way. (*Pause*) You will never understand. You have never pledged everything you had to the cause of all, the way we had" (p. 20). Sujata is such a brainless mother, that she understands neither the social movements nor her son. She confesses, "Brati was the soul of my life, yet I knew him so little" (p. 21). But Nandini points out the importance of the responsibility of parents in understanding their children, i.e. sons. She says, "It's deadly time when people do not belong to one another by virtue of kinship or ties of blood. Everyone remains a stranger these days to everyone. It's a crime to allow this to persist. It's an obligation these days to know one's son" (p. 21).

Nandini's comment on this lack of integrity and honesty on the part of the parents and their inability to set a model for the younger generation forms part of social criticism offered indirectly by Mahasweta Devi. Nandini tells Sujata, "It's for you to take the first step. Isn't it your obligation to set a model for the younger generation to follow? Why do you demand loyalty by virtue of relationship? Why don't you try to earn it by virtue of your integrity? You won't be honest, won't forge relationships and then you put the whole blame on us" (p. 21). Thus, there is lack of understanding and communication between the older generation and the younger one due to ideological differences and clash of personalities. Nandini instantiates it clearly, "Brati came from a household of a certain kind, he hated his father, Sanchayan, Dipu and Smaran came from a smug high middle class. Somu, Laltu and Bijit belonged to apolitical, poor refugee homes. Mani and Kushal had parents involved in leftwing politics. But they all shared one common feature: the children and the parents were strangers to one another" (p. 21).

Because of the betrayal of the whole group by Anindya, Nandini is arrested on the next morning and tried and tortured in the cell. Nandini is cross-questioned by the Police Inspector, Saroj Pal, who exposes her lies, shows her the photos of her comrades like Somu, Bijit, and Brati. He opines that Anindya is "an excellent chap. He loves his country, his society" (p. 24). He tells her that her parents would have to pay for her stubbornness. He further reveals the truth, "They've all left you in the lurch and are cooperating with us" (p. 24). Then Saroj Pal tortures Nandini by pressing the burning cigarette to her cheeks twice thereby proving the inhuman practices of the Indian Police Department.

Nandini's stay in the prison-cell has given her a traumatic experience, which she can never forget. She tells Sujata, "I won't be able to tell you all that happened after. (*Pause*) The sores on the skin have healed, but I'll never be normal again.... After what I went through in prison, every man approaching me seems to be a policeman" (p. 25). Disagreeing with the complacency of Sujata, Nandini reacts strongly, "No. No. No. No. It was never quiet, nothing is quiet. Nothing's changed. Thousands of young men rot in the prisons without trial, they're denied the status of politicals, and yet you'd say it's all settled down again? Torture continues with greater sophistication and more secrecy and yet you'd say it's all quiet?" (pp. 25-26). Then Nandini bursts with righteous anger at the ignorance and complacency of mothers like Sujata, "How can you be so smug and complacent? With so many young men killed, so many imprisoned, how can you wallow in your complacency? It's your 'all right with the world, let's go on nicely' that frightens me most. How can you carry on with your *pujas*, concerts, cultural festivals, film festivals, poetry fests?" (p. 26). Then Nandini shows her right eye blinded by the gleam of thousand watt lamps and suspects that she might be arrested once again. When Sujata wants to visit her again, Nandini points out the futility of the visit by showing the contrast between Sujata and herself, "No. What do you gain of coming to me? You live with your past. I have to harness my present, and think of the future" (p. 26). Sujata feels a bit hurt by Nandini's unwillingness to welcome her. She also remembers that Somu's mother had suggested to her not to visit her on account of social disapproval. These events, of course, hurt Sujata, but at the same time they awaken a sense of guilt in her of not having tried to 'understand' her own son. She, therefore, wants to punish herself. Her repentance, of course, indicates her awakening. She tells Nandini, "I won't go to Somu's mother again. I won't come to you. I won't go the places where Brati exists. May be that's my punishment for not knowing Brati" (p. 27). Obviously, the belated awareness is better, though bitter, than the bliss of ignorance.

Even when the engagement party of drinking is full swing, Sujata remembers her son, "Brati, I spent the whole of the day with you, and I can't forget myself now to carry out my duties" (p. 27). She remembers further, "Brati's fingers, his eyelids, how cold they are to the touch. Nothing can be colder. I was with Brati the whole day" (p. 27). Even when the other members of the family and the relatives are enjoying their liquor, Sujata, like a typical mother broods over her son. It easily testifies to the mother's filial attachment. But yet her husband attributes his son's death to "bad company, bad friends, the mother's influence" (p. 29), which is very ironical and shows that he has not understood his own wife properly.

When the daughters are dancing along with their friends, Saroj Pal, the Police Inspector drops in for a minute, conveys his best wishes to Tony and Tuli and rushes away in the police van. Sujata broods over her son and the likes of him,

> Still in uniform? Still on duty? Mass action in Baranagar? (*Turns to the dancers, all absorbed in their whirling movements.*) Still the Black Maria, the revolver in the holster, the helmeted policemen within the van? Where's the job this time? Where will the siren screech? Where will the streets resound to the pounding boots, the threatening van? Where will bullets pierce the wind? Where—again? Where will Brati run to? Where? (*Addressing the audience*) Why don't you speak? Speak for heaven's sake, speak, speak, speak, speak! How long will you endure it in silence? Where's the place where there's no killer, no bullets, no prison, no vans? (*Goes round the stage.*) Where can you escape it all, Brati, in Calcutta, in West Bengal, from north to south, from east to west? You can't be on the run any longer, Brati. Brati, come back. I found you today, Brati. If the siren screeches again, if the vans race, and Saroj Pal chases another young man somewhere, you'll be lost again. (*Pointing to the audience, and the dancers*) Corpses, stiffened corpses, all of you! (*Pointing to herself*) And I myself? Did Brati die so you could carry on in your cadaverous existence, enjoying and indulging in all the images of the world, all the poetry, the red roses, the neon lamps, the mother's smile, the child's cry, forever, till infinity? Do the living die, only to leave the world to the dead to enjoy? No! Never! (*The dancers break off from the dance, and stand in an immobile row at the back of the stage, with Dibyanath and the Kapadias.*) Let this No of mine pierce the heart of this city, rise to the skies, be borne on the winds over the whole state to every nook and corner. Let it set the past, the present, and the future atremble. Let it tear down the happiness of everyone cooped up in his own happy happiness. (*Pause*) Brati... (*She falls down. Pause. The rest break their freeze and rush up to her.*)

Then Dibyanath shouts out that Sujata's appendix has burst. She has died with deep frustration about the loss of her son and a sense of horror about the police violence and atrocities. Thus, the mother-son relationship has continued in a mystic way even after the death of the son. Although the mother is ignorant, apolitical and almost brainless, she has a lot of filial attachment to her son and tries to understand him and his Naxalite activities inspired by a noble cause, by listening to his surviving companions. Mahasweta Devi has obviously presented in a subtle fashion the excruciating agony of motherhood undergone by Sujata. Although she is just a mother of 1082 for the inhuman police department, she is an embodiment of boundless cordiality and concern for her son, and proves the dictum that there is no greater well-wisher than the mother in the world.

Apart from this main theme of mother-son relationship in the play, there are a few minor themes, which are treated satirically by the playwright. For example, on the day of Tuli's engagement, Mrs. Kapadia (Tuli's future mother-in-law) talks about her faith in a holy man. She says, "The moment I saw the Swami, my dear, a light flashed within me. We met at the San Francisco airport, and he said, My dear daughter, meet me at Miami. Just think of it, how did he know that I was going to Miami beach?... And from that moment itself he has been my guru. America has discovered the Swami, just as it had once discovered Vivekananda. Now India will recognize the Swami" (p. 27). Mrs. Kapadia and others, who participate in the party by drinking liquor and dancing shows that they are not orthodox Hindus, but Westernized ones. But Mrs. Kapadia's faith in the Swami looks contradictory to her pseudo-Westernization. It also throws light on the Indians' intellectual slavery. For example, India recognizing a Swami (or any great man for that matter) only after he is discovered by America is an example of Indian's lack of confidence in themselves and lack of competence in judging the worth of their own people. They always need a certification from the West.

Referring to Brati's death, Mrs. Kapadia tries to console Dibyanath with her sleek spirituality, "There's nothing to grieve for. The Swami says, there's no death. It's only the body that dies, the soul lives on. Your body will die. And then your souls will meet in heaven" (p. 29). Mrs. Kapadia even tries to offer whisky to Sujata, who declines it gently. Mrs. Kapadia's whisky and her faith in the Swami and Heaven highlight the contradictions of her personality. The playwright seems to have a dig at the Americanization of modern Indians and their philosophy of convenience.

Another piece of satire may be seen in the case of Bengali poets, who claim to be rebellious in their poetry, but never so in actual poets. When Mrs. Kapadia is introduced to a young poet, Dhiman, she compliments him on being a poet. Then Jyoti, under the alcoholic influence, describes the poet's thematic concerns, "Dhiman writes sob stuff on the twenty thousand men rotting in the prisons.... When Brati died, he was whining over Bangladesh. Now when everything's under control, he writes about them, from his pigsty of safety" (p. 28). The satire becomes more pronounced when Jyoti replies to Amit, "That friend of yours? He's a washed out poet! He cultivates the rich to booze off them. And you blow him up as the rebel poet! What was your poet up to, when my brother was killed?" (p. 28). Obviously, Jyoti has pointed out the opportunism, miserliness, and cowardice of the poet, who, far from being a socio-political activist, remains content in being a rebel poet only in black and white. By contrast, Brati plunged into socio-political action and fought and fell for a noble cause.

One of the conspicuous ironies of the play is that Brati is killed on his birthday itself. Again it is on Brati's birthday as well as death anniversary that Tuli's engagement is fixed. It is again on the same day that Sujata dies of appendix. These coincidences hold mirror to the irony of human life itself.

As for the technique of the play, it may be said that it is quite modern in that it is not based on any indigenous folk theatre of Bengal or any other part of India. It looks like a modern British or American play in its structure. The technique of mixing the present and the past seems to be quite fresh in the play. For example, the play begins in the present and then shifts to the past and comes back again to the present. Thus, the flashback scenes come as part of the memories of characters. Somu's Mother and Nandini remembering Brati's activities, and

Nandini's torture by Saroj Pal, the Police Inspector are flashback scenes linking the past with the present. Sujata's memories being played on the tape-recorder show the past events or thoughts. Such experimentation with the theatrical technique easily brings to our mind similar experiments made in Arthur Miller's plays. Although the play is relatively a short one, it is packed with serious thought about the socio-political reality of Bengal in particular and India in general. The language is generally terse without any sentimentality, but yet it attains poetic intensity at times. The significant contribution of Mahasweta Devi lies in the fact that this play makes the reader/spectator think seriously about the burning problems of contemporary Indian life.

Work Cited

Devi, Mahasweta *Five Plays*, Tr. Samik Bandyopadhyay, Calcutta: Seagull Books, 1999. (All the references are to this edition.)

• • • • •

23

The Absurd Drama in Kannada

The absurd literature, especially drama, started in Europe in the 50s of the twentieth century, grew in an abundant fashion and now become part of the main stream of literature. The absurd literary movement was not a systematic movement with a common purpose and a clear philosophy or ideology. The important writers of the absurd literature like Jean Paul Sartre, Albert Camus, Samuel Beckett, Arthur Adamov, Eugene Ionesco, Jean Genet, Harold Pinter, Edward Albee, Fernando Arrabal, N.F. Simpson, Gunter Grass and others hailed from different nations. For example, Beckett was from Ireland, Ionesco was Romania, Adamov was from Russian Armenia, Albee was from America; Pinter and Simpson were from England, Gunter Grass was from Germany, and Arrabal was from Spain. Likewise their mother tongues were also different from one another. Some of these writers happened to live in France and wrote in French quite accidentally. They came under the influence of existential philosophy, which was becoming very popular during troubled times after the world wars. They were influenced by the writings of the French authors like Sartre and Camus and their worldview and began to write in their own way by following their own techniques. French was the mother tongue of Jean Genet and he, therefore, wrote in his mother tongue. But it is a matter of surprise to know that even Beckett, Ionesco, and Arrabal and others wrote their works in French, although it was not their mother tongue. But they had not given any label to the kind of writing they had done in French. But it was a critic called Martin

Esslin, who studied these works systematically, discerned a common principle among them and labeled it as The Theatre of the Absurd in 1961. Since then the title of the absurd has stuck to this kind of literature, which spread to the other European countries and America.

The word 'absurd' has been used in different branches of knowledge. Originally, the word 'absurd' belongs to musicology and means 'cacophony'. In mathematics, the method of working out the sums is called 'surds' and by implication 'absurd' means anything that is 'unsystematic' or 'chaotic'. In logic, the word 'absurd' means something 'illogical' or 'irrational'. In aesthetics, it means 'irrelevant' or 'asymmetrical'. It has other lexical meanings like 'irrelevant', 'meaningless', 'useless' and 'ridiculous', etc.

Though the concept of the absurd was recognized as part of existentialism earlier, it was systematically discussed by Albert Camus for the first time in his *The Myth of Sisyphus* in 1942. According to him, the modern man could not achieve harmony with the external world and therefore the human life has become purposeless. Due to the purposelessness of life all our acts appear to be meaningless and create a metaphysical anguish in us. It is this metaphysical anguish, which forms the foundation of the Literature of the Absurd. The absence of ideals or their destruction creates disillusionment in us. It is such themes that are depicted in the plays of Beckett, Adamov, Ionesco, and Jean Genet; and also in the plays and novels of Sartre and Camus. These writers articulated the illogical element of life in the traditional, logical manner in their works. In other words, they expressed their absurd vision of life in a systematic technique. But the absurd playwrights who came after them expressed the absurd vision of life through the absurd technique itself. The playwrights of the second group went a step ahead and made their drama absurd both in theme and in technique. That is why Martin Esslin discusses only the playwrights of the second group in *The Theatre of the Absurd* (1968). Since the absurd plays of the second group are more complex in their nature, the characteristic features of these plays are discussed here in some detail.

Then what is the specialty of these absurd plays? The answer to this question may be given as follows. The element of dream and fantasy occupy great significance in the absurd drama as in poetic-drama. But one striking difference between the two is that whereas the language in poetic drama is refined and poetic, that in the absurd drama is quite crude. Not merely that. The language in the absurd drama loses its supremacy and becomes rather secondary. That is because language cannot be relied upon totally, as it has lost its communicative power. Since there is no concordance between our speech and the stated meaning, the absurdity between the two becomes blatant. As Martin Esslin points out the 'psychic distance', which Bertolt Brecht wants to achieve in his plays, becomes more conspicuous in the absurd drama.

The strands of the absurd vision of life are traceable to the French philosopher Nietzsche's *Thus Spoke Zarathustra* (1883) in which he presented his thesis that God was dead on a particular day. This idea was not merely the individual belief of Nietzsche, but the common belief of all the Europeans. Once it is believed that God is dead, and then the entire human life becomes purposeless, illogical, chaotic, and absurd. Man has to search for the purpose or meaning of life in such a dark, Godless world.

It is exactly this search for meaning that happens to be the central thematic concern of the absurd drama. When the external world loses it meaning, and the art forms lose their relevance, man begins to struggle to search for and understand the fundamental meaning, the supreme ideals and the norms of behaviour.

Since the absurd drama presents the tragic vision of disappearance of fundamental values or certainties, it comes in a way nearer to the religious quest. The protagonist or the author of the absurd drama sees some indescribable force or energy, which is equivalent to God (in the absence of God), sings about it, laughs at it or cries over it. Thus, he expresses his sense of wonder at and fear about the cosmos like the primeval man. He immerses himself in the dream world in order to escape from the mechanical life.

In the absurd drama we find the picture of the loss or oblivion of fundamental values and man's experience of nausea as a consequence of the worldliness and mechanical nature of life. It is this experience of the meaninglessness of life that Albert Camus presents in his *The Myth of Sisyphus*. According to Camus, the behaviour of people and their manners look like meaningless mimes. Camus compares this situation to somebody talking over the phone behind the glass walls of the booth. We can see only the lip movements and gestures of hand of such a man but we cannot hear his words. According to Camus, in the modern world we feel disgusted or nauseated by man's exhibition of inhumanity. We find only such experiences depicted in the absurd drama.

Since man in the modern world has lost his faith in religion, no value of life enjoys any certainty. Consequently, man has to live an uncertain life. Having lost his faith in God, he has been searching for alternative values of life elsewhere. The external situations and circumstances of the world look absurd and make him depressed and disgusted with life. That is why he abandons them and starts searching for something other than God for spiritual and psychological shelter and security. For example, Beckett's *Waiting for Godot* presents man's encounter with Time and his perennial waiting for Godot. Gilbert's plays depict man's continuous waiting for something or the other from birth to death.

Though the absurd drama presents the themes of alienation, loneliness, lack of communication and death, etc. and therefore looks absurd and like a child's play, it seems to return to the realm of the religious by trying to present the eternal truths of myths. The Greek Drama, the Medieval Mystery Plays and the Parables of the Baroque Drama offer us a picture of man caught in the mysterious and dangerous world and his effort to wriggle out of it.

But one conspicuous difference between the Greek Drama and the Absurd Drama is that whereas the life depicted in the Greek Drama had a commonly accepted philosophical foundation, the absurd drama does not have any common and systematic philosophy or ideology. The absurd philosophy believes in the view that human life has no systematic philosophy about it. In the absurd world nobody is bothered to explain or understand the divine design or *lila*. The absurd drama presents the dreams, fantasies, and fears of man when he delves deep into his inner self. Hence, the vision of life depicted in the absurd drama is more and more personal or private. Man's inability to adjust himself with the external world and the privacy of this vision happen to be the central thematic concerns of the absurd drama.

Since the absurd drama presents the picture of man's inner life, it concentrates on man's essential situation or condition and not interested in showing the problems of the external world, or narrating the external events or man's fate or heroism or ideology. There is no chronological or systematic picture of events, but it presents the picture of the human condition. Hence, the language in the absurd drama is not logical or rational, but is based on some patterns of imagery. No traditional kind of moral problem is presented there.

Since the absurd drama depicts the subjective vision of the playwright, the characters of these plays have no concreteness of the real world. Since there is no conflict or encounter between two individuals in them, it is not possible for us to consider them as 'drama' in the traditional sense. The purpose of the absurd drama is not to narrate story or teach a moral lesson but to present a few patterns of poetic imagery interwoven with subpatterns of imagery. This interweaving of poetic imagery in the absurd drama may be compared to a musical orchestra creating a complex impression on the mind of the spectators. In this sense, the absurd drama comes very near symbolic or imagistic poetry. Critics like Martin Esslin explain the absurd drama mainly through an analysis of such poetic images ingrained in them. The vision of life presented in them is not a 'fluid' one but rather 'static' one. Hence, it may be compared to a still picture rather than a motion picture. Time seems to be frozen in them.

The absurd drama may be said to be the extreme opposite of naturalistic drama. Here the vision of life is presented here is emotional one rather than intellectual. Hence, it may create many contradictory feelings in the spectators. The absurd dramatist abandons the intellectual language and resorts to the intuitive or musical language.

In the 'literary' drama verbal language enjoys the supremacy, but in the anti-literary drama like circus and Music Hall Theatre the verbal language is reduced to the minimum thereby giving scope for other elements of drama like gesture, stage properties, etc. It symbolizes the modern world wherein the verbal language has lost its communicative power and sanctity by becoming stale and failing to articulate the real or deeper experiences of man.

The absurd drama arouses the deeper psychic forces in man thereby liberating him from the unconscious fear and horror and awakening the integrative forces or energies in him. In his encounter with the deeper forces within him man attains a new awareness of his identity.

Since the modern man finds only contradictions, splits (or schizophrenia) and fragments in the external world, he suffers from a sense of dilemma. Hence, the absurd drama presents such a split or fragmented life. That is why the spectator cannot understand it easily. He has to piece together the fragments of the absurd vision and integrate them creatively to understand them properly.

In the modern world human life is characterized by many contradictions and attitudes along with some kind of madness. Though many social groups profess to be secular opens, yet they try secretly for the welfare of only their own groups. Thus, there is schizophrenia in the society, which is depicted by the absurd dramatist. This schizophrenia is very much present in the society and not in the mind of the absurd playwright.

The absurd drama offers a therapeutic treatment to the spectator by presenting the picture of disintegrated life, which destroys the human soul. Just as the Greek drama offers an emotional purgation by presenting man's struggle with Fate or Divine power, the absurd drama also provides a similar purgation of emotions by presenting the absurdity of modern human life and offers him a therapeutic treatment. For example, when Beckett's *Waiting for Godot* was performed in the presence of the prisoners in the city of San Quentin, the prisoners enjoyed the play wholeheartedly simply because the prisoners knew the importance of 'waiting' and the attendant sorrow better than the ordinary spectators.

The absurd drama does not present any issue or problem and its solution. In some absurd plays, the theme introduced in the early scenes goes on becoming more and more prominent, whereas in some other plays there is a circular structure and the play ends after where it began. In the traditional drama, the spectator can easily guess what may happen next. But in the absurd drama the spectator cannot what is happening right now on the stage, let alone guessing what may happen next. The events may not happen according to some logic of probability, but they may happen in the most unexpected way. Far from offering any answer to solution to the spectator, the absurd dramatist provokes him how to ask questions. After the performance is over, the spectator may piece together the thematic fragments of the play and be able to see a holistic image or vision hidden behind them. The presentation of such a complex pattern of imagery can offer a deep aesthetic pleasure to the spectator by its multidimensionality and suggestivity.

Though the language in the absurd drama may look apparently simple and foolish, it is not so at a deeper level. There is a lot of difference between madness in real life and the madness presented in the absurd drama. The so-called madness presented in the absurd drama is controlled by the artistic and dramatic rules. That is why it is not easy to write a good absurd play. The absurd vision of the dramatist becomes intelligible to the spectators only if he (the dramatist) has experienced the fears, dreams, and obsessions deeply in his heart. Otherwise, it remains a private madness of a mental patient.

Since the absurd vision of the dramatist is based on the psychological truth, it does not concern itself with social, political or objective picture of life. The absurd drama is, therefore, apolitical and anti-ideological. It stresses the truth of experience of the inner self. The success of such an absurd play depends upon the genius, the depth of experience and refinement of taste possessed by the playwright. Far from presenting a ready-made philosophy, the absurd playwright discovers his vision of life directly and experimentally in writing or composing his play. All the religions of the world have their own philosophical frameworks and ritual practices. Obviously, rituals are nothing but the enactments of the philosophies of their respective religions. In this sense, the absurd plays may be compared to the religious rituals.

From another point of view the vision of the absurd dramatist is near to the modern scientific outlook. All the myths, religions, and mystic experiences succeed in understanding the mystery of the universe, science does not believe in these attempts. According to scientific attitude, it is not possible to understand the world or universe completely. The scientist tries to understand the mystery of the universe at least partially only through inference, experiment, and hard effort. Many of the truths or mysteries of the universe still remain outside the ken of human understanding. The scientist believes that his limited knowledge of the world is surrounded by darkness. The absurd drama also presents man's groping in this darkness and suffers from depression and anxiety. As Camus says, man has no choice of freedom to escape from this dark world. That is the bitterest truth of his life. As the philosopher Democritus says, "There is no truth other than the void". Beckett repeats the same view again and again.

One similarity between the religious and mystic experience and that of the absurd dramatis is that both of them dwell in the truth of the void, which is beyond the ken of language. But the religious man attains fulfillment and spiritual liberation, whereas the absurd dramatist experiences frustration and anxiety. Whereas the experience of the religious mystic is affirmative, that of the absurd dramatist is negative. Both of them dwell on the edge of their experience or energy. That is why the language they employ is beyond the ken of logic. Both of them use distinct kind of poetic imagery. While the religious mystic experiences 'bliss' and 'liberation', the absurd dramatist feels depressed and anxious and through these very experiences, he becomes hardened and strengthened to face the life with a sense of laughter.

***

The absurd drama and fiction in Europe is enriched by the works of famous writers like Jean Paul Sartre, Albert Camus, Samuel Beckett, Arthur Adamov, Eugene Ionesco, Jean Genet, Gunter Grass, Harold Pinter, and Fredric Simpson. In spite of their individual differences among them, they share a common belief in the existential absurdity of life, which is characterized by the human predicament, meaninglessness, purposelessness, estrangement, loneliness, anxiety, lack of communication, and lack of choice, etc. It is not necessary to discuss their works in detail here. Our purpose in this article is to understand the Kannada absurd drama against the background of the European absurd drama.

***

The absurd literature, especially drama in Kannada, emerged as one of the ramifications of *navya* or modernist literature, which was directly influenced by the modern Western literature. But it had a snail's pace. Playwrights like Girish Karnad, Na. Ratna, Chandrakant Kusanur, Chandrashekhar Kambara, Chandrashekhar Patil, P. Lankesh, Poornachandra Tejaswi, Chaduranga and Arya have contributed their mite to the tradition of absurd drama in Kannada. Their plays attracted man elite spectators by their freshness and novelty, shocked and irritated the traditional spectators and puzzled the uneducated spectators completely. Such plays have been performed only in some select cities like Dharwad, Hubli, Bijapur, Bengaluru, and Mysore. As there is a yawning gap between the professional theatre and the amateur theatre, the number of spectators, who can watch the performances of both kinds of drama, is very limited. The traditional spectators, who can enjoy the professional (company) plays throughout the night, cannot enjoy the plays of Sriranga and Kailasam even for three hours. That is because they are disappointed not to find any song, dance or crude language or innuendos. When it comes to the absurd drama, the traditional spectators simply cannot understand what is happening on the stage and ignore it totally by considering it as fool's play. Hence, it may be said that the Kannada absurd plays are written by the intellectual playwrights for the intelligent or elitist audience. That explains the highly limited number of people, who are interested in reading or watching them on the stage. These playwrights had kept the Kannada absurd drama alive in the 1970s and 1980s, but now it has almost become defunct in the twenty-first century.

A common feature of the absurd drama in Kannada is that it is the technique rather than the vision of life presented in it that is absurd. The metaphysical absurdity, which is the basis of the European absurd drama, cannot be found in the Kannada absurd drama. That is because in India our belief in religion and God, in the theory of *karma* or fate has not disappeared completely, though it has relaxed to some extent. The problems of contemporary India like sexual freedom, communal discrimination, quest for political power, exploitation, and poverty, etc., can be discussed and solved socio-politically and presented systematically through the medium of art. But the Kannada dramatists deliberately resort to myths and present their view of life through the absurd pattern of images and symbols, to understand which the readers or spectators require a special kind of orientation.

The Kannada absurd dramatists may be divided into two groups. One, some playwrights express their absurd vision, i.e. thematic content through absurd language and technique. Girish Karnad belongs to this group. Such playwrights may be described as existentialist playwrights (like Sartre and Camus). Two, some playwrights present the absurd thematic content through the absurd language and technique. Na. Ratna, P. Lankesh, Kusanur, Patil and others belong to the second group. Some plays of these playwrights may be discussed in brief in the following paragraphs.

Girish Karnad has written many famous plays so far, among which only *Tughlaq* and *Hayavadana* may be labeled as absurd drama. In *Tughlaq* (1964), the element of absurdity is blatantly visible in the eponymous hero. It shows how a very intelligent man can be a foolish man as well. Girish Karnad has depicted the life of such an absurd protagonist in a very systematic and rational language and technique. In other words, the presentation of the absurd mind of the protagonist is ridden with contradictions. We can clearly make out from Tughlaq's language that we cannot understand his mind. His language is characterized by contradictions and paradoxes rather than by unintelligible words or illogical and irrational babblings. The development of the personality of Tughlaq and his characterization is very logical, although we cannot understand his absurd mind.

Tughlaq is depicted in the play as a dreamer. As his kingdom is inhabited by both Hindus and Muslims, he does not want to be mistaken to be pro-Muslim king. Inspired by the Platonic philosophy, he wants to achieve a balance between Hindus and Muslims. But unfortunately the subjects of his kingdom do not care for his ideal due to their selfish motives. Whereas the Muslims hate him for his soft corner for Hindus and considering them as his brothers thereby exempting them from the payment of *jizya* tax, the Hindus suspect that he being a Muslim king cannot give them the right kind of protection. Thus, Tughlaq, who wants to achieve a balance between Hindus and Muslims, is unfortunately disliked and suspected by both the parties. Far from employing politics to protect the religion, he employs religion to achieve a political balance. For example, he invites Sheikh Imamuddin to his kingdom and restarts the practice of prayer that had been discontinued for the last five years. By this gesture he wants to demonstrate to the Muslims that he is an ardent lover of Islam. But at the same time he sees that nobody turns up for prayer by appointing the soldiers to scare them away from there and that the prayer-ground remains empty. Here Tughlaq's use of a religious priest for his political game looks absurd from the point of view of the common man.

A dreamer, Tughlaq becomes a failure in solving the practical problems of life. Talking like a poet, enjoying the beauty of stars, he plays the role of a god like Jesus and Lord Krishna and thinks that he can solve all the problems of his subjects. But the irony of his life is that he can talk like an omniscient God, but he cannot control everything in life like an omnipotent God. Thus, he appears like a mental patient suffering from the delusion of grandeur. A man, who knows all the problems of his kingdom, cannot understand how people of his own religion like Aziz take the guise of Hindus and deceive him by their double-dealing. Likewise he is so innocent and foolish as not to detect how the people of his kingdom mint the fake currency by misusing his administrative machinery when he introduces copper currency in his kingdom. Hence, his decisions and deeds turn out to be quite absurd due to the yawning gap between his dream and practical wisdom.

Tughlaq appoints Shihabuddin to manage the affairs of the kingdom during his absence, but after returning to the kingdom, he learns that Shihabuddin has betrayed him and stabs him to death mercilessly. Similarly, when his stepmother gets Nazib killed for Tughlaq's own good, he declares her deed as treachery and that treachery is worse than adultery and orders her to be stoned publicly to death. The punishment that he wants to give to Aziz, who has shattered his dreams, is to promote him as the sovereign of the Deccan. All these deeds of Tughlaq are, obviously, are contradictory and absurd. He behaves as strangely as Caligula, though he is not as cruel as the latter.

In Tughlaq's life we can see two kinds of absurdity. Firstly, there is a conspicuous gap between his dream and practical wisdom. He lacks the omnipotent power of God to materialize his great dream. Secondly, there is no concordance between him and his contemporary society. That is because the people of his kingdom do not belong to one homogeneous group or culture but to two contradictory cultures like Hindus and Muslims. One religion or culture tries to destroy or violate the ideals of the other religion or group. For example, Aziz succeeds in shattering the ideals of Tughlaq by exploiting his love of Hindus. Similarly, he makes Tughlaq helpless by murdering Ghiasuddin Abbasid, the Muslim religious leader. It is this cultural contradiction between Hinduism and Islam that contributes to the absurdity to the events in the play. Consequently, Tughlaq is finally defeated by history. That is because Tughlaq wants to transform his high dream into reality and to achieve something that is impossible and absurd. The playwright has depicted the absurd behaviour of Tughlaq by employing intelligible language and logically convincing technique.

Hayavadana (1971) another absurd play by Girish Karnad depicts the fundamental problem of sex in human life. The playwright has borrowed the theme of this play from the sixth tale of *Betala Panchavishati* and Thomas Mann's long short story, *The Transposed Heads*. The frustration of man's incompleteness and his attempt to overcome it are depicted symbolically here. The central problem in the play is whether it is man's head or body, which is important for a woman and which of the two a woman desires more or whether she wants to combine both of them. In order to delineate such a fundamental and philosophical problem, it becomes inevitable for the playwright to violate the law of probability. Devadatta and Kapila severing their heads in front of the goddess; and later their recovery of life when Padmini exchanges their heads—events like this are, obviously mythical in nature and therefore look improbable and absurd from a realistic point of view. But they undoubtedly symbolize the higher truths of life and the dilemmas they create in the minds of the characters and the attempts of the characters to overcome them. Once we accept this central improbability, all other events happen quite logically. The dialogues are quite logical and intelligible.

Devadatta represents the head or intellectuality and heart or emotion, whereas Kapila represents body along with its beauty and strength. Padmini, who is a symbol of sexuality according to Vatsyayana's *Kamasutra*, secretly desires Kapila's body though she is formally married to Devadatta. But she cannot express her desire due to her fear of the society. Initially, she disdains Kapila as a wild boar, but gradually she grows to like his physical strength and beauty. Her accidental exchange of their heads in the temple of the goddess fulfils her secret desire but creates a new problem for her—the problem of belonging. Whereas Devadatta with Kapila's body claims Padmini to be his wife, Kapila with Devadatta's body claims her to be his wife. Devadatta argues that it is the head, which decides the identity of man, and therefore, Padmini belongs to him, who has Devadatta's head. But Kapila argues that Padmini has cohabited with the body of Kapila, she belongs to Kapila, who wears Devadatta's head. Thus, the dichotomy between body and mind is problematized in the play. Padmini is utterly puzzled by the confused identities of the two men. Finally, she chooses to accept Devadatta (with Kapila's body) as her husband and gives birth to a baby boy.

But as years go by, both Devadatta and Kapila regain their original qualities. So far Kapila has lived with a sense of hatred for Devadatta and Devadatta has lived with a sense of fear. But neither of them can live without Padmini. Hence, they kill each other by stabbing. Then Padmini gives her son to the Bhagavata asking him to send him into the custody of Sabara.

The dolls' talking like human beings is quite absurd from the realistic point of view, but symbolically they are inevitable as they act as means of externalizing the inner dream of Padmini. Similarly, Hayavadana's talking like a human being, though he has the form of a horse is absurd. His playing with Padmini's son by making him sit on his back and losing his human voice and resuming his whinnying shows the process of his completion as a horse. Karnad's vision that everyone is suffering from a sense of incompleteness and quests after completeness is quite serious and logical and systematic. But the technique of expressing this philosophy is partially absurd. And the language is perfectly logical and intelligible.

***

Na. Ratna, who belongs to the second category of absurd playwrights, is an important writer, because his plays happen to be absurd both in content and in technique and therefore puzzle the reader or spectator a lot. But yet we can perceive the symbolic truth ingrained in them. In his *Ellige* (*Where to*?), there are seven characters, none of which has any proper name. For examples, the characters like the elder, the younger, the young lady, a young man 1 and young man 2 are the personae of the play. As their very names suggest, they do not seem to belong to Kannada Land. But on the contrary, they symbolize the fundamental human problems. At the beginning of the play the younger one and the elder one are going to somebody's house in some town. But the names of the town or the person to whose house they are going is not particularized. On the way, they see a wall. Whereas the younger one crosses the wall by jumping over it, the elder one cannot jump over it and suffers on that count. Here the wall is not a real one, but it symbolizes the hindrances in the path of life. The play begins on a realistic level and then suddenly leaps to the symbolic level, which looks quite absurd. But the symbolic level presents the fundamental questions of life. For example, when one is treading the distant path, what if one dies on the way? Such question suggests the eternal human anxiety about death. Even when the two persons set out on their journey to meet somebody, on the way they cannot locate the address as it is written in *modi* script. Thus, they lose their way but they happen to meet two lovers, who have also lost their way but they seek their help in finding their own path. Thus, the whole situation is absurd but yet it is symbolic and may be applied to the entire human life. But finally they do not know where exactly they are going.

The play is not intelligible on the realistic plane, but it may be understood on the symbolic plane. The language also loses its logicality and intelligibility smacks of the dream world, thereby creating an impression of the absurd. On the whole the message of this play seems to suggest that man has no clearly defined goal nor does he know the exact path leading to that goal.

Na. Ratna's *Gode Beke Gode* (*Do you want a Wall?*, 1973) is also symbolic in its action and language. There are only four characters, which are anonymous. When the play begins, 'one' man and 'another' man are hawking a glass wall, "Do you want a hot and fresh wall?" This act of selling the wall is very absurd on the realistic plane but can be understood on the symbolic plane. Normally, a wall of bricks, or stones or mud or wood allows man some privacy for his being naked or behaving, as he likes; protects him from the sight by others and gives him a limited freedom. But the wall offered for sale here is one of glass, which is transparent. Though it can protect man from wind and rain, it cannot protect man from other's eyes and hence cannot give him the real privacy. As it is a means of showing one's private behaviour to others it is difficult to sell or buy it. The glass wall thus symbolizes the modern man's loss of privacy. We can extend the symbolic meaning of the glass wall further. It represents the transparency of the inner thoughts and feelings of man, which may be so dirty and ugly that by revealing them to the public we may suffer the loss of our prestige, dignity and honour.

There are other meanings also to the glass wall. This wall has been found unexpectedly by one man and he invites another man to sell it together. But both of them are suffering from loneliness. As both of them are on two sides of the wall, they cannot communicate with each other. Though the transparency of the wall gives them an impression that they are very near to each other, they are distanced from each other because of their contact being blocked by the wall.

Normally, a wall is fixed permanently in a particular place. But the wall in the play is a mobile one and hence it has made the modern man to be continuously on the move and never giving him a sense of fixedness or permanence. Instead of the wall protecting them, it is they, who have to protect it constantly and prevent it from breaking. Thus, the glass wall subverts all our expectations about it and looks quite absurd. The language also is quite absurd in keeping with the central theme.

Bonte (*The Rag Doll*, 1973) happens to be the most odious and strange/weird play among the absurd plays of Na. Ratna. The playwright has tried to present an elevated symbolic truth by selecting an improbable theme from the realistic point of view. Though there are eleven characters in the play Husband and Wife are anonymous. As they have lost a child, they are dreaming of begetting another. Accordingly, the Husband instructs milkman to order a cobbler to stuff the dead body of the child with straw. Accordingly, the doll gets ready. Now both Husband and Wife make arrangements to celebrate the birthday of the baby and invite friends like Shennai couple, Kumar and the Doctor, who come and offers gifts to them by mistaking the doll to be a live child, partake of the meal. When they toss the child affectionately, the leg of the baby dashes against the leg of a chair and wounded. The Doctor, therefore, gives an injection to the baby. They spend some time chitchatting. Later they put a few eggs in a toy-hen, and make it lay eggs by pressing its belly. While repeating this play the eggs fall beneath the table. Then all the grown up people duck below the table like children to pick up the eggs. The play ends with this event.

In this play, people mistaking the doll as the real baby is very absurd. But its symbolic meaning is very serious and psychologically valid. By milking the cow by seeing the face of the baby and by mistaking the dead baby or doll for the live baby the Wife has a feeling of motherhood and a sense of fulfillment. Thus, the play offers the psychological truth. Though the Husband knows that his baby is dead, he wants to create an illusion about the reality of the baby for his wife and make her happy thereby being happy himself. The celebration of the birthday of their baby is nothing but an enactment of their wishful dream.

The acts like bathing the baby, tossing it in the air and playing with it are all natural instincts common to a woman or mother. When the priest comes to their house he remains doubtful about whether he should perform the birth rites or funeral rites of the baby. This event shows the height of absurdity. At the end of the play the grown up people duck beneath the table and behave like children. This act also symbolically expresses the psychological almost Freudian truth that man, however grown up he may be, wishes to become a child again.

One can the meaning of this play and read a religious truth also in it. The belief in the doll as the real baby shows the Faith Therapy offered by religion. Just as we willingly believe or mistake the cow-dung icon of Ganesha to be the God and worship Him thereby attaining a psychological and spiritual satisfaction and giving a direction to our action and giving a meaning to our life.

As the characters mistake the dead baby to be a live baby or the absence to be the presence, the language that they employ is replete with humour. Those, who have come to celebrate the birth of a baby being to remember their past lives and discuss theme like death, Lord Yama, and rebirth, etc. This incongruence creates a thick atmosphere of the absurd in the play.

Chandrakant Kusanur has written many absurd plays out of which only two may be discussed here. His *Vidusaka* (*The Comedian*, 1971) happens to be an Indianized version of Beckett's *Waiting for Godot*. 'Death' and 'waiting' are the central thematic concerns of this play. The characters in this play have no proper names. Six characters come on the stage, whereas three characters speak from behind the curtain. Three characters are waiting for Krura (the cruel man). Then there comes an old man on a wheel chair and dies by vomiting blood. Then the old man's daughter asks Vidusaka as to who is responsible for the death of her father. Then she asks him, "Sir, do you love me?" Such behaviour looks quite absurd. When the three persons feel bored by waiting for the arrival of Krura, they start telling stories. The first man tells a story in which there is a king, who conducts the *putrakameshthi yajna* without being aware of his own impotence and his queen mistakes the maidservant's baby as her own. Then the baby grows into a young prince and lusts after his own mother and feels ashamed of himself after realizing his sin. All these events are quite absurd. Then the second man tells a story of Sayakka and Deyakka. When Deyakka grows proud and conceited she is subjected to the wrath of Goddess Laxmi and becomes extremely poor. Both these stories are the ones that are narrated during the month of *Shravan*.

The telling of these two stories is, obviously, to while away their time during their waiting for Krura. Krura is clearly a symbol of death. After the story telling is over, Vidusaka comes and learns that all the three persons are missing and the chairs are empty. There is a cap lying beneath one of the chairs. On the cap is written, "Krura had come here." When Vidusaka takes the cap and wears it he dies by crying weirdly.

The play conveys the message that it is inevitable for man to live his life waiting for the death. Though death is certain, the time of death is unknown. Man, who is in the expectation of death, finds life to be rather boring and meaningless. Vidusaka undertakes the task of laughing and making others also laugh in order to forget the boredom and meaninglessness of life. His laughter consists of absurd dialogues.

None can fail to see the deep influence of Beckett's *Waiting for Godot* on this play. Krura is an Indianized version of Godot. Though Vidusaka is rooted in the Indian culture, he does not represent the contemporary society of India. Hence, the employment of an antiquated character is not quite relevant. The playwright could have used a modern character for the purpose.

Kusanur's *Halla, Kolla, Niru* (*River, Valley, Water*, 1970) delineates the theme of treachery. There are three anonymous characters like A, B, and C. Each one of them boasts oh his virtue and comments on the vices of others. These three characters represent three points of view. Each one of them misunderstands the other and abandons or betrays him for that reason. The play stresses the psychological examination of the reasons for this treachery or betrayal. When the play begins, A, B, and C sit in the cane chairs and begin to talk absurdly. It is through this absurd conversation that the playwright shows certain psychological states. The dialogue turns from mosquitoes to love, to head, and to plans, etc. The characters articulate their sorrow and frustration in life. For example, B trying to pass a thread through the eye of the needle suggests that man does not do everything with a purpose. B suggests further that man is entangled like a string in the spool and suffers. The absurdity of this play depends mainly on its dialogues. The little action that is found in this play shows that B and C hoist A on their shoulders. Though A sits on their shoulders, he refuses to give them the piece of sugarcane that he holds in his hand. Angered by A's refusal, B and C download A on the floor. When A requests them again for help, they lift him up and suspend him by his hands from the hooks in the ceiling. Though this action appears to be absurd from the realistic point of view, its symbolic meaning is quite obvious. The moral of this play is that everybody goes up in life by the help of others and forgets them afterwards thereby proving himself to be ungrateful. Once a man becomes notorious for his ingratitude, then nobody would come forward to help him. Even if people pretend to help him they see to it that no good comes out of that help.

Chandrashekhar Kambara has written many plays, among which two plays like *Chalesh* and *Narcissus* belong to the tradition of the absurd theatre. *Chalesh* (*A Man with Sunglasses*, 1971) depicts the pitiable life of Govinda, who cannot afford to pay the rent for his house. The extreme poverty of Govinda offers a realistic foundation to the play, but his effort to wriggle out of the problem assumes symbolic dimension, which gives the element of absurdity to the play. Govinda, who is an actor in the Gubbi Company, wants to escape from the torture of moneylenders and therefore wears a goggle so that they may not recognize him. It is this goggle (with dark glasses) that becomes a symbol of his protest and fight against his poverty. It becomes a superstructure of dream or utopia built on the foundation of bitter poverty. Govinda's histrionic talent helps him a lot in this playacting. He wears the goggles and addresses his wife as 'Devi' and in turn she addresses him as 'Aryaputra.' Thus, they talk like a king and a queen of the folk drama. Their dramatic talk looks humorous as well as absurd.

When Govinda is enjoying himself in this dream world, the owner of the house, Nanjayya comes there and shouts at him and asks him to pay off the rest instantly. But Govinda begins to boast about himself in a false way in order to wriggle out of the situation. Whereas Nanjayya talks on a realistic level, Govinda does so on a symbolic level thereby creating an atmosphere of absurdity and discordance between two levels. Govinda, who has no ability to clear the rent, indulges in conceited talk and poetic self-praise, which add to the absurdity of the play.

Nanjayya does not care for Govinda's conceited talk and shouts at him to clear the rent. Then Govinda hits upon another plan of wriggling out of the problem. He lies that one of his sons has become a minister and that he is coming there within an hour along with his wife and driver. Temporarily, this lie becomes the truth. Then within ten minutes his son, Shankar, his daughter-in-law Sarasu and his driver, Hushappa come there and try to help him out of the trouble from Nanjayya.

Though Govinda escapes from the trouble temporarily with the help of this lie, later he gets himself entangled in its net. His son and so-called minister, daughter-in-law and the driver refuse to go away from his house although Govinda declares repeatedly that they are not related to him in any way. Not only that. They even become messengers of Lord Yama for him. They become the owners of the house, try to kill him and begin to dig a grave in his bedroom. But Govinda goes on becoming stronger by this absurd experience. But unfortunately his wife, Kashibai dies by shock of her husband's so-called death. Then Govinda becomes utterly lonely and helpless like a dog. But as the playacting of the three guests becomes too much for him, Govinda gives up his own playacting and escapes from the net of lies. Now he is able to bear the sorrow of his wife's death, although he is deeply aggrieved. Thus, Govinda, who is an actor, gives up his playacting and returns to the real world. His histrionic talent helps him to protest against his poverty and the consequent humiliation and his desire to become a rich man. The events in this play change from the realistic level to the symbolic and again return from the symbolic level to the realistic ones thereby adding up to the element of absurdity to the play.

Kambara's *Narcissus* (1971) is an absurd play with a complicated symbolic pattern. Though the language of the play is borrowed from the real life, the behaviour of the characters and the manner of events happening in it are symbolic and absurd at the same time. Just as Narcissus of the famous Western myth, falls in love with his own image reflected in the water of a pond, Nani, the eponymous protagonist of this play is in love with a girl called Gita, but he renames her as Sudha, writes a love-letter to her and forces her to come to his house. He talks very foolishly with her. He feels frightened when he learns that her husband, who is a Police Sub-Inspector, is standing outside his house. As Gita tries to escape from his house, Nani drags her by her face as if she is a corpse. Then there arrives a Jogati. Bhimya asks the Jogati to sleep with Nani, but Nani fails to recognize her. Then Nani gets angry by listening to the Jogati's requests and asks Bhimya to neck her out. By that time, Gita's husband, who is a Police Sub-Inspector, comes there and arrests Nani.

Though the title of the play is borrowed from the Greek myth, the characters and events are all Indian. Narcissism suggests the universal quality of self-praise or that mental state. Nani has been searching for his alter ego or other self in somebody. Now he wants to find that other self in Sudha, who is a married woman and whom he has renamed as Sudha. He loves her and therefore wishes to attract her in the ambit of his love. This shows his protest against the social norms. But he has no ability to violate the social norm. He treats Sudha cruelly when she tries to go away from him. His behaviour borders on sadism.

Nani, who wants to have sex with Sudha without her husband's knowledge about it, fails to enjoy sex with the Jogati, who is a professional prostitute. Not merely that. When she is possessed by the goddess Yellamma and begins to dance before him he shoots her to death. Thus, Nani does not succeed in satisfying his sexual hunger. Finally, Gita's husband comes there and arrests him.

The message of this play is that whenever a man indulges in limitless self-love he has to have an encounter with the society and whenever he violates the norms of the society, he is punished properly by it. Bhimya, who is a servant of Nani, provides a sharp contrast to him. Whereas Nani is an idealist, Bhimya is a practical person. Whereas Nani protests against the social norms and gets punished by the society, Bhimya accepts the social reality and enjoys his life within the limits. For example, Bhimya, far from going behind married women (like Nani) invites the Jogati and satisfies his sexual itch. Similarly, he is invited by the Police Sub-Inspector and offered a job of a police constable.

There is a lot of difference between Nani's alter ego and the Jogati's alter ego. Nani's other is an essence of his vices; whereas the Jogati's other is the holy goddess. For the Jogati, her prostitution is part of the divine service and hence she has not guilt consciousness about her sexual sin.

Nani and Bhimya playacting the roles of Gita's mother-in-law and her husband brings to our mind Jean Genet's play, *The Maids*, wherein two maidservants playact the roles of a mistress and a servant in the absence of their mistress.

Chandrashekhar Patil has written many plays, half of which are absurd. His *Appa* (*Father*, 1970) is a short but a very beautiful lyrical absurd play. Basava, the protagonist of the play, is a boy of six years and the son of a prostitute. Not knowing the identity of his father, he is subjected to ridicule and humiliation in the society. He wants to know from his mother the name of his father. A similar theme is depicted in Strindberg's play, *The Father*. But the main difference between the two plays is that the protagonist of Strindberg's play is a grown up young man, who is aware of the social norms, but the protagonist of Patil's play is an innocent boy. He is ridiculed and insulted in his school and lane by other boys about his father. He, therefore, pesters his mother and wants to know who his father is. His identity crisis and his innocence have been articulated lyrically by the playwright. He tells his mother how the other day the gowda of the village invited him, offered him tea and gave him ten rupees and said that he (Basava) was like his own son. The mother is shocked by Basava's report. She, therefore, wants to distract his attention by narrating a folk tale to him. She knows that neither her son nor she can get the exact answer to the question as to who his father is. She refers to a folktale of a flower with petals of different colours and nobody knows which seed has begotten which petal. But the boy Basava is not able to understand the symbolic meaning of the folktale.

The absurdity presented in this play is partial in the sense that it is absurd only from the boy's point of view and not from the mother's. The spectators know quite well that it is natural for a prostitute to conceal the name of the father of her child. Since prostitution is a socially approved institution, the spectators do not consider it as absurd. But it appears absurd only when looked at from the boy's point of view. The protagonist is a representative of many such forlorn children. The intention of the playwright is only to highlight the crisis of identity of the son of a prostitute and not explore the cause and consequences of such a profession. But the absurd technique employed by the playwright is very successful.

Kunta, Kunta, Kuravatti (*The Lame Man of Kuravatti*, 1970) is another interesting absurd one-act play. There are only three anonymous but typical characters like the Lame Man, the Blind Man, and the Deaf Man. The play conveys the message that every one of them has been struggling to attain or possess that quality or ability that he lacks in him. As they are always obsessed with their deficiencies, they wish to fulfil their dreams as and when possible. Though all the three of them wish to operate with other for their happiness, it is not possible for them to do so. Though they express their lacunae and the consequent frustration, they cannot understand the others. Consequently, their language appears to be quite absurd and comic. For example, the Lame Man dreams of wear the finely polished Bata shoes. The Blind Man dreams of wearing a wrist-watch and the cooling glasses and the Deaf Man dreams of enjoying listening to classical music. Their mutual misunderstanding indicates the lack of communication among them creates a lot of humour on the stage.

Though the play is a short one, it presents the universal tendency of man to long for that which he does not have with him. It also shows the truth that since each man's lacunae are different from the others' they cannot communicate successfully among themselves due to the impossibility of a common language.

P. Lankesh has written eight plays, among which his *Teregalu* (*The Waves*, 1967) is said to be a good absurd play. Cruelty happens to be the main thematic concern of the play, which is structured systematically, but its language has an occasional absurdity in it. The protagonist of this play is anonymous and represents every man. The three visitors, Kitti, Vitti, and Kanthi, who come to his house, claim to be his former students. One of them is tall, the second is of average height and the third one is short. They start enquiring into his crimes and expose the ugly reality masked by his exterior appearance. As the action of the play proceeds, out respect for the protagonist goes on decreasing. Finally, it is revealed that the protagonist is a criminal, who has become the owner of the house after killing its former owner. His outward gentlemanliness and respectability conceal his vices like adultery, deceptiveness and murderousness, etc. All the three visitors expose his crimes, playacting the roles of the jury and declare death sentence for him. The protagonist loses our sympathy completely at the end of the play.

The person, who has killed the former owner of the house and become its present owner, is an embodiment of corruption so rampant in the modern society. He has killed his conscience by compromising with life and been leading a luxurious life. The three persons, who expose his former crimes, play the role of detectives and easily bring to our mind the Furies of the Greek Drama. The cruelty that the three visitors show in punishing the criminal creates a sort of balance to the former cruelties indulged in by him. That is why we do not feel sad when we learn that he is sentenced to death sentence by hanging. The events exposing the crimes of the contemporary society are structured quite logically and systematically, but the element of absurdity is found only in the dialogues. The questions and answers are directly aligned with each other. The questions that are asked on the realistic level are answered on the fantastic or symbolic level. Similarly, the cluster of sentences or words uttered by some characters are not logically intelligible ones, but are clustered together according to the psychological law of association of ideas. References to the mortal world, Delhi, Harapanahalli and Nijalingappa, etc., have no logical connection in-between them, but show the working of the minds of the characters and contribute to the element of absurdity on the verbal level thereby confounding and confusing the mind of the spectators.

The three visitors like Kitti, Vitti, and Kanthi, who expose the protagonist's crimes, ridicule them and finally turn out to be the jury and dismiss his case rather indifferently and pronouncing the death sentence on him. This is, obviously, an absurd technique. The so-called spies changing their roles into those of the jury on the stage itself—such action is not to be found in the traditional Kannada drama.

***

Poornachandra Tejaswi's *Yamala Prasne* (*The Twin Question*, 1964) is a short but beautiful absurd play. Though the events in the play are the products of the Indian social condition, the manner of assembling them is quite absurd. At the beginning of the play two friends Ramesh and Hemant come pushing their motor-cycle, which had developed some mechanical trouble. Like many Indian intellectuals they compare their vehicle to the chariots of the Kurukshetra battle. They try hard to start the vehicle. The wayfarers also come to help them by kicking the pedal, but the more they try to repair it, the more it grows problematic. The spare parts of the vehicle become loose and fall on the ground. The vehicle, obviously, becomes a symbol of modern life, wherein things fall apart and the center cannot hold. By that time a police constable comes there, enquires about an anonymous dead body lying nearby and charges the two persons with the crime of murder. Thus, connecting the two unconnected parties like the two friends and the dead body is very absurd. The point of view of Hemant and Ramesh and that of the policeman are contradictory to each other and each point of view tries to cancel the other one.

When the policeman is trying to charge them with the crime of murder, a young lady happens to come there and tells the policeman that the dead body is lying there since the morning thereby exonerating the two persons. After this problem is solved a gardener comes there and starts begging for money in order to conduct the funeral of the anonymous dead body. Ramesh suggests that the dead body may be taken to the government hospital; the gardener tells him that the dead body has been brought from the government hospital itself. Such reversals of expectations create and element of absurdity and humour in the play and suggest the tragedy of poverty at a deeper level. Though the gardener's attempt to exploit the death of another man for earning his own livelihood is really pitiable, though apparently it looks very humorous. From the gardener's point of view, the entire mortal world is like a moratorium. Nobody can deny that. The message of the play seems to be that man has to keeping trying to understand life even after experiencing the absurdity of it. The events like the mechanical trouble of the motor-cycle, the policeman trying charge them with the crime of murder, and the gardener using the situation to his own advantage are not individually absurd, but their coincidence at the particular spot is absurd. This combination of events gives us a picture of disoriented life. Death-consciousness is very intense in this play. Even those, who wish to live their life, beautifully and meaningfully cannot escape from the death consciousness. The playwright has satirized the contemporary society through the absurd technique in a subtle way. For example, the policeman's professional suspicion and inhumanity are satirized by the playwright in a subtle way.

***

Rajagopal Arya has written many children's plays. His *Bayalu Alayadolago* (*Is Space within the House?*, 1977) is a full-length absurd play. Here both the events and dialogues are absurd and therefore confound the reader/spectator. There are seven characters bearing the Bengali names. At the beginning of the play, Ashukosh and Dada are discussing how they came into the temple. Different people have come to this temple and got trapped into it. Its walls are as thick as a mile. The door of the temple opens only inside and not outside like a trap. All those, who are entrapped in this temple, have been repenting over their sins and crimes. This temple easily resembles the Yaksa Town in Rabindranath Tagore's *Red Oleanders*. The temple, far from kindling a devotional feeling or divine consciousness in the people, has turned out to be a prison house, a trap, a cage or a labyrinth. One can only enter it, but can never come out of it. It easily brings to our mind Dante's Inferno. The absurdity of the play may be seen in its satirical story itself. Like in Samuel Butler's *Erewhon*, the normal values of the world have been reversed here. The virtues of normal life are considered as 'vices' in this temple. Conversely, the vices of normal are considered as 'virtues' in this temple. Ashutosh is shocked to learn from Krittika herself, that she, whom he had loved earlier, has now turned out to be a prostitute. Though Ashutosh has worked hard for his party, he is betrayed by his own party members. He has even forgotten his name since his arrival here and become Virup. The priest in this temple has become a dictator, who sacrifices his prisoners to ingratiate his deity. Far from killing them himself, he gets one prisoner killed by another prisoner. He enjoys sex with the prostitute, Krittika. Though she was a beloved of Ashutosh in the past, he has no control over her now.

The prisoners of this temple not only repent over their sins and crimes, but also re-enact their dreams. They have to be sacrificed to the deity as per the order of the priest. They cannot escape from a small ventilator because the ventilator turns out to be a magnifying glass.

Though the events of this play apparently happen on a realistic level, they can be better understood on the symbolic level. Here the temple and the priest symbolize the inevitability and universality of the religion and religious exploitation. Religion has a great control over the human life in countless aspects. The satire in the play suggests the moral that religion, far from giving man the experience of wholeness and holiness, gives him only an experience of emptiness. The language of the dialogues looks absurd, but the overall philosophy of the play happens to be satirical.

***

Chaduranga's *Ilibonu* (*Rat-Trap*, 1972) is another important absurd play. There are only three characters, which are anonymous: The Climber, the Digger, and the Wife. They do not represent any particular caste, religion or region, but are typical, universal, and symbolic.

Ilibonu presents the essential human predicament. The action of the play happens not on the realistic plane but on the symbolic plane. The events happening here violate the law of probability and follow the logic absurdity. The dialogues are, therefore, absurd. The events happen here as in dreams and go on hopping from one idea to the other according to the law of association of ideas. The rat-trap is the central image of the play, successfully symbolizing man's 'bondage' or 'imprisonment'. Because of the image of the rat-trap, the play assumes the dimension of poetic drama. In the Hindu philosophy, especially Vedanta, the parrot in the cage symbolizes soul's imprisonment in the human body. The parrot in the Hindu philosophy symbolizes the individual soul. The parrot is bewitching to look at and provides a lot of pleasant entertainment to man. But Chaduranga seems to have deliberately chosen the rat to symbolize the ugliness of modern human life. He wants to convey the message that the modern man has been trapped in the mortal world like a rat in a trap and been suffering due to his lack of choice and predicament. He cannot escape from it in spite of his constant effort to do so. Thus, the absurd conflict between man's desire to escape from the bondage and the impossibility of escape assumes universal dimension.

For example, the Climber and the Digger represent two contradictory tendencies found in the human society. The Climber wants to climb the ladder and go up, whereas the Digger wants to dig the earth and go down deeper into the earth. Thus, both of them happen to be ambitious, dreamers, and idealists. But there is a gap between their desires and accomplishment. For example, although the Climber tries repeatedly to climb the ladder, either he slips down because of the slipperiness of the rungs, or because the rungs break down under his weight. He slips down, squirts his legs and keeps on moaning out of pain. Similarly, the Digger tries to dig the pit, but is prevented from doing so because of the rainwater rushing into the pit. Thus, even if their dreams are not fulfilled, they cannot sit idle, but have to continue their efforts, though mechanically.

We may interpret these characters and their action in a variety of ways. For example, the Climber symbolizes the ascent and superhuman or divine element; the Digger symbolizes descent and the subhuman or animalistic instinct. But man, especially the modern man can become neither god nor beast totally, but has to suffer in the in-between state, which is the greatest irony of his life. Since both the characters symbolize the two contradictory tendencies, they are complementary to each other. One may compare them to the characters of Shakespeare's *The Tempest*. Whereas the Climber resembles Ariel, the Digger resembles Caliban. But the conspicuous difference between Shakespeare's play and Chaduranga's is that in the former there is an omniscient and omnipotent character, Prospero, who can reconcile the functions of Ariel and Caliban, but in the latter, there is no such reconciliatory power.

Ilibonu conveys the message of uncertainty of the purpose of human behaviour and the unpredictability of events in life. Similarly, Chaduranga has shown how marriage, like life, has become a bondage. The estrangement between husband and wife is shown by the playwright through the character of the Wife. The Wife comes in search of her husband, the Climber and talks affectionately with him, but he pretends to not to know or recognize her. Here the Climber enacts his dream of escape from the marital bondage and responsibility. As he rejects her openly, she mistakes the other man, the Digger to be her husband. The Wife, here may be taken to be an archetype of a wife, who is in search of a husband. When the Climber rejects her, she requests the Digger to be her husband. This event shows that a wife wants a husband or a woman wants a man, no matter who he is.

But the two men wish to escape from the marital responsibility and the worldly life on the earth. But the Wife acts as *maya* and tries to entangle them in the worldly life. She wants to attract and drag them into the rat-trap of worldly life and take care of them. Just as they see a rat-trap in the real life, they seem to be trapped in that rat-trap on the symbolic level. They are afraid that she may put the garland of flowers prepared by her around their necks. Although she does not put the garland around their necks, they are bound by her symbolically. She offers them *kodubale* (horn-ring) to attract them towards her. Here the *kodubale* by its shape symbolizes the female genitalia, and therefore stands for her sexual magnetism. When she orders them to get up and collect and bring in dry faggots for the oven, they oblige her helplessly.

Thus, they are trapped into the rat-trap completely. Thus, the events as well as the dialogues are absurd on the realistic level, but can be understood on the symbolic level.

***

The absurd dramatists of Europe started writing their plays in the 40s of the twentieth century, reached the peak of success in 1950s and 1960s. They wielded a lot of influence on the younger writer. But by the end of 1960s the absurd movement began to dwindle. Thus, the absurd movement originated within a short time, reached its glory quickly and then disappeared into the traditional drama tradition. But within its short span, it contributed its distinctive vision of life to the world of drama. It taught the playwrights how to dramatize the surprising and shocking inner dreams, fantasies, and nightmares of man and present them on the stage.

The number of absurd dramatists in Kannada is very limited. Even they have either stopped writing such plays or turned their attention to other kinds of drama. The main reason for this negligence is that these absurd plays are meant for the elitist audience. Even the so-called intellectual spectators will read or watch these absurd plays only out of curiosity and not out of deep love for them. Nowadays with the emergence of postmodernist literary movements like *Dalit* (Subaltern) and *Bandaya* (Resistance) Literatures the writers have turned their attention to the portrayal of socio-political issues. In a way the days of the absurd drama are over in Kannada literature. But it should be remembered that the absurd drama added a symbolic and poetic dimension to the Kannada drama and refined the literary taste and sharpened the sensibility of the audience by their freshness and deep and serious reflection about life. Likewise, they have become great challenges to the drama directors and their histrionic talent.

Works Cited

Artraud, Antonin, *The Theatre and Its Double*, New York: Grove Press, 1955.

Arya, *Bayalu Alayadolago*, Dharwad: Manohar Granthamala, 1977.

Beckett, Samuel, *Waiting for Godot,* London: Methuen & Co., 1970.

Brown, John Russell, *Modern British Dramatists*, New Delhi: Prentice Hall of India, 1980.

Brustein, Robert, *The Theatre of Revolt*, Boston, 1965.

Camus, Albert, *The Myth of Sisyphus*, Harmondsworth: Penguin Books, 1942.

Chaduranga, *Ilibonu*, Mysore: Suruchi Prakashan, 1972.

Coe, R.N., *Ionesco*, London: Oliver Boyd, 1961.

Coe, R.N., *Beckett*, London: Oliver Boyd, 1964.

Eliade, Mircea, *Myths, Dreams and Mysteries*, London: Havill, 1960.

Eslin Martin, *The Theatre of the Absurd*, Harmondsworth: Penguin Books, 1961.

Frye, Northrop, *Anatomy of Criticism*, Princeton: Princeton University Press, 1957.

Gascoigne, Bamber, *Twentieth Century Drama*, London: Hutchinson & Co., 1970.

Giraddi, Govindaraj, *Nataka Sahitya mattu Rangabhumi*, Heggodu: Akshara Prakashan, 1989.

Hinchcliffe, Arnold P., *The Absurd*, London: Methuen & Co., 1972.

Kambara, Chandrashekhar. *Nelasampige*, Hampi: Kannada University, 2004.

Karnad, Girish. *Karnadara Samagra Natakagalu*, ed. G.S. Amur, Dharwad: Manohar Granthamala, 2009.

Kurtakoti, Kirtinath, *Asangata Natakagalu*, Dharwad: Karnataka Vidyavardhaka Sangha, 1977.

Kusanur, Chandrakant. *Muru Asangata Natakagalu*, Heggodu: Akshara Prakashan, 1970.

Lankesh, P. *Elu Natakagalu*, Bengaluru: Patrike Prakashan, 1972.

Lankesh, P. *Natakadalli Navyate*, Bengaluru: Bengaluru University, 1972.

Naikar, Basavaraj, *Kannada Asangata Natakagalu*, Gulbarga: Gulbarga University, 1991.

Naikar, Basavaraj, *Asangata*, Bengaluru: Karnataka Sahitya Akademi, 2002.

Nayak, Ha. Ma. and Sindhuvalli A. Eds. *Hosa Samvedaneya Natakagalu*, Mysore: Suruchi Prakashan, 1986.

Macquarrie, John, *Existentialism*, New York: Penguin Books, 1978.

Marulasiddappa, K. *Adhunika Kannada Nataka*, Bengaluru: Ankita Pustaka, 2002.

Patil, Chandrashekhar. *Champa Natakagalu*, Bengaluru: Sankramana Prakashan, 2002.

Ratna, Na. *Gode Beke Gode mattu Bonte*, Dharwad: Manohar Granthamala, 1973.

Taylor, John Russell, *Anger and After*, London: Methuen, 1962.

Tejaswi, Purnachandra. *Yamala Prashne*, Heggodu: Akshara Prakashan, 1964.

Titus, Harold H. *Living Issues in Philosophy*, New Delhi: Eurasia Publishing House, 1968.

• • • • •

24

Symbolic Imagery in *Red Oleanders*

That Rabindranath Tagore's drama is symbolic drama is incontrovertible. Though Tagore's genius was essentially poetic, he could not help employing his poetic methods and devices in non-dramatic form also. Tagore's drama is not an exception to this. Whether Tagore was influenced by the Symbolist Movement of France directly or indirectly is not known for certain. But the fact that he made use of his imagination, i.e. image-making faculty wherever he could, is no doubt accepted by one and all. Though the use of symbols and image is common in poetry, it may encroach upon the dramatic area especially if the writer happens to be a practitioner in a variety of literary forms. Thus, Tagore infused his drama with that poetic symbolism or imagery, which is the special feature of poetry. He achieved his characterization in his plays through symbolic imagery. The use of symbols and images is necessitated either by the inadequacy of the realistic things and characters to convey the writer's vision of life or by the temperament of the writer specially inclined towards this habit or by the desire to sugarcoat the bitter truth of life and moral edification through delight. The use of symbols is very common in the plays of Shakespeare, W.B. Yeats, O'Neill, Arthur Miller, and in the Noh Plays of Japan. What then is a symbol? "A symbol in the broadest sense of the term," says M.H. Abrams, "is anything, which signifies something else." The symbols used by the writer may be personal or private; or they may be natural or artificial; or religious or secular. In spite of the critical recognition of the symbolism of Tagore's drama, no attempt has been made so far to analyze them in detail in the manner in which Miss Caroline Spurgeon has done the Shakespearean imagery. A study of the images of symbols of any writer will no doubt help us to visualize the map of his imagination. An attempt in this direction has been made in the following analysis.

The first symbol that strikes our attention is the setting of the play itself, which serves as a metaphor. The Yaksa Town itself is the symbol of the modern, mechanized civilization encouraging highly bureaucratic and almost dictatorial forms of government, which delights in dehydrating the people. Besides the Yaksa Town, the inhabitants of the kingdom are also symbolic. The characters sometimes oscillate between the symbolic and the allegoric. The king, who is the Head of the Government, is naturally the symbol of the supreme authority. The king happens to be controlled by the negative laws of the Yaksa Town. The king, who is traditionally known as the well-wisher of the subjects, or the guardian of Truth or justice or the human representative of the Absolute is reduced to being self-imprisoned in the jail of his own tyranny. He has to wield his power through the governmental machinery consisting of the hierarchical order of officers like the Governor, the Assistant governor, and the Headman, etc. The king and his political machinery represent the suppressive government but upon the pursuit of material wealth, the inimical group of characters like Nandini, Ranjan, Professor, Kishor, and Bishu among others represent the idealistic philosophy of life. The idealist set of characters has become misfits in the Yaksa Town. Thus, these symbols (sometimes mere allegories) hold mirror to the contemporary Indian society and signify Tagore's dissatisfaction with the mechanical life, which had no place in it for the spiritual values at all.

Apart from the symbolic setting and characters, *Red Oleanders* has many symbolic aspects and references, which throw light upon the issues of not merely contemporary life but the timeless also. They enhance the poetic meaning of the play and make significant contribution to the structure of the play. The play consists of diverse kinds of symbols like the floral, the animal, the aquatic, the geographical, the mythological, the cosmic, the political, the domestic, the human, the natural, and the economic symbols.

The floral imagery is the dominant symbolic imagery as is evidenced by the very title of the play. The symbolism of flowers is variously interpreted by different schools of thought. The traditional school interprets the flowers as the symbols of spiritual happiness. The flower in the religious literature of the West is a very common and popular phenomenon. The flower, which takes the diverse Western forms like rose, jasmine, lily or bluebell, assumes the form of a lotus in India. In our play, the red oleander does the function of the Rose Maiden of the European literature. Like the Rose Maiden, Nandini, the red oleander also acts as an Awakener of the morally and spiritually slumberous. The flower symbolizes Bliss or Ananda for the school of Sri Aurobindo. The other school, i.e. the Freudian school interprets the flower as the symbol of sexuality as it generally resembles the shape and performs function of the procreative organs of the female species. Tagore has employed the floral symbol in the play not in the Freudian sense, but in the traditional sense. Flowers are the symbols of spiritual beauty in the play. That is why Kishor tells Nandini, "I must steel sometime from my digging and digging of nuggets to bring out flowers to you" (p. 1). Of all the flowers, especially red oleanders are the most wanted ones in Yaksa Town, which means that spirituality is very rare in the materialistic society there. Kishor says to Nandini, "You said you *must* have red oleanders. I am glad they're hard to find in this place. Only one tree I discovered after days of search, nearly hidden away behind a rubbish heap" (p. 2). Thus, red oleander acts as symbol and as metaphor at different times. The colour of the oleanders also has some significance. The oleanders are *red* ones. The red colour has different meanings in different contexts. Red may suggest blood, danger, prostitution, etc. But in the play under discussion red colour has the conventional moaning and it, therefore, conveys the spiritual beauty. In fact, it easily reminds us of Burn's "My love is like a reared rose". We may detect the element of danger also in the redness of oleander. Nandini meets her death at the end of the play. It symbolizes the truth that it is dangerous to be beautiful in this world. Till

Professor rightly says, "in that red there is not only beauty but also the fascination of fear" (p. 8). Nandini herself vouches for the beauty of red oleanders. She says, "Ranjan sometimes calls me Red Oleander. I fear that the colour of his love is red,—that red I wear on my breast and on my arms" (p. 9). Another kind of flowers of some significance in the play is *Kunda* flowers, which are white. 'White' may suggest purity, spirituality, simplicity, and cleanliness in different contexts. But white in the present play suggests royalty. That is way Nandini tells the king, "I have brought you a garland of white *Kunda* flowers" (p. 11). Another symbol connected with flowers is, of course, the garland, which signifies the spiritual union of Nandini and Ranjan.

The ecological images also have a place in the play. The image of grapes symbolizes the helplessness of the human beings in Yaksa Town. The king of this region wants to have a pervert enjoyment of the sight of his own destructive action. He says, "Then like a squeezed bunch of grapes with its juice running out from between the gripping fingers if I could but hold you tight with these two hands of mine" (p. 5). Fruits in Yaksa Town, far from being handled elegantly are squeezed and crushed and not enjoyed in the real sense. Naturally, the contextual meaning of fruits happens to be that of objects meant to be wasted rather than to be utilized in the proper sense. Thus, everything in Yaksa Town tends to be misused.

The union of strength and tenderness is shown in an arboreal image. Whereas Ranjan is compared to a big tree, Nandini is compared to a tiny bird inhabiting therein. Nandini tells Bishu about her experience with her lover, "It was as if he were a thousand-year-old banyan tree, and I a tiny little bird when I lit on a branch of his and had my little swing, his needs must have felt a thrill of delight to his very marrow. I loved to give that bit of joy to that lonely soul" (p. 42).

The aquatic images, which are few in number, symbolize the negative tendencies of human beings. The hypocritical tendency of people in power, the sleek and sophisticated appearance hiding the dangerous and beastly nature is symbolized by the crocodile's teeth. Tagore's irony is very clear here. When Chandra wrongly complements the 'niceness' of the authorities like the

Governor, Bishu rightly points out, "Yes, nice and polished like the crocodile's teeth, which fit into one another with so thorough a bite that the king himself can't unlock the jaw, even if he wants to" (p. 29). The misleading quality of hypocrisy of the men in power is revealed in Bishu's words, "Crocodiles teeth begin by smiling and end by biting" (p. 34). The positive nature of love between Nandini and Ranjan is to be seen in another aquatic image of vehicle. Nandini loves Ranjan very deeply and truly. The concordance of the two souls is to be clearly seen in her declaration, "I love Ranjan as the rudder in the water might love the sail in the sky, answering the rhythm of wind in the rhythm of waves" (p. 42).

The geographical or natural images are many in the play and testify to the author's love of Nature. Tagore's poetry contains abundant natural imagery. The river, for example, has the conventional meaning in the play. It symbolizes the union of the opposite qualities of life like beauty and destructiveness. Nandini compares Ranjan to a river.... She says, "My Ranjan's strength is like that of your river, Sankhini,—it can laugh and yet it can break" (p. 6). Another geographical image of a desert is used in the play to denote the destructive imperialism of the Yaksa Town authorities. Thus, possessiveness and destructiveness go hand in hand. The king tells Nandini, "I am parched, I am bare, I am weary. The following thirst of this desert licks up one fertile field after another, only to enlarge itself—it can never annex the life of the frailest of grasses" (p. 16). Far from being the symbol of magnanimity and sublimity the geographical imagery has a negative meaning. The mountain assumes self-destructive quality symbolizing the life-weariness and self-destructiveness of the extreme power embodied in the king. He tells Nandini, "One day, Nandini, in a far off land, I saw a mountain as weary as myself. I could not guess that all its stones were aching inwardly. One night I heard a noise, as if some giant's evil dream had moaned and moaned and suddenly snapped asunder. Next morning I found the mountain had disappeared in the chasm of a yawning earthquake. That made me understand how overgrown power crushes itself inwardly by its own weight" (p. 17).

The animal imagery has the conventional meaning in *Red Oleanders*. Man's inhumanity to man is symbolized by the beast. In Yaksa Town, men want to involve others in danger and see and enjoy the fun instead of feeling pity or compassion. They are thrilled and elated by the sight of others' suffering. Bishu rightly points out, "They have a big beast inside them, that's why the heads are not lowered by the indignity of man, rather the inner brute's tail swells and wags with pride at man's downfall" (p. 77).

The bird imagery is used in the play to denote both positive and negative meanings. Birds usually symbolize the concept of freedom. They are symbolic of transcendental beauty and spiritual freedom in Shakespeare. They act as ambassadors of celestial world. In *Red Oleanders*, birds signify different meanings. The caged-bird is the best symbol of the imprisonment of true freedom. The people of Yaksa Town cannot enjoy even the holidays because they are imprisoned in their kingdom. Phagulal clarifies the difference between the native places of the people and the Yaksa Town, "Freedom itself was enough for the holidays in our village. The caged-bird spends its holidays knocking against the bar. In Yaksa Town holidays are more of nuisances than work" (p. 20). The conditioned nature of the people of Yaksa Town is also symbolized by the caged-bird. Even when they are allowed to go to their native villages, the inhabitants of Yaksa Town rush back to it as they are conditioned by the mechanical life. Bishu points out, "If you go there today you will fly back here tomorrow, like a caged-bird to its cage, hankering for its drugged food" (p. 25). The accidental entrance of people into the Yaksa Town is symbolized by the bird pierced with an arrow. Bishu describes how he was brought into the kingdom, "Just as a bird on the wing is brought to the ground by a chance arrow, so did she bring me down to the dust" (p. 40). This reveals the truth that people have not come here of their accord but are brought in much against their willingness. They have been condemned to stay here and suffer with others. The bird called Blue-throat or *nilakantha* and its feathers are symbols of good omens. They are the heralds of good tidings of Ranjan's arrival. Nandini's faith in the auspicious nature of bird-wings is complete. She says, "Everyday a pair of blue-throats come and sit on the pomegranate tree in front of my window...if a feather from the wings of Blue-throats finds its way into my room, then I will know my Ranjan is coming. This morning, as soon as I woke, I found a feather on my bed.... When I meet him I shall put this feather on his crest" (p. 54). Bird has the spiritual meaning and acts as the vehicle of the glad tidings of the celestial world. Whereas the birds signify positive meanings to Nandini and her group, they hold negative meanings to the king's political machinery. For them birds, instead of symbolizing spirituality, are the signs of negation. The Governor accuses Nandini of having ensnared Bishu by her magic. He was so long content to be quietly burrowing away underground like a worm. "It's you who taught him to spread the wings of death" (p. 74).

The architectural image of chamber is used to symbolize the spiritual secret of life. Speaking of the king's contempt for the scientific approach, the professor says, "He says it only burgles through one wall to reveal another behind it, and never reaches the inner chamber of the Life spirit" (p. 59). Again the image is a romantic and worn out one.

Many are the human images in the play, which are symbolic of the negative values of life in Yaksa Town. The hand, which the king wants to stretch out and clasp Nandini, is terribly frightening. The hand here naturally symbolizes the incompleteness and partialness of principles, which terrify people. Comprehensiveness and right perspective will give man confidence and courage. Unfortunately, Yaksa Town is known for its incomplete and partial philosophy of life, which paralyzes the lives of human beings there. Addiction to liquors, especially wine, is one of the human weaknesses indulged by the people of Yaksa Town. In order to forget their misery and drudgery they are compelled to be addicted to wine. Whereas the men are used to the real wine, the women, as Bishu says: "are endowed with the wine of gold, even worse than their husbands" (p. 35). The human image of babies is employed by the dramatist to symbolize wickedness of the authorities there. Babies, usually, are symbols of innocence, harmlessness, and divinity etc. But in *Red Oleanders* the conventional meaning is reversed and the babies are made to represent the wickedness and crookedness of the powerful fellows. The image of children has Freudian undertones. The Doctor rightly says, "These big men are big babies. They must have plenty of play. When they get tired of one game, if you don't supply them with another, they'll break their toys" (p. 80). The tendency to play with the lives of the helpless is satirized through this image. The mud-and-shoes image is employed to signify the unimaginable servility of the sycophants in Yaksa Town. Nandini cannot help remarking on Phagulal to his face, "so you too admire the Governor, as the mud beneath his feet admires the sales of his shoes" (p. 91).

Though very few, the economic images are predominant in the play as they symbolize the very philosophy of the Yaksa Town, which happens to be callous materialism. The ridiculous exaggeration of the importance of the dead wealth called gold and the unimaginable attachment to that metal is symbolized by the people ever digging the gold nuggets. The dwellers of Yaksa Town want to have and not be gold. They prefer the having mode rather than the being mode. The professor points it out very clearly, "You'll see our tunnel diggers creeping out of the holes like worms, with loads of things of need. In this Yaksa Town all our treasure is of gold, the secret treasure of the dust" (p. 3).

Political images, so inevitable in a political satire, symbolize the negative values of life encouraged directly or indirectly by the bureaucratic government of the Yaksa Town. Net is the most conspicuous image symbolizing the barrier between the ruler and the ruled. The door of the king's palace is blocked with a net, which prevents the subjects from having direct access to him. It also symbolizes the self-imprisonment resultant upon his tyrannical rule. This net becomes a powerful symbol in the play. The king's own door is fixed with a net. Nandini accuses the professor, "You hide your king behind a wall of netting" (p. 4). The professor himself knows, "Nandini too lives behind a network of scholarship" (p. 5). The net tends to be imperialistic. "So the net is spreading farther and farther", and binds everybody inextricably. Net thus holds mirror to the worst form of bureaucracy. The chains are also important political symbols of the curtailment of human freedom. But the ironical fact is that the chains, instead of restricting their life, give them the real, spiritual freedom. Bishu, when imprisoned, declares, "These chains will bear witness to the truth of my freedom" (p. 76). Another important political image is the flag symbolizing the political tyranny of the king. The king, after realizing the futility of power minus human affection decides to put an end to his foolish power by breaking the flagstaff. Not only that, he would join hands with others breaking the prison walls. So the King says, "I too am out for breaking. Behold the first sign—my broken Flagstaff" (p. 99).

Mythological and ritualistic images are many in the play. Most of them naturally happen to be Indian. Essentially, a poet as Tagore is, he cannot help using the mythological references. The sacrificial lamb is one of the dominant ritualistic images, and is used to symbolize the callous selfishness and cruelty of the authorities or officers in Yaksa Town. It also symbolizes the authorities exploiting the helpless by reducing the whole beings to fragments and pieces. Phagulal says, "Our mad Bishu says: to remain whole is useful only for the lamb itself; those who eat it prefer to leave out its horns and hooves, even object to its bleating when butchered" (p. 21). The exploiter's unwillingness to allow the exploited even to articulate their sorrow is beautifully satirized through this ritualistic image. Another mythological image of hell rightly describes the nature of Yaksa Town. Not that the Yaksa Town has no beauty in it, nor that the inhabitants therein have no ability to see that beauty. It is not so much the absence of beauty as the inability to comprehend it that makes the Yaksa Town so horrible. Bishu says, "I know the atmosphere of this place breeds contempt for beauty. There must be beauty even in hell; but nobody there can understand it, that's their cruellest punishment" (p. 23). The helpless victims of the Yaksa Town easily resemble the creatures of Plato's caves or those of Dante's hell. The image of tortoise is another important feature of the Indian mythology. The helpless people, who have to suppress themselves in order that others may attain the conspicuous heights of power, are compared to the tortoise. Gosai's ironical interrogation contains the answer, "Are they not the very incarnation of the sacred Tortoise of our scripture, that held up the sinking earth on its back? Because they meekly suppress themselves underneath their burden, the upper world can keep its head aloft" (p. 31). The dead frog is another mythological image symbolizing the living death of the inhabitants of Yaksa Town. They seem to have learnt the art of meaningless living or existentialistic life from the frog. As the king says, "Once upon a time this frog got into a hole in a stone, and in that shelter it existed for three thousand years. I have learnt from it the secret of continuing to exist, but to live it does not know. Today I felt bored and smashed its shelter. I've thus saved it from existing forever" (p. 47). The men in power frightening the powerless and deriving pleasure out of that is satirized through the mythological image of playacting the role of a demon. Nandini jokes about it to the king, "You seem to take pleasure in seeing people frightened at you. In our village plays Srikantha takes the part of a demon; when he comes on the stage, he is delighted if the children are terrified. You are like him" (p. 50). Nandini uses another mythological image to symbolize the magnanimous strength and beauty of Ranjan. For her Ranjan is "Like a man from the epics—his forehead like the gateway of a tower, his arms like the iron bolts of some inaccessible fortress" (p. 41).

Cosmic images also have a place in the play. The half-ness of things is satirized through the cosmic image. In Yaksa Town, there is neither complete darkness nor complete illumination. It is this half-ness of things, or value-system that confuses the people. The professor explains this properly, "All creatures fear an eclipse. The shadow Demon, who lives in the gold caves, has eaten into it. It is not whole itself, neither does is allow anyone else to remain whole" (p. 8).

In the entire play, there is only one musical image, i.e. that of lyre, a musical instrument. The people of Yaksa Town are the most unmusical fellows and hence the irrelevance of music for them in their business-like life. In the society ruled by materialistic philosophy spiritual things or arts have no value, and would become the butts of ridicule. Nandini, who is an embodiment of beauty and tenderness, becomes a redundant thing like a musical instrument. The professor says, "In this Yaksa Town there are governors, foremen, headmen, tunnel-diggers, scholars like myself, there are policemen, executioners and undertakers—altogether a beautiful assortment. Only *she* is out of element. Midst the clamour of the market place she is a tuned-up lyre" (p. 59).

Thus, the variety of images shows the contrast between the materialistic and spiritualistic values and adds to the poetic beauty of the play.

References

Abrams, M.H. *A Glossary of Literary Terms,* Third Edition, Madras: Macmillan Co. of India, 1979, p. 168.

Desai, S.K. "Symbolism in Tagore's Plays" in *Critical Essays on Indian Writing in English.* Ed. M.K. Naik et al. Madras: Macmillan and Co. of India, 1977, p. 165.

Bayley, Harold, *The Lost Language of Symbolism*, Vol. II. London: William and Norgate, 1952, p. 231.

All the quotations in this article are from of *Red Oleander.* Madras: Macmillan and Co. of India, 1980.

• • • • •

25

Disintegration of the Family in *Halfway House*

Although modern Indian drama is quite rich in various Indian languages, unfortunately very little of it is available in English translation. It is high time for Indian scholars and publishers to turn their attention to the translation of regional drama into English for giving it a pan Indian and even international recognition, which it rightly deserves. Mohan Rakesh, who has been one of the leading figures of the Hindi drama, has tried to hold mirror to the contemporary society of India in many of his plays. *Halfway House* (1999) offers a microscopic picture of the decadence of a middle-class family in a metropolis and shows the transition of values in the changing society of India. Many critics have rightly pointed out the influence of Shaw and the Absurd dramatists on Mohan Rakesh, though it is neither advisable nor possible to quantify the influence. Yet it should be remembered that Mohan Rakesh was so deeply rooted in the Indian soil that the influence of foreign playwrights could have been only peripheral.

It is true that the changing values of life in the Indian society have created many existential problems for man. But there is a conspicuous difference between the European existentialism and the so-called Indian existentialism. The European existentialist predicament was the result of a metaphysical angst caused by the loss of faith in God. The death of God certified by Frederick Nietzsche had created a metaphysical vacuum in Europe in the first part of the twentieth century. But this kind of metaphysical vacuum is not possible in India, which is a land of many religions and philosophies. The existential dilemmas of Indians are mostly social, economic, and moral rather than metaphysical. Therefore, the absurdity of the European kind cannot be expected in the Indian life.

Halfway House may be described as an existential play in the Indian context. It offers a picture of the decadence of a bourgeois family in a metropolis of the twentieth-century India. It shows the disintegration of the institution of marriage and family and hints at the various factors contributing to the negative process. The extended metaphor of the house is built up all through the play. Generally speaking, a house is a place where the blood relatives live together peacefully, homogeneously, and harmoniously. Such a house is indeed heavenly. As Sarvajna, the famous saint-poet of seventeenth-century Karnataka says:

> If you have a cozy house,
> A little gold for expenses,
> And an understanding wife,
> Then set fire to Heaven.
> Sarvajna.

An ideal home consists of economic security, matrimonial harmony and understanding and the unity among the members of the family contributing to the general peace and happiness of life. Your own home will be a Heaven. Sarvajna has described the ideal conditions of a domestic Heaven. By placing Mohan Rakesh's picture of the halfway house against the backdrop of an ideal home suggested by Sarvajna, one may understand how far it conforms to or falls short of the ideal.

Right from the beginning to the end of the play, the picture of the house projected by the dramatist is a negative one. As we proceed with the reading or watching of the play, various aspects of reality begin to show up. The entry of the woman into the house after her return from the office sets the negative tone of the play. Obviously, she returns tired after a long day's work in the office and easily feels irritated to find that the house is not kept clean and tidy, "Whenever I come back, the house is in a mess" (p. 7). The initial dialogues of the first scene itself reveal the difference in the nature of the house. Far from being a patriarchal family, it strikes us as a matriarchal family, the chief reason for which is the economic one. Instead of the man or husband being a breadwinner, there is a woman or wife in the present family, who is the breadwinner. The man or husband being a non-earning member is reduced to a helpless position and is insulted and taken for granted by all the members of the family. Thus, the traditional roles of the father and the mother are reversed here and, therefore, the 'power' of the house is shifted from the father to the mother, thereby converting the family from the patriarchal to the matriarchal system at least partially. The economic factor, i.e. earning the livelihood, which has given a special responsibility and power to the woman, has concurrently reduced the husband to the level of dependence and helplessness. That is why the husband is of no count for the wife. The wife, because of the power of being the breadwinner, asserts herself in the routine matters of domestic life.

She is unhappy with her husband for not having been practical in his business partnership in the past. She complains that he was made to invest some money in a company with his partner Juneja but ultimately put to great loss, though Juneja had his usual profit. Mohan Rakesh indirectly shows the evils of modern business partnerships, uncertainties of profit and the risk involved in the whole system. In a way, Mahendra easily brings to our mind Willy Loman of Arthur Miller's *Death of a Salesman*. Like Loman, Mahendra is a failure in life and undergoes an experience of metaphorical death. That is why he complains that nobody cares for him or respects him in the house and that he is used as a 'mere stamp of respectability.' He says sadly as well as angrily, "I am of no use, of no use at all. I'm only an idler...to be kicked and bullied just as you please. Can anyone tell me why I should stay here?" (p. 26). Thus being an economic non-entity in the family makes him suffer from a feeling of estrangement. "I am responsible for ruining my life, your life, all our lives! And I still stick to this house, because I'm a parasite, because I like living off my wife" (p. 27). He suffers from a sense of constant humiliation in the family. One may easily notice the irony involved in his name. 'Mahendra', which means the Great Lord Indra, the mythical god known for wealth, luxury and glory provides a sharp contrast to Mahendra, who is known for his utter poverty, humiliation, and helplessness.

Poverty dogs the family in many details. For example, the younger girl complains that she has no money to spend on her tiffin, "If I am hungry in school, I've no money to buy anything. And at home it takes hours to heat the milk" (p. 20). Likewise she complains that she does not want to be insulted by her teacher for not taking the skeins of thread to the school, "The same thing happened once again in the needle-work class. Miss said, ...if you don't get me the skeins of thread today either, I won't go to school any more. Miss told me in front of the whole class" (p. 21). The younger girl is thus unhappy with her mother for not providing the necessary comforts and amenities of life. The unhappiness of the girl is obviously because of the overall poverty of the family. The boy quit the college halfway and got a job with Air Freeze Company: But he left his job within six weeks. Now he has been leading a jobless life like his father and is a burden on the family. He buys a tin of cheese mainly because he could buy it on credit and even makes a phone call on credit. Thus, the economic burden of the family is aggravated by the joblessness of two men in the house. That explains why the mother feels the pinch very acutely, "The burden of this house is so great that I need someone to share it with me. I can't manage it alone. Your father lost all our money, and has been idle ever since" (p. 41). It is in order to lighten the economic burden that she invites her boss Singhania to her house and requests him to help her son to get a suitable job. Thus, the entire family is paralyzed by the economic deficiency and consequently converted into a metaphorical 'hell'.

The economic factor has indirectly given rise to other problems in the family. Unlike the traditional housewife, who is confined to her home and is obedient to her husband, Savitri is educated as well as employed. The position of a working-woman has given her the right to assert herself. Being a new woman and a city-bird, she wants to have sexual freedom not enjoyed by the traditional Hindu wife. Although she invites her boss Singhania to her house under the pretext of requesting him for a job for her son, her behaviour is not approved by her husband or by her son.

The boy does not want to get a job through the mother's boss, "I don't want a job. Not through that fellow anyway" (p. 28). He dislikes Singhania for various reasons. Among the mentionable reasons two can be seen. The boy dislikes him because "he doesn't even have the sense to button up his trousers after.... If he hadn't been your boss, I would have booted him out that day. Lolling on the sofa and scratching himself in the groin! His thoughts stray in one direction, his eyes in another, and I'm supposed to guess that he's addressing me" (p. 29).

Like a modern liberated woman, Savitri does not believe in the sanctity of chastity. Her sexual promiscuity is combined with her ambition. She is deeply interested in material comforts, status, position, and wealth. That is why she has had four lovers in the past. She always felt a great temperamental incompatibility with her husband and therefore sought the company of other men like Juneja, Shivjeet, Manoj and finally Jagmohan. Juneja narrates the history of Savitri's extra-marital life very clearly, "... it was obvious even then that you didn't consider Mahendra to be the man with whom you could spend your life...every year you've tried to free yourself by looking around for another man! In the beginning I was one of these men.... After me, you were enamoured of Shivjeet...his university degree, his trips abroad, or whatever. In reality he interested you only because...he was not Mahendra.... Then you met Jagmohan, you admired him for his excellent contacts, his smart way of life, his generosity" (p. 73). But in spite of having these love affairs, Savitri was never happy with anyone of them nor did she stick to anyone of them. Savitri was indeed shocked when her own lover Manoj married her daughter Binni. Her affair with different men is strongly resented by Mahendra and her son. So far she has not shown the courage to elope with anyone of her lovers. But now that Jagmohan, her last lover, has come back to Delhi, she wants to go away with him for good. The son, who is fed up with her oscillation between marital and extra-marital loyalties, wants it to be decided once for all, "High time the situation changed!... I want the whole business to be decided one way or the other" (pp. 45-46). But the problem is not to be solved so easily, because of the complex nature of life itself. When Savitri goes out with Jagmohan and desperately requests him to accept her as a life-partner, he refuses to do so. Thus, her route of escape from the matrimonial hell is mercilessly blocked by her fate. She is condemned to continue her life in the matrimonial hell much against her wishes. The frustration is caused by the sense of incompleteness of her husband. Like her husband, she also provides a sharp contrast to the mythical Savitri, who wanted to save her husband from the clutches of death. Unlike the mythical figure, Savitri constantly quarrels with and complains against her husband.

Whereas Savitri has suffered for not taking a drastic step in her extra-marital affairs, her older daughter Binni has been suffering for taking a very drastic step in eloping with Manoj, the lover of her own mother, thereby aggravating the suffering of the mother. In spite of her marrying a man of her choice, she has not been able to live happily with him. Unable to live with him any longer, she has returned to the parental home, thereby adding to the anxiety and liability of the family. Thus, both the mother and the older daughter provide two extremes of sexuality but share in the suffering qualitatively.

Sexual curiosity or obsession seems to be an important ingredient in the make-up of the young people in the family perhaps because of the wrong role models provided by the mother and the older daughter. This aspect of the family holds mirror to the slackening of Hindu morality in the changing urban society of India. If the elders indulge in sexuality openly, the younger ones do so secretly or vicariously. For example, Kinni reads the Memoirs of Cassanova on the sly by stealing it from her elder brother. Likewise, she is interested in discussing with her friends the sex-life of others' parents. Similarly, the son has been courting a girl called Varna, working at the Udyog Centre. Besides the economic and sexual problems, the temperamental differences among the members of the family also aggravate the unhappiness of the family. Savitri, for example, is a very ambitious woman, who wants her husband to be strong in mind and body, successful in his business, earn a lot of money for the family and be a glamorous person. She, therefore, complains that Mahendra has no personality or strength of character or self-confidence. She explains it to Juneja, "Let me tell you about the reality I know. Why does one get married? In order to fulfill a need,...an inner... void, if you like; to be self-sufficient...complete. But that's not why Mahendra got married! The object of his existence is...as if...he were there only to fill in the gaps in the lives of others" (p. 69). But when she is disappointed with him, she tries to seek those things in her lovers. But even there, she has not been able to have lasting relationship because of the uncertainties and contingencies of middle-class life. She has a bit of Lady Macbeth's ambition in her, but like a Lawrentian heroine she goes on searching for perfect matrimonial happiness, but gets frustrated at every step. She is not able to solve the problems of her life because of her ambition and desire for pomp and glory and by refusing to accept the contingencies of life with a sense of yogic resignation. Far from accepting her fate and making the best of the reality of her life, she pines for what is not. When she cannot escape from the bondage of matrimony and family, she suffers from a sense of being trapped in it. The Hindu philosophy teaches the great lesson that when the objective world cannot be changed; one has to make one's own life meaningful only through subjective change and sublimation of feelings. Savitri is obviously incapable of such adjustment of life, because of her complaining temperament. The objects of her complaint may change, but the complaints remain the same. It is the negative approach of Savitri, which is pointed out by Juneja, "Whether you were a child or not, you used to speak in the same way you do now. That day you pulled Mahendra to bits you said he was a wimp, had no backbone.... But the names of the people who had made him so were different then. You put the blame on his parents" (p. 72). Juneja further analyses her mind very clearly, "The point is that if any of these men had been a part of your life instead of Mahendra, you would still have felt that you had married the wrong man. You would still have encountered a Mahendra, a Juneja, a Shivjeet or a Jagamohan and thought and reacted in the same way. Because the meaning of life to you is how many different things you can have and enjoy at the same time. One man alone could never have given them to you, so no matter whom you married, you would always have felt as empty and as restless as you do today" (p. 74). Savitri's search for completeness or over-ambition is comic as well as tragic at the same time. She feels angry and helpless at the same time and has no courage either to have sublimated reconciliation with her fate or to snap her relationship with the family. She, therefore, remains an embodiment of frustration.

The same temperamental hauteur can be seen in her older daughter Binni also. But there is a slight difference between their modes of action. Whereas Savitri has a Hamletizing tendency, Binni has a Macbethizing tendency. Binni has been bolder than her mother in taking quick and hasty decisions and suffers as a consequence. After having married Manoj, lover of her mother, she has come back to her parents, as she could not get on well with her husband due to temperamental incompatibility and Catherine-like defiance. As she herself explains it. "He speaks with such assurance that...that I start...I start despising myself. I feel like...like smashing everything around me. Like defying him in a way that would...enrage him. He likes my hair long, so I want it cut He doesn't like me to work, so I want to have a job. Anything to torment him! But I can't do it. And when I realize this, I feel so crushed that...I cut myself off from him for days on end" (p. 19). But in spite of being bolder than her mother, Binni suffers from the feeling of being trapped in the mechanical repetition of the pattern of frustration. "But then, slowly, we start treading the same weary path. Everything happens in the same way…until we reach the same abyss once again" (p. 19). Binni, like her mother, is trapped in the emotional hell of the family. The cause of Binni's frustration and estrangement is to be sought in the subjective world rather than in the objective world. "What reason? A cup of tea spilt from his hand or a short delay when he returns from work? These little things are not really reasons; they become reasons. A strange sort of feeling mounts up within me and spreads like poison through my whole being. Everything I touch or see or hear becomes distorted and I stand helpless and fearful under the spell of a destructive fate. But Mama, I don't know why...I just can't see why! It happens unasked, unforeseen. It...it...tortures me till I think I'm going mad. And in the end? In the end he too turns against me and says...that...it is from the house I have taken something with me which prevents me from being natural" (pp. 17-18). Binni, like her mother, puts the blame on the house or on others in the moments of anger. But the cause of their anguish is rooted in themselves, in their temperament although they are not able to understand it.

Like the older girl, the younger girl is also adamant and defiant in nature and, therefore, adds to the irritability of the domestic atmosphere. Kinni is very cheeky and argues with elders disrespectfully. She complains about her loneliness in the house after her return from school when nobody is there to talk with her. When her mother asks her as to why she tore the book, she answers disrespectfully, "It got torn. What can I do? The same thing happened again in the needle-work class" (p. 21). When the mother suggests that they can talk about it later on, she retorts, "You're always telling me to talk later on" (p. 21). When the mother talks disdainfully about her and her Miss, she snaps, "Then why don't you take me out of school? I could also loaf around all day like Shoki" (p. 21). Instead of addressing her elder brother as Ashok, she calls him Shoki. That is why the older girl complains about her, "Mama, you really have turned her into a cheeky little brat!" (p. 21). She refuses to go to school on some pretext or the other and reports the secrets of Ashok to the parents. Similarly, she has a habit of scandal-mongering and discussing the sexual matters with her friends like Surekha thereby earning the wrath of their parents. She starts crying when people do not oblige her. When somebody calls her a child affectionately, she retorts, "Yes...I'm a big girl. Sometimes I'm told I am a child...sometimes a big girl" (p. 61). She calls her older sister and other members of the family "lumps of clay" and exhibits her mannerlessness and hysterical behaviour. She is, therefore, slapped by the mother and locked in a room. But she also bolts the door from inside to rebel against the mother. Kinni is thus a typical representative of adamant and cheeky girls, who are uncontrollable and who aggravate the tension in the family and make the domestic hell more intolerable than it normally is.

Mahendra also suffers partially due to his peculiar temperament. Though once upon a time he was a successful business partner, now he has fallen on bad days due to the cut-throat competition in the commercial world. The present economic poverty has reduced him to the level of a nonentity and affected his mind and heart adversely. He feels hurt to notice that he commands no respect from anybody in the family, especially his wife, who questions his very manhood, "For how many years have I been bearing the burden of life? And for how many years have I been looking after this family? And despite that, what have I come to...that everyone answers me back, is rude, disrespectful, and impertinent. What is my status in this house? Silent acceptance, perpetual snubs, constant insults, is that all I deserve after so many years?" (pp. 25-26). He is unhappy to know that he is regarded "only as a stamp of respectability, to be used when the need arises" (p. 26). It is true that economic poverty has reduced him to a non-entity, but he has no strength of the soul to face the situation boldly. He suffers from inferiority complex, self-pity, and self-accusation, "I am of no use, of no use at all. I'm only an idler...to be kicked and bullied just as you please. Can anyone tell me why I should stay here?...I'm responsible for ruining my life, your life, all our lives. And I still stick to this house, because I'm a parasite, because I like living off my wife, because...I know I'm like dry rot in this house, eating away at its very foundations" (pp. 26-27).

Mahendra is a failure as a husband not only because he is not the breadwinner now, but also because of his psychological dependence on others. He is incapable of taking independent decisions about life and seeks help and guidance from others. Savitri complains, "Ever since I've known, I've always found him leaning on someone or other. Particularly on you. He's never been able to do anything without asking you. If we want to buy something, he must ask you. When he wanted to marry me, he had to ask you. He can't even breathe without asking you.... And what has been the result? That he's never had any confidence in himself! The test for everything in his life has been you. Whatever you think, want, do, he too must think, want and do. Why? Because you are a man. And he? He's not even half a man!" (pp. 68-69). Mahendra seems to have neglected his own family in his eagerness to make his friends happy. This is indeed a very grave deficiency in any householder. Savitri is right when she complains about it to Juneja, "His friends need him to pass their own leisure hours. No party is fun without Mahendra. His main job is to keep his friends happy. And not only is it his main job, but it should also be the only concern of his family" (p. 70).

Although Mahendra has been a very meek husband now, he had been very dominating and cruel to his wife in the past. Savitri sees a contradiction in his admirable public behaviour and his private cruel behaviour. She complains, "That same Mahendra, who smiles meekly among his friends, becomes a fiend when he comes home. One never knows when he may scratch one's eyes out or drink one's life-blood. One day he makes a bonfire of his clothes in anger. Another day he sits on my chest and bangs my head against the floor" (p. 71). It is on account of his extremities and contradictions that he is disdained by his wife.

Another feature of his personality is his helplessness in dealing with his wife's extramarital affairs. Although like any husband with self-respect he dislikes his wife's lovers, he does not have the courage to oppose them openly or the generosity to ignore them. On the contrary, he talks only ironically about them and indulges in self-pity. Similarly, he has neither the patience to stay with the family nor the courage to go away from there. When he goes away from the house in a fit of anger and stays with Juneja, he comes back again to his house because he says he loves his wife in spite of temperamental clashes. Because of his eccentricities, he creates a psychological hell for himself as well as for others.

Mahendra's son has also been an extension of his personality. The son, like his father, has been a failure in his education and job. He is not serious about anything in life. He has no clearly defined goal or desire for any achievement. As his mother complains against him, he is "only interested in three things... in sleeping all day, in cutting out those pictures and...taking out things from home" (p. 30). Otherwise he will loaf around in the city or chase a girl or read pornographic books. Although his mother seriously tries to help him by getting him a job through the influence of her boss, he does not understand her motherly concern for him. On the contrary, he puts embarrassing questions to his mother about the boss. He does not want to get a job through the influence of Singhania. Further, he draws a cartoon of Singhania and makes fun of him after the latter's departure from their home. Like his father, he is useless. He does not understand the sacrifices made by his mother for the family. Although he himself is a useless boy, he questions everybody in the house about his or her past and present actions. Through his cheekiness and comic approach, he aggravates the atmosphere of the multi-dimensional hell called their family.

Thus, all the five members of the family suffer from economic, sexual, and temperamental problems and undergo the experience of hell caused by incompleteness, fragmentation and the resultant frustration. The tension between the desire to escape and the inevitable bondage to harsh reality continues in a repetitive circle. All the members of the family are disoriented from one another for various reasons, but seem to be trapped in the prison of the house. *Halfway House*, thus, presents the predicament of the modern man in the Indian context and offers a picture of a family on the brink of disintegration. Although existentialistic dilemma and the human predicament form the theme of the play, the theme itself cannot be described as absurd. On the contrary, it is the technique of the play, which has certain elements of the Absurd drama. Even the dialogues are quite logical and sensible in their style. There is nothing mysterious or inexplicable about the problematic of the play. That there is no harmony or alignment of interests and goals among the members of the family or that they have no freedom of choice is clear enough.

The Absurdist technique of *Halfway House* may be seen in its static nature. The principle of indirection seems to be the dominant technical feature of the play. For example, there is very little direct physical action in the play whereas the indirect action is comparatively more. The characters constantly refer to the past to understand the cause of their frustration in the present. In other words, the present seems to be haunted by the ghost of the past. There is more talking than doing in the present. The principle of indirection may be seen in the revelation of characters' hidden motives also. This is an epistemological problem in the play. Almost all characters in the play do not reveal their nature *through* their actions, but are revealed or interpreted by others. Mahendra is interpreted or explained by Savitri. Binni is explained by Savitri and by the boy. Kinni is explained by the boy and vice versa. Mahendra and Savitri are explained by Juneja. Many times these explanations or interpretations are exaggerated or negativized on account of their own subjective prejudices and eccentricities. Everyone explains the other from his/her own point of view and never has the willingness or imagination to interpret the other from the other's point of view. Thus, they come out with half-truths and are incapable of arriving at the whole truth.

Reference

Rakesh, Mohan, *Halfway House*, Tr. Bindu Batra, Ed. Dilip K. Basu, Delhi: Worldview Publication, 1999. (All the references to the text are from this edition.)

• • • • •

26

Existential Vision in *Evam Indrajit*

Badal Sircar (1925-2011) has been accepted as one of the important playwrights of India. A Civil Engineer and Town Planner by profession, he has enriched the Indian drama with many of his Bangla plays like *Baki Itihas* (*Remaining History*, 1965), *Pralap* (*Delirium*, 1966), *Tringha Shatabdi* (*Thirtieth Century*, 1966), *Pagla Ghora* (*Mad Horse*, 1967), *Evam Indrajit* (*And Indrajit*, 1968), and *Shesh Nei* (*There's No End*, 1969) dealing with contemporary Indian themes. In addition to being a playwright, Badal Sircar was also a producer, who formed his group "Shatabdi" and produced a number of plays—including some of his own and those adopted from other languages. Initially, he produced his plays on proscenium stages, but later gave it up and resorted to angamancha (theatre in the round). "His concern was the pointlessness of existence, compounded by a sense of associative guilt and responsibility in maladjusted persons belonging to the urban middle class in a world of increasing violence and inhumanity."[1] Most of his plays have been translated into many Indian and foreign languages and staged successfully. "With the performance of Sircar's *Evam Indrajit* in Bengali in Calcutta in September 1965, theatre practitioners all over India became aware of a major talent and a major play. The play provided for them the shock of recognition. It was about the Indian reality as they knew it; it was a theatrically effective and crystallised projection of all the prevalent attitudes, vague feelings and undefined frustrations gnawing at the hearts of the educated urban middle class."[2] "In Bengal, the contradiction was resolved at a certain level with the middle classes aligning themselves with the left forces. In other parts of the country, the best elements in the middle classes were opting for the armed forces or the administrative services. Evam Indrajit is in some ways about the residue; the residue consists of those who have failed to adjust, align and ceased to aspire and also those who are enmeshed in the day to day struggle for survival" (p. iv).[3]

Since the playwright wants to highlight the existential dilemmas of the middle class youth of Bengal, he has created four characters like Amal, Vimal, Kamal, and Nirmal, who are not far different from one another. The setting is, of course, Bengal, although the exact city is not mentioned by the playwright. Although the action of the play is deceptively realistic in bits, the organisation of this action is not realistic but romantic, philosophical, arbitrary and defies the law of probability. The life of Amal, Vimal, Kamal, and Nirmal lived by them is not only represented by the playwright but is also commented upon by the Writer, the mouth piece of the dramatist. Thus, there is an alternation of participation and observation and/or interaction all through the play. Badal Sircar has given a meta-dramatic dimension to Evam Indrajit by introducing the character of a Writer, who wants to write a play about the life of the educated urban middle class people, but who finds it rather difficult to do so on account of his own poverty of experience and the emptiness of the lives of his characters. The Writer is, obviously, the mouthpiece of Badal Sircar himself, through whose perspective the life of the four characters is viewed. The action of the play does not conform to the law of probability and hence not convincing on the empirical level. Since Badal Sircar is deeply influenced by the existential philosophy and the Absurd Theatre of the West, he has tried to superimpose it on the Indian, especially Bengali life—not the whole of it, but a small chunk of it. This superimposition of a Western philosophy born out of the human predicament in the European contest on a small chunk of Bengali society appears to be quite absurd. Whereas the existential predicament of the European man is caused by the disturbing objective events like world wars destroying the human faith in the metaphysical centre, i.e. God, the existential predicament seen in the life of four characters like Amal, Vimal, Kamal, and Nirmal appears to be more subjective or self-made than objective. Hence, it appears to be rather arbitrary and unconvincing than culturally feasible and acceptable.

Badal Sircar has chosen to portray three phases of human life—student life, employment, and married life, which are equivalent to the first two stages of Hindu life, i.e. bachelorhood (*brahmacharya*) and householder's life (*grihasthashrama*). The picture does not cover the third and the fourth stages of forest-dwelling (*vanaprastha*) and ascetic life (*sanyasa*). Thus, only the first two stages of human life are presented through the direct action of the play. But the Writer within the play lets his philosophical imagination a free play to embrace the whole of life (implying all the four stages of life) which forms part of the ideological dimension of the play. It may be said that all action in the play is seen through the Writer's reflection. Thus, the action of the characters is framed within the philosophical reflection of the Writer. Hence, the action of the play, which violates the law of probability, runs on the axis of existential philosophy of the Western kind. What is very surprising is the fact that neither the Writer nor the characters show any acquaintance with Hindu philosophy, although all of them happen to be Hindus. The betrayal of utter ignorance of Hindu philosophy and the flaunting of the Western existential philosophy is indeed tantamount to absurdity. Whereas absurdity is tolerable, the absurdity of absurdity is very intolerable. But once this basic problem is recognised and conveniently ignored in line with Coleridge's 'willing suspension of disbelief' the play may be understood and interpreted in a coherent manner.

The play opens meta-dramatically with the Writer, who is obsessed with a desire to write a good play. He is not bothered even about his food. But ironically enough, in spite of his high seriousness of intention, he is not able to produce a substantial or significant play due to his poverty of experience. "What shall I write? Who shall I write about? How many people do I know? And what do I know about them?" (p. 3). The Writer is indeed caught in a paradoxical situation. He cannot write about the suffering masses, as he has no first-hand experience about them. But the people around him whom he knows quite well do not provide solid and eventful material for his play. “I’ve written many plays. I want to write many more. But…I know nothing about the suffering masses. Nothing about the toiling peasants. Nothing about the sweating coal-miners. Nothing about the snake charmers, the tribal chieftains or the boatmen. There is no beauty in the people around me, no splendour, no substance. Only the undramatic material—Amal, Vimal, Kamal and Indrajit” (p. 8). The names of characters like Amal, Vimal, Kamal, and Nirmal (Indrajit) sound alike. The phonetic similarity of these names indicates that lack of distinctive qualities in them and shows their ordinariness. They are like any Tom, Dick, and Harry. The playwright presents the school life of these four characters and enables the Writer to make his observations about it. Amal, Vimal, Kamal, and Indrajit attend the classes in the school mechanically and learn the rudiments of Physics, Poetry, and Prose. But they cannot understand the subjects wholly. Their juvenile interest is confined to certain popular things like cricket, film, physics, politics, and literature. But they are not deeply interested in their education. They are tired of the student life and want to escape somewhere. As Indrajit confesses to the Writer, “I’m tired of being a student” (p. 10). He does not know what to do because he has no clear goal and direction in life. He says, “I don’t know. Sometimes I just want to run away.... Some place, you know, somewhere far away…outside—beyond” (p. 10). Although they are not deeply interested in the educational process, they have to face the examination rather mechanically. The Writer feels that their life is “totally undramatic. You can’t make a play out of these people. It isn’t possible” (p. 12). He articulates the mechanicality of their life in a song made of cardinal numbers:

One – two – three
One – two – three – two – one – two – three
One – two – three – two – one – two – three
Four – five – six
Four – five – six – five – five – four – five – six
Four – five – six – five – four – five – six
Seven – eight – nine

Seven – eight – nine – eight – seven – eight – nine
Seven – eight – nine – eight – seven – eight – nine. (p. 11)

The four young men going to school, attending classes and taking examinations mechanically is symbolised by the Writer's numerical song.

The Writer observes the college life of Indrajit and others. After the learning is over, they have to take their examination. After the examination, they have to go in search of jobs for their livelihood. The process is repeated in a cyclic fashion. The Writer, therefore, articulates his view pontifically, "One – two – three! Amal, Vimal, Kamal. And Indrajit. And Manasi. From home to school. From school to college. From college to the world. They are growing up. They are going round. Round and round and round. One – two – three – two – one. Amal, Vimal, Kamal, and Indrajit" (p. 19). The Writer sees some connection between the daily round of human life and the cosmic cyclicity, "The sun, which rises every morning rose today as usual, and he is now setting. And in that corner, there between the branches, is the orange moon" (p. 20). The sunrise followed by sunset and the moonrise followed by moonset, obviously, indicates the mechanical rhythm of cosmic life providing a parallel to the mechanical roundedness of human life.

Then the Writer decides to write an interesting play about the love affair between Indrajit and Manasi as he considers it to be an 'immortal dramatic theme…' (p. 16). He observes their life and even talks to Indrajit and is rather disappointed to learn that Indrajit hates the rules of the society and wants to marry his cousin Manasi, although it is not permitted by the society as it is tantamount to incest. Indrajit hates the rules of the society that make a widow like Leela suffer at the hands of her parents-in-law and a seven year boy earn his living by polishing shoes. He wants to escape from the restriction of rules. He tells Manasi that he wants to "Bring down all these walls, which surround us" (p. 21). The Writer makes his observations like an existential philosopher, "Indrajit and Manasi. They've come a long way. A long way? Have they really come? Or they just going round and round? Round and round? They can get married. Again the same round again. They may not get married. Again the same round. One – two – three – four – three – two – one. It's all a question of going round and round. The answer is a circle – a zero. That's why no one asks the whole question. They cut it to suit their size. The answer they get is—life. A different sort of life for each man" (p. 25). Having pointed out the mechanicality and roundedness of life, the Writer advises the characters to make their life meaningful by escaping from the circle and living the present life and by experiencing the eternity in the present moment. "One moment, one single moment. Deny that circle. Deny that going round and round. Deny the whole question. One moment, one moment in the present. Life. And let's not add this life in other lives. For that will lead us to the whole problem again—resulting in a zero. Let us save this life. Let us save this one moment in the present—that is life" (p. 26).

The Writer observes that all the four characters go through the round of life by trying hard to get some jobs after completing their graduation. They attend the interviews, which are simply absurd and farcical. The Writer makes his philosophical observation, "Amal retires. His son Amal takes up a job. Vimal is ill. His son Vimal takes up a job. Kamal is dead. His son Kamal takes up a job. And Indrajit. And Indrajit's son Indrajit. There on the pavement is a seven-year-old boy with a box in his hand and a baby in his arms. There—on the pavement near him is a woman. Her name is Leela. Her husband died of TB. Beyond there is an orange sky under which Manasi wants to love life. Life. So many loves. So many parts and bits and parcels and pieces and molecules and atoms and they mix and mingle and move and turn and go round and round till they become a giant ferries wheel. And I have to write about them. I have to put into language the drama of these atoms going round and round. But language is senile and words are battered and maimed" (p. 28). The Writer not only points out the mechanical cyclicity of life (of the four characters), but also expresses his own difficulty in writing a play about their mechanical life. The Writer cannot be said to be totally pessimistic. In spite of the mechanical aspect of life and the fragmented nature of human self, the Writer believes in the possibility of making life beautiful and meaningful. "I am divided. I am broken into pieces, into atoms. I'm a symphony composed of atoms" (p. 29). He desires to overcome his fragmentation and achieve unity of life by becoming a symphony of atoms. His deep-seated affirmative view of life and optimistic note is articulated in his song:

> The earth is crushed, but it's still alive
> The century's old, but it listens still,
> All lights go off,
> A whisper in chorus in the dark. (p. 29)

The human life may be defeated but it is not destroyed as it is still alive. The twentieth century life may be old, but still it listens to man's voice. In spite of the overwhelming darkness, man may hear an assuring whisper. As this song bears out, life is not as empty and meaningless as the people (Amal, Vimal, Kamal, and Nirmal) think.

The second act shows the mechanical round of the office work. The Writer comments, "From home to school. From school to college. From college to the world. The world is an office. Like this one. A lot of business is transacted here—very important business. A lot of people work here—Amal, Vimal, Kamal and Indrajit" (p. 30). Now the three characters have finished their graduation and become employees in offices and parents at home. The office life is again characterised by mechanical repetition of certain acts like hurrying to the office, ordering the peon to get some tea, keeping files, dictating letters, getting the boss's signature, etc. The Writer, who observes their office life comments on it, "After the files, tea. The files. Then snacks. Then files. Then tea. Then files. Then train—bus—train" (p. 32). The four characters are not able to think seriously about life. But the Writer is free enough to think about the fragmentation of his self and his desire for the attainment of wholeness. His quest for wholeness may be seen in his cogitation, "I sit with the part and think of the whole. I sit in the dust and think of the earth. And I screen the dust that is the earth that is crushed. Why? Are the seeds of life mixed with the dust? But the earth is crushed, the sky is barren and the century nods in senile stupor. But I still sit and think. I still think of Man, the whole Man and the fragments of my consciousness are still searching—searching for something else" (p. 34).

The Writer thinks philosophically and expresses it poetically. But his philosophical level does not match his Auntie's mundane and practical level. She cannot understand his deeper. Disturbing questions and crisis of identity. When he asks her, "I am wondering…who are we?" (p. 34), she answers in a very casual way. "What's there to think so much about in that? You are you. Who else?" (p. 34). When he asks her, "But what are we?" she answers very sleekly, "You are all bright pieces of gems, that's what you are. You've got good degrees, good jobs!" (p. 34). But when he asks the third and most difficult question, "Why are we? I mean why are we here? She tries to silence him with her practical answer, "Oh, shut up. Why shouldn't you be here? You haven't done any harm to anyone, have you?" (p. 35). She considers his questions as simply stupid. The Writer is awakened to the deeper metaphysical questions about his identity, the purpose of his life and his role in and relevance to the cosmos. Such fundamental questions form the core of all religions and philosophies of the world—not excluding the *Vedantic* one. But the Auntie, who lives on the practical level ignores his disturbing questions as stupid and suggests a very practical solution, "Why don't you get married? Why shouldn't you? Everyone get married. Why shouldn't you?" (p. 35). She opines that "You should be all right if you get married" (p. 36). The Writer again pontificates, "Yes! Marriage! Birth, marriage and death. But, then marriage and then death" (p. 36). He again notices the cyclicity of human life. In marriage also he sees a cyclic pattern—first bride and bridegroom, then husband and wife; then father and mother—in the lives of Amal, Vimal, and Kamal. Indrajit is the only exception to this pattern. He could not marry Manasi as she did not want to violate the norms of the society by committing incest. Indrajit talks with Manasi like a philosopher. Although the earth and the human life on it appears to be very insignificant in the vast solar system, yet he believes in the value of his life. "But there are times when I think life is vast. When I forget how ephemeral my life is in the total flow of time—a mere second. I forget that my existence is a pointless particle of dust. I start believing that nothing is more valuable than my life in the world" (p. 41). Manasi, who has a lot of gusto for life, believes in making the most of it. "I may be a germ, but still I seek, seek without shame. The audacious assertion of life claims immortality in its brief spark" (p. 41).

The humdrum life of the characters continues. Amal is frustrated in his job. "I'm working in this rotten ABC Company. I've wasted my life there. Six years as the Senior Assistant. Yet they have taken a Madrasee Babu as the Assistant Manager.... This is the day of the Madrasees. We Bengalis will die at the hands of other Bengalis.... I'm fed up with life" (p. 42). Vimal is transferred to Ranchi. He has sent his son to La Martiniere School. He is muddling along. Kamal is so busy with the problems of his life that he has given up his hobbies like playing the mouth organ. He is involved in a business deal and Insurance agency. Indrajit wants to go abroad, especially London and try for a job. He feels that there is no improvement in his life. He has realised the futility of arguments and feels tired. "I just feel tired—exhausted. I just do what I feel like doing at the moment" (p. 45). The Writer speaks for the experiences of the four characters when he sings:

I am tired—I am very tired.
Let all these rapid questions be.
Let all these rapid questions be.
In the mute enveloping darkness let me just go to sleep.
What's the use of all these words?
Why fling arguments in the wild winds?
I am sick of reasoning now...
I am very tired. (p. 45)

The life-weariness felt by the characters is part of the existential predicament of the Western or European Man. Badal Sircar's perception of life seems to be deeply influenced by the Western existential philosophy untouched by the Indian philosophy, although the locale is very much Indian.

In the third act, Amal, Vimal, and Kamal play cards and discuss their frustrations. Amal is unhappy about his inability to get a promotion and his family illness. Vimal is unhappy about the terrible condition of his living quarters and his son's failure in the examination. Kamal is unhappy about his business, which is bad and about the death of his father. They have received a letter from Indrajit from London that he has completed his degree successfully. They think that foreign degrees have great value in India. The Writer makes his philosophical observation about the existential cyclicity, the tragedy of knowing and the inevitability of dreaming. "Calcutta, Bhopal, Bombay, Jullunder, Meerut, Udaipur, Calcutta, London. Everything goes round and round like a wheel. Still it's not a proper wheel, it's a spiral. And that precisely is the tragedy—the tragedy of knowing. I catch something. And just when I understand it, it suddenly ends and I throw it away. Then again I grab at something else. Still the hope for a sudden, unexpected, wonderful happening doesn't die. One continues to feel that this isn't all. Sometime something must happen to fill the world with a dazzling light, throwing the past into obscurity. What a silly dream. The sleep ends—but not the hangover of the dream" (p. 48). The Writer feels that nothing exciting happens in life. The boredom of life is articulated by Indrajit, "Whatever I wished to have, I have got. But there is no sense of achievement—that is the bitter truth" (p. 49). Being disillusioned and bored with life, Indrajit wants to find happiness in death. "Dying! That is the greatest happiness" (p. 49). He has also realised the truth that he has no faith in life, which is essential for the attainment of happiness. "One needs faith to live. Faith in God, faith in fortune, faith in man, faith in work, faith in revolution, faith in oneself—faith in love. Tell me which of them is alive in me today?" (p. 49). He further confesses that he being one among a million, his life is a lie and a farce. He does not want any false consolation and blindfold of faith. His life is marked by bleakness and boredom:

> Keeping afloat
> Clutching at a piece of straw
> Life resting on a wretched faith
> Of a believer.
> The land is blurred
> In a grey mist of sighs,
> The bright realms beyond the clouds
> Are lost in lies
> In this love sojourn.

So take away the crutches
Of false consolation!
Take away the blindfold of faith
From the eyes!
Get drowned!
Go under and see
How far is the bottom!
How deep!
Man moves;
Man is the strangest of creatures.
He builds his house on the rocks
In the depth of the seas. (p. 50)

Indrajit's song shows that he wants to face the naked reality of life with all its challenges and insecurity.

Indrajit has now returned from London to Calcutta thereby completing the circle. Having begun his journey from Calcutta, he ends it by returning to the starting point. He has married not his cousin Manasi, but another woman, who is also called Manasi. One may understand that Manasi is an equivalent of *maya* or the female principle. Man needs to marry some woman or the other no matter who she is or what her name happens to be. All women are Manasis for the playwright. Having married a different Manasi (which is a necessity) Indrajit does not feel any excitement about it. "My wife looks after the house. I work in the office. My wife goes to a film. I go with her. My wife goes to her parents' house. I eat in a restaurant. She comes back. I go marketing" (p. 54). His humdrum life proves to him the principle of repetition of the past in the future and that nothing exciting or meaningful happens. "I walk between the rails of the railway line. It's straight line. I look back—the iron rails meet in a point far away. I look ahead—the same two iron rails meet in a point far away. The further I move the more the points move too. What is behind is ahead. There is no distance between the past and the future. What's there in the past is in the future as well" (p. 55). Though he is tired, he has to keep on walking as there is no escape from it. "The same old road...I walk and walk and walk. Keep on walking. And yet is there no escape?"

(p. 55). The Writer philosophises about Indrajit and such others' experience. He iterates that there is no escape from the empty and meaningless life. Human life is marked by fatigue or weariness, emptiness of language and communication and sickness and the death within man.

All the words of music
Of crashing cymbals,
All the dazzling lights
Sick with drunkenness
You know the multicoloured shroud
That covers the rotting corpse
You know all that's there before
Is only a garland
Of flowers that have been
You know I end here
I am dead
Within me.
And yet why do I insist
That I go on?
For there is—Oh! Yet there is
No escape! (p. 56)

The chain of images in the song testifies to the element of sickness, futility, waste, and death, which are the dominant strands of existential philosophy. Almost all the characters in the play seem to be dead within. One is easily reminded of Eliot's words, "I had not thought death had undone so many!" All the characters in the play have to keep on walking on the road of life and carry on simply because there is no escape. Life happens to be a continuous chain of anxieties. When one problem is solved, another crops up. Man has to keep on struggling for better things and security not only for himself, but for his children. Man is thus forcibly engaged in the struggle for survival. Amal, for example, wants to take a correspondence course and pass a Diploma so that he may get the Associate Membership of the Institute and even become the Manager by way of promotion. Vimal is busy getting all sorts of loan and cement permission in order to build a house. "if one builds a house now, one will have a roof over one's head in old age. Besides one has to think of one's children" (p. 57). Kamal is engaged in some business, but he lacks the necessary capital. And he has to maintain his six children for which he needs a lot of money. Thus, all these three characters have some hope, ambition and dream of achieving something, but Indrajit does not have that romantic quality. He confesses, "The light never came. The sky didn't burn. I could not leave the solid earth" (p. 58). Now that he has accepted his ordinariness, he cannot dream any longer. He is no more Indrajit, but mere Nirmal engaged in the business of mechanically living. He has to continue to live simply because he cannot die. He has realized that there is no choice of any kind or escape. His existential dilemma is summarised by the Writer, "Walk! Be on the road! For us there is only the road. We shall walk. I know nothing to write about—still I shall have to write. You have nothing to say—still you will have to talk. Manasi has nothing to live for—she will have to live. For us there is only the road—so walk on. We are the cursed spirits of Sisyphus. We have to push the rock to the top—even if it just rolls down" (p. 59). He says further that man has no hope because he knows the future, which is not different from the past. "We must, we must, we must. We must live. We must walk. We know no sacred places. Yet we must go on with the pilgrimage.... There's no respite" (p. 60). He articulates the existential dilemma of Indrajit in the concluding song:

And hence
There's no end.
There's no hope
Of fulfilment
By the holy shrine
At journey's end.
Forget the questions,
Forget the grief
And have faith
In the road—
The endless road.
No shrine for us,
No God for us,

But the road,
The endless road. (p. 60)

Although the rock tends to roll down the mountain, Sisyphus has been condemned to push it up perpetually. He has to indulge in the struggle in spite of the knowledge of its futility. Like Vladimir and Estragon in Beckett's *Waiting for Godot*, who go on waiting for Godot, although they are not sure of his arrival, Indrajit has to keep on walking on the road, although there is not God or shrine to be found at the end of the journey. He has to keep on walking continuously as he is not sure of his destination.

The Writer also happens to be part of the existential situation in which his characters are caught. The dramatic and the meta-dramatic elements are intertwined. The Writer confesses, "True, I am not succeeding with the play. But don't you see I am trying my best. A play—a play about Amal, Vimal, Kamal? And Indrajit?" (p. 49). He shares his difficulty with Manasi, "Tell me, how can you write a play about someone, who sees life realistically and dreams about it romantically?... The more I tie him up in a plot, the more he escapes; says it isn't real. The more lines I write for him, the more he stands outside them. Says they are not real. Oh! He knows too much—altogether too much" (p. 50). Just as the human life to be depicted in the play is an existential wheel or circle, the Writer's play also happens to be circular in its plot. "Well, you see, in this play there isn't much difference between the beginning and the end. It's a circular play" (p. 52). Like his characters, who have no choice except to keep on walking on the road, he has to continue his effort to write the play. "I know nothing to write about—still I shall have to write" (p. 59).

The existential and absurd vision ingrained in the play is articulated through certain significant metaphors like those of wheel, circle, parallel railway track, cycle, spiral, zero, atom, trap, journey, tree of knowledge and Sisyphus, which in turn hold up a picture of limbo or hell. Commenting on the intellectually alive urban middle class of Bengal, Satyadev Dubey says that some of them aligned themselves with Marxist/Leftist forces. "In other parts of the country, the best elements in the middle classes were opting for the armed forces or the administrative services. *Evam*

Indrajit is in some ways about the residue; the residue consists of those who have failed to adjust, align and ceased to aspire and also those, who are enmeshed in the day-to-day struggle for survival" (Introduction, p. II). Although Indrajit belongs to the group of Amal, Vimal, and Kamal, he suffers from the tragic awareness of his ordinariness and his failure to achieve something like spiritual fulfilment on account of his lack of faith. But Manasi provides a binary opposition to Indrajit as she has faith in life and accepts life with all its ugliness and contingencies. Indrajit is the eternal question mark seeking an answer.

Although the existential and absurd vision of *Evam Indrajit* is interesting in itself, one wonders if it is relevant at all to the Indian situation. The plot construction is very arbitrary and defies the law of probability. The characters have no substantial life-like individuality. The interconnection between the Writer and the characters happens to be a clever trick, though a new experiment in theatrical field. The most conspicuous element that is absent in the play is the Indian, especially the Hindu epistemology. Although the names of the characters like Amal, Vimal, Kamal, and Nirmal remind us of the Bengali locale, one wonders why the Writer (surrogate of Badal Sircar) fails to understand them, i.e. characters and situations from the perspective of Hindu philosophy, for example, agnosticism or *charvakavada*. Applying the epistemological tool of Western existentialism to the Indian context is as absurd as uncalled for. The Writer in the play (surrogate of Badal Sircar) is crass ignorant about the Hindu philosophy and seem to be snobbish enough to be Westernised in his (borrowed) thinking and interpretation. That is exactly the reason why the characters and events in the play are not sufficiently convincing. The Writer repeatedly commenting upon the characters and events takes away the quality of suggestivity and makes it very literal, obvious, and sickening. This is the result of grafting an alien worldview on a native condition of life by totally neglecting the native tools of interpretation. The play disturbs the sensitive reader more by its irrelevance than by its relevance. It is possible to disagree with the Writer's interpretation of the events in the play at every stage and to offer an alternative, i.e. native Indian, Hindu interpretation. Moreover, the character of the Writer himself is redundant because the vents in the play should be autonomous and self-explicatory and not need a commentary by the Writer from the European perspective.

Notes

1 Badal Sircar, *Evam Indrajit* in *Three Modern Plays*, Fifth Impression, Delhi: Oxford University Press, 1996. (All the page references are to this edition.)

2. Kiranmayi Raha, *Oxford Companion to Indian Theatre*, ed. Anand Lal, New Delhi: Oxford University Press, 2004, p. 449.

3. Satyadev Dubey, *Introduction* to *Evam Indrajit*, *Three Modern Plays*, Fifth Impression, New Delhi: Oxford University Press, 1996, p. IV.

• • • • •

27

The Nature and Evolution of *Saṇṇãṭas* in North Karnãṭaka

Saṇṇãṭas (which means Small Plays) are very popular in North Karnãṭaka and are used in contrast to *Doḍḍãṭas* (Big Plays). Both these plays are part of *ã Bayalãṭa* (Open Air Plays) or *Aṭṭadãṭas* (Stage Plays). A systematic history of this folk drama is not yet available in Kannada due to the deplorable lack of historical sense in Karnãṭaka as well as India. The field of folklore in Kannada is still in the explorative stage and hence no clear-cut history of folk arts or drama has been available. Most of the articles and booklets written in Kannada are piece-meal and not integrated with other material related to it directly or indirectly. As for English books on the same subject, unfortunately there are no books at all except a rare few. Recently, the folklore studies has been gaining ground and becoming popular because of the institutional training and recognition of the subject in the universities of Karnãṭaka and due to the special interest and efforts of Kannada professors in the universities and colleges. Until recently folklore studies was not recognized as a standard subject to be taught, learnt or studied or researched into. But nowadays it has been recognized institutionally because of the influence of foreign universities.

Saṇṇãṭa may be said to be a poor man's or proletarian art-form. *Saṇṇãṭa*, which means a small play, is called so simply because of its simplicity of stage requirements, simple costumes, realistic dialogues, and social problems of the common man as distinguished from the grand mythological themes, gorgeous costumes, grand stage settings, elevated language of dialogues, and the depiction of heroic sentiment or *vīra rasa*. Since *Saṇṇāṭa* is played with the help of a small drum called *dappu*, it is also known as *Dappināṭa* (Drum Play). The folk artist holds the small drum in his left hand and plays upon it with his right hand thereby producing short rattles.

Scholars are united in their common opinion about the origin and possible evolution of this form of small play. Since *Saṇṇāṭa* is also known as *Dappināṭa* or a drum play, it becomes easy for us to conjecture that *dappu* was widely used by the singers of *gīgī* songs and *lāvaṇi* songs and hence *Saṇṇāṭas* must have been evolved out of these *gīgī* songs by dialogues and action being added to them in-between. This is borne out by the close similarity of themes between *gīgī* songs and *Saṇṇāṭas*. Thus, the form of *Saṇṇāṭa* must have been the result of the conversion of audible (*śravya*) art into spectacular art (*dṛśya*).

Saṇṇāṭa, which means 'a Small Play,' may be contradistinguished from *Doḍḍāṭa*, which means 'a Big Play.' Both these forms of play belong to the Eastern Mode (*Mūḍalapāya*) tradition of folk theatre. Though both of them are part of folk tradition, one conspicuous contrast between the two may be noticed. Whereas *Doḍḍāṭas* deal with grand themes which are generally mythological and consequently the costumes of the characters are simply grand, gorgeous, and spectacular and the language used by the characters is grandiloquent, stylized, and elevated and poetic accompanied by loud and deafening instrumental music of horizontal double-headed drums (*Mṛdaṅga*) and clarinets (*Shahnāi*) and even by leg-harmonium.

The characteristic features of *Saṇṇāṭa* provide a sharp contrast to those of *Doḍḍāṭa*. As its very title suggests, everything in *Saṇṇāṭa* is or happens to be on a small scale due to the paucity of financial resources, time, and patience on the part of organizers and audiences. The themes of *Saṇṇāṭas* are, generally, erotic (*śṛṅgāra*), devotional (*bhakti*) and comic (*hāsya*) as against the grandeur of heroic (*vīrarasa*) sentiment depicted in *Doḍḍāṭas*. The erotic and devotional sentiments are deeply connected with the social life of the people. Hence, *Saṇṇāṭas* are nearer to the hearts of the common man, the farmers, the villagers, and the proletariats.

In accordance with the popular themes of love and devotion, the stage of *Saṇṇāṭas* is also quite small and simple. It does not require a large stage spacious enough for the dance of gods and demons, but a relatively small stage of about 30 × 20 feet made of wooden boards, bamboos, and tarpaulins. A simple white or mono-coloured curtain at the back of the stage will be sufficient. The audience does not expect anything colourful and gorgeous on the stage.

Similarly, *Saṇṇāṭas* require less time than *Doḍḍāṭas* for performance. Generally, a *Saṇṇāṭa* may take about three to four hours (barring the exceptionally lengthened performances), but *Doḍḍāṭa* requires an entire night of about 9 to 10 hours.

The costumes worn by characters are as simple as their daily wear and are not expensive, grand, and antique. The characters speak not the grand and stylized language of *Doḍḍāṭas*, but employ the colloquial dialect of northern Karnāṭaka, which is known for its raciness, robustness, and ruggedness. Since the dialectal language is shared by the characters and the audience, the artistic communication will be very easy and fast. The response of the audience will be quick and spontaneous.

Music

Dappu or small one-headed drum is the main percussion instrument used in *Dappināṭas*. *Dappu* is a small version of tabor. It is not originally an Indian instrument, but has come from Persia. The word '*dappu*' is derived from the Persian instrument called 'duff.' The Marathi people happen to be experts in playing this instrument. It is used in most of the *gīgī* and *lāvaṇi* songs. The songs employed in *Dappināṭas* are not classical songs but short couplets (though repeated) especially suited to the rhythm that can be produced on *dappus*. The tunes are typically folksy and quite interesting. The player of *dappu* keeps on wandering all about the stage playing his instrument.

The other instruments used in *Dappināṭas* happen to be cymbals made of brass, which produce a tingling or rattling sound as required. A wind instrument called *pungi kayi* (gourd-pipe) was used in the early days, but nowadays it has been replaced by normal harmonium or leg-harmonium. Nowadays, the folksy tunes are replaced by classical tunes because of the influence of classical Hińdustãni music in northern Karnãţaka especially in the professional theatre known as Company Drama. Similarly, nowadays *dappu* is replaced by a pair of *tablã* and *đagga* drums and cleverly adapted to the requirements of *Saṇṇãţa* tunes.

Songs are quite common in *Saṇṇãţas* as also in *Dođđãţas*. But the songs in *Saṇṇãţas* are sung to the accompaniment of small flat one-sided drum called *dappu*. Hence, the plays are called *Dappinãţas* (*Drum Plays*) named after the main percussion instrument used in it. At the intense moments the characters resort to songs and soar high in the sky of poetry. Then the same theme of the song is spoken in the form of prose-dialogue. Thus, prose-dialogues are interspersed with numberless songs. And songs are accompanied by light or rigorous dance by the characters. Music occupies more than half of the Saṇṇãţa performances.

The Front-Chorus (*Mumméḷa*) and the Back-Chorus (*Himméḷa*) occupy an important role in *Saṇṇãţas*. These choruses introduce, or comment on or sympathize with or link up the events of the play thereby contributing to the cohesion and comprehensibility of the theme of the play. There is a good deal of similarity between these choruses of *Saṇṇãţas* and those of Greek tragedies. They also contribute to the community vision of life and the choric element.

The language used by the characters in these *Saṇṇãţas* is dialectal and colloquial, which has its own beauty and rhythm. As this dialect is spoken by the major portion of the audience, there is sure to be quick communication between the characters and the audience. It is not stylized, artificial, and grandiloquent like in *Dođđãţas*.

As already shown, the erotic or the devotional themes are predominant in *Saṇṇãţas*, most of the plays have the titles suggestive of their themes. For example, many plays have the suffix, 'Kalyãṇa' in their titles. 'Kalyãṇa' means marriage (of some lady). The plays with devotional themes are simply named after the famous saints like Tirunīlakaṇṭha, Allamaprabhu, and Kabīradāsa and so on.

There are also social and contemporary themes dealt with in some *Saṇṇāṭas* like exploitation of the poor by the rich; of women by men; of the natives by the foreigners and so on.

The *Saṇṇāṭas* are very popular in certain districts of northern Karnāṭaka like Dhārwāḍ, Beḷagāvi, Vijayapura, Kalaburagi, and Bīdar.

Thematically, *Saṇṇāṭas* may be classified into two categories like devotional and social. The devotional plays may be further classified into Śaiva and Vaiṣṇava groups. The devotional themes are very popular in *Saṇṇāṭas*, because devotional tradition was very strong in Karnāṭaka right from the twelfth century. The devotional tradition may be divided into two groups: one, Śaiva and two, Vaiṣṇava popularized by *Śaraṇas* and *Haridāsas* respectively. The *Saṇṇāṭas* were evolved with a didactic purpose of popularizing these two devotional traditions. Whereas the Śaiva tradition highlights the supremacy of Lord Siva and the Vaiṣṇava tradition highlights the supremacy of Lord Viṣṇu as the targets of their devotion. Whereas the twenty-five frolic plays of Lord Śiva, sixty-three ancestors, the *Śaraṇas* of the twelfth century and the histories of local saints provided the raw-material for the Saṇṇāṭas of Śaiva tradition, the stories of the *Rāmāyaṇa*, the *Mahābhārata*, the *Viṣṇu Purāṇa*, and *Bhāgavata* provided the themes for the *Saṇṇāṭas* of Vaiṣṇava tradition. Hence, these *Saṇṇāṭas* were known as *Śaraṇaratas* (*Śaraṇa* Plays) and *Dāsarāṭas* (*Dāsa* Plays). These two broad categories of *Saṇṇāṭas* are exemplified by particular plays with specific heroes or protagonists. For example, the plays like *Kārikālamme, Tirunīlakaṇṭha, Nijaguṇa Śivayôgi*, and *Hémaraḍḍi Mallamma* belong to the tradition of Śaiva devotion, the plays like *Śrī Kṛṣṇa Pārijāta* and *Rādhānāṭa* (Rādhā Play) belong to the Vaiṣṇava tradition.

There is some confusion about the *Śaraṇaratas* and *Dāsarāṭas* and their themes and performers. *Śaraṇaratas* may deal with the lives of twelfth-century *Śaraṇas*, but they are not necessarily staged by the distinct troupes devoted to only such Śaiva themes. Similarly, the *Dāsarāṭas* may deal with Vaiṣṇava themes, especially those of *Daśãvatãra*. But the performers of *Dãsarãṭas* are not Haridãsas, but professional artistes called *dãsas* belonging to lower castes (of singers) in the society. Their main aim is to provide entertainment and humour. Dr. Basavaraj Malashetti has enumerated many types of *dãsas* like *Golladãsa*, *Holedãsas*, *Ambigadãsas*, *Puttadãsas Rãdhã*, *Ramadãsas*, and *Kabbéradãsa*. Śrĩ Betageri Krishnasharma has enumerated other kinds of *dãsas* like *Chhatredãsas*, *Beđadãsas*, *Holedãsas*, and *Đombadãsas*. These *dãsas* belong to lower castes and known for their singing talent in addition to other professions for their livelihood. Sri Betageri Krishnasharma, a senior scholar, opines that most of the *dãsas* live in some villages of Vijayapura and that there is no connection between these entertaining *dãsas* and *Haridãsas* of Vaiṣṇava tradition. The troupes of these *dãsas* were maintained by the Hindu kings of middle ages. They had to accompany the military during war time and entertain the soldiers during their leisure. In course of time this group of entertainers (*dãsas*) entered the Mahãrãshtra military life to provide entertainment to the Marathi soldiers and their performances came to be known as *Tamãśa*. Again a folk playwright from Basaragi village wrote his *Rãdhãnãṭa* (Rãdhã Play) in imitation of *Tamãśa*. This opinion of Betageri Krishnasharma is quite perceptive, but needs to be verified by folklore scholars with necessary fieldwork.

Origin

Dappinãṭa seems to have become prominent in Northern Karnãṭaka in the latter part of the nineteenth century. These plays in the first phase were called *Dappinãṭas* (Drum Plays) as they were performed to the accompaniment of small, flat, one-sided percussion drum held in the left hand and struck by the right hand fingers. These plays abounded with a series of folk songs interspersed with dialogues and action.

In the second phase, these *Dappinãṭas* came to be known as *Saṇṇãṭas* (*Small Plays*) and developed their theatrical techniques like a good stage, costumes, and relevant themes and so on. According to the common opinion of elders, the ancestry of *Dappinãṭas* does not go beyond 1860, but it had established itself firmly around 1900.

Some senior scholars like Dr. M.G. Biradar put forth the view that the *Dappināṭas* must have emerged out of the famous *gīgī* and *lāvaṇi* songs, which were very popular in Northern Karnāṭaka. For example, there was a *Haradési-Nāgési* tradition of singing in which men and women sang in mutual competition to argue for the male superiority and the female superiority respectively. This auditory art was later converted into spectacular, dramatic art when the songs were interlarded with dialogues and action, accompanied by other stage properties like costumes, curtains and sceneries, etc. This kind of transformation is quite possible and stands to our reason.

As a result of such transformation from the audible *gīgī* and *lāvaṇi* recitation to the spectacular performance of *Saṇṇāṭa*, new playwrights like Hasansab of Iṅgaḷagi village, who composed the first *Saṇṇāṭa* entitled *Rādhānāṭa* (Rādhā Play). Hasansab was both a singer of *gīgī* and *lāvaṇi* songs and a composer of the first *Saṇṇāṭa* mentioned above. Many other singers of *gīgī* and *lāvaṇi* songs composed many *Saṇṇāṭas* in imitation of Hasansab's practice. The origin of *Saṇṇāṭas* cannot be traced easily for lack of recordation and documentation. But it seems to have evolved gradually by the addition of instrumental music, dance, action and gesticulation, and dialogues.

It seems to have borrowed the use of *dappu* from *gīgī* recitation, dialogue from *Haradési-Nāgési* tradition, dancing style and theatrical technique from *Tamāśa* and music from the Company Drama respectively in accordance with its requirements. It seems to have assimilated these elements harmoniously into a new form of folk-drama called *Saṇṇāṭa* and refined it in course of time.

First Phase

Historically speaking, *Saṇṇāṭas* may be classified into two phases: first and second. The first phase consists of the period from the beginning to the second decade of 20th century. The *Dappināṭas* of this period were basically musical plays (operas) and the dialogues were not fixed but improvised extempore by the actors. The old play-scripts begin with a prayer to Lord Gaṇapati, the Warder of all the hurdles, followed by a preparatory song, which introduces the theme of the play in a nutshell, and addresses the audience directly. Such preparatory or introductory songs are conspicuous by their absence in the second phase. *Kaḋlimaṭṭi Station Mãster, Saṅgyã-Bãḷyã* and *Rũpaséna* belong to the *Saṇṇãṭas* of the first phase.

Second Phase

The second phase of *Saṇṇãṭas* seems to have begun with *Tĩrunĩlakaṇṭha* composed around 1920 by Nĩlakaṇṭhappa Pattãr (endearingly called Pattãr Master), who hailed from Kãdaravaḷḷi (or Kãdroḷḷi) village of Bailahongala taluka. This religious *Saṇṇãṭa* is also known by an alternative title, *Kãdroḷḷi Ata* (Kãdroḷḷi Play). Nĩlakaṇṭhappa is said to have been trained in the Company Drama (or Professional Theatre), which had emerged in Northern Karnãṭaka then. Similarly, he was deeply influenced by the teachings of Vedantic philosophy by a famous Vedanti, Adrisappa of Kãdroḷḷi village. The ideal combination of theatrical experience and philosophical knowledge of Vedanta helped Nĩlakaṇṭhappa to compose the religious/philosophical *Saṇṇãṭa*, entitled *Tĩrunĩlakaṇṭha*, named after one of the sixty-three Śaiva saints of Tamilnãḋu. This *Saṇṇãṭa* happens to be a distinct play with a mixture of elements of standard literature and folk literature. The songs of this play were deeply influenced by the music of professional Company Drama and assumed a new shape. Nĩlakaṇṭhappa seems to have composed nearly 25 plays of this type.

Another playwright, Yallappa Munonni (who was a school teacher by profession) composed some plays like *Mãyi Ãta* (*Allamaprabhu*), *Nijaguṇa Sivayũgi* and *Kabĩradãsa*, etc., under the pen-name Śivãnaṅda Kavi. These plays are composed in the tradition of Nĩlakaṇṭhappa Pattãr. Thus, these two playwrights, Nĩlakaṇṭhappa Pattãr and Śivãnaṅda Kavi started and consolidated the tradition of *Saṇṇãṭas* of the second phase. Other playwrights, who were influenced by those of the second phase, have composed the well-known plays like *Chellãḷanãṭa*, *Dharmadévate*, *Basavaṅta-Balavaṅta*, *Kaḋlimaṭṭi Station-Mãster*, and *Viśwãmitra*, etc., continued the tradition of the second phase.

Hasan Sãhéb may be accepted as the father of *Rãdhãnãṭa* (Rãdhã Play), because he composed his play before Babuji Kumbar of Basaragi village (of Chikkôđi *taluka* of Beḷagãvi district) could compose his *Rãdhãnãṭa*. A group of actors like Nabisab (of Taḷewãđi village of Basavana-Bãgewãđi *taluka*), Shivanand Hiremath, Imam Sãhéb of Sagareddi village (of Shahapur *taluka* of Gulbarga district) popularized Hasan Sãhéb's *Rãdhãnãṭa* by their countless performances. If the ancestry of Hasan Sãhéb's *Rãdhãnãṭa* is accepted, then the sequence of first phase and second phase as classified by Malashetti has to be abandoned and altered. In that case, Hasan Sãhéb's *Rãdhãnãṭa* and its tradition becomes the first phase; Babuji's *Rãdhãnãṭa*, Rãyappa Pattãr's *Saṅgyã-Bãḷyã*, *Rũpaséna*, and *Kađlimaṭṭi Station-Mãster* belong to the second phase; and Nĩlakaṇṭhappa Pattãr's *Tirunĩlakaṇṭha* and other plays of that tradition belong to the third phase.

The original *Rãdhãnãṭa* composed by Hasan Sãhéb underwent a few changes subsequently in the hands of his disciples like Ladlesh of Iṅgaḷagi and the latter's disciple, Nabisãb. The characters like Dũti, Sakhãrãm Tãtyã, Chimaṇa, and Galpoji (belonging to the *Tamãśa* tradition of Mahãrãshṭra) found in the *Rãdhãnãṭa* of Nabisãb were conspicuous by their absence in Hasan Sãhéb's original *Rãdhãnãṭa*. The three types of characters like Chimaṇa, Galpôji, and Sakhãrãm Tãtyã, so common in *Tamãśa*, have entered the Kannada version of *Rãdhãnãṭa*.

Gradually, some changes took place in the performance of *Rãdhãnãṭas*. For example, the heavy dose of philosophy gave place to the discussion of worldly matters; dialogues became more important than songs. Because of these changes Nabi's version of *Rãdhãnãṭa* became extremely popular. The songs in the original version of *Rãdhãnãṭa* by Hasan Sãhéb resembled *gĩgĩ*-songs, but now they have lost their original nature and come under the influence of the songs of *Saṅgyã-Bãḷyã* and *Śrĩ Kṛṣṇa Pãrijãta*.

***

According to the veteran folklorist, Dr. Mallikarjuna Latthe, there have been more than three to four hundred *Saṇṇãṭas*, which were and are performed in Karnãṭaka, although most of them are not unfortunately published in book form. They remain in the form of play-scripts only in the houses of the artistes or playwrights or their descendents. The two most prominent *Saṇṇãṭas* like *Saṅgyã-Bãḷyã* and *Śrĩ Kṛṣṇa Pãrijãta* have been translated by the present writer on a national and international level.

From the thematic point of view these *Saṇṇãṭas* may be classified into three categories like (i) social *Saṇṇãṭas*; (ii) historical *Saṇṇãṭas*; and (iii) mythological *Saṇṇãṭas*.

Arabarãṭa, *Saṅgyã-Bãḷyã*, *Kãshibãyi*, *Rũpasingh*, *Kaṭṭi Chenna*, *Balavaṅta-Basavaṅta*, and *Gulbakãvali* happen to be the prominent and well-known social *Saṇṇãṭas*.

Kabĩradãsa, *Allamaprabhu*, *Akkamãhãdévi*, *Kanakadãsa*, *Sindhoor Laxmaṇa*, *Saṅt Tukãrãm*, *Kittũr Chennamma*, *Saṅgoḷḷi Rãyaṇṇa*, *Keḷadi Chennamma*, *Beḷavaḋi Mallamma*, and *Hémaraḋḋi Mallamma* happen to be some of the famous historical *Saṇṇãṭas*.

Likewise, *Śrĩ Kṛṣṇa Pãrijãta*, *Harischaṅdra*, *Rãdhãnãṭa*, *Satyavãna Savitri*, *Bhakta Prahlãda*, and *Vĩra Abhimanyu* happen to be some of the prominent and well-known mythological *Saṇṇãṭas*.

***

Here we may examine three prominent social *Saṇṇãṭas* briefly for the benefit of western readers.

Saṅgyã-Bãḷyã

Saṅgyã-Bãḷyã is a social *Saṇṇãṭa* written by Nĩlakaṇṭhappa Pattãr of Bailawada village, has been very popular all over Karnãṭaka even now. It deals with the illegal and secret adulterous relation between Gaṅga, wife of Vĩrabhadra, a jeweller and an unmarried youth, Saṅgappa (or Saṅgyã), unexpectedly discovered by the husband, Vĩrabhadra. Unable to bear the stigma on the family honour, due to his wife's adultery, Virabhadra forcibly takes the help of Bãḷappa, a crony of Saṅgyã and succeed in murdering him treacherously thereby seeking revenge upon his cuckolder. Earlier to that he has already driven out his wife and sent her back to her parents' home after confiscating all of her gold ornaments.

This play happens to be very popular in northern Karnāṭaka due to the combination of dialogues, songs, and dance, which naturally adds to the theatrical effect. It easily brings to our mind the Elizabethan tragedy of blood and horror. In the initial phase of its performance in the early part of 20th century puritanical people and respectable men and women were hesitant to witness its performance.

There has been a critical controversy about whether it is based on historical facts or just an imaginary theme. As there are no written records about such events, the controversy has remained unsolved yet. But still the play may be enjoyed as a story of crime and punishment with its incontrovertible social and moral relevance. The play offers a challenge to the modern feminists of both moderate and radical school.

(Some scholars like Dr. M.M. Kalburgi think that the play, *Saṅgyā-Bāḷyā* was not based on real facts of history but a vindictive act on the part of the folk playwright, Pattār Master, who was in love with Gaṅgā and who was frustrated by Gaṅgā's rejection of his love and therefore took revenge upon her by writing a play to denigrate and blackmail her maliciously. In order to set the matter right, Dr. Kalburgi himself wrote a corrective version entitled *Khare Khare Saṅgyā-Bāḷyā* (*Authentic Saṅgyā-Bāḷyā*) and got it staged at Dhārwāđ and other places. Obviously, it is meta-dramatic in its nature.

Dharma Sāmrājya or *Satya Samśôdhane* is another important social *Saṇṇāṭa* written by Nīlakaṇṭhappa Pattār.

Kaṭṭi Chenna

Kaṭṭi Chenna is a social *Saṇṇāṭa*, which deals with Chenna's heroic struggle against the Chief of the village, the Gowđa and the local constabulary, when his family honour was at stake. He goes on escaping from the police to a number of places like Betageri, Sogala Hill, Julagatti, Kurubagatti, and Shivapura. Chenna's heroic struggle has been a matter of great appreciation and admiration with the local people of the place wherein Chenna moved about. Chenna's idealism and his belief in the family honour are highlighted in this social play.

Śrĩ Betageri Krishnasharma mentions a few other social *Dappinãṭas* like *Dunđya-Mõdin* (later modified as *Manamõhana-Kuśãla*), *Sãhukãrana Ãta* (*Play about a Richman*), and *Chanđrachũđa-Satyaśĩla*.

Sangoḷḷi Rãyaṇṇa

Similarly, *Sangoḷḷi Rãyaṇṇa* (*Rãyaṇṇa of Sangoḷḷi*) is a political *Saṇṇãṭa*, which is very popular in the wide region surrounding Kittur (which was once a famous kingdom). It presents the heroic struggle of Rãyaṇṇa, the bodyguard of Rãṇi Chennamma of Kittũr kingdom, against the authorities of the East India Company around 1824 and the guerilla war in which he engaged himself until he was treacherously betrayed to the British Government by his own people and finally hanged to death. This *Saṇṇãṭa* is naturally inspiring because it whips up the feeling of patriotism in all the Indians.

Sometimes *Saṇṇãṭas* are known by the main theme depicted in them. For example, some of them are known as *Śaraṇarãṭa* (*Śaraṇa Plays*) and *Rãjãnãṭas* (*Rãjã Plays*) and *Bãvãnãṭa* (*Bãvã Play*). Whereas *Śaraṇarãṭas* dealt with the lives of VĩraŚaiva *Śaraṇas* and *Rãjãnãṭas* deal with the lives of kings.

One may say that the mythological themes do not fit in with the requirements of *Saṇṇãṭas*. But one may see many historical-political themes are deal with in them. For example, *Kittũru Chennamma*, *Sangoḷḷi Rãyaṇṇa*, and *Keḷadi Chennamma*, etc., are a few of historical *Saṇṇãṭas*, but the number of historical *Saṇṇãṭas* is very small.

Geographical Distribution

The folk theatre like *Dođđãṭas* and *Saṇṇãṭas* were very popular in northern Karnãṭaka. Bellay district is said to be the centre of *Dođđãṭas* whereas, *Śrĩ Krisna Pãrijãta*, a distinct form of devotional *Saṇṇãṭa* was popular in the districts of Vijayapura and Bagilukote and along the banks of Ghataprabha and Krishna Rivers. Similarly, other social *Saṇṇãṭas* were said to be popular in the *taluka* of Bailahongala.

Interaction between Karnãṭaka and Mahãrãshtra

Though the northern Karnãṭaka and southern Mahãrãshtra are separate States now, they have a common culture with a mixture of Kannada and Marathi languages. Hence, there was mutual interaction and influence of one literature and culture on another. For example, Lord Vitthala of Pandarapura is known in Mahãrãshtra as 'Kãnađãvu Viṭṭhala.' The deities like Khaṇđoba, Yellamma and Śãkãmbari are found in both the States. Mangalavede in Mahãrãshtra was connected with the life of Basavéśwara of Karnãṭaka in the twelfth century. Similarly, a group of followers of Sant Jńãnéśwara of Mahãrãshtra had settled down in Karnãṭaka (especially at Dambala town). The original place of Éknãth of Mahãrãshtra was in Karnãṭaka. Similarly, the great poet of Mahãrãshtra, Muktéśwara spent his childhood days in Karnãṭaka. The ancestors of Dr. D.R. Bendre, the Jńãnapĩṭh Awardee in Kannada were Mahãrãshtrians.

Vishnudas Bhave and Annasãheb Kirloskar were responsible for the birth and growth of modern Marathi theatre. But there was a deep influence of Kannada folk theatre on these two writers. Whereas Vishnudas Bhave's plays were like the Marathi versions of Kannada *yakṣagãnas*, the plays of Annasãheb Kirloskar were deeply influenced by the Kannada *Pãrijãta* and Turamuri Sesagiriraya's *Śakuṅtalã*. For example, the characters or actors and actresses singing their own songs (not somebody lending their voice), and women performing the roles of female characters (and not men) owe their practices to the influence of Kannada *Pãrijãtas*.

There is a close relation between the popular Marathi *Tamãśa* and the Kannada *Rãdhãnãṭas* and *Dãsarãṭas* and *Pãrijãta*. For example, the characters like Gulpõji, Chimaṇã and Dũti found in Kannada *Rãdhãnãṭas* resemble the characters like Kṛṣṇa, Rãdhã, and Mausi found in Marathi *Tamãśa* plays. Similarly, the spiritual debate of *Kalgi-Turã* is found incidentally in *Tamãśa* but extensively in *Rãdhãnãṭa*.

Some critics like Malashetti argue that the encounter between Gopala and Gollati in Kannada *Saṇṇãṭas* is borrowed from the *Tamãśa* tradition of Mahãrãshtra. The character of Dũti in Kannada *Saṇṇãṭas* is parallel to that of Mausi in *Tamãśa* as both of them are addressed as females, though dressed in male garments.

The *Tamāśa* tradition is believed by some scholars to be started in the seventeenth century itself during the Peshwa rule. But there is a critical controversy about who influenced whom: whether Karnāţaka or Mahārāshtra. This fact is yet to be verified and finalized by scholars of both the languages with the help of field work and written records.

Need for Improvement

Most of the time, the *Saṇṇāţas* are performed by the folk artistes in rural areas only. These folk artistes are generally illiterate and therefore violate the rules of relevance, decency and etiquette in their performances. Hence, the performances are many times rather crude and rough in their presentation. There is a great need for improvement or refinement of this art by the folk artistes. They require a talented scholar like Dr. Shivarama Karanth. The *Saṇṇāţas* need to be performed by educated artistes for educated audience so that there may be a conspicuous improvement in the use of dialogues and language in general and refinement in the histrionic gestures also.

Generally, the performances of *Saṇṇāţas* begin about 10.00 at night and end only about or after sunrise. This long-drawn performance may be tolerated by the rural audience, but certainly not liked by the educated audience of the cities. As a result of this long-drawn performance the theme gets diluted and the performance keeps on dragging unnecessarily. Hence, there is a need for cutting the time of dancing and music to the absolute minimum and paying more attention to the advancement of the theme. Similarly, long and irrelevant pontificatory/spiritual/philosophical dialogues may be reduced to the minimum so that the plays may gain in dramatic effect. There is a lot of repetition in the dialogues of *Saṇṇāţas*. For example, the Bhāgavata says something, which is repeated by Mari Bhāgavata and again by some character. This repetition, tolerated by the illiterate rural audience cannot be tolerated by the educated urban audience at all. So these repetitions may be avoided as far as possible without damaging the effect of the scenes. Similarly, some songs, originally inserted into the play just to elongate the time of performance, may be mercilessly removed in the interest of dramatic intensity.

Thus, the all-night performance of the *Saṇṇāṭas* should be reduced to just three hours performance so that the plays may be more cohesive, intense, and impressive.

The costumes in *Saṇṇāṭas* should be used according to the requirements of the theme. The absurdity of the male character addressed as Dūti (female messenger) should be avoided by clothing the character in female garments like sari and blouse only. Otherwise the absurdity continues to be jarring on account of its irrationality.

The stage for *Saṇṇāṭas* need not be made of wooden boards only, but the solid stage of cement easily available nowadays on the school campuses or temple complexes may be used for the performances. The torches fed with oil in the early days may easily be replaced by modern electric lighting arrangement. In the early days, when loudspeakers or amplifiers were not available in India, the actor and actresses had necessarily to raise their voice and speak their dialogues and sing their songs at the highest pitch in order to be heard by the audience in the open-air theatre.

Instead of the characters shouting at the top of their voice may be made to speak at their natural tone and pitch with the help of mikes and amplifiers.

More importance should be given to histrionic talent than to mere dialogues. For example when one character is speaking something, the other characters should be responding to it with gestures and postures, though not directly answering them.

The selection of actors and actresses should be made according to the needs of the theme and nature of the characters. Male characters should behave like men and female characters should behave like women. Nothing should be artificial. Male characters acting the role of female characters should be positively avoided.

Too much of realism or naturalism should be avoided in the performances of *Saṇṇāṭas* and some scope should be given to the exercise of imagination of the audience. For example, Nijaguṇa, the eponymous hero removes his royal garments and burns them publicly on the stage before donning the ascetic robes. The actual burning of clothes is not required at all. The detachment of the protagonist from the worldly life may be shown through dialogues rather than from disconcerting acts on the stage.

The humour provided by Bhãgavata and Dũti in *Saṇṇãṭas* should be within the bounds of decency, relevance, and reason. Their humorous dialogues should not be inordinately lengthy and out of tune with the main theme of the plays.

The *Saṇṇãṭas* should be directed by well-trained Drama Directors systematically through workshops and training courses. Nothing should be *ad hoc* and unsystematic, and chaotic. Strict discipline should be followed at every stage of the performance.

Another thing, the most important one, is that the traditional *Saṇṇãṭas*, which are still in the form of mental or oral texts, should be reduced to black and white and be printed and published after testing their cohesiveness in actual performances by removing the unnecessary frills and diversions, which might have crept into the oral texts due to the illiteracy of the actors and actresses in the bygone days.

Not only that. The best performances of these *Saṇṇãṭas* should be recorded through video tapes or cassettes for the benefit of future generations.

Works Cited

(English)

Gargi, Balavant. *The Folk-Theatre of India.* Washington: University of Washington Press, 1966.

Mathur, J.C. *Drama in Rural India.* New York: Asia Publishing House, 1964.

Naikar, Basavaraj. *The Folk Theatre of North Karnãṭaka*, New Delhi: Authors Press, 2012.

Naikar, Basavaraj. Tr. *Pattãr Master's Saṅgyã Bãḷyã: A Tale of Love and Betrayal*, London and New Delhi: Minerva Press, 2004; Chennai: Macmillan & Co. Pvt Lit., 2008.

Naikar, Basavaraj. Tr. Tammanna of Kulagodu, et al., *Śrĩ Kṛṣṇa Pãrijãta*, Bengaluru: CVG Books, 2016.

Ranganath, H.K. *The Karnãṭaka Theatre.* Dhãrwãḍ: Karnatak University, 1960.

(Kannada)

Biradar, M.G. *Janapada Samôlokana*, Kalaburagi: Chitkala Prakashana, 1981.

Boralingaiah, H.C. *Karnāṭaka Janapada Kalegaḷa Kôsha*, Hampi: Prasārāṅga, Kannada Visvavidyalaya, 1996.

Chidananda-Murthy, M. *Gramīṇa*. Bangalore: Bapco Prakasana, 1977.

Durgadas, K.R. *Baḷḷāry Jilleya Bayalāṭagaḷu*, Belagavi: Samata Prakasana, 1996.

Hiremath, Basavalingayya and Vishweshwari. Eds. *Saṇṇāṭada Swarūpa*, Kittūru: Bhushana Prakasana, 1998.

Hiremath, R.C. *Janapada Sāhitya Darśana*, Part I. Dhārwāđ: Karnatak University, 1974.

Imrapur, Somashekhara, *Janapada Vijñāna*. Dhārwāđ: Chetana Prakasana, 1979.

Ittannavar, Śrī rama, *Śrī Kṛṣṇa Pārijāta: Oṅdu Adhyayana*. Bilagi: Vini Prakasana, 1991.

Kalburgi, M.M. *Mārga*. Vols. II and I. Bangalore: Naresh and Company, 1988.

Kambar, Chandrasekhar, *Uttara Karnāṭakada, Janapada Raṅgabhūmi*. Dhārwāđ: Manvantara Prakasana, 1965.

Kittur, Krishnamurthy et al. *Gulbarga University Research Journal* (Kannada), Vol. I, No. 1. Gulbarga: Gulbarga University, Prasārāṅga, 1988.

Krishnasharma, Betageri, *Kannađa Jānapada Sāhitya*, Dhārwāđ: Prasārāṅga, Karnatak University, 1976.

Latthe, M.S. *Bayalāṭada Sārathi*. Mutanal: Mallasarja Prakasana, 1978.

Latthe M.S. *Janapada Kavicharite*. Dhangapur: Basavantarao Malipatil Memorial Publication, 1980.

Latthe, M.S. *Janapada Samsôdhanātmaka Barahaguḷu*. Kalaburagi: Patil Dal Mill, 1980.

Latthe, M.S. *Kannada Yatre*, Kalaburagi: S.B. Patil Dal Mill Prakasana, 1980.

Lokapur, Balasaheb. *Śrī Kṛṣṇa Pārijāta: Mūru Upanyāsagaḷu*. Bagilukote: Seminar Committee, 1995.

Malashetti, Basavaraj, *Uttara Karnāṭakada Bayalāṭagaḷu*. Dhārwāđ: Prasārāṅga, Karnatak University, 1983.

Marulasiddappa, K. *Ādhunika Kannađa Nāṭaka*, Bengaluru: Ankita Pustaka, 2002.

Police-Patil, Basavaraj. *Hyderãbãd-Karnãṭakada Saṇṇãṭagaḷu*, Gulbarga: Prasãrãṅga, Gulbarga University, 1999.

Sunkapur, M.S. *Sivananda Kavi's Allamaprabhu* (Bayalata). Dhãrwãḍ: Prasãrãṅga, Karnatak University, 1973.

Sunkapur, M.S. *Janapada Sãhitya Darśana,* Part II. Dhãrwãḍ: Prasãrãṅga, Karnatak University, 1976.

Sunkapur, M.S. *Janapada Sãhitya Darśana,* Part III. Dhãrwãḍ: Prasãrãṅga, Karnatak University, 1978.

Timmapur, H.I. *Saṇṇãṭagaḷu*. Dhãrwãḍ: Prasãrãṅga, Karnatak University, 1999.

• • • • •

28

Shadow Plays in Karnataka

Origin

Shadow Play or Leather-Puppet Play is believed to have originated in India and migrated to other countries of the world. "Hindu kings conquered Java in the first century A.D. and ruled for 1,500 years. During this long period of time Javanese life became Hinduized. Malay-Polynesian deities, which had counterparts in the Hindu pantheon, took on the corresponding Hindu names, and the shadow plays figures henceforth showed them dressed in the Indian *dhoti*. When there were no such Hindu counterparts for the Malay-Polynesian deities, these deities retained their Malay-Polynesian character and their shadow play figures continued showing them dressed in the Malay-Polynesian *sarong*. In the course of time the number of shadow play figures was increased by the addition of characters taken from Hindu mythology."[1] This kind of folk theatre is said to have been prevalent in India even before the beginning of the Christian era. There are said to be references to the Shadow Plays in Sanskrit as well as regional literatures. For example, there are said to be references to the Shadow Play in Kautilya's the *Arthashastra*, Vyasa's the *Mahabharata* (1500 *sloka*), Harshavardhana's *Naisadha Charitre* (XVIII, 13) mentions that King Nala invited the Puppet-Players and arranged a puppet-show in the Hall of Entertainment (*Pramoda Bhavana*). Rajasekhara, a Kannada poet of 11th century mentions in the fifth Act of his play *Bala Ramayana* that there was a puppet-players, who was playing the puppets of Sita and her maidservant Sindhurika and that

Ravana mistook the puppet-Sita to be the real one and touched it only to be disappointed. Gunadhya's *Kathasaritsagara* of the 12th century mentions how Somaprabha, the daughter of Silparaja presented her friend Kalyanasena with a box of puppets. Ratnakaravarni's *Bharatesa Vaibhava* points out the presence of puppet-players among the visitors to Emperor Bharata's court. There are references to the Shadow Play in the *vacanas* of *saranas*, who lived in the twelfth-century Karnataka and in the *kirtanas* of Kanakadasa in sixteenth-century Karnataka. Cennabasava, one of such *saranas*, makes a reference to the Shadow Plays or Leather-Puppet plays in one of his *vacanas*. Kaliketa Bommayya, another *sarana* of the same galaxy is said to have been a *killiketa*, i.e. professional shadow-play artist.

There was said to be a *virakta* called Santa, the puppet-player (Gombeyadisuva kayakada Santa) during the reign of Emperor Srikrisnadevaraya (1419-46). Kanakadasa, one of the famous Haridasas of the same period refers to the puppet-play by saying that the whole cosmos is engaged in a puppet-play.

There is a reference to 'Kalaketa' in *Basava Purana*, which is interpreted variously by different scholars. Dr. L. Basavaraju (in his Preface to *Sivadasa Gitanjali*, p. 38) opines that the Kalaketa Bommayya used to entertain the devotees by performing the role of Virabhadra and conduct the *dasoha* out of the money collected through his *kayaka*. But there is no clear reference to any Shadow Play here.

There are references to Shadow Plays in Dhanapala's *Tilaka Manjari*, Vidyaranya's *Pancadasi*, Palkurike Somanath'a *Panditaradhya's Carita* and the *kirtanas* of Kanakadasa and Purandaradasa.

The Shadow Theatre enjoyed royal patronage during the reign of Rastrakutas, Kadambas, Calukyas, and Hoysalas, especially that of Vijayanagara Emperors.

The Indians believe in the divine origin of all arts. In spite of such romantic belief by people in general, the scholars have continued to debate whether the Shadow Play preceded the Puppet Play or vice versa or whether the puppet theatre preceded the human theatre.

Evolution of Shadow Theatre

Shadow Play happens to be one of the best forms of folk art. Being a professional art, it has employed all the techniques of attracting the popular attention to itself. One may notice a sort of evolution in the history of this art. Broadly speaking, two phases could be deciphered in its evolution. In the first phase, the transparent and figural cutouts were employed. Then as years went by, the cut-out puppets were made to move their limbs like hands and legs. Later the theme, technique and music of *yaksagana* were incorporated into the shadow play. In the second phase, the shadow play was based on ballads (*lavanis*) and epics like the *Ramayana* and the *Mahabharata*. Both the forms of shadow play are luckily prevalent in Karnataka, although it is very difficult to decide which of them preceded the other. Whether one form was the logical consequence of the other or whether both of them grew simultaneously but independently is yet to be researched into.

How?

One is curious to know as to how the Shadow Play must have come into existence in India. The picturesqueness and multicoloured nature of the Shadow Play helps us to establish some connection between the folk-paintings, which preceded this theatre. For example, in ancient India, people had the habit of getting the walls of caves and temples painted; or getting woven picturesque clothes and gifting them away to temples; or getting the pictures of favourite gods painted on wooden boards. Similarly, they had the habit of getting a series of pictures connected with a single theme drawn or painted on a roll of cloth and exhibiting them to the public on proper occasions. Such practice could be seen in Vedic, Jain, and Buddhist traditions. (Chilvin Norris, a French scholar opines that '*Patakatha*' or 'Canvas Story' is older than the Sanskrit Drama. A Jain *Purana* entitled *Kuvalayamala* mentions the fact that a Jain monk used to offer his religious discourses with the help of a roll of pictures. Similarly, there are references to '*Patacitra*' or 'Canvas Picture' in Buddhist literature and to '*Yama Pata*' in Sanskrit *Puranas*.)

The Jain volume of palm leaves entitled *Mahadhavala* is modelled after the folk painting and drawing. There are references to '*citrapata*' (canvas of pictures) in the Old Kannada prose work, *Vaddaradhane* by Sivakotyacarya and Pampa's *Adipurana*. In the *Mahabharata*, there has been a tradition for centuries of entertaining people during the Navaratri festival with the help of a canvas of pictures and to the accompaniment of *Bhagavata-Vina*. The nomadic community of Rajasthan called '*Thakurs*' has cultivated this art as a hereditary one. The '*Garoda*' people of Gujarat employ a scroll of pictures called '*Bapuji ki Padacitra saruli*' to propagate the heroism of their kings and the greatness of the Jain *tirthankaras*. Similarly, the roll of pictures measuring three feet in width and thirty feet in length are said to be available in Bengal, Bihar, Orissa, and Andhra Pradesh (especially Telangana area).

Killiketas

The directors of leather-puppet plays are called '*killiketas*' in Belgaum, Dharwad, Bijapur, and Bellary districts and '*katabas*' in Gulbarga district and '*Gomberamas*' or '*Chitra Marutis*' in old Mysore area. They are also called by different names like *Sillekyata*, *Katabujata*, *Kolukyata*, *Astrikyata*, *Kalikyata*, *Bundekyata*, etc. The members of *killiketa* community are the professional artists of this folk-theatre. The meaning of the word '*killiketas*' is interpreted variously. Some scholars guess that it must have been directed from '*kilu katha*' (vulgar story). The artists, who must be narrating low or vulgar stories originally must have later come under the influence of *Yaksagana Bayalatas* and taken to the narration of stories from the *Ramayana* and the *Mahabharata*. H.K. Ranganath has illustrated this in his *The Karnataka Theatre*. The Puppet-Theatre is known by different names in different geographical locations of India. It is called *Kataputali* in Hindi, *Kalasutri Bihayi* in Marathi (Maharashtra), *Tolu Bommalata* in Telugu (Andhra Pradesh) *Killikyatara Ata*, *Gombi Ata* and *Gomberamara Ata* in Kannada (Old Mysore), *Katabara Ata* in Bijapur and Gulbarga districts and as *Mandyana Ata* in some parts of Karnataka.

A correct historical picture of the tradition of Shadow Play is available in the *Gazetteer of Bombay* (Vol. XXIII) prepared in 1884, which contains some solid information about *killiketas* (pp. 196-201). According to it, *killiketas* were also called *katabas* and the ancestor of *killiketas* happened to be a *ksatriya*, who accompanied the Pandavas during the latter's exile. According to Edgar Thurston, "The *Killikeyatas* are a Marathi-speaking people, who amuse villagers with their marionette shows in the Telugu and Canarese countries" (*Castes and Tribes of Southern India*, Vol. III, Delhi: Cosmo Publications, 1975, p. 293). As S.M. Natesa Sastri says, "Their profession is enacting religious dramas before the village public (whence their name, meaning buffoon). The black *kambli* (blanket) is their screen, and any *mandapa* or village *chavadi*, or open house is their stage. Night is the time for giving the performance. They carry with them pictures painted in colours on deer skins, which are well tanned, and made fine like parchment. The several parts of the picture representing the human or animal body are attached to each other by iron wires, and the parts are made to move by the assistance of thin bamboo splits, and thus the several actions and emotions are represented to the public, to the accompaniment of songs. Their pictures are in most cases very fairly painted, with variety and choice of colours. The stories chosen for representation are generally from the *Ramayana* and the *Mahabharata*, which they however call *Ravanyakatha* and *Pandavakatha*—the stories of Ravana and the Pandavas" (*Indian Review*, VII, 1906, Quoted by Thurson, p. 293). Thurson further says that the dead of these *killikyatas* are buried in a seated posture and that some of their women are engaged as professional tattoers.

All the *killiketas* know Kannada and have no traditional story to prove that they migrated to Karnataka from Andhra Pradesh. It, therefore, means that they had settled down in Karnataka for long. They use a mixture of Kannada and Marathi at home. They follow a rule of their community that they must tour the country at least once in three months. However, if they cannot tour, they are expected at least to change their oven in the kitchen from one place to another. The men-folk go for fishing during the daytime, but perform the Shadow Play during the nighttime. These *killiketas* possess lands in Bagilukote, Badami, Hunagund and other places gifted to them in the past. But they do not cultivate them by themselves. After the introduction of the Law of Disarmament and Prohibition against Deforestation, the people of these areas invite and hire the *killiketas* to kill the pigs, which ruin the crops in the fields. The *killiketas* have many sub-sects among them, decided by their specific professions. They follow many rituals ranging from birth to death.

An important piece of information given in the *Bombay Gazetteer* happens to be a *sannad* dated Fasali Year 930 (1520 or 1521 AD) given to the *killiketas* by the Second Sultan of Bijapur. Ismail, the Second Sultan of Adilshahi family of Bijapur is said to have ruled from 1510 to 1534 AD. These historical facts prove that the Shadow Plays used to be performed by *killiketas* by 1520 AD. Since they had land grants, they must have had good social status also. The *Gazetteer* mentions that there was no change in the lifestyle for the past two or three centuries. This takes their ancestry still further back.

The *Gazeteer* of Belgaum published by the Old Bombay State mentions (p. 196) that *killiketas* have migrated in groups from Kolhapur and Satara of Maharashtra to Karnataka. The *Gazetteer* of Bijapur district mentions that their domestic language was Marathi with a mixture of Kannada.

The *Mysore Castes and Tribes* (pp. 513-35, 1930) offers detailed information about the *killiketas*. It says that the *killiketas* used to get land grants from the rulers for their entertaining service. The book also refers to an interesting story about the ancestor of *killiketas*. The *killiketas*, so runs the story, were originally the agriculturists of Maharashtra. One of their women had maintained an illegal relation with a goldsmith called Kattare Kalachari. Even after the adultery was publicly known, she lived with him and bore seven sons to him. Consequently, she was excommunicated and did not know how to earn her livelihood. The lover, i.e. Kalachari, therefore, taught her the art of cutting the leather-puppets, singing, and entertaining through which she could earn her livelihood. Thus, they formed a caste of their own, joined in by their relatives also. Later they migrated group by group to the southern parts of the country like Karnataka.

Ancestry/Comparative Picture

Though one may guess the ancestry of the Shadow Play with the help of the word '*killiketas*' and their autobiographical information, one cannot fix a cutout date for its ancestry. Some scholars opine that there are evidence to prove that the Shadow Theatre was prevalent in Andhra Pradesh as early as the third century BC. It had reached its height during the reign of Satavahana, Pallava, Calukya, Kakatiya dynasties and during the reign of the kings of Vijayanagara and Tanjavuru. It travelled to South East Asia along with the Indians, who migrated to those places through the coastal cities like Kalinga, Jeemani, Korangi, and Vadre. But there can be another method of deciding its ancestry by comparing it with similar art found in Siam, Indo-China, Jawa, and Bali. Though such plays are performed in these countries by Muslims, the themes happen to be Indian. This theatre must have gone there at some point of history when they were ruled by the Emperors of South India. A Chola King bearing the title 'Gangaikonda' (perhaps Rajarajendra Chola, 1012-44 AD) is said to have ruled over these countries when the Shadow Theatre migrated there.

Some scholars conjecture that the Shadow Theatre must have migrated from the coast of Andhra Pradesh to Southeast Asia; that the Arabs must have taken it from Jawa to Arabia; and that it must have migrated from Arabia to Syria, Turkey and North Africa. They further opine that the ancient Indian saints and philosophers must have used the Shadow Plays for the propagation of religion and moral edification. Though this art developed into a means of entertainment later, it never gave up its basic didactic purpose (Shyam Parmar: *Traditional Folk Media in India*, 1975).

The Stage

For the preparation of the leather puppet-stage, the puppeteer requires four bamboo poles for fixing in the earth at Four Corners and four bamboo poles for connecting them at the top corners. The three sides, except the front and top, are covered with a mat or with coconut fronds. Then a black blanket and a white *dhoti* are required for the performance of leather puppets. The stage is decorated with mango leaves, which is believed to be a sign of auspicious-ness.

The stage required for the performance of small leather-puppets by the puppeteer in a sitting position is generally of six feet in height and eight feet square. The front position of the stage is fixed with an immaculately white *dhoti* of three and a half feet width for a curtain. Below the *dhoti*, a black blanket of one and a half feet width is fixed.

The puppeteers sit inside the stage behind the black blanket, but they are not visible to the audience on account of the black curtain. A wick lamp or electric lamp is hung behind the puppeteers. When they hold the leather-puppets between the lamp and the white curtain, the puppets cast wonderful multi-coloured shadows on the white curtain thereby creating a magical world for the audience. Most of the puppeteers including singers, instrumentalists and helpers belong to the same caste of *killiketas* and to the same family.

But the stage required for the performance of life-size or bigger than life-size puppets is quite different from that of small puppets and resembles almost the stage of folk-theatre (*bayalata*). Whether the puppets are big or small, the puppeteer has to be an expert in handling the leather-puppets very dexterously. On the whole, the performance of small leather-puppets is said to be far more attractive than that of big ones. Such performances are sure to capture the attention of folk audiences.

The location for the stage or performance of the leather-puppets may be any place convenient to it. Referring to *killiketas* and their performances, S.M. Natesh Shastry says, "Their profession is enacting religious dramas before the village public. The black *kambali* is their screen, and any *mandapa* or village *chavadi* or open house is their stage. They carry with them pictures painted in colours and deer skins, which are well tanned and made fine like parchments" (*Indian Review*, VIII, 1906). He has also referred to the way in which the different parts of the pictures are joined with thin wire and how the parts are made to move with the help of very thin sticks, how they exhibit their dexterity in controlling the puppets, how their singing was accompanied by instrumental music and how the themes were borrowed from epics like the *Ramayana* and the *Mahabharata*.

The maximum duration of a leather-puppet play or shadow play is of three hours. The puppeteer camps in a village for about a fortnight along with his troupe. From the first day of his camp, the people of different lanes of the village invite him (by offering him *vilya*) to perform the thematic events of their choice in the next few days. Thus both the puppeteer and the villagers schedule the calendar of performances carefully and see that there is no repetition of themes in that village. In fixing the dates of shows, both the parties take care to see that the series of performances follow some chronological order or a principle of thematic continuity. For example, the first show in a village depicts the theme of Kauravas poisoning Bhima; the second show would depict the chess play between Kauravas and Pandavas. The next show would depict the exile of Pandavas. The next show would depict the killing of the demon Kamsa and the last one would depict the war of Kuruksetra. Thus, all these shows put together would offer an overview of the *Mahabharata*. Mr. Keshappa of Kakanur village of Badami *taluka* of Bagalkot district has the ability to present the main episodes of the *Mahabharata* in twenty-one shows on twenty-one nights. Each play has a patch of humour for about fifteen to twenty minutes for the entertainment of people.

The number of camping days may range from fifteen to thirty days or even to a couple of months in different villages. On the last day, the puppeteer offers a free show in front of the village temple, as a mark of gratitude to his patrons, who have paid him in cash or kind for so many days. The next day he would leave the village along with his troupe for the next village.

Preparation and Painting of Leather-Puppets

The main substance with which the leather-puppets are made is the animal hide, especially that of deer or goat. But the general opinion of these artists is that deerskin is the best suited to this purpose on account of its transparency and durability. But in the border area between Karnataka and Andhra Pradesh even buffalo-hide is used for the preparation of big size, i.e. life-size puppets.

The leather-puppeteers used to get the deer skin mainly by hunting the animals. Sometimes the *gowdas*, i.e. village chiefs used to hunt the animals and donate their hides to puppeteers and ask them to prepare the puppets in memory of their (donors') ancestors. Sometimes they used to buy the animals hides and donate them to the puppeteers.

After acquiring the animal hide, the puppeteer has to take the responsibility of seasoning it, cutting it into required shapes and sizes and painting them appropriately. He has to follow a very careful method of seasoning the animal hide in order to make it transparent as well as durable. He would first soak the hide in water, then scrape off the hairs and sundry it. Now the hide looks likc a transparent paper or glass. Then he would carve the outline of the required picture on it with a sharp bodkin-like instrument and cuts it off separately.

There are two types of leather-puppets: one, comprehensive puppets containing the figures of man, chariot, charioteer and weapons; two, individual puppets whose hands, trunks, legs and hands are prepared separately and joined together to facilitate the easy movements of limbs.

Whether the puppets are comprehensive or individual, the method of preparing them is the same. The puppeteer has to carve the outlines very carefully and pierce tiny or relatively big holes to create the impression of ornaments (including even crests).

The next stage is of painting the puppets. The paints are also prepared by the puppeteers themselves. In the earlier days, such paints were prepared out of roots, leaves, barks and fruits of trees. But later, paints had to be bought from shops. The puppeteers have to select only the prominent and durable colours, which are bewitching to the eyes. The colours like red, black, and yellow are used prominently. Though such colours painted on the leather-puppets may look rather dull, they look very attractive when they are held against the light. The painted puppets are dried the shade and never in the sunlight lest the colour should fade.

In the earlier days, the entire puppets used to be sewed to small bamboo sticks with the help of which the puppeteers used to play them. Here the entire puppets were to dance. The movement of limbs was not possible. But later more flexibility was introduced into the preparation of leather-puppets. Three parts of the body like neck; chest and waist are sewn to a bamboo stick to make them look erect. Then head, hands, thighs and legs are sewn with a string separately thereby facilitating their movements. If the puppets are small, the puppeteer has to sit behind the curtain and perform the play. If the puppets are of life-size, then he has to stand upright to perform the play.

The time when such flexible puppets came into existence is not known precisely. But it seems possible that there was some influence of string-puppets upon them. But these things cannot be proved on account of lack of evidence.

The neat preservation of these leather-puppets is also an art. The puppeteer has to see that the puppets do not grow dry or brittle. He has, therefore, to apply to them some kind of liquid prepared by him out of roots and leaves. If properly preserved like this, the leather-puppets may last for more than hundred years. After the performance is over, the puppeteer keeps the puppets neatly arranged in a bamboo box called '*bavali*', which is held in high reverence by him.

The preparation of new leather-puppets is not an easy task. First of all it is a very costly affair and the artists, who can paint these puppets, are not easily available. Therefore, the old puppets have to be used for the old themes. This is the opinion of Kakappa of Kakanur.

Text and Performance

There are no written texts for the leather-puppet performances. The themes are orally transmitted from generation to generation. These artists have a reverential attitude towards their art. Every New Moon Day and Full Moon Day, they offer *puja* to the leather-puppets. Similarly, at the beginning of each play they offer prayers to Lord Ganesa and the village deity. After the prayer is over, the puppeteer explains the theme of the play briefly and prays to Lord Ganesa to ward off all the possible hindrances for the performance. (One may easily see the parallels between the leather-puppet shows and the *bayalatas*.) Then he thanks and praises all the people of the lane and their leaders, who have arranged the show with contributions from among themselves.

The literature of leather-puppet theatre is transmitted orally and hardly reduced to the written text. It consists of both prose and poetry. The puppeteer, who is a professional artist, knows his prose dialogues by heart. His eloquence is highly appreciable. His mastery over his voice, his ability to produce a variety of tones is remarkable. He cannot achieve originality in his prose dialogues every day. The songs sung by him are mostly composed by others and borrowed by him to suit the needs of the theme. But he goes on adding to the humour of the play by learning new jokes, proverbs, and sentences after the gap of a few months.

Sentiments

The sentiments of heroism (*vira*), pathos (*karuna*), and humour (*hasya*) are commonly depicted by the leather-puppet theatre. Whenever the feelings of the characters reach high intensity, the prose dialogues culminate into beautiful songs sung to the accompaniment of musical instruments thereby capturing the hearts of the audience. The humorous element is depicted through ironical and satirical remarks and sometimes through absurd combination of thought and rhymes. Introducing humorous interludes right in the midst of the main theme is a characteristic feature of the leather-puppet performances. The humorous dialogues between the *killiketa* and his coquettish beloved, Bangarakka entertain the audience. Many times humour is tinctured with obscenity. The puppet, i.e. *killiketa* attracts the attention of the audience with his peculiar shape, black complexion, snub-nose, thick lips, potbelly, and crooked hands and legs.

Themes

Generally, mythological themes from the *Ramayana* and the *Mahabharata* and the *Bhagavata* and other narratives are selected for leather-puppet performances. But nowadays even historical and social themes are depicted. The stories connected with mythical heroes and events like Vira Abhimanyu, Babhruvahana,

Kichakavadha, Dashavatara, Parijata, Bhasmasura, Yayati, Rati-Kalyana, Girija-Kalyana, Sita-Swayanvara and Bhisma Vijaya, etc. are depicted by the Shadow Plays. There is a common habit of exchanging themes between Shadow Plays and *Baayalata* folk plays. Some adventurous troupes have been able to present Shadow Play performances on the lives of Basaveswara and Mahatma Gandhi.

Nowadays Shadow Theatre is used by the Government of Karnataka for propagandistic purpose of popularizing the government politics and projects like literacy campaign, green revolution, health education, family planning, and awareness about AIDS.

Language

The language employed by the puppeteer is neither the standard one nor the folk one, but a golden mean between the two. It is occasionally peppered with descriptive patches and figures of speech. The puppeteer does not care for the purity of language or thought. On the contrary, he can mix the profound with the profane, the ancient with the modern, the classical with the realistic, Sanskrit with English and so on for the sole purpose of entertaining the audience. The abundant use of abusive words like whoreson, son of a bitch, curses and proverbs are the common features of the language of Shadow Plays.

A distinct feature of the Shadow Plays of Hyderabad-Karnataka happens to be the regional variety of language used in them. The major language employed in them is Kannada, but it is always mixed with either Telugu or Marathi or even Urdu in order to attract the audiences of the border areas of Karnataka, Maharashtra, and Andhra Pradesh.

Dialogues

The chief value of a leather-puppeteer lies in his (mono-actor like) ability to utter a variety of dialogues of different characters by producing a variety of tones according to the situation. The audience think that the dialogues of different characters are spoken by different people, but the fact is that it is only the puppeteer sitting behind the curtain, who produces a variety of sounds and tones—like the heroic and the pathetic, the turbulent and the serene, the male and the female, the written and the colloquial, the old and the young.

While the puppeteer is speaking the dialogues from behind the curtain, the *tabla* (vertical drum) player sitting outside the curtain, will be responding to the former with his affirmative tags like 'yes', 'yes' and interrogative tags like 'What happened next?' and 'Is that so?'.

Music

Music is an inevitable part of puppet theatre. But there cannot be a simple answer to the question as to what kind of music is employed in this theatre. On the whole, three kinds of music are employed by different troupes. Some troupes employ purely folk music; some, semi-folk music and some others, standard (or classical) music. In the early days, the members of back-chorus used to play *dholu* or *dholak*, but later *dholu* was replaced by the horizontal drum called *maddale* due to the influence of *bayalata* theatre. Similarly, in the early days, they used to employ a drone-box called '*pavari*', but later on it was replaced by the harmonium. But cymbals have continued to be employed in the present as in the past. A majority of puppeteers and members of back-choruses cannot afford to learn music systematically and rigorously due to their crushing poverty.

Superstitions

There are many religious, cultural, and social superstitions attached to the leather-puppet theatre of Karnataka. Some people believe that they can get rains for their village by arranging a performance of the leather-puppet play. Some others believe that they can have the disease of their cattle cured by arranging a performance of such plays. Sometimes people used to get the leather-puppets of Rama, Sita or Krishna prepared and donate them to the director of puppet-theatre in memory of their elders or ancestors. The open praise of such donors by the director would elicit further donations by other donors.

Geographical Variations

The leather-puppet theatre is found in every part of Karnataka except the coastal and rainy belt of the State. It is a domestic art and the puppets are multi-coloured. But the puppets of other States are only black and white.

The leather-puppets of northern Karnataka are not very big. They measure one and a half or two feet in height. The heroes represented by these puppets wear a cap, have a beard, hold a sword in hand and ride elephants or horses. There seems to have been the Muslim influence on the making of these puppets. The legs of these puppets are not flexible but immovable. The entire puppets are made to dance. The puppet player sits behind the curtain whereas the interpreter sits outside and interprets the story to the audience. Women join as back-chorus to the other male singers.

The puppets of southern Karnataka are slightly bigger than those of the north (yet of middling size). The main feature of these puppets happens to be that the legs and hands of these puppets are flexible or movable. Therefore, the movements of such puppets are more dexterous and attractive than those of the immovable ones. Even the difficult actions like cutting the throat or other limbs (especially legs and hands) of the enemy can be shown through these puppets.

The leather-puppet theatre tradition of Andhra Pradesh and Karnataka border is very different from that of interior Karnataka, in that the puppets of the former are of life-size in height and multi-coloured. This naturally requires a big stage and a good deal of ability on the part of the director, who cannot sit but has got to stand and control the puppets.

Troupes

Dr. Shivaram Karanth suspected that there might not be more than four or five troupes of *killiteta* performers. But recent facts discovered by the folk scholars show that there are a number of troupes in Karnataka, which are not properly discovered, counted, and recorded. According to present calculation, there are said to be about 300 troupes of leather-puppet performers and about twenty-five troupes of string-puppet performers in Karnataka.

Some of the troupes of leather-puppet performers are said to be found in the villages like Akkihebbala, Tyapenahalli (near Nagamangala), Kadabahalli (near Bellur), Markonahalli, Ketuhalli (near Ramanagar), Mudugere, Bommalatapuram, Belagallu (Bellary district) and Binkadakatti and some villages of Belgaum, Dharwad, Hassan, Mandya, Mysore, and Gadag districts, etc.

We may have a glimpse at some well-known leaders of leather-puppet troupes in order to know the variety of methods and manners of performances. For example, Gomberama Hombayya has a repertoire of more than thirty-three '*prasangas*' (thematic units or events) connected with the *Ramayana* and the *Mahabharata*. His troupe takes a series of five nights for the performance of a few select events of the *Mahabharata* story.

His troupe has about five hundred leather-puppets equally divided by his four sons. All the members of the family except children know the dialogues of all the characters to speak according to the contexts. They have got to get a curtain cloth of nine elbows-length only through begging. They decide the direction of the stage according to the astral time (*tithi*) and the theme of the play. Whenever the elderly man in the family cannot earn enough through such performances, his sons separate from him and start earning their own livelihood from their own independent performances. This is how the tradition has been kept up.

There is a family of *killiketas* in Gosabala village of Belgaum district, who have a land grant in recognition of their profession. They perform a leather-puppet play about the Pandavas on the day of Kartik.

Bharamaappa and his family from Yadramanahalli gave a performance of an event of the *Ramayana* at the Kannada Department of Karnatak University, Dharwad in October 1984. The performance began with a praise of Lord Ganesha and Goddess Sharada followed by the meeting between Golla (milkman) and Gollati (milkmaid). This is the influence of the *sannata* (Small Play) entitled *Sri Krisna Parijata.* There are also traces of the influence of the Jaina *Ramayana*. Bharamappa's domestic language is Marathi. He learnt the art from his maternal grandfather, maternal grandmother, and uncle, Basappa of Morageri. He used to employ the leather-puppets belonging to his ancestors. The *shanubhoga* of the village had offered him a land grant in recognition of his art.

Bharamappa offers his own interpretation of the folk-myth of Jokumaraswami. According to him, Kyatappa is born earlier than Jokumara. His wife Bangarakka is naked. Kyatappa has a tuft of hair on his head and is a hero in the village. *Killiketa* is a director. Bharamappa has a right to perform his puppet-shows in thirty-three villages. He gets his gifts from the villagers during the harvesting season. While receiving these gifts from the farmers, he utters the good wishes in a set poetic style.

According to Bharamappa, *killiketas* are of two kinds: one, domestic and two, fishermen. They worship the domestic deities like Huligemma, Yallamma, Kolashanta, Tipperudraswami, Kottureshа, Maddanaswami and Goni Basappa, etc. They worship the leather-puppets on the festival days of Dasara and Ugadi. According to Bharamappa, the troupes of leather-puppets are available in villages like Odakalagi (Kudligi *taluka*), Garaga (near Maremmanahalli), Anakunti (Ranebennur *taluka*) and Hatti (Mulgund *taluka*). Once Bharamappa visited Russia for arranging performances by his troupe.

The parents and grandparents of Sayabanna Satabara of Gulbarga used to perform leather-puppet plays, though he has not learnt this art formally. But he has donated more than a hundred leather-puppets to Gulbarga University for preservation in the folk museum. Sayabanna's ancestors hailed from Devanagaon of Bijapur district.

Shankara is a '*kataba*' from Uduchana village of Afzalpur *taluka* of Gulbarga district. He performs the leather-puppet plays like his father and uncle. His relatives stay in Salotagi village of Bijapur district and have thousands of leather-puppets in their possession.

Bhimappa of Bommanakheda village of Chincholi taluka, Bapu Kshetri and his son Rachu Kshetri and Maruti Uppar of Maindaragi village and Ramachandra of Karur village of Alanda taluka are well-known leather-puppet players.

Rachu Kshetri and Maruti Uppar of Maindaragi village have written a *sannata* (Small Play) entitled *Arabara Ata*. Both of them happened to be good leather-puppet performers also. Whereas Rachu was an expert in singing, Maruti was an expert in playing *dappu* (small flat drum). They were also known for their creativity in adapting the *Arabara Ata* (*A Play about Arabs*) to the leather-puppet theatre and achieved great popularity by giving performances of the same play in villages and towns like Madana-Hipparagi, Nimbaragi, Akkalakot, and Maindaragi. Later the same theme was adapted to the *Gondaligya* narrative performances also. Both of them happened to be disciples of a Muslim saint called Gaibi Pir.

Once upon a time Raichur district was known for leather-puppet theatre. Krishnappa of Kurdi village of Manvi *taluka* was an expert leather-puppet performer. He is known as Sillikyata Krishnappa. Even in his advanced age, he has been performing and teaching his art to a number of disciples. In 1986, he was honoured with an Award by the Janapada and Yakshagana Academy of the Government of Karnataka.

Similarly, Doddabalappa of Moranalli village of Koppala district and Doddabharamappa of Yadravi village of Hagaribommanahalli *taluka* of Bellary district were also honoured with Awards by the Janapada and Yakshagana Academy of the Government of Karnataka. It is a matter of pride for India that Doddabharamappa visited Germany and earned the appreciation of the German audience for his leather-puppet shows.

Belagallu Viranna happens to be an important shadow-puppeteer, who has settled in Bellary and who has continued this art through his family tradition. He has been awarded the Karnataka Rajyotsava Prasasti, Karnataka Janapada Academy Prasasti and Janapadasri Prasasti in recognition of his excellent performances of leather puppets all over Karnataka and even beyond the State.

Gunduraj is another leather-puppeteer, who has settled in Huvinahalli Kavali in Hassan district. He has been engaged in the preparation of puppets, singing in the back-chorus and playing the puppets in collaboration with his father Gombe Ramayya right from his fifth year. He has been giving thousands of performances of other arts like playing on the harmonium, *Harikatha* and *Bhagavata* recitals. He has been honoured with the Karnataka Janapada Academy Award and many awards from many cultural associations. He has leather-puppets in his possession, which are about three hundred years old.

These artists, Belagallu Viranna and Gunduraj have been performing inside as well as outside Karnataka. The leather-puppets prepared by these artists have been exported to many foreign countries like Italy, England, America, Africa, and Korea.

The Puppet Land of Bangalore and Ranga Putthali employ the puppets for the expression of dream element. Putthalika troupe of Kolkatta has adapted *Ali Baba and Hundred Thieves* to leather-puppet theatre.

Need for Modernization

The leather-puppet theatre is neglected these days because of the onslaught of modern technological means of entertainment like film, television, radio, audio and video shows, etc. The villagers, who have come under the influence of such modern media, do not show much interest in inviting the leather-puppet troupes to their villages. Some of the puppeteers have, therefore, been directing their art to propagandist programmes of the Government of Karnataka like family planning, pulse polio removal AIDs and cancer, rural development, national pension scheme and literacy, etc. On the whole, the leather-puppet theatre is on the verge of death. The precious art can be preserved only with the entry of educated people into the world of folk art, encouragement by organizations dedicated to folklore and the public patronage for the folk-artists.

Encouragement

It is a matter of satisfaction to note that the Government of Karnataka has been recognizing the talent of leather-puppet performers and encouraging them with prestigious awards. The five major universities in Karnataka (at Dharwad, Gulbarga, Mysore, Mangalore, and Bangalore) have been showing keen interest in the folklore studies. But the urgent need of the hour seems to be a willingness to introduce the practical training about the leather-puppet performance as a separate course in the post-graduate departments by appointing well-known artists in the field as it is done in the universities of England, America, Canada and other European countries. Similarly, the Department of Kannada and Culture should create and maintain a database of all the artists (living and dead), their troupes and tools for the encouragement of further research in the field.

Note

1. Ulbricht, H. *Wayang Purwa*. Kaula Lampur: Oxford University Press, Reprint, 1972, p. XV.

• • • • •

Select Bibliography

English

Gargi, Balavant. *The Folk-Theatre of India.* Washington: University of Washington Press, 1966.

Mathur, J.C. *Drama in Rural India.* New York: Asia Publishing House, 1964.

Ranganath, H.K. *The Karnataka Theatre.* Dharwad: Karnatak University, 1960.

Kannada

Biradar, M.G. *Janapada Samalokana,* Kalburgi: Chitkala Prakasana, 1981.

Boralingaiah, H.C. *Karnataka Janapada Kalegala Kosha,* Hampi: Prasaranga, Kannada Visvavidyalaya, 1996.

Chidananda Murthy, M. *Gramina.* Bangalore: Bapco Prakasana, 1977.

Durgadas, K.R. *Ballary Jilleya Bayalatagalu*, Belagavi: Samata Prakasana, 1996.

Hiremath, R.C. *Janapada Sahitya Darsana,* Part I. Dharwad: Karnatak University, 1974.

Imrapur, Somashekhara, *Janapada Vijnana.* Dharwad: Chetana Prakasana, 1979.

Ittannavar, Srirama, *Sri Krisna Parijata: Indu Adhyayana.* Bilagi: Vini Prakasana, 1991.

Kalburgi, M.M. *Marga.* Vols. I and II. Bangalore: Naresh and Company, 1988.

Kambara, Chandrasekhar, *Uttara Karnatakada, Janapada Rangabhumi.* Dharwad: Manvantara Prakasana, 1965.

Krishnasharma, Betageri, *Kannada Janapada Sahitya*, Dharwad: Prasaranga, Karnatak University, 1976.

Latthe, M.S. *Bayalatada Sarathi.* Mutanal: Mallasarja Prakasana, 1978.

Latthe, M.S. *Janapada Kavicharite.* Dhangapur: Basavantarao Malipatil Memorial Publication, 1980.

Latthe, M.S. *Janapada Samsodhanatmaka Barahagulu.* Kalburgi: Patil Dal Mill, 1980.

Malasetty, Basavaraj, *Uttara Karnatakada Bayalatagalu.* Dharwad: Prasaranga, Karnatak University, 1983.

Marulasiddappa, K. *Adhunika Kannada Nataka*, Bengaluru: Ankita Pustaka, 2002.

Police-Patil, Basavaraj, *Hyderabad-Karnatakada Sannatagalu*, Gulbarga: Prasaranga, Gulbarga University, 1999.

Sunkapur, M.S. *Janapada Sahitya Darsana,* Part II. Dharwad: Prasaranga, Karnatak University, 1976.

Sunkapur, M.S. *Janapada Sahitya Darsana,* Part III. Dharwad: Prasaranga, Karnatak University, 1978.

• • • • •

Index